$595

Larry S. Wdonal

PROBING AMERICA'S PAST

PROBING AMERICA'S PAST

A Critical Examination of Major Myths and Misconceptions

VOLUME II

THOMAS A. BAILEY

Stanford University

D. C. HEATH AND COMPANY
Lexington, Massachusetts   Toronto   London

FOREWORD

Young people enrolled in college today have almost invariably taken elementary and secondary courses in United States history—or at least have been exposed to them. Yet many college textbooks do little more than retrace the nation's past in broader outlines and greater detail. My major purpose in writing this volume has been to encourage the student to *probe* more deeply. He is especially invited to examine critically the more important myths, legends, misconceptions, misinterpretations, other dubieties and misstatements of American history.

The material is organized to stand on its own feet; the brief prologues of each chapter provide an overall historical background. Yet I hope that the book will also prove useful as a supplement or complement to the standard surveys, especially the short ones.

My analysis is particularly concerned with why and how the picture got out of focus. Naturally I have been forced to omit many myths of minor importance or relegate them to footnotes. False beliefs about America's past have now become so numerous that a full analysis would fill many volumes. I realize, of course, that modern scholarship has discredited many of these untruths but they continue to linger in the older textbooks and in the public mind.

Traditional accounts are the ones that naturally attract the greatest encrustation of myth. My approach therefore follows the conventional chronological pattern of political, diplomatic, military, and economic history. Nevertheless I devote considerable attention to social phenomena, especially race problems, where they significantly affect the mainstream.

One of my basic purposes is to stimulate thought and provoke discussion. This aim partly explains why the numerous subheads all appear in the form of questions, even though some of these cannot be answered with finality. My hope is that readers will develop an appreciation of how American history has been warped in the past so that they may be on their guard in the present. They should come away with a deepened awareness of the complexity of the historical process, the prevalence of pitfalls, and the folly of making easy generalizations.

I am under heavy obligation to a host of scholars (including graduate students) for their papers, articles, and books, many of which are listed in the footnotes and bibliographies. I am especially indebted to Don E. Fehrenbacher, Carl N. Degler, George D. Bullock, and Philip A. Feldman for having critically read (I hope without incriminating themselves) all or substantial parts of the manuscript. Stephen M. Dobbs, the chief collaborator, prepared a detailed critique of the manuscript, checked the footnotes and bibliographies, and meticulously proofread the galley sheets.

Thomas A. Bailey
Stanford University
Stanford, California

CONTENTS

26 Wilson and the Return of the Democrats   514

27 Waging Neutrality, 1914–1917   530

28 America in World War I   559

29 Wilsonian Peacemaking   578

1ˢᵗ test

30 Harding and the Era of Normalcy   599

31 Coolidge and Pseudoprosperity   614

32   Hoover and the Great Depression   633

33   The New Deal and the New Neutrality   657

2ⁿᵈ test

37 The Korean Conflict and Its Aftermath   765

38 The Eisenhower Interlude   783

39 Kennedy and the New Frontier   801

21

Reconstruction
North and South

President Lincoln consistently maintained that the rebellious South had not really left the Union. His successor, Andrew Johnson, enlarging upon Lincoln's proposals, recognized new governments in the Southern states when they had satisfied certain preconditions, including the renunciation of secession and the abolition of slavery. By December 1865, ten of the eleven "wayward sisters" had accepted these stipulations. But Congress, seizing control under the leadership of Radical Republicans, barred the Southerners from their seats in the House and Senate. New and more stringent conditions for "readmission" were then imposed, including ratification of the Fourteenth Amendment, which, among various provisions, conferred citizenship on the Negroes.

President Johnson, himself a Southerner, favored a more lenient policy. When repudiated at the polls in the Congressional elections of 1866, he encouraged the secessionist states to reject the Fourteenth Amendment, and all but Tennessee did. An angered Congress thereupon forced military reconstruction on the South in 1867. Under the jurisdiction of the U. S. Army, new governments were set up in the defiant states. They were required to ratify not only the Fourteenth but also the Fifteenth Amendment, which entitled the Negro to vote. Although the attempt by Congress to remove President Johnson by impeachment failed in 1868, military reconstruction dragged on and was formally completed by 1877. Yet, in a sense, it has never been completed and must rank as one of America's great failures.

WHY IS RECONSTRUCTION
A REVISIONIST BATTLEGROUND?

In the years after the Civil War most Southern historians wrote of Reconstruction with an understandable bias. Their view was that while the Northerners on the whole had fought honorably, they had reconstructed the ex-Confederacy dishonorably. They had not only disfranchised a host of educated whites but had enfranchised a horde of uneducated blacks, who had then proceeded to stage a travesty of government under the leadership of scheming Northern "carpetbaggers." Such mismanagement was to Southerners living proof that the blacks were incapable of participating usefully in government, whether in casting the ballot or in holding office. Nothing good could come out of the Negro–carpetbag–scalawag governments, the argument ran, and the conservative whites — the "redeemers" — finally felt justified in using the brutal methods of the Ku Klux Klan to rescue the South from misrule by their former bondsmen.

Southern historians received a strong assist from the novelists, notably Thomas Dixon, a North Carolina Baptist clergyman, who published *The Clansmen* in 1905. It was brought to the screen in D. W. Griffith's pioneer classic melodrama, "The Birth of a Nation" (1915), one of the most famous cinemas of all time. The Reconstruction Negro was portrayed as ignorant, bestial, and lustful, slavering after white women; the Ku Klux Klansmen were knights in white sheets, flogging and murdering to restore order and virtue.

Not surprisingly, the best-known histories of Reconstruction were written by Northern historians in the victorious North, and the most famous of them established a pattern early in the twentieth century. Perhaps the most influential writer was James Ford Rhodes, whose chapters on Reconstruction in his multivolume work appeared from 1904 to 1906. More significant at the academic level was Professor W. A. Dunning of Columbia University, who trained a whole school of scholars and who published an important synthesis of the postwar decade in 1907.[1] Historians of the Rhodes-Dunning school generally argued that the South had done the North a terrible wrong by forcing a Civil War on it. But they also felt that the North had visited a grievous injustice on the South by forcing the odious Negro–carpetbag Reconstruction on the "decent" ex-Confederates. The two wrongs more or less canceled

---

[1] W. A. Dunning, *Reconstruction, Political and Economic* (1907).

each other out. Thereafter the graying "Billy Yanks" and "Johnny Rebs" could take increasing pride in their Civil War and celebrate it with annual jamborees.

Early in the twentieth century a few black historians, conspicuously Dr. W. E. B. Du Bois and Dr. Carter G. Woodson, were arguing that the Negro was not innately inferior. They concluded that his ineptitudes during Reconstruction, when he was unprepared for his sudden new responsibilities, should not be held against him. On the whole, these historians contended, he had contributed constructively in passing desirable reformist legislation in the so-called black-and-tan legislatures. But such views encountered much resistance or indifference from white historians.

By the 1950s, if not earlier, the intellectual climate had undergone a marked change. Old white supremacist doctrines of racial inferiority had fallen into disrepute among anthropologists, ethnologists, sociologists, and historians. Following the momentous desegregation decision of the Supreme Court in 1954, the nation found itself caught up in a civil-rights revolution. White historians were making fairer assessments of the role of the Negro, as well as of his white associates and backers, during the ordeal of Reconstruction.[2]

WAS RECONSTRUCTION CONFINED TO THE SOUTH?

The Reconstruction Era is often described as something unique in American experience. Actually, every war the nation has fought has been followed by a period of reconstruction — readaptation, replacement, retooling, and restoration. This was notably true after the Revolutionary War, World War I, World War II, and the Korean War.

Experience with reconstruction was not confined to the South. The entire nation had been sucked into the war, to a greater or lesser extent. Readjustment — social, cultural, political, economic, constitutional — was inevitable in the rest of the Union as well as in the South, though in the North to a less painful degree. Lincoln's exercise of war powers had aroused the jealousy of Congress, and in the tug-of-war for a reassertion of authority the South was trampled underfoot.

Reconstruction is often portrayed as almost purely political —

[2] A convenient summation of revisionism may be found in Kenneth M. Stampp, *The Era of Reconstruction, 1865–1877* (1965). See also Larry Kincaid, "Victims of Circumstance: An Interpretation of Changing Attitudes Toward Republican Policy Makers and Reconstruction," *Jour. of Amer. Hist.*, LVII (1970), 48–66.

the reestablishment of a normal relationship between the seceded South and the successful North. This process was important and headline catching, but other aspects were hardly less significant. Economic reconstruction in the South required a restoring of devastated areas and a putting of the cotton-based economy back on its feet. Social reconstruction primarily meant adjusting the unchained black to his new status, especially in his relations with the whites. Cultural reconstruction involved rebuilding ruined schools and churches while grappling with the problem, among others, of educating vast numbers of illiterate Negroes (and also whites).

The impression that life somehow ground to a halt in the South during this era of agony is thoroughly misleading. Life always goes on, as it even did during the Black Death of the fourteenth century, which killed about three-fourths of the population of Asia and Europe. In the South men worked and played; they sinned and prayed; they married and begot children. One prominent historian has stated that "Despite strange doings in statehouses, Southerners usually lived as quietly and as normally during Reconstruction as in any other period of the South's history."[3] No one can deny that in many parts of the South, especially the isolated mountain valleys, no Yankee bayonet was seen, no Klansmen donned sheets, and life went its monotonous way. But this was certainly not the case in the most populous areas, where Negroes were concentrated and where political turmoil and violence were commonplace.

DID RECONSTRUCTION EVER END?

Reconstruction was in effect but a continuation of hostilities by other means. It was a kind of civil war, fought for political control and social dominance, and waged between white supremacist conservatives and white Radical–Republican–Negro forces. There were grave disorders, including wholesale murdering, large-scale rioting, and occasional pitched battles, complete with artillery and with small armies on each side. Overall hundreds were killed (mostly Negroes), thousands were wounded, and at times statewide race wars seemed inevitable. If this was "normalcy" for the South, the prewar life of the region must have been turbulent indeed.

As a matter of fact, reconstruction began long before the war ended, conspicuously in conquered parts of the South, and still goes on. The persistence of the white–black antagonisms and the sporadic cross-

---

[3] F: B. Simkins, in Howard H. Quint, et al., eds., Main Problems in American History (1964), II, 2.

burnings by besheeted Klansmen are cases in point. Some of the marginal land knocked out of production by the war has never been returned to agriculture but has reverted to forest.

WAS RECONSTRUCTION
DESIGNED PRIMARILY AS PUNISHMENT?

A persistent complaint of the South was that the Yankee victors treated the vanquished with a brutality seldom if ever found in the annals of civilized peoples. Never before, Southerners pointed out, had black ex-slaves been placed over their former white masters.

At the outset we must remember that the South had been devastated and prostrated by the war. Even if the wayward states had been welcomed back on the prewar basis, except for slavery, they would have passed through an ordeal of social and economic adjustment.[4]

All things considered, the South was lucky to get off as well as it did. One can think of no unsuccessful rebellion in history, conducted on such a vast scale, that was followed by such lenient punishment. There was no head rolling. Only one Southerner was hanged for alleged brutalities: the Swiss-born head of the notorious Andersonville prison. By pre-1861 standards, thousands of Confederates probably could have been executed for treason. The Constitution clearly stipulates that "Treason against the United States, shall consist only in levying war against them, or in adhering to their enemies, giving them aid and comfort." [5]

Yet the "traitors" received only a slap on the wrist. Most of the Confederate leaders were rather speedily pardoned and restored to their full civil rights. There was no wholesale confiscation of private property, quite in contrast with the fate of tens of thousands of Loyalists during and after the American Revolution. Much Southern acreage was sold for unpaid taxes, as during the Great Depression of the 1930s, but that was something else. Congressman Thaddeus Stevens urged confiscating the estates of the lordly planters, and turning their land over to the ex-slaves as payment for unrequited sweat. But Americans are basically conservative in their attitudes toward private property, and though the Negroes needed land desperately, the Stevens scheme was shelved.

[4] A half-century later, the Germans complained that they were prostrated by the reparations burden of $32 billion imposed by the victorious Allies of 1918. What really prostrated them was the war, which had cost them about $100 billion. The reparations were a last straw.

[5] Art. III, Sec. 3. In Virginia, in 1676, twenty-three men were hanged following Bacon's Rebellion. During and following the Canadian uprising of 1837–1838, some fifteen rebels were executed and several score were transported.

No leading ex-Confederates were exiled, quite in contrast with the customary practice. But hundreds of Southerners, unwilling to face the music, including a possible noose, exiled themselves to Mexico, Brazil, Venezuela, and other foreign lands.

The Yankee victor not only declined to confiscate property and impose reparations, but he even tried to help his fallen foemen back onto their feet. Private benefactions from the North to the South, inadequate though they were, totaled millions of dollars in the postwar years. This is not the usual treatment accorded unsuccessful rebels.

Ironically, the South brought many of its woes upon itself. Overflowing with bitterness and remembering great victories, many Southerners were never completely convinced that they had been beaten. Many still cling to that belief.[6] Conquered but not subdued, they clamored to be taken back into the Union (which they had sought to break up) and be given all the privileges which an American is entitled to under the Constitution (which they had spurned). Some of them, naively enough, even expected financial compensation for their liberated slaves.

The vanquished South almost certainly would have come off far better if it had thrown itself on the mercy of the victors, saying, "You beat us in a fair fight; now do what you will with us." The defeated Japanese in 1945 were much more clever. They swallowed, or pretended to swallow, the large doses of "democlasie" administered by General MacArthur, the Yankee Mikado. They were farsighted enough to perceive that the more cooperative they were, the sooner the conqueror would leave. This is precisely what happened: Japan emerged with a "soft" peace treaty in 1951 that would have been unthinkable in 1945. But the South expected and even demanded lenient treatment, and when it was not forthcoming, embarked upon a shortsighted, even suicidal, course.

WAS JOHNSON CRUCIFIED FOR LINCOLN?

Critics have often charged that President Andrew Johnson was politically crucified for Abraham Lincoln. This view assumes that if Lincoln had lived, he would have suffered exactly the same fate as Johnson — as ex-President Truman was wont to say.

It is fruitless to explore this "iffy" question at length: we simply

---

[6] Southern schoolchildren have often been puzzled to know how the South could have lost the war if it had won most of the important battles — that is, in the earlier phases.

have no way of finding out. We do realize that Lincoln's soft-on-the-South policy had already met stiff opposition in Congress from the radical Republicans, who were determined that the war-provoking Southerners should do penance for their sins. Lincoln would have had further troubles with a Congress that was determined, as postwar Congresses usually are, to regain usurped powers. But to assume that a seasoned statesman of his tact, flexibility, prestige, and proven ability would have floundered into the impeachment quicksands runs counter to all that we know about him. Above all, he was a victorious presidential leader — and victory has a way of silencing criticism.[7]

Shocking though it may seem, some vengeful Republicans of Radical persuasion were secretly pleased by Lincoln's assassination. A few of them were not too successful in concealing their satisfaction; they were confident that they could bend the ex-tailor Andrew Johnson, the Tennessee hillbilly, to their will.

Many die-hard Southerners spontaneously rejoiced when they heard of Lincoln's assassination, much as some Dixiecrats later exulted over the murder in Dallas of President Kennedy, a friend of civil rights for blacks. Lincoln had been built up as the archfoe — as the man who had kept the meat-grinding war going to the last corpse. If he had been willing to cry quits at any time, the South would have made good its effort to establish an independent, slavery-based republic. Perceptive Southerners, on the other hand, were quick to realize that Lincoln's death was a calamity. President Andrew Johnson, to be sure, was a Tennessean and a former slaveholder, but he was branded an apostate. He was also — or had been — bitterly hostile to the Southern aristocracy which had engineered the secession exodus. Better a Lincoln with "malice toward none" than a Johnson with his malice toward many.

President Lincoln is not cherished in the South as he is elsewhere in America. The civil rights struggle in the 1960s, which involved a belated attempt by the North to implement the Emancipation Proclamation ("The New Reconstruction"), added nothing to his stature among militant Southerners. A generation or so ago the first task of many pupils in Southern white schools was to rip from their history textbooks (often published in the North) the picture of "Old Abe." For many years Tennessee was the only one of the "wayward eleven" states of the Confederacy that regularly observed Lincoln's birthday — and Tennessee was the only one to escape the rigors of military Reconstruction.

[7] For a recent downgrading of Lincoln's differences with the Radicals, see Hans L. Trefousse, *The Radical Republicans: Lincoln's Vanguard for Racial Justice* (1969); also Herman Belz, *Reconstructing the Union: Theory and Policy during the Civil War* (1969).

WAS JOHNSON A PRESIDENTIAL MISFIT?

Andrew Johnson's reputation has undergone a roller-coaster course of ups and downs.

White supremacist Northern historians at the turn of the century, conspicuously Rhodes and Dunning, wrote him off as an inept, uncouth, bullheaded misfit who failed to hit it off with Congress. The Radical Republicans, so this interpretation runs, seized control and, under carpetbagger–Negro auspices, imposed bayonet reconstruction on the South. The net result was untold woes for the gallant ex-Confederates, who deserved better treatment.

Then came a remarkable rehabilitation. The historian–lawyer James Schouler, after an examination of the Johnson manuscripts, emerged with a more charitable interpretation in 1914. In 1929–1930 three favorable biographical studies were published by R. W. Winston, L. P. Stryker, and G. F. Milton, plus the impassioned *The Tragic Era*, by the Democratic spellbinder and journalist, Claude G. Bowers.[8] Johnson now appeared as an able, dedicated, intelligent, and much-maligned statesman, who stood like a rock for constitutional principles, but who was nearly railroaded out of the White House by diabolical Radical Republicans.

The atmosphere of the 1950s and 1960s, during which the issue of civil rights for Negroes was making headlines, prompted a downward reassessment of Johnson, who had once been a small-scale slaveowner and hence a "racist." Several important books emerged in which the "Tailor President" again appeared as narrow, tactless, brittle, and responsible for many of the woes that the South endured during the postwar years.[9] He was generally condemned not so much because he had botched Reconstruction for the whites as because he had bungled it for the blacks, who to this day have not fully recovered from the searing experience.[10]

It now seems clear that Johnson at best was a rough diamond, ill suited to quiet the storm into which he was propelled by Booth's bullet. Never a Republican (he was a lifelong Democrat), the ex-tailor

---

[8] The anti-Republican bias of some of these books, notably that by Bowers, has been attributed to a desire to discredit the then current Republican administration of Herbert Hoover. In 1928 Bowers had delivered the keynote address at the Democratic convention in Houston, where Hoover's opponent, Al Smith, was nominated.

[9] See particularly Eric L. McKitrick's *Andrew Johnson and Reconstruction* (1960).

[10] See Albert Castel, "Andrew Johnson: His Historiographical Rise and Fall," *Mid-America*, XLV (1963), 175–184.

had been put on the Union (Republican) ticket with Lincoln in 1864 to attract Democratic votes and sew up the election. He had appeared drunk at the vice presidential swearing-in ceremonies in 1865, although he was not reputed to be a heavy drinker and although this disgraceful exhibition seems to have been partly the result of illness. A Constitution-worshiper (he was buried with a copy of the document for a pillow), he proved inflexible in his strict interpretation of states' rights — and in truth states' rights received a bad beating during Reconstruction. The Radical Republicans limited by Congressional legislation the jurisdiction of the Supreme Court, which did not distinguish itself during this era by standing up boldly against the legislative arm.[11] If the Radicals in Congress had been able to remove Johnson, they might next have attempted to beat the Supreme Court into complete submission.

WAS JOHNSON'S RECONSTRUCTION POLICY WISE?

President Johnson's early course is puzzling. Venomous against the Southern white aristocrats, he at first breathed fire and hemp, while Radical Republicans in the North applauded. Then, experiencing a softening of the heart, he adopted in substantially modified form Lincoln's lenient proposal for reconstructing the wayward states.[12] He was prepared to welcome them back into the Union (and Congress) as though nothing much had happened, except for the abolition of slavery. He even encouraged them to resist the less lenient terms of the Radical Republicans.

Johnson's policy was nonmalice, but it was also nonwisdom. The recent war had cost over 600,000 lives, to say nothing of untold wealth. After four blood-spattered years, the Northern victors were unwilling to permit the vanquished to reenter Congress on equal terms — with twelve more votes than they had enjoyed when they seceded. (The Negro now counted as five-fifths, not three-fifths, of a man in apportioning representation.) In siding with the ex-rebels against their conquerors, Johnson was asking for trouble, and he got it.

The newly created all-white Southern governments, without

[11] The timidity of the Court has been generally overstressed; it dealt rather vigorously with some nonreconstruction issues. For recent scholarship see Stanley I. Kutler, *Judicial Power and Reconstruction Politics* (1968).

[12] W. B. Hesseltine argues that Lincoln's various proposals for reconstructing the South had all failed, and that he was probably without a plan when shot. (But this does not mean that he could not have evolved one.) *Lincoln's Plan of Reconstruction* (1960). Lincoln, unlike certain Radical Republicans, held that the Southern states had never left the Union. He was later upheld by the Supreme Court in 1869 (Texas *v.* White).

Negro enfranchisement and without ex-Confederate disfranchisement, elected a large contingent to the new Congress, which assembled in December, 1865. Impenitently, they chose the Vice President of the defunct Confederacy (A. H. Stephens), four ex-Confederate generals, five ex-Confederate colonels, several ex-Confederate officials, and a number of former members of the Confederate Congress. Of course, one of the problems of the postwar South was to find able white leaders who had not been tarred by the brush of secession.[13] Outraged by this so-called Southern defiance, the Republican Congress excluded the entire body of "whitewashed rebels" from their seats, pending a more chastening probationary period.

President Johnson, deadlocked with the Radical-lead Congress, finally appealed to the country for support during an undignified and disgraceful stump-speaking tour in 1866. The ensuing Congressional elections returned a two-thirds anti-Johnson majority to both houses of Congress, which now claimed a mandate to impose its will on the South. Actually the result was not much of a mandate for anything: in many contests the choice was between a Radical, anti-Johnson Republican, on the one hand, and an ex-Copperhead, pro-Johnson Democrat, on the other. Many voters held their noses and voted Republican.

DID JOHNSON DESERVE IMPEACHMENT?

Johnson was finally impeached by the House in 1868 and tried by the Senate on the impeachment charges.[14] The bill of indictment was flimsy and partly trumped up. Its most damaging accusation was that the Chief Executive had violated the recently passed Tenure of Office Act, which forbade the President to remove Senate-confirmed appointees without the consent of the Senate. Johnson, believing the Act to be unconstitutional, deliberately violated it in the hope of getting a test case before the courts. The Supreme Court inferentially decided, fifty-eight years later, that Johnson was right in principle on this particular issue.[15] At all events, the President escaped with his political life when the Senate failed by one vote to secure the requisite two-thirds majority. Several more

[13] In reconstructing postwar Germany after 1945, American officials encountered a similar problem in trying to find responsible and able Germans who had not been tainted with Nazism.

[14] Because Johnson was not removed from office, the error persists that he was never impeached.

[15] The case was Myers v. United States (1926), and involved the removal of a postmaster in Portland, Oregon, by President Wilson in 1920.

negative votes for Johnson might possibly have been scraped together if they had been needed.[16]

"Old Andy" Johnson was obviously not guilty of "high crimes and misdemeanors," as prescribed by the Constitution, and hence did not deserve removal. The Machiavellian schemes of the Radicals merited a stern rebuke, and the outcome was a victory for sound government and for preservation of the traditional checks and balances. No President since then has ever been confronted in the Senate with a two-thirds majority of the opposing party, but this does not mean that he never will be, or that a hostile bipartisan coalition cannot be formed against him.

Andrew Johnson's stature as a President is probably higher today than it deserves to be. The American people on the whole are generous, and sympathy for the embattled ex-tailor merges with a kind of guilt complex over his "dirty deal." The blunt truth is that far from being a leader who led, he first lost his temper, then the Congress, and then control of the situation. He was right some of the time, and inflexible most of the time, but he failed to achieve a lenient reconstruction of the South largely because of his own narrowness and folly. At the outset, the Congress was far from united on any course of action, and if Johnson had been able to exercise tactful leadership, he almost certainly would have come closer to success.

HOW RADICAL WERE THE RADICAL REPUBLICANS?

The Radical Republicans in Congress, able to command a two-thirds majority by attracting non-Radicals, finally imposed a harsher reconstruction policy. In so doing they abolished the existing state governments, already set up under the Lincoln–Johnson plans. These regimes were white only and were heavily permeated with ex-Confederates.[17] Pro-Southern historians have long complained that the Radical Republicans not only overthrew well-functioning white regimes, but substituted malfunctioning black-and-white rule. As a result, the charge continues, these legislators actually interrupted one of the most promising phases of reconstruction. What stuck in the throats of many Southerners

[16] None of the seven "recusants," or Republicans who voted to acquit Johnson, was ever returned to a public office, though the story that they were "hounded" out of public life does not seem well founded. R. J. Roske, "The Seven Martyrs?" *Amer. Hist. Rev.*, LXIV (1959), 323–330.

[17] Some of the new constitutions drawn up by the white Southerners contained forward-looking provisions regarding public education — for whites only.

was the fact that, having accepted Johnson's terms in good faith, they were required to begin all over and endure the much less generous terms of Congress. To the South this was like changing the rules after the game had started.

Much misunderstanding exists about the Radicals, who were determined to reconstruct the South severely or radically. They never boasted a majority in either House of Congress, although their leadership proved so aggressive, like that of the War Hawks in 1812, that they created the impression of majority rule.[18] Nor were they as purposeful or united as often portrayed. Their unity consisted of a determination to deal firmly, not to say iron-fistedly, with the South, and create there a strong Republican party.

What the Radicals had primarily in mind when they fashioned a stringent reconstruction policy is not easy to discover. Some had single motives; others had a half dozen or so motives.

Probably some Radicals sought vengeance primarily. The term "Vindictives" has been applied to them, and properly so, but it hardly fits a number of the others.

Some Radicals were eager to create a viable Republican party in the South so that later Congresses would continue to pass Republican-backed legislation. The danger was ever-present that potential Democratic majorities, bolstered by Southern members, might even repeal Republican laws enacted since 1861. These measures included the high tariff acts and the Homestead Act, which the Republicans had enacted after the South had seceded from both Congress and the Union.[19]

Beyond question some Radicals, such as Representative Thaddeus Stevens, were idealistically vengeful, though certain scholars claim that Stevens hypocritically used the blacks as political stooges.[20] Ex-abolitionist Radicals such as Senator Charles Sumner were so deeply committed to the Negro cause that the sincerity of their idealism is

[18] Some historians argue that the phrase "Radical reconstruction" is misleading because the Radical leaders had to compromise with Republican moderates to secure much of their legislation. See David Donald, "Reconstruction," in John A. Garraty, ed., *Interpreting American History* (1970), *I*, p. 353.

[19] The old thesis of Charles A. Beard and Howard K. Beale that Northern business supported Radical reconstruction for its own ends is weakened by the proven disunity among these elements. See Stanley Coben, "Northeastern Business and Radical Reconstruction: A Re-examination," *Miss. Valley Hist. Rev.*, XLVI (1959), 67–90. Many businessmen felt that Radical reconstruction interfered with their business in the South. No consistent pattern of voting on economic matters in the Senate by identifiable Radicals was found in Glenn M. Linden, " 'Radicals' and Economic Policies: The Senate, 1861–1873," *Jour. of Southern Hist.*, XXXII (1966), 189–199.

[20] The more recent biographies of Thaddeus Stevens (by Ralph Korngold) and Benjamin Wade (by H. L. Trefousse) stress higher motives.

difficult to challenge.[21] Sumner, and others of like mind, believed that the freedman needed the ballot for his own protection against resentful white ex-Confederates. Similarly, Negro votes were evidently required to erect safeguards against vengeful ex-Confederates determined to deal sternly with Southern whites ("Tories") who had remained loyal to the Union.

Thaddeus Stevens, as noted, urged the redistribution of acreage among the ex-slaves. He pressed this scheme with such persistency that the more conservative Radicals breathed a sigh of relief when he died in 1874, before Reconstruction formally ended. In the end, the landless Negro emerged with relatively little land, much of it inferior soil from the public domain. The "forty acres and a mule," which cruel rumor had led blacks to expect as a gift, turned out to be scanty acres and no mule.

Leading Radicals, despite their professed concern for the ex-slave, actually did little for his physical betterment. Some, while promoting his cause, cherished a dislike for him. Negroes in the South today might well be better off if their so-called friends, in their zeal to line up votes, had been less self-seeking and more self-restrained. Radicals and their associates did manage to force into the federal Constitution two epochal amendments — the Fourteenth and Fifteenth — but for about a century these enactments rang hollow. The intended results might have been achieved by other means more satisfactorily and more permanently if the North had been willing to move less hastily. In some respects deferred amendments — assuming that they could have passed later — would have been better than dead-letter amendments.[22]

WERE THE CARPETBAGGERS NORTHERN VULTURES?

Hate-laden epithets, such as "carpetbagger" and "scalawag," [23] have occupied a prominent place in the textbooks, and have further distorted the Reconstruction picture. Standard dictionaries define a carpetbagger

---

[21] Sumner, a flaming idealist, was the most conspicuous Radical in the Senate, but he had relatively little influence on the men who framed the major reconstruction legislation. Some of it he opposed, and he "gravely objected" to the Thirteenth, Fourteenth, and Fifteenth Amendments. See David Donald, *Charles Sumner and the Rights of Man* (1970), pp. 9, 241, 432.

[22] A differing view is held by a leading revisionist, Kenneth M. Stampp, who contends that the Fourteenth and Fifteenth Amendments "make the blunders of that era, tragic though they were, dwindle into insignificance." *The Era of Reconstruction,* p. 215.

[23] The term "scalawag" was evidently first used to describe runty livestock, but came to connote a mean fellow. In this sense it antedated Reconstruction and was commonly used in western New York as early as 1848. M. M. Mathews, ed., *A Dictionary of Americanisms on Historical Principles* (2 vols., 1951), *II*, p. 1465.

as "a [white?] Northerner in the South after the Civil War especially seeking private gain under the reconstruction governments." Legend has a pack of villainous and impoverished Northern "jackals," with their possessions stuffed into small carpetbags, descending upon the impoverished South and seeking what they could devour.

Many men undeniably came down from the North, including hundreds of ex-Union soldiers who had admired the fertile soil, flowering foliage, and warm climate while marching through enemy country. Some were poor but others brought investment capital, which they frequently lost in orange groves and other unfamiliar ventures. (This partly explains why so many of them finally sought salaried political office.) But if these newcomers devoted themselves to bettering the economy of the community while attempting to better their own, they were not unwelcome, especially if they brought their families and did not get involved in the struggle for Negro rights. Such men were not regarded as true carpetbaggers at all by contemporary white Southerners. A modern scholar has proposed as a new definition, "white Northerners who went South after the beginning of the Civil War and, sooner or later, became active in politics as Republicans." [24]

Some white Southerners, needing Yankee money for their dollar-dry land, openly advertised for white Northerners of substance. A few of the so-called carpetbaggers were men of wealth, and they had a large hand in launching such worthy enterprises as the great iron works of Birmingham and Chattanooga.

Other new arrivals came in response to other motives. Many were free Negroes [25] (often disliked by the white carpetbaggers) who came down to help their own people while helping themselves. Notable in this group of "black carpetbaggers" were college-educated Hiram R. Revels (a one-time barber) and B. K. Bruce, the only two Negroes to sit in the United States Senate until 1967.[26] A number of the white newcomers went South with no intention of becoming involved in politics but were sucked into the controversy. Some of them were dedicated schoolmen or "school marms," hated and even abused by the whites because they taught Negroes — something widely forbidden by law in slavery days. There were even carpetbaggers-in-reverse, including

[24] See R. N. Current, "Carpetbaggers Reconsidered," in D. H. Pinkney and T. Ropp, eds., *A Festschrift for Frederick B. Artz* (1964), p. 144. See also his *Three Carpetbag Governors* (1967). The word "carpetbagger," still in use, was applied to Robert F. Kennedy, a longtime resident of Massachusetts, when he ran successfully for the U. S. Senate in New York in 1964.

[25] By Websterian definition these Northern Negroes could be carpetbaggers but contemporary white Southerners usually made them a part of a despised trinity: carpetbaggers, scalawags, *and* "niggers."

[26] Senator Edward W. Brooke was elected from Massachusetts in 1966.

residents of war-torn Virginia who moved north into Maryland, where better economic opportunities beckoned.

If the Northern carpetbaggers had only migrated west to improve their lot, as many Americans were doing, they would have been hailed as sturdy, westward-moving pioneers, the backbone of the nation. Some of them, for example, undecided between Kansas and Arkansas, finally chose Arkansas. But by going south they were branded, especially in Southern textbooks, as "tramps" and "vandals."

WERE THE "SCALAWAGS" TRAITORS?

The so-called scalawags have also been unfairly blackened. They were white men whom the ex-Confederates regarded as traitors because they supported the Washington government and its reconstruction policies.

Thousands of so-called scalawags were respectable white Unionists, largely in the mountainous areas, who had consistently favored the Northern cause before and during the war. To them, the Confederates were the renegades and traitors. From the viewpoint of the North, but not of most white Southerners, these loyal citizens were praiseworthy. In fact, the Washington government set up a claims commission to indemnify them for property seized by the Confederacy during the war.[27]

Countless additional scalawags were former Whigs, from the upper crust of Southern society. They had provided powerful opposition to the Democrats before secession; they had supported the Confederacy lukewarmly if at all; and they were naturally disposed to join the Republican coalition, which before the war had taken over the remnants of the Whig party, including Abraham Lincoln. Many if not most of the former Whigs, some of them ex-Confederate leaders, were thoroughly respectable. During Radical Republican reconstruction they held the balance of power in certain localities, but most of them ultimately moved over into the Democratic camp.

Some scalawags were unabashedly ex-Confederate, ex-Democratic turncoats. Suffering from war weariness, they perceived the wisdom of cooperating with the inevitable; they realized that by working from within they would have a better chance of softening Republican reconstruction. They preferred the order of military rule to the disorder

---

[27] F. W. Klingberg, *The Southern Claims Commission* (1955). The physically abused and proscribed Unionists in the South resembled the abused and proscribed Loyalists of the American Revolution. Both were loyal to their central government and were partially indemnified after the war by an official claims commission. The basic difference is that the Southern Unionists finally came out on the winning side.

of continued strife. In this category could be found no less a figure than General James Longstreet, one of the key subordinates of General Lee at the Battle of Gettysburg and elsewhere.[28]

WAS SUDDEN EMANCIPATION AN UNMIXED BLESSING?

Overnight emancipation of the slaves, though perhaps inevitable as a war measure, was a dubious boon. Thousands of footloose freedmen died of exposure, hunger, and disease. Emancipation in other lands, such as Britain's Jamaica in the 1830s, was often preceded by a period of apprenticeship, but even this had produced grave hardships. Yet the abolitionists had strong grounds for arguing that the only way to learn responsibility under freedom is to exercise freedom, just as the best way to learn to swim is to get into the water. As events unhappily turned out, in all too many instances freedom for the Negro meant freedom to starve. In prewar Savannah, the death rate of blacks had been lower than that of the whites; after the war the figures were reversed.[29]

The greatest desires and needs of the Negroes were education and land. Both were to have been provided under the Freedman's Bureau (short for Bureau of Refugees, Freedmen, and Abandoned Lands). Authorized on March 3, 1865, by act of Congress, this agency was headed by the kindly General O. O. Howard,[30] "the Christian General." The Bureau initially did commendable work in feeding, educating, and adjusting blacks, but it fell into disrepute in the South because of corruption and its attempts to build up a Republican–Negro political machine. As for "abandoned lands," the Bureau distributed some inferior acreage to blacks but most of it was eventually retrieved by the original owners.

Free or cheap acreage no doubt would have helped the freedman, but here his abolitionist friends failed him. Once they had achieved their supreme goal of freedom for the Negro, they showed no comparable zeal for his betterment, whether political, social, or economic. As ill luck would have it, the ex-bondsman slipped into the quicksands of quasi-bondage; in many cases he was not as well off as he had been under slavery, especially if he had been attached to "massa's" Big House.

[28] An analogy is provided by the aged Marshal Pétain of France who, in 1940, collaborated with the German conquerors in setting up a puppet Vichy regime, presumably in the hope of serving France by mitigating the blow of defeat.

[29] R. S. Shryock, "The Nationalistic Tradition of the Civil War: A Southern Analysis," South Atlantic Quar., XXXII (1933), 294–305.

[30] While head of the Freedman's Bureau, General Howard was instrumental in founding Howard University in Washington, D. C., today, as then, a leading institution for blacks.

Yet land, even if distributed, would not have been a cure-all. Black farmers would have encountered serious problems in the best of circumstances, for most of them were without training, capital, and equipment.

Prewar plantations tended to remain largely intact, at least temporarily. Neither the poor Negro nor the poor white benefited at the outset from the economic upheaval to the degree that one might suppose.[31] Substantial improvement in land redistribution came a decade or so later. Even so, freed blacks and poor whites alike tended to sink deeper into the virtual peonage of sharecropping.

WERE THE BLACK CODES UNJUSTIFIED?

The notorious Black Codes of 1865–1866 were passed by the white Southern legislatures to keep the Negro "in his place" (on the plantation) and to provide a dependable labor supply. These laws were nothing new. Before the war they had been enacted to control the slave; now they were modified to control the "free" Negro. Many Northerners saw little difference between the new Black Codes and the old ones; and in truth there was little in some of them. Among all the ill-advised actions of the South after Appomattox, few did more to arouse resentment in the North than the Black Codes. Especially offensive were those that required the Negro to be sold into forced labor for breach of contract or to pay off a fine. Had the North in fact won the war if the freedman was to be plunged back into quasi-slavery?

Some kind of legislation, much less harsh than the Black Codes and designed to insure a stable labor supply, probably was needed. But the South bent the bow too far, for it still did not realize that it had lost a war that in large part was fought to free the slave. Some blacks regarded freedom as freedom from work and flogging, and many of them naturally took off to drink deep of their newfound liberty. But countless thousands, habituated to the plantation routine, preferred to stay, and their former white masters wanted them to remain — "in their place" — as cheap and reliable labor.

Freed Negroes on the whole behaved far better than one might have expected, considering the lifelong resentments built up under the lash. Despite some instances of violence, their record was admirable

---

[31] Similarly, the confiscated Loyalist estates of the American Revolution were slow in being broken up and placed in the hands of small farmers. See H. B. Yoshpe, *The Disposition of Loyalist Estates in the Southern District of the State of New York* (1939).

when compared with that of the blacks in the Congo following the hasty withdrawal of former Belgian overlords in the 1960s. Most ex-slaves evidently had no desire to force their way into white society, and even after they had attained some political power in the Reconstruction legislatures, few of them tried to make themselves socially equal with their former masters.

WERE SOUTHERN LEGISLATURES BLACK DOMINATED?

Few aspects of Reconstruction history are more colored with falsification than the doings of the Negro–carpetbag–scalawag legislatures. White supremacist politicians and historians have traditionally exaggerated the buffooneries of these bodies, which allegedly proved that the blacks were incapable of either voting or governing. The story is too often told in terms of black and white, literally, rather than of the predominant greys.

Many Negroes served in the Reconstruction legislatures, but in only one, that of South Carolina, were they ever in a majority. Even then they numerically controlled only the lower house, largely because the resentful whites had boycotted the polls. Blacks never "dominated" any legislature; leadership was generally left to white men, whether carpetbaggers or scalawags. The part played by ex-slaves was normally that of followers and henchmen; without the support of white Republicans they could not have enjoyed even this role. Some of the Negro legislators were surprisingly well educated and able, especially those former freedmen who had attended schools and colleges abroad or in the North.[32]

Some of the ex-slave legislators were illiterate, and this understandable fact has received much publicity. One Southern newspaper referred to "gibbering, louse-eaten, devil worshipping barbarians." But a contemporary observer could easily find uneducated or semiliterate white men in Southern legislatures, or for that matter in Northern ones. An ill-educated Negro who spoke and understood English was probably better stuff potentially for citizenship than were many of the tens of thousands of illiterate whites from Europe who, unable to speak English, were pouring into America during the postwar years.

[32] James S. Pike, the famous Northern ex-abolitionist journalist, published a classic account in 1874 of the scandalous antics of the black-and-white South Carolina legislature (The Prostrate State). R. F. Durden, in his James Shepherd Pike (1957), has shown that Pike was moved by an animus against the Grant administration to exaggerate Negro legislative buffooneries. But one must be careful not to conclude that there was no truth whatever in the picture he presented.

WERE THE SOUTHERN LEGISLATURES CORRUPT?

Carpetbag–Negro legislatures of the era were undeniably guilty of much extravagance and considerable corruption. This too was regrettable. Two wrongs do not make a right, but such was the postwar "Era of Good Stealings," both North and South, that extravagance and corruption were probably as widespread in the North as in the South. The unsavory Tweed Ring in New York City almost certainly stole more money than all the Reconstruction legislatures combined: there was more to steal. Nor was corruption a monopoly of any one party or race. When the Republican white–Negro legislatures were finally ousted, and replaced by lily-white Democratic legislatures, corruption by no means ceased. In some states it increased. Graft proved to be bipartisan, biracial, bisectional, and bicameral.

Ex-Confederates complained bitterly about the burdensome taxes voted by the Negro–carpetbag–scalawag legislatures. These levies bore heavily on some temporarily disfranchised whites — that is, ex-rebels proscribed by the Fourteenth Amendment and the state constitutions. But the extent of disfranchisement has been overblown. Much of the white nonvoting was due either to apathy or to a stubborn boycott of the polls as a protest against "damnyankee" reconstruction.

Taxes were indeed increased by the "black-and-tan" legislatures, some of whose members owned no real estate. But such levies had generally been low before the war, especially as compared with those in the Northern states, where the costs of free public education were high. Now that the Negro was no longer a slave, the state had to provide for his social welfare, from education to incarceration. (Under slavery, he had received a flogging; under freedom, he received a jail sentence.) Moreover, the devastation caused by the Yankee "vandals" had to be repaired: bridges, schools, courthouses, and other public buildings. When all these charges are totted up, we must conclude that the tax burdens imposed by the new legislatures were not egregiously high, either on an absolute basis or in relation to Northern outlays.

Low income rather than high taxes was the real problem. Impoverished planters in many cases simply did not have the money with which to pay such levies, and tens of thousands of acres were sold under the sheriff's hammer. At one time about one-fifth of Mississippi was advertised for tax sales. Some carpetbag legislators undoubtedly voted higher levies on land in the hope that it could be bought up for a song, by themselves or scheming friends. Relatively few Negroes acquired these cheap acres at the sheriff's sales: they had earned only a few dollars and they were inclined to spend irresponsibly those that they had. Slavery had not bred habits of thrift.

WERE THE NEW LEGISLATURES INEPT?

Perhaps the grossest distortion of all is the accusation that the corruption-riddled Reconstruction legislatures passed no measures worthy of memory and many worthy of infamy. White supremacists, without examining the record, could easily arrive at this conclusion, for out of ignorance, inexperience, extravagance, and favoritism could surely come only evil. Moreover, alleged evidence that the blacks had demonstrated an incapacity for good government provided further justification for excluding them from all government.

In point of fact, the black–carpetbag–scalawag regimes struck many laudable blows for better government.[33] Some of the new state constitutions, adopted by conventions in which Negroes sat, were admirable documents. Indeed, in some instances they were copied copiously from democratic Northern models. Most of these charters were retained by the ex-Confederates, in whole or substantial part, when they regained the driver's seat.

The "clownish" legislatures themselves, to the annoyance of white supremacists, passed many commendable laws. In the prewar era, the South had lagged behind the rest of the nation in forward-looking social and economic legislation. (Much of the blame lay at the door of slavery.) The new legislatures made a determined attempt to catch up with the nineteenth century, and they substantially succeeded when they passed overdue laws for public schools, poorhouses, insane asylums, and other social services. Much of this progressive legislation was retained by the Democratic white South when it returned to power. Many Southerners concluded, with a wry face, that what was good for the blacks could also be good for the whites.

We must also note that the Negro legislators, especially at the outset, were not conspicuously vindictive in imposing penalties on their former white masters. In Mississippi the black members of the legislature petitioned Congress to remove political disabilities from the Confederates; in some of the states the black–carpetbag regimes did a creditable job of administering public affairs. And the Negroes elected to Congress — 22 between 1870 and 1901 — did not perform disgracefully, although on the whole their contributions were not spectacular.

[33] See the pioneer revisionist article by W. E. B. Du Bois, "Reconstruction and Its Benefits," *Amer. Hist. Rev.*, XV (1910), 781–799.

Ironically, many Southern whites were glad to see them go to Washington so that the Northerners might get a dose of their own medicine.[34]

On balance, Southern whites were probably not so much disturbed by what their ex-slaves did as they were by the fact that ex-slaves were doing it — that is, exercising political control. Hypocritically, the federal government in the North, then as later, was conspicuously remiss in appointing qualified Negroes to public office. Even the carpetbaggers and the scalawags were not completely happy over the black instruments that they had to employ, and in 1868 the white Radicals and Conservatives in the Georgia legislature banded together and rashly expelled them — temporarily.

HOW SEVERE WAS MILITARY RECONSTRUCTION?

From 1867 to 1877 reconstruction went forward with federal bayonets, which white Southerners long resented. The brutal truth is that they asked for what they got. Breathing defiance, they spurned reconstruction based on the Fourteenth Amendment, which would have been relatively velvet-gloved. An outraged Congress then lowered the boom with military reconstruction.

Martial law in the United States in time of peace — but was this peace? — is clearly contrary to the spirit, if not the letter, of the Constitution. But during these hectic days the Supreme Court was discreet enough not to arouse unduly the impeachment-minded Radicals in Congress.

Revisionist historians have complained in recent years that too much emphasis has been given to the presence of glittering bayonets. They assert that *only* 20,000 Yankee troops were deployed in all the South to support reconstruction; that these soldiers were stationed only in key spots; and that their number was trifling when compared to the 1,000,000 or so under arms at war's end. The truth is that 20,000 men constituted virtually the entire United States army at the time, exclusive of the forces needed to protect the frontier against Indians. In the eyes of bitter ex-Confederates the presence of *one* Yankee bayonet guarding the polling places was an indignity. The "blue-belly" invaders were reinforced by thousands of Negro militiamen, who, even when

---

[34] Negro historians praise the decorum and accomplishments of the Negro members of Congress; white historians have been prone to speak of them as troublemakers or the tools of their Radical masters. A fair judgment would seem to be that they did routine work that was creditable in view of the numerous handicaps under which they worked. See S. D. Smith, *The Negro in Congress, 1870–1901* (1940).

well behaved, piled indignity on indignity by their very presence.[35] Indicative of their widespread employment is the fact that the governor of South Carolina, a corrupt carpetbagger from Pennsylvania, undertook to arm 20,000 of them before his reelection in 1870.

Federal troops were undoubtedly arbitrary and tough, but such was their nature. Even so, the governments and courts operating under military rule were fairer than commonly supposed, as was generally true of British rule over colonial peoples in the heyday of Empire. There were even some complaints from carpetbaggers and blacks that ex-Confederates were too friendly with the Yankee soldiers; and after the Radical civilian governments took over and the federal troops departed, many Southerners remembered nostalgically the law and order imposed by the military.

The prolonged presence of the federal troops has likewise been exaggerated, although in the eyes of militant ex-Confederates one day of military occupation was one day too much. Tennessee escaped military reconstruction altogether by prudently embracing the Fourteenth Amendment. In the other ten states, the military regime lasted from about three to ten years, and only two stubborn states, Louisiana and South Carolina, brought on themselves the extreme penalty of ten years. The average term of occupancy was much less.[36]

A maximum possible disfranchisement of ex-Confederates was not generally enforced even under military reconstruction. The Democratic whites were simply outvoted by the Republican whites and their black cohorts. Not until the Negro vote was intimidated or destroyed did the tide turn in favor of the Democratic "Redeemers."

HOW EFFECTIVE WAS THE KU KLUX KLAN?

White Democrats ("Redemptionists") in the South finally seized control of "their government" by violence — "organized mayhem." Bursting with indignation over what they regarded as a travesty of decent rule, they employed the doctrine, so familiar to later-day Communists, that the end justifies the means.

The Ku Klux Klan (KKK), contrary to popular fancy, did not

[35] Negro historians speak well of the black militia and their "playful pranks"; white historians are more prone to stress their indiscipline, insolence, and rowdyism. There can be no doubt that their presence helped precipitate a number of bloody clashes and incipient race wars. See Otis A. Singletary, *Negro Militia and Reconstruction* (1957).

[36] For testimony that the army discharged its disagreeable duties creditably, see James E. Sefton, *The United States Army and Reconstruction, 1865–1877* (1967).

spring into being as a protest against Negro–carpetbag rule. It was organized in Tennessee in 1866, nearly a year *before* Congress passed military reconstruction, partly as a prankish social organization and partly to discipline "uppity" ex-slaves. It was then expanded to over-throw the Northern–Negro regimes. Seldom emphasized is the fact that it was spurred along its bloody path by rival Union Leagues, complete with secret rituals, which the Yankees organized among the black Re-publicans.[37]

Night-riding and besheeted white "restorationists," preying on Negro fears and superstitions, persuaded countless thousands of freed-men not to participate in government or even to vote. When mild in-timidation failed, the enforcers resorted to the lash, the torch, the tar kettle, the castration knife, the noose, and the bullet. Hundreds of blacks were brutally murdered in attacks or in mass lynchings, as were a few white Republicans. The most luridly publicized of the night-riders represented the Ku Klux Klan, although the Knights of the White Camellia were more numerous. There were also dozens of other groups using terrorism. (Some of the outrages were no doubt committed by criminals who, as "bogus Klansmen," simply donned sheets.) The Klan was officially and temporarily curbed by iron-toothed Congressional laws, but it assumed other forms — such as rifle clubs ("Mother's Little Helpers") — and continued what was essentially guerrilla warfare.[38]

Deadly though terrorism was in reducing unwanted votes and voters, economic reprisals were probably equally effective. Negroes who participated in political activity lost their jobs, just as some black "free-dom marchers" in the South during the 1960s were photographed by police and then dismissed.

DID THE 14TH AMENDMENT INSURE CIVIL RIGHTS?

A noteworthy effort to protect the Negro's civil rights was the Four-teenth Amendment (1868), which attempted to make the freedman a citizen — a second- or third-class citizen as events proved. This safe-guard, like the Thirteenth, was in a broad sense illegal — if there can be such a thing as an unconstitutional constitutional amendment. The Southern states ratified it under duress and at a time when Congress

[37] James E. Sefton, "A Note on the Political Intimidation of Black Men by Other Black Men," *Ga. Hist. Quar.*, LII (1968), 443–448.

[38] The Force Acts of 1870–1871, though belated, were reasonably effective in curbing the Klan until 1874, when Northern apathy and Southern defiance contrived to make them virtual dead letters. Everette Swinney, "Enforcing the Fifteenth Amendment," *Jour. of Southern Hist.*, XVIII (1962), 202–218.

did not regard them as states. Without their votes, the requisite three-fourths of the states could not be lined up; hence they were forced to approve the amendment before they could return to the Union fold.[39]

Actually the Fourteenth Amendment proved to be a cruel hoax as far as the Negro was concerned. For generations it was flagrantly violated in the South, and it further contrived to raise up a nation of scofflaws. For more than a century the black was forced to struggle for his full civil rights under the Amendment. But in one unexpected quarter it proved to be a resounding success. The federal courts later held that a corporation was a legal "person"; and since no "person" could be deprived of his rights without "due process of law," the Fourteenth Amendment was effectively used by giant corporations to prevent the states from imposing regulatory controls on them. Charles and Mary Beard in 1927 gave wide currency to the view, earlier expressed by ex-Senator Conkling in 1882, that this language was deviously inserted into the Amendment to shield big business. But the so-called evidence supporting this conspiracy thesis is flimsy at best.[40]

DID THE 15TH AMENDMENT ENFRANCHISE NEGROES?

The Fifteenth Amendment, adopted in 1870, does not guarantee to anyone the right to vote. Under the federal Constitution, the individual states established qualifications for voters. The Fifteenth Amendment stipulates that no one shall be *denied* the vote because "of race, color, or previous condition of servitude [slavery]."

Like its sister Fourteenth Amendment, the Fifteenth Amendment was forced on the South, or at least on four of the still unreconstructed states, as a precondition for ending military reconstruction. It was likewise extorted under duress, and in this sense it was unconstitutional in spirit. It was obviously designed by Republicans in Congress to preserve the Negro vote in the South against that day when the ex-Confederates would return to power, rewrite their constitutions, and disfranchise the blacks. (Provision had already been made for the Negro vote in the new state constitutions set up under military rule.)

To a degree, the ballot was forced on the illiterate or semi-literate black by Republican whites in the North. Concern for their

[39] The representation in Congress of those Southern states that denied the Negro the vote was to have been reduced by the Fourteenth Amendment, but this provision was never enforced.

[40] See Charles A. Beard and Mary Beard, *The Rise of American Civilization* (1927), II, 112–113; J. B. James, *The Framing of the Fourteenth Amendment* (1956); Howard J. Graham, *Everyman's Constitution* (1968), Chs. I, II.

own political power coincided with consideration for the welfare of the freedmen. Some Negro leaders had been demanding the vote from the outset, arguing that the ballot itself was a "schoolmaster." But we may doubt that the great mass of ex-slaves panted for this boon, even assuming that they knew what it was. (Some even deposited their marked ballots in mailboxes or in hollow trees.) Many Northern leaders contended, including President Lincoln, that gradual suffrage for educated and propertied Negroes would be better for all concerned. Southerners were quick to point out that Northern states, while forcing Negro suffrage and officeholding on the South, conspicuously and hypocritically denied both the ballot and the office to their tiny black minority.[41]

Southern whites did not object so much to the Negro's voting as they did to his voting with the white "renegade" and "interloper" to lord it over them. They probably would have welcomed the black vote if it could have been used to dislodge the carpetbag–scalawag regimes. This conclusion is borne out by what happened when the last supportive federal bayonets were withdrawn in 1877 and "home rule" was restored. For about two decades longer some Negroes sat in Southern legislatures, and many blacks continued not only to vote but to vote the Democratic ticket. But in the 1890s Populism, an agrarian reform movement sweeping the Plains states, invaded the South, where the Negroes potentially held the balance of political power. These black pawns could no longer be counted on to support the white ruling class; hence the whites decided to rob them of their vote. This was done by stuffed ballot boxes, literacy tests (unfairly administered by whites to the advantage of whites), and similar trickery. By the turn of the century the Negro vote in the South was virtually eliminated, and it did not again emerge as a factor of consequence until about a half century later.

Jim Crow — the symbol of segregation — was perhaps more a child of the 1890s than of the Reconstruction 1870s.[42] For about two decades after emancipation considerable numbers of blacks, though by no means all, sat beside whites in public conveyances, restaurants, and theaters. But disfranchisement in the 1890s brought its twin brother, ironclad segregation. Ironically, later generations of white Southerners

[41] After the desegregration decision of the Supreme Court in 1954, Southerners complained bitterly that the North forced *de jure* integration on them while retaining *de facto* segregation in its schools.

[42] Jim Crow, a song-and-dance Negro character played by blackfaced Thomas D. Rice of New York ("the father of American minstrelsy"), was immensely popular in minstrel shows beginning approximately 1830. C. Vann Woodward, *The Strange Career of Jim Crow* (2nd rev. ed., 1966) is the standard work. The first edition, published in 1955, left the false impression that there had been little or no Jim Crowism in the South before the 1890s. Actually there had always been some segregation, and there had been some Jim Crow laws during Reconstruction.

would not tolerate the same intimate contacts which many of their fathers had taken for granted for a generation or so after the Civil War. Jim Crowism even went so far as to provide separate Bibles in the courts for the witnesses to kiss. Thus the "counter-Reconstruction" engineered by the Southern whites finally achieved complete success, with "separate but equal" facilities that were always separate but seldom equal.

DID THE MONROE DOCTRINE SAVE MEXICO FROM FRANCE?

Military reconstruction, although virtually completed during President Grant's eight years, was inaugurated under President Johnson. But there was much more to the ex-tailor's administration than reconstruction. The second half of his troubled term was brightened by twin triumphs in foreign affairs. In the same year, 1867, two monarchical flags left the mainland of the Americas permanently: those of Tsarist Russia and Napoleonic France.

Behind the smoke screen of Civil War, the theatrical and ambitious Napoleon III had played a dangerous game. He challenged the Monroe Doctrine frontally by placing his puppet, Maximilian of Austria, on the throne of once-republican Mexico. This synthetic regime, which lasted about four years, finally collapsed when Napoleon withdrew supporting French troops and left Maximilian to face a Mexican firing squad.

Americans have taken much pride in the belief that pressure from Washington, backed by one million battle-hardened veterans, brought about the humiliation of Napoleon III. But the story is not that simple. Various additional pressures were operating, including the cost of the adventure to thrifty French taxpayers, the rise of a powerful Germany under Bismarck, and the relentless guerrilla warfare waged by the Mexican patriot Juárez (with United States support). America's Civil War army had been largely demobilized, but another potent force could have been mobilized if needed.[43]

Napoleon's spectacular challenge to the Monroe Doctrine — the most dangerous up to that point in its history — resulted in a complete vindication of that Doctrine. But the oddity is that Secretary of State Seward, in his diplomatic interchanges with Paris, did not once mention Monroe by name, even though the implications were clear. This critical episode taught a lasting lesson. If the United States has enough power and is willing to wield it, Washington does not have to invoke the doctrines of long-dead Presidents. When the nation has the Big Stick, it

[43] See Henry Blumenthal, *A Reappraisal of Franco–American Relations, 1830–1871* (1959).

can speak softly and get results; when it has no effective muscle, it can shout loudly and get no results.[44]

DID THE AMERICANS REALLY WANT ALASKA?

The purchase of Alaska (then called Russian America) was a happier tale, with a less melodramatic ending. Like Louisiana in 1803, this vast expanse virtually fell into America's lap. In later years the Communist "line" was that the stupid Tsar had been gulled by the fast-talking Yankees, and that since the transaction was therefore illegal, the territory should be handed back.

Actually the Russians were looking for a convenient purchaser on whom to unload Alaska, for they found it costly to maintain and difficult to defend. In the event of another Anglo–Russian war, the powerful British fleet probably would seize it. The Tsar possibly could have sold Alaska to England, thus rounding out Canada, but he had no desire to strengthen his archfoe. He much preferred to bolster Britain's chief rival in the Western Hemisphere. The Russians therefore dangled the Alaskan bait before the overeager expansionist, Secretary of State Seward, who seized the hook with voracity and signed a purchase treaty with celerity.

Seward's zeal was not shared by the American people. They were not in an expansionist mood after the blood-draining Civil War, and many of them did not have the foggiest idea where Alaska was. Why spend good money for walrus-covered icebergs? But once Seward had signed the treaty, America could not affront the Tsar by hurling this ice-covered liability back into his teeth — the same Tsar who presumably had helped save the Union by scaring off French and British interventionists with his two fleets in 1863.[45] So the Senate approved the treaty and the House passed the appropriation of $7,200,000, albeit under protest and with some Russian gold exchanging hands for necessary votes.[46] Many reluctant Americans were willing to gamble that the dubious "bargain" would "pan out" — as it ultimately did.

[44] When President Kennedy forced the Soviets to withdraw their missiles from Cuba in 1962, he did not invoke the Monroe Doctrine against this frontal challenge. But he wielded the (nuclear) Big Stick, and the Russians backed down.

[45] For this Russian myth, see above, pp. 394–395.

[46] The rumor has gained some currency that $1,400,000 of the total purchase price of $7,200,000 was an under-the-table payment by the United States for the expenses of sending the Russian fleets to America in 1863. See A. W. Lane and L. H. Wall, eds., *The Letters of Franklin K. Lane* (1922), pp. 260–261. This tale is without foundation, though further credited in Drew Pearson and Jack Anderson, *U. S. A. — Second-Class Power?* (1958), p. 303.

President Johnson's harassed administration was thus credited with two memorable strokes in foreign affairs — Mexico and Alaska — and Secretary of State Seward deserves a lion's share of the praise.[47]

DID THE BLACKS WIN THEIR FREEDOM?

The illusory nature of overnight liberation was perhaps never better expressed than by Frederick Douglass, the famed ex-slave, abolitionist, orator, and journalist, who wrote in his memoirs (1882):

> Though slavery was abolished, the wrongs of my people were not ended. Though they were not slaves, they were not yet quite free. No man can be truly free whose liberty is dependent upon the thought, feeling, and action of others, and who has himself no means in his own hands for guarding, protecting, defending, and maintaining that liberty. Yet the Negro after his emancipation was precisely in this state of destitution.
>
> The law on the side of freedom is of great advantage only where there is power to make that law respected. I know no class of my fellow men, however just, enlightened, and humane, which can be wisely and safely trusted absolutely with the liberties of any other class. Protestants are excellent people, but it would not be wise for Catholics to depend entirely upon them to look after their rights and interests. Catholics are a pretty good sort of people (though there is a soul-shuddering history behind them); yet no enlightened Protestants would commit their liberty to their care and keeping.
>
> And yet the government had left the freedmen in a worse condition than either of these. It felt that it had done enough for him. It had made him free, and henceforth he must make his own way in the world, or, as the slang phrase has it, "root, pig, or die." Yet he had none of the conditions for self-preservation or self-protection.
>
> He was free from the individual master, but the slave of society. He had neither money, property, nor friends. He was free from the old plantation, but he had nothing but the dusty road under his feet. He was free from the old quarter that once gave him shelter, but a slave to the rains of summer and the frosts of winter. He was, in a word, literally turned loose, naked, hungry, and destitute, to the open sky.
>
> The first feeling toward him by the old master classes was full of bitterness and wrath. They resented his emancipation as an act of hostility toward them, and, since they could not punish the emanci-

[47] See Glyndon G. Van Deusen, *William Henry Seward* (1967).

pator, they felt like punishing the object which the act had emancipated. Hence they drove him off the old plantation, and told him he was no longer wanted there. They not only hated him because he had been freed as a punishment to them, but because they felt that they had been robbed of his labor.

An element of greater bitterness still came into their hearts: the freedman had been the friend of the government, and many of his class had borne arms against them during the war. The thought of paying cash for labor that they could formerly extort by the lash did not in any wise improve their disposition to the emancipated slave, or improve his own condition.

Now, since poverty has, and can have, no chance against wealth, the landless against the landowner, the ignorant against the intelligent, the freedman was powerless. He had nothing left him but a slavery-distorted and diseased body, and lame and twisted limbs, with which to fight the battle of life.[48]

WHO WON THE NORTH–SOUTH STRUGGLE?

No doubt the North won militarily, but in many respects it finally lost the war after the war, when the fighting was continued in other guises. The Northerners were able to gain general acceptance of their version of the war and its causes; the white Southerners were able to win general acceptance of their version of reconstruction and its tragedies.

Ex-Confederate conservatives, in the role of Bourbon[49] "Redeemers," ultimately secured complete control of all the state governments when the last supporting Yankee bayonets were withdrawn in 1877, as was seemingly inevitable. None of the federally reconstructed state governments endured more than nine years, and they all fell again into the hands of the same white ruling class that had brought on secession. Southern stubbornness finally beat Northern high-handedness.

One is tempted to say that the South was never completely reconstructed, but that it continued to live as a section apart. Governed for a time by an outside power, it continued to bear many of the marks of a colonial province, whether economically, politically, culturally, or psychologically. The great Chicago fire of 1871 was greeted with much satisfaction in Yankee-scorched Dixie: one prominent Southerner gleefully remarked, "the wind is in our favor." As the only great section

---

[48] *Life and Times of Frederick Douglass* (1882), pp. 458–59.

[49] The exiled Bourbons of France, finally returned to power after the French Revolution, were so reactionary as to cause cynics to say, "A Bourbon never learns and never forgets."

since 1783 ever to feel the heel of the conqueror, the South has been conspicuous in movements for military preparedness, particularly when Hitler was on the loose in the 1930s and early 1940s.

The Southerners lost their slaves but gained freedom from the burdens of slavery, while retaining the whip hand over former bondsmen. The blacks slipped into a state of peonage, then disfranchisement, then segregation — all three. During and after the World War of 1914–1918, hundreds of thousands of Negroes left for the North, partly propelled from the South and partly attracted by more promising economic opportunities in the North. They brought intensified racial problems to cities such as New York, Chicago, Detroit, and Los Angeles, to the not-too-secret satisfaction of many Southerners.

What came to be known as the solid South solidified into a Democratic stronghold for several generations. Southern members of Congress, elected from "safe" districts, rose by seniority to the chairmanships of powerful committees. There they could promote legislation favorable to the South, bottle up bills desired by the North, or filibuster to death bills reported to the floor of the Senate. They exercised influence in grotesque disproportion to the voting population of the states that they represented. With the coming of the Democrats to power in 1933 under Franklin Roosevelt's New Deal, vast industrial and defense establishments, backed by federal funds, blossomed forth in Texas and elsewhere in Dixieland.

These latter-day developments did much to quiet the chronic, and not altogether groundless, complaints of Southerners that they had long been kept in a state of economic vassalage. They resented exploitation by Northern capital (timberland bought for fifty cents an acre and then ravaged), as well as discrimination in banking practices and railroad rates. They deplored the century-old necessity of selling their agricultural products in a low-priced world market and having to buy their manufactured goods in a high-priced market — the result of Yankee-imposed tariffs. Yet even before Franklin Roosevelt's New Deal, a change was taking place, for thousands of cotton spindles had left New England to seek Southern climes, where they would enjoy proximity to cheap fiber, cheap land, cheap labor, and cheap water. Yankee New England clearly lost the textile war.

Nor did Calhounism expire in the South. Nullification reigned anew, as the Fourteenth and Fifteenth Amendments were universally flouted. States' rights and the ancient doctrine of state interposition against the federal government really never died and were revived conspicuously following the desegregation decision of the Supreme Court in 1954. In the subsequent battle over equality for Negroes, the rebel yell rose again, the KKK rode again, and the Stars and Bars were again widely displayed, in one state capital higher than the Stars and Stripes. A states' rights presidential candidate (Thurmond) carried four Southern states in 1948; another (Wallace) carried five Southern states in 1968.

The "Rebellion" collapsed in 1865, but a rebellious spirit survived. Today all eleven states of the former Confederacy (plus Kentucky) observe the birthdays of President Jefferson Davis and General Robert E. Lee.

ADDITIONAL GENERAL REFERENCES

J. G. Randall and David Donald, *The Civil War and Reconstruction* (rev. ed., 1969); K. M. Stampp, *The Era of Reconstruction, 1865–1877* (1965); R. W. Patrick, *The Reconstruction of the Nation* (1967); Avery Craven, *Reconstruction: The Ending of the Civil War* (1969); J. H. Franklin, *Reconstruction: After the Civil War* (1961); E. L. McKitrick, *Andrew Johnson and Reconstruction* (1960); W. R. Brock, *An American Crisis: Congress and Reconstruction, 1865–1867* (1963); La Wanda and J. H. Cox, *Politics, Principle, and Prejudice, 1865–1866* (1963); W. A. Dunning, *Reconstruction, Political and Economic, 1865–1877* (1907); H. K. Beale, *The Critical Year* (1930); David Donald, *Charles Sumner and the Rights of Man* (1970); E. M. Coulter, *The South During Reconstruction, 1865–1877* (1947); F. B. Simkins, *The South, Old and New* (1947); P. H. Buck, *The Road to Reunion, 1865–1900* (1937); H. L. Trefousse, *The Radical Republicans* (1969); R. P. Sharkey, *Money, Class and Party: An Economic Study of Civil War and Reconstruction* (1959); W. E. B. Du Bois, *Black Reconstruction in America, 1860–1880* (1935); J. M. McPherson, *The Struggle for Equality: Abolitionists and the Negro in the Civil War and Reconstruction* (1964); Robert Cruden, *The Negro in Reconstruction* (1969); Fawn Brodie, *Thaddeus Stevens: Scourge of the South* (1959).

22

Politics from Grant to Harrison, 1869-1889

The two decades from 1869 to 1889 were years of Republican ascendancy in Washington, except for the last four, when the Democrats returned to power. In 1869 the Republicans elevated to the presidency the politically inexperienced war hero, General Grant, who, despite a scandal-ridden administration, continued to be popular enough to win reelection overwhelmingly in 1872. True to tradition, the Grand Old Party remained committed to big business, the protective tariff, and a heavy-handed reconstruction of the South.

President Hayes succeeded Grant in 1877, but only after an electoral contest with the Democrat Tilden that was bitterly fought and heatedly disputed. Republicans and Democrats alike were guilty of gross irregularities. One high price that Hayes paid for Democratic acquiescence in his election (the "great fraud") was to promise to withdraw supportive bayonets from the two remaining carpetbag governments in the South: Louisiana and South Carolina. Happily he managed to restore a degree of respectability to the scandal-tainted Republicans, and on the whole gave the country an honest and courageous administration.

After another tight election the Republican James A. Garfield was sent to the White House in 1881, only to be fatally shot nearly five months later by a deranged and disappointed office seeker. Vice President Chester A. Arthur, a New York politician who unexpectedly met the challenge of his high responsibilities, presided over the implementation of the landmark Pendleton Civil Service Reform Act of 1883.

Grover Cleveland, a leading Democrat, assumed the Presidency in 1885, after defeating James G. Blaine, the perennial Republican aspirant, in an agonizingly close contest. One of Cleveland's greatest achievements was to restore confidence in the capacity of "the party of the Rebellion" to govern. With his various veto messages and his sensational appeal for reforming the tariff, he demonstrated a rare brand of political courage. Yet he was defeated for reelection in 1888 by the Republican nominee, Benjamin Harrison, though only by a narrow margin and as the result of various mischances.

WAS GRANT A COMPLETE FAILURE AS PRESIDENT?

There can be no doubt that in statecraft Grant was inexperienced and naive, and that posterity would think better of him if he had not ventured out beyond his depth into the whirlpool of public affairs. But if one is to apportion blame, one cannot avoid pointing an accusing finger at the American people. They displayed a lack of political maturity that matched Grant's when they drafted yet another war hero for this exalted office. He was twice nominated unanimously by the Republican national convention and both times won the ensuing election by a substantial margin. In 1880 the unwritten third-term barrier narrowly kept him from the Republican nomination and probable election: he led all other rivals on the first thirty-five ballots. If he was a disaster as President, the voters evidently did not think so. Writing to Congress in his "farewell apology" address, he candidly acknowledged the mistakes of inexperience without confessing failure.

Moral standards had broken down, primarily as a result of the Civil War, and corruption was rampant. The "eight long years of scandal" probably would have existed with or without Grant, though perhaps in a less acute form. Several of the worst episodes associated with the era had developed before the silent general entered the White House. But they came to a head during his presidency and reflected grave discredit on him, especially the Crédit Mobilier railroad scandal (which involved the bribery of certain Congressmen) and the Tweed Ring in New York (which was entirely a municipal grafting operation on an imperial scale). To blame Grant for these misdeeds would be as logical as to blame him for the great Chicago fire, which raged in 1871 during his first administration, or the Custer "massacre," which occurred in 1876 at the hotly contested battle with the Indians at the Little Big Horn River in Montana.[1]

---

[1] George Custer had fallen into disfavor with Grant; and a desire to redeem himself probably accounted in part for his rash attack. He knew that the enemy was

Grant admittedly made some bad appointments, as all Presidents do, including Lincoln, but more than most. In his case he showed a misplaced sense of loyalty in covering up for his subordinates, as President Truman later did, when they were caught with their hands near the cookie jar. A notorious instance was the involvement of his private secretary in the Whiskey Ring scandal, which involved robbing the Treasury of revenue. Grant also showed an inexcusable lack of delicacy by being seen in public with a pair of financial buccaneers, Fisk and Gould, prior to their disruptive attempt in 1869 to corner the gold market during a memorable "Black Friday" on Wall Street.

The war hero in a politician's coat was saved from some costly blunders by others. He proposed to recognize prematurely the Cuban insurgents in 1869 during their struggle against Spain but was quietly spared this embarrassment by Secretary of State Fish. Grant's determined attempt to annex Santo Domingo, partly in response to pressure from American speculators, was blocked by the United States Senate, with Senator Sumner playing a leading role.

Congress deserves much of the credit or blame for what happened during these troubled years. It failed to support the feeble civil service commission that it had authorized, though Grant mildly recommended reform. It passed legislation in 1871 designed to crush the opposition of the Ku Klux Klan to military reconstruction. And in 1872 it voted amnesty for practically all those ex-Confederates excluded from office by the 14th Amendment.

Despite the scandal-cursed administration, life did go on. Grant stood foursquare for sound money, and the nation rode through the cyclical Panic of 1873 (which could not be blamed on the White House). In an exhibition of courage, the General vetoed an inflationary money bill in 1874, and the next year Congress voted to resume the redemption of paper currency with specie (effective 1879). Under Grant's aegis, military reconstruction was almost completed; the nation continued to bulge awesomely westward; the industrial machine roared at an increasingly impressive rate. Peace was preserved, despite grave danger of war with Britain (*Alabama* claims) and with Spain (the *Virginius* affair).[2]

---

far more numerous, and he unwisely divided his command into three units, which, as might have been anticipated, failed to synchronize their movements. His detachment of some 250 men was wiped out. A large body of literature has sprung up dealing with the alleged blame of various participants. See Edgar I. Stewart, *Custer's Luck* (1955).

[2] The *Virginius*, registered under the U. S. flag but secretly owned by Cubans, was carrying arms to the Cuban insurgents. It was seized on the high seas by a Spanish warship, following which some fifty men on board, including Americans, were shot as pirates. Diplomacy finally effected an amicable solution.

Grant was clearly one of the most inept of the Presidents, but not even he was a complete failure.[3]

WERE THE BRITISH
GOOD SPORTSMEN IN THE "ALABAMA" CASE?

During and after the Civil War the Northerners developed a deep bitterness toward Britain over the pro-Southern lapses of the London government. The most burning grievance of all was the failure of the British authorities to exert themselves to prevent Confederate commerce destroyers such as the *Alabama*, openly built in England, from escaping to sea and ravaging Yankee shipping. Many Northerners believed that the sympathy and aid, direct or indirect, thus received by the South lengthened the war by at least two years. Senator Sumner of Massachusetts delivered a sensational speech in Congress on April 13, 1869, in which he declared that this prolongation increased the bill for damages to more than $2 billion. Such preposterous demands chilled all hope of settlement.

At length the British, thanks in part to the skillful diplomacy of Secretary of State Hamilton Fish (perhaps Grant's luckiest appointment), signed the epochal Treaty of Washington in 1871. Among its numerous provisions, Britain agreed to submit Washington's demands to arbitration, under terms that would almost guarantee the payment of some *direct* damages to America for the ravages of the Confederate raiders. This is precisely what happened when the designated arbitral tribunal, meeting in Geneva in 1872, assessed the London government $15,500,000. The award was more than enough to take care of the most valid Yankee claims.

Why did Great Britain, the number one naval power, consent to an arbitration in which she was bound to lose? Was it because the British conscience was so deeply troubled by official negligence during the Civil War years as to want to make amends?

There were clearly some English liberals who felt that their government had been criminally negligent in this sorry business, and they wanted to wipe the slate clean. But probably more important was the realization that the London officials had created a dangerous precedent. In the end, it might boomerang upon their own shippers, who possessed the largest merchant marine in the world. Henceforth, when

---

[3] See John A. Carpenter, *Ulysses S. Grant* (1970) for one of the more convincing efforts to rehabilitate Grant as President.

the British were at war with some small and landlocked power, what was to prevent their enemy from buying or building raiders in the United States which would sally forth to ravage Great Britain's commerce? There were thousands of Irishmen in America who hated England fiercely enough to contribute funds to such ventures, and even to man the ships themselves.[4]

Britishers were happy to have this damaging precedent erased from the books by the Geneva tribunal, although not overjoyed at being assessed $15,500,000 for their laxness. If, in the future, unfriendly nations should seek to harm Britain by permitting such unneutral activity, they might be restrained by the knowledge that they would ultimately be presented with an immense bill for damages.

WAS THE TREATY OF WASHINGTON A CLEAR GAIN?

The landmark Treaty of Washington (1871), concluded between Britain and the United States, was in some respects more important for its by-products than for its provisions. By establishing the Geneva Tribunal, it created a milestone in the troubled history of international arbitration. By arranging for the settlement of several vexatious disputes, it dispelled ominous war clouds and inaugurated a new day in Anglo–American relations. And by generating a more favorable atmosphere, it made possible the dismantling of Canadian border fortifications, thereby extending to land the principle of disarmament on the Great Lakes established by the Rush–Bagot Agreement of 1817.[5]

But on a dollar-and-cents basis the final settlements proved disappointing to many Americans. Those red-blooded patriots who had backed indirect damages to the tune of $2 billion or more felt that the $15,500,000 awarded was small potatoes indeed.

Additionally, the Treaty of Washington made provision for a commission of three men to consider general claims on both sides. This body met in Washington from 1871 to 1873. It disallowed all American claims, while awarding damages to Britain in the sum of $1,929,819, most of which represented the seizure of British merchant ships as a result of illegal Union blockade practices.

---

[4] See F. E. Gibson, *The Attitudes of the New York Irish toward State and National Affairs, 1848–1892* (1951); Thomas N. Brown, *Irish–American Nationalism, 1870–1890* (1966). In 1881 the Irish–American inventor, John P. Holland, built an operable submarine with Irish Fenian funds. Launched in the Hudson River, it was designed to destroy the British fleet. *Dictionary of American Biography*, IX, p. 145.

[5] C. P. Stacey, "The Myth of the Unguarded Frontier, 1815–1871," *Amer. Hist. Rev.*, LVI (1950), 1–18.

Negotiators of the Treaty of Washington had also arranged for compensation to Britain (actually the Canadians) for continuing to grant fishing privileges to the Americans. A commission of three men met in Halifax in 1877 and awarded the British $5,500,000, despite heated American protests.

By these two adverse decisions, the $15,500,000 allotted to the United States at Geneva was watered down to a net of about $8 million. But this figure was vastly smaller than the cost of a full-dress war between the two nations. The outcome was a gain for peace and sanity.

DID GREELEY DOOM THE LIBERAL REPUBLICANS?

Reformist dissatisfaction with the Republican party over the scandals of the Grant administration inspired the Liberal Republican revolt in 1872 — one of the few significant third-party movements in American history. Its primary goals were civil service reform and a more lenient reconstruction of the South.

One often reads that the Liberal Republican nominating convention, meeting in Cincinnati, fell into the hands of scheming politicians. They allegedly manipulated the conclave of starry-eyed cranks and came up with the nomination of an erratic and outspoken newspaper editor, freakish-appearing Horace Greeley. The assumption is that Grant might have been beaten for reelection if this convention had only chosen an outstanding statesman, like the coldly reserved Charles Francis Adams, son of President John Quincy Adams and grandson of President John Adams.

Adams was unquestionably able, but he was not an ideal vote-getter. Aside from aloofness, he was burdened by his family heritage, which was anti-Jackson and anti-Democratic and consequently unappealing to the Western masses. Regarded as an England-lover (he had been U. S. Minister in London during the Civil War), he repelled hundreds of thousands of Irish–American voters. He did not even have the full support of the anti-Grant malcontents in his own Massachusetts, and he had given no positive word that he would accept the nomination if tendered. In these circumstances one is surprised that he fared as well as he did in the balloting at Cincinnati: [6]

---

[6] After the sixth ballot was taken, Greeley led Adams by a narrow margin, but a shift of votes promptly made the count 482 to 187. Edward Stanwood, *A History of the Presidency* (1898), p. 344.

	1st	2d	3d	4th	5th	6th
Charles Francis Adams, Mass.	203	243	264	279	258	324
Horace Greeley, N. Y.	147	245	258	251	309	332
Lyman Trumbull, Ill.	110	148	156	141	81	19
B. Gratz Brown, Mo.	95	2	2	2	2	0
David Davis, Ill.	92½	75	41	51	30	6

It is evident that Greeley was in strong contention as a candidate from the outset and that the convention chose him in the belief that he would poll more votes than Charles Francis Adams or any of the other hopefuls. He was an eccentric appearing man; he supported radical causes such as women's rights; and he had shown erratic judgment as an editor. But he had also displayed moral courage by signing Jefferson Davis' bail bond and urging a warm handclasp across the North–South "bloody chasm." He staged an active public-appearance campaign (which was unusual for presidential candidates in that day), speaking to large audiences and delivering with effectiveness a number of speeches with substantial intellectual content. As the influential editor of the New York *Tribune* for many years, he had become a household word, and he was able to capitalize on his fame.

Probably no nominee trotted out by the Liberal Republicans could have defeated Grant. There is little reason to believe that Charles Francis Adams, or even some other candidate, would have done substantially better than the badly beaten Horace Greeley.[7]

WAS "THE CRIME OF '73" CRIME OR COLLUSION?

In 1873 Congress passed a law formally dropping the standard silver dollar from the list of coins minted by the Treasury. The ostensible reason was that for some years the western miners of silver bullion had not been presenting it for coinage because it was worth more in the commercial market. In 1872 the metal in a dollar brought $1.03.

By 1876 the price of silver had sagged badly, owing largely to increased production in the West. A renewal of the coinage of bullion into the old standard dollar would have profited the miners, but now this outlet was closed. For more than two decades the cry "The Crime

[7] See M. T. Downey, "Horace Greeley and the Politicians: The Liberal Republican Convention of 1872," *Jour. of Am. Hist.*, LIII (1967), 727–750.

of '73" rose from the throats of Westerners, debtors, and others with a stake in the wholesale coinage of silver. The implication was that the gold-standard men, working hand in glove with the gold-standard British, had entered into some kind of conspiracy in Congress to rob the silverites and enrich the bondholders, at a time when this dark deed would pass unnoticed.

Actually the basic facts reveal no dark conspiracy. By 1872 the officials in the Treasury Department, with abundant data in their possession, could forecast the imminent upsurge of silver production and the subsequent cheapening of the metal. They feared that a debasing of the currency with subpar dollars would result in serious inflation and hence would damage both the public credit and the creditor class. These experts also believed that the United States would be on sounder ground if, like Britain, it adopted the gold standard. The Treasury Department made its information available to certain interested Congressmen, notably Senator Sherman of Ohio, Chairman of the Senate Finance Committee. The bill that demonetized the dollar passed in 1873, after protracted debate in several sessions of Congress, and with the support of many members from the silver states who were not fully aware of what they were doing.

"The Crime of '73" was clearly not a crime.[8] It could better be called "The Collusion of '73." There were conspirators, of a sort. They did not advertise fully and candidly the economics of the situation and the imminent overproduction of silver. But their collusion, despite later charges of dishonesty, was not designed to line their own pockets but to strengthen the public credit. In this they evidently succeeded.[9]

WAS TILDEN "ROBBED" OF THE PRESIDENCY?

One of the few clear aspects of the confused presidential election of 1876 is that Samuel J. Tilden (Democrat) polled about 250,000 more popular votes than Rutherford B. Hayes (Republican). Yet the special Electoral Commission, by a strictly partisan vote of 8 to 7, awarded Hayes every one of the twenty electoral votes in dispute (involving four states). Hayes was declared the winner, 185 to 184.

[8] In the eyes of many Liberal Republicans, the real "crime of 1873" was the second inauguration of Grant.

[9] Allen Weinstein, "Was There a 'Crime of 1873'?: The Case of the Demonetized Dollar," *Jour. of Amer. Hist.*, LIV (1967), 307–326; Allen Weinstein, *Prelude to Populism: Origins of the Silver Issue, 1867–1878* (1970); W. T. K. Nugent, *Money and American Society, 1865–1880* (1968).

There have been two other presidential elections in which the loser polled a substantially larger popular vote than the winner. These occurred when J. Q. Adams defeated Jackson in 1824–1825, and when Harrison bested Grover Cleveland in 1888. With the Electoral College subject to inequities, the popular-vote winners in all three cases were the victims of an antiquated system.

When three of the Southern states in 1876 presented conflicting sets of returns, they created a situation for which there was no relevant law or constitutional directive. The American people are to be commended, in a situation which might have produced a new Civil War, for having devised a solution through the temporary bipartisan Electoral Commission of fifteen.[10]

Neither side came into or out of the contested election with completely clean hands. The Republicans undoubtedly were the beneficiaries of many fraudulent votes.[11] The Democrats in the South frightened away from the polls countless black (Republican) voters by threats, violence, and outright murder. Possibly enough Negroes were thus "bulldozed" to account for Tilden's popular plurality.

HAS THE COMPROMISE OF 1877 BEEN UNDERRATED?

For many years scholars believed that after the Electoral Commission had been formed (in itself a compromise solution), the electoral deadlock was broken by a simple concession. Hayes, the story goes, promised that when he became President he would withdraw the last interfering federal troops from the South. Two Republican carpetbag governments, those in South Carolina and Louisiana, were then being supported by Yankee soldiers. Their departure would mean that the Democrats would gain control. Eager though the Democrats were to rule in Washington, they were to some extent mollified by the promise of a rapid return to home rule in these two states.

[10] The fifteenth member was to have been an independent Supreme Court justice with Democratic leanings, David Davis of Illinois. But at the eleventh hour he accepted election to the Senate, and his departure left only Republicans on the high court from which to draw the fifteenth member. There is reason to believe that Mr. Justice Bradley, on the Electoral Commission, decided to cast the crucial vote for Tilden, but at the last minute changed his mind. C. Vann Woodward, *Reunion and Reaction: The Compromise of 1877 and the End of Reconstruction* (rev. ed., 1956), pp. 167, 172–174.

[11] Further evidence that Tilden was "robbed" in Florida appears in J. H. Shofner, "Florida in the Balance: The Electoral Count of 1876," *Fla. Hist. Quar.*, XLVII (1968), 122–150.

Modern scholarship, especially that of C. Vann Woodward, has revealed that the wirepulling behind the scenes was much more complex.[12] Over a period of many weeks informal negotiations resulted in a number of "understandings" between the Republicans and the Tildenites. Hayes would be permitted to take his seat, despite the blatant partisanship of the Electoral Commission, in return for the reassignment of the troops, plus other assurances. He would have to appoint a Southern Democrat to his Cabinet, permit the awarding of a considerable number of the federal offices to Democrats, and show a friendly attitude toward Southern needs, especially financial grants for internal improvements, including railroads.

Many of these alleged promises were not kept, conspicuously those regarding internal improvements, but overall the Compromise of 1877 must rank as one of the major political achievements of American history.[13] In 1861 the Northern Republicans and the Southern Democrats were unable to agree on the Crittenden Compromise, and the Civil War came; in 1877 they were able to compromise, and another Civil War may have been averted. The memory of the previous one was too fresh.

DID HAYES "WITHDRAW" TROOPS FROM THE SOUTH?

In April, 1877, President Hayes issued orders for "withdrawing" the troops that were supporting the Republican carpetbag governments in South Carolina and Louisiana. The Democrats speedily proceeded to take over both regimes, while many Republicans in the North bitterly criticized Hayes for this "betrayal" of the Republican cause.

Much misunderstanding exists about the so-called "withdrawal" of federal troops. The impression still prevails in some quarters that not a single federal soldier could be found in the entire South after 1877. As a matter of routine, both before and after the Civil War, federal garrisons were maintained in the South, and still are. They were there primarily to provide coastal defense against foreign foes, to man the forts guarding such seaports as New Orleans and Charleston, and especially to protect the western frontier against hostile Indians.

When Hayes entered the White House in 1877 there were about 25,000 federal troops scattered throughout the South, mostly on the

[12] Woodward, *Reunion and Reaction.*
[13] For a discounting of the Woodward thesis and a reemphasis on the overriding importance of the pledge regarding troops, see Rembert W. Patrick, *The Reconstruction of the Nation* (1967).

frontier of Indian-beset Texas. When he left office in 1881 there were substantially the same number. In the case of South Carolina and Louisiana the troops were withdrawn from the vicinity of the buildings housing the state governments and redeployed to places where they could no longer be used to prop up regimes that did not enjoy popular support. If large-scale violence had occurred, these soldiers could have speedily returned, without having to march all the way from north of the Mason-Dixon line.[14]

WAS PRESIDENT HAYES A PARAGON OF INTEGRITY?

Rutherford B. Hayes, though personally honest, became President as the result of what was probably the most dishonest presidential election in American history — dishonesty that was generously shared by the Democrats and his own Republican party. Though he ran behind his opponent by thousands of popular votes, he was elevated by the compromise Electoral Commission, and he believed himself both legally and morally entitled to his high office.

Impartial observers can hardly deny that Hayes brought a new aura of respectability and integrity to the White House, with the aid of his prohibitionist wife, "Lemonade Lucy" Hayes. Swept away was the fetid atmosphere of the blowsy, horsey, greedy crowd that had surrounded Grant. Substantial progress was made toward needed civil service reform in the politics-riddled New York Customs House. Hayes stood foursquare for sound money and in 1879 (January 1) presided over the restoration of the gold standard (voted by Congress under Grant). Henceforth the legal-tender paper currency of the Treasury could be redeemed with specie.

Hayes has perhaps been overpraised for two acts of political courage. One was appointing as postmaster general David M. Key, a Southerner who was also a Democrat and an ex-Confederate officer — to the chagrin of resolute Republicans. The other was restationing the federal troops, after which the Democratic Solid South solidified for several generations.

Both of these acts of courage were less courageous than they seemed. They were evidently carried out in response to solemn pledges given during the behind-the-scenes bargaining that made possible Hayes'

---

[14] Clarence C. Clendenen, "President Hayes' 'Withdrawal' of the Troops — An Enduring Myth," *South Carolina Magazine of History*, LXX (1969), 240–250. Some troops were withdrawn from the South on a temporary basis for action against Northwest Indians and Eastern strikers.

election through the Compromise of 1877. It would almost certainly have caused an uproar among Democrats if he had backed out on these commitments. Indeed the storm of criticism probably would have been about as great as that which did arise from the Republicans, most of whom were not privy to the backstairs bargain. To quiet the outcry, Hayes handed out a number of federal jobs to Republicans who were thrown out of state offices following the so-called withdrawal of the troops.

Taking care of such displaced politicians was not unethical and was perhaps unavoidable. Much less defensible was Hayes' action in rewarding with federal jobs the Republican members of the Louisiana Returning Board who had, with tainted hands, been responsible for turning the state — and the presidency — to him.[15] But that was how the game of politics was played, and to some extent is still played.

WAS PRESIDENT GARFIELD A MARTYR?

On July 2, 1881, after nearly four months in office, Garfield was fatally shot by Charles J. Guiteau, a mentally deranged lawyer and office seeker who was evidently a paranoid schizophrenic.[16] After lying in agony through the long, hot summer, the President died on September 19, nearly eighty days after the shooting. His prolonged suffering, combined with anxiety for his recovery, contributed to the stereotype of "The Martyr President."

We ordinarily define a martyr as one who gives his life or endures great suffering for a belief, a principle, or a cause. Every President who dies in office in a sense is a martyr to his high office and the cause of representative government. But this senseless murder by a deranged assassin hardly deserves to be described in such high-flown terms.

At the time of the assassination the ruling Republican party was being torn by two factions: the old-guard "Stalwarts," with Senator Conkling of New York a kingpin, and the half-reformist "Half-Breeds," with James G. Blaine and James A. Garfield as prominent leaders. When the Stalwarts failed to nominate ex-President Grant for a third term in 1880, the convention finally turned to Half-Breed Garfield on the 36th ballot, to the acute dissatisfaction of Senator Conkling. In an unsuccess-

[15] Hayes also rewarded the clerks of the Louisiana Returning Board, plus various relatives of those involved. The historian Rhodes calls these appointments "the greatest blot on his administration." J. F. Rhodes, *A History of the United States from the Compromise of 1850* (1906), VII, 289.

[16] Charles E. Rosenberg, *The Trial of the Assassin Guiteau* (1968), xiii.

ful attempt to mollify the Stalwarts, the convention chose for the Vice Presidency a New York spoilsman named Chester A. Arthur. Ironically, President Hayes had dismissed him from the Collectorship of the Port of New York in 1878 for objectionable political activity.[17]

Upon entering the White House, President Garfield appointed the Half-Breed Blaine (a bitter enemy of Conkling) his Secretary of State, and removed from the coveted office of Collector of the Port of New York a meritorious appointee of President Hayes. To turn the knife in the wound, Garfield chose for this ripe political plum in the state of New York a bitter enemy of Conkling, the senior Senator from New York. A frightful quarrel resulted. Conkling resigned in a huff from the Senate and sought vindication through reelection by the New York legislature in Albany. Within its walls he openly lobbied, backed by the personal support of Vice President Arthur. In the midst of this unseemly quarrel over spoilsmanship, Guiteau shot Garfield, allegedly boasting, "I am a Stalwart. Arthur is now President of the United States."[18]

Garfield did not, martyrlike, willingly sacrifice his life for civil service reform. But his death shocked the nation into doing something about an evil that had spawned such a tragedy. His death in these circumstances was undoubtedly a service to his reputation, for his few short months in office had not given promise of a strong presidency.

DID CONGRESS REALLY FAVOR
THE PENDLETON CIVIL SERVICE ACT?

Garfield's murder, combined with the notoriety attached to monetary assessments extracted from federal office holders, aroused the public to the point where Congress was compelled to act. Various state elections in the autumn of 1882 revealed an angry mood, especially the gubernatorial victory in New York of a civil-service reformer, Grover Cleveland, by a margin of nearly 200,000 votes. In the Congressional elections that same fall the Democrats turned a Republican majority of 147 to 135 in the House into a thumping Democratic majority of 197 to 118.

---

[17] Recently revealed documents show that Arthur, who managed the campaign in New York, became deeply involved in "dirty politics," including the extortionate assessment of contributions from officeholders who feared for their jobs. T. C. Reeves, "Chester A. Arthur and the Campaign of 1880," *Pol. Sci. Quar.*, LXXXIV (1969), 628–637.

[18] The arresting officer reported him as saying quietly while leaving the scene of the crime, ". . . Arthur is President, and I am a Stalwart." Shortly before the shooting Guiteau wrote that the deed was designed to "unite the Republican party and save the Republic." *Ibid.*, pp. 4, 41.

Conspicuous among the losers were prominent spoilsmen. The way the political tide was running, the Republicans, who still controlled the House until March 1883, would lose the presidency to the Democrats in 1884 (as they narrowly did). With civil service reform suddenly popular, the Republicans would do well to get on the reformist bandwagon. In short, a primary concern of the Congress that passed the Civil Service Reform Act was winning the election of 1884, not achieving genuine reform.

In this atmosphere the Republicans strove to pass a Civil Service Reform Act by early 1883. They could thus "freeze" into their offices a number of Republican appointees who had long been fattening on federal patronage. Ironically, the Democrats, many of whom had urged civil service reform during the long years of Republican officeholding, began to have second thoughts. If they won the presidency in 1884, they would not want to have their hands tied.

The Pendleton Civil Service Reform Act of 1883 was finally approved with bipartisan support by a Republican Congress in January 1883. It passed the Senate with relatively little debate or amendment and with only five dissenting votes, all Democrats. (Seven more Democratic Senators went on record as opposed.) The House disposed of the bill in about thirty minutes by a vote of 155 to 47, with considerable opposition from the Democratic South.[19] Congress gulped down this bitter medicine with a wry face but did not lick the spoon.

One reason why the Pendleton Act generated so little overt opposition was that, like so many historic "firsts," it was relatively weak. But it did establish the principle of a merit system and it did provide foundations for improving the federal civil service. A three-man Civil Service Commission was charged with the responsibility of administering competitive examinations. Such tests would be required of those whom the President designated as in the classified service. (President Arthur classified about one-tenth of all federal employees; about seventy-five years later the fraction had increased to about nine-tenths.) The Pendleton Act also outlawed the vicious practice of levying "job insurance" assessments on federal office holders.

One curious feature of the Pendleton Act is that it was endorsed by the ex-spoilsman, President Arthur, who subsequently showed commendable vigor in implementing it. Shocked by the death of President Garfield, he generally rose above the unsavory political connections

---

[19] See Ari Hoogenboom, *Outlawing the Spoils: A History of the Civil Service Reform Movement, 1865–1883* (1961), pp. 246–249.

that he had earlier established with the New York "Stalwarts," and gave the country a respectable administration.

HOW NEW WAS THE NEW IMMIGRATION?

In 1882, under President Arthur, another red-letter law was passed which, for the first time, restricted general immigration by excluding paupers, convicts, and defectives.[20] Foreign nations had been prone to dump their undesirables on America.

This pathbreaking statute revealed a growing concern over what has been called the "New Immigration," which was distinguished by a marked increase in the 1880s of immigrants from southern and southeastern Europe. Yet the new immigration was hardly "new," because a sprinkling of such people had been arriving since early days, even though they were not to form a majority of all newcomers until near the turn of the century. Many of them, perhaps one-fourth, were birds of passage who returned after they had "made their pile" or wanted to see the Old Country once more.

English-speaking immigrants from the British Isles and Nordic types from northern and western Europe had been generally welcomed. Usually Protestants, they were easier to assimilate than the non-Nordic and Catholic immigrants from southern and eastern Europe. But whether in the long run the "new" arrivals made less good citizens is a question that can never be satisfactorily answered. As for the charge that immigrants in the nineteenth century generally exploited the country, one can say with complete assurance that countless thousands of them were cruelly exploited as laborers in dangerous mines and disease-producing factories. In the case of the New Immigration, which was notoriously abused, we may doubt if most emigrants improved their economic lot by making the move. Many merely swapped slums. But their children usually enjoyed opportunities that would have been lacking in the homeland.

Immigration has always been, and continues to be, a major theme in the American experience. As early as the colonial era, tens of thousands of Germans, among others, reached what is now the United States,

---

[20] In 1882 the Chinese were excluded for ten years (later extended), as a result of Sinophobia which found expression nationwide, not solely in the West. Stereotypes developed regarding the dirt, disease, perfidy, barbarity, and strangeness of heathen "Mongolian" coolies. See Stuart C. Miller, *The Unwelcome Immigrant: The American Image of the Chinese, 1785–1882* (1969).

and in proportion to earlier comers represented a stream roughly comparable to the heavy immigration from Europe in the late nineteenth century.

Newer arrivals, with their lower standard of living, tended to produce larger families. If the millions of immigrants who arrived in the late nineteenth and early twentieth centuries had never emigrated, the earlier comers might possibly have kept their birthrate higher and the population of the United States might be approximately what it is today. The original 60,000 French Canadians have, by their birthrate alone, increased their numbers proportionately to a greater degree than have the people of the United States, immigrants and all.

The concept of a "melting pot," in which the peoples of all races and climes would be fused into a common type, has proved somewhat illusory. Various ethnic groups, including the Polish-Americans and some German-Americans, have tenaciously clung to much of their national identity. A better figure of speech would be a salad bowl, in which the ingredients form a whole but in which one can recognize pieces of tomato, cucumber, and lettuce.

DID THE REVEREND BURCHARD DEFEAT BLAINE?

The presidential election of 1884, in which the Republican idol James G. Blaine ran against the Democrat Grover Cleveland, proved to be a dramatically close one, as were most of these quadrennial canvasses from 1876 to 1896. Blaine would have won if he had carried New York State, which he lost by 562,005 to 563,154, or a margin of 1,149 votes. In short, a shift of 575 votes to Blaine would have sent him, instead of Cleveland, to the White House.

In the closing days of the campaign in New York City, Blaine was present at a gathering where the Reverend Samuel D. Burchard, a Presbyterian clergyman and a Republican, publicly branded the Democrats as the party of "Rum, Romanism, and Rebellion." The weary candidate, who may have been mentally composing his reply, did not immediately react to this insulting alliteration.[21] In the circumstances, silence seemed to give assent. Democrats gleefully plastered the state (and the nation) with the damaging malediction, "Rum, Romanism, and Rebellion," which many voters falsely attributed to Blaine himself.

[21] Several years later Blaine explained privately that he had heard Burchard but, since few others had, he decided not to direct attention to the barb. D. G. Farrelly, " 'Rum, Romanism and Rebellion' Resurrected," *Western Pol. Quar.*, VIII (1955), 262–270.

This concept was not original, although Burchard's expression of it may have been.[22] Moreover, there was a large element of truth in it; and nothing, the proverb tells us, hurts like the truth. Southern Democrats had engineered secession in 1860–1861, and during the Civil War they had enlisted the sympathy of Northern Copperhead Democrats. Irish immigrants, who were heavily Roman Catholic, had from early days favored the Democratic party, which was generally more friendly to poor foreigners than its rivals. And the downtrodden Irishmen were notoriously inclined to drown their many sorrows in whiskey (not rum).

Burchard's boomerang was particularly damaging to Blaine because he, unlike most other Republican presidential nominees, had a special appeal to the Irish vote: his mother was a Catholic and his sisters had been brought up in that faith.[23] This insult to the religion of his mother almost certainly alienated at least 575 Irish–American votes, or enough to cost Blaine the White House.

But the Burchard blunder has too often been overstressed. In a close presidential election, any one of a dozen or so oversights, mishaps, or slips of the tongue may be enough to turn the tide one way or the other. This was as true in 1884 as it was in President Kennedy's victory of 1960, when the Irish–Catholic vote again played a significant role.

In the state of New York alone any one of the following could have accounted for Blaine's loss of the necessary few votes: (1) the bitter, knife-in-the-back enmity of his Republican rival, Senator Roscoe Conkling; (2) the fund-raising "millionaires' dinner" in New York City at which Blaine was present on the eve of the election; (3) the Prohibition ticket, which drew off many normally Republican votes; (4) the election-day rain in upstate New York which discouraged many Republican farmers from hitching up their horses and driving to the polls; and (5) allegedly fraudulent Democratic votes.

Nationwide, other factors conspired against Blaine's success. The business recession of 1884 had a depressing effect on the fortunes of the Republican party — the "ins." The "Mugwumps" or independent-minded Republicans threw their support behind Cleveland. Finally, suspicions as to Blaine's honesty, growing out of allegations that he had used public office for private profit, continued to act as a roadblock to

[22] In 1876, when Tilden's election seemed assured, the future President James A. Garfield was writing privately that the Republicans had been defeated "by the combined power of rebellion, Catholicism, and whiskey. . . ." R. G. Caldwell, *James A. Garfield* (1931), p. 251.

[23] Blaine's father was a Protestant. By a compromise arrangement not uncommon then, the girls were reared as Catholics and the boys as Protestants. D. S. Muzzey, *James G. Blaine* (1934), p. 5.

the White House. Living on a lavish scale that did not seem justified by his visible means of support, he was never able to satisfy the public and many historians that the charges of corruption were completely groundless.

WAS GROVER CLEVELAND A "PROFILE IN COURAGE"?

President Cleveland, a man of strong principles and stubborn convictions, was generously endowed with a high degree of moral courage. As a young bachelor-lawyer, he became sheriff of Erie County, and in line of duty hanged with his own hands two murderers, thus becoming known as "The Buffalo Hangman." Elected mayor of Buffalo on a reformist platform, he made many enemies and came to be dubbed "The Veto Mayor." Untainted by connection with the Democratic machine in New York City, he was elected reformist governor of the state, and earned the epithet "The Veto Governor." One of his most widely criticized but most courageous acts was to veto a bill lowering the fare on the elevated railroads of New York City from ten cents to five cents. He acted in the well-justified belief that this popular bill was a flagrant violation of the state's contractual obligation to the carriers.

As a reformer with high principles, Cleveland was nominated for the presidency at Chicago by the Democrats in 1884. Many members of the party were weary of the old war horses, and in seconding the nomination General Bragg declared pointedly that we "love him most for the enemies he has made."

But the high ethical principles of the Democratic Cleveland fell under a cloud when the news leaked out during the campaign that he was supporting an illegitimate boy, now eight years old and born to a widow, Mrs. Maria Halpin, to whom he had been attentive during his bachelor days in Buffalo. An ordinary politician would probably have "lied like a gentleman," but Cleveland's response was "Tell the truth!" This was probably the wisest course politically because only the truth could combat the scandalous exaggerations and falsifications that his political enemies were broadcasting.

The facts are that this liaison appears to have been Cleveland's sole serious departure from the path of virtue, and that rumors of this "woman scrape" were being circulated at the time of his nomination. He conceded that he had been intimate with the widow, although he never acknowledged that the child was his own. Several other men had been paying court to the lady about the same time, and this circumstance probably accounts for his relative indifference to the future of the child.

An explanation began to go the rounds that as a bachelor he was bravely "covering up" for a married man — a theme that was later developed at length in a popular novel by Paul Leicester Ford, entitled *The Honorable Peter Sterling* (1894). At all events, there evidently had been no seduction and no promise of marriage, but there had been an acceptance of responsibility and assumption of child-support payments for the boy's upbringing.[24] Democrats made the best use they could of the argument that Cleveland's private immorality (temporary and long past) was less reprehensible than Blaine's public dishonesty in money matters (allegedly still continuing).

While President, Cleveland strove manfully for reform and economy in government. As a nonveteran who had supported his widowed mother during the Civil War and had paid for a substitute to go in his place, he incurred the wrath of the veterans when he vetoed scores of private pension bills, as well as the Dependent Pension Bill of 1887. Not surprisingly, he came to be known as "Old Veto" or "The Veto President."

Despite his reputation for inflexible courage, Cleveland bent to political expediency during his first administration in two conspicuous instances. One was when he yielded to the Democratic clamor for offices by permitting the ousting of thousands of Republican incumbents by Postmaster General Adlai Stevenson, Sr. The other came in 1887, when he ordered the return of captured Confederate flags, only to be forced to rescind his action in the face of a tidal wave of protest, especially from outraged Northern veterans.

DID HARRISON'S ELECTION MANDATE A HIGHER TARIFF?

Bothered by a growing surplus in the Treasury from customs duties, President Cleveland tried to persuade Congress to reduce the tariff. His initial suggestions ignored, he exploded a bombshell in 1887 when he sent to Congress a state of the union message that dealt exclusively with the need for lowering existing rates. His political advisors had urged him not to rock the boat and jeopardize his (and their) chances of reelection, but the high-principled Cleveland plunged ahead. After his defeat at the polls in 1888, the Republicans, who had made "free trade" the burning issue of the campaign, declared that they had received a mandate from the voters to raise customs duties. They acted on this

[24] The child was ultimately removed from an orphanage, adopted by a family in western New York, and became a distinguished professional man. Allan Nevins, *Grover Cleveland* (1932), pp. 165–166.

assumption when a Republican Congress passed the high McKinley tariff bill of 1890.

If one party wins a majority or even a plurality of the popular vote in an election, it can with some plausibility claim a mandate. But the election of 1888 was fairly close, and Cleveland, though losing in the Electoral College, polled about 100,000 more votes than his rival. If any party was to claim a mandate, the Democrats were in a stronger position than their opponents, at least on the popular basis.

We should note, moreover, that there are always dozens of issues in any national election, most of them secondary or minor. In 1888 the national platforms discussed such issues as civil service reform, the admission of Chinese laborers, pensions, the disposal of the public domain, Mormonism, states' rights, the trusts, the coinage of silver, and other matters. Where the issues were so numerous and the results so close, one can hardly say that the outcome was a mandate on any one of them.

Did Cleveland lose the election, as commonly supposed, because he courageously (bullheadedly?) forced the tariff question upon the public and laid himself open to the charge of being a "free-trader"? (Clearly he was advocating a tariff for revenue rather than the British brand of free trade.) The election results do not add much support to the allegation that Cleveland's stand on the tariff cost him the election. In a number of the states where manufacturing was important, and a protective tariff presumably desirable, Cleveland ran well. He carried Connecticut, though with a slightly reduced vote over 1884. In various localities where manufacturing was strong, including New Jersey, he showed greater strength than four years earlier, although in other places his vote fell off.[25]

In view of these contradictory statistics, we must be chary of blaming Cleveland's tariff message for his defeat. Some of his defenders have argued that his gravest mistake was not in sending the message but in delaying it until late in 1887, too late for the Democratic campaign of tariff "education" to have its full effect.

DID SACKVILLE-WEST COST CLEVELAND REELECTION?

During the losing Cleveland campaign of 1888 a resident of Southern California, George Osgoodby, born in America of British parents, wrote

[25] Details appear in Nevins, *Grover Cleveland*, p. 441; Svend Petersen, *A Statistical History of the American Presidential Elections* (1963), pp. 51–56.

to the British Minister in Washington, Lionel Sackville-West, asking for confidential advice as to how to vote in the forthcoming presidential election. The indiscreet Briton should have ignored the inquiry, or should have replied that a foreign envoy cannot properly interfere in the domestic concerns of the country to which he is accredited. Instead he dispatched a labored reply, naively marked "private."

Osgoodby, who signed himself as British-born Charles F. Murchison, held back publishing the letter, fearful of Democratic reprisals. He was finally persuaded by Republicans to turn it over to a local newspaper, which gleefully published it on October 18, 1888, three days later.[26]

This diplomatic indiscretion was political dynamite. It impugned the good faith of President Cleveland in the current difficulties with Britain over Canadian fisheries; yet it stated in effect that the interests of England would be best served by a vote for Cleveland. The luckless minister made matters worse by granting an interview to the press, which quoted him, he claimed, in garbled form. Hundreds of thousands of Irish–American voters, heavily concentrated in New York, hated the British and normally supported the Democratic ticket. Sackville-West's implication that a vote for Cleveland was a vote for England almost certainly forced thousands of irate Irishmen into the Republican camp, at least for this election.

A snowstorm of telegrams descended on Washington, demanding that Cleveland send the "damned Englishman" home. The President waited briefly and then yielded to this overwhelming pressure in an act that does not square with his image of seldom bending the knee. Sackville-West was stupid, indiscreet, and blundering, but his was a private letter, not a public declaration. By the ordinary procedures of diplomacy and international law, a protest should have been lodged with London, following which the British, after a leisurely investigation, almost certainly would have recalled the inept envoy. But all this would take time, and the election was only a few days away. So Sackville-West was bundled off home, and the British showed their displeasure over this hasty act by not appointing his successor until Cleveland had left the White House some months later.

Cleveland lost New York State, and with it the election, by 14,373 votes out of more than 1,300,000 cast. A shift of 7,187 ballots would have brought him victory, and almost certainly at least this many

[26] T. C. Hinckley, "George Osgoodby and the Murchison Letter," *Pacific Hist. Rev.*, *XXVII* (1958), 359–370. Osgoodby appears not to have been encouraged by the Republican managers, as alleged, to write the entrapping letter in the first place.

Irishmen were alienated by Sackville-West's letter.[27] A blundering Presbyterian minister, the Reverend Mr. Burchard, had helped to bring Cleveland victory over Blaine in 1884 with his "Rum, Romanism, and Rebellion" indiscretion. A blundering British minister, Lionel Sackville-West, helped to bring Cleveland defeat in his contest with Harrison in 1888 when he indiscreetly penned his letter to Osgoodby. In politics, as in football, the "breaks" have a way of evening up.

ADDITIONAL GENERAL REFERENCES

L. D. White, *The Republican Era, 1869–1901* (1958); John A. Garraty, *The New Commonwealth, 1877–1890* (1968); H. Wayne Morgan, *From Hayes to McKinley: National Party Politics, 1877–1896* (1969); Allan Nevins, *Hamilton Fish: The Inner History of the Grant Administration* (1936); John A. Carpenter, *Ulysses S. Grant* (1970); R. G. Caldwell, *James A. Garfield: Party Chieftain* (1931); W. B. Hesseltine, *Ulysses S. Grant* (1935); Irwin Unger, *The Greenback Era* (1964); Harry Barnard, *Rutherford B. Hayes and His America* (1954); C. Vann Woodward, *Reunion and Reaction* (rev. ed., 1956); Allan Nevins, *Grover Cleveland* (1932); J. R. Hollingsworth, *The Whirligig of Politics: The Democracy of Cleveland and Bryan* (1963).

[27] The Democratic candidate for governor of New York, David B. Hill, won reelection on the same ticket which brought defeat to Cleveland. The common charge that this result was due largely to stab-in-the-back machine politics is not well founded. See Herbert J. Bass, *"I Am a Democrat": The Political Career of David Bennett Hill* (1961), pp. 121–125.

23

The Ferment
of the Nineties

Returning to power under President Benjamin Harrison in 1889, the Republicans managed to eliminate the bothersome surplus in the Treasury, largely by a lavish disbursement of pensions to Civil War veterans. The administration also made an inflationary concession to the debt-burdened farmers and to the Western states by passing the Sherman Silver Purchase Act of 1890, thus obligating the Washington government to buy 4,500,000 ounces of silver monthly. The same Congress approved the pioneering Sherman Antitrust Act of 1890.[1]

The Republicans, who interpreted their presidential victory in 1888 as a mandate to boost the tariff, enacted the high McKinley Bill in 1890. Ensuing public dissatisfaction was largely responsible for a Democratic landslide in the Congressional elections that autumn. The increasing agrarian discontent also found vent in the rapid spread of the People's (Populist) party, which had emerged in the early 1890s[2] *and which nominated a presidential candidate in 1892, General James B.*

---

[1] The few teeth of the Sherman Act were weakened by the courts (seven of the eight prosecutions under President Harrison failed); trusts continued to multiply; and the original legislation was not markedly strengthened until 1914, with the passing of the Federal Trade Commission Act and the Clayton Antitrust Act, plus subsequent regulatory measures.

[2] The term "Gay Nineties," reflecting a type of entertainment then prevalent, was a misnomer. The era was one of prolonged agricultural depression and financial stringency, which plagued tens of millions of farmers, laborers, and businessmen. See R. M. Wik, "The Gay Nineties — Reconsidered," *Mid-America*, XLIV (1962), 67–79.

Weaver. He ran third, behind the victorious ex-President Grover Cleveland (Democrat) and the incumbent President Harrison (Republican), whose cause was hurt by the bloody Homestead steel strike in Pennsylvania.

Financial panic in 1893 brought new woes to President Cleveland, who sweated out a troubled second administration. The free-silver wing of the Democratic party, seizing control in 1896, nominated William J. Bryan for the presidency. He lost to the Republican William McKinley in one of the most heated and colorful election campaigns in American history.

DID SECRETARY BLAINE OVERSHADOW HARRISON?

By 1889 James G. Blaine, a glamorous presidential aspirant since 1876, was clearly the uncrowned king of the Republican party. President Harrison, evidently envious of such popularity, could hardly avoid giving him the choicest appointive position within his gift, the Secretaryship of State, which Blaine had held briefly in 1881 under Garfield. The country expected a "spirited" foreign policy under the once-dynamic "Jingo Jim" Blaine. He shone most brightly in playing host to the first Pan-American Conference, held in Washington, D. C., in 1889, but the results of this wordy conclave were minimal. He also arranged in 1892, after considerable bluster, for the settlement by arbitration of a dispute with the Canadians and British over the slaughter of America's Alaska seals outside the three-mile limit. But the outcome was more a victory for the preservation of peace than for the preservation of the seals.

Americans had come to expect more of a saber-rattling performance from Blaine than they received. He was now older, somewhat dispirited, and unwell. When a crisis arose with Chile in 1891 over the killing of several U. S. sailors in uniform by an enraged mob, Harrison, rather than Blaine, was the jingo. The President had worn the American uniform in the Civil War, and Blaine had not ("invisible in war, invincible in peace"). It was the Secretary of State who had to restrain his chief, rather than vice versa. In the end the Chileans were forced to eat humble pie, which left a long and bitter aftertaste.

Four days before the Republican National Convention met in Minneapolis in 1892, Blaine brusquely resigned his Secretaryship of State, allegedly because of a last-minute flareup of his presidential fever. Harrison seemed relieved to have his ambitious underling depart, even though Blaine had fallen somewhat short of overshadowing his chief.[3]

On a man-to-man basis, Harrison was one of the coldest personalities ever to occupy the White House, although this trait has perhaps been overdrawn. Disappointed office seekers in particular could long remember his fishy eye. But as a resourceful and eloquent public speaker, he proved effective with large crowds, in a day when orators had no microphones or amplifiers. His administration was respectable, and the first "billion dollar Congress" (the 51st) ground out some significant legislation, including the Sherman Antitrust Act and the McKinley Tariff Act of 1890.

WERE THE RAILROAD MAGNATES AS KNAVISH AS ALLEGED?

Farmers in the Plains States were undoubtedly depressed during much of the 1880s and 1890s, whether as a result of low prices, overproduction, poor harvests, locusts, drought, inept management, crippling mortgages, or other handicaps. Their natural impulse was to blame the railroads — America's first billion-dollar industry — as the financial ogres that were crushing them by charging supposedly excessive rates.

Railroading in the post–Civil War years was not the moneymaker it was commonly supposed to be, although promoters such as Jay Gould and Cornelius Vanderbilt reaped millions through stock manipulations and reorganizations. Vanderbilt in particular vastly improved the New York Central. But most of the lines, especially those in the thinly populated West, went into receivership or experienced other serious financial difficulties, especially in panic years. The enormous fortunes reaped from the railroads — especially the Union Pacific and the Central Pacific — were most easily amassed by the insiders who built the lines through construction companies, notably the scandal-ridden Crédit Mobilier in the case of the Union Pacific. From government loans and other sources these builders paid themselves tens of millions of dollars in extravagant charges for laying the rails. But operating freight and passenger cars through scantily populated Western states was not a lucrative business.

Much of the profit that the railroads subsequently made, and are making today, came through exploiting the mineral and other resources of the areas granted to them by the government for construction. These

[3] Harry J. Sievers, *Benjamin Harrison: Hoosier President* (1968), p. 225.

giveaways of the public domain were harshly criticized in later years as wholly unnecessary. But the fact remains that much of the land was worthless until the railroads arrived, and they would not come without some financial inducements. Besides, millions of acres were recovered by the government when the terms of the grants were not fulfilled.[4]

Popular fancy to the contrary, rates on the railroads did not rise consistently in the 1880s and 1890s; in fact, during the three decades prior to 1900 the trend was almost uninterruptedly downward.[5] Accusations that the railroad stocks were "watered" (deliberately inflated in value), and that the railroads were overcapitalized, were often all too true. Such overcapitalization was used as justification for the established rates.

Railroad operators often granted secret rebates of a part of their freight charges to favored shippers, notoriously to Rockefeller's oil empire. But these "kickbacks" could be justified on the grounds that wholesale lots were shipped rather uniformly over the year, with resultant economies to the railroad. Much less defensible was Rockefeller's practice of securing secret drawbacks or rebates on the payments for freight made by his competitors. Ingenious practices such as charging more for a short haul than a long haul seemed vicious, but in most cases such rates were made possible by the absence of competing lines or alternate water routes.[6] Charging "what the traffic will bear" is an ancient principle of the marketplace.

WAS THE INTERSTATE COMMERCE ACT EFFECTIVE?

By 1887 the railroads were in a chaotic state, with about 1,500 separate lines. Many were losing money in ruinous rate wars resulting from cutthroat competition; there were even some instances of railroads haul-

---

[4] Maps showing in black ribbons the immense amount of territory granted by the federal government to the railroads are misleading because the 640-acre sections on each side of the track alternated in checkerboard fashion. Also such maps often do not take into account the acreage finally forfeited. See R. S. Henry, "The Railroad Land Grant Legend in American History Texts," Miss. Valley Hist. Rev., XXXII (1945), 171–194; also commentary in ibid., XXXII (1946), 557–576. P. W. Gates, "The Railroad Grant Legend," Jour. of Econ. Hist., XIV (1954), 143–146, demolishes the myth that the government lost nothing by donating the land because the price of the remaining alternate sections was allegedly doubled.

[5] William Z. Ripley, Railroads: Rates and Regulation (1912), pp. 411ff. One should note that the prices of farmers' crops fell proportionately even lower.

[6] Transportation by water was generally cheaper in the 19th Century; a vast amount of oceangoing bulk cargo was still going under sail as late as 1880, even though the steamship was in common use for passengers before the Civil War. See Douglass C. North, Growth and Welfare in the American Past (1966), p. 110.

ing freight on their own tracks and paying for the privilege of doing so. The common practice of "pooling" or raising the rates in a competitive area and then putting the profits into a common pool, subsequently shared, was not a satisfactory answer.

In 1887 Congress, prodded by a long-suffering public, passed the Interstate Commerce Act, which applied only to interstate railroads. It provided that charges should be reasonable and just (although no provision was then made for rate-fixing by the Interstate Commerce Commission). The statute also outlawed discriminatory rates (relating to persons and places); it forbade drawbacks, rebates, pooling, and charging more for a short haul than a long haul over the same line. Although a weak and ineffective law, the Interstate Commerce Act was a historic foot in the door of government regulation, and it paved the way for subsequent legislation with adequate muscle.

Many of the railroad operators supported some kind of regulation that would bring order out of disorder, but others strongly opposed the measure that emerged. Yet a number of directors, especially those connected with the weaker railroads, favored the Interstate Commerce Act.[7]

WERE THERE "ROBBER BARONS" IN THE GILDED AGE?

The term "robber barons" came to be applied to the great American captains of industry in the several decades after the end of the Civil War. This epithet was seized upon successively by the Populists, the Muckrakers, the Progressives, and others. In the late 1920s and early 1930s the unflattering designation was further popularized by the liberal historians Vernon L. Parrington and Charles and Mary Beard. It had a special appeal during the Great Depression of the 1930s, when the big bankers and businessmen served as convenient scapegoats, and when Matthew Josephson's journalistic exposé, The Robber Barons (1934), achieved great popularity and notoriety.[8]

---

[7] Edward A. Purcell, Jr., "Ideas and Interests: Businessmen and the Interstate Commerce Act," Jour. of Amer. Hist., LIV (1967), 561–577. See also Gabriel Kolko, Railroads and Regulation, 1877–1916 (1965).

[8] Charles and Mary Beard concluded that the industrial giants were men who had worked their way up from the economically lower strata of society, but subsequent research has shown that most of these tycoons came from native-born, nonfarming, upper- or upper-middle class families, with an impressive number having had a high school or college education. See William Miller, "American Historians and the Business Elite," Jour. of Econ. Hist., IX (1949), 184–208. A convenient historiographical survey is Hal Bridges, "The Robber Baron Concept in American History," Business Hist. Rev., XXXII (1958), 1–13. See also Peter Jones, ed., The Robber Barons Revisited (1968).

Robber barons were medieval nobles who profited from robbing their neighbors, holding prisoners for ransom, or exorting high fees from travelers passing through their domain. The captains of American industry engaged in price wars, but the consumer was the beneficiary, at least in the short run. These magnates did import contract labor from Europe (although this was a relatively minor part of their manpower); they did work their men long hours; and they did strive to keep wages low. But even harsher conditions prevailed in a number of other countries.

No one can deny that many if not all of these industrialists were guilty of sharp practices. But the era was one of dog-eat-dog in the scramble for riches, and ethics for the business world were far from standardized.[9] Governor Nelson Rockefeller, grandson of the oil king John D. Rockefeller, was quoted as saying that his grandfather did not break any laws but that a lot of laws were passed on account of him. The most ruthless of the business tycoons "robbed" one another by mercilessly crushing competition; extorted rebates and drawbacks on shipments over the railroads; corrupted courts, politicians, and legislatures (which were all too ready to be bought); "watered" their stock or manipulated the stock market; ravaged natural resources; disregarded the welfare of the consumer; fought the unionization of labor; and employed spies and thugs, some of whom resorted to arson and dynamite.

WERE THE "ROBBER BARONS" BENEFACTORS?

There were in general two kinds of industrial barons: the builders and the wreckers. Railroad promoters such as Daniel Drew were manipulators and wreckers; railroad kings such as Henry Villard, Leland Stanford, and James J. Hill, though all grew immensely wealthy, actually built lines and consolidated economic empires by marshaling accumulations of capital, much of it foreign.[10] Carnegie was called the "Steel King," but he had no monopoly on steel, any more than Rockefeller had on oil. Many of these giants improved the quality and quantity of their products by industrial statesmanship, which involved eliminating waste, reducing price fluctuations, insuring a steady flow of raw materials, and

[9] The Federal Trade Commission Act was not passed until 1914, and to this day the Federal Trade Commission has its hands full policing business ethics.

[10] When the railroad tycoon, W. H. Vanderbilt, remarked, "The public be damned," he may have meant that there was more to running a railroad than pleasing passengers. Edward C. Kirkland in J. A. Garraty, ed., *Interpreting American History* (1970), *II*, 17.

introducing technical improvements. The "barons" passed on to the consumer the economies of large-scale production. Some of them were not chasing money solely for money's sake but were enjoying a fascinating game. Many of them paid good wages and sustained a high level of employment. A number of them, notably Rockefeller, lived exemplary private lives. Some of them used their money to pioneer in tangential or even unrelated areas. Leland Stanford, one of the builders of the Central Pacific railroad, made significant contributions to higher education, horse breeding, wine production, and the development of the moving picture.[11]

American science, education, medicine, and other disciplines have benefited immeasurably from the "loot" amassed by these "greedy" robber barons. The Rockefeller and Carnegie fortunes, to name only two, formed an important portion of American private philanthropy, which has been conducted on an unprecedentedly munificent scale (partly to escape taxes). Rockefeller and Carnegie brought their organizational genius to the task of giving away usefully hundreds of millions of dollars. The Rockefeller program for wiping out hookworm in the South, launched in 1909, proved to be sensationally successful, and it was only one of many such ventures.

By the 1950s and 1960s the views of many historians had shifted perceptibly. There was a tendency among them to regard the best of the great entrepreneurs more as "industrial statesmen" than as robber barons.[12] But even statesmen are prone to be devious.

DID THE POPULISTS FAIL COMPLETELY?

The Populist party (officially known as the People's party) mustered its greatest strength in the presidential election of 1892, when its candidate, General James B. Weaver, won 22 electoral votes from six Western states. It proved to be one of the few third-party political groups in American history to break into the Electoral College. Its strongest support came from the Great Plains and the Rocky Mountain area, where

---

[11] See Norman E. Tutorow, *Leland Stanford: Man of Many Careers* (1971).

[12] Allan Nevins, the biographer of John D. Rockefeller, concluded in 1954 that these industrial statesmen, by building up America's economic might, should be credited with having won World War I and World War II. "Should American History Be Rewritten?" *Saturday Review*, XXXVII (1954), 48–49. This thesis is not completely persuasive. These entrepreneurs could not have been looking that far ahead, and it is entirely possible that American industry would have become approximately as strong, if not stronger, under a less free-wheeling economy.

its demand for the free coinage of silver struck a responsive chord among people whose prosperity was partly derived from mining that precious metal.

Among the many grievances of those malcontents who swelled the Populist ranks one must list falling agricultural prices, poor credit and marketing facilities, crop failures at home, and bumper competitive crops abroad.[13] Low prices were due in part to deflation, and a major objective of the Populists was to inflate the currency with the "unlimited coinage" of silver in the ratio of sixteen ounces of silver to one ounce of gold. These goals had a strong appeal in the South, but memories of Republican reconstruction kept many possible bolters securely in the Democratic fold. Even so, in their high-water election of 1892 the Populists won 36 percent of the popular vote of Alabama, 23 percent of that of Texas, and 19 percent of that of both Mississippi and Georgia, with scattered support in other states of the South.

The Populists suffered the fate of most third parties when their most attractive principles were ultimately borrowed by either or both of the two major parties. This political larceny was conspicuous during the heyday of the Progressive movement, which flourished in the first two decades of the twentieth century.

At one time or another, Populist spokesmen advocated the following, all of which in time were wholly or partially attained: a flexibly sound currency system; a lower interest rate on farm mortgages; tax reform designed to ease the disproportionate burden on the poor; a graduated income tax (finally authorized by the 16th Amendment of 1913); control of the trusts; government regulation of railroads; postal savings facilities; the conservation of land and natural resources; the right of labor to organize; limitations on the issuance of antilabor injunctions; the eight-hour workday; restrictions on immigration; the secret Australian ballot; improved voter registration laws; the initiative and the referendum; direct primary elections; presidential preference primaries; the recall of public officials, even judges; and the direct election of U. S. Senators by the people rather than the legislatures (finally authorized by the 17th Amendment of 1913).[14]

All these proposals and others were not necessarily original

---

[13] For a discussion of the adverse effect of good grain crops abroad, and for evidence that from 1865 to 1900 prices for farm products fell less than the general price level see North, *Growth and Welfare*, Ch. XI.

[14] See John D. Hicks, "The Persistence of Populism," *Minnesota History*, XII (1931), 3–20. Among Populistic schemes never adopted one should list the "free and unlimited coinage of silver and gold" at the ratio of 16 to 1; government ownership and operation of all railroads; and government ownership of the telephone and telegraph systems.

with the Populists. Yet seldom if ever in American history has any party in so short a time had the satisfaction of seeing so many of its principles enacted into law or written into the Constitution. In the twentieth century, owing in large part to Populistic pressures, the people came to rule in greater measure than they had in the nineteenth century.

WERE THE POPULISTS ANTI-SEMITIC?

In the 1950s and the 1960s a heated controversy developed among certain American historians over the allegation that the Populists were anti-Semitic. There can be no doubt that scattered references were made by Populist newspapers and orators to grasping Jewish moneylenders — Shylocks and Rothschilds — but these barbs can easily be misinterpreted.

The Populists, whose leading spokesmen emerged in the Great Plains West, were agrarians caught in the squeeze between low prices for their crops and high interest rates on their mortgages. Many of their creditors were moneylenders in the East or in England. These debtors were basically anticapitalist and antiplutocrats, and this meant anti-Wall Street, antibanker, and antiurban Easterner. When the Populists directed their venom at usurious bankers, they were often criticizing moneylenders who just happened to be Jews. The international Jewish banking house of the Rothschilds, with a base in England, was frequently condemned. But we should note that non-Jewish capitalists, especially Britons, were likewise assailed. Hereditary Anglophobia made easier an animus against both British bankers and Jewish–English bankers.

There was unquestionably some anti-Semitism among the Populists, as there was among the rank and file of white Christians all over America. But this sentiment was far from being a major concern of the Populists, many of whom showed a tolerant attitude toward various ethnic groups.[15] Historians should avoid the pitfall of concluding that anticapitalism was synonymous with anti-Semitism.[16]

One does not have to look far for evidence of some anti-Semitism outside Populist ranks. During the free-silver Democratic

[15] For evidence that the people of Kansas, a hotbed of Populism, generally respected the Jews in their midst, see W. T. K. Nugent, *The Tolerant Populists* (1963), pp. 109–110.

[16] For evidence that the "incidence of Populist anti-Semitism was infinitesimal" see Norman Pollack, "The Myth of Populist Anti-Semitism," *Amer. Hist. Rev.*, LXVIII (1962), 76–80. Stress on anti-Semitism appears in Richard Hofstadter, *The Age of Reform* (1955), pp. 77–81.

convention of 1896 that nominated William J. Bryan for the Presidency, frenzied delegates were heard to shout, "Down with gold! Down with the hook-nosed Shylocks of Wall Street! Down with the Christ-killing gold bugs!" [17] Unjust charges that Bryan himself was anti-Semitic hurt his candidacy in the New York area, where he ran poorly.

WERE SUGAR MEN BEHIND THE HAWAII REVOLUTION?

Missionaries and traders from the United States had sailed out to the tropical Kingdom of Hawaii early in the nineteenth century. By 1893 Americans or American-descended residents had come to dominate the economic life of the islands, especially the production of sugar. Their prosperity suffered a staggering blow when the McKinley Tariff of 1890 placed Hawaiian sugar on an unfavorable basis. If the islands could only be annexed to the United States, they would enjoy all the privileges of the American sugar producers. This fact was so obvious that when revolution against the native monarchy occurred in 1893, cynics were quick to claim that the uprising was "of sugar, by sugar, and for sugar." Actually many of the leading cane growers in Hawaii were dubious about annexation or opposed to it. For one thing, the contract-labor laws of the United States would probably be invoked to cut off the supply of cheap Oriental field hands.[18]

Economic motives were undoubtedly present, but on a larger scale. The hereditary Hawaiian dynasty, headed by Queen Liliuokalani, was extravagant, corrupt, and capricious. It was understandably resentful of the way white foreigners, especially those from the United States, had taken over so much of the wealth of the islands. The Americans would be more secure in their property holdings, not to mention their lives and liberties, if they could come under the protecting folds of the Stars and Stripes.

DID THE U.S. CONNIVE AT THE HAWAIIAN REVOLUTION?

Early in 1893, when Queen Liliuokalani attempted to establish an autocratic new constitution by royal edict, the whites (mostly Americans)

---

[17] New York *Sun*, Sept. 16, 1896, as quoted in Paolo E. Coletta, *William Jennings Bryan: Political Evangelist, 1860–1908* (1964), pp. 141, 191.

[18] W. A. Russ, Jr., "The Role of Sugar in Hawaiian Annexation," *Pacific Hist. Rev., XII* (1943), 339–350.

rose in revolt. They appealed for help to the notoriously proannexa-
tionist U. S. Minister in Honolulu, John L. Stevens, who promptly summoned some 150 armed men from a nearby warship. They were landed
ostensibly to protect American lives and property, but most of them
were stationed where they could help to overawe the Queen.

Minister Stevens was guilty of additional irregularities. The day
after the uprising, he hastily extended formal recognition to the new
revolutionary regime, though unauthorized to do so. Less than two
weeks later he proclaimed Hawaii a protectorate of the United States,
hoisted the American flag, and wrote to the State Department urging
formal annexation before the British seized the prize. All this was completely unauthorized by Washington.

Three days after the United States troops were landed, a
"Hawaiian" commission (four Americans and one Englishman) was
hurrying to Washington to arrange for a treaty of annexation. When
the pact was finally submitted to the Senate, only two weeks of Harrison's administration remained, and the question of annexation carried
over into Cleveland's administration. Delay was caused in part by the
heated public debate over the wisdom of acquiring overseas real estate:
the nation was not yet ripe to lurch down the uncertain road of imperialism, as it did five years later.

President Cleveland, who suspected that a powerful Uncle Sam
had gravely wronged a weak native queen, withdrew the treaty from
the Senate and ordered an investigation. The inquiry revealed that a
strong majority of the population did not wish annexation, and that the
coup probably would not have succeeded without the unauthorized
intervention of Minister Stevens. But since Cleveland could not properly use force on the new, white-dominated Hawaiian Republic, it remained precariously independent, pending a change of heart (and of
administration) in Washington.[19]

WAS GROVER CLEVELAND A STRIKEBREAKER?

In the presidential election of 1892, when the Populists made their most
formidable bid, ex-President Cleveland defeated the incumbent President Harrison and the Populist candidate General Weaver by a comfortable margin. (Cleveland's earlier campaign for a lower tariff had
evidently borne belated fruit.) Within a few months after the new ad-

[19] A scholarly summation is Merze Tate, *Hawaii: Reciprocity or Annexation*
(1968).

ministration took office, the financial Panic of 1893 struck with devastating force, presenting the White House with a series of vexatious problems. Among them was the Pullman railroad strike, which precipitated one of the most controversial episodes of Cleveland's troubled career.

In 1894, at the height of the panic, the wealthy Pullman Palace Car (sleeping car) Company reduced the wages of its workers by 25 percent, without reducing the relatively high rents of the company-owned houses in the model town of Pullman, now in Chicago. The American Railway Union, headed by the militant Eugene V. Debs, refused in sympathy to handle Pullman cars, thereby tieing up many key railroads. Interstate commerce, including the transit of mails, was undoubtedly disrupted, although the strikers expressed a willingness to carry mail on non-Pullman cars. The governor of the state, John P. Altgeld ("the Eagle Forgotten"), insisted that the state troops could handle the situation.

Cleveland's Attorney General, hot-tempered Richard Olney, a prominent railroad attorney and a director of one of the railroads involved, was a rock-ribbed conservative.[20] After winning the acquiescence of President Cleveland, he arranged for the issuance of a federal injunction forbidding interference with the transit of mails. The next day (July 3, 1894) he induced President Cleveland to send United States troops to Chicago. Debs was indicted by a federal grand jury for interfering with the mails and interstate commerce; he was ultimately sentenced to six months in prison for contempt of court as a consequence of defying the injunction. The strike was finally broken by this armed intervention from Washington, but not until bloody clashes and wholesale destruction had taken their toll.

Governor Altgeld stoutly maintained that Cleveland's dispatching of troops, without a request from the Illinois authorities, was an unconstitutional invasion of states' rights. He insisted that the situation had been under control, that there had been no serious disorders, and that extreme violence had broken out only after the federal forces were dispatched. But the Supreme Court, with several of its members former railroad attorneys, unanimously upheld the right of the Washington government to intervene in order to free interstate transportation and to insure transit of the mails (In re Debs, 1895).

Whatever the legalities, it seems clear that a bitterly antilabor

---

[20] In a jealous fit he had permanently barred his daughter from his home after she had married a dentist whom he had found acceptable as a suitor. Henry James, Richard Olney (1923), p. 19.

Secretary Olney had misrepresented basic facts to the President.[21] If he had not done so, Cleveland might have delayed acting, or he might not have acted at all, in which case the President would not have been cast in the role of strikebreaker. In some respects the chief antagonists were not Pullman, Debs, or Cleveland, but Governor Altgeld and Secretary Olney. Altgeld, a man of great compassion for the working class and other victims of injustice, was a leading liberal who might have been the Democratic nominee for President in 1896 if he had not been born in Germany. Olney, a champion of the propertied interests, deplored lawlessness and disorder, and he instinctively turned to the iron fist as a means of restoring order.

DID CLEVELAND MISHANDLE THE VENEZUELA DISPUTE?

The boundary between Venezuela and British Guiana had been a source of recurrent dispute since at least 1840, or more than half a century. London had shown some willingness to accept a compromise line, but in 1887 the Venezuelans abruptly broke off diplomatic relations. Moreover, they employed a skilled propagandist in the United States, William L. Scruggs. This agent proved to be remarkably effective in promoting the Venezuelan side of the controversy to Cleveland and his Secretary of State Olney, the brusque and undiplomatic former Attorney General.

British officialdom was annoyingly indifferent. This dispute was a trivial affair when compared with other imperial headaches, and London wanted no interference by a third party. The Cleveland–Olney duo thereupon decided to force a showdown. Olney fired off a long and labored note to the British Foreign Office in 1895 arguing that Britain's unwillingness to arbitrate the (extreme) claims of Venezuela constituted a violation of the Monroe Doctrine. The United States, he arrogantly insisted, was so dominant in the New World that its "fiat" was "law" on those subjects to which it confined "its interposition." [22]

London's reply, after a maddeningly long delay, was a flat rejection of outside intervention. Cleveland, his dander up, responded by sending a bombshell message to Congress. He urged that the United States appoint a commission to determine where the disputed boundary should run and then, if necessary, sustain it by force.

---

[21] Allan Nevins, *Grover Cleveland* (1933), pp. 611ff. President Hayes had used federal troops to control the railway strikers of 1877, but only at the invitation of the state authorities.

[22] *Foreign Relations, 1895, I,* 558 (Olney to Bayard, July 20, 1895).

So overwhelming was the popular response that critics accused Cleveland of electioneering. Whether consciously or not, he was appealing to widespread anti-British feeling, especially among the Irish–Americans, on the eve of a presidential election in which the reigning Democrats would be bitterly blamed for the current economic depression. At a time when American silverites were blaming hard times on gold-standard Britain, Cleveland had chosen Britain as a convenient whipping boy.

The President's two-fisted reapplication of the Monroe Doctrine was grotesquely out of line with any previous interpretation. If Cleveland and Olney had declared that Britain, by bulging her boundary line over into Venezuela, was violating the noncolonization clause of the Monroe Doctrine, they would have been on sound though weaker ground. But instead they took the startling position that any European interference in the New World, even by powers already there, would be regarded as an unfriendly act in violation of the Monroe Doctrine.

WAS THE VENEZUELA BLOWUP BENEFICIAL?

Rather than go to war with the United States, London reluctantly backed down and consented to arbitration of the Venezuelan boundary. With several modifications, the arbiters granted the British essentially what London had been claiming all along, thus proving, as the Foreign Office had long argued, that Venezuela's pretensions had been extravagant in the extreme.

At the height of the crisis, war between America and Britain seemed a real possibility. It was averted in part because the people of Great Britain did not want to fight anybody over a faraway stretch of jungle land, and in part because the rising might of Germany posed a threat nearer the British Isles. Cleveland may well have been bluffing. At least he undertook no serious war preparations, even though the British navy, which was vastly stronger than that of the United States, could presumably have ravaged the American coasts.

Admirers of Grover Cleveland have long applauded his resolute handling of the Venezuela boundary affair. Although risking war, he forced the disputants to arbitrate a running-sore dispute, and thus promoted peace. He jarred the British into recognizing the need for cultivating better relations with America, especially in view of growing German rivalry in Europe. Many Latin Americans appreciated Uncle Sam's concern for their sovereignty, and the Monroe Doctrine seemed to be strengthened by his reaffirmation.

On the other hand, the financial world was badly jolted, as the stock market collapsed and recovery from the current financial panic halted.[23] Europeans voiced renewed dissatisfaction over American pretensions under the Monroe Doctrine, while Canada and many Latin Americans feared dominance by a powerful neighbor whose "fiat" was "law" in this hemisphere. Although Cleveland was a foe of the imperialism that came in 1898, he may have quickened the impulse to imperialism by his stirring defiance of the British lion two years earlier. And the new era of British–American friendship would probably have arrived in 1898 anyhow, given Britain's need for friends, without his having skated so perilously to the edge of war.

A detached observer would probably conclude that the uproar over Venezuela was unnecessary, and that with more patience and tact the problem could have been solved amicably without the lush harvest of ill will. The President's ablest biographer concludes that Secretary Olney, blunt and bellicose, led his chief astray, as he had in the handling of the Pullman strike.[24]

WAS BRYAN UNKNOWN WHEN NOMINATED IN 1896?

The traditional accounts indicate that William Jennings Bryan, an obscure ex-Congressman who had recently been defeated in Nebraska for the U. S. Senate, came out of nowhere at the Democratic convention in Chicago. He swept the assemblage off its feet with his "extemporaneous" "Cross of Gold" speech, and won the nomination solely on the strength of this inspired effort.[25]

Actually Bryan in 1896 was widely known as the most eloquent champion of free silver in the country. Although only thirty-six years old at the time (one year past the constitutional minimum for the Presidency), he had served two terms in Congress, where he had de-

[23] The financial world was not, as once thought, unanimous in opposition to Cleveland, and there is reason to believe that he was in some degree motivated by a desire to protect American commercial interests under the Monroe Doctrine. See Walter LaFeber, "The Background of Cleveland's Venezuelan Policy: A Reinterpretation," *Amer. Hist. Rev.*, LXVI (1961), 947–967. Yet it would appear that commercial motivation was not the dominant one in provoking a showdown; the stake in Latin American trade was relatively small. See N. M. Blake, "Background of Cleveland's Venezuelan Policy," *ibid.*, XLVII (1942), 259–277.

[24] Nevins, *Grover Cleveland*, p. 640. It is interesting to note that Venezuela, in 1968, revived its ancient claims against Guyana, which, as an independent member of the British Commonwealth, had replaced British Guiana in 1966. See *New York Times*, Aug. 14, 1968.

[25] See James A. Barnes, "Myths of the Bryan Campaign," *Miss. Valley Hist. Rev.*, XXXIV (1947), 367–404.

livered sensationally eloquent speeches on the tariff and the currency. In the months preceding the convention, he had presented hundreds of lectures on free silver in dozens of states to tens of thousands of people. While not generally regarded as the probable Democratic candidate, he himself believed that he would be nominated, as did a few others. If the silverites secured control of the Chicago convention (which they did), he was almost certain to be seated as a delegate from Nebraska (which he was), and he would be permitted to make a speech (he was known as the most formidable possible challenger of the "gold bugs").

Everything worked out as Bryan had planned. He insisted that he was nominated not only by his tremendous "Cross of Gold" speech but by what he called the "logic of the situation." He was never a "dark horse" in the sense of being disregarded in the early balloting: he actually ran second to Richard P. (Silver Dick) Bland of Missouri before winning out on the fifth ballot. None of his other dozen opponents in the balloting, virtually all of them "unknowns" today, could conceivably have staged as effective a campaign as he did.

As for Bryan's speech being "extemporaneous," he had already presented essentially the same arguments to scores, if not hundreds, of audiences throughout the country.[26] After making a few introductory remarks by way of adjustment to the occasion, he launched into his superlative effort without having to worry unduly about the phrasing or what he was going to say next. It was probably the most effective convention speech ever delivered in the United States, but it was not primarily extemporaneous.[27]

DID BRYAN COME NEAR WINNING IN 1896?

Bryan claimed after the election that if he could have rearranged 19,446 votes in six close states, he would have won by one electoral vote.[28] Roughly the same calculation can be made about many close presidential elections, but it is equivalent to saying that if one team had received all the "breaks" in a football game and its opponents none, the lucky team would have won.

Statistically, the election of 1896 was not even close, certainly

[26] David Starr Jordon recalled that essentially the same speech was delivered to the students of Stanford University, and that "we were not impressed with the profundity of the discourse. . . ." *The Days of a Man* (2 vols., 1922), I, 477.

[27] Bryan wrote, shortly after the event, "A portion of the speech was extemporaneous, and its arrangement entirely so, but parts of it had been prepared for another occasion." W. J. Bryan, *The First Battle* (1896), p. 206.

[28] Coletta, *Bryan*, p. 192.

not when compared with most canvasses since the Civil War. McKinley triumphed with 271 electoral votes to 176, with 51 percent of the popular vote to 46 percent for Bryan, and with a popular plurality of nearly 600,000 votes. If Bryan could have reversed the results by arranging some 19,000 votes, the minority rather than the majority would have won.[29]

Every close election campaign abounds in "ifs." If the balloting had occurred in August, when the Bryan tide was cresting, McKinley might well have been defeated. If the price of wheat had not risen sharply in the last few weeks of the canvas; if the Republicans under Mark Hanna, their National Chairman, had not spent money so lavishly in their campaign of "education"; if Hanna's "slush fund" had not bought "phantom votes"; if the Gold (Cleveland) Democrats had only supported the ticket; if Bryan had only spurned the Populist endorsement; if the Republicans had not threatened workers with loss of jobs, manufacturers with loss of contracts, and mortgagors with loss of mortgages; if the urban laborites (who wanted to be paid in sound dollars) had supported Bryan more strongly; if the solvent farmers had only voted Democratic (farmers who owned their land without mortgage were inclined to vote Republican) [30] — if all these adverse circumstances had only operated in Bryan's favor, he probably would have been elected.

Free silver was unquestionably the leading issue of the campaign, but there were many others, including the tariff and antilabor injunctions.[31] The results were hailed by the Republicans, despite their 51 percent popular vote, as a mandate to enact legislation placing the country inflexibly on the gold standard. We may doubt that they had a genuine mandate, but in any event they illogically interpreted the result as a directive to raise the tariff (in the Dingley Act of 1897). Not until March 1900, some three years after McKinley's gold-bug victory, were the Republicans able to enact the Gold Standard Act. By that time enough silverite members had left Congress to make possible this legislative triumph.

---

[29] With 6,516,722 votes, Bryan attracted more support than any previous presidential candidate, winner or loser. But McKinley polled 7,113,734.

[30] Farmers in the upper Mississippi Valley were normally Republican anyhow, and Bryan's failure to make serious inroads among the solvent farm owners of this area not only cost him the election but undermined the theory that the campaign was basically an agrarian–industrial clash. Gilbert C. Fite, "Republican Strategy and the Farm Vote in the Presidential Campaign of 1896," *Amer. Hist. Rev.*, LXV (1960), 787–806.

[31] To the embarrassment of the Republican high command in the presidential election of 1896, candidate McKinley had earlier shown considerable sympathy for free silver. H. Wayne Morgan, *William McKinley and His America* (1963), pp. 154–155.

WAS SILVER MONEY DISHONEST MONEY?

One charge leveled against the Bryanites in 1896, as well as against free-silverites of an earlier day, was that silver money was "dishonest." If the free and unlimited coinage of silver was instituted, debtors would be able to pay off their creditors with dollars that were worth about fifty cents — or so the argument ran.

Precious metals, in human terms, cannot be dishonest, though men can put them to dishonest use. In the case of money in the post–Civil War decades, the basic problem was one of deflation. If a farmer borrowed $1,000 at a time when wheat was worth a dollar a bushel, he in effect was agreeing to pay back 1,000 bushels of wheat. If the price of wheat had dropped to 50 cents a bushel at the time his mortgage fell due, he would have to "pay back" two thousand bushels of wheat, or twice as much (plus interest) as he had borrowed. The indebted farmer, with much logic, argued that this arrangement was unfair and dishonest.[32]

During periods of inflation, as during the War of Independence, the process was reversed. Then debtors could with relative ease pay their debts "without mercy," while creditors fled, rather than be forced to accept depreciated money. In such circumstances those who had loaned good money complained that they were being paid off in "dishonest dollars." The only way this problem can be solved is to devise some scheme by which the purchasing power of the dollar will remain constant.

We may conclude that the free-silverites of 1896 were not necessarily dishonest or honest but were victims of an economic squeeze from which they sought escape by using the lever of free silver. Bryan's overshadowing emphasis on this weapon has obscured the fact that basically he was a reformer who was seeking to improve the plight of the masses. He sincerely believed that they were the victims of the privileged classes, buttressed by an inflexible currency.[33]

Would the country have been ruined if Bryan had been elected? He was branded a crackpot and a lunatic, but one may doubt if any catastrophe would have occurred. The stock market no doubt would have dropped, and certain international bankers would have been hurt.

[32] The effect of this hypothetical situation was mitigated by the fact that many mortgages ran for about three and a half years, and often could be renewed on more favorable terms. North, *Growth and Welfare*, p. 141.

[33] As Secretary of State in 1913, Bryan had a large hand in persuading Congress to accept the Federal Reserve Act, which added immensely to the flexibility of the currency.

But Bryan would not have been able to institute free silver in the face of a Republican Congressional majority, which would control the Senate for at least four more years. By that time, returning prosperity and the increased supply of gold (which eased deflation) might have made impossible the adoption of 16 to 1 by Congress. By 1898, the slogan "Free Silver" was eclipsed by "Free Cuba."

At all events, Bryan accepted defeat with something of a sense of relief, partly because he realized that he could not have made his views prevail for at least four years with a hostile Congress.[34]

WAS CLEVELAND A SUCCESSFUL PRESIDENT?

Cleveland was unique in being the only President to serve a second full term after an interval had separated his two stints in office. They were about as unlike as two administrations could be. During the first one, although confronted with a Republican Senate that offset a Democratic House, he could point to a number of legislative achievements of a nonpartisan nature. The list includes the Presidential Succession Act of 1886 (stipulating the line of succession in the event of the President's death); the Electoral Count Act of 1887 (to prevent the kind of deadlock that had developed between Hayes and Tilden in 1876–1877); the repeal in 1887 of the Tenure of Office Act of 1867 (thereby enabling the President to dismiss at will Senate-confirmed appointees); and the Interstate Commerce Act of 1887 (aimed at curbing abuses by the railroads).

In his first term Cleveland also brought the issue of fraud forcefully to the attention of the country by vetoing the Dependent Pension Bill and numerous private pension bills. Bothered by the mounting surplus in the Treasury, he launched a campaign of education aimed at reducing high tariff schedules. His record also showed some progress in civil service reform, in conserving natural resources, and in building a modern steel navy. Although defeated for reelection in 1888, he polled a plurality of the popular vote.

Retiring to New York City to practice law after his defeat, Cleveland became associated with a wealthy class, and his innate conservatism deepened. During these years radicalism throughout the country increased, with the Populist movement peaking in the early 1890s, and the ex-President found himself increasingly out of step with the times. Returning to the White House in 1893, he was pleased to have a Congress

---

[34] Coletta, *Bryan*, p. 190.

controlled by his own Democratic party. But the irony is that his legislative achievements were less noteworthy in his second term than in his first, even though Democrats mustered a majority in both Senate and House during the first two years. In the midterm elections, late in 1894, the Republicans regained both houses by a landslide.

At the outset of his second administration, Cleveland stirred up a storm when he tried to do right by the deposed Liliuokalani, ex-Queen of Hawaii. Then came the devastating Panic of 1893, and Cleveland's controversial efforts to mitigate its blight by engineering a repeal of the Sherman Silver Purchase Act and by borrowing immense reserves of gold from the Wall Street bankers for the Treasury in a series of highly criticized transactions. His strenuous efforts at tariff reform netted the unsatisfactory Wilson–Gorman Bill, which, in the interests of party harmony, he rather weakly allowed to become law without his signature.[35] He broke the back of the Chicago Pullman strike in 1894 by sending in federal troops, with dubious warrant, and he came close to precipitating war with Britain over the Venezuela–British Guiana boundary. He atoned in some measure for this belligerency by refusing to get involved in the Cuban rebellion on the side of the insurgents (that perplexity was left for President McKinley). He also made further progress in civil service reform through an extension of the classified service, and he struck a blow for conservation of land through the Carey Desert Land Grant Act of 1894.

Despite his creditable record, Cleveland received an unprecedented slap in the face near the end of his second term. The free-silver Democratic Convention in Chicago, by a vote of 564 to 357, rejected a resolution approving his administration. Cleveland left office with the Treasury surplus gone and his party disrupted, defeated, and demoralized. Sixteen years were to pass before another Democrat would become President (Woodrow Wilson), although he polled only 41.8 percent of the popular vote. Thirty-six years were to elapse before a Democratic candidate (Franklin Roosevelt) would receive more than 50 percent of the popular vote.

Historians commonly rate Cleveland, the conservative, as a "Near Great" President. Admittedly he was more forthright, stubborn, and courageous than most, but much of his achievement was on the negative side: in not approving pension legislation, in not annexing Hawaii, in not intervening in Cuba, and in not supporting the silver

---

[35] In addition, Cleveland had aroused the Senate by writing to a member of the House that an abandonment of Democratic low-tariff principles would mean "party perfidy and party dishonor." Allan Nevins, ed., *Letters of Grover Cleveland, 1850–1908* (1933), p. 355.

inflationists. His most conspicuous single effort in the area of aggressive leadership related to tariff reform, yet the Wilson–Gorman Act of 1894 was so foreign to his wishes that in effect he repudiated it. Ironically, the most redeeming feature of this unsatisfactory law — a federal income tax — was knocked out the next year by an adverse ruling of the Supreme Court. (Not until 1913 was such a levy made possible under the 16th Amendment.)

Historians can applaud Cleveland's courage and dogged devotion to duty, while regretting that he was unable to rack up a larger number of constructive achievements.

ADDITIONAL GENERAL REFERENCES

Harold U. Faulkner, *Politics, Reform and Expansion, 1890–1900* (1959); F. A. Shannon, *The Farmers' Last Frontier: Agriculture, 1860–1897* (1945); G. C. Fite, *The Farmers' Frontier, 1865–1900* (1966); John D. Hicks, *The Populist Revolt* (1931); John F. Stover, *The Life and Decline of the American Railroad* (1970); G. R. Taylor and I. D. Neu, *The American Railroad Network, 1861–1890* (1956); Thomas C. Cochran, *Railroad Leaders, 1845–1890* (1953); Allan Nevins, *Study in Power: John D. Rockefeller* (2 vols., 1953); Matthew Josephson, *The Robber Barons* (1934); Norman Pollack, *The Populist Response to Industrial America* (1962); Allan Nevins, *Grover Cleveland* (1932); Robert D. Marcus, *Grand Old Party: Political Structure in The Gilded Age, 1880–1896* (1971); S. L. Jones, *The Presidential Election of 1896* (1964); R. F. Durden, *The Climax of Populism: The Election of 1896* (1965); P. W. Glad, *The Trumpet Soundeth: William Jennings Bryan and His Democracy, 1896–1912* (1960); Louis W. Koenig, *Bryan* (1971); P. W. Glad, *McKinley, Bryan, and the People* (1964); Margaret Leech, *In the Days of McKinley* (1959); H. W. Morgan, *William McKinley and His America* (1963).

24

The Spanish-American War and After

Inaugurated in March 1897, President McKinley inherited oppressive problems, notably Cuba. There the Spaniards had been attempting for two years to stamp out a new rebellion by employing ruthless methods. American antipathy to Spain, fanned by the "yellow press," reached dangerous dimensions when the U. S. battleship Maine was blown up in Havana harbor in mid-February 1898. After Spain failed to make satisfactory concessions to the rebellious Cubans, Congress formally precipitated war in April 1898.

The U. S. navy, better prepared than the army, destroyed two Spanish fleets, one at Manila on May 1, 1898, and the other near Santiago, Cuba, on July 3, 1898. A small American army landed in Cuba, amid great confusion, and successfully fought the Spaniards in several sharp engagements.

Beaten Spain agreed to an armistice in August 1898, fortunately for the disease-decimated American army in Cuba. By the terms of the Treaty of Paris, approved in 1899, the United States acquired Puerto Rico, Guam, and the Philippines. Cuba was given nominal freedom, though kept in Yankee leading strings for many years. The American electorate seemingly, but illusorily, approved the new policy of overseas imperialism by resoundingly reelecting McKinley over Bryan in 1900.

In annexing the Philippine Islands, America annexed a bloody insurrection which technically dragged on from 1899 to 1902. Already a world power in 1898, the United States now emerged as a great power, with a significant new stake in the Far East. Secretary John Hay's efforts to protect American economic interests in China through an Open Door policy, proclaimed in 1899–1900, met only limited and temporary success with the other major nations.

WAS McKINLEY A PUPPET PRESIDENT?

Cartoonists and other mythmakers did the amiable President McKinley a grave disservice. They portrayed him as a weak puppet, manipulated by Wall Street and the trusts, as personified by a domineering and bloated Mark Hanna. Vice President Theodore Roosevelt has often been quoted as saying that McKinley had "the backbone of a chocolate eclair," [1] because he would not yield to the clamor of the crowd and rush into war with Spain. Yet backbone was needed to resist the pressure of inflamed opinion and not throw the issue into the lap of Congress.

McKinley was a seasoned politician, administrator, and legislator. He provided Congress and his Republican party with effective leadership, more so than most of his predecessors. Like George Washington, he was slow in making up his mind but firm in his decisions. He finally recommended war with Spain after prolonged deliberation, which involved carefully weighing the alternatives and listening to the voice of public opinion, as all leaders in a democracy should. He decided to retain the Philippines by the same process. Perhaps he blundered in taking these faraway islands, but when a decision had to be made, McKinley was capable of showing decisiveness. With a headline-catching Secretary of State, John Hay, McKinley was the first Chief Executive to provide active world leadership, ranging from Cuba to Hawaii to Guam to the Philippines to China.

DID DE LOME INSULT McKINLEY?

Even a diplomatist is entitled to private opinions, and Minister Dupuy de Lôme, ably representing Spain in Washington, wrote a confidential letter to a personal friend in Havana, probably late in 1897. It was stolen from the post office in Havana by an insurgent spy and turned over to Hearst's New York *Journal*, which, conniving at theft, published it on February 9, 1898. The resulting uproar hastened the drift toward an open break.

---

[1] This sneer has also been attributed to ex-Speaker T. B. Reed, but in neither case has it been documented. The most scholarly biography of McKinley is H. W. Morgan, *William McKinley and His America* (1963).

Alluding to a recent message to Congress by McKinley, De Lôme described the President as "weak and a bidder for the admiration of the crowd, besides being a would-be politician who tries to leave a door open behind himself while keeping on good terms with the jingoes of his party."

There was much truth in De Lôme's observations, for McKinley was both a servant and molder of public opinion. Moreover, these epithets were not nearly so harsh as those that were being hurled at the President by a war-thirsty press, including those journals that demanded drastic action for this insult to the Chief Executive. A demand for De Lôme's recall was forthwith presented to Madrid, which had already received the Minister's resignation.

De Lôme had committed no real sin but he had violated the diplomatist's eleventh commandment, "Thou shalt not be found out." His most damning statement, generally overlooked at the time and later, was a recommendation that Madrid use duplicity in proposed commercial negotiations with the United States. If Spanish officials could resort to bad faith in this area, what reason was there to believe that they were negotiating in good faith for a settlement of the Cuban crisis? Increasingly McKinley and his advisers were being driven to the conclusion that war was the only viable alternative.[2]

DID SPANIARDS BLOW UP THE BATTLESHIP "MAINE"?

On February 15, 1898, only six days after the De Lôme letter made the headlines, the second-class battleship *Maine* provided a supersensation by exploding in Havana harbor, with the loss of some 260 officers and men. The destruction of this warship was undeniably one of the major precipitants of the war — perhaps the major precipitant. Yet to this day we do not know, and probably shall never know, how she was blown up or by whom.[3] The assumption was widespread in America that perfidious Spain had done the dastardly deed, while the proud Spaniards bitterly resented this affront to their honor.

An impartial investigation by a disinterested body was never made; Washington flatly rejected Spain's offer to arbitrate. There was one official Spanish investigating commission, and although it was not allowed near the wreck lest it tamper with the evidence, it concluded

[2] H. W. Morgan, "The De Lôme Letter: A New Appraisal," *Historian*, XXVI (1963), 36–49.
[3] This conclusion is reached in John E. Weems, *The Fate of the "Maine"* (1959), pp. 171, 177–178.

that there had been an internal (accidental) explosion. Two official U. S. investigations were undertaken, in 1898 and 1911, both conducted completely or partially by the Navy Department, a party at interest. They found for an external explosion (which meant a submerged or partially submerged mine), although the conclusions of the two American investigations were somewhat contradictory. The 1911 examination, which involved constructing a coffer dam around the wreck and pumping out the surrounding water, revealed some metal plates bent inward, but this evidence is not conclusive. There were two explosions, the second possibly being the powder magazines; and plates can be bent into curious and inexplicable shapes by internal suctions or buckling under the weight of a sinking ship.

An internal accidental explosion might have resulted from spontaneous combustion in the coal bunkers, defective electrical wiring (it was then in a primitive state), or some other mischance. Mysterious explosions have occurred in time of peace on warships on dozens of occasions.[4] Cuban Communists now contend that the Americans blew up the ship themselves so that they would have an excuse to fight Spain and "enslave" Cuba in the golden chains of Wall Street. This absurd allegation assumes that responsible officials in Washington were guilty of wholesale murder and that they would destroy a formidable warship on the eve of war with a Spain that was alleged to have a slightly stronger navy. If this was the purpose, the destruction of an old Civil War ironclad in Havana harbor would have served about as well.

Other hypotheses have all been debated. Cuban insurgents may have blown up the ship to bring America into the war on their side. Headstrong Spanish subalterns may have taken matters into their own hands. Yet both of these explanations involved a considerable number of persons, and the risk of detection, in view of the watch being kept by the *Maine*, would have been great. Besides, complete secrecy would have been most difficult to maintain, especially for more than seventy years.

Also improbable is the hypothesis that Spanish officials in Cuba, acting under orders from Madrid, deliberately blew up the vessel. Spain was trying by every honorable means to avoid war, not trigger one. Nervous Spanish officials in Cuba fully realized that America was only

---

[4] In 1936 I arranged for a questionnaire to be sent to the sixty prominent Cubans listed in *Who's Who in Latin America*. Asked to choose among the various theories, nineteen responded. They were overwhelmingly of the opinion that the explosion was of an internal accidental nature and that this view was also held by a majority of the Cuban people. Details appear in Joseph E. Alder, "The *Maine* Incident," unpublished Master's Thesis, Stanford University (1936).

90 miles away, while Spain was 3,000 miles away and "God was high in the heavens." Yet war hysteria swept the United States, while the masses irrationally seized upon the most improbable explanation of all.

COULD McKINLEY HAVE AVERTED WAR WITH SPAIN?

Early in 1898 Washington proposed, preliminary to an amicable adjustment of the Cuban problem, that Madrid grant an armistice to the insurgents and revoke the order herding rebel civilians into concentration camps.[5] A third condition, involving eventual United States mediation and possible independence for Cuba, was put in a less imperative category.[6] Spain yielded to the first two American demands by revoking reconcentration orders and directing an armistice *at the discretion of the commander of the army.*

On April 11, 1898, two days after Spain had made these hope-giving concessions, McKinley sent his message to Congress recommending a declaration of war. The assumption is common that he deliberately forced a conflict on Spain after Madrid had capitulated to American terms.

Only two of the three conditions were involved. The offer of an armistice to the insurgents was rather vague and also meaningless. The Cuban rebels had announced that they would accept no such concession, and hence the war would grind on. The third condition, involving eventual U. S. mediation and Cuban independence, was ignored.

It was clear to McKinley that Spain was unwilling to give up Cuba, and that the rebellion would drag on indefinitely. Tens of thousands of Cubans would die; disease might spread to the United States from the island pesthouse; and American trade and financial interests would continue to be damaged. Public opinion was ripe for intervention after the blowing up of the *Maine,* and if the Republican administration did not fight Spain, the Democrats could well win the Congressional elections of 1898 and the White House in 1900, under the banner of

---

[5] In 1896, finding that the civilians succored the *insurrectos*, General Weyler inaugurated the policy of herding the populace behind barbed wire enclosures. In the absence of proper hygienic precautions, the victims died like flies; hence the so-briquet "Butcher" Weyler. As in all internecine conflicts of this magnitude, there were atrocities on both sides. After America became involved in the Philippine insurrection in 1899, she adopted reconcentration policies that bore an unpleasant resemblance to those of "Butcher" Weyler. The British in South Africa resorted to similar measures with atrocious results during the Boer War (1899–1902).

[6] E. R. May, *Imperial Democracy* (1961), p. 154.

"Free Cuba" rather than "Free Silver." To Republicans like McKinley the breakup of the rest of Spain's empire was preferable to the breakup of the Grand Old Party.

McKinley might have stood out against war to the end if he had not been convinced that fighting Spain would solve a seemingly insoluble problem which involved humanitarianism, national honor (the *Maine*), and international investments and trade. Successful warfare was presumably in the best interests not only of the country but of the Republican party as well.

DID THE YELLOW JOURNALS BRING ON WAR?

William R. Hearst, the newspaper tycoon, is said to have boasted that it cost him $3 million to bring on the war with Spain. This is one of those statements which may never have been uttered but which, if uttered, should not be taken seriously. It ascribes to one individual too much credit for having unleashed forces which had already gathered immense momentum.

Hearst, with his New York *Journal*, and Joseph Pulitzer, with his New York *World*, were rivals in "yellow journalism" who successfully built up circulations by featuring sensational reporting. Cuba's insurrection, with its atrocity stories, was made to order for them. The truth about the concentration camps was bad enough, but the more jingoistic journals resorted to exaggeration, misrepresentation, and downright falsification. Lurid pictures supplemented blaring headlines.

Many sober editors throughout the land did not imitate the tactics of Hearst and Pulitzer, but others did.[7] Whether or not war with Spain could have been avoided if there had been more responsible journalism is a question that can never be answered with complete confidence. The De Lôme insult, the blowing up of the *Maine*, indignities to American citizens in Cuba, the deaths of thousands of innocent women and children in concentration camps — all these were provocative facts needing no journalistic embroidery.

Senator Proctor of Vermont visited four of the six provinces of Cuba, and then solemnly delivered a devastating speech on the floor of the Senate (March, 1898). He reported confirmation of the common estimate that out of a population of 1,600,000 Cubans, a total of 200,000

---

[7] See G. W. Auxier, "Middle Western Newspapers and the Spanish–American War, 1895–1898," *Miss. Valley Hist. Rev.*, XXVI (1940), 523–534.

had died within a few months of starvation and disease caused by mistreatment. This widely reported speech greatly reinforced the impact of the yellow journals.

DID BIG BUSINESS FORCE WAR WITH SPAIN?

In 1936 Julius W. Pratt published an impressive monograph which argued that the business community, which feared the unsettling influence of war, had strongly opposed the steps that led to the clash with Spain. America's annual trade with Cuba amounted to about $100 million; its investments to $50 million. In 1963 Walter LaFeber sharply challenged Pratt's view by citing a number of spokesmen for business, finance, and commerce who favored hostilities.[8] Where does the truth lie?

In the absence of modern polling techniques, and even with them, it is hazardous to generalize about so elusive a phenomenon as public opinion. But if any one fact emerges with clarity from this confused era, it is that public sentiment generally favored a war to evict the Spaniards from Cuba and end the inhumanity of their repressive measures. Within this great body of citizenry, there was the business community: some of its members favored intervention, others did not. What the rough percentages may have been, we shall never know. It is unlikely that the business world, clearly divided on this question, was alone capable of exerting enough pressure on McKinley to persuade him that war with Spain was in the national interest. The heavier pressure evidently came from the great body politic. Actually some of the largest American investors in Cuba favored Spain's efforts to crush the insurrection; having secured their concessions from Spanish authority, they feared complete loss to successful rebels.

After the shooting started, and imperial plums such as the Philippines began to fall into America's basket, the business community perked up. It began to show much greater unanimity on the desirability of expanding foreign markets and investments in a colonial empire controlled by Americans. Cuba, however, was to be free, for reasons relating to both idealism and dollars.[9]

[8] See J. W. Pratt, *Expansionists of 1898* (1936); Walter LaFeber, *The New Empire* (1963).
[9] Congress put itself formally on record through the Teller Amendment, when voting for intervention in Cuba, as guaranteeing the freedom of Cuba, to the bewilderment of land-grabbing European imperialists. America was fighting to free, not enchain Cuba; besides, American sugar interests did not want the lush island to come inside the U. S. tariff wall. There was also considerable fear that Spain

DID McKINLEY AUTHORIZE THE PHILIPPINE ATTACK?

Young and superenergetic Theodore Roosevelt, on fire for war, was Assistant Secretary of the Navy. The legend is that one day (February 25, 1898) when his superior was absent, he cabled instructions to Commodore Dewey, commanding the Far Eastern squadron in Chinese waters, to attack the Spanish fleet in the Philippines in the event of war with Spain. Acting solely on Roosevelt's orders, Dewey delivered magnificently on May 1, and McKinley woke up, the tale further relates, to find the Philippine island archipelago on his hands. A Chicago newspaperman reports the President as saying that before Dewey's victory he could not have told within 2,000 miles "where those darned islands were." [10]

There is a kernel of truth in this hoary story. Theodore Roosevelt did manage to put Commodore George Dewey, a fighting man, in command of the Asiatic squadron, and did cable orders to be in readiness to strike the Spanish fleet. But the plan for attacking the Philippines had been worked out in 1896 within the Navy Department the year before Roosevelt arrived in Washington.[11] McKinley was advised as early as September 1897 of the proposed blow; the Secretary of the Navy twice discussed with him the orders for Dewey; and the President approved the final directive sent to the Commodore on April 24, 1898,[12] one week before the battle in Manila Bay. McKinley would have been an ill-informed man indeed if he could not have told within 2,000 miles where those "darned islands" were.

WAS DEWEY'S VICTORY A PRAISEWORTHY ONE?

Dewey, with a fleet of six fighting ships, sailed boldly at night into Manila Bay, although it was falsely rumored to be mined. On May 1, 1898, during several hours of firing, he destroyed the entire Spanish fleet of a dozen or so third-rate vessels, with no loss of life on the American side and with minimal damage to his own command. Few naval

---

would attempt to transfer Cuban financial liabilities to the United States. P. S. Holbo, "The Convergence of Moods and the Cuban–Bond 'Conspiracy' of 1898," *Jour. of Amer. Hist.*, LV (1968), 54–72.

[10] H. H. Kohlsaat, *From McKinley to Harding* (1923), p. 68.

[11] There was nothing sinister about having these "contingency" war plans. Major nations routinely work them out for possible foes.

[12] J. A. S. Grenville and G. B. Young, *Politics, Strategy, and American Diplomacy* (1966), Ch. X; May, *Imperial Democracy*, p. 244.

victories have been more complete, and the rapture of the American public was unrestrained.

Dewey's daring foray proved not so daring as it seemed at first sight, even though the enemy had shore batteries and some torpedo boats. The probabilities are that he knew Manila Bay was not mined: Consul General Williams, who reported to Washington that it was not, joined Dewey's fleet shortly before it left Chinese waters, and in all likelihood so informed the commander. Moreover, the Spanish fleet, badly outgunned, was grossly overmatched. All of the ships were small, and almost all were antiquated and inefficiently served. One of the vessels, with machinery in disrepair, lay immobile, and such of its guns as could be brought to bear were pointed out to sea. The Spanish losses were some 380 killed and wounded.

So much can go wrong in a military or naval operation of major proportions that Dewey clearly took certain risks, but the odds, in the light of hindsight, were strongly in his favor. As events turned out, he probably was closer to destruction from the guns of a gathering German fleet than from those of the Spaniards.

DID THE BRITISH SAVE DEWEY FROM THE GERMANS?

Dewey had smashed the Spanish ships but had to wait in the harbor for troops from America with which to capture fortified Manila. The city was also under attack from the Philippine insurgents. During this long and anxious delay, foreign warships began to assemble in the Bay, presumably to evacuate imperiled nationals from Manila and to observe events. The colony-hungry Germans, with an eye to picking up the Philippines should the Americans not annex them, gradually assembled a stronger fleet than Dewey's — under the circumstances a grave discourtesy. The stiff-necked German commander, arguing that Dewey was attempting to enforce an illegal blockade of the harbor, chose to ignore American regulations. At one point Dewey lost his temper and threatened to shoot it out. The German commander finally got the message and in July 1898, the atmosphere cooled appreciably.

By August 13, 1898, American troops and supplies had finally arrived in sufficient numbers to mount an assault on Manila, which surrendered after a kind of mock battle designed to salvage Spanish honor. On the day of this final attack, the two major British warships stationed themselves to the north of Dewey's bombarding fleet of eleven ships, between Dewey and the reduced German squadron of three vessels.

Hence the utterly groundless legend took root that the Germans were about to blow Dewey out of the water, and that the British, by speedily intervening, saved the Americans from destruction.

It is undeniable that the British, seeking allies, were unusually friendly to the Americans at Manila. But the documents reveal that Dewey was then in no danger from the Germans, and that the British made their leisurely move for the purpose of observing the effect of the American bombardment.[13]

DID DEWEY TRIGGER THE ANNEXATION OF HAWAII?

From 1893 to 1898 the paradisiacal Hawaiian Islands, spurned by President Cleveland, had remained outside the gates. The United States would not take them as a gift from the ruling regime, even though there was some risk that the British or the Japanese might scoop them up.

Then came the Spanish–American War, with Commodore Dewey's stunning victory over the Spanish fleet at Manila Bay, May 1, 1898. He urgently needed supplies for his fleet, as well as troops to assault the fortifications of the city. Hawaii was by far the most useful coaling and provisioning way station, although supplies could have been sent with more difficulty by the shorter but fogbound Alaska great-circle route. The conviction rapidly developed that America would have to annex Hawaii to succor Dewey, whom a grateful nation could not abandon in his hour of victory.

Actually the islands did not have to be annexed to be used as a supply base. The government of the tiny republic was openly and flagrantly violating its neutrality by selling needed supplies. It reasoned that if it compromised itself sufficiently by these acts of unneutrality, the United States, as a point of honor, would have to go through with annexation if the Hawaiians were not to face the wrath of Spain alone.[14]

On the wave of a help-Dewey sentiment, a joint resolution for the annexation of Hawaii slid through Congress by an overwhelming vote, in July 1898, and the idyllic islands were at last firmly under American control. Basically more important than short-run assistance to Dewey was the desire to possess Hawaii as a first-line defense of the Pacific Coast. From this point of view, the islands seemed destined to

[13] T. A. Bailey, "Dewey and the Germans at Manila Bay," *Amer. Hist. Rev.*, XLV (1939), 59–81.
[14] T. A. Bailey, "The United States and Hawaii during the Spanish-American War," *Amer. Hist. Rev.*, XXXVI (1931), 552–560.

be in American rather than in Japanese or other foreign hands. Such a need had been obvious to naval experts for decades, and the Spanish–American War provided a pointed and effective object lesson.

HAVE THE ROUGHRIDERS BEEN OVERPRAISED?

The most highly publicized cavalry regiment of the Spanish–American War was the "Rough Riders," [15] organized by Leonard Wood as colonel and Theodore Roosevelt as lieutenant-colonel (later full colonel). This colorful outfit, ranging from ex-cowboys to ex-polo players, ran heavily to tough, two-fisted characters. In the confusion of embarking in Florida, all their horses were left behind (except a few for the officers), as well as about half of the men. Though trained to function on horseback, the Rough Riders became known as "Wood's weary walkers."

Some 16,000 American troops were landed near Santiago, Cuba, of which only about 500 were horseless Rough Riders. They ran into heavy fire in charging uphill against entrenched Spaniards, suffering serious casualties and receiving indispensable support from Negro units, notably the crack 10th Cavalry. Abandoning his horse, Roosevelt advanced recklessly on foot, firing his revolver while bullets whistled past him.[16] He gained further publicity by writing a book, *The Rough Riders*, which did not play down his heroics. He believed himself deserving of the Congressional Medal of Honor for exposing himself so rashly to enemy fire, and he pulled wires during subsequent years in a vain effort to secure it.

Undoubtedly the Rough Riders fought bravely, but they received a disproportionate amount of the glory because of the headline-conscious Roosevelt. One of his proud but dubious boasts was that his outfit suffered much heavier casualties than any of the other five volunteer regiments.

WAS SANTIAGO A GLORIOUS AMERICAN VICTORY?

Early in the war a small and wretchedly ill-prepared Spanish fleet, under the command of a protesting Admiral Cervera, was ordered to the West

---

[15] The name "Rough Riders" had been applied to various units as far back as the Civil War.

[16] Whether Roosevelt charged up San Juan Hill or Kettle Hill is a subject of controversy. At the time he consistently spoke of Kettle Hill, but later referred to the San Juan hills. Theodore Roosevelt, *An Autobiography* (1913), pp. 241–242.

Indies. Upon arriving short of coal, it was promptly bottled up in the
Cuban harbor of Santiago by a vastly superior American naval force.
As the American army closed in from the rear, Cervera was ordered to
escape, although he insisted that such a course was suicidal. On July 3
he suddenly emerged from the harbor, and in a long running fight his
weaker and fewer ships were all destroyed, with a loss of some 600 killed.
The pursuing Americans suffered no damage of consequence, while
losing only one life. As Captain Philip of the *Texas* reportedly remarked, "Don't cheer, boys; the poor devils are dying." [17]

Santiago was an exhilarating victory for the Americans, but
the odds against the Spaniards diluted the taste of triumph. Admiral
Sampson, the American commander, happened to be several miles away
when the enemy made its break, and his second in command, Admiral
Schley, participated more actively in the fighting. An unseemly and
protracted dispute developed between the partisans of these two men as
to who deserved the more credit for the victory. Someone aptly remarked that there was glory enough for all.

WAS THE SPANISH WAR A "SPLENDID LITTLE WAR"?

John Hay, soon to become famous as Secretary of State, wrote in 1898
that the Spanish–American War was a "splendid little war." It was
splendid in the sense that it was short, spectacular, and successful, with
no serious setbacks for American arms. The two naval victories, at
Manila and Santiago, were about as complete as such actions could
possibly be, and losses to the victor were trifling. Spain was heavily
overmatched in these two battles in guns and ships, and such handicaps,
combined with inefficiency and inadequate preparedness, contributed to
her undoing. Even so, American marksmanship and tactics left much to
be desired. When the four destroyed Spanish cruisers near Santiago
were officially examined, evidence was found of only 122 hits, although
the pursuers had fired 9,433 shots. Efforts were made in subsequent
years to improve American marksmanship.

Military operations in Cuba were difficult, and at times the
outcome was seriously in doubt. America was grossly unprepared for
fighting in the tropics, and the confusion, mismanagement, and bungling
that went into this campaign almost defy belief. Soldiers suffered acutely
from the heat (woolen uniforms designed for Montana winters), inade-

---

[17] Cuban insurgents, notoriously uncooperative with and unappreciative of their
American deliverers, shot down some of the Spanish survivors making their way
to shore.

quate or putrid food ("embalmed beef"), and disease, including yellow fever and malaria. If the Spaniards had not surrendered when they did, this "army of invalids" might well have melted away. In the entire war over 2,000 men died of disease, or more than five times the battle deaths.

The Spaniards had an estimated 200,000 troops in Cuba; the Americans landed only some 16,000. Fortunately for the invader, Spanish ineptitude far eclipsed that of the attacker, and Spain managed to put into the Santiago area a force that was not significantly larger than the American army.

DID GOD TELL McKINLEY TO TAKE THE PHILIPPINES?

In November 1899, more than a year after he decided to annex the Philippines, President McKinley conferred with a delegation of fellow Methodists in the White House. More than three years later, early in 1903, one of the members allegedly present, General James Rusling, published in the *Christian Advocate* (January 22) a lengthy verbatim account of what McKinley had supposedly said. Among other revelations, the President declared that, in making the decision to keep the Philippines, he had got down on his knees to seek divine guidance and had received some kind of inner revelation.

In the absence of an expert shorthand reporter or a phenomenal memory, one is puzzled to understand how General Rusling could have remembered McKinley's exact words, even the same day he heard them, much less three years later. Further suspicion is thrown on this tale by a book that Rusling had earlier published in 1899, in which he had Lincoln report, in suspiciously similar language, a prayerful experience on the eve of the Battle of Gettysburg.[18]

It is improbable that McKinley's remarks were recorded with complete precision, and the story of the prayer might well have been fabricated. But McKinley was a devout man, and the alternatives which he weighed were all currently being discussed. They probably had gone through his mind, with or without divine guidance.

To take or not to take the Philippines was a question that presented many choices, all of them bad from the point of view of the United States. If McKinley abandoned the islands to the "brutal" Spaniards, he would prove faithless to the principle involved in freeing Cuba. If he turned the Philippines adrift, anarchy might develop or Germany might gobble them up, thereby possibly touching off a war

[18] See Robert H. Ferrell, *American Diplomacy* (rev. ed., 1969), pp. 402–405.

in which America would be involved. If he took only the main island, Luzon, Germany might seize the others, thus outflanking the American position and rendering it untenable. There seemed to be no safe or honorable choice but to take the whole group. The United States could then "civilize" the islands (missionary elements applauded) and uplift the natives (commercial and manufacturing interests approved), and perhaps ultimately give the Filipinos independence when they had demonstrated that they could stand alone. McKinley had his ear to the ground, whether or not he was attuned to the Almighty, and public opinion seemed to oppose the hauling down of "Old Glory." Prayer probably played a minor role, if that, in the whole episode.

DID AMERICA PROVOKE THE PHILIPPINE INSURRECTION?

The misgoverned Filipinos, emulating the misgoverned Cubans, had risen in revolt against Spain as recently as 1896, under the leadership of Emilio Aguinaldo. The Spanish officials succeeded in coming to terms with the insurgents by buying off their leaders, and in the aftermath Aguinaldo found himself exiled on the Asiatic mainland. Dewey arranged for him to return after the Battle of Manila Bay for purposes of organizing the insurgents once again against Spanish authority.[19] The American admiral, though seeking an ally against a common enemy, later denied having made any promises of independence. But it seems improbable that the Filipinos would have cooperated with the Americans in overthrowing Spanish misrule if they had not been led to believe, tacitly if not explicitly, that they would be given control of their own destiny. They had before them the precedent of the Teller Amendment of 1898, which had specifically promised the Cubans their freedom less than two weeks before the Battle of Manila Bay.

Filipino charges of bad faith led to increasing bitterness and friction. If Congress had been willing to make a specific pledge that the Philippines would be granted their liberty as soon as order was restored, the terribly costly and prolonged insurrection against the Americans probably could have been avoided. A resolution to this effect was postponed by Congress until after the insurrection began in February 1899. Then the proposal was defeated by a narrow margin. The humanitarianism that had prompted a war to free Cuba was evidently dampened by the spirit of commercialism and imperialism generated by the victorious clash of arms.

[19] *Autobiography of George Dewey* (1913), pp. 245–246.

WAS THE PHILIPPINE INSURRECTION A MINOR WAR?

The "splendid little" Spanish–American War, reckoned one of America's major conflicts, lasted some four months; the Filipino insurrection lasted some thirty-eight months, before dribbling off into desultory shooting.[20] The invasion of Cuba had involved some 16,000 American troops; the brief assault on Manila some 20,000 American troops.[21] Yet more than 120,000 U. S. soldiers were finally engaged in the Philippine war, and the casualties (killed, wounded, and dead from disease) exceeded those of the Spanish–American War by about 1,500.

Warfare in the Philippines was large-scale, prolonged, and costly, both in blood and treasure. Nor was it "splendid." Scant glory was derived from battling these shadowy and half-naked natives fighting in defense of their liberties, with Uncle Sam cast in the ugly role of the oppressor.

Atrocities were inevitable. As Americans had learned when fighting Indians, and were later to relearn in Vietnam, when one's adversary resorts to savage tactics, one is pulled down more or less to his level. The barbarities of Filipino guerrillas, sometimes practiced against their own people, provoked retaliation in kind. Shocking tales filtered back to America of the use of the "water cure" torture and other expedients to extract information from reluctant prisoners. Following the surprise and massacre of an entire company of forty-eight American regulars, General Jacob ("Hell-Roaring Jake") Smith issued orders (not carried out) to kill every male over ten years of age on the island. The subsequent reaction of world opinion to such lurid publicity did much to blacken the good name of the United States.

WAS THE ELECTION OF 1900 A MANDATE ON IMPERIALISM?

In 1900 the Democrats renominated Bryan on a platform which declared that McKinley's imperialism was the overshadowing issue. They lost the election by a relatively wide margin, and the Republicans forthwith claimed that they had received a mandate to continue with their imperialistic policy of retaining the Philippines. In short, the public al-

---

[20] Captured in 1901, Aguinaldo died in 1964, in his 94th year, after having collaborated with the Japanese invaders in World War II.

[21] By prearrangement with the Americans, the Spaniards put up token resistance to the Americans in order to avoid capture by the embittered insurgents.

legedly voted approval of annexation. This interpretation has found its way into numerous textbooks, from which it has not been completely dislodged.

There was never a national poll (or even a public opinion poll) on whether the American people wanted to cut loose from the Philippines, and the election of 1900 was not a substitute for such a referendum.[22] There is no official machinery in a general American election for registering the popular will on a single issue. If there were, the alternatives could be put clearly and the vote counted fairly.

A presidential election can hardly be a referendum on any single issue, particularly of foreign policy. In 1900 the voters were asked to vote the Republican ticket (McKinley) or the Democratic ticket (Bryan). Many Republicans who disliked imperialism supported McKinley because they were more fearful of Bryan's free silver heresies. Some Democrats who opposed overseas ventures voted for Bryan because they were more worried about Republican policies regarding the tariff, trusts, and the gold standard. The Democrats claimed that imperialism was the "paramount" issue; the Republicans insisted that the "paramount" issue was Bryanism — that is, what a triumphant Bryan would do to prosperity, the full dinner pail, full employment, and national finance. One of the big questions in 1900 was: What *is* the paramount issue?

To add to the confusion, there were scores of issues set forth in the national platforms, and there were 10 different parties or political groups. What a majority of the voters thought about the Philippines will never be known, certainly not from the vote for Bryan or McKinley. The issue of imperialism, already hashed over for more than two years, had grown stale by 1900. There was no question of taking or not taking the islands: that issue had been decided when the Treaty of Paris was approved by the Senate in February 1899.[23] The Philippines were already on America's hands and had been for more than a year and a half. If the electorate, in a clear-cut referendum, had been asked its views on several possible alternatives, it probably would have voted to free the

[22] T. A. Bailey, "Was the Presidential Election of 1900 a Mandate on Imperialism?" *Miss. Valley Hist. Rev.*, XXIV (1937), 43–52.

[23] The approval of the treaty had supposedly been swung by Bryan's inducing a few key Democratic Senators to vote affirmatively. He argued that America had the islands already and that the quickest way to free them was to take them from Spain and give them their liberty. Critics believed that Bryan's strange conduct grew out of his needing the issue of imperialism with which to tar the Republicans in 1900, for the free silver issue of 1896 was dead. For evidence that Bryan's influence with the Senate was probably not decisive and that he wanted to get the issue of imperialism out of the way, see Paolo E. Coletta, *William Jennings Bryan: Political Evangelist, 1860–1908* (1964), pp. 233–237.

islands after a satisfactory degree of stability had been restored. (The insurrection was still raging and would continue for about a year and a half.)

HOW OPEN WAS HAY'S OPEN DOOR?

The year 1899 was a milestone in America's Far Eastern policy. Secretary John Hay, fearing that foreigners would carve up defenseless China to the detriment of American economic interests, presented identical notes to the major powers in which he urged them to honor the principles of the Open Door.[24] This formula provided that within its leasehold or sphere of interest in China each foreign nation would permit a substantially free flow of trade. In short, let America share in the exploitation. Although the powers on the whole responded with conditional or evasive answers, Hay boldly proclaimed the Open Door to be in effect.

Hay widened his theater the next year when he called for the principal nations to respect the territorial integrity of *all* China and permit commercial equality in "all parts" of China, not merely within foreign leaseholds or spheres of interest. This time he did not call for formal acceptances: he probably feared similarly evasive answers.

For several decades the policy of the Open Door — a fair field and no favors — was generally respected by the powers, but not because they feared John Hay or the frowns of the United States. They were so suspicious of one another that they would not permit any one nation to secure an undue advantage.

As a legal principle, the concept of an Open Door was an ideal dating back to early American trade with China. It continued to be both a phrase and a legal fiction rather than a binding principle in international relations. Not until 1922, when the Washington Conference was in session, did nine of the powers (the Nine Power Treaty) formally sub-

---

[24] Scholars concerned with an economic interpretation of history have stressed in recent years — perhaps overstressed — the impact of commercial and financial interests on the shaping of U. S. policy in the Far East. The older accounts are inclined to play up strategic and humanitarian considerations, including missionary endeavors. The commercial view is presented in Thomas J. McCormick, *China Market: America's Quest for Informal Empire, 1893–1901* (1967). The traditional view of exaggerated expectations of a huge Chinese trade appears in Paul A. Varg, *The Making of a Myth: The United States and China, 1897–1912* (1968). A persistent myth is that America's trade with China or investment stake there was ever of major dimensions. In the best years the trade figures were about 3 percent of America's total exports and the investment statistics were comparably small.

scribe to the Open Door. Germany and Russia, outcasts of World War I, were not among the signatories.

In 1931, when Japan went on a rampage in China's Manchuria, the Open Door received a swift kick in the panels. Continued war in the Far East, combined with the Communist takeover of China in 1949, destroyed whatever validity the policy possessed as regards the former Celestial Empire. But the United States, with varying degrees of success, has through most of its national history sought to achieve the goal of nondiscriminatory commerce (the open door) among the trading nations of the world.

DID AMERICA BECOME A WORLD POWER IN 1898?

For many years the fallacy prevailed that the Spanish–American War was a coming-out party for a new world power. Until then, so we are told, the United States had been of little or no consequence as an international force. But, with a series of smashing triumphs in 1898, the Republic for the first time burst out on the hemispheric stage.

A world power is one that carries sufficient weight to make its influence felt in a positive way in the world balance. If one accepts this standard definition, the United States was a factor of considerable consequence from the day of its official birth, July 1776.[25] The French were sufficiently interested in adding the maritime and military strength of America to their own as to make a hard and fast military alliance with the new Republic in 1778, and then to fight side-by-side with it.

Until 1914 the great powers of Europe formed a kind of exclusive club — Britain, France, Germany, Russia, Austria–Hungary, Italy — and they were loath to recognize the upstart United States as a world power. They could deploy more military strength in Europe than America could, but America could deploy more strength in North America, particularly by the time of the Civil War, than any one of them could or would.

By the 1890s the United States was the second most populous of the white nations (behind Russia) and had built up an industrial establishment, particularly with steel, that placed it at or near the forefront of the powers. The American navy was being modernized, and the army, though small, could be expanded with a vast pool of man-

[25] See T. A. Bailey, "America's Emergence as a World Power: The Myth and the Verity," *Pacific Hist. Rev.*, XXX (1961), 1–16.

power, wealth, and other resources. The Spanish–American War merely demonstrated, to observers who had eyes to see, that the United States had for some time been a *world* power and was entitled to admission to the ranks of the *great* powers. Yet many Europeans, even Adolf Hitler as late as World War II, would not concede that America was a world power. But their saying so did not alter obvious realities.

ADDITIONAL GENERAL REFERENCES

Foster R. Dulles, *America's Rise to World Power, 1898–1954* (1955); H. W. Morgan, *William McKinley and His America* (1963); E. R. May, *Imperial Democracy* (1961) and E. R. May, *American Imperialism: A Speculative Essay* (1968); Walter LaFeber, *The New Empire* (1963); J. W. Pratt, *Expansionists of 1898* (1936); W. A. Russ, *The Hawaiian Republic, 1894–1898* (1961); Merze Tate, *Hawaii: Reciprocity or Annexation* (1968); W. A. Swanberg, *Citizen Hearst* (1961); Frank Freidel, *The Splendid Little War* (1958); Walter Millis, *The Martial Spirit* (1931); Bradford Perkins, *The Great Rapprochement* [with Britain] (1968); R. L. Beisner, *Twelve Against Empire: the Anti-Imperialists, 1898–1900* (1968); E. B. Tompkins, *Anti-Imperialism in the United States: The Great Debate, 1890–1920* (1970); David Healy, *U. S. Expansionism: The Imperialistic Urge in the 1890s* (1970); Tyler Dennett, *John Hay* (1933); A. W. Griswold, *The Far Eastern Policy of the United States* (1938).

25

The Roosevelt–Taft Era

After President McKinley's assassination in September 1901, Vice President Theodore Roosevelt succeeded to the presidency and proceeded to provide flamboyant leadership. In his first (partial) term, he mediated a prolonged coal strike, initiated a sweeping program of conservation, launched a "trust-busting" crusade, settled the Alaska boundary dispute with Canada, and negotiated a treaty with Panama for constructing the isthmian canal. In the presidential election of 1904 Roosevelt snowed under the Democratic nominee, colorless and conservative Alton B. Parker.

Thus elected "in his own right," T. R. (as he was called) partially rewrote the Monroe Doctrine to justify intervention in the Caribbean republics; successfully mediated the Russo–Japanese War in 1905; surmounted crises with Japan arising from attempts by California to exclude coolies; and eased tensions in the Pacific by sending the battleship fleet around the world. Immensely popular with the masses, he could have been nominated and elected for a second full term. Instead he chose to turn over the helm to his hand-picked successor, William Howard Taft, who in 1908 handily defeated Bryan, who by now was a three-time loser.

Roosevelt's act was a difficult one to follow. Taft blundered by supporting too enthusiastically an unsatisfactory tariff revision and by backing Secretary of the Interior Ballinger, who seemed to be anticonservationist. The new President continued with considerable success the "trust-busting" of his predecessor, and his Congresses ground out a considerable amount of constructive legislation. But the Republicans were convulsed by a revolt of the insurgent-progressives within the party, and by a call for Roosevelt to wrest leadership from a Taft who allegedly had fallen under the domination of the conservatives. Roosevelt headed the newly formed Progressive party in 1912 in an effort to unhorse his successor, but the result was to insure a victory for Woodrow Wilson, the liberal Democratic candidate.

WAS THEODORE ROOSEVELT RADICAL OR CONSERVATIVE?

Conservatives within Republican ranks — men such as Mark Hanna — regarded the accession of Roosevelt ("that damned cowboy") with horror. They feared that they had a wild-eyed radical on their hands.

In truth Roosevelt was a relatively mild liberal reformer, whose bluster was worse than his bite. He may not have been the greatest of the Presidents, but he was certainly the noisiest. His favorite saying was "Speak softly and carry a big stick; you will go far," both in domestic and foreign affairs. If he had a formidable navy, he could deal quietly with weaker powers and get results; if he had no military muscle, he could shriek and nothing much would happen. In point of fact, T. R. often rewrote the proverb to read, "Shout loudly and carry a big stick." His egoism, bellicosity, showmanship, exhibitionism, and unconventionality combined to project him into the public eye. One result was that he seemed to be accomplishing more than the record revealed.

As a liberal with the brakes partly on, Roosevelt could be categorized as a radical conservative or a conservative radical, a kind of middle-of-the-roader. He advocated many reforms, but being a practical man he would often settle for half a loaf. He was not one to butt his close-cropped head vainly against a stone wall. He operated as a safety valve to let off discontent. Like his distant cousin, Franklin Roosevelt, he may have headed off full-scale socialism by advocating mild forms of socialism.[1]

WAS ROOSEVELT A FRIEND OF THE NEGRO?

In October 1901, after scarcely a month in the White House, T. R. invited to dinner the distinguished Negro educator, Dr. Booker T. Wash-

---

[1] Roosevelt became more radical after leaving the presidency. While campaigning for reelection in 1912, he went so far as to advocate the popular recall of judges and of judicial decisions at the state level. This latter proposal was especially shocking to conservatives. See his speech of Feb. 21, 1912, at Columbus, Ohio. *Senate Docs.*, 62 Cong., 2 sess., XXXVI, No. 348, pp. 14–15.

ington.[2] (The President had already sought his counsel on a judicial appointment.) The white South was outraged; various reprisals were visited on Negroes; and the cause of racial harmony suffered a sharp setback. Recognizing that he had made a political mistake, Roosevelt invited no more black people to dinner while he was President.

T. R.'s handling of the Brownsville affair evoked an even greater uproar. In August 1906, men from three Negro companies of U. S. infantry, stationed at Fort Brown in Texas, allegedly shot up the town about midnight. One man was killed and a policeman was wounded. A subsequent official investigation revealed that many white Texans resented the presence of the black troops, who had been subjected to various indignities and who supposedly had vented their wrath in this murderous fashion. Since the presumably guilty soldiers would not confess or inform on one another, Roosevelt ordered all men of the three companies discharged "without honor" from the service, with a forfeiture of their pensions and other benefits. About 160 blacks were thus dismissed, including many veterans who had served long and creditably, six of them holding the coveted Congressional Medal of Honor. None of the group was ever formally tried.

Senator Foraker of Ohio, championing the blacks, advanced with considerable plausibility the theory that white civilians had done the shooting. They had then scattered empty army cartridges earlier retrieved from a firing range, thus implicating the Negro soldiers.[3] Apparently realizing that he had acted with undue harshness, Roosevelt softened his order somewhat, and some of the discharged men were ultimately readmitted to the army. The incident is one that Roosevelt chose not to mention in his lengthy *Autobiography* (1913). Belatedly, in 1972, the army cleared the records of the soldiers involved.

[2] As head of the Negro Tuskegee Institute in Alabama, Booker T. Washington had long advocated industrial training as a means of gaining self-respect and economic independence for blacks. He believed that economic equality should precede agitation for social equality with whites. The more radical Negro leaders, conspicuously Dr. W. E. B. DuBois, branded Washington a "White Man's Negro," and wrote him off as an "Uncle Tom." It would appear that this judgment was unduly harsh. Moreover, the fictional Uncle Tom was not a bootlicker. A more recent attempt at a balanced appraisal is John P. Flynn, "Booker T. Washington: Uncle Tom or Wooden Horse," *Jour. of Negro Hist.*, LIV (1969), 262–274. In successfully seeking to please both whites and blacks in the interests of the blacks, Washington wore various masks and deviously resorted to secretiveness, misinformation, and espionage. L. R. Harlan, "Booker T. Washington in Biographical Perspective," *Amer. Hist. Rev.*, LXXV (1970), 1581–1599.

[3] Joseph B. Foraker, *Notes of a Busy Life* (1916), II, 290–291. John D. Weaver, *The Brownsville Raid* (1970) is a popularized account favorable to the blacks.

WAS ROOSEVELT A TRUST-BUSTER?

The Sherman Antitrust Act of 1890 had done little to discourage the formation of gigantic business combinations. Roosevelt's three predecessors had brought only eighteen legal actions against them, or fewer than two a year on the average. Roosevelt, in about seven years, instituted forty-four actions, or about six a year. His determination to revive the half-dead Sherman Act made headlines, conspicuously with the Northern Securities Case in 1902. Cartoonists made merry with their portrayal of the Rough Rider, Big Stick in hand, flailing away at the trusts.

Roosevelt did "bust" a few trusts, but these potent combinations continued to multiply rapidly during his administration. He was at pains to declare that he did not oppose all large combines. He would tolerate good trusts but frown on bad trusts; he was not so much hostile to monopoly as to the evils of monopoly. Yet the salutary results that he achieved were not commensurate with the clatter he stirred up. In point of fact, his lackluster successor, President Taft, brought ninety legal actions against the monopolistic organizations in four years, or more than twice as many as Roosevelt in about half the time.

But in saying that T. R.'s role as a trust-buster has been overplayed one must in all fairness add certain essential facts. He breathed new life into a Sherman Act which had been slowly dying, and he established a precedent for the more numerous prosecutions under Presidents Taft and Wilson. He also helped arouse the public to an awareness of this oppressive problem. And some of his more sensational suits, particularly the dissolution of Standard Oil of New Jersey in 1911, were initiated under his administration but adjudicated under Taft.[4]

WAS ROOSEVELT THE FIRST CONSERVATIONIST?

T. R. was by no means the first conservationist: men such as John Wesley Powell, intrepid explorer of the Colorado River, had already been attempting as early as the 1870s to alert the American public to the magnitude of the environmental problem. In 1900 Congress passed a law authorizing the President to withdraw from sale or settlement mil-

---

[4] Some of the trusts dissolved did not suffer seriously from reorganization. In 1911, after the dissolution of Standard Oil of New Jersey, the stock of the company rose in value. Harold U. Faulkner, *The Quest for Social Justice, 1898–1914* (1931), p. 119.

lions of acres of government land containing coal and other subsurface minerals.

Roosevelt threw himself into the conservation crusade with characteristic vigor and showmanship; he was an Easterner who had come to know the West as a cattle rancher. During his presidency he set aside more than 148 million acres for national forests, more than 80 million acres of mineral lands, and about 1,500,000 acres of water-power sites. In 1907 he established the Inland Waterways Commission to study transportation congestion, and this step forward led to a famous White House Conservation Conference the next year.

Roosevelt's campaign for irrigation and flood control, as well as the preservation of forests, soil, water resources, and wild life, accomplished much good. It deserves to rank with, perhaps outrank, such an achievement as starting the Panama Canal. Later generations, increasingly concerned with environment, owe much to the Rough Rider for having given the early movement Rooseveltian momentum.

DID T. R. "BIG STICK" THE KAISER IN VENEZUELA?

In 1902 the British, German, and Italian governments undertook to compel an irresponsible Venezuelan regime to settle claims for defaulted debts and injuries to their citizens. The Germans notified the State Department of their intention to bring pressure and were informed that the Monroe Doctrine would not be involved, provided that there was no occupation of territory.

Given a go-ahead, the European powers established a joint blockade, seized or sank several Venezuelan gunboats, and bombarded some coastal fortifications. In these operations the Germans appeared to be unnecessarily harsh. Within a short time the Venezuelan government proposed arbitration, with the support of the United States, and the issues were amicably settled.

In several of his presidential letters in subsequent years Roosevelt made clear that he was bursting with some big secret. In 1915–1916, after Germany had brutally invaded Belgium in World War I, he released his tale. It was a lurid one involving a secret ultimatum to the Kaiser to pull out, under threat of being thrown out by Admiral Dewey's Caribbean fleet. Scholars have found no written evidence of such an ultimatum in the German archives, and hence have expressed much skepticism. Some believe that Roosevelt, who tended to magnify his deeds with repeated telling, created the story out of whole cloth in the bitter anti-German atmosphere of World War I.

It is possible that Roosevelt may have exerted some kind of behind-the-scenes pressure on Berlin, perhaps informally — or at least he convinced himself that he did. German representatives in the United States on three occasions reported relatively mild warnings. If Roosevelt fabricated the dramatic story, he evidently formulated the main outlines several years before he left the White House. It is also clear that he rather menacingly concentrated the American fleet in the Caribbean, and this in itself may have been warning enough.[5]

DID ROOSEVELT PLOT THE PANAMA REVOLUTION?

Roosevelt urgently wanted an isthmian canal started, specifically at Panama, then a part of Colombia. The State Department finally negotiated a canal treaty in 1903, but the Colombian Congress rejected it, finding the monetary terms unsatisfactory. (The payment was to have been $10 million down and $250,000 a year.) Roosevelt thereupon denounced the Colombians as highwaymen who were blocking the march of civilization.

Naturally the Panamanians, who had unsuccessfully rebelled on numerous occasions, feared that the United States would now build the canal in Nicaragua. They consequently revolted again, set up a republic on November 3, 1903, and three days later — with indecent haste — Roosevelt extended recognition to the new republic. Shortly thereafter the United States signed a treaty with Panama that permitted construction of the canal.

Colombia claimed that she had been grievously wronged, and her position was strengthened when Roosevelt indiscreetly boasted, in a speech in Berkeley (California) in 1911, "I took the canal zone. . . ." During his lifetime he fought all proposals to recompense the Colombians, but after he was dead and oil (coveted by Yankee promoters) was discovered in Colombia, Congress voted a heart-balm indemnity of $25 million.

Did Roosevelt, as often charged, have an active hand in the plot

---

[5] A full version of the episode, rather favorable to Roosevelt, appears in Howard K. Beale, *Theodore Roosevelt and the Rise of America to World Power* (1956), Ch. 6. A careful examination of American and foreign newspapers has found no support for the heroic Roosevelt tale. Paul S. Holbo, "Perilous Obscurity: Public Diplomacy and the Press in the Venezuelan Crisis, 1902–1903," *The Historian*, XXXII (1970), 428–448. Yet presumptive evidence of some kind of Rooseveltian pressure is presented in E. B. Parsons, "The German-American Crisis of 1902–1903," *The Historian*, XXXIII (1971), 436–452.

that led to the Panama revolution? No convincing evidence has yet come to light that he did. But, consciously or not, he abetted the plotters in Washington. His loud and vehement utterances encouraged the conspirators to go ahead in the belief that the United States would send warships to prevent the Colombian army from landing and crushing the rebellion. This is precisely what happened.

The ancient Treaty of 1846 with Colombia (then New Granada) obligated the United States to preserve the "perfect neutrality" of the isthmus so as to protect "free transit." This stipulation was obviously designed to safeguard Colombia against invasion by some foreign power, and not to be used *against* Colombia herself. In any event, Roosevelt intervened with a display of armed might and the revolution was a success. The moral position of the United States in this affair was not above reproach.

WAS A REVOLUTION NECESSARY FOR A CANAL?

Roosevelt took the position that since Colombia held up the vital treaty, there was no possibility of constructing an isthmian waterway unless he supported the Panamanian revolutionists.

The truth is that there were many feasible routes across the isthmus, and the one that had long been considered the most desirable lay across Nicaragua. This republic was already independent; hence no revolution was needed. The Nicaraguans were eager to come to an agreement with the United States. By the terms of legislation already passed by Congress, Roosevelt was directed to negotiate with Nicaragua if he failed to secure an agreement with Colombia "within a reasonable time and upon reasonable terms." Some legalists were already arguing that Roosevelt was required to turn to Nicaragua after his rebuff at the hands of Colombia.

But T. R. was desperately eager to be "elected in his own right in 1904," and he coveted the glory of starting the canal. Negotiations with Nicaragua might take time and cost more. Moreover both he and the American public were being subjected to clever propaganda by a new French canal company, whose predecessor had earlier started the waterway at Panama. Having failed, it was now trying to unload its holdings on the United States for $40,000,000.[6] Lobbyists for the de-

---

[6] C. D. Ameringer, "The Panama Canal Lobby of Philippe Bunau-Varilla and William Nelson Cromwell," *Amer. Hist. Rev.*, LXVIII (1963), 346–363.

funct concern raised the bogey of earthquakes and volcanic activity in Nicaragua, and these reports evidently influenced both Roosevelt and the American Congress.

The chief lobbyist for the French company, Philippe Bunau-Varilla, did more than help engineer the Panama revolution and salvage the $40,000,000 for his company. He managed additionally to have himself appointed minister from the infant Republic of Panama to Washington, although he was a French citizen. The result was that he hastily negotiated a treaty which the Panamanians have long regarded as most unfair and ungenerous, and under which they have chafed since 1903.

If Roosevelt had been more patient and the election of 1904 had not been so imminent, a practicable canal could have been constructed in Nicaragua without the rich harvest of ill will in Colombia and Panama. If he had been willing to sweeten the terms offered Colombia by another $15 million, the pact might well have been ratified by Bogotá without further delay. As it was, the United States ultimately paid an indemnity of $25 million, after much unpleasantness.[7]

WAS THERE EVER AN ALASKA BOUNDARY ARBITRATION?

For many years the Canadians had claimed a generous portion of the Alaska panhandle — a strip of territory which would give them the heads of the main inlets. After years of controversy, an agreement was reached in 1903 between London and Washington for setting up a tribunal consisting of "six impartial jurists of repute." Roosevelt appointed three Americans, none of whom was a "jurist" of "repute" and all of whom were of dubious impartiality. The British King chose two Canadians, plus one eminent British jurist, Lord Alverstone, Lord Chief Justice.

Roosevelt blustered behind the scenes, threatening to occupy the disputed area with troops (this could only mean war) if the tribunal did not run the boundary to his satisfaction. Such pressures almost certainly got to Lord Alverstone, who, faced with an awesome responsibility, voted with the three Americans in upholding the main claim of the United States. The Americans were jubilant; the Canadians were outraged.

A true arbitration is one in which either party runs the risk of losing. In this case Roosevelt could get no worse than a tie vote because the three Americans ("impartial jurists of repute") were determined

<hr>

[7] See D. C. Miner, The Fight for the Panama Route (1940).

from the outset to support the position of the United States. T. R.'s none-too-subtle use of the Big Stick on Lord Alverstone evidently got results but, as in the case of Panama, at the cost of much ill will.[8]

DID ROOSEVELT REWRITE THE MONROE DOCTRINE?

After the Venezuelan episode of 1902–1903, Roosevelt became increasingly apprehensive of European debt collectors. If they came — Germany was especially feared — they might stay. If they stayed, they would violate the Monroe Doctrine and threaten the United States, which would then be obligated to throw them out. This would mean shooting, and shooting would mean war.

If the United States would not permit the European creditors to collect, Roosevelt felt that he had a moral obligation to arrange for the collecting. He would take over the customs houses, which were a ready source of revenue and graft, and then allocate a portion of their income for European debts. In this way he could keep both the Europeans and trouble on the other side of the Atlantic.

The first beneficiary — or victim — of this arrangement was the Dominican Republic, which in 1904–1905 consented with some reluctance to the supervision of Big Brother from the North. But the scheme worked; the debts were collected; and the creditor nations kept away.

Monroe's original Doctrine had warned the European powers to stay out. Roosevelt's version meant, "We'll go in so that you will keep out." This, in effect, was standing the original dictum on its head, and only by strained logic can one call it a true corollary. It was in essence a brand new doctrine of interventionism.[9] But Roosevelt was clearheaded enough to perceive that the American public would accept his formula more readily if he attached it to an ancient and honored name.

WAS THE BATTLESHIP CRUISE A STATESMANLIKE GESTURE?

In 1907–1909 President Roosevelt, hoping to impress Japan and the other powers, sent the American battleship fleet of sixteen ships (essentially all that were available) on a trip around the world, including Japa-

[8] T. A. Bailey, "Theodore Roosevelt and the Alaska Boundary Settlement," *Canadian Hist. Rev.*, *XVIII* (1937), 123–130.

[9] See the chapter (VI) "Non-Intervention Becomes Intervention," in Dexter Perkins, *The Monroe Doctrine, 1867–1907* (1937).

nese waters. He regarded this successful 46,000-mile cruise, completely without precedent, as his most important contribution to world peace.

The visit of the fleet undoubtedly gave the Japanese an opportunity to stage a welcoming demonstration which cleared the air and enabled the two nations to ease some of their tensions through the Root–Takahira agreement of 1908. Other powers were impressed by this large-scale maneuver, while the ability of the United States to uphold the Monroe Doctrine in the Americas was dramatically advertised. Yet, as more recent studies have further shown, this global naval demonstration was a gigantic gamble, as dangerous as it was unnecessary. All's well that ends well, the saying goes, but the rash venture could easily have ended in complete disaster.

The sixteen war vessels were obsolescent because the launching of Britain's all-big-gun *Dreadnaught* in 1906 had rendered other battleships inferior, including Britain's. The American warships, although none broke down badly, revealed grave technical defects, and two of them had to be replaced after the fleet rounded South America and reached San Francisco, en route to the Orient. Both the ships and their quarreling officers were too old. The Americans were fatally dependent on accompanying foreign colliers, which would have been withdrawn, in conformity with neutral obligations, if the United States had tangled with Japan in Far Eastern waters. In such an event the fleet without fuel would have been helpless.

The Japanese were not overawed: in fact, the British were betting on them in the event of a clash in East Asia. Although America's overall naval strength was superior to that of Japan, the Japanese could bring more to bear in their own waters. Shortly after the sixteen battleships left Japan, the Japanese paraded 123 of their warships of all classes, many victoriously battle-tested in 1905 against Russia, in a line twenty miles long.[10]

DID ROOSEVELT DESERVE THE NOBEL PEACE PRIZE?

In 1906 Roosevelt was awarded the Nobel Peace Prize, presumably for his part in arranging for the Russo–Japanese peace conference, near Portsmouth, New Hampshire.[11] There, after much behind-the-scenes

[10] See Robert A. Hart, *The Great White Fleet* (1965).

[11] The delegates actually met at the Kittery navy yard in Maine, just across the river from Portsmouth, New Hampshire. A recent summation is Eugene P. Trani, *The Treaty of Portsmouth* (1969), which praises T. R.'s stellar accomplishment as only "momentary" (p. 159).

pressure, the two belligerents finally agreed to terms that ended the gory war of 1904–1905.

Roosevelt's part in this episode was greatly to his credit. The Japanese, who had been exhausting their manpower in beating the Russians, secretly asked him to serve as a mediator. He had no relish for this task, knowing that the role of the umpire is thankless. But he concluded that bringing the carnage to a speedy end was in the national interest. If either one of the contestants collapsed, the balance of power in the Far East would be dangerously overbalanced in favor of the other, presumably to the detriment of America's commercial and strategic interests. So Roosevelt consented to serve as mediator. When neither Japan nor Russia came out of the conference with as much as desired, he earned the lasting ingratitude of both.

Despite this signal contribution to peace, Roosevelt was not a man of peace. He loved war, rejoiced in the whine of bullets, and believed that fighting was necessary to strengthen and preserve virile virtues.[12] His public and private glorification of arms finds no parallel in the statements of responsible men high in American public life. He had his glorious hour with the Rough Riders; and perhaps the bitterest disappointment of life was the flat refusal of President Wilson to permit him to raise a volunteer division, with himself in command, for service in France against the Germans in 1917–1918. William Howard Taft, a true man of peace, wrote privately in 1911, "The truth is he [T. R.] believes in war and wishes to be a Napoleon and to die on the battlefield."[13] All things considered, conferring the Peace Prize on Roosevelt was somewhat like awarding a medal for bravery in battle to pacifist Mahatma Gandhi.

WAS ROOSEVELT A SUPERIOR PRESIDENT?

Roosevelt was a great personality, a great showman, a great exhibitionist, a great egoist, a great activist, a great controversialist, a great self-glorifier, a great preacher of the moralities, a great popular idol, a great politician, a great opportunist, a great vote-getter. But was he a great President?

The legislative output of his Congresses was not especially

[12] In June 1897 Roosevelt had told a Naval War College audience at Newport: "Peace is a goddess only when she comes with sword girt on her thigh. . . . No triumph of peace is quite so great as the supreme triumphs of war." Quoted in H. F. Pringle, *Theodore Roosevelt* (1931), p. 172.

[13] H. F. Pringle, *The Life and Times of William Howard Taft* (2 vols., 1939), II, 748.

noteworthy, even though his own Republican party retained control.[14] His relations with that body at times were badly strained, especially at the end. His reformist achievements did not measure up to his reformist zeal, even though his crusade for conservation enjoyed noteworthy success. A few trusts were "busted" but vastly more were formed during his "reign." Despite his notorious bellicosity, he did go out of his way to avoid a war with Japan, conspicuously by patching up difficulties with the Californians over Japanese immigration and by sacrificing Korea in 1905 to Nipponese imperialism. His record in world leadership was impressive: for the first time the United States operated on the global stage in the grand manner, with battleships and all.

But Roosevelt's impetuosity and capacity for deviousness left some black marks.[15] His handling of the Brownsville affray resulted in a grievous injustice to many Negro soldiers; his role in the Panama revolution, although not that of a direct conspirator, sullied the national character; his so-called arbitration of the Alaska boundary was a travesty of arbitration; his liberties with the Monroe Doctrine in the Dominican Republic were a perversion of Monroeism that greatly worsened the "Bad Neighbor" Policy.

If Roosevelt had been less self-righteous and better balanced, he would have been a greater President, but then he would not have been the uninhibited Theodore Roosevelt.

WAS PRESIDENT TAFT A REACTIONARY?

William H. Taft, whom Roosevelt hand-picked as his successor, is often branded a reactionary — or at best a deep-dyed conservative. Here the historian becomes involved in the use of terms that can only be rather loosely defined.[16] Yet it seems reasonable to conclude that Taft, though

[14] Significant legislation included the Elkins Act (1903) and the Hepburn Act (1906) for regulating railroads; the Newlands Reclamation Act (1902); and the Pure Food and Drugs Act (1906).

[15] Aside from Roosevelt's handling of the Panama affair and the Alaska boundary dispute, to mention only two questionable episodes, one may note his role in connection with the seizure of a presumed American citizen, Jon Perdicaris, by the Moroccan bandit Raisuli. Although arrangements had already been made for the release of Perdicaris, and although grave doubts then existed as to his naturalization (he was of Greek birth), Roosevelt arranged for the dispatch of the stirring and politically profitable cablegram, "Perdicaris Alive or Raisuli Dead." H. E. Davis, "The Citizenship of Jon Perdicaris," *Jour. of Mod. Hist.*, XIII (1941), 517–526. The State Department later ruled that Perdicaris had been an American citizen at the time of the incident.

[16] Some historians in more recent years have argued that the Progressive movement was not really progressive at all: it was primarily in the hands, they claim, of middle class conservatives, including businessmen.

a conservative by upbringing, legal training, and judicial temperament, was a mild liberal as regards social reform. The Roosevelt–Taft years experienced the cresting of the Progressive reform movement — reform in American social, political, and economic life — and the portly Taft was unable to keep up with the bandwagon. Lagging behind, he seemed by comparison more reactionary than he actually was.

Taft's course in relation to the Payne–Aldrich Tariff of 1909 is often cited as proof of his innate conservatism. Actually it is further evidence of his penchant for foot-in-mouthism. The basic facts are simple. The Republican platform had rather ambiguously promised to revise the existing high tariff, and the assumption was, though not stated specifically, that the changes would be substantially downward. Taft fought hard for reasonableness in the schedules that Congress was preparing, and when he managed to bring about somewhat lower rates than at one time had seemed possible, he finally signed the measure with something approaching relief.[17]

The President's next step was to go out on the stump and defend the Payne–Aldrich tariff. But the public had been led to expect much lower rates. Taft should have said that, while he did not particularly like the new law, it was the best that he could wheedle from a reluctant Congress. Instead, at Winona, Minnesota, in a hastily prepared speech, he declared, "On the whole, I am bound to say that I think the Payne bill is the best bill that the Republican party ever passed." Strangely enough, this statement was basically true, at least from the standpoint of a staunch Republican. It was the first major Republican tariff ever to bring a downward revision, even though a modest one.

WAS TAFT A PROGRESSIVE?

In the area of conservation Taft did commendable work. He withdrew extensive oil lands from sale and created vast new national forest reserves. But these forward steps are largely obscured by a furious dispute involving his Secretary of the Interior Ballinger and his Chief Forester Pinchot in connection with the private exploitation of natural resources.[18] Ballinger, in accord with the strict letter of the law, threw open to sale certain public lands that he regarded as unlawfully withdrawn under

---

[17] S. D. Solvick, "William Howard Taft and the Payne-Aldrich Tariff," *Miss. Valley Hist. Rev.*, L (1963), 424–442.

[18] The story is told anew in James Penick, Jr., *Progressive Politics and Conservation: The Ballinger–Pinchot Affair* (1968). Pinchot appears to have been largely motivated by politics.

Roosevelt. Pinchot, a devoted conservationist, struck back. Partially in the interests of administrative efficiency, Taft supported his chief subordinate, whom Progressives judged, rather mistakenly, to be working against the public welfare. Not until March 1911, more than a year after the storm broke, did Ballinger resign, leaving an unfortunate anticonservationist aftertaste.

As a trust-buster, Taft, as already noted, "busted" many more trusts than Roosevelt, although some of the prosecutions had been launched under his predecessor, and although he received less popular acclaim for his achievements. Trust-busting had become old hat.

On the whole, Taft's record as a progressive does not pale to nothingness when compared to that of Roosevelt, despite certain political blunders. During Taft's troubled four years, Congress established further control of the railroads through the Mann–Elkins Act. It also created a postal savings bank and a parcel post system. Responding to the President's recommendation, it passed the Sixteenth Amendment (income tax), which was ratified by the requisite number of states in 1913.

A strict constructionist, Taft was trained as a jurist, and his great ambition was to sit on the Supreme Bench. He did not enjoy politics, as T. R. did: the whole business made him "sick," he often complained in his private letters. But his ambitious wife and brothers prodded him into political life, during which he reluctantly turned down an appointment to the Supreme Court four times. After leaving the presidency, he was finally named Chief Justice in 1921, and in that capacity he was successful and happy. One is surprised to find that as President he performed as well as he did in a job he so thoroughly disliked and for which he was temperamentally unsuited.

WAS TAFT "GUILTY" OF DOLLAR DIPLOMACY?

The stigma of Dollar Diplomacy has long, and somewhat unfairly, been attached to Taft. In the popular mind it meant the use of foreign policy, backed by the tax-supported U. S. Marines and Navy, to enlarge and protect the investment abroad of private American capital, particularly that of Wall Street. The objects of such attention were usually "backward nations" such as Nicaragua and the Dominican Republic.

This kind of dollar diplomacy was not unique with the United States, and it was not particularly new. By 1898 the investments of Americans in Cuba, for example, had amounted to about $50 million and largely accounted for the zeal that some investors displayed for intervention. Taft merely inherited a situation which he felt bound to recognize. Even so, as William Jennings Bryan pointed out in 1913, dollar diplomacy involved serious inequities. American investors would sink their money abroad, in response to high interest rates which in turn reflected a high rate of risk. Then the bankers would clamor for sending in Marines to remove the risk.

Taft promoted a more defensible type of dollar diplomacy with considerable enthusiasm and some success. It was to reverse the operations of the old "gunboat policy" and induce investors to pump their dollars into strategically critical areas, such as the countries near the unfinished Panama Canal. If American bankers did not, German and other foreign investors might come in. Serving as "fronts" for their governments, they might set up potential military or naval bases which would jeopardize the isthmian waterway. In short, have the dollars of private investors support the national interest, rather than have the nation support the dollars of the private investors.[19] Or, as Taft put it in a message to Congress, the scheme was one of "substituting dollars for bullets."[20]

WAS THE 1912 NOMINATION "STOLEN" FROM T. R.?

Having anointed Taft his successor, Roosevelt gradually became disenchanted with him. A succession of disturbing developments indicated that the new leader was not faithfully carrying out Rooseveltian policies; he seemed to be consorting with reactionaries and alienating the friends and stalwart supporters of T. R.

An incident which helped to induce Roosevelt to challenge Taft for the presidential nomination occurred in 1911, when the administration brought suit against the U. S. Steel Company as a monopoly. The story went back to 1907 when, during the sharp "Wall Street Panic," Roosevelt had permitted the huge company to purchase, at what turned out to be a bargain price, the assets of the Tennessee Coal and Iron Company. Taft, a member of the Cabinet, had then acquiesced. But now he was having his administration sue, partly on the grounds that the acquisition of the Tennessee company had created a monopoly. The Supreme Court finally ruled against the government in 1920, thus

---

[19] The dollar diplomacy of the Taft era involved principally private funds. The so-called dollar diplomacy of the years after World War II, amounting to more than $100 billion in foreign aid, involved money from the Washington Treasury and hence from the pockets of the taxpayers. Communist spokesmen have seized upon the cliché "Dollar Imperialism."

[20] Cong. Record, 62 Cong., 3 sess. (Dec. 3, 1912), p. 9.

upholding Roosevelt. But T. R. was outraged by Taft's about-face and by this reflection on the correctness of the original decision. Hell had no fury like a Roosevelt whose conduct was being publicly questioned by a presumed friend and beneficiary.

Progressive elements within the Republican party were seeking a candidate who could dislodge Taft, and for a time the reformist Senator La Follette of Wisconsin seemed like a promising candidate. After he had made an intemperate and overlong speech to the periodical publishers in Philadelphia, the Progressives claimed that he had broken down. They thereupon dumped him in favor of Roosevelt. La Follette, while pleading weariness on this occasion, claimed that he had been used as a front runner so that the Rough Rider might charge in and seize the banner. The truth seems to be that Roosevelt had much greater voter appeal and that the Progressives wanted a winner.[21]

When the Republican nominating convention convened in Chicago, T. R. was clearly the overwhelming favorite with the rank and file of the party. In the thirteen states that held primaries, Roosevelt had won 278 votes, Taft 48, and La Follette 36. But this was not enough. In most of the states, including those in the Democratic Solid South, boss-controlled conventions had chosen Taft delegates. They now occupied the driver's seat. This, ironically, was the same boss-dominated steamroller that Roosevelt had been happy to use in engineering the nomination of his successor four years earlier. The shoe was now on the other foot, and when the Taft forces organized and controlled the convention, the Rough Rider directed his supporters to walk out.

Crying "naked theft," Roosevelt and his followers took steps to organize a third party — the Progressives — with the primary objective of defeating Taft. The election of the Democratic candidate, Woodrow Wilson, was thereafter a foregone conclusion if the Democrats could only hold their ranks intact.

It is perfectly plain that Taft's nomination was technically a legal operation. Roosevelt may have won the popularity contest in the primaries, but the incumbent had the machine-made votes, and that was what counted when the roll was called. This sort of thing had happened before and it has happened since.[22]

---

[21] La Follette conceded that he "was not at my best," owing to strenuous campaigning, but he denied that he had suffered a breakdown and gives evidence to support his view. See *La Follette's Autobiography* (1960 edition), p. 259.

[22] Senator Goldwater's nomination by the Republicans in 1964 was achieved by the votes of delegates chosen by machine-manipulated state conventions and was unpopular with liberal Republican voters.

DID BRYAN ENGINEER WILSON'S NOMINATION?

Dr. Woodrow Wilson, after a disruptive quarrel with Dean West over the graduate school, had been forced out of the presidency of Princeton in 1910, only to land on his feet with a nomination for the governorship by the Democrats of New Jersey. Eighteen days after leaving his college post he was elected. Earlier a strong conservative, he had gradually become a flaming progressive and had attracted much attention nationally by his crusade for the democratization of education at Princeton.[23] As governor of New Jersey, he had routed the politicos who had put him into office, and had given the boss-ridden state a sheaf of legislative reforms that thrust him into the front rank of the progressive parade. The Democratic liberals saw in Wilson the leader who could take them to the White House, while defeating both Taft and Roosevelt in a three-cornered race.

A favorite of the Bryanites and other Democratic regulars was Speaker Champ Clark of Missouri, an old-line political wheelhorse given to alcoholic excesses. He nevertheless had about 435 delegates pledged to support him when the Democrats met in Baltimore in 1912, whereas Wilson had about 245. On the tenth ballot the crucial delegation from populous New York plumped for Clark, who then had 556 votes, or far more than a simple majority. A two-thirds vote was needed to nominate under the existing Democratic procedures, and not since 1844, when the two-thirds rule was adopted, had a candidate failed to receive the nomination after having amassed a majority.

On the fourteenth ballot, William Jennings Bryan, who as a delegate from Nebraska was pledged to Clark, dramatically shifted to the progressive Wilson, on the alleged grounds that he could not support a candidate backed by New York's Wall Street interests and Tammany Hall. (There were those who felt that he was hoping for presidential lightning to strike him a fourth time.) On the 46th ballot Wilson was nominated.

Bryan's role in supporting Wilson, although of considerable importance, has clearly been overplayed. The big breaks came on the 42nd ballot when Illinois delivered its large bloc of votes to Wilson, and when the Democrats backing Senator Underwood of Alabama flocked to

---

[23] Wilson came to overplay the extent to which he had been contending for democratization in promoting his educational reforms at Princeton. Arthur S. Link, *Wilson: The Road to the White House* (1947), pp. 75–77.

Wilson on the 46th.[24] Bryan's chief contribution seems to have been his highlighting the need to nominate a progressive not beholden to Wall Street.[25]

DID ROOSEVELT HOPE TO WIN IN 1912?

In the three-way contest of 1912, Wilson's election was about as much of a foregone conclusion as anything can be in politics. The simple arithmetic was that if the majority Republican party split its vote between two candidates, as it did, the Democratic hopeful would come in under the wire. The Princetonian won a smashing victory in the electoral college, 435 votes to 88 for Roosevelt and 8 for Taft. Curiously enough, Wilson polled only 41.85 percent of the popular vote, and his 6,301,254 votes were fewer than Bryan secured in any one of his three losing campaigns, 1896, 1900, and 1908, even though the population of the country had increased by more than 20 million since 1896.

Roosevelt had consented to run in the forlorn hope that he could attract enough progressive votes from the Democratic camp. He might have succeeded if the Democrats had nominated a man other than the progressive Wilson, as they almost did in backing Champ Clark. Significantly, Roosevelt accepted the Progressive nomination *after* Wilson had been nominated by the Democrats, and hence knew that he faced an uphill battle.

If the Rough Rider had little or no hope of winning himself, then he must have run largely to keep Taft out of the White House and oust the reactionary bosses. He must have found the prospect of a progressive Wilson in the White House more palatable than that of a "disloyal" Taft, but as his hatred of the Princetonian mounted in ensuing years, he probably had second thoughts.

Roosevelt was again tendered the Progressive nomination in 1916, but he spurned it, leaving the Progressive party which he had founded forsaken, leaderless, and doomed to die. He had no stomach for splitting the Republican party again and guaranteeing to Wilson a second term in the White House. This so-called betrayal of a cause behind which Roosevelt had marshaled so many dedicated followers was one of the more questionable decisions of a controversial career.

[24] The scholarly evidence is summarized in P. E. Coletta, *William Jennings Bryan: Progressive Politician and Moral Statesman, 1909–1915* (1969), Ch. 3.

[25] Louis W. Koenig, *Bryan* (1971), p. 496.

ADDITIONAL GENERAL REFERENCES

Henry F. Pringle, *Theodore Roosevelt* (1931); W. H. Harbaugh, *Power and Responsibility* (1961); Howard K. Beale, *Theodore Roosevelt and the Rise of America to World Power* (1956); Eugene P. Trani, *The Treaty of Portsmouth* (1969); F. R. Dulles, *America's Rise to World Power* (1955); G. E. Mowry, *The Era of Theodore Roosevelt, 1900–1912* (1958); J. M. Blum, *The Republican Roosevelt* (1954); G. W. Chessman, *Theodore Roosevelt and the Politics of Power* (1969); S. P. Hays, *Conservation and the Gospel of Efficiency, 1890–1920* (1959); Elmo Richardson, *The Politics of Conservation* (1962); Richard Hofstadter, *The Age of Reform* (1955); E. F. Goldman, *Rendezvous with Destiny* (1952); Gabriel Kolko, *The Triumph of Conservatism, 1900–1916* (1963); Robert H. Wiebe, *The Search for Order, 1877–1920* (1967); Raymond A. Esthus, *Theodore Roosevelt and Japan* (1966) and *Theodore Roosevelt and the International Rivalries* (1970); C. E. Neu, *An Uncertain Friendship: Theodore Roosevelt and Japan, 1906–1909* (1967); G. E. Mowry, *Theodore Roosevelt and the Progressive Movement* (1946); Henry F. Pringle, *The Life and Times of William Howard Taft* (2 vols., 1939); Walter V. and Marie V. Scholes, *The Foreign Policies of the Taft Administration* (1970); A. S. Link, *Wilson: The Road to the White House* (1947).

26

Wilson
and the Return
of the Democrats

*Determined to implement his New Freedom program for the American
people, Wilson dramatically revived the ancient practice, abandoned in
1801 by weak-voiced Thomas Jefferson, of appearing before Congress
to deliver his various messages. So effective was his dynamic leadership
that the members responded with an unprecedented legislative output.
It included a drastically revised tariff, a new Federal Reserve banking
system, and a tightening of controls over the trusts and other instruments of monopoly.*

*In foreign affairs Wilson likewise pursued high ideals. He in-
duced Congress to honor its treaty obligation to Britain by repealing the
discriminatory toll arrangements for the Panama Canal; he refused to
recognize the murder-tainted government of President Huerta in Mexico;
and he attempted to undo the much-criticized Dollar Diplomacy of the
preceding Taft administration.*

*To Wilson's distress, his lofty ideals did not always square with
realities, and he did not succeed conspicuously in reversing Dollar
Diplomacy. Ironically, it reversed him. U. S. Marines were used extensively to protect American property, despite the protests of the
"natives" in Nicaragua, Haiti, and the Dominican Republic. Wilson's*

good intentions toward Mexico resulted in two undeclared but strictly limited wars with that resentful neighbor. Yet Wilsonian idealism permitted the Mexican revolution against despotism to run its course, despite the clamor of American investors for occupying the entire country.

WAS WILSON AN IMPRACTICAL IDEALIST?

No doubt Wilson was an idealist in the sense that he had noble ideals for himself, for his countrymen, and for humanity in general. But this is not to say that he was a dreamy-eyed visionary. Although a pacifist in the sense of loving peace and hating war, he was not an extreme or doctrinaire pacifist. Reared in the war-ravaged South, he had seen enough of the results of fighting to want no part of it. Yet when the Germans began to sink American shipping indiscriminately on the high seas in 1917, he sent a ringing war message to Congress and emerged as the spectacularly successful leader of a great crusade against German militarism.

Wilson's idealism, highlighted by his fight for the League of Nations in 1919, has obscured the fact that he was a gifted and unusually successful practical politician. Schooled in the harsh arena of academic politics as president of Princeton, he was never defeated for public office: he won the governorship of New Jersey once and the presidency of the United States twice. He had a penchant for appealing over the heads of the political bosses and the legislators to the sovereign people ("the appeal habit"), and until his physical collapse in 1919 he enjoyed marked success in these endeavors. He also had a flair for epigrams, such as "It must be a peace without victory" and "The world must be made safe for democracy." [1] Some of these phrases were twisted out of context and used to embarrass him.

Wilson was a visionary in the sense that he had a vision of a better tomorrow and worked tirelessly with the tools at hand to attain it. This singleness of purpose was the mark of a great leader. He pleaded guilty to being an idealist: in a speech at Sioux Falls, South Dakota, while on his tragic tour for the League of Nations in 1919, he said, "Sometimes people call me an idealist. Well, that is the way I know I am an American. America . . . is the only idealistic nation in the world."

---

[1] The origin of the expression "A war to end war" has been erroneously attributed to Wilson. In 1914 the British author Herbert G. Wells published a book entitled, *The War That Will End War.*

WAS WILSON UNABLE TO COMPROMISE?

A common misconception persists that Wilson was constitutionally unable to compromise, and that this weakness accounts for his failure to
get his League of Nations past the tomahawks of the Senate in 1919–
1920.

Wilson was undeniably a stubborn man and a fighter for what
he conceived to be right. He had descended from a long line of Scotch
Presbyterians, who traditionally have been difficult to push around. At
Princeton University he probably could have survived his battle with
Dean West over the Graduate School by some kind of face-saving
compromise, yet he chose to go down with colors flying. He ultimately
found himself seeking a new job, which turned out to be the governorship of New Jersey.

Nonetheless, Wilson's so-called inflexibility, at least before 1919,
has been grossly overplayed. No man can go far in democratic politics —
and Wilson got to the very top and stayed there eight years — if he
insists on having his own way all the time. Politics is the art of the
possible, and compromise is an essential ingredient in achieving the possible. "All government," declared Edmund Burke in 1775, "is founded
on compromise and barter." Seldom, if ever, has any major controversial
legislation passed the United States Congress that was not the result
of some give and take.

Wilson could compromise, and did on many occasions, notably
during the Paris negotiations of 1919, when he reluctantly accepted a
Treaty of Versailles that was a bundle of compromises. But he was
clearly more willing to compromise on means than on principle.

WAS WILSON WARPED BY PARENTAL DOMINATION?

Posthumous psychoanalysis is a dangerous bog, yet in recent years
several writers have conspicuously undertaken to explain Wilson's controversial behavior in terms of an Oedipus complex caused by resentment against his father. The theory is that Wilson locked horns with
Dean West at Princeton and with Senator Henry Cabot Lodge in the
Senate because he was subconsciously responding bitterly to memories
of a stern and dictatorial parent.[2]

[2] A. L. and Juliette L. George, *Woodrow Wilson and Colonel House* (1956),
advanced the father-domination thesis with considerable persuasiveness and re-

No one can deny that Wilson's father, a Presbyterian clergyman, was a strong personality, and that he became the lad's taskmaster, counselor, and comrade. Yet the evidence is overwhelming that Wilson admired and loved him. Woodrow's numerous letters to him are filled with expressions of affection that ring true, and later in life he brought his aged father to Princeton to live with him.

Wilson's stubbornness and bitterness toward Dean West and Senator Lodge can be plausibly explained on rational grounds that would rule out a father fixation. President Franklin Roosevelt had a domineering and doting mother; President Kennedy had a domineering and dictatorial father. As Presidents, both men stubbornly resisted assorted adversaries, and, as in the case of Wilson, the explanation of their attitudes can be plausibly found in causes other than parental domination.

WAS BRYAN A MISFIT AS SECRETARY OF STATE?

President Wilson was under heavy obligation to name William Jennings Bryan as his Secretary of State in 1913. The silver-tongued orator was not only the uncrowned king of the party and the leader of its most important faction, but he had been partly responsible for Wilson's winning the presidential nomination at Baltimore. The President-elect, as something of an intellectual snob, had no admiration for Bryan's intellect, but he perceived that so prominent a Democrat would be less troublesome, as one humorist put it, "in his bosom than on his back." [3]

It is true that Bryan could boast of no experience in diplomacy or international law (as was true of most of his predecessors), but the record shows that he did much creditable work as Secretary of State. He loyally supported his chief in the attempt (not too successful) to reverse Dollar Diplomacy in Latin America and the Far East; he strongly backed Wilson's determination to let the Mexican people have their revolution; he labored earnestly to salve Japanese sensibilities regarding discrimina-

---

straint. Sigmund Freud and William C. Bullitt, *Thomas Woodrow Wilson: A Psychological Study* (1966), went overboard in a thoroughly untrustworthy hate-Wilson book that is riddled with gross errors and unprovable assumptions. Freud (the famous psychiatrist) and Bullitt disagreed on their interpretation, so Bullitt published the book after his collaborator's death. No one can be sure what Freud really believed. One conclusion is inescapable: both men had long hated Wilson, and they obviously had pooled their prejudices. For a devastating critique of the book by the leading Wilson authority see Arthur S. Link, "The Case for Woodrow Wilson," *Harper's Magazine*, CCXXXIV (1967), 85–93.

[3] As early as 1904 Wilson confided to a friend that although Bryan had caught the finer aspirations of American life, "the man has no brains." R. S. Baker, *Woodrow Wilson: Life and Letters* (1931), *III*, p. 203.

tion by Californians against landowning by Oriental immigrants; and he negotiated some thirty conciliation or "cooling-off" treaties with most of the leading nations. These pacts might have proved useful if World War I, erupting as it did in 1914, had not spread into a global conflagration.

Bryan's reputation as Secretary was blackened by a barrage of ridicule. A lifelong teetotaler, he undertook to ban alcoholic beverages from official functions — "grape juice diplomacy." As a perennial lecturer on the Chautauqua circuit, he felt the need to supplement his salary by going out at critical times to speak on peace and kindred subjects from the same platform that was occupied by vaudeville performers. He made a number of bad appointments to the foreign service by rewarding old supporters, whom he indiscreetly called "deserving Democrats" — to the derisive and hypocritical glee of "resolute Republicans," who had long been doing the same thing. Yet the record reveals that in some respects Bryan was no worse a spoilsman than some of his Cabinet colleagues or than Wilson himself.[4]

Bryan's long commitment to peace was such that when Wilson took a bellicose tone in response to Germany's sinking of merchant shipping in 1915, the great orator felt obligated to resign from the Cabinet. Condemned as a pacifist and pro-German, he found himself pilloried for giving aid and comfort to Berlin by sensationally advertising this division within the official family in Washington.

Bryan perhaps served most usefully as Secretary of State in acting as the administration's chief lobbyist with Congress. There he was able to exert invaluable influence with loyal supporters, many of whom had voted for him three times, in facilitating the passage of Wilson's New Freedom legislation. In particular, Bryan's help in shepherding through Congress the epochal Federal Reserve Act was of major importance.

Whether as a public official or as a private citizen, Bryan was a man of deep sincerity and no little perceptiveness. He lived to see many of the reforms he had advocated written into law, some of them by the rival Republicans, who freely borrowed his ideas.[5] With good reason he once quipped that he was the only man who could govern the country by losing elections.

---

[4] See Paolo E. Coletta, *William Jennings Bryan: Progressive Politician and Moral Statesman, 1909–1915* (1969), Ch. 4.

[5] Bryan's was one of the most important voices agitating for what became in 1913 the 16th Amendment (federal income tax); in 1913 the 17th Amendment (direct election of U. S. Senators); in 1919 the 18th Amendment (prohibition of alcoholic beverages); and in 1920 the 19th Amendment (woman's suffrage).

HOW NEW WAS WOODROW WILSON'S "NEW FREEDOM"?

The slogan "New Freedom" was attached by Wilson and his followers to the liberal philosophy of government that they championed during the campaign of 1912. Although not a particularly new concept to the country, it was relatively new to Wilson. In 1910, when the New Jersey bosses nominated him for governor, they regarded him as a conservative who would not upset the economic and social applecart.

But Wilson had changed rapidly and within a short time became a flaming liberal. Once known as an enemy of "Bryanism," of government regulation of industry, and of the restrictive practices of labor unions, he executed what amounted to an about-face. In a series of eloquent speeches, which were later published under the title *The New Freedom* (1913), he set a new course. He pleaded for a more humanitarian spirit in both government and business; for political reforms that would return power to the people; and for breaking the grip of selfish and privileged interests, including the trusts. He passionately believed that the alarming growth of monopoly had rendered obsolete the Jeffersonian concept of noninterference from Washington. Going beyond mere regulation, he argued that the national government should embark upon a positive program to insure social justice and equal opportunity for all.

Clearly this "New Freedom" was hardly new. Its basic philosophy goes back at least to the Populists and other protestors of the nineteenth century, and from there to the Muckrakers, Insurgents, and Progressives of the first decade of the twentieth century. The tradition continued on in Franklin Roosevelt's New Deal, Truman's Fair Deal, Kennedy's New Frontier, and Johnson's Great Society.

In 1910, during the preliminaries of the campaign of 1912, Theodore Roosevelt, growing increasingly radical, had preached his New Nationalism, most spectacularly in a speech at Osawatomie, Kansas (John Brown's old home). In urging greater control over private property, T. R. advocated the "general right of the community to regulate its use to whatever degree the public welfare may require it."

Roosevelt's New Nationalism was an outgrowth of his "Square Deal" and a precursor of the New Freedom, which Wilson enunciated about two years later. Both men were in basic agreement about ends — that is, individual freedoms combined with social and economic justice. The chief difference was in means. Roosevelt would actively use government to safeguard and protect the individual. Wilson rejected such an approach as paternalistic: he would use government to eliminate monopoly and injustice so that the citizen could achieve and enjoy his new freedom with a minimum of supervision.

WAS THE CLAYTON ANTITRUST ACT A MAGNA CARTA?

Wilson's inspirational leadership resulted in an extraordinary legislative output by his first Congress, the 63rd. Among major enactments were the Underwood Tariff Act of 1913 (a substantial downward revision); [6] the Owen-Glass Federal Reserve Act of 1913 (establishing greater flexibility of currency and stability in banking); [7] the Federal Trade Commission Act of 1914 (designed to restrict unfair practices by corporations engaged in interstate commerce); and the Clayton Antitrust Act of 1914.

Obviously the Clayton Act added some new teeth to the gums of the old Sherman Antitrust Act of 1890, but in general it proved disappointing to the foes of the trusts. The Senate severely weakened the House version, and Wilson failed to insist on a stronger bill, because he placed heavy reliance on the regulatory possibilities of the new Federal Trade Commission. Here also disappointment lay ahead.

The courts, broadly interpreting the Sherman Antitrust Act, had regarded labor unions as combinations in restraint of trade and hence subject to prosecution. As a result of efforts to remove this liability, the Senate did make a gesture when it wrote into the Clayton Act a pious declaration that "The labor of human beings is not a commodity or article of commerce." But the statute made few changes of any consequence in existing restrictions regarding unions, antilabor injunctions, and contempt-of-court judgments. With unwarranted enthusiasm, Samuel Gompers, longtime head of the American Federation of Labor, hailed the new law as the "Magna Carta" of labor. The brutal truth is that rulings by conservative courts in subsequent years removed much of the protective covering for the "poor working stiff." Not until the era of Franklin Roosevelt's New Deal did a new day really dawn for labor, most conspicuously with the National Labor Relations Act (Wagner–Connery Act) of 1935.

[6] Wilson believed that lobbyists for the trusts were scheming to disembowel the bill, and he supposedly forced them to retreat with a ringing appeal to the people. For evidence that the trusts were rather indifferent, see Frank Burdick, "Woodrow Wilson and the Underwood Tariff," *Mid-America*, L (1968), 272–290.

[7] Many of the biggest bankers, though later favoring the final enactment, opposed the Federal Reserve Act initially proposed.

WAS THE CANAL TOLLS-EXEMPTION A TREATY VIOLATION?

Britain and America, as ancient rivals for world trade, had long cast covetous eyes on the proposed trans-isthmian water routes. In 1850 they compromised their differences in the Clayton–Bulwer Treaty, which firmly committed both nations to the joint control and protection of the projected waterway.

Half a century later the British were under pressure to reduce their overseas commitments in the face of Germany's rising might. The resulting Hay–Pauncefote Treaty of 1901, between the United States and Great Britain, left the Americans with a free hand to build, manage, and fortify the canal. But there was one clearly worded restriction:

> The canal shall be free and open to the vessels of commerce and of war of *all nations* observing these Rules, on terms of entire equality, so that there shall be no discrimination against any such nation, or its citizens or subjects, in respect of the conditions or charges of traffic, or otherwise. [Italics added.] [8]

As the costly Panama Canal neared completion (opened in 1914), many taxpayers in the United States began to have second thoughts about yielding equal privileges to foreigners. Yankee engineering genius had succeeded where the French had failed; the construction had proved enormously expensive; and countless citizens felt that American coastwise traffic, such as that flowing from the Atlantic to the Pacific Coasts, ought to be exempted from paying tolls. Foreign shipping was barred from coastwise commerce anyhow, and the tolls exemption would force competing transcontinental railroads to lower their rates and hence benefit the American consumer.

During the presidential campaign of 1912, the platforms of the Democratic and Progressive parties had both favored tolls exemption for coastwise oceanic traffic. Candidate Woodrow Wilson had then rather hastily approved this concession. In August 1912 Congress wrote the exemption into law, thereby drawing a vigorous protest from London. The British were quick to perceive that the cost of servicing toll-free American coastwise traffic would have to be shared by all foreign maritime nations, with a consequent rise in charges. But the position of the legalists in Washington was that the reference in the treaty to commerce being open to "all nations" on equal terms applied to "all *other* nations,"

---

[8] W. M. Malloy, *Treaties . . . 1776–1909* (2 vols., 1910), *I*, p. 783.

even though such terminology was not used. This legalistic hairsplitting was supported by President Taft and Secretary of State Knox, both of them distinguished lawyers.[9]

The exemption voted by Congress was evidently a violation of the letter and spirit of the Hay–Pauncefote Treaty of 1901, even though no formal ruling was ever obtained from the Hague Court or some other disinterested tribunal. Britain's suggestion of arbitration under the Anglo–American Treaty of 1908 met with a cold shoulder from the United States Senate. President Wilson, a man of honor, reversed himself after coming to the White House and decided to press for repeal. He reasoned that the stronger the nation, the heavier its obligation to keep the strict letter of its commitments, and that honorable conduct regarding the tolls would strengthen the credibility of the Republic's foreign policy all over the world. America, he felt, was too great to act small.

DID EXEMPTION REPEAL INVOLVE A SECRET DEAL?

Wilson realized that a fight over repeal would arouse the Irish–Americans and other Britain-haters within his own Democratic party, and consequently he held back until the Underwood Tariff and the Federal Reserve Act were safely in the fold. Then, on March 5, 1914, he appeared before a joint session of Congress to urge repeal. He made what many observers thought was a veiled reference to his troubled relations with Mexico: "I ask this of you in support of the foreign policy of the administration. I shall not know how to deal with other matters of even greater delicacy and nearer consequence if you do not grant it to me in ungrudging measure." Afterwards he explained to newsmen that he had been referring to American foreign policy in general, and not relations with any particular country.[10]

The myth quickly developed that Wilson made a secret "deal" with the British to the effect that they would support his Mexican policy in return for his bringing about a repeal of the tolls exemption. This charge was in fact made at the time by critical Republicans and certain England-haters. On the surface there seemed to be some truth in it, especially in view of the visit to Washington, in November 1913, of

[9] The United States and Great Britain both signed the treaty and if "all nations" had meant "all other nations," then Britain would have been entitled to ask for special privileges also.

[10] See Arthur S. Link, *Wilson: The New Freedom* (1956), pp. 304–314, for full details.

Sir William Tyrrell, who discussed current difficulties. Although Tyrrell was only an unofficial envoy, he did receive assurances that Wilson would work for repeal of the tolls exemption at the strategic time. The records of the London Foreign Office that were opened in the 1960s reveal no evidence of a secret "deal" regarding Mexico. Obviously the British, albeit lukewarmly, were going along with Wilson's hands-off-Mexico policy, and they continued to do so despite grave irritation over the canal-tolls controversy. The President's problem was to retain, not gain, Britain's cooperation.

Wilson's upright course was highly pleasing to the British. When repeal was achieved in June 1914, less than two months before the great guns began to boom in Europe, the last outstanding Anglo–American dispute of any consequence was erased. In the more relaxed atmosphere following Wilson's public plea for honorable conduct, the British renewed their general arbitration treaty with the United States — a renewal previously in doubt — and later in 1914 signed a new conciliation treaty with Washington.[11]

Unhappily, Wilson's desire for an "ungrudging" reversal was not fully met. While repealing the exemption as an act of grace rather than as a matter of right, Congress passed an amendment reserving the privilege of exempting American coastwise ships at some future date from paying tolls. To the British this reservation seemed like an ungracious threat, but it was soon forgotten and never employed.

DID WILSON REVERSE DOLLAR DIPLOMACY OR VICE VERSA?

Like many other leading Democrats, Wilson had been highly critical of Taft's Dollar Diplomacy. Among the most spectacular of the new President's early announcements were jolting declarations that his administration would not support American bankers in Latin America or in China. Yet President Taft had encouraged Wall Street to invest in both of these areas.

Like Thomas Jefferson, Wilson soon discovered that theory and practice do not always jibe. Concern for the dollars of American investors alone probably would not have produced a reversal. But two developments in 1914 helped change viewpoints. One was the completion of the Panama Canal, together with an increased sensitiveness to strategic threats in the Caribbean. The other was the outbreak of

---

[11] See W. S. Coker, "The Panama Canal Tolls Controversy: A Different Perspective," *Jour. of Amer. Hist.*, LV (1968), 555–564.

World War I, which involved the danger of hostile submarine bases in the same general area.

It so happened that the Taft administration had been negotiating a dollar-diplomacy treaty with Nicaragua. The pact was so favorable to the United States that Secretary Bryan and Wilson, despite their commitment to idealistic goals, decided to complete it. Among other advantages, the United States would secure a perpetual option on a trans-isthmian canal route, and pay a mere $3 million (much of which was ultimately channeled to big bankers in New York City). Bryan even tried to force into the pact a proviso permitting intervention, much in the manner of the Platt Amendment for Cuba, but the Senate balked, thus delaying ratification until 1916.

The Bryan–Chamorro Treaty with Nicaragua also impinged upon the sovereignty of neighboring Costa Rica, El Salvador, and Honduras. They all appealed to the Central American Court of Justice, created in 1907 under the sponsorship of Washington. The three plaintiffs won their case, but both Nicaragua and the United States ignored the decision. As a consequence, the Court of Justice, for which there had been high hopes, collapsed.[12]

In 1912, the year before Wilson took office, Taft landed American Marines in Nicaragua to protect American lives and property. The troops remained there without interruption for the next thirteen years, eight of them Wilson's dollar-diplomacy years.

Riotous disorders in the tiny black nation of Haiti (the second oldest republic in the Western Hemisphere) also brought the Marines to protect American lives and property in 1915. They stayed uninterruptedly for two decades. Haitian patriots ("bandits") resented this paternalism, and the Marines shot scores of them in the process of "pacifying" the country in the interests, critics charged, of The National City Bank of New York.

Dollar Diplomacy, Wilson style, ran a somewhat similar course in the neighboring Dominican Republic. Theodore Roosevelt had introduced custom-house control in 1904–1905, and when this proved inadequate, the Marines were landed in 1916. They remained for eight years, most of them under a military government established by the U. S. Navy Department. As in Haiti, many dissenters were shot during the course of "pacification."

On the whole, Dollar Diplomacy reversed Wilson rather than vice versa. After announcing that he would not support American investors in Latin America or China, he proceeded to do so. In Latin

---

[12] T. L. Karnes, *The Failure of Union: Central America, 1826–1960* (1961).

America particularly he went much beyond any of his predecessors, including Taft and Roosevelt. In 1913 he bluntly told the bankers that he would not back them in a six-power consortium in China; four years later he urged them to go into a four-power consortium. In all of these reversals he persuaded himself that the national interest (as well as the outside world) was being best served.

In 1918, after America entered the World War, Wilson proclaimed self-determination for subject peoples as one of his most important Fourteen Points. Critics such as ex-President Roosevelt were quick to suggest that if he meant to practice what he preached, he would pull American Marines out of Nicaragua, Haiti, and the Dominican Republic. The inhabitants could then enjoy their full liberties under self-determination.[13]

DID WILSON'S MEXICAN POLICY SQUARE WITH HIS IDEALS?

The Mexican people had long suffered from despotic government. For thirty almost unbroken years — from 1877 to 1911 — iron-man Porfirio Díaz had ruled, and during this era foreign investments in Mexican mines and other properties had increased to about $2 billion. More than half of this sum was held by Americans. Long-repressed revolution erupted in 1910–1911; Díaz was forced to flee to France; and a liberal visionary, Francisco Madero, became the head of a democratic government. After scarcely more than a year he was murdered in 1913 during a coup headed by his leading general, Victoriano Huerta, who proceeded to make himself president-dictator. Many of the leading powers promptly accorded him official recognition, including Britain, Germany, France, Italy, and Japan.

A pressing question before Wilson when he became President was whether or not to recognize the Huerta regime. In the past the standard American practice had been to accord official recognition to established governments, regardless of how they came into power. But Wilson was unwilling to extend the right hand of fellowship to "butcher" Huerta. His heart went out to the ragged and oppressed Mexican masses, whose badly needed revolution had been aborted; he abhorred government-by-murder and would have no dealings with the head murderer. Among various blessings, he wanted the poor peons to enjoy constitutional liberties and a proper share of the great landed estates.

[13] Theodore Roosevelt's diatribe in Kansas City *Star*, Oct. 30, 1918.

Wilson's conscience was all the more troubled by evidence that the holdover American ambassador in Mexico City, who heartily favored the stability of the new despotism, was probably privy to the murder plot. Speaking like the ex-professor he was, Wilson told a visiting British emissary in 1913, "I am going to teach the South American republics to elect good men." [14] He was especially determined not to intervene in Mexico in the interests of American investors, some of whom had lost their lives and many of whom had lost their property during the revolutionary disorders. The pressure from the business community for military intervention became almost unendurable.

As events turned out, Wilson's Mexican policy was beset with a long series of frustrations and contradictions. Huerta simply would not respond to the President's formal demand in 1913 that he resign, and the relationship devolved into a personal vendetta between the ex-professor and the ex-revolutionary. We can only surmise what Wilson would have said if Huerta had demanded his resignation after taking office with only a 41 percent plurality in the election of 1912. A leading Republican journalist, George Harvey, asked pointedly, "What legal or moral right has a President of the United States to say who shall or shall not be President of Mexico?"

As fate would have it, Wilson, the apostle of peace and idealism, twice waged an undeclared war on Mexico. The first occasion was the assault on Vera Cruz in 1914; the second was General Pershing's pursuit of Villa in 1916–1917. A full-dress war with provisional President Carranza, who succeeded Huerta in 1914, was averted by the narrowest of margins. A major deterrent was the imminence of America's large-scale embroilment with Germany in World War I.

Yet in two respects Wilson's Mexican policy deserved commendation. He resisted full-scale armed intervention in the interests of American investors, who kept up a constant clamor. And he permitted the Mexican masses to have their revolution, which, after more chaos, eventually brought an end to generations of despotism.

WAS WILSON JUSTIFIED IN INTERVENING AT VERA CRUZ?

In 1912 President Taft had clamped an embargo on shipments of American arms to Mexico, but early in 1914 Wilson lifted it to permit munitions to flow to Huerta's rivals. Wilson also stationed American

[14] B. J. Hendrick, *The Life and Letters of Walter H. Page* (1923), *I*, 204.

warships off the Mexican seaport of Vera Cruz to block the transit of foreign weapons to the established regime.

A trifling incident was now inflated to major proportions. A small, unarmed party of men in a whaleboat from one of the American warships went ashore at Tampico to secure gasoline, inadvertently entering a restricted area then threatened with rebel attack. Although under cover of the American flag, they were arrested and marched through the streets, but soon were released with a profuse oral apology from the military governor. Yet the American commander in these waters, Rear Admiral Henry T. Mayo, was not satisfied. Without authorization from Washington he immediately demanded a formal apology from the military governor, the severe punishment of the officer responsible for the "outrage," and the hoisting of an American flag on shore to the accompaniment of a twenty-one gun salute.

Such terms were grotesquely out of line with the so-called affront to American honor, and Huerta balked at the absurdity of thus recognizing the flag of a government that refused to recognize him. The pacifist President Wilson and his pacifist Secretary of State Bryan could have disavowed Admiral Mayo, who had acted impulsively. But, aside from embarrassment, there were complicating factors. Red-blooded patriots (many of them investors) were most vocal about upholding the national honor;[15] Wilson was looking for an excuse to topple the bloody-handed Huerta; and a German merchantman, loaded with arms for Huerta, was about to enter the Mexican port of Vera Cruz.[16]

In this crisis atmosphere, Wilson sought authorization from Congress to use armed might to uphold American rights and secure a redress of grievances. Such permission was promptly voted. American forces bombarded and occupied Vera Cruz on April 21, 1914, with a loss of 19 Americans killed and 71 wounded, and of about 126 Mexicans killed and 195 wounded. Such a brutal invasion united Mexican opinion behind the teetering Huerta, while bringing the two nations to the edge of a full-fledged war.

[15] In 1914 Wilson was not too proud to fight at Vera Cruz, but the next year, following Germany's sinking of the British passenger liner *Lusitania*, with a loss of 128 American lives, he told an audience in Philadelphia (May 10, 1915): "There is such a thing as a man being too proud to fight. There is such a thing as a nation being so right that it does not need to convince others by force that it is right." The two offenses were not comparable, but the decision to use force in 1914 was doubtless influenced in large part by the weakness and proximity of Mexico.

[16] Wilson's principal biographer believes that Wilson was not frank in making so much of the Tampico affair. A. S. Link, *Woodrow Wilson and the Progressive Era* (1954), pp. 123–124. See also Robert E. Quirk, *An Affair of Honor: Woodrow Wilson and the Occupation of Vera Cruz* (1962).

Wilson was rescued from this ugly predicament by the offer of the ABC Powers (Argentina, Brazil, and Chile) to mediate the dispute. A meeting was held at Niagara Falls, Canada, but its recommendations were not accepted by Mexico. In the end Huerta's moral and military position deteriorated; he fled the country in July 1914, and his rival Carranza became provisional President of Mexico. American forces then withdrew from Vera Cruz.

The Tampico incident and the Vera Cruz occupation cast Uncle Sam in the role of a supersensitive bully. Mexicans would not soon forget this incursion. Not only was it an act of aggression difficult to justify, except as an excuse for strong-armed action, but it was further marred by futility. The German ship laden with arms for Huerta simply moved down the coast and landed the weapons at another Mexican seaport.

WAS THE PERSHING EXPEDITION A FAILURE?

Venustiano Carranza, the new Mexican President, and Francisco Villa, the so-called Robin Hood bandit, were bitter rivals for power. Wilson, badly misjudging Villa's character, had early supported his rebellion against Carranza, but in the end recognized the Carranza regime. Presumably to show his bitterness toward the United States and create trouble for his successful rival, Villa decided to strike a bloody and spectacular blow at the hated Yanquis. He also needed to replenish his supplies.

In the early morning darkness of March 9, 1916, a band of approximately 400 Villistas attacked and sacked the American border town of Columbus, New Mexico, leaving behind some seventeen dead Americans, civilian and military. A punitive expedition under General Pershing was hastily organized to pursue Villa's force, and according to the legend, bring him back "dead or alive." The Pershing expedition, though encountering difficult terrain and other obstacles, penetrated about 300 miles into Mexico with considerable speed, but did not capture Villa. As war impended with Germany in 1917, and as the Carranza government grew increasingly hostile to the large-scale American presence, the entire expedition was withdrawn, supposedly in complete failure.

Unvarnished facts present a different picture. Villa's attack actually resulted in a staggering defeat; the small contingent of American troops quickly rallied and within a few hours killed the extraordinary total of 130 of the attacking force, or about one-third of its number, to say nothing of the wounded. The pursuing army that finally assembled under General Pershing (ultimately some 12,000 men all told) was not under orders to bring Villa back "dead or alive" (a favorite phrase of the journalists). The official mission was to be completed when Villa's band, or bands, were known to be broken up.[17]

Pershing's expedition was successful in its broad objective. Villa, though hotly pursued, reportedly wounded, and almost captured, was not brought back, but his forces were shattered and scattered. Neither he nor any other Mexican leader ever thereafter mounted a really serious attack across the American border.

In retrospect one must conclude that General Pershing was confronted with no easy task in assembling widely dispersed American troops and launching a large-scale invasion through mountains and deserts in the face of both rebel and federal antagonists. There were in fact two bloody clashes with Carranza forces. Much disorganization was inevitable, and the results were disappointing. The Imperial German government clearly was not impressed with Yankee military prowess as it completed its plans to push America into the World War with an unrestricted submarine campaign. On the other hand, the training that the small American army received was invaluable in preparing for the large-scale European operation that lay ahead, while the emergence of "Black Jack" Pershing as a first-rate commander was one of the more memorable by-products of this much misunderstood operation.

ADDITIONAL GENERAL REFERENCES

A. S. Link, *Woodrow Wilson and the Progressive Era, 1910–1917* (1954) and *Wilson: The New Freedom* (1956); Arthur Walworth, *Woodrow Wilson* (2 vols., 1958); J. A. Garraty, *Woodrow Wilson* (1956); J. M. Blum, *Woodrow Wilson and the Politics of Morality* (1956); R. S. Baker, *Woodrow Wilson: Life and Letters* (8 vols., 1927–1939); P. E. Coletta, *William Jennings Bryan: Progressive Politician and Moral Statesman* (1969); Kenneth J. Grieb, *The United States and Huerta* (1969); Peter Calvert, *The Mexican Revolution, 1910– 1914: The Diplomacy of Anglo–American Conflict* (1968); P. E. Haley, *Revolution and Intervention: The Diplomacy of Taft and Wilson with Mexico, 1910–1917* (1970); H. F. Cline, *The United States and Mexico* (1953).

---

[17] Clarence C. Clendenen, *The United States and Pancho Villa* (1961), p. 251. German agents, who were active, may have urged Villa to attack; certainly they wanted the United States to become bogged down in a war with Mexico. F. J. Munch, "Villa's Columbus Raid: Practical Politics or German Design?" *New Mexico Hist. Rev.,* XLIV (1969), 189–214.

27

Waging Neutrality,
1914-1917

When Europe burst into flames in the summer of 1914, the official position of Washington was neutrality, although evidently most Americans were overwhelmingly pro-Ally. The State Department protested vigorously against the unorthodox British blockade of Germany, but finally acquiesced in it, primarily because it took few, if any, lives. Gradually America became enmeshed in the Allied cause through immense private loans and the shipment of vast quantities of munitions.

Imperial Germany, seeking to break the strangling British blockade, resorted to submarine attacks on merchant shipping. This new type of warfare, to achieve maximum effectiveness, involved the inhumanity of sinking without warning. American lives and property were inevitably destroyed, dramatically in the sinking of the British liner Lusitania in 1915. During ensuing months Wilsonian diplomacy induced Berlin partially to leash the submarine, but on January 31, 1917, the German government proclaimed unrestricted submarine warfare against essentially all shipping in the stipulated war zones. Wilson, still hoping to avoid hostilities, severed diplomatic relations in the vain hope that Berlin was bluffing.

In mid-March, 1917, the Germans sank four unarmed American merchant ships without warning, in two cases with heavy loss of life. Germany was now making war on the United States, and Wilson felt bound to ask Congress to formalize the conflict that Berlin had forced upon the Republic. The German decision to use the submarine ruth-

lessly was the immediate precipitant of hostilities, although many factors or "causes" contrived to bring Germany to this brink of desperation. And numerous additional considerations persuaded the American people to regard the U-boat attacks as a virtual declaration of war.

WAS GERMANY RESPONSIBLE FOR STARTING WORLD WAR I?

As the critical year 1914 dawned, the peace of Europe was still precariously preserved by the delicate balance between two systems of alliances. The three Central Powers consisted of Germany (the strongest of the group militarily), Austria–Hungary (a ramshackle collection of ethnic groups), and Italy (an undependable ally). The Triple Entente embraced France (with a large and well-trained army), sprawling Russia (with the most manpower of all), and Great Britain (with the most potent navy afloat).

The spark that touched off the European powder magazine was fired at Sarajevo by a Serbian patriot, who assassinated Francis Ferdinand, heir to the throne of Austria–Hungary, in June 1914. (Slavic Bosnia, desired by Slavic Serbia, had been annexed by Austria–Hungary in 1908.) As far as immediate responsibility for a localized clash was concerned, neighboring Serbia bore a heavy burden of guilt. The assassination was planned by its Chief of Intelligence, who provided the arms, and its prime minister probably knew in a general way what was being plotted.

Next in the chain reaction of responsibility was Austria–Hungary. Alarmed by Serbia's excitation of her Slavic minorities, she rashly presented an ultimatum that would impose impossible demands on her offending neighbor, even at the cost of war, whether localized or general. Russia, backing her sister Slavic protégé, Serbia, abruptly ended all possibility of a strictly localized conflict by prematurely mobilizing her massive army, which, though formidable, was unwieldy and ill-equipped.[1]

Germany erred grievously in giving blank-check support to her only dependable ally, Austria–Hungary, thereby encouraging the stern demands on Serbia. In this respect Berlin bore the heaviest responsibility for turning a two-nation dispute into a world war. As soon as the slow-moving Russians began to mobilize their troops, the Germans felt that they had to strike at the French through Belgium, knock France out of

[1] Revisionist historiography regarding war responsibility is treated in W. I. Cohen, *The American Revisionists* (1967).

the war, and then shift their armies eastward to meet the ponderous Russian attack. Otherwise they feared that they would be "encircled" and crushed in a two-front assault.

French responsibility for the general conflagration was less direct, although France might have exerted strong pressure on her Russian ally to delay mobilization. Certainly many French nationalists, with Russia about to strike Germany in the rear, welcomed this opportunity to attack their neighbor and regain Alsace-Lorraine, seized by the Germans in 1870–1871.

British responsibility was perhaps the least direct. The London Foreign Office, which feared German occupation of the cross-Channel ports, might have restrained Berlin by proclaiming at the outset that an attack on France by way of Belgium would inescapably bring Britain into the conflict. As it was, Great Britain did not declare war on Germany until several hours *after* the Germans had declared war on France and had begun their invasion of Belgium. The neutrality of this tiny country had been guaranteed by the European powers in 1839, but the German Chancellor blunderingly referred to the pact as a "scrap of paper."[2]

Germany's lunge into Belgium (undertaken while the Russians were already invading Germanic East Prussia) was interpreted by many Americans as proof positive that Berlin had not only plotted the war but was solely responsible for it. Allied propaganda ceaselessly played up this assumption. When the fighting ended, the Germans were forced to sign the Treaty of Versailles, which declared that Germany and her allies were guilty of "imposing" hostilities on the Allies.[3] Most Germans did not believe this, and Adolf Hitler made effective use of the "war guilt lie" during his spectacular rise to power and in his successful attempt to throw off the Treaty of Versailles. Under him, Germany deliberately launched World War II by attacking Poland in 1939, and this assault seemed to prove, though actually it did not, that Germany was similarly guilty in 1914.

[2] The British Ambassador in Berlin, Sir Edward Goschen, reported to London on August 4, 1914, his recollection of the words of Bethmann-Hollweg, the German Chancellor: "Just for a word — 'neutrality,' a word which in wartime has so often been disregarded, just for a scrap of paper — Great Britain is going to make war." This unfortunate phrase was used with telling effect by Allied propagandists. Many shocked Americans were unaware that their own government had treated scores of treaties with Indian tribes as "scraps of paper."

[3] The specific wording of Article 231 follows: "The Allied and Associated Governments affirm and Germany accepts the responsibility of Germany and her allies for causing all the loss and damage to which the Allied and Associated Governments and their nationals have been subjected as a consequence of the war imposed upon them by the aggression of Germany and her allies."

WAS AMERICA NEUTRAL DURING THE NEUTRALITY PERIOD?

America, with its immense immigrant population from various "Old Countries" in Europe, was a "menagerie of nationalities." German–Americans and anti-British Irish–Americans naturally sided with Germany; Anglo–Americans and Franco–Americans favored Britain and France. On August 18, 1914, President Wilson issued an appeal urging his people to be "impartial in thought as well as in action."

This, taken literally, was a most difficult prescription. The individual citizen can control his actions but hardly his thoughts. An inescapable fact is that the great majority of the American people were evidently pro-Ally from the beginning. For one thing, Germany had appeared to be the wanton aggressor by bursting into Belgium (in an alleged effort to avoid a Franco–Russian "encirclement"). In occupying that tiny country, the Germans used brutal methods, such as the shooting of hostages, to suppress civilian resistance. Moreover Germany, with the saber-rattling Kaiser Wilhelm II often in the headlines, had been a commercial and imperial rival of the United States for several decades, and German imperialism, militarism, navalism, and illiberalism had proved offensive to a more democratic America.[4]

As for the Allies, despotic Russia had few friends in the United States, but conspicuous in the Allied camp were the French and British. France was an old friend who had helped America win her independence; the debt-to-Lafayette feeling was still strong; and France had obviously been brutally assaulted by Germany. The British, who had become increasingly friendly to the Americans near the turn of the century, were the cultural creditors of the United States. Both peoples were bound together by a common heritage of language, law, literature, tradition, and blood, and the United States could not stand by unconcerned if England were being overrun by German goosesteppers.

WAS WILSON NEUTRAL IN THOUGHT AND ACTION?

President Wilson tried hard to steer a genuinely neutral course, and in considerable measure succeeded. Although greatly annoyed by British seizures of American ships and other restrictive practices, his basic sym-

---

[4] See C. E. Schieber, *The Transformation of American Sentiment Toward Germany, 1870–1914* (1923).

pathies were with the Allies. On one occasion in private he burst out, "England is fighting our fight."

Wilson's mother was born in England, and his grandparents on both sides came to America from the British Isles. As a youth he greatly admired English thinkers, especially the economist Walter Bagehot, and tried to pattern himself after British statesmen, especially William E. Gladstone. In later life he spent a half dozen or so summers in the British Isles, with scant attention to the Continent, roaming about the beautiful countryside and drinking in the atmosphere of Wordsworth and Shelley.

All things considered, Wilson did remarkably well in holding his pro-Ally sympathies in check. He received little pressure in the opposite direction from his Cabinet, which was generally pro-Ally and which contained one member, Secretary of the Interior Lane, who was Canadian born. The most conspicuous exception was Secretary Bryan, who was more truly neutral than his pro-Ally colleagues. They naturally regarded him as pro-German.

Bryan resigned in June 1915, fearful that President Wilson was going to push America into war over the *Lusitania* sinking. He was succeeded by Robert Lansing, who moved up from a subordinate position in the State Department. Wilson was inclined to think of him as something of a glorified clerk, but he proved to be strongly pro-Ally and exercised a much stronger hand in shaping anti-German policies than was recognized at the time.[5]

WERE THE GERMANS ALONE GUILTY OF ATROCITIES?

Germany, as the apparent aggressor, fought most of the war in foreign countries, with the inevitable interruption of their civilian life. (The one noteworthy exception was an early Russian invasion of East Prussia which was devastatingly repulsed, but not until the "barbaric" invaders had been accused of many atrocities.) In Belgium and northeastern France, where the heaviest fighting of the war occurred, libraries, schools, and cathedrals were damaged or destroyed, and civilians were forced into labor camps or executed when caught fighting without uniforms. Altogether, more than 5,000 of them are estimated to have lost their lives.

This heavy-handed German occupation of "poor little Belgium" was harsh enough, but Allied propagandists improved on the gory tales

---

[5] D. M. Smith, *Robert Lansing and American Neutrality, 1914–1917* (1958).

spread by rumor. Accusations that the Germans crucified Canadians, skewered infants with bayonets, used corpses of soldiers for soap, and routinely cut off the breasts of Belgian maidens and the hands of Belgian babes were all later shown to be hoaxes. Indeed the amputation of childish hands without immediate medical assistance would have resulted in speedy death by bleeding.[6]

While spreading such lurid tales, the Allied censors, who controlled news coming to America over the cables, were careful to see that reports of the misbehavior of their soldiers were given scant publicity. Allied troops ultimately occupied a portion of Greece under conditions roughly comparable to Germany's violation of Belgium's neutrality, but Americans took little notice of this incursion, partly because it was not pursued with Germanic thoroughness and ruthlessness.

In truth, during all armed clashes of any size atrocities occur—and on both sides. War in itself is the greatest atrocity of all, and "humane warfare" is a contradiction in terms. Soldiers are trained to kill, and in the heat of battle are often less than gentlemanly. Prisoners are commonly shot if they cannot be taken along or if their release would imperil security. Certainly the American record is not lily-white. In slaughtering Indian men, women, and children, in torturing Filipinos during the Philippine insurrection, or in shooting women and children in Vietnam, the Americans have earned their share of world disapprobation.

DID ALLIED PROPAGANDA DRAG THE U. S. INTO WAR?

In the years after World War I, and particularly in the neutrality-conscious 1930s, a theme popular is some quarters was that Uncle Sam had been "suckered" into the conflict against Germany by Allied propaganda.

Unquestionably Allied propagandists, especially the British, were extremely active in the United States, whether in the press, on the plat-

---

[6] There was undoubtedly some rape in Belgium, as there has traditionally been by conquerors, but its incidence was probably overplayed. In 1944 when the Americans invaded France, there were instances of attacks on French females by their liberators, and when the Russian soldiers occupied enemy Vienna and Berlin, raping occurred on a wholesale basis. Lord Bryce, well known in America, lent his name to an official British report in 1915 which combined rumor, fiction, and truth in a devastating compilation. For atrocities see James M. Read, *Atrocity Propaganda, 1914–1919* (1941) and H. C. Peterson, *Propaganda for War: The Campaign Against American Neutrality, 1914–1917* (1939). Although not designed as pro-Nazi propaganda, Peterson's book was widely distributed in America by the Germans as a warning against being gulled again by Allied propaganda.

form, or in the mails. The Republic was deluged with words and pictures which played up German atrocities and underscored the menace of "Hunnish" imperialism, militarism, and barbarism. All this undoubtedly had some effect in further poisoning the American mind against the Central Powers, but its overall impact is impossible to measure.

Several basic facts must be kept in mind. One is that the Americans were already strongly biased in favor of the Allied cause as soon as the war started and long before the propagandists could shift into high gear. Another is that the Germans launched a counter-propaganda campaign in the United States which emphasized British interference with American shipping and mails, while deploring the inhumanity of selling shiploads of munitions to the Allies for making German widows and orphans. But German propagandists were weakened by being thrown on the defensive and by having to justify the aggressive–defensive acts of the Fatherland.[7]

In truth, the Allies did not need to manufacture propaganda because lurid headline events were damaging enough in themselves. The ruthless invasion of Belgium, despite the "scrap of paper," was a fact, even though the Germans were aiming to burst out of what they deemed an iron ring and even though they requested permission to pass through, with a twelve-hour deadline.[8] The sinking of the *Lusitania* by the Germans, with the loss of more than a thousand civilians, was a fact, even though the ship was carrying munitions to the enemy. The shooting ("judicial murder") of an English nurse in Belgium, Miss Edith Cavell, was a fact, even though she had helped more than a hundred Allied soldiers to escape through German lines and even though her execution in 1915 was justified by the German military code.[9] The

[7] See F. A. Bonadio, "The Failure of German Propaganda in the United States, 1914–1917," *Mid-America*, XLI (1959), 40–57. Contrary to a number of other writers, Arthur S. Link, the foremost Wilson scholar, believes that the German propaganda was "shrewd and subtle," and that on the whole the German effort "was larger than the British." See J. A. Garraty, ed., *Interpreting American History* (1970), II, 126–127. The "subtlety" of German propaganda largely disappeared when, less than a year after the war's outbreak, the German agent, Dr. Albert, left his brief case full of secret papers on a New York elevated train. The vast collection in the Hoover Institution (Stanford University) contains about twice as many Allied propaganda pieces as German.

[8] Berlin promised, should permission to pass be granted, to guarantee the independence and integrity of Belgium and ultimately pay an indemnity. But the Belgians decided to go to war rather than accept this encroachment upon their sovereignty. Twenty-seven years later, in 1941, Hitler burst into Belgium with no advance notice whatever.

[9] The French shot more than a half dozen women spies, including the famed Dutch seductress, Mata Hari. But she was neither an English woman nor a nurse, and had been engaged in a much older female profession. Miss Cavell, who could have taken refuge in legal technicalities, naively confessed, thereby implicating eight others. Read, *Atrocity Propaganda*, pp. 210–213.

propaganda effect of the *Lusitania* sinking and of the Edith Cavell execution more than offset any military advantage that the Germans may have gained from these harsh, if technically justifiable, acts.

DID AMERICAN BANKERS INVOLVE THE U. S. IN WAR?

In the neutrality-conscious 1930s, numerous critics in America accused the Wall Street bankers of having had a large hand in pushing the nation into war in 1917 to salvage their immense loans to the Allies. Indeed, no one can deny that such lendings were huge and that some of the leading financiers were pro-Ally. During the so-called neutrality period private bankers advanced $2.3 billion to the Allies, mostly secured by good collateral, but only $27 million to Germany, which was regarded as a poor risk.

Such loans were perfectly legal, although onesided and largely for the purchase of munitions in America. Undoubtedly they did violate the true spirit of neutrality. On the other hand, they did contribute greatly to national prosperity, while lifting the Republic out of the depression doldrums of 1913–1914. For economic reasons, if for no other, the administration in Washington permitted such transactions to go forward with at least its tacit blessing.

To argue that a handful of bankers forced the United States Congress to declare war in order to save their investments is to credit them with vastly more direct influence than they had. These loans represented the savings of many Americans, and if the Allies had been visibly collapsing, these investors, as well as the bankers themselves, would no doubt have brought considerable pressure to bear on the administration to intervene.[10]

Actually, in February and March 1917, when Germany began her unrestricted submarine campaign and Wilson broke diplomatic relations with Berlin as a prelude to war, the country was not aware that the

[10] During the Nye Committee investigation of 1934–1936, much was made of the somewhat hysterical telegram that Ambassador Page sent from London to the State Department, March 5, 1917, stating that America would have to go to war to save Allied credit and preserve her export trade. But this plea came more than a month *after* Wilson had severed relations with Germany. For telegram see *Foreign Relations, 1917*, Suppl. 2, vol. I, 516–518. Page had become so notoriously pro-British by this time that President Wilson was ignoring him. The Ambassador's greatest influence had come earlier, when he had privately encouraged the British to continue the blockade practices against which the United States government was strongly protesting. Someone has caustically observed that Page was a fine ambassador: the only question was which country was he representing? See Ross Gregory, *Walter Hines Page* (1970).

Allies were losing. They were, in fact, thought to be winning. Not until after Congress declared war did German U-boat sinkings shoot up to terrifying proportions, and not until after the United States entered the conflict did the Allies reveal in confidence how close they were to the end of their tether.

WAS AN OLD-STYLE
BLOCKADE FEASIBLE IN WORLD WAR I?

The conventional blockade sanctioned by international law as of 1914 was relatively simple. The blockading nation (Britain) would station its warships closely off the coast of the blockaded enemy (Germany), and intercept all ships coming or going.

But the old methods did not fit the new conditions of World War I. A warship blockading close in was a sitting duck for modern long-range artillery and particularly for the submarine. The British, pleading the "unique" or "peculiar" conditions of the conflict, took extraordinary liberties with traditional freedom of the seas, as conceived of by Americans. The Royal Navy would intercept neutral ships, shepherd them into port, and then in a leisurely manner search them for contraband destined for the enemy, whether directly or through neighboring neutrals such as Denmark and Holland.[11] The British arbitrarily defined contraband to include even foodstuffs that might be used, even circuitously, to support the armed forces. Yet the old rules had held contraband to be the materials of war, such as weapons and ammunition. Britain's justification was that in an all-out conflict virtually all basic commodities were in some way related to the clash of arms.

The British were not completely arbitrary in their seizure of contraband-carrying American merchant ships. In many cases Britain would pay for the cargo of cotton, meat, wheat, and other commodities, but because of delays and other drawbacks, the American shipper would not make the maximum profit. Clearly he was not as well off as he would have been if allowed to reach the lucrative markets that would have been open to a neutral carrier under the ancient rules of international law.

---

[11] This interdiction of shipments going by indirect routes to a belligerent was perfected by the Americans during the Civil War (the doctrine of "continuous voyage"). Neutral cargoes of contraband to the Confederacy by way of neutral ports were seized on the high seas. The British then acquiesced in and later improved upon this practice during World War I. The blockade problem is treated in Marion C. Siney, *The Allied Blockade of Germany, 1914–1916* (1957) and Alice M. Morrissey, *The American Defense of Neutral Rights, 1914–1917* (1939).

In perfecting the blockade of Germany, Great Britain mined much of the North Sea (after alleging an earlier German sowing of illegal mines in open waters), and forced all neutral shippers to stop at British ports for scrutiny. If they were not carrying objectionable cargo, they would receive sailing directions that would carry them safely through the minefields. Without such guidance, they could have tried to bull their way through with an almost certain prospect of destruction. Late in February 1915, two American merchant ships, the *Evelyn* and the *Carib*, reportedly carrying cargoes for Germany, struck mines in the North Sea and sank, with the loss of one man in the first mishap and three in the second.[12] The mines were presumably, though not certainly, British.

Blocking off and systematically mining a large area of the North Sea was a flagrant violation of international law as interpreted by Americans. One is therefore greatly surprised to find that Washington never lodged an official protest with London. More than two years later the State Department merely reserved American rights.[13] Yet, indicative of double-standard neutrality, Washington had promptly and sternly protested against the submarine zone around the British Isles proclaimed by Germany on February 4, 1915.

WAS THE BRITISH BLOCKADE ILLEGAL?

Long-range British blockade practices were certainly unorthodox, as judged by time-honored international law. Legalists can still argue as to whether or not Britain was justified in resorting to these tactics in retaliation against alleged German malpractices (for example, sowing mines in the open seas) or because of the "unique" or "unusual" conditions of this conflict. At all events, Washington vigorously protested against the British blockade as illegal, though finally and grudgingly acquiescing in it. If the Americans had chosen to back up their protests with naval escorts (the United States then had the third strongest navy in the world), the British almost certainly would have had to back down. They could ill afford a new foe as powerful as America, and they certainly would be foolish to quarrel with their chief munitions depot.

It is entirely possible that the United States would have taken a stronger position if the American people had not been sympathetic

---

[12] *Foreign Relations, 1915*, Suppl., 339–340. Mines sank ships without warning, in contrast to the submarine, whose torpedo at least left a telltale wake.
[13] *Ibid., 1917*, Suppl. 1, 519–520 (Feb. 19, 1917).

toward the Allies, and if the Wilson administration and key members of
the diplomatic corps, such as Ambassador Page in London, had not been
pro-Ally as well. If Washington had forced the British to abandon their
unorthodox blockade practices, the German High Command might have
felt that it could win the war without resorting to the unrestricted submarine campaign which ultimately forced the United States into the abyss
in 1917. As events turned out, Washington pursued a fateful double-
standard policy toward the rival blockades.

DID THE MUNITIONS TRADE PROVOKE GERMANY TO WAR?

When war erupted in Europe in 1914 (as later in 1939), the United States
was wallowing in an economic depression. Immense orders from the
Allies for munitions helped to pull the nation out of stagnation and onto
a plateau of prosperity.

Germany and the other Central Powers believed passionately
that the huge American trade in war materials with the Allies was unneutral, as indeed it was in spirit, if not in fact.[14] The United States
rapidly became the principal overseas supplier of munitions to one set
of belligerents. Even so, the Americans would have been quite willing to
sell comparable amounts to the Central Powers if the British blockade
of Germany had not prevented deliveries. The sale of war materiel by
a neutral was clearly sanctioned by international law; in fact, the
Germans themselves had engaged in this ugly traffic while a neutral in
past wars.

When the great conflict erupted in 1914, Germany, as a highly
industrialized nation, was well prepared to supply herself with munitions. But the British had counted on control of the seas in the event of
a general war, and on consequent access to the arms factories of America.
Washington could quite legally have clamped an embargo on the export
of military hardware, as a number of smaller nations did to conserve
their scanty supplies or for other reasons. But such a restriction would
have worked so heavily to the advantage of a prepared Germany, and
to the disadvantage of an unprepared Britain, as to amount to unneutrality.

By the time the Wilson administration came squarely to grips
with this problem the prosperity of America was too intimately tied in
with the Allied munitions trade to permit a stoppage. An embargo would

---

[14] See C. J. Child, "German-American Attempts to Prevent the Exportation of
Munitions of War, 1914–1915," *Miss. Valley Hist. Rev.*, XXV (1938), 351–368.

have been unfair to the Allies; unrestricted sales to Britain and France would prove to be unfair to Germany and her associates. But continued shipments meant continued prosperity, and no politically conscious administration would deliberately choose a course that would plunge the country back into a depression. Besides, Americans generally wanted the Allies to win. Hence dollars and desires alike dictated the profitable course of least resistance and wide-open munitions shipments.

Germany and her allies were greatly angered by the sale of arms to their enemies, who thus escaped defeat while inflicting maddening losses on their foes. The misconception is common that the Germans launched their all-out submarine campaign in 1917 primarily because they wanted to stop the shipments of American munitions. If so, then the United States brought the war on itself by continuing this profitable if disagreeable business.

Official documents now reveal that in 1917 Berlin launched its submarine campaign for the purpose of knocking England out of the war by cutting off *all* commerce, including food. The German High Command reasoned that the British Isles would be starved out in at least six months, long before the United States could raise an army and send it to Europe. Meanwhile America could not help the Allies much more than she was already doing with mountainous cargoes of munitions and other materiel.[15]

DID THE MUNITIONS MAKERS PUSH THE U. S. INTO WAR?

During the 1930s, when Congress was attempting to legislate "permanent" neutrality, the charge was frequently heard that American munitions makers had been responsible for pushing the nation into the conflict. Taking heed of this so-called "lesson" of history, the legislators in 1935, 1936, and 1937 passed acts forbidding or severely restricting shipments of munitions to the belligerents. Loans were likewise forbidden.

To say that American munitions makers shoved the Republic into the conflict is to grant them far more persuasion with Congress, which declared war, than they could possibly have possessed. To say that their shipments angered the Germans to the point that Germany pushed America into the war is to exaggerate the importance of the arms trade in 1917, as we have just noted.

[15] See Ernest R. May, *The World War and American Isolation, 1914–1917* (1959), Ch. XVIII.

Why should American munitions makers, so their defenders argue, have prodded the nation into the slaughter? They were making indecent profits as it was, and their unpublished slogan might well have been "Neutrality Forever," or as long as Allied funds and credits held out. Armed hostilities would raise the specter of government controls, excess profits taxes, renegotiated contracts, and various other annoyances and encumbrances. During the period of the Senate Nye Committee investigation in the 1930s, representatives of huge companies such as Du Pont soberly testified that they preferred the steady profits of peacetime, with fertilizers and chemicals, to the boom-and-bust business spawned by war.[16] A skeptical public refused to believe them.

Contrary to a widely believed Marxist myth, the New York Stock Exchange has generally reacted unfavorably to rumors of war and favorably to prospects of peace. Significantly, on July 31, 1914, as hostilities were erupting in Europe, the Stock Exchange was so severely depressed that it temporarily closed for the first time since the financial crisis of 1873.

WAS THE GERMAN SUBMARINE WARFARE UNLAWFUL?

In attempting to establish a counter-blockade of the British Isles, Berlin resorted to submarine warfare for the first time in history on a considerable scale.[17] Under the hoary rules of international law, the German submersible would have to emerge, force the neutral merchantman to heave to, and send out a boarding party to examine the suspect and its papers for evidence of contraband destined for the foe. An enemy craft of any kind was always subject to seizure. But if it was neutral, and if it was transporting contraband of war to one's antagonist, it could be seized, manned by a prize crew, and sent on to a German port for adjudication. Under certain circumstances, a neutral freighter carrying contraband to one's adversary could be lawfully sunk or burned (as could an enemy merchantman), but not until the passengers and crew had been taken aboard the attacking vessel or otherwise placed in a position of safety. This did not mean small boats in the open and stormy sea, far distant from land or succoring ships. An enemy warship could, of

[16] See John E. Wiltz, *In Search of Peace: The Senate Munitions Inquiry, 1934–1936* (1963).

[17] The Confederates used primitive submarines against the Yankee blockade; they managed to sink one enemy ship and damage another. Both attacking vessels were lost.

course, be sunk at any time without warning and without concern for survivors.[18]

Embattled Germany soon found that the submarine could not be used effectively as a commerce destroyer if the practices established by sailing-ship international law were followed to the letter. A skeleton crew could not be put aboard the merchantman because the tiny submarine, with its small complement of men, had no sailors to spare. If it had, how could it have sailed its victim through the British minefields and blockade for scrutiny by a German prize court? If the underseas attacker chose to torpedo the ship, it had no room on board for the passengers and crew, many of whom were potential saboteurs.

In the early stages of the war, the Germans made some attempt to abide by the ancient rules.[19] The submarine would emerge and fire a warning shot across the bow of the suspected merchantman as a signal for it to heave to for visit and search. (The enemy ship often flew a neutral flag—even the Stars and Stripes—as a ruse of war.) The intended victim could follow one of several courses: heave to; put on a burst of speed and escape (the surface speed of the submarine was less than that of fast steamers); open fire on the fragile submersible with a six-inch gun (by 1915 many British merchantmen were so armed); or steer directly at the vulnerable attacker and destroy it by ramming. The London government offered rewards to captains who would ram enemy submersibles, and this honor was soon claimed by several bold mariners. In addition, the British used warships disguised as merchantmen to entrap the unsuspecting U-boat.

After some intended victims had turned and escaped, and after several submarines had been stove in by enemy merchantmen, the German officials concluded that the old rules of warfare simply did not fit the new weapons. They therefore decided that where a contrary course seemed hazardous, the submarine would be justified in sinking

[18] In 1936 the powers (including Germany) subscribed to the London Protocol, further spelling out international law: "In particular, except in the case of persistent refusal to stop on being duly summoned, or of active resistance to visit or search, a warship, whether surface vessel or submarine, may not sink or render incapable of navigation a merchant vessel without having first placed passengers, crew, and ship's papers in a place of safety. For this purpose the ship's boats are not regarded as a place of safety unless the safety of the passengers and crew is assured, in the existing sea and weather conditions, by the proximity of land, or the presence of another vessel which is in a position to take them on board." Stephen Heald and J. W. Wheeler-Bennett, *Documents on International Affairs, 1936* (1937), p. 633.

[19] At the outset of the war the Germans had only a half dozen or so submarines available. If they had waited until they had several score before opening up, they might have knocked Britain out of the conflict. By beginning on such a small scale, they gave the enemy time to develop effective antisubmarine techniques.

without warning, and without regard for the lives of passengers and crews.[20]

This new policy was shockingly inhumane, but Berlin justified it on the grounds that the "peculiar" or "novel" circumstances of the war warranted a departure from the old rules. The Germans pointed out that the British, alleging "peculiar" and "novel" conditions, had sharply modified international law by establishing an "illegal" blockade and by blocking off the high seas with minefields. To be sure, this policy did not take the lives of innocent noncombatants because the neutral merchant ships heeded the blockade. But many innocent lives would have been lost if the neutrals had attempted to force their way blindly through the British minefields in the North Sea, while also trying to feel their way through the German submarine blockade. An essential difference between the two hazards was that the neutral shipper had a good chance to slip through the submarine blockade, whereas he had virtually no chance of avoiding the British minefields without sailing directions.

WAS GERMANY'S ALL-OUT SUBMARINE WARFARE JUSTIFIED?

A crucial difference between the "liberties" that the British took with international law and those taken by the Germans was that Britain's blockade confiscated property (often paid for), while Germany's U-boat took lives (which could not be satisfactorily paid for). World opinion was shocked, but such condemnation did not greatly concern Berlin. By 1916 the United States was the only considerable power remaining neutral, and it had a contemptibly small army that could not even catch Pancho Villa.

The Germans were involved in a desperate struggle, brought on by menacing foes, or so they believed. Enemy navies, chiefly British, had thrown around them a "starvation" blockade which ultimately brought on serious food shortages. The Germans had on hand a weapon which they believed could establish a counter-blockade of Britain and starve her out. Should they use their U-boat with maximum effectiveness (which meant sinking without warning)? Or should they muzzle it and quietly lose the war, as they had an excellent chance of doing if they could not break the Allied blockade?

---

[20] Under the old rules, a resisting merchantman or one attempting to escape after being warned to stop was equated with an enemy warship, which could lawfully be sunk without warning.

Certain British spokesmen declared, during and after the conflict, that if the tables had been reversed, Britain would never have resorted to so unsporting a tactic as unrestricted submarine warfare. Such restraint seems highly unlikely, because few nations will deliberately lose a war when they have at hand a weapon which they think will win it or hasten its end and save the lives of their own people. America dropped two atomic bombs on Japan in 1945 for the same reason that Germany employed her ultimate weapon—to win the war.[21]

From a strategic standpoint, the Germans erred not so much in exploiting the U-boat ruthlessly as in employing it in such a way in 1917 as to force the United States into the war. They grievously underestimated the speed with which "America the Unready" could raise an effective fighting force and send it to Europe.

Germany used the submarine and lost World War I; she used it again and lost World War II. A reasonable conclusion would seem to be that nations resorting to the submarine as their chief naval threat are doomed to defeat. Actually Germany came perilously close to overcoming Britain in both conflicts. Historically the submarine has been a relatively cheap naval weapon, and there is no guarantee that it will not be on the winning side in a future conflict.[22] The enormous subsea fleet built up by the Russians after World War II, with the United States in second place numerically, is in itself a mute testimony to the menace of this type of craft.

DID GERMANY HAVE REASON TO SINK THE "LUSITANIA"?

In February 1915 Berlin announced that it would establish a submarine war zone about the British Isles and attempt to sink all *enemy* ships, whether warships or merchantmen, armed or unarmed, found within that

---

[21] In 1936, as already noted, the nations of the world, including Germany, signed the London Protocol barring the sinking of unresisting merchant ships without warning and without adequate provision for the safety of passengers and crew. On the first day of World War II in 1939, the Germans sank without warning the British passenger ship *Athenia*. When the United States entered World War II in 1941, American submarines promptly began to destroy an enormous amount of Japanese merchant shipping without warning. In general, belligerent nations involved in an all-out war will be bound by international law only insofar as they deem it to their advantage to do so. They take into account such factors as world public opinion (especially if there are powerful neutrals whose support is desired) and possible reprisals. Shooting prisoners, for example, is a generally unprofitable game that two can play.

[22] The submarine proved its effectiveness as an American weapon against the Japanese in World War II.

area. Neutrals, of course, might be sunk by mistake. The official announcement stated that this step had become necessary as retaliation
against the "illegal" British blockade, in which the neutral nations were
acquiescing.

Ship after ship went plunging to the bottom. The ninety-first,
the crack British *Lusitania*, was torpedoed without warning on May 7,
1915, while nearing the Irish coast, with the appalling loss of 1,198
men, women, and children. Of those who lost their lives, 128 were
Americans.[23]

Berlin claimed that the vessel had been warned, although not in
the orthodox fashion. First there had been the announcement of the
German war-zone in February, then the repeated sinkings (twenty-two
while the *Lusitania* was en route), and finally the publication in the New
York press of an official general warning on the day that the *Lusitania*
sailed. There had still been time, although a change was inconvenient,
for the American passengers to transfer to a slower and less luxurious
U. S. liner. It had ample room; it sailed two hours later; and it arrived at
Liverpool.

German spokesmen truthfully charged that the *Lusitania* was
carrying munitions. Its manifest listed 4,200 cases of small arms ammunition, plus 1,250 empty shrapnel cases and other nonexplosive contraband. But the nature of the cargo has no bearing on the rule that an
unarmed and unresisting passenger ship must not be sunk without warning and without proper provision for the safety of passengers and crew.[24]

Berlin claimed that the *Lusitania* was transporting a body of
Canadian troops (hence a troopship) and was armed with powerful guns.
No credible evidence has ever been forthcoming that the vessel was
carrying an organized body of uniformed soldiers; no reliable witnesses
among the scores who later testified ever reported seeing mounted
cannon. Washington at one juncture took the position that, since
passenger ships and merchantmen had traditionally carried guns to fight
off pirates and other foes, the presence of *defensive* armament did not
convert passenger liners into warships. But a defensive weapon against

[23] The misconception lingers in some quarters, largely because of the heavy loss
of American life, that the *Lusitania* was an American ship. Prior to the sinking of
this British Cunarder, the Germans had attacked several American vessels, including
the *Gulflight*, which was torpedoed on May 1, 1917, with the loss of three lives.
This, technically, was a more serious offense against the United States than the
sinking of a British ship, even though fatalities were fewer.

[24] There was a second explosion, which accounted in part for the extraordinarily
rapid sinking of the ship (18 minutes), and which may have been caused by
nonlisted explosives or the possible explosion en masse of the ten or eleven tons
of powder in the small-arms cartridges. See T. A. Bailey, "The Sinking of the
Lusitania," *Amer. Hist. Rev.*, XLI (1935), 54–73.

enemy cruisers was an offensive weapon against submarines, which were so fragile that one well-placed shot would destroy them.

From one point of view the *Lusitania* was an offensively armed ship, and hence subject to destruction without warning. The British captain was carrying specific orders, as the Berlin government knew many merchant ships were, to ram on sight any enemy submarine. The prow of the speedy *Lusitania* could so easily crush the hull of the attacking submarine that the captain of the smaller craft would have been foolhardy if he had shown himself.[25]

Whatever the technical justification, the practical justification admits of little argument. Weapons are used to win wars, not lose them, and the sinking of the *Lusitania* was a great propaganda defeat for Germany. It outraged world opinion, stimulated America's preparedness campaign, and further predisposed Americans to favor the Allied cause. Many commentators have gone too far in saying that the *Lusitania* brought the United States into the conflict; indeed, Congress waited almost two years before passing the war declaration. But the *Lusitania* was clearly related to the state of mind that caused America to accept the German challenge when it finally came in 1917. The 4,200 cases of small arms ammunition never reached Germany's foes, but the Fatherland probably would have been better off if they had.

COULD AMERICANS LEGALLY SAIL ON BELLIGERENT SHIPS?

American citizens had a perfect legal right, according to the old rules of international law, to sail into submarine-infested waters on belligerent British and French passenger ships. Two serious attempts were made by Congress early in 1916 to pass legislation forbidding such travel, but President Wilson used his influence to have them squelched. He argued that if the nation renounced the right of its citizens to engage in such travel, such a retreat would herald a breakdown of the whole "fine fabric" of international law. Secretary Bryan believed that the State Department should warn American citizens against such travel,

---

[25] Contrary to legend, the *U 20* was not lying in wait for the *Lusitania;* it had only three torpedoes left and was returning to Germany from an unspectacular cruise when the speeding *Lusitania* unexpectedly changed course and came within deadly torpedo range. The London government was criticized for not sending out destroyer escorts, but there were not enough such craft to go around, and the British had confidence that the *Lusitania's* speed was protection enough. An unauthorized German devised a commemorative medal showing the *Lusitania* bristling with guns; Allied propagandists struck off about 250,000 replicas of it. Arthur Ponsonby, *Falsehood in War-Time* (1928), p. 125.

especially since American and other neutral passenger ships were available. But Wilson was unyielding, even though he had been willing to admonish Americans to stay out of the Mexican war zone.

The Germans feared that the loss of American lives would seriously involve them with the United States. Their cautious attitude explains in part why they published their general warning advertisement (its printing was delayed by mischance for a week) on the day the *Lusitania* sailed. Such interference in the domestic affairs of a foreign nation was a serious diplomatic irregularity which the Germans could justify only by the unwillingness of Washington to face up to reality.

Americans who were traveling to England for business or pleasure assumed the grave risk of involving their own country in war with Germany by thus "committing suicide." They had a perfect legal right to do so, but they were just as dead when drowned as if they had been in the wrong. And the consequences for their own countrymen were frightening.

One anomaly is that what President Wilson regarded as dishonorable in 1915 became acceptable by legislation in the 1930s. By the neutrality legislation passed during that era, Congress forbade American citizens to travel on belligerent passenger ships. If such a statute had been on the books in 1915, none of the 128 Americans who lost their lives on the *Lusitania* could have been legally on board.

WAS THE "SUSSEX" LESS IMPORTANT THAN THE "LUSITANIA"?

After protracted negotiations with Berlin, the German government finally agreed that no more unresisting passenger ships would be sunk without warning, provided that they did not offer resistance or attempt to escape.

In March 1916 a German U-boat commander, evidently thinking he had sighted a warship, torpedoed (but did not sink) a French cross-Channel passenger steamer, the *Sussex*, with about eighty casualties, including several injured Americans. Misinformed by the navy officials, the German Foreign Office at first denied responsibility, and this apparent duplicity angered Wilson. He instructed the State Department to deliver a virtual ultimatum to Berlin. Unless Germany renounced the sinking of unresisting merchantmen and passenger ships without warning, the United States would have no choice but to sever diplomatic relations—a step which in those days was an almost inevitable prelude to war.[26]

[26] The *Sussex* crisis is fully treated in A. S. Link, *Wilson: Confusions and Crises, 1915–1916* (1964).

Berlin reluctantly acceded to the American demand, but added a "string"—namely that Washington must bring pressure to bear on the Allies to relax their "illegal" "starvation blockade." Wilson accepted the qualified concession but rejected the "string."

Diplomatically, the *Sussex* was by far the most important ship of the war as far as America was concerned. Wilson had secured what he regarded as an important concession—temporarily. But he had made the mistake of restricting his freedom of maneuver by handing the Germans what amounted to a blank-check declaration of war. If they should see fit to renew their inhumane attacks without warning, he would be honor bound to break diplomatic relations. And that would almost certainly mean war.

SHOULD WILSON HAVE PUSHED PREPAREDNESS EARLIER?

From the beginning there was a strong feeling in America that the Allies would win the war, for they enjoyed vastly superior resources and manpower, as well as naval supremacy. Nothing happened comparable to the later collapse of France in 1940 to shake the American people out of their complacency.

A small group of war-minded citizens, conspicuous among them Colonel Theodore Roosevelt, foresaw the possibility of a German victory or American involvement. They therefore launched a spirited campaign for preparedness. The existing regular army numbered only about 100,000 men, and the navy, though large, was not at the peak of efficiency.

Wilson, a pacifist at heart, at first opposed the preparedness agitation, which, to be sure, was then the voice of a minority. Not until about a year after the outbreak of war in Europe had raised alarming danger signals did he reverse his position, and not until November 4, 1915, more than three months later, did he come out publicly in support of preparedness. As the result of a vigorous popular campaign, Congress voted in 1916 to increase the size of the army and to enlarge the navy with an unprecedented appropriation for 156 new vessels in three years.[27]

With the wisdom of hindsight we can see that Wilson erred in not throwing himself enthusiastically behind the preparedness move-

[27] The army bill was woefully inadequate for what lay ahead, and when war came the regular force had not been substantially increased. The navy bill, with its emphasis on big battleships rather than on antisubmarine craft, resulted in the partial construction of many ships that were not needed in World War I. Many of those nearing completion were scrapped as a result of the Washington Conference of 1921–1922.

ment from its early beginnings. He could wield no Big Stick when the German warlords decided to push America into the abyss early in 1917. If he had managed to accumulate a respectable army, with adequate maritime transportation, in addition to a formidable antisubmarine fleet, the Germans might not have forced the United States into the fray. When the crunch came, they felt that they had little to fear and much to gain by an unrestricted submarine campaign.

WHY DID WILSON WIN REELECTION IN 1916?

The presidential election of 1916, during which Wilson ran for a second time, proved to be one of the closest in American history. The Republican nominee, Charles Evans Hughes, in assailing Wilson's lack of firmness with Britain, naturally appealed to the German–American vote. On the other hand, ex-President Roosevelt's bellicose condemnation of the President's alleged spinelessness toward Germany was a dubious asset to the Republicans, one of whose chief problems was to win back the Progressives who had deserted to follow the Rough Rider in 1912. Wilson's forward-looking record regarding the tariff, trusts, and banking had swung many of the former Progressives over to the Democratic camp. Labor generally was happy with Wilson, who in mid-campaign had approved a controversial act granting an eight-hour day to railroad workers. The country was enjoying war-spawned prosperity, and it was at peace, a condition which appealed strongly to the woman vote. (Wilson carried ten of the twelve states in which female suffrage had been established.)

A clever slogan, "He Kept Us Out of War," almost certainly won the election for the Democrats. Wilson evidently did not devise it; [28] he did not use it in his speeches; and he did not make a definite promise not to enter the conflict at some time in the future. But he did stress the theme of past and prospective peace in his campaign addresses, and he did insist that he would continue policies to attain that end. The slogan was a historical fact rather than a specific pledge, though widely regarded as such. The irony is that when Wilson was inaugurated President for the second time, on March 4, 1917, he had already broken

[28] The officials of the Democratic National Committee in 1916 claim to have contrived the phrase, "With honor, he has kept us out of war." This was shortened in the campaign literature to "He Kept Us Out of War." A. S. Link, *Woodrow Wilson and the Progressive Era, 1910–1917* (1954), pp. 242–243n. There is some reason to believe that Wilson was annoyed by the use of the slogan, which was an implied pledge for the future.

relations with Berlin preparatory to a Congressional declaration of war the next month.

As the early presidential votes rolled in, Hughes evidently had swept the East, which was industrialized, antilabor, and anti-Progressive.[29] Wilson retired for the night relieved that the burden of four more years probably had been lifted. But as the more progressive Middle West and West were heard from, optimism grew that Hughes' early lead might be overcome. When California, the last doubtful state, was belatedly counted with its 13 electoral votes, Wilson had won by a margin of 277 to 254, although his popular plurality was much greater: 9,129,606 to 8,538,221. But he was still a minority President because of the substantial, though reduced, third-party vote for the Socialists and the Prohibitionists.

DID CALIFORNIA SWING THE ELECTION OF WILSON?

Wilson carried California by 3,806 votes out of a total of 999,551 cast; a shift of 1,904 ballots would have won the state and the election for Hughes, 267 electoral votes to 264. Hughes lost as the result of a series of blunders. Among various miscues, his Old Guard managers on several occasions contrived to keep him from meeting and greeting California's favorite son, Governor Hiram W. Johnson, the Progressive of 1912 who in 1916 was seeking a Senate seat as a Republican. (He had been Theodore Roosevelt's vice presidential running mate during the party-splitting Bull Moose campaign of 1912, and the Old Guard conservatives never forgave him.)

The most costly mischance occurred when Hughes made a brief stop at a hotel in Long Beach, California. Not realizing that Governor Johnson was staying there, he failed to meet the ex-Bull Mooser. Johnson could have courteously made known his presence but, feeling vengefully bitter against Hughes's Old Guard managers, chose not to do so. This "forgotten handshake" was interpreted by Johnson's numerous followers as a deliberate affront. It almost certainly drove more than several thousand Progressive voters into the Wilson camp, thereby costing the Republicans the election. While Hughes was losing Cali-

---

[29] The legend is that early the next morning a reporter called at Hughes' hotel with bad news but was sent away by the candidate's son with the explanation that, "The President could not be disturbed." The newsman allegedly retorted, "When he wakes up tell him he's no longer President." The story is completely apocryphal. See the "official" biography by Merlo J. Pusey, *Charles Evans Hughes* (2 vols., 1951), I, p. 361.

fornia by some 3,000 votes, Johnson, running for U. S. Senator on the same Republican ticket, *carried* the state by nearly 300,000 votes.

In a big-score football game won by one point, the player who scores the first touchdown is as important as the one who registers the last, even though the late scorer ordinarily receives more acclaim. Three other states were carried by Wilson with narrower pluralities than in California, but the Golden State is credited with having swung the election to him because its votes were the last crucial ones to be counted.[30]

Such heavy emphasis on "He Kept Us Out of War," both in California and nationwide, was not lost on the Berlin officials. A logical conclusion was that America might not fight if Germany launched an unrestricted submarine campaign.

WAS THE U-BOAT PROCLAMATION A WAR DECLARATION?

During the nine months following the *Sussex* crisis in 1916, relations between the United States and Germany remained relatively tranquil. Tensions between America and Britain increased. The British had greatly angered the Americans by detaining and searching the mails, while allegedly filching trade secrets from them. London also published a blacklist of German-tainted firms in the United States with which His Majesty's subjects were forbidden to trade.[31] In private Wilson referred bitterly to the "poor boobs" in England and favored building a navy bigger "than hers and do what we please." One of the curiosities of these months is that Germany and the United States, each in its own way, were contending with Britain for freedom of the seas.

Then like a bombshell came the announcement by Berlin, on January 31, 1917, of unrestricted submarine warfare. When fully effective, the German submarines would sink, or try to sink, all shipping, enemy or neutral, found within the war zones established around the British Isles and in the Mediterranean Sea. As a concession that

[30] A change of 29 popular votes in New Hampshire (43,779 for Wilson to 43,723 for Hughes), of 1,766 in New Mexico (33,693 for Wilson to 31,163 for Hughes), and of 868 in North Dakota (55,206 for Wilson to 53,471 for Hughes) would have cost Wilson the election. These three states had 12 electoral votes, enough to insure a Hughes victory. Svend Petersen, *A Statistical History of the American Presidential Elections* (1963), p. 81.

[31] The State Department based its protest to London against the blacklist on the grounds of international morals rather than international law, for the British were clearly within their rights in forbidding their own subjects in time of war to engage in certain activities. In World War I and World War II the Americans not only adopted the blacklist but greatly expanded and refined it.

amounted to an insult, Berlin would permit one American ship a week to sail to and from an English port, with stipulated restrictions.[32]

This proclamation was in effect a declaration of war by Germany on the United States: it was a filling in of the blank check that Wilson had handed Berlin in the *Sussex* ultimatum. The German High Command assumed that Washington would respond by declaring war, but counted on knocking England out in a few months, as almost happened, long before America could throw an effective fighting force into Europe. Berlin was taking a calculated risk, evidently well justified by the military situation. But these calculations did not work out well, largely because antisubmarine techniques were perfected and because the United States was able to recruit, train, and transport an army far more expeditiously than Berlin had thought possible.

Much learned ink has been spilled on the subject of why the United States fought Germany. Just about the simplest possible answer is that Germany began assailing the United States, and the sovereign American republic, with its high sense of honor, did not have much choice but to fight back.[33] The war declaration passed by Congress clearly bore the fearsome trademark, "Made in Germany." All this is so evident that some historians, in the usual "flight from the obvious," have sought more complex explanations.

WAS ZIMMERMANN'S NOTE A PROPER CAUSE OF WAR?

Wilson was profoundly shocked by the German announcement of unrestricted submarine warfare, but he nourished the flickering hope that

---

[32] One often reads that in January 1917 Germany "reopened" unrestricted submarine warfare. This is not precise. The original announcement, that of February 4, 1915, contained a restriction: only *enemy* shipping would be attacked, but neutrals might be sunk by mistake. The final announcement declared war (February 1, 1917) on *all* shipping, and hence was unrestricted, except for the trivial concession made to the United States. *Foreign Relations, 1915*, Suppl., p. 94; *ibid.*, 1917, Suppl. 1, pp. 100–102.

[33] Norway, Sweden, Denmark, and Holland, all important maritime nations, remained neutral throughout World War I, though suffering much more damage to their shipping from ruthless German submarine attacks than did the U. S. But they were so weak militarily that they would only worsen their condition by fighting. As a consequence, national honor was subordinated to continued neutrality and prosperity. The United States chose the sword, partly because it had an excellent chance to vindicate its rights by helping to defeat Germany. In 1968 North Koreans fired upon and captured a U. S. Navy intelligence ship, the *Pueblo*, killing one member of the crew, injuring others, and holding both the ship and the eighty-two survivors for nearly a year. This was a far more serious affront to the flag than any of the incidents involving U. S. ships before April 1917, but America did not declare war. It already was deeply involved in the Vietnam fighting, and drastic action to recover the eighty-two prisoners could well result in their deaths and those of tens of thousands of other American servicemen as well.

the desperate warlords of Berlin would not do what they announced they were going to do. He promptly severed relations, as he was morally bound to do after the *Sussex* ultimatum. Yet he was determined to wait for an "overt act" before he would ask Congress to recognize the state of war that Germany was forcing upon his people.

During these anxious days America was driven closer to the brink by the fantastic Zimmermann note. The German Foreign Secretary, Arthur Zimmermann, had cabled instructions to the Minister in Mexico City as to what should be done *in the event of hostilities* with the United States. The envoy should seek an alliance with Mexico, holding out the bait of recovering Texas, New Mexico, and Arizona. He was also to induce Japan, ironically one of the Allies, to change sides and join the scheme.

All great nations have, or ought to have, contingency plans to guide them should war come with potential enemies. There was nothing unlawful or particularly sinful about planning an alliance with Mexico, which was on bad terms with the United States and in a position to cause the Americans considerable embarrassment during the imminent German–American war. But the note was intercepted and decoded by the British, who turned it over to the Washington authorities. They, in turn, published it.[34]

Zimmermann's note caused a sensation, in some respects greater than that of the submarine announcement, especially in Texas and the Southwest, which had no desire to be given back to the Mexicans. The effect was further to predispose the American people to accept the challenge to war that the Germans had flung into their teeth. Wilson himself was especially angered by Berlin's duplicity.

WHY DID AMERICA FIGHT?

While waiting for the Germans to commit an overt act, Wilson sought authorization from Congress to arm merchant ships. But he was thwarted by a filibuster conducted, in the President's bitter words, by a little group of eleven "willful men" — some of them pro-German. The truth is that most of the wordage in this debate came from supporters of

---

[34] Zimmermann compounded his offense by clumsily admitting the authenticity of the telegram, when he could have "lied like a gentleman." Many Americans would have believed that the message was a fabrication of the Allied propagandists, and Washington could not have offered proof without betraying the secrets of British intelligence. See Barbara W. Tuchman, *The Zimmermann Telegram* (1958). Zimmermann sent a follow-up telegram on February 5, 1917, instructing the German minister not to wait for a declaration of war but to act "even now."

the bill, many of whom wanted to force a special session of Congress so they could keep a closer eye on Wilson's conduct of foreign policy.[35]

In mid-March 1917 the "overt acts" came with a vengeance when four unarmed American merchant ships were sunk by the Germans on the high seas, with the loss of some thirty-five lives. Deeply distressed, Wilson went before Congress and asked for a formal acceptance of the state of war that Germany had "thrust" upon the United States. He did not ask for a declaration against Austria–Hungary, Bulgaria, and Turkey, all allies of Germany, because they were not making war by sinking American shipping.[36] The "thrusting" of war was the same formula used by President Polk regarding Mexico in 1846, and to be used by President Franklin Roosevelt regarding Japan after Pearl Harbor in 1941. All three leaders asked Congress to acknowledge the hostilities that had come from the aggressive acts of an enemy.

Some writers have loosely argued that Wilson decided to fight Germany, and some have even stated that he declared war on Germany. Only Congress can formally declare hostilities, as it did. As for going to war with Germany, one must again note that Germany went to war with the United States and that the American nation reluctantly and belatedly acknowledged that assault. Technically it was no less an assault than that at Pearl Harbor in 1941.

As the crisis finally developed in 1917, one can say with considerable assurance that Wilson did not "go to war" with Germany primarily because of pressure from advisors, the business world, the bankers, the munitions makers, the propagandists, or pro-Allied partisans. He did not go to war because he was pro-Ally; though pro-Ally, he distrusted Allied war aims, open and secret. He did not go to war to preserve the old balance of power, although he personally preferred a kind of stalemate "peace without victory" that would hold Germany in check through a balance of power.[37] He did not go to war because he wanted to establish a League of Nations or have a seat at the peace table. In fact he did not initiate hostilities at all.

Once the conflict had been "thrust" upon the United States, Wilson was willing to accept it. It presented an opportunity for bringing the conflict to a speedier end, for insuring to the United States a hand in the final settlement, and for providing an opportunity to establish a peace-preserving League of Nations.

[35] Richard Lowitt, "The Armed-Ship Bill Controversy: A Legislative View," *Mid-America*, XLVI (1964), 38–47.

[36] Not until December 7, 1917 did Congress declare war on Austria–Hungary. It never declared war on Bulgaria or Turkey.

[37] On this theme see E. H. Buehrig, *Woodrow Wilson and the Balance of Power* (1955).

SHOULD WILSON HAVE TRIED "ARMED NEUTRALITY"?

Some eminent scholars have maintained that Wilson did have a choice. He could have instituted an "armed neutrality," rather than asking Congress formally to recognize the hostilities that had been "thrust" upon the Republic.

The record is clear that Wilson did briefly try an "armed neutrality." [38] Following the successful filibuster by the little groups of "willful men" and others in the Senate, he found authorization in a near-forgotten statute. About four armed merchant ships were sent to sea between March 16 and April 6, 1917, when Congress declared war.[39] The four merchantmen which were sunk in mid-March 1917, and which triggered the declaration of war by Congress, were all unarmed. But a clash between the nation's armed ships and German submarines was inevitable, with or without a declaration of war.

When the armed merchant ships of one nation begin shooting back at the submarines of another, there no longer is an "armed neutrality." Whatever America was experiencing in 1917 was armed but it was not neutrality: it was undeclared war.

As events shaped up, Wilson had his choice between limited hostilities and a global conflict. He chose to recommend the latter, evidently because the so-called armed neutrality not only could not insure freedom of the seas but was leading inexorably to a larger clash.

DID AMERICA "RUSH" INTO WAR?

During World War II, after Nazi Germany had knocked France out in 1940 and had Britain reeling from submarines and aerial bombers, certain American publicists and propagandists misread history. They argued that the United States should enter the conflict, as it had done in 1917, to save the collapsing Allies, to protect the North Atlantic shipping lanes, and to avert an imminent attack on North America if Germany should emerge triumphant.

[38] In his war message of April 2, 1917, Wilson said: "Armed neutrality is ineffectual enough at best."

[39] Official unpublished records made available to me by the Department of the Navy show that three of the four ships provided with guns and gun crews were passenger liners of the American Line sailing from New York, plus a schooner from Georgia. None had a brush with a German submarine before April 6, although the New York was damaged by a mine, presumably German, while entering Liverpool harbor.

As previously noted, the war declaration of 1917 did not come until after Germany had forced it on the Republic by an unrestricted submarine campaign. America did not rush in to save the Allies: she did not then know how badly off they were. With illusory successes on the Western Front and in the Middle East in March 1917, they were supposed to be winning. America did not go to war to save the North Atlantic shipping lanes. Submarine sinkings had been going on since February 1915—more than two years—and they were not only an old story but they were not particularly alarming. Prior to the unrestricted campaign of February 1917, German U-Boats had been destroying about 150,000 or so tons of shipping a month, a figure within the replacement capacity of the Allies and neutrals. Not until later in April, after America entered the war, did sinkings of Allied and neutral merchantmen shoot up to the alarming total of nearly 900,000 tons. This threat of disaster was brought under control only after the British reluctantly adopted, partly in response to American urgings, the convoy system and other antisub devices.[40]

The United States went in to save the Allies, primarily in its own interests, but it did not rush. On January 31, 1917, Germany announced her unrestricted submarine campaign, effective the next day. Wilson waited more than two months before asking Congress, on April 2, 1917, for a declaration of war. This delay did not reflect a conviction that the Allies were in desperate straits.

America did not "rush" into the war because it feared attack by an embattled Germany in the not-distant future. To be sure, Germany's aggression against Belgium and her strong military tradition were played up by Allied propagandists. They implanted considerable fear and further disposed the American people to accept hostilities after war had been forced upon them. But many naval experts knew better, even if the lay public did not. Germany's powerful surface fleet, constructed with limited coaling capacity and designed for short cruises in the Baltic Sea and the North Sea, was not prepared to cross the Atlantic and attack the strong U. S. navy and shore batteries in American waters. Even so, the prospect of coexisting with a Europe dominated by Imperial Germany was not an attractive one, and the prospect of halting German imperialism made the declaration of war in 1917 more palatable to the American Congress.

---

[40] On paper, the convoy system should not have worked, but it did. It was adopted largely because the alternative was a certain loss of the war. For the role of the American Admiral W. S. Sims, see E. E. Morison, *Admiral Sims and the Modern American Navy* (1942), pp. 347ff.

ADDITIONAL GENERAL REFERENCES

A. S. Link, *Woodrow Wilson and the Progressive Era, 1910–1917* (1954), *Wilson: The Struggle for Neutrality, 1914–1915* (1960), *Wilson: Confusions and Crises, 1915–1916* (1964), and *Wilson: Campaigns for Progressivism and Peace, 1916–1917* (1965); E. R. May, *The World War and American Isolationism, 1914–1917* (1959); K. E. Birnbaum, *Peace Moves and U-Boat Warfare* (1958); C. C. Tansill, *America Goes to War* (1938); Charles Seymour, *American Diplomacy during the World War* (1934) and *American Neutrality, 1914–1917* (1935); Daniel M. Smith, *The Great Departure: The United States and World War I, 1914–1920* (1965); Carl Wittke, *German–Americans and the World War* (1936); *War Memoirs of Robert Lansing* (1935); John M. Cooper, Jr., *The Vanity of Power: American Isolationism and the First World War, 1914–1917* (1969).

28

America in World War I

The American people, although accepting war with considerable reluctance, finally worked themselves into a high pitch of enthusiasm under the spell of Wilsonian idealism. But the Washington government, which remembered that it had been "neutral" for more than two years and that it was upholding high ideals, treated the remaining neutrals with unexpected tenderness.

The navy had been designed as the first line of defense—that is, near the American coasts. It was not prepared for a war against Germany in far-off waters. The army, though slightly enlarged, had not been increased to a formidable force, despite the belated preparedness, agitation, and legislation of 1916. At the time of America's war declaration there was little thought of sending an immense body of troops to France, but the needs of the Allies [1] for manpower soon became so pressing that several million soldiers were hastily raised by conscription. Meanwhile the Allies held back the Germans.

Not until more than a year after Congress declared war did substantial numbers of American troops begin to arrive in France, there eventually to participate in the final decisive drives. These inexperienced warriors fought with great dash, but they suffered heavy losses while gaining less ground than anticipated. Among various obstacles

---

[1] The United States, traditionally suspicious of alliances, never became an Ally but, at Wilson's insistence, an Associate of the Allies; hence "the Allied and Associated Powers."

were uncertain transportation, inadequate supplies, rough terrain, and dug-in defenders.

Facing imminent defeat in October 1918, Berlin sought a "soft" peace based on Wilson's Fourteen Points. After tense negotiations, the Germans were formally granted this concession before signing the armistice of November 11, 1918. The German army was beaten, though it had much fight left in it. It was also stabbed in the back by a revolution in the Fatherland caused largely by an awareness of impending military defeat.

Meanwhile, in 1917–1918 Russian Bolsheviks seized power, vowing eternal hostility toward the capitalist world, including conspicuously the United States. They then proceeded to take their nation out of the conflict. For reasons relating primarily to keeping Russia in the war, America became involved in two small armed interventions, one at Archangel (northern Russia) and the other in Siberia. Both of them deepened mutual suspicion and distrust.

WAS PUBLIC OPINION UNITED AGAINST GERMANY?

The Congressional vote on the war resolution of April 1917, was 82 to 6 in the Senate and 373 to 50 in the House, for a total of 56 negative votes. This was a larger percentage of opposition than that mustered against America's other declared wars, except in 1812.[2] In view of the high enthusiasm and remarkable unity with which the nation fought in 1917–1918, such dissent is often overlooked. Most of it sprang from the German–American and Scandinavian–American immigrant centers of the isolationist Middle West, while only one negative vote came from the industrialized East, that of a Socialist member from New York. Easterners had a large stake in the success of the Allied cause, both in trade and in investment; and they were nearer the conflict and more worried about the possibility of an attack by the Germans. The East was also the section that had been more enthusiastic about fighting Germany after the *Lusitania* outrage than the Middle West or the Far West.

A mustering of 56 negative votes in Congress at a time when the Germans were obviously attacking the United States, as well as all other maritime neutrals, is significant. Many German–Americans felt that

[2] The votes on the Mexican War resolution, the Spanish–American War resolution, the World War II war resolutions (Germany, Japan, Italy) were virtually unanimous, while the vote in 1812 was 79 to 49 in the House and 19 to 13 in the Senate. For opposition to the war in America (1917–1918) from Socialists, pro-Germans, I.W.W.s and others, see H. C. Peterson and G. C. Fite, *Opponents of War* (1957).

Germany was plainly within her rights, morally if not legally, in striking back at the starvation blockade of Britain with a similarly illegal counter-blockade. In view of these circumstances, highly vocal pro-Germans believed that the United States should bar its citizens and ships from the war zones—a concession that Wilson had fought as dishonorable but which became honorable by act of Congress in 1939.

Congressional critics in 1917 were moved by additional arguments. Some felt betrayed because they believed that Wilson had broken the pledge implicit in his winning slogan, "He Kept Us Out of War." Others did not take seriously the menace of a victorious Germany. Many Congressmen were motivated by hereditary Anglophobia and by the deep-rooted isolationist tradition against foreign intercession by a militarily unprepared America.

There almost certainly would have been more dissent if Congress had realized that it would be required to send overseas an army of two million men. This was an eventuality not even faintly envisaged by most Americans when war was declared.

DID AMERICA GO TO WAR FOR DEMOCRACY?

As far as immediate precipitants were concerned, the German U-boat, as earlier noted, was clearly the chief culprit in forcing the Republic into the abyss. But Wilson could hardly whip the American people up to a crusading pitch with the slogan: "The World Must Be Made Safe Against the Submarine." Hence the battle cry "Make the World Safe for Democracy" sprang from Wilson's war message.[3] The implication was not that America should force popular government, American style, on the entire globe. On the contrary, the aggressors should be so curbed that people desiring self-rule could safely enjoy it. Another popular slogan, not coined by Wilson but widely used, proclaimed that the nation was fighting "The War to End War."

Inevitably, as is so often the case, the major precipitating cause of the war (the submarine) became lost to sight while the American people enthusiastically pursued more lofty objectives—battling for democracy and to end war. If the Republic was fighting for such goals, then these must have been the "cause" of the fighting—at least in the popular view and even in the minds of some later historians.[4]

[3] Wilson had said, "The world must be made safe for democracy."

[4] The extent to which some historians warped their historical standards to provide the government with patriotic propaganda against the enemy became something of a scandal. See Harold Josephson, "History for Victory: The National Board for Historical Service," *Mid-America*, LII (1970), 205–224.

This supplanting of the real causes by official objectives—as was conspicuously true of the War of 1812—has spawned much misunderstanding. It also led to postwar disillusionment and renewed isolationism. When the war to end war had ended, wars had not ended: about a score were being waged in various parts of the world. In succeeding decades, with the rise of Communist and right-wing dictators, the world became even less safe for democracy than it had been when the great conflict erupted.

DID AMERICA HIGH-HANDEDLY VIOLATE NEUTRAL RIGHTS?

While still the foremost neutral, the United States had taken a leading role in upholding neutral rights, though more emphatically against Germany than Britain. After becoming a belligerent, Washington allegedly turned its back on the principles it had formerly upheld. The Counselor of the Department of State allegedly told a visiting Briton in the spring of 1917: ". . . It took Great Britain three years to reach a point where it was prepared to violate all the laws of blockade. You will find that it will take us only two months to become as great criminals as you are." [5]

As a matter of fact, America did not violate the rights of neutrals in a wholesale fashion. It did acquiesce in the British blockade, and it did cooperate in rationing shipments to nations adjacent to Germany, such as Holland and Denmark, from which commodities slipped into the enemy camp. But such rationing was not illegal, only disagreeable. The United States did adopt the expanded British definition of contraband, and it did play the major role in laying an antisubmarine mine barrage across the North Sea from Britain to Norway.[6] But as regards both of these allegedly unlawful innovations Washington only reserved its rights during the earlier diplomatic controversies with Britain.

Washington did adopt the commercial blacklist against enemy-connected firms in neutral countries, but its initial protest to Britain on this subject had been based on international morals, not international law. In applying this new economic weapon the United States was neither so sweeping nor so ruthless as Britain.

[5] Counselor Polk in 1941 denied that he had made this statement. See T. A. Bailey, *The Policy of the United States Toward the Neutrals, 1917–1918* (1942), pp. 1–2.

[6] The mine barrage, consisting of some 70,000 contact mines (56,000 laid by Americans) neared Norway's three-mile territorial waters about August 5, 1918. Rather than violate a weak neutral's sovereignty by completing the barrage, the United States waited about two months while inducing the Norwegian government to close the gap itself. Meanwhile, German submarines presumably continued to slip out to sea. *Ibid.*, pp. 410–420.

In short, the United States was unexpectedly deferential to the neutrals: such clear-cut infractions as occurred were clearly minor and infrequent. Nor was Washington in any rush, for its actions generally followed delay and debate. One reason for not engaging in the objectionable Allied blockade practices was that the British were handling the problem effectively without urgently needing further help. Moreover, active cooperation with them in seizing neutral ships would jeopardize the claims that American shippers already had lodged against the London government.[7]

WAS THE U. S. NAVY WELL PREPARED FOR WAR?

If ever a nation had ample warning that it might be drawn into hostilities, it was the United States. Whether as colonials or as nationals, the American people had never avoided involvement in any one of the previous seven wars that had featured a contest for control of the seas. This titanic conflict had hardly begun in 1914 when even casual observers could see that the neutrals, whether strong or weak, were going to be caught in the middle of a lethal contest between the British blockade and the German submarines.

We have already noted Wilson's belated conversion to preparedness, and to the enactment of legislation in 1916 designed to strengthen the armed forces. As for the navy, one grave mistake was the continued emphasis on big battleships. If there was a real possibility that America would clash with Britain, such a program made sense; but considering pro-Ally sentiment in America, this eventuality seemed remote. If the nation was going to fight Germany, then small antisubmarine craft would be desperately needed. The British battleship fleet was substantially superior to that of Germany, which, following the inconclusive battle of Jutland in 1916, never again tried a head-on entanglement with Britain's main force.

America's naval strategy was based on the mistaken notion that big battleships would be needed to fight German battleships in the Western Atlantic, probably the Caribbean. This concept was totally unrealistic. Even if the British fleet had been destroyed, the exhausted Germans would have had their problems in mounting an attack in

[7] In 1926 the assistant to the Secretary of State prepared an exhaustive report in which he concluded that only 11 of the 2,658 pending claims against Britain were meritorious. Many had already been settled by the British; others were vague, involving trifling amounts, or enemy aliens seeking American protection. *Ibid.*, pp. 480–481. These figures indicate that the hardship on American shippers inflicted by the British blockade was much exaggerated.

Caribbean waters, far distant from their home base. Many of their ships were designed, as regards fuel capacity, for cruising in the Baltic Sea and North Sea.

After the United States entered the conflict, much of the construction on big battleships authorized by the act of 1916 had to be suspended. Highest priority was given to antisubmarine craft. Although Britain was in desperate shape from shipping losses to the submarines in the last weeks of April 1917, the first flotilla of U. S. destroyers did not reach the British Isles until May 4, almost exactly a month after the declaration of war. The navy was reluctant to spare antisubmarine craft that could defend American coasts against U-boats and German battleships; it simply was not ready to wage the kind of war that its foe was fighting.[8]

WAS A LARGE
OVERSEAS ARMY PLANNED FROM THE OUTSET?

When Congress voted for hostilities in April 1917, the public had little or no expectation of sending a considerable army to France, partly because there was no considerable army to send. Many Americans envisaged a limited-liability war. Armed merchantmen and vessels of the U. S. navy would seek to destroy the U-boats. Then, when the Germans were willing to recognize America's right to a free sea and stop warring on the nation's merchant shipping, Washington could make peace with Berlin, leaving the Allies to continue the war on land for their own selfish objectives.[9]

But to the surprise of the Americans, the Allies soon revealed that they were scraping the bottom of their manpower barrel, and they indicated that if they went under, the United States would eventually succumb to Germany. The ill-fated offensive of General Neville in France collapsed in April 1917, some two weeks after America declared war, and widespread mutinies convulsed the French army. Fortunately for the Allied cause, the Germans were not aware of this near-fatal crumbling. Late in April 1917 separate diplomatic missions, one from Britain and one from France, arrived in Washington to reveal in confidence the alarming straits of the Allies. As a result of their pleas, the Wilson

[8] See Harold and Margaret Sprout, *The Rise of American Naval Power, 1776–1918* (1939), Ch. 19.

[9] For contemporary documentation of this point see the bibliographical note in T. A. Bailey, *Woodrow Wilson and the Lost Peace* (1944), p. 331.

administration reluctantly reached the decision to dispatch overseas an army which ultimately numbered some 2,000,000 men, and which helped turn the tide toward victory.

WHY WAS CONSCRIPTION DELAYED SO LONG?

Not until six weeks after Congress had voted the war resolution did that body pass the Selective Service (Draft) Act, following protracted and often heated debate. This foot-dragging is astonishing when one remembers how desperately the Allies needed men, and how close was the race between disaster and victory. The basic reason why Congress did not "rush" to pass a draft law was the same reason why it did not "rush" to pass a declaration of war. Congressmen did not then know how near the Allies were to defeat.

Delays in Congress were also partially due to ex-President Roosevelt's request for authority to raise a volunteer division, with himself as commander. He was violently anti-German; he gloried in war; he could have attracted an enthusiastic throng of volunteers; and the French, their morale shattered by the collapse of the Neville offensive, desperately wanted him to come with reinforcements and inspire them with new life.

But Wilson and his subordinates snubbed the gallant colonel. Now 59, Roosevelt was rheumatic, afflicted with tropical fever, half deaf, and blind in one eye. He had never commanded more than a regiment, in a horse-and-saber war some twenty years earlier. This was a modern, impersonalized, barbed-wire and trench conflict, of prodigious proportions. Roosevelt would draw off the cream of the officer material, which was badly needed for the army about to be drafted. He would be the first of a number of political generals, such as had vexed Lincoln, for Roosevelt's example would cause other ambitious leaders to spring forward. In the Spanish–American War the fight-thirsty colonel had proved to be headstrong and insubordinate, and having been presidential Commander-in-Chief would not add to his manageability. He could do more good at home writing articles and making speeches to bolster morale. So ran the administration arguments, which, when backed by hard-nosed military men, had conclusive force.

Remembering unfortunate experiences with conscription both North and South during the Civil War, Congress was much concerned with the un-American, arbitrary, autocratic nature of a draft. Why conscript tens of thousands of German–Americans to kill their kinfolk?

Even Britain had waited eighteen months before resorting to conscription, and she was under the gun. What would it profit a nation to Prussianize itself in an attempt to fight Prussian militarism?

In the end the Selective Service Act was passed, designed to *select* able-bodied men of draft age to serve in such occupations, whether military or civilian (through deferments), as would best sustain the war effort. Registration Day for the draft came on June 5, 1917, two months after Congress declared war.[10]

WAS THE AMERICAN ARMY PROPERLY TRAINED AND EQUIPPED?

The German High Command, when it unleashed submarine warfare on the United States, had counted on the inability of the Americans to raise an effective fighting force in time. Even if they were able to raise one, where was the maritime transportation to ship it and supply it?

To the amazement of the Germans, the United States, though starting virtually from scratch and with a Selective Service Act passed six weeks *after* war was declared, sent more than two million soldiers abroad before the shooting stopped. Yet not until the spring and summer of 1918, after more than a year, did the "doughboys" begin to reach France in formidable numbers. General Pershing, to be sure, paraded through Paris on July 4, 1917 with some 14,500 troops, but this was merely a token contingent, designed largely to bolster French morale with a visible promise of much more to come.

America's achievement was a remarkable one, but it would not have been possible without major help from Britain and France. The Allies provided about 54 percent of the shipping, mostly British, that brought over the American Expeditionary Forces (A.E.F.).[11] Preferring to use the cargo space for men rather than materiel and supplies, the Allies furnished much of the equipment, including tanks, howitzers, rifles, machine guns, and especially a French artillery piece, the famed 75.

Such hasty training as the American troops received was not adequate for the task at hand. (President Wilson later declared that the

---

[10] The delay would have been even longer if Secretary of War Baker, keeping the secret from Congress, had not daringly (and illegally) authorized the printing and shipment of the millions of necessary forms even before the Selective Service Act was passed. See Frederick Palmer, *Newton D. Baker: America at War* (2 vols., 1931), pp. 212ff.

[11] Only one Europe-bound troop transport (*Tuscania*) was sunk by the enemy; five were torpedoed on the way back, two of which made port.

army was raised so quickly because it was trained to go only one way—forward.) Though strong on spirit and confidence, the troops were weak in experience and leadership. Many of the units were given supplementary training by Allied officers when they reached France, after which they were commonly assigned to "quiet" sectors.

The first sizable encounter with veteran German troops came at Seicheprey, April 20–21, 1918. Achieving a surprise in the fog, the enemy inflicted a temporary defeat on the raw 26th Division by taking a toll of about 500 casualties and bagging 187 prisoners.[12] But in many subsequent engagements the draftees, acquiring experience with each new contact, acquitted themselves creditably. Even so, the heavy losses of 10 percent casualties in the final Meuse-Argonne offensive (120,000 out of 1,200,000 men engaged) were due in large part to inadequate training and improper adaptation to German tactics.

DID BLACK AMERICA CONTRIBUTE TO VICTORY?

Approximately 300,000 Negroes were drafted to fight the war for freedom and democracy. (All-white Southern draft boards granted exemptions generously to fellow whites.) About two-thirds of the black draftees were assigned to labor battalions and other unglamorous service, often to their dissatisfaction. Some of the combat outfits, especially those brigaded with the French, won many decorations for bravery. The Negro recruits proved generally impervious to German propaganda, which emphasized lynchings at home; and when the shooting stopped they were eager to return to America, there to rejoin families and friends. The experience of being treated as equals by the French, who had long ignored the "color line," did not wean the black Americans away from their primary allegiance.

As far as Negroes were concerned, the home front was far from tranquil. War industries in the North and economic hardship in the South pulled or propelled tens of thousands of blacks to the Northern cities, where they did much to ease the labor shortage resulting from the all-out war effort. But the influx of Negroes created new tensions, with a consequent outburst of race riots, lynchings, and other outrages both during and after the war. The flareup in East St. Louis in July 1917,

---

[12] John J. Pershing, *My Experiences in the World War* (2 vols., 1931), *II*, 16. An initial contact with German troops in World War II, at Kasserine Pass in Tunisia, February 1943, resulted in a sharp but temporary setback for the Americans. See Dwight D. Eisenhower, *Crusade in Europe* (1948), Ch. 8.

less than two months after Congress declared war, cost the lives of some 40 blacks and eight whites, to say nothing of many injuries and extensive property damage.

The prejudices of Southern whites against black soldiers, especially those carrying rifles, were not easy to overcome, and the stationing of Negro draftees in the South led to ugly incidents during the war. The worst outburst came in Houston, Texas in September 1917. Goaded beyond endurance by the white police and citizenry, black soldiers of the 24th Infantry killed seventeen whites, as a consequence of which thirteen Negroes were hanged and many others were imprisoned. .

When one considers the ever-present evidence that lynchings and other forms of racial discrimination were not going to be eliminated by this war of high ideals, one can only marvel that the blacks generally supported their country with as much loyalty as they displayed.

SHOULD THE U. S. HAVE MAINTAINED A SEPARATE ARMY?

The Allies, desperately short of manpower and fearing an overpowering German spring drive in 1918, sought to integrate American troops with existing units. Their arguments were that the setting up of a separate sector manned by a U. S. army would consume valuable time, deprive the Allies of needed replacements, and jeopardize the inexperienced American forces.

Backed by the administration in Washington, General Pershing fought tenaciously for a separate army under the overall command of Marshal Foch.[13] The American was thinking of the morale of his forces and the pride that would suffuse them (and the people back home) if he saved his men from a piecemeal parceling out. He no doubt was aware that a victorious United States army, with himself in command, would be more satisfying to the national ego (and his own) than a victorious Allied army fleshed out with American troops.

In reading Pershing's memoirs, one is impressed with his having fought and won three great battles. The first was with Washington for the necessary supplies and equipment. (This he narrowly won, because his army, in the final great drive, was consuming materiel at such an

---

[13] On March 26, 1918, in the teeth of the great German spring offensive, the Western Allies agreed on a coordinator-in-chief rather than a commander-in-chief, Marshal Foch. He was to have strategic direction of military operations, with tactical direction left to the British, French, and American armies, and with each commander-in-chief of these armies vested with the right to appeal to his government should he feel that Foch's orders endangered his force. See Pershing, My Experiences, I, 363, 376–377.

alarming rate that the armistice came as a lifesaver.) The second battle was with Allied headquarters for the preservation of a separate army. Pershing finally secured command of a sector reaching from the French right wing to Switzerland and containing rugged, desperately defended terrain. The third great battle—at times it seemed almost secondary— was with the German foe.

So it was that Pershing retained an American army and held an American sector, although two divisions were loaned to the French in Belgium, and a number of units, including Negroes, were brigaded with the French. His arguments about homeland pride and morale no doubt were valid, but many more small American detachments could have been earlier employed in the depleted Allied armies. The Germans drove within forty miles of Paris in May 1918, and were checked by the narrowest of margins. If a breakthrough had been achieved because of Pershing's stubbornness, and if Paris had been taken and France knocked out of the war, the separate-army decision could have been fatal.

DID THE U. S. WIN THE WAR FOR THE ALLIES?

Americans were traditionally regarded by foreigners as braggarts, and the outcome of World War I accentuated this trait. A common boast was that the Allies had been fighting the Germans fruitlessly for about four years; then the "Yanks" arrived in numbers, and in about four months the Germans hoisted the white flag. A barbed quip was that A.E.F. (American Expeditionary Forces) meant "After England Failed." This sneer was resented by the British, and especially by the Canadians, whose total casualties approximated those of their giant neighbor, even though their population was about one-twelfth that of the United States. The soldier deaths of the British were about twenty times those of the United States; those of France and Russia were even greater.

The Allies held back Germany for about two and a half years before the United States declared war. They then carried on for another year while the Americans were hastily recruiting and training a conscript army. The "Yanks" did not see action on any considerable scale until late in May 1918, when the 1st Division captured Cantigny and the 3rd Division helped turn the tide at Château Thierry, on a broad front that hotly engaged several million Allied troops. In July 1918, in the second battle of the Marne, the U. S. had 300,000 "doughboys" in an extended operation which marked the beginning of a permanent German retrograde movement.

In the great Allied advance of September to November 1918,

Pershing's army was engaged in the Meuse-Argonne offensive. Progress, at first satisfactory, soon slowed down disappointingly, for the Germans had emplaced numerous machine guns in a wooded area and took a heavy toll of the inexperienced Yankee attackers. The hasty redeployment of American troops for this drive had resulted in snarling lines of supply and communication, with subsequent shortages and confusion. The Lost Battalion of Major Whittlesey was not lost—his location was well known—but it plunged too far ahead. Surrounded by German troops, it sustained heavy casualties, and suffered without food and virtually without water for about 100 hours.[14] Farther to the north the British made more satisfactory progress; it was they who broke through the Hindenburg line.

Clearly the United States did not win the war single-handed but helped mightily in turning the tide. The Republic's entrance into the conflict gave a boost to drooping Allied morale, while depressing German spirits. Shipments of American supplies were stepped up. The navy did yeoman work in helping to contain the German battleship fleet, and particularly in providing destroyers and other smaller craft for curbing the German submarine menace. American manpower, with the promise of more to come, helped to impress the German generals with the hopelessness of their cause and with the necessity of suing for peace.

WERE THE FOURTEEN POINTS ORIGINAL WITH WILSON?

In various public addresses, President Wilson had expressed in rather abstract terms the principles for which he believed the Allies were fighting. By early January 1918 the crisis called for more specific and pointed affirmations. The Russian Bolsheviks, after long demanding a "peace without annexations or indemnities," had ripped open the Tsarist archives and exposed to the world the secret treaties made by the Allies for parceling out the territorial booty of their enemy. A dramatic move was needed to offset the moral black eye thus given to the Allied cause, while encouraging Russia to remain in the war.

Wilson responded magnificently when he appeared before Congress on January 8, 1918, to deliver his Fourteen Points address. In three

[14] On October 21, 1918, Premier Clemenceau, who disliked Pershing's stubbornness, wrote to Marshal Foch saying that unless the American general subordinated himself to Foch and showed more activity, an appeal should be made directly to President Wilson, presumably in the hope of replacing Pershing. Foch did not accept the suggestion. For text of letter see T. B. Mott, *Twenty Years as Military Attaché* (1937), Ch. XXV.

subsequent speeches, he set forth additional points, for a total of about twenty-three.

Contrary to a popular belief, the Fourteen Points were hardly original with Wilson. Three days before this memorable address, David Lloyd George, the British Prime Minister, had partially stolen Wilson's thunder by a speech in which he emphatically mentioned the President's basic Fourteen Points, except three: open covenants, openly arrived at; a lowering of international trade barriers; and freedom of the seas. Britain, with her powerful navy, was unwilling to recognize a free sea.[15] Oddly enough, a week before Lloyd George's speech, the Bolsheviks issued a statement of aims which included all of the three points not mentioned by the British Prime Minister.

In short, Wilson codified the best of announced war aims, including some proclaimed by the Germans and Bolsheviks, and added a few of his own.

DID THE FOURTEEN POINTS DISARM GERMANY?

Showered upon Germany and German trenches by balloons, shells, and other media, the Fourteen Points undoubtedly helped undermine the morale of a weary and hungry Germany. Especially seductive to German Poles was the promise of an independent Poland. Germany in general was attracted by freedom of the seas (of which Britain had long been mistress), and the removal of economic barriers among the nations. Many Germans feared economic reprisals at the end of the conflict.

In October 1918, with their lines in France buckling under massive Allied assaults, the panicky German generals induced the Berlin government to approach Wilson with the suggestion of a peace based on the Fourteen Points. After delicate negotiations, the Allies finally agreed to propose an armistice on this basis, with two exceptions. The British held out for a reservation on freedom of the seas, and the French secured an elucidation to the effect that the restoration of territory evacuated by Germany should include reparations for damages to civilian property. One basic problem was that the Allies had never accepted the Fourteen Points as their war aims, although they had been willing enough to acquiesce in them as instruments for weakening the enemy.

Germany was finally promised a peace that would be based on

[15] Wilson doubted that his Fourteen Points speech was necessary following Lloyd George's speech. Charles Seymour, ed., *The Intimate Papers of Colonel House* (1928), *III*, 341.

the Fourteen Points, with the two exceptions noted. This agreement, which Berlin formally accepted, has come to be known as the pre-Armistice contract. Under the Armistice of November 11, 1918, the Germans were partially disarmed and rendered incapable of successfully resisting an Allied invasion. Seven months later they were forced to sign peace terms in which many of the Fourteen Points did not appear completely intact, if at all. The defeated Germans filled the air with cries of betrayal.[16] In a very real sense the Fourteen Points disarmed Germany, although a forcible disarmament was seemingly inevitable within a matter of months.

WERE THE GERMAN ARMIES STABBED IN THE BACK?

A twin legend quickly developed, later exploited by the Nazis during their rise to power more than a decade later. It was that the German armies (a) were never defeated but (b) were stabbed in the back by the politicians and other dissident groups.

Superficially there was much substance in these charges. The German armies finally surrendered on French and Belgian soil, not on that of the Fatherland. By the terms of the Armistice the beaten soldiers retained their rifles, as well as about half of their heavy artillery, machine guns, and other materiel. They marched home with bands playing and colors flying to be welcomed as conquering heroes who had for more than four years fought off an invasion of Germany, and who in this sense had won the war.

The evidence is conclusive that the German armies were defeated and that their surrender was only a matter of fighting through to the bitter end. One should remember that from September 29 to November 3, all three of Germany's allies—Bulgaria, Turkey, and Austria–Hungary —signed armistice agreements and dropped out of the war, thereby exposing the Fatherland's flank. Much pointless bloodshed and destruction were averted by the partial and then virtually complete disarmament of Germany, as achieved through the Armistice.

But in a sense the German armies were stabbed in the back. The naval personnel at Kiel mutinied on November 3, 1918 rather than engage in hopeless sorties, and from there revolution spread like wildfire to

---

[16] The Germans themselves were to some extent to blame for their own "betrayal." During the pre-Armistice negotiations they had an opportunity to seek a more specific definition of the Fourteen Points and to suggest reservations, but they concluded that vagueness would operate to their advantage. See *The Memoirs of Prince Max of Baden* (1928), II, 39.

Berlin. Yet the naval mutiny and subsequent revolt did not defeat the army; these behind-the-lines outbreaks occurred primarily because the generals had confessed defeat and inevitable destruction.

General Pershing regretted that unconditional surrender was not demanded, for he was certain that the Germans would have been compelled to yield, admittedly after much more bloodshed. If this had been the case, the legend of nondefeat would have had more difficulty in taking root, and the lesson that aggression had not paid would have been more fully learned by potential German aggressors.[17]

DID AMERICA PROVOKE BOLSHEVIST HOSTILITY?

In March 1917, three weeks before Congress declared war, a revolution in Russia overthrew the despotic Tsarist regime and substituted a quasi-democratic government. The United States promptly extended formal recognition (March 22), and thus became the first of the great powers to do so.

Satisfaction in the United States over the upheaval in Russia had many roots. Traditionally antimonarchical and prodemocratic, Americans normally greeted with enthusiasm the downfall of tyranny and the enthroning of democracy anywhere.[18] America was about to enter upon a crusade to make the world safe for democracy, and she would have been embarrassed by the presence of the Tsarist black sheep in the Allied camp. Besides, democracies were supposed to fight harder, and the Russian military effort in the common Allied cause was suffering fatally from disorganization, demoralization, and decimation. Wilson, in his war message, greeted the new Russia as "a fit partner for a League of Honor."

But in October 1917 a Bolshevik coup overthrew the new government. Vladimir Lenin and Leon Trotsky emerged as the two most important leaders in establishing a Communist regime. Far from extending prompt recognition, Washington waited sixteen years, during which relations between the two governments remained embittered. The legend has gained wide acceptance that the Bolsheviks became unfriendly to America because America had first been unfriendly to them, and that if Washington had only extended the right hand of fellowship, the Bolsheviks would not have become a menace to the capitalist world.

---

[17] Pershing, *My Experiences, II,* 368–369. The controversy over Germany's 1918 *conditional* surrender, based on the Fourteen Points, was in mind when Roosevelt and Churchill, in January 1943, demanded "unconditional surrender" at the Casablanca conference.

[18] Cynics once remarked that the Americans approved of every revolution except their own — the Civil War.

Actually the Bolshevist[19] leaders proclaimed their undying hostility to the capitalist world—of which the United States was the most potent exemplar—before, during, and after their coup. The overseas republic offended them by merely existing. Before leaving New York to play his revolutionary role, Trotsky urged his followers in America to keep on organizing until they were able "to overthrow this damned rotten capitalistic government." In December 1917, a few weeks after the Bolsheviks seized power, the new Communist regime appropriated 2,000,000 rubles for the use of its agents abroad in promoting world revolution.[20]

There was little reason for the Wilson administration to make haste in recognizing the Russian revolutionists. Large question marks were raised by their avowed hostility to capitalism, by their repudiation of debts to Western nations incurred by the Tsarist regime, and by their wholesale outrages against the propertied classes, including the shooting of Tsar Nicholas II and his entire family. Wilson, as a strong noninterventionist and self-determinist, was willing to wait for the dust to settle in the hope that a more democratic regime would emerge. Why prejudice relations with such a government, or interfere with its birth, by a premature recognition of Moscow?

If Russia withdrew from the war, as the Bolsheviks contrived to do in 1918, hundreds of thousands of veteran German troops would be released for the Western front (as they were). Germany for the first time would have a marked superiority there in manpower (as she did). Bolshevik leaders had proclaimed a policy of immediate peace with "No annexations, no indemnities" before they engineered their successful coup, and soon after it they issued a decree putting this policy into effect. Why should the United States and its Allies assist Russia in unilaterally dropping out of the desperate conflict against Germany by extending the warm hand of recognition to the Bolshevik regime? In the eyes of the Americans and their Allies, the Soviet leaders had betrayed a sacred commitment to the common Allied cause.

DID AMERICA INTERVENE IN RUSSIA'S CIVIL WAR?

There was a strong, if somewhat illusory, tradition of Russian–American friendship in the nineteenth century, based largely on a common distrust of Britain. This tradition has been primarily responsible for the myth

---

[19] Ironically, Bolshevik means "a member of the majority," and the revolutionaries never attained this status.

[20] See T. A. Bailey, *America Faces Russia* (1950), p. 238.

that the United States has never had an armed clash with Russia. The fact is that American troops shot it out with Russian armed forces on Russian soil in two theaters from 1918 to 1920.

At Archangel, in northern Russia, an Allied expedition appeared in the late summer of 1918, some six months after the Bolsheviks had formally taken their country out of the war. Ostensible objectives of the invaders were to encourage local resistance to the Germans and to prevent immense quantities of military supplies from falling into hostile hands. As time wore on, the invaders increasingly cooperated with the counterrevolutionaries (Whites) against the Bolsheviks (Reds), as was perhaps inevitable in the circumstances. In short, the military goal was to keep as much of Russia in the war against Germany as long as possible to ease German pressures on the Western front.

After prolonged urgings by the Allies, Wilson was finally induced to contribute some 5,000 troops, under British command, to the ill-starred Archangel venture. Not fully informed of the grandiose Allied plans, he conceived of the American mission as having the primary aims of safeguarding military stores and rendering such aid as the Russians found acceptable, without interfering in their internal affairs. But this armed support for the dissident Whites led ultimately to clashes with the Bolshevik Reds, during which the American forces sustained some 500 casualties. Following much dissatisfaction in the United States over involvement in this undeclared war, American troops were withdrawn in July 1919.[21]

WAS THE SIBERIAN INTERVENTION ANTI-BOLSHEVIK?

From 1918 to 1920, the United States joined an Allied expedition in Siberia, committing about 9,000 men. President Wilson embarked upon this venture with extreme reluctance, after long delays, and under heavy pressure from the Allies. His motivation for ordering participation is not completely clear. Seeking above all to defeat Germany, he seems to have been prompted by a desire to keep military supplies from falling into Bolshevik hands, while assisting in the rescue of some 45,000 marooned Czech soldiers who were presumably fighting their way across Siberia to join the Western Allies. Wilson evidently also had in mind preventing the Japanese imperialists from getting too strong a foothold in Siberia and Manchuria, thereby jeopardizing America's Open Door policy. General Graves, commanding the American con-

[21] For this episode see L. I. Strakhovsky, *Intervention at Archangel* (1944).

tingent, was under strict orders to avoid any involvement in Russia's internal affairs.

Japan's participation was necessary, for she had a large number of troops conveniently near, and she was evidently preparing to go it alone. Washington assumed, without a firm commitment, that the Japanese and American forces would be approximately equal. But Japan ultimately increased her contribution to 72,000 men, about eight times that of the Americans.

As at Archangel, the American Siberian venture did not work out as Wilson had hoped. In keeping open the trans-Siberian railroad for the assistance of the Czechs, the Allied force kept it open for the shipment of supplies to the anti-Bolshevik elements, thereby becoming involved, contrary to instructions, in the Russian civil war. Hostile Russian forces exchanged fire with the American troops, thirty-six of whom were killed, to say nothing of the wounded.[22]

The Bolshevik Reds were angered because Wilson intervened at all; the anti-Bolshevik Whites, as well as the British and French, were embittered because he did not intervene enough; the Japanese were offended because United States forces were obviously trying to thwart their desires for expansion; and American citizens were aroused against this seemingly purposeless war prosecuted without the sanction of Congress for more than a year after the great conflict in Europe had ended. A fact that the Bolsheviks did not appreciate is that Wilson opposed the dismemberment of Russia, and to the extent that he may have checked the Japanese, he prevented it.

Soviet leaders have never allowed their people to forget that their country was twice invaded by the imperialistic and capitalistic United States, at Archangel and in Siberia. They avoid pointing out that both expeditions would never have occurred if there had not been a German war, from which Russia had unilaterally withdrawn, leaving her Western allies in the lurch. They also fail to note that Wilson did his utmost to avoid interference in Soviet internal affairs, that the American forces mounted no campaign in Siberia against Bolshevik elements, and that Wilson was evidently determined to thwart Japanese designs on Soviet territory.

A Soviet conviction that the intervention was anti-Bolshevik is not surprising in view of the fact that many Americans, with the silence of Washington encouraging them, believed this interpretation themselves and wanted to believe it. Japan was one of the Allies, and an

[22] War Department, Annual Reports, 1919 (3 vols., 1920), I, 25.

announcement of actual anti-Japanese intentions would have hurt the Allied cause.[23]

When negotiations for the recognition of Russia were being consummated in Washington in 1933, some thirteen years later, the Soviets were prepared to press claims for damages arising out of the American participation in the Siberian venture. After the Russian negotiator, Maxim Litvinov, was permitted to examine certain American documents, he abandoned the Siberian claims. According to Secretary of State Hull, the official records proved that the United States troops had been there, not for imperialistic purposes, but "to ensure the withdrawal of the Japanese, who had a far larger force in Siberia with the intent to occupy it permanently." [24] This issue thus died a diplomatic death but continues to live a propaganda life.

ADDITIONAL GENERAL REFERENCES

F. L. Paxson, *America at War* (1939); Edward M. Coffman, *The War to End All Wars: The American Military Experience in World War I* (1968); Harvey A. DeWeerd, *President Wilson Fights His War: World War I and the American Intervention* (1968); Mark Sullivan, *Our Times*, Volume V (1933); P. W. Slosson, *The Great Crusade and After, 1914–1928* (1930); E. E. Morison, *Admiral Sims and the Modern American Navy* (1942); J. R. Mock and Cedric Larson, *Words that Won the War* (1939); H. C. Peterson and G. C Fite, *Opponents of War, 1917–1918* (1957); H. N. Scheiber, *The Wilson Administration and Civil Liberties, 1917–1921* (1960); B. M. Baruch, *American Industry in the War* (1921); George F. Kennan, *Soviet–American Relations, 1917–1920* (2 vols., 1956, 1958).

---

[23] Betty Miller Unterberger, *America's Siberian Expedition, 1918–1920* (1956), p. 233. This excellent study is especially strong on the anti-Japanese aspects. See also the same author's "President Wilson and the Decision to Send American Troops to Siberia," *Pacific Hist. Rev.*, XXIV (1955), 63–74, which summarizes much of the above study, and her edited *American Intervention in the Russian Civil War* (1969).

[24] *The Memoirs of Cordell Hull* (2 vols., 1948), I, 299.

29

Wilsonian Peacemaking

After appealing fruitlessly for the election of a Democratic Congress to back him, Wilson left for Paris in December 1918, as head of the American peace delegation of five negotiators. His attempts to force the League of Nations into the Treaty of Versailles succeeded, but in achieving his goals he was forced to compromise away, in whole or in part, many of his Fourteen Points. Yet he hoped that a strong League of Nations, with America playing its proper role, would eventually iron out inequities in the peace settlement.

Returning home with the completed pact, Wilson found the atmosphere at first favorable, for public opinion seemingly supported the Treaty. But the Republican opposition in the Senate, headed by Henry Cabot Lodge, adopted delaying tactics in a successful attempt to divide and confuse the country.

A frustrated Wilson, though weary and ailing, finally decided to appeal to the people in a transcontinental barnstorming campaign. Instead of staying in Washington and making enough concessions to the Republican moderates in the Senate to achieve ratification, he embarked upon this hazardous gamble. On the return trip from the Pacific Coast he collapsed and henceforth directed the fight for the Treaty from a secluded sickbed.

Senator Lodge and his colleagues added fourteen reservations (later fifteen) to the resolution of ratification, but Wilson spurned any such dragging anchor. He urged the Democratic minority in the Senate to block the treaty with these restrictions attached, and this they loyally and blindly did. Wilson hoped to make the presidential election of 1920 a "solemn referendum" in favor of an unreserved League, but the Republican opposition swept to victory under Harding. Henceforth the issue was dead as far as America was concerned.

WAS POLITICS "ADJOURNED" DURING THE WAR?

Wilson had been reelected President in 1916 after a bitterly partisan campaign. Republican businessmen in particular resented the liberal program that the ex-professor had forced through Congress, and they were determined at all costs to regain the White House in 1921.

America's declaration of war against Germany in April 1917 called for a high degree of national unity, and to a considerable extent politics took a back seat. After all, both Democratic and Republican soldiers were being drafted to fight the enemy. Republicans in Congress, on the whole, supported the war measures of the Democratic administration with commendable loyalty. At times the so-called opposition party was more united in its support, notably of the conscription bill, than were the quarreling Democrats.

On May 27, 1918, when Congress was preparing to go home and "mend fences" for the upcoming primary elections, Wilson again appeared before that body. Appealing to its sense of duty, he declared that "politics is adjourned," for he had in mind a nonpolitical summer session for Congress.[1] To have proclaimed politics "adjourned" for the duration of the war would have been worse than futile: politicians can no more avoid playing politics than they can avoid breathing.

Wilson had an unwanted genius for coining phrases that could be wrenched out of context and widely misconstrued. The assumption somehow took root that he had "adjourned" politics for the duration, that the Republicans had acquiesced in this declaration, and that he broke the political truce with respect to the Congressional elections of 1918.

Politics was never "adjourned" during the war, although there were periods of relative quiescence. The most embittered Wilson-haters among the Republicans, notoriously ex-President Theodore Roosevelt, were ceaselessly scheming to regain the seats of power.

[1] Seward W. Livermore, *Politics Is Adjourned* (1966), pp. 135–136.

WAS WILSON'S OCTOBER APPEAL A BLUNDER?

Normally the party controlling the White House loses some Congressional seats in the midterm elections. Wilson, who did not enjoy too comfortable a majority in either house of Congress, naturally feared the traditional setback. If he lost control of the legislative arm, he would not be able to speak so authoritatively at the peace table, and consequently he might fail to secure a just and durable peace crowned by the League of Nations.

After much indecision, Wilson issued his famous "October Appeal" (October 25, 1918). He called not for the election of Senators and Representatives who would back him up at the peace table, but for the election of Democrats. A less blunt and partisan approach would almost certainly have caused less of a furor.

A chorus of condemnation immediately burst from the Republicans. Wilson had seemingly broken the so-called politics-is-adjourned pledge or truce. Moreover, he was accused of having taken a step wholly without precedent in asking for the election of men of his own party. In point of fact, President McKinley, on October 11, 1898, some two months after the armistice with Spain, had made a speech in which he had called openly for a Republican Congress. This earlier "October Appeal" had not aroused comparable fury; indeed it had received the warm endorsement of Theodore Roosevelt, who later in 1918 was condemning Wilson's manifesto.

Various Presidents since 1918 have unabashedly pleaded for a Congress of their own party. As recently as 1970 the Republican President Nixon embarked upon a strenuous speechmaking campaign, with controversial results, in his unsuccessful efforts to wrest control of both houses of Congress from the entrenched Democrats.

Wilson erred not so much in breaking a nonexistent truce or precedent as in taking an unnecessary gamble. He asked bluntly for a Democratic Congress. The Republicans in the ensuing election carried both houses by relatively narrow margins, especially the Senate.[2] If Wilson had issued no appeal, he could have waved aside the results as the normal midterm reaction against the party in power. But by flatly

---

[2] The Senate was now to contain 49 Republicans and 47 Democrats; the House 240 Republicans and 190 Democrats. The Republicans picked up 30 seats in the House, or about the normal midterm administration setback. Of course no one can prove that Wilson would not have lost more ground if he had not issued the October Appeal.

staking his prestige on the October Appeal, he suffered a stinging set-back when the country seemingly repudiated him. When he journeyed to Paris to make the peace, he was the only leader of a major power present not entitled to be there; that is, if one considered the American legislative majority as equivalent to a parliamentary majority.

SHOULD WILSON HAVE REMAINED HOME?

Two weeks after his electoral "repudiation," Wilson announced that he was going to attend the Paris Peace Conference as head of the American delegation. Critics, mostly Republicans, immediately cried out that he should stay at home, attend to pressing domestic business connected with demobilization, and cable instructions to his representatives at the Peace Conference. Unhurriedly, without personal pressures, he could thus engineer a better treaty. Wilson, his foes claimed, was a rank amateur in diplomacy, and when he got his feet under the same table with the white-spatted and frock-coated European diplomatists, they would "slicker" him out of about everything except the Washington Monument.[3]

But Wilson was hardly an amateur diplomat, although he had never come up through the professional service. He had learned something about diplomacy as president of Princeton University and as governor of New Jersey. For more than five years he had been director-in-chief of American foreign policy, and with relatively weak Secretaries of State he had kept the most important threads in his own hands. His earlier interchanges with the Germans and the Allies, in connection with the Armistice agreement, had revealed him to be a master negotiator. Indeed America had no comparable practitioner of diplomacy in the large, except possibly Theodore Roosevelt, who was to die in a few weeks.

Isolationist sentiment was still deeply entrenched in America, and precedent-worshippers were quick to note that no previous President had ever set foot on European soil during his term.[4] One oddity is that

[3] The myth must be discarded that the American delegation in Paris was naive and ill informed. Shortly after America entered the war, about 150 experts were gathered into The Inquiry, which prepared hundreds of detailed reports on specific problems of prospective peacemaking. These reports and many of these experts were available in Paris, making the Americans the best informed, probably, of any of the delegations. But an overburdened Wilson did not make use of as much of this assistance as was ideally desirable. See Lawrence E. Gelfand, *The Inquiry: American Preparations for Peace, 1917–1919* (1963).

[4] President Theodore Roosevelt had gone to Panama in 1906 to see "the dirt fly," but this journey was in the Western Hemisphere; the Canal Zone was an American leasehold in perpetuity; and Panama was a virtual puppet of the United States.

Wilson was pilloried for doing what many of his successors were to do; [5] in fact, a President today would be condemned for not actively serving as the nation's leader in overseas "summit conferences." Wilson was a generation ahead of his time.

There was much point to the argument that Wilson would be beaten down by the daily pressure and exhausting labor in Paris. After he had said "no" enough times to men whom he had come to know personally, the impulse would be strong to say "yes" occasionally, even to the wrong demands. But the problems were so complicated and so vexatious, and rapid progress was so essential, that doing business by cable would have been slow and awkward. There are strong reasons for believing that the Treaty of Versailles emerged a fairer pact because Wilson was there in person to use his enormous prestige to combat the nationalistic and imperialistic aims of the other great powers. [6]

DID WILSON ORIGINATE THE LEAGUE OF NATIONS?

An impression somehow lingers that the concept of a League of Nations was original with Wilson, and that he rammed its Covenant down the throats of his associates at Paris.

The germs of an international peace-keeping concert of nations may be traced at least as far back as the Italian poet, Dante (1265–1321). Many Americans had been more enthusiastic about the League idea than Wilson, and this group initially included Senator Henry Cabot Lodge. In Europe, particularly England and France, a number of distinguished minds had been focusing on the notion of collective security. Wilson was an ardent if belated convert.

At Paris, the American President was named chairman of the Commission on the League of Nations, which in 10 after-hour meetings struck off the draft that was presented in tentative form to the Conference. It consisted primarily of a piecing together of earlier Wilsonian outlines with the drafts formulated by a large number of European thinkers. [7] In short, the League of Nations was far from being Wilson's

[5] Most of Wilson's successors, notably Roosevelt, Truman, Eisenhower, Kennedy, Johnson, and Nixon, traveled enormous distances to confer with national leaders on foreign soil.

[6] It has often been said that America wanted nothing at Paris except peace — and did not get that. The United States indeed sought no territory at Paris and subsequently no reparations, except for the costs of the Rhineland army of occupation. But it did want security against future attacks by aggressors, and in the end did not achieve even that.

[7] T. A. Bailey, *Woodrow Wilson and the Lost Peace* (1944), p. 188.

original creation, but he adopted it, made it peculiarly his own brain-child, and fought for it to the last ditch.

One must not conclude that Wilson literally forced the League upon his European associates. Many of them thought that it would do no harm, might do some good, and would at the same time humor Wilson and the rich Americans. Much of the most serious opposition came from those critics who felt that the League should not be incorporated in the Treaty of Versailles as Section I, and that it should be put aside until completion of the more pressing business of making peace with the fallen foe.

DID WILSON SACRIFICE HIS FOURTEEN POINTS FOR THE LEAGUE?

It will be recalled that during the war Wilson had enunciated some 23 points or principles, popularly known as the Fourteen Points. Germany had laid down her arms late in 1918 on the basis of a pre-Armistice contract that guaranteed a peace based on these points, with two reservations, one on freedom of the seas, the other on reparations. At Paris, Wilson was forced to compromise on a number of these issues, and to some extent he yielded in the hope that the League of Nations, his capstone point, would ultimately iron out injustices.

Wilson's critics have contended that only about four of the twenty-three points and principles emerged completely intact from the Peace Conference. This assessment is hardly fair. It assumes that because a point was only 90 percent achieved it was not achieved at all. The League of Nations was to handle freedom of the seas and disarmament, and when this organization failed to do so, Wilson was blamed. Moreover, several of the points related to Russia and Turkey, both of which were in such chaos that the peacemakers, including Wilson, could exercise no control over them.

A fair analysis does much to support the view of Secretary of State Lansing, one of the American delegates at Paris and no blind admirer of Wilson. He subsequently testified that, insofar as circumstances would permit, the Fourteen Points were "substantially" carried out.[8] But this legalistic justification brought scant comfort to the Germans.

[8] *Senate Docs.*, 66 Cong., 1 sess., no. 106.

DID WILSON FAIL AT PARIS?

As the premier world leader, President Wilson had raised up such extravagant expectations that even modest success as a peacemaker would have been regarded as failure or near-failure.

Wilson did persuade the victorious Allies to adopt the League of Nations (they had wanted to postpone it) and insert it into the text of the peace treaty as Section I (they had wanted a separate instrument). He did induce the imperialistic powers to take over the colonies of the vanquished, not as conquests but as mandatories of the League — a seemingly idealistic solution that ultimately became thinly disguised imperialism. Wilson did support the creation of an independent Poland, the restoration of Belgium to its people, and the reacquisition of Alsace-Lorraine by the French, thereby partially fulfilling his dream of self-determination, implicit in the Fourteen Points.

Wilson won a further victory for self-determination when he induced the French to yield their demands for the German Rhineland in return for two security treaties, which he and the British Prime Minister respectively signed. Both statesmen pledged their nations to come to the aid of France if she should again be the victim of "unprovoked" aggression. The United States Senate withheld its approval, and France felt betrayed.[9]

Wilson was not the only leader at Paris forced to compromise. All the other leading statesmen were compelled to accept half-loaf solutions that they did not find completely appetizing.

WERE WILSON'S SETBACKS AT PARIS DUE TO ILLNESS?

Critics have charged that Wilson would have accomplished more at Paris if his mind had not been clouded by illness. Some rumormongers have even given currency to the charge that he was suffering from an advanced case of syphilis.

The record is clear that at a critical juncture, early in April 1919, Wilson was stricken with a high fever, a racking cough, vomiting,

---

[9] See L. A. R. Yates, *The United States and French Security, 1917–1921* (1957). President De Gaulle of France had before him the lesson of the American betrayal when he pursued an anti-American course in the 1960s. In traditional European diplomacy the failure of a nation to ratify a formally signed treaty was regarded as a breach of faith.

diarrhea, and insomnia. So sudden was the onslaught that his physician at first suspected poison but finally diagnosed the illness as influenza. A recent examination of the evidence by a prominent neurologist, Dr. Edwin A. Weinstein, points to a cerebral vascular occlusion (blood clot in the brain).[10]

Wilson had a long and complicated record of many illnesses before and after reaching the White House. Evidence of brain damage may be found in 1896 (when he incurred partial paralysis of a hand); in 1906 when he suffered temporary blindness of the left eye (later reduced to impaired vision); and in 1908 (when he was again afflicted by partial paralysis of a hand). Dr. Weinstein concludes, pursuing the pattern of brain damage further, that in April, 1919, at the Peace Conference, Wilson sustained "a lesion in the right cerebral hemisphere extending to include deeper structures in the limbic-reticular system." [11] The later massive stroke, with paralysis of one side of the body and face and impairment of speech, came in September 1919, following his exhausting oratorical campaign for the League. He remained a permanent semi-invalid.

Wilson's conduct during the peacemaking years, 1919–1920, indicates brain damage, including irrational stubbornness, irritability, groundless suspicions, forgetfulness, and other symptoms. Considering his background of ill health, one must conclude that at Paris he did remarkably well.

WAS THE TREATY OF VERSAILLES A BAD PEACE?

The pact negotiated in Paris but signed at Versailles proved to be one of the most abused and least perused treaties in history. It is widely regarded as a failure because it did not keep the peace: World War II erupted twenty years later.

One is surprised that any kind of treaty, good or bad, came out of the Paris Conference, in view of the chaotic conditions in Central Europe, the need for haste to stave off Bolshevism, and the necessity for compromise. The pact actually included many commendable features, including the League of Nations Covenant, the mandates system, and the liberation of certain ethnic minorities from unwanted overlords. From the general peace settlement there emerged a map of Europe which

---

[10] Edwin A. Weinstein, "Woodrow Wilson's Neurological Illness," *Jour. of Amer. Hist.*, LVII (1970), 341.
[11] *Ibid.*, 342.

more nearly followed ethnic lines than any of its predecessors. But unfortunately these ethnic changes in some cases cut across lines of
communication and transportation.[12]

A basic fault of the settlement was that it fell between two
stools. A victor may have peace or he may have vengeance, but he is
not likely to derive both from the same agreement, any more than one
can simultaneously secure milk and beefsteak from the same cow. A
mild peace of accommodation may permit the vanquished to forget his
wounds and establish harmonious relationships with the victor, as was
conspicuously the case with the treaty finally concluded with Japan in
1951.[13] A harsh peace of vengeance, such as the punitive terms imposed
by Germany on France in 1871, will keep alive a spirit of revenge and
sow the seeds of a new war to reverse the results of the old one. The
Treaty of Versailles was harsh enough (thanks to the embittered French
and their European Allies) to infuriate the Germans, while mild enough
(thanks to Wilson's idealism) to ensure that the fallen foe would not be
"permanently" enchained.[14]

A bad treaty in the hands of just men may be reasonably successful; a half-good treaty in the hands of vengeful men will almost
certainly fail. Much depended on the wisdom, forbearance, and vision
of the statesmen who were charged with implementing the Treaty of
Versailles. The rickety edifice known as the peace settlement was to be
erected on a four-pillared structure, with Uncle Sam providing one of
the pillars. When the fourth prop was never emplaced, the topheavy
structure teetered for twenty years and then collapsed. A sound super-
structure can be erected on a three-legged stool, but not on a four-
legged chair that has lost one leg.

The Germans had been promised a peace based on the Fourteen
Points, but they did not get it. They accepted the Treaty of Versailles
under duress, and it turned out to be a different pact from the one they
had signed, largely because the United States retreated into isolation
and left Europe to "stew in its own juice."

One example will suffice. The key Reparations Commission was
to decide upon the specific amount of damages to be wrung from
Germany. America was to be represented on this body, but when the
Senate failed to approve the Treaty, control fell into the hands of the
understandably vengeful French and Belgians. Germany was thereupon

[12] See Paul Birdsall, *Versailles Twenty Years After* (1941).
[13] One should note that because of a six-year delay, passions on both sides had
cooled off.
[14] A victorious Germany probably would have imposed a harsher peace, if we
may judge by the Treaty of Brest-Litovsk that she imposed on Russia in 1918.

assessed the astronomical sum of $32 billion, only a relatively small portion of which she ever paid — and that under protest.

DID WILSON LIE ABOUT THE SECRET TREATIES?

Upon returning from France with the Treaty of Versailles, Wilson consented to meet with the all-important Senate Foreign Relations Committee. Although he answered many questions in detail and with evident candor, he was less than truthful in one response. Asked if he had known in advance of the notorious secret treaties that the Allies had negotiated among themselves for partitioning the territory of the enemy, he stated flatly and repeatedly that he had not learned of them before reaching Paris.

This, of course, was not true. Wilson's prior knowledge can be well established by various documents, including Point 1 of the Fourteen Points, regarding open covenants. We remember that this principle had been specifically designed to offset the unfortunate effect of the publication by the Bolsheviks of the secret treaties found in the Tsarist archives.

Why Wilson did not tell the truth remains a mystery. Shortly before his first inauguration he had remarked to Colonel House that a man was justified in lying if the honor of a woman or an issue of public policy were involved. While president of Princeton he had testified in 1910 that he had not read a booklet written by Dean West for which he, himself, had written a laudatory preface.[15] Possibly this untruth and the one about the secret treaties resulted from some kind of blockage stemming from recurrent brain damage, beginning in 1896.[16] Perhaps, with the Treaty of Versailles under heavy fire, he found himself in the position of a doctor who feels that he must tell "white lies" for the patient's good.

DID POLITICS KILL THE TREATY IN AMERICA?

President Wilson evidently returned from Paris in an uncompromising mood: too much compromise, he probably felt, had already gone into the Treaty. He had managed to engraft his partially borrowed brainchild, the League of Nations, upon the pact as its very first section.

---

[15] Arthur S. Link, *Wilson: The Road to The White House* (1947), p. 70.
[16] Weinstein, "Woodrow Wilson's Neurological Illness," p. 333.

This precious League was so intimately tied in with accompanying sections that, in his view, it could not be cut out without killing the entire instrument. Such a step, he felt, the Senators would never dare to take.

The Senate was narrowly controlled by the Republicans, with Senator Henry Cabot Lodge of Massachusetts as Chairman of the powerful Foreign Relations Committee. The Treaty of Versailles would have to be approved by a two-thirds vote of the Senate, and Wilson had been unwise in not deferring to that body before, during, and after the Paris negotiations. He not only did not invite any Senators to join him on the American commission of five,[17] but he did not even seek the advice of the Senate in advance of the Conference. In addition, he had asked only one Republican, a minor figure at that, to serve on the Peace Commission, even though the Republicans, in the light of the recent Congressional elections, were the majority party in both houses of Congress. The Senate in general and the Republicans in particular felt snubbed.

Given little or no opportunity to write the treaty in Paris, the Republicans felt that they were entitled to do a little rewriting in Washington. This they attempted, first with amendments (which presumably would have required a resummoning of the entire Peace Conference), and then with reservations. These were to be appended to the resolution of ratification as an expression of America's understanding of how she had bound herself. In general they reserved the nation's rights under the Monroe Doctrine and in regard to controlling armaments, tariffs, immigration policy, and other functions of a sovereign state. In their final form these stipulations, initially fourteen, were known as the Lodge Reservations.

Wilson hated Lodge (the feeling was mutual), and he flatly refused to accept a resolution of ratification with the Republican-supported Lodge Reservations formally attached. But he was willing to accede to rather similar interpretive reservations worked out with the Democratic minority in the Senate.

Both sides were playing politics in the League fight, although at times the Republicans seemed to be the only offending party. The Democrats realized that such an achievement as a completed Treaty of Versailles, with its hope-giving League of Nations, would be an impressive feather in their cap as they approached the presidential election of 1920. They might be able to put another Democrat in the White House. Many Republicans feared that Wilson was prepared to defy

[17] To have invited a Senator or Senators would have caused much embarrassment because Senator Lodge, whom Wilson disliked, would have been regarded as the number one choice.

the two-term tradition and run again in order to make sure that "his" League of Nations would get off to an auspicious start. Partly with control of the White House in mind, a hard core of Democrats in the Senate steadfastly supported Wilson's opposition to the Lodge Reservations.[18]

Rival Republicans, with the election of 1920 also in view, had no desire to assist their opponents. They felt that if they could "Americanize" and "Republicanize" the treaty by adding safeguarding reservations, they would gain credit with the voters and consequently eject the Democrats from power in 1920. This attitude does much to explain the ensuing deadlock.

DID LODGE'S RESERVATIONS "EMASCULATE" THE TREATY?

Wilson insisted that Lodge's reservations would "emasculate" the entire treaty and hence should be voted down in favor of somewhat comparable Democratic reservations that would not. But the record indicates that the invalid in the White House grossly exaggerated the importance of the Republican reservations, particularly after he collapsed with brain damage and was kept in seclusion.

About ten of the original fourteen Lodge Reservations related primarily to the Covenant of the League of Nations, which quantitatively was a relatively small part of the lengthy Treaty of Versailles. The remaining reservations touched rather inconsequentially on the rest of the whole instrument.

Wilson may have felt that if he swallowed Lodge's reservations the Republicans would come up with more, and then again more. But this was a game that could be played only once without the danger of a backlash effect. Certainly one reason why Wilson was unwilling to accept these reservations was that, in his view, the other four major powers (Britain, France, Italy, and Japan) would turn them down. We shall never know for certain what they would have done because they were not given that opportunity. Wilson himself took this heavy responsibility on his own shoulders. So essential was American adherence for the success of the League of Nations, and so necessary was Uncle Sam's financial support for the rehabilitation of Europe, that with some

---

[18] A poll of newspaper editors by state on the League issue in the spring of 1919 bears a striking resemblance to the Democratic electoral vote in the subsequent presidential election of 1920. See map in T. A. Bailey, *Woodrow Wilson and the Great Betrayal* (1945), p. 47. It is interesting to speculate that if there had been a 22nd Amendment (approved in 1951), the issue of a third term for Wilson would have been removed, and the Treaty might have been ratified.

grumbling these four powers might have accepted: France and Italy almost certainly, Britain probably, and Japan possibly.[19]

Senate reservations, as distinguished from amendments, were an old story in American history, going back well into the nineteenth century. Altogether they have been employed in about two dozen significant instances, involving both multination and two-nation pacts. They have been attached to two additional treaties of peace since Versailles, that of 1921 ending the war with Germany, and that of 1951 ending the war with Japan.[20]

In general, Senate reservations fall into two categories. The first reserves the right of the nation to retain its own policies without interference, such as the Monroe Doctrine and control of immigration. The second reserves the right not to become involved in foreign military action without the consent of the Senate or the entire Congress. In short, safeguards for American sovereignty.

Significantly, the Senate had only recently revealed its concern with sovereignty. In 1911 President Taft, a Republican, had negotiated general arbitration treaties with Britain and France, and when the Senate proposed to amend them, he embarked (like Wilson) on a personal appeal to the country, and (like Wilson) failed to overbear the Senate. That body, with the Republican Senator Lodge as leader, so amended the pacts that a disgruntled Taft refused to go through with ratification (as in effect Wilson was later to do). President Wilson would have done well to heed recent history when he adopted an unyielding attitude toward the Senate majority, now Republican.[21]

Ironically, in 1945 a number of the Lodge Reservations to the League of Nations were written, implicitly or explicitly, into the Charter of the United Nations. This refinement may account in part for the action of the Senate in approving the document without a serious attempt to attach American interpretations.

SHOULD WILSON HAVE TRIED HARDER TO COMPROMISE?

The Treaty of Versailles probably would have been approved in America without the League of Nations, which Wilson had forced into it. The League dragged down the Treaty, and Article X of the League dragged

[19] In November 1919 the Lodge Reservations required the written approval of at least three of the Big Four Powers; in March 1920 they required only the silent acquiescence of all the nearly 30 Allied and Associated Powers.

[20] In 1926 the Senate approved adherence to the World Court, but attached five reservations, one of which was so fundamental to the working of the court that its members rejected it and the United States never did join. See D. F. Fleming, *The United States and the World Court* (1945).

[21] James E. Hewes, Jr., "Henry Cabot Lodge and the League of Nations," *Proceedings of the American Philosophical Society*, CXIV (1970), 245–255.

down the League. This was the proviso that America would have a moral obligation to aid any League member victimized by external aggression. Wilson declined to weaken this guarantee, and Lodge, who felt with good reason that such a pledge was one that America would not or could not always honor, refused to make any such unreserved commitment.[22]

Wilson did try to reason, collectively and individually, with the Republican Senators. With the wisdom of hindsight we may conclude that he should have yielded more ground in his attempts to win over a few of the dozen or so mild-reservationist Republicans.[23] The Republican party controlled the Senate by a margin of two members and hence was able to attach all of the Lodge Reservations by a simple majority vote, although a two-thirds vote was necessary to approve the entire treaty. If Wilson had been able to convert six of the moderate Republicans and add them to the 43 dependable Democrats, he would have had a working majority. Not only could this simple majority have voted down all Republican reservations, but it could have added the milder interpretive reservations of its own that Wilson approved.

Instead of staying in Washington and trying to compromise with the moderate Republicans, the President embarked upon a barnstorming appeal to the country. This was a desperate gamble, for he was already in a state of near exhaustion. Moreover, such a campaign was obviously futile. Even if he had been able to persuade the voters to turn out of office all of the Republicans up for reelection who favored the Lodge Reservations, he still would not have had the necessary two-thirds majority for ratification.[24]

DID WILSON BLOCK RATIFICATION OF THE TREATY?

In November 1919, and again in March 1920, the treaty came up for approval. Both times it failed of a two-thirds vote, whether with reserva-

[22] *Ibid.*, 245–255. Lodge's opposition to universal commitments was consistent with his earlier record.

[23] Kurt Wimer, "Woodrow Wilson Tries Conciliation: An Effort that Failed," *Historian*, XXV (1963), 419–438. Wilson did make more of an effort to win over the moderate Republicans than is generally supposed, but he evidently was unwilling to go far enough.

[24] Wilson seems not to have been fully aware of this obstacle because, at one point after his collapse, he privately drew up an abortive scheme calling upon the Senators who opposed him to resign and stand for reelection. (The "appeal habit" again.) If a majority of them lost their seats, he would resign, as would the Prime Minister of Britain if he lost his majority. This proposal reveals both Wilson's desperation and his clouded judgment, for no Senator in his right mind would ever bow out at the behest of the President. See Kurt Wimer, "Woodrow Wilson's Plan for a Vote of Confidence," *Pennsylvania History*, XXVIII (1961), 279–293; Bailey, *Woodrow Wilson and the Great Betrayal*, pp. 214–215.

tions or without reservations. On both occasions Wilson, a secluded paralytic substantially removed from reality, sent word to the Democratic minority to reject the resolution of ratification with the hated Lodge Reservations appended. Enough Democrats faithfully followed his bidding to bring about the negative results.

Wilson expressed the wholly unrealistic hope that with the Lodge Reservations spurned the way would be cleared for an unreserved approval of the pact. But his Democratic minority was simply unable to muster enough strength. By the time of the second vote, in March 1920, most clearheaded observers realized that the alternatives were either a treaty with the Lodge Reservations or no treaty at all. Wilson preferred no approval to a half-hearted approval, and he counted on the country to bring about the desired result by subjecting the treaty to what he called a "solemn referendum" in the upcoming election of 1920. But the old obstacle still remained: not enough opponents of Wilson's views were up for reelection to make possible the desired change.

As it turned out, the treaty with the Lodge Reservations was defeated because Wilson insisted on such a defeat, in the hope that a ratification more to his liking could be subsequently secured. He hoped to throw the onus for the defeat in the Senate on the Republican majority, not on himself.

Some critics have blamed the two-thirds rule for the frustrating outcome. But Wilson insisted that if the Senate approved the treaty with the Lodge Reservations, he would not carry through ratification. The ultimate obstacle was the President rather than the two-thirds rule. He demanded approval on his terms or — as events turned out — not at all; he asked for all or nothing, and got nothing.

DID SENATOR LODGE DEFEAT THE TREATY?

At the time, and even later, many critics accused Lodge of being the chief architect of the treaty's defeat. This is probably true if one qualifies the statement by saying that he contrived to bring about rejection of an *unreserved* treaty. But, as events shaped up, he at least appeared to be trying to push the treaty through, with his reservations appended, thus creating the deadlock with Wilson.

There is solid evidence that Lodge was willing to go even further than he did in softening his reservations, but he was brought up short by the "irreconcilables" within his own party.[25] He felt that a

---

[25] The "irreconcilables" were fourteen Republicans and two maverick Democrats who were opposed to the treaty, whether reserved or unreserved. The group con-

disastrous split in Republican ranks, like that of 1912, had to be avoided at all costs. There is also testimony that Lodge worked out a compromise with a go-between for Colonel House, who arranged to send the draft on to the White House. No response of any kind was forthcoming.[26]

DID WILSON SERIOUSLY SEEK A THIRD TERM?

Wilson not only wanted a "solemn referendum" on the League in the impending presidential election of 1920, but he regarded himself as the one standard-bearer who could lead his party and his cause to victory. He definitely angled to have his name placed before the Democratic convention in San Francisco, but his friends quashed the effort. Counting heavily against him were his ruined health, his lost prestige and popularity, the century-old two-term tradition, and the virtual certainty of defeat.[27]

The magnitude of Wilson's self-delusions is astonishing. He evidently believed that he not only could win a third nomination and election but lead the nation vigorously into the League of Nations, all with more than one-third of the Senate against him. Such unrealistic notions more than suggest that his mind was not functioning normally. Although he seemed bright enough on occasion, his face and side were still paralyzed, his once penetrating voice was muffled, and his brain evidently could not sustain prolonged and meaningful exertion. Both he, his family, and close advisors rejected the disagreeable truth that his mind had been affected, although the bodily paralysis and thickness of speech were telltale symptoms of brain damage. As a prominent physician has written in this context: "Denial of illness, or anosognosia, literally lack of knowledge of disease, is a common sequel of the type of brain injury received by Wilson." [28]

WAS HARDING NOMINATED IN A SMOKE-FILLED ROOM?

A misconception persists, reinforced by subsequent personal and political scandals, that Harding was a semiliterate political "nobody."

---

tained isolationists, realists, and idealists, several of whom were sympathetic toward the idea of a League but were not willing to support this one. See Ralph A. Stone, *The Irreconcilables* (1970).

26 See Stephen Bonsal, *Unfinished Business* (1944), pp. 274–275.

27 Kurt Wimer, "Woodrow Wilson and a Third Nomination," *Pennsylvania History*, XXIX (1962), 193–211.

28 Weinstein, "Woodrow Wilson's Neurological Illness," p. 346.

He was boosted into the White House, so the tale goes, by a clique of Senate bosses who planned to use him as their puppet.[29]

As a United States Senator from Ohio, Harding was a well-known figure in the Republican party. A spread-eagle orator of the old school, he had been chosen to give the stirring keynote address at the Chicago convention in 1916 that nominated Hughes. Big, handsome, warm-handed, "folksy," and kindly, he loved dogs and people. Although not regarded as an intellectual heavyweight, he had won the goodwill, if not the friendship, of a host of politicians within the party. He was not a completely dark horse because he secured 65½ votes on the first ballot in 1920, and then slowly built up his support. After the front-runners — General Wood, Governor Lowden, and Senator Hiram Johnson — fell into complete deadlock and killed one another off, the convention turned to Harding as a compromise. A backslapping politician, he profited from being the second or third choice of a large number of delegates.

During the late evening of the first day of balloting fifteen or so leading Republicans, mostly Senators but including two ex-Senators and two non-Senators, wandered in and out of journalist George Harvey's suite in the Blackstone Hotel. A few of them were influential in their state delegations. They informally discussed various possibilities into the early morning, and even summoned Harding to ask him if there was any blot on his record that would disqualify him as a candidate. He asked for ten minutes to review his past and then solemnly declared that there was not.[30] Word then somehow leaked out that the Senate bosses favored Harding, and partly as a result the Ohioan received the nomination on the tenth ballot.

In truth, there was no nomination in the smoke-filled hotel room. Of the fifteen or so leading Republicans present, only about two expressed themselves as wholeheartedly favoring Harding. Most of the others either opposed his nomination outright, were lukewarm, or had other favorites of their own.

---

[29] This story evidently started when Harry M. Daugherty, Harding's campaign manager, made the flippantly offhand remark to reporters that his candidate would be nominated at 11 minutes after two in the morning by a dozen or so weary men sitting around a table. Samuel H. Adams, *The Incredible Era* (1939), p. 130. Many if not most hotel rooms at political conventions in this era were smoke-filled, including the convention hall. See also Randolph C. Downes, *The Rise of Warren Gamaliel Harding, 1865–1920* (1970).

[30] Rumors then concerned an affair with Nan Britton and the possibility of a Negro strain in the Harding line. This latter accusation, difficult to prove, played a role in the ensuing campaign. The Negro charge and others are developed fully in Francis Russell, *The Shadow of Blooming Grove: Warren G. Harding in His Times* (1968).

DID SENATE BOSSES CONTROL THE CHICAGO CONVENTION?

There were about 1,000 perspiring delegates in the Chicago convention hall, many of them eager to pay their mounting hotel bills and catch the next train for home. To say that they were controlled by the handful of perplexed men who drifted in and out of Harvey's room in the Blackstone Hotel is to tax one's credulity.

When word got out that Harding was the choice of the party's leaders, the Senate bosses naturally wanted to claim credit for what happened, even if they had not achieved it. In so doing, they would have more influence at the White House. But Harding was nominated primarily because he was regarded as the most "available" candidate. He was a well-known figure; he hailed from politically potent Ohio; [31] he was an acceptable compromise choice; and he could presumably win for the ticket. Through his popular call for a return to "normalcy," he had already appealed strongly to a war-weary and strife-torn America.

If further proof were needed that the Senate bosses did not control the convention, it may be found in the nomination of the Vice President. The Senate leaders evidently wanted one of their number: Senator Lenroot of Wisconsin. But the convention, dominated by conservatives if not by Senate bosses, took the bit in its teeth and stampeded to Governor Calvin Coolidge of Massachusetts. The colorless New Englander had become a national hero overnight as a result of allegedly crushing what appeared to be a Bolshevik-type uprising at the time of the Boston police strike, nine months earlier. His telegraphed response to Samuel Gompers of the American Federation of Labor had an enormous appeal to the law-and-order citizenry: "There is no right to strike against the public safety by anybody, anywhere, any time."

The facts are that Coolidge had apathetically permitted the situation in Boston to deteriorate alarmingly; that the Mayor of Boston had taken the initiative in breaking the strike with armed force; that Coolidge resorted to decisive action only *after* the strike was broken; and that his immortal words to Gompers were sent three days *after* the Mayor had brought the uprising under substantial control. Thus the "silent" Coolidge was the lucky beneficiary of credit that belonged elsewhere, primarily because he managed to dispatch a few ringing

---

31 "When in doubt, take Ohio," was a time-worn political aphorism. Myths about Harding's nomination are set forth in Andrew Sinclair, *The Available Man* (1965).

words at a time when the country wanted resolute action taken against near-anarchy.[32]

WAS THERE EVER A
"SOLEMN REFERENDUM" ON THE LEAGUE?

Meeting in wind-swept San Francisco, the Democrats nominated James M. Cox for the presidency and Franklin D. Roosevelt for the vice presidency. (In promoting his own prospects, Wilson contrived to ruin those of his son-in-law, William G. McAdoo.) The platform endorsed a League safeguarded by mild reservations, and candidate Cox loyally supported the Wilsonian League.

The Republican platform, highly ambiguous on the League issue, was so worded that both opponents and proponents of Wilson's scheme could stand on it. Harding wobbled all over his spacious platform but finally came out against the League in its existing form. Instead he would approve a vague (and soon-forgotten) substitute known as an Association of Nations. In short, not a Democratic League but a Republican Association. Thirty-one prominent Americans, mostly leading Republicans, issued a manifesto assuring the nation that the surest way to get into the League was to support Harding. The Republican "irreconcilables" argued that the surest way to stay out was to support Harding.

To say that the campaign was confusing is to put it mildly. Many voters, regarding the League as a dead issue, were more concerned with returning to "normalcy" under Harding. They were weary of Wilsonian idealism, do-goodism, moral overstrain, and European quarrels. The country may have registered something of a mandate to go back to the "good old days," but it certainly could not return a mandate for or against the League. The only way to hold a true plebiscite is to have the people vote "yes" or "no" on a given question, as the Swiss did in joining the League.[33] There were so many issues that the voter was simply unable to register his views on the single one of the League by voting for Harding or Cox. Indeed, much of the pro-Harding vote was anti-Wilson.

Harding was swept into the White House by a plurality of some 7,000,000 votes. Wilson had asked that the election be made a "solemn

---

[32] The story of the police strike is well told in Donald R. McCoy, *Calvin Coolidge* (1967), Ch. 9.

[33] This was evidently the only "solemn referendum" held anywhere in the world. D. F. Fleming, *The United States and the League of Nations, 1918–1920* (1932), p. 418.

referendum" on the League, and the results seemed to be a solemn repudiation.[34] The Democrats insisted that there had been no true referendum, and many of them urged that there be one in the next presidential election, that of 1924. But the Republicans replied that Wilson had asked for a solemn referendum and he had received one — a cold shoulder for the League. The victor traditionally interprets the election results as he likes, and the trumpets of victory drown out the protests of the loser. No sane candidate consents to rerun a race that he has already won. Thereafter Republican politicians, awed and misled by Harding's 7,000,000 plurality, generally shunned the League issue, while public interest and support faded away.

As events turned out, Wilson condemned his newly born "brainchild" to death by forcing it to run in an electoral campaign in which it could not possibly receive a clear-cut endorsement. Public opinion polls, as we know them today, did not then exist. But the probabilities are strong that a majority of the voters favored the treaty with some kind of reservations rather than entering the "League trap" without some kind of safeguards.

WAS WILSON A GREAT PRESIDENT?

Academic historians, preponderantly sympathetic Democratic liberals, have traditionally acclaimed Wilson as one of the "great" Presidents, along with Washington, Jefferson, Lincoln, and Franklin Roosevelt.

If we ignore the problem of comparing with precision the greatness of different men living in different times and facing problems with differing degrees of complexity — i.e., comparing apples with oranges — we encounter an additional perplexity in the case of Wilson, and that is his anemic record after his collapse. He was an invalid or semi-invalid during the last year and a half of his eight years.[35]

Wilson's leadership in 1913–1914 in driving through Congress

---

34 Wilson had early developed the "appeal habit" as president of Princeton, governor of New Jersey, and as President of the United States. His appeals over the heads of the duly constituted authorities to their constituents had brought unusual success in his early dealings with Congress, but his luck ran out with the October Appeal of 1918. Thereafter he failed at Paris in his appeal over the heads of the Italian delegates to the Italians, over the head of the Senate to the American people during his barnstorming campaign of 1919, and over the head of the Senate in his appeal for a "solemn referendum." Colonel E. M. House, Wilson's erstwhile stellar advisor, branded this last appeal as "incredibly unwise."

35 For an assessment of these problems, see T. A. Bailey, *Presidential Greatness* (1966), especially pp. 310–312. Civil libertarians have been critical of Wilson's harsh treatment of dissenters during the war and of his Attorney General's prosecution of Reds after the President's collapse.

his sweeping domestic reforms was truly amazing. His diplomatic record had much to commend it, although he did not "keep us out of war." Perhaps the task was hopeless. His war leadership was outstanding, although his overemphasis on ideals brought about the seemingly inevitable "slump in idealism" when the shooting stopped. His record as a peace negotiator in Paris, though marred by inevitable compromise, was much better than many of his critics would concede. Yet in getting the nation into peace he was much less successful than getting it into war. His personal vendetta with Lodge and his refusal to compromise further (possibly because of earlier brain damage) were accentuated by his massive stroke in September 1919. His resignation then would have been better for his reputation and the country, and probably would have resulted in a speedy approval of the treaty with some kind of Republican reservations attached.

But Wilson lingered on, a pathetic shell of the once dynamic statesman. Without power to lead constructively, he nevertheless possessed the power to obstruct effectively. His appeal for a "solemn referendum" was bound to produce misleading results, as it did.

In short, there were two Wilsons: the one before his fateful collapse, and the one after. The first had many of the attributes of greatness; the second, an invalid, did not. To what extent the second canceled out the first will always be a matter of speculation.

ADDITIONAL GENERAL REFERENCES

A. J. Mayer, *Politics and Diplomacy of Peacemaking* (1967); N. G. Levin, Jr., *Woodrow Wilson and World Politics* (1969); A. S. Link, *Wilson the Diplomatist* (1956); T. A. Bailey, *Woodrow Wilson and the Lost Peace* (1944) and *Woodrow Wilson and the Great Betrayal* (1945); D. F. Fleming, *The United States and the League of Nations* (1932); Herbert Hoover, *The Ordeal of Woodrow Wilson* (1958); Ferdinand Czernin, *Versailles, 1919* (1964); Paul Birdsall, *Versailles Twenty Years After* (1941); Harold Nicholson, *Peacemaking, 1919* (1933); S. P. Tillman, *Anglo–American Relations at the Paris Peace Conference of 1919* (1961); L. E. Gelfand, *The Inquiry: American Preparations for Peace, 1917–1919* (1963); J. A. Garraty, *Henry Cabot Lodge* (1953); W. M. Bagby, *The Road to Normalcy: The Presidential Campaign and Election of 1920* (1962).

30

Harding and the Era of Normalcy

Candidate Harding had appealed to the mood of the country in 1920 with his call for a return to the good old days of what he termed "normalcy." [1] *To a considerable degree he delivered. His administration negotiated separate treaties of peace with the defeated enemy while carrying forward the work of reconstruction at home. Not completely isolationist, Harding extended backdoor cooperation to the infant League of Nations, but this was about all that American public opinion would then tolerate.*

The Harding administration deserves credit for the results — naval and diplomatic — of the Washington Conference on the Limitation of Armament in 1921–1922. Many Republicans, their consciences perhaps pricked by the defeat of the League, sponsored this gathering as a "peace conference." Presumably it would bring about the arms reduction that had been envisaged under the League of Nations. The disarmament aspects of the Washington conclave did not work out as optimists had hoped, but this failure was more the responsibility of Harding's successors than his own.

Harding worked earnestly at his job, made some excellent appointments to his Cabinet, avoided domination by the Senate, and grew perceptibly in office. But he was betrayed by rascally subordinates, who

---

[1] Linguistic purists hooted at Harding for having "coined" this word rather than using "normality." Actually "normalcy" was to be found in the *Oxford English Dictionary*, which uncovered a usage in mathematics as early as 1857.

engulfed his administration in a cesspool of scandal that indelibly black-ened his name.

DID THE UNITED STATES "BETRAY" EUROPE?

The most pressing unfinished task before the new Harding administration in 1921 was to make peace with the fallen foe. Two attempts at approving the Treaty of Versailles under Wilson had brought only defeat and frustration. In the interests of restoring international trade to normalcy, if for no other reason, the state of war had to be brought to an official end.

Congress first passed a joint resolution in 1921, similar to the one already vetoed by President Wilson, declaring hostilities terminated. Washington then proceeded to negotiate three separate treaties: with Germany, Austria, and Hungary. These instruments claimed for America the advantages, but none of the responsibilities, contained in the original peace settlements. Thus the United States turned its back on its associates in the recent war against the Central Powers, and left Europe to its own devices.

America's lone-wolf course was condemned in some quarters as a "betrayal," which is commonly associated with gross treachery, like that of Benedict Arnold.[2] But the word also means "to disappoint the expectations of" and "to mislead." In this milder sense, "betrayal" describes much of what happened. President Wilson, speaking in good faith for his nation, "misled" the Allied powers into thinking that America would ratify the Treaty of Versailles and join the League of Nations. The victors consented to accept certain unpalatable provisions of the treaty and the League in the expectation that the Republic would honor the commitments of its spokesman. When it refused to do so, Europe's high hopes were disappointed, and the late Associates felt both misled and betrayed.

SHOULD THE U. S. HAVE STAYED OUT OF WORLD WAR I?

As events turned out, America sent a huge army to Europe at the urging of the Allies, helped to crush the "Hun," and then ran out on her moral

---

[2] The theme of "betrayal" is discussed in the last chapter of T. A. Bailey, *Woodrow Wilson and the Great Betrayal* (1945). Using the "treacherous surrender" concept of "betrayal," Charles A. Beard attacks at length the milder connotation used in the above cited book. See his *American Foreign Policy in the Making, 1932–1940* (1946).

commitments under the abortive French Security Treaty and the League of Nations. Having left Europe in a shambles, Washington made separate terms with the fallen foe. Critics were reminded of the householder who ran to the assistance of his neighbor, beat off the robbers, and then went home, leaving the victim bleeding on his living room floor.

Europeans have since argued that if the Americans were not going to assume the responsibility of succoring Europe and averting another World War, they should have kept out altogether. The Mother Continent, the argument ran, knew its problems best. If the Americans had not come in and turned the tide, then the Europeans might have worked out a stalemate peace of some sort that would have averted the rise of Hitler.

All this is speculation. The Allies were certainly delighted to have the "Yanks" join the fray on their side, with or without obligations as to the future. Whether, in the absence of America, the Germans or the Allies would have won, or a stalemate peace could have been hammered out, no one knows. About all we can say with certainty about subsequent developments is that the United States, with the power to do so, was shortsighted in not shaping European events to its own advantage. Instead, it retired behind its ocean moats and permitted Europe to drift into the whirlpool, with the almost virtual certainty that America would ultimately be sucked in again.

WOULD A U. S.-SUPPORTED LEAGUE HAVE INSURED PEACE?

Architects of the League of Nations had assumed that the United States, as the principal founding father, would both join and uphold the new world organization. But this was never done. As a result, the League was lamed at birth, though not completely crippled, by the nonadherence of the richest and most powerful nation.

America's self-exclusion had clearly demonstrable effects. One related to disarmament, or more properly arms limitation, which the League was supposed to engineer. With a great power such as the United States on the outside, the League was never able to achieve its goal. Perhaps it would have failed in any event, partly because it excluded in its early years a temporarily disarmed Germany and an ideologically menacing Russia.

Another weakness of the League to which America's nonmembership contributed involved economic sanctions against wrongdoers under Article XVI. Whenever a possible application arose, the point was invariably raised that a boycott against an offending nation would be useless. America, so the argument ran, would not be bound by it and probably would undercut the League by continuing to trade with the boycotted country.[3]

In short, the nonmembership of the United States provided a convenient excuse for fainthearted nations to shun a courageous course. This reasoning came to the fore conspicuously in 1931, when the Japanese warlords might have been stopped in Manchuria, and again in 1935, when Italy's Mussolini might have been halted in Ethiopia.

But to say the League was hamstrung from the start by the nonadherence of the United States is not to say that a League fully backed by Washington would have averted World War II. The later history of the United Nations, operating under the shadow of nuclear incineration, does not give completely reassuring support to such a thesis. If the members of the old League had acted resolutely and in harmony, they might have checked the rising tide of aggression. But working at cross-purposes, fearing to make a false step, and distrusting America's reaction, they permitted the League to die.

WERE THE REPUBLICAN 1920s ISOLATIONIST?

A myth has developed that because the United States turned its back on Europe, it was neither interested in nor involved with affairs across the Atlantic.

But the League of Nations and its agencies were too important to ignore, even though fourteen of its early communications to the State Department, partly through inadvertence, remained unanswered temporarily. Washington kept itself informed by unofficial observers in Geneva, the site of the League, and by 1930 had participated in more than forty League conferences. These were presumably all nonpolitical, relating to such problems as the control of opium and obscene publications. By 1931 the United States had five permanent officials stationed in Geneva, all authorized to represent American interests as they related to the League.

In 1926 the Senate voted 76 to 17, on President Harding's recommendation, to join the judicial arm of the League known as the World Court. But the traditionally suspicious Senators attached five reservations, one of which proved unacceptable to the other nations.

[3] This actually happened in relation to Italy when the League imposed limited sanctions. H. B. Braddock, "A New Look at American Policy during the Italian–Ethiopian Crisis, 1935–1936," *Jour. of Mod. Hist., XXXIV* (1962), 64–73.

In the end the United States never joined, although American internationalists made a final effort in 1935.

Even if America had been isolated from Europe politically, it certainly was not economically.[4] During the 1920s Wall Street bankers invested hundreds of millions of dollars in Europe, conspicuously in Germany. Much of this money was used to build new factories which, ironically, were later employed to manufacture Hitler's sinews of war. The United States also contributed unofficially to a lightening of Germany's reparations burden through the Dawes Plan (1924) and the Young Plan (1929).

Economic involvements are among the deepest. A factory that is built with American money in Germany cannot easily be withdrawn, although an army of occupation can be, as one was in 1923.

WAS THE U. S. RESPONSIBLE FOR FRENCH INSECURITY?

France had been invaded by the Germans thrice within a century, with the 1914 invasion being the most devastating of all. She had lost about a million and a half men, to say nothing of the crippled. Shell-shocked, fearful, and vengeful, she was determined that the Germanic invader should not come again. (He was to come again in 1939.)

French security was to have been insured by the treaties of guarantee signed in France by Wilson and Lloyd George in 1919 — instruments which committed the Americans and British to come to the aid of France if again attacked by the German aggressor. The United States Senate refused to act on this pact, with the result that the British were automatically released from their obligations.[5]

The French were also to be protected by collective security under the League of Nations. When the United States declined to join the League, thereby weakening that organization, France felt even more naked before her old enemy.

Abandoned by America and Britain, and left to their own devices, the French decided that they would have to provide for their own security. They consequently embarked upon a rearmament program which gave them, until at least the mid-1930s, the strongest army in

---

[4] The theme of economic involvement is developed more fully in William A. Williams, "The Legend of Isolationism in the 1920s," *Science and Society*, XVIII (1954), 1–20. For evidence that the author carries his thesis too far, see R. J. Maddox, "Another Look at the Legend of Isolationism in the 1920's," *Mid-America*, LIII (1971), 35–43.

[5] See L. A. R. Yates, *The United States and French Security, 1917–1921* (1957).

Western Europe. France's unwillingness to limit armaments on land made impossible any satisfactory international progress in that direction, and her continued maintenance of a powerful military establishment did much to provoke the Germans. Hitler finally threw off the shackles of the Treaty of Versailles in the 1930s and rearmed.

One must be careful not to blame Uncle Sam for all of Europe's woes, but America's contribution to French fears was substantial. It had a direct relation to the failure of arms limitation in the 1920s and 1930s, and ultimately to the emergence of a rampageous Hitler.

WHO DESERVES CREDIT FOR THE WASHINGTON CONFERENCE?

Harding's administration has often been praised for a monumental achievement in staging the Conference on Limitation of Armament — known in popular shorthand as the Washington Disarmament Conference. This latter designation was misleading. No great nation was then seriously interested in disarming itself completely; the main purpose of the conclave was to *limit* arms in various categories, on land as well as on sea. When statesmen spoke of *disarmament* in the 1920s and 1930s, they almost invariably meant arms *limitation*.

Harding had relatively little to do with summoning the Conference. The primary initiative was taken by Senator Borah of Idaho, one of the "irreconcilables" unalterably opposed to the Treaty of Versailles, with its built-in League of Nations. The President was more or less prodded into issuing the invitations, and he acted partly to head off the British, who evidently were preparing to make the first move. Harding ostensibly had only a small hand in the Conference itself, aside from ceremonial speeches. But he did give Secretary Hughes close and constant support, and he did help to shepherd the resulting treaties through the Senate.

Dominant among the Americans at the Conference was Secretary of State Hughes. Harding had named him to his Cabinet, along with Secretary of Commerce Hoover, in the teeth of considerable opposition to both nominees from the Senate oligarchy. During the 1920 campaign Harding, clearly conceding that he was no intellectual giant, had promised to add to his Cabinet the "best minds." He delivered when he named Hughes and Hoover.[6] But regrettably these were offset by two designing

[6] Hughes and Hoover had signed the statement of the "Illustrious Thirty-One" during the campaign of 1920, certifying that the election of Harding would promote entrance into the League. Both men were heavily criticized for not raising a row in

minds: Secretary of the Interior Fall (a popular appointment) and Attorney General Daugherty.

DID THE WASHINGTON
"DISARMAMENT" CONFERENCE DISARM?

Originally the plan was to reduce armies as well as navies at Washington, but the French, with their understandable security psychosis, interposed an insuperable roadblock. They logically argued that security
would have to precede disarmament, not vice versa.[7]

All hopes of limiting smaller craft such as submarines ran afoul
of French fears. In concentrating on land defense against Germany,
France had allowed her navy to fall behind. Although the Allies had
suffered grievously from German U-boats during the recent war, the
French wanted no restrictions on submersibles, largely because of their
African colonies. Submarines were the poor nation's weapon, and the
French, in the event of a future war with Germany, would want to use
them to help convoy black troops from Africa across the Mediterranean
to fight for France.

The most significant naval restrictions that the conferees could
agree on at Washington related to capital ships: battleships and battle
cruisers.[8] As events turned out, the three leading naval powers —
America, Britain, and Japan — consented to destroy scores of large
vessels, built or being built, thus leaving their capital ship strength in
the ratio of 5-5-3, with tiny Japan on the small end of the ratio. France

---

the Cabinet and holding Harding to this commitment. But the election results were
generally, if erroneously, interpreted as a mandate against the League; the Senate
"irreconcilables" were menacing watchdogs; and public opinion was increasingly
drifting away from the League, even with reservations. In these circumstances,
Hughes concluded that there was no point in disrupting the administration by
pressing for the seemingly impossible. See Robert K. Murray, *The Harding Era*
(1969), p. 137.

[7] Several fallacies clouded popular judgment in this era. One was that armaments
were the disease, rather than the symptoms of the disease — insecurity. Another
was that a clear distinction could be made between offensive and defensive weapons:
about everything depends on the use to which they are put. Another was that naval
disarmament was largely a matter of arithmetic. Actually, no two nations had precisely the same defensive needs, whether for colonies, lines of communication, home
defense, or whatever. Finally, the belief was common that the second-best navy is
like the second-best hand in a poker game, that is, worthless. Yet smaller fleets have
often been capable of defending local waters or diluting the enemy's naval strength.
Moreover, the second-best hand in a poker game has often taken the "pot" with
successful bluffing. On this general subject in relation to the Washington Conference see Harold and Margaret Sprout, *Toward a New Order of Sea Power* (1940).

[8] As defined at Washington, a capital ship was a warship, not an aircraft carrier,
exceeding 10,000 tons or carrying guns larger than eight inches in caliber.

and Italy each came out with 1.67. There was also to be a ten-year holiday in the construction of unauthorized capital ships, as well as an upper limit on the size of aircraft carriers.

In response to the charge that Uncle Sam scrapped brand new battleships in return for the scrapping of blueprints by the other powers, several facts should be noted.[9] All three leading powers were obligated by the Five Power Naval Treaty to sacrifice not only uncompleted battleships but also battleships in existence. The United States gave up somewhat more tonnage than the others. But it scrapped no newly completed battleships, only old ones, while consenting to junk eleven that were being belatedly built under the Act of 1916. To have completed these would have cost hundreds of millions of dollars; hence the United States gave up only potential supremacy at a time when the taxpayers were evidently unwilling to continue the burden. The hope was that the other powers would follow America's lead, but this they did not do. Thus the folly of "disarmament by example" was painfully impressed upon the American public.

WAS THE WASHINGTON CONFERENCE USELESS?

Disappointing progress toward arms limitation at Washington gave the work of the conferees a blacker eye than it deserves. Although no limit was placed on armies or smaller naval craft, substantial limitations were imposed on the bigger and costlier ships. These restrictions not only took much of the fever out of the dangerous arms race but saved the taxpayers in five countries enormous sums of money.

The United States, evidently regarding naval limitation as an accomplished fact, failed to build up in the unrestricted categories. Meanwhile, the other nations opened up a lively race in submarines, cruisers, destroyers, and other noncapital ships. What they were doing was no secret, and if Uncle Sam refused to build up allowable strength, he had only himself to blame, not the Washington Conference.

Paradoxically, the greatest success of the so-called disarmament conference probably lay in areas other than arms limitation. Mounting tensions between Japan and America were greatly eased by two important diplomatic understandings in Washington. One was the Four

---

[9] The illusory results of conclaves such as the Washington Conference inspired the humorist Will Rogers to remark, "The United States never lost a war or won a conference." America did not win the War of 1812, the Korean War, or the Vietnam War, and she has done remarkably well in a considerable number of international conferences.

Power Treaty of 1922, involving the United States, Britain, Japan, and France. It provided a vague substitute for the existing Anglo–Japanese Alliance, which many Americans regarded as an intolerable pistol aimed at them. The new pact weakly called upon the four powers to consult together "as to the most efficient measures" when their interests in the Pacific were threatened. The Nine Power Treaty of 1922, for the first time in a formal multination agreement, affirmed the principles of the Open Door for China.[10]

This general diplomatic air-clearing in the Pacific and in East Asia may have helped to postpone war with Japan for about twenty years.

WAS TEAPOT DOME AN INDEFENSIBLE TRANSACTION?

Such is the perversity of human nature that Harding's administration, like Grant's, is perhaps best remembered for its postwar scandals. The newspaper press and muckraking books made so much capital of these revelations that the President's name was permanently tarnished. Before the dirt settled, his former Secretary of the Interior (Fall) was jailed; his Attorney General (Daugherty) was twice saved by hung juries; several other responsible officials were imprisoned; and a few corrupt harpies committed suicide.

Much of Harding's trouble grew out of ill fortune or faulty judgment in picking associates, especially those of the overpublicized "Ohio Gang." He himself was never directly implicated in any of the financial irregularities uncovered. In the months before he died, the colossal grafting of Colonel Charles R. Forbes, director of the Veterans' Bureau, was revealed — about a quarter of a billion dollars all told — and an angry Harding forced the resignation of this dishonest official in February 1923. The President should have instituted legal prosecution or a Congressional investigation. But reacting like a true politician who feared unfavorable publicity, he tried to sweep the unsavory mess under the rug. Following a Congressional exposé after Harding's death, Forbes was found guilty of defrauding the government and was sentenced to two years in a federal penitentiary.

Further corruption uncovered after Harding's death was even more sensational, and involved the Teapot Dome scandal. Oil reserves for the Navy had been under the control of the Navy Department, but

[10] See T. H. Buckley, *The United States and the Washington Conference, 1921–1922* (1970).

Secretary of the Interior Fall persuaded Secretary of the Navy Denby and President Harding to have them transferred to his jurisdiction. Both Harding and Denby evidently believed they were acting in the national interest. The argument was that private exploiters were sinking wells adjacent to the naval reserves and draining off the oil. Besides, the navy needed refined oil in storage — rather than crude petroleum in the ground — as well as pipelines and fuel tanks in strategic places, especially Pearl Harbor.

Secretary Fall, after secretly receiving some $400,000 from two millionaire oil men, Harry F. Sinclair and Edward L. Doheny, leased to them the precious oil reserves entrusted to his care. Concessions in the Wyoming reserves (popularly called Teapot Dome after a domelike rock) went to Sinclair, and those in the Elk Hill reserves in California to Doheny.

If the financially-pinched Fall had been an honest man, the leases would have had much justification. The enormous oil tanks that Doheny built at Pearl Harbor were of crucial importance in the Pacific war that came with Japan in 1941. But the bribing of Fall brought the whole transaction into disrepute.[11]

After a series of trials, Fall wound up in jail for taking a bribe, while juries failed to convict the two alleged bribe givers, Sinclair and Doheny. Sinclair, having hired agents to "shadow" one of the juries, was charged with contempt of court and sentenced to prison for six months.[12]

DID HARDING DIE OF A BROKEN HEART?

Harding died in a San Francisco hotel, August 2, 1923, while returning from a wearisome transcontinental trip by way of Alaska. Many writers have assumed that he succumbed to a broken heart, knowing that many of his trusted appointees had betrayed him and that he had failed completely as President.

There can be little doubt that Harding was deeply disturbed by the scandals already uncovered, notably Forbes' looting of the Veterans'

[11] Fall had a common Western distaste for preserving natural resources, and one scholar concludes that his "leasing policy was not simply a response to bribery." If it had been, he probably could have secured $2,000,000 instead of $400,000. Burl Noggle, Teapot Dome: Oil and Politics in the 1920's (1962), p. 213.

[12] Sinclair also drew a fine of $1,000 and a sentence of three months in prison for contempt of the Senate in refusing to answer questions. All told, he remained in jail for six and one-half months, thus giving the lie to the saying that one cannot put a million dollars in jail. The New York Times, Nov. 11, 1956, 1:3.

Bureau, and by other evidence of irregularities. Fortunately for his peace of mind, he was spared Teapot Dome and the other nests of iniquities. Yet current worries unquestionably imposed an additional strain on him, although a "broken heart" is a rather meaningless term.

Actually, Harding was not a well man when he left Washington for Alaska and points south.[13] He was much overweight; his blood pressure was high; and he had been suffering for some time from a heart condition. Returning to San Francisco, he took to his bed, contracted pneumonia, and evidently died of apoplexy. At least this is what his five reputable physicians reported.

Human nature responds avidly to conspiratorial theories, and the rumor gained ground that Harding was deliberately poisoned, perhaps by a jealous wife who knew of his various infidelities.[14] There is no credible evidence to support such a theory.

HAS HARDING BEEN UNJUSTLY MALIGNED?

Upon winning the presidential nomination against great odds, Harding was regarded as supremely lucky. He would have been a happier, healthier, and more reputable man if he had never reached for the coveted prize. The only one of the three Republican Presidents of the "Roaring Twenties" to be accounted genuinely lucky was Calvin Coolidge, who came in at the right time and left shortly before the Great Depression descended.

Harding was tainted by the scandals that erupted during his lifetime and smeared by those that gushed forth after his death, notably Teapot Dome. The Democratic investigators in Congress had a field day in exposing the misdeeds of Harding's Republican associates, so much so, in fact, that the public wearied of sensation. In some quarters the prosecutors were more condemned than the prosecuted.

Especially damaging to Harding was the conduct of his Attorney General and political mentor, Harry M. Daugherty, the small-town lawyer from Ohio. The conduct of his office fell under suspicion before Harding's death. In two subsequent trials for financial irregularities,

---

[13] Ironically, the broken Woodrow Wilson not only outlived the seemingly robust Harding by six months but attended his funeral services.

[14] An early medical report stated that Harding's digestive upset, which may have been a heart attack, was caused by eating some tainted crab meat. This probably stirred up the rumors of deliberate poisoning. The thoroughly unreliable Gaston Means, in The Strange Death of President Harding (1930), intimates that a vengeful Mrs. Harding poisoned her husband and points to the numerous deaths about this time, probably coincidental, of persons in the Harding family or close to Harding.

Daugherty refused to take the stand and testify on the grounds that as a lawyer he had privileged information which presumably would incriminate Harding. This successful attempt to hide behind the shroud of an old friend and a deceased President shocked the nation. The former Attorney General was finally let off when two juries failed to agree, and he could boast that "No charge against me was ever proved in any court." [15] One reason was that some of the key evidence had been conveniently destroyed, presumably with Daugherty's knowledge or connivance.

A handsome, 46-columned memorial to Harding was completed in Marion, Ohio in 1927, but no prominent official could be persuaded to dedicate it. President Coolidge — "Cautious Cal" — warily sidestepped this assignment. Rather belatedly, President Hoover journeyed to Marion in June 1931 for the dedication, and there tastelessly touched on the Harding scandals by observing that the President had been betrayed by crooked friends and associates.

In 1927 Miss Nan Britton, a young woman from Marion, Ohio, published a scandalous book, *The President's Daughter*. She alleged that Harding, then a U. S. Senator, had begotten her baby in 1919 during a prolonged liaison which had lasted even into the presidency. She was unable to prove a paternity case because, she claimed, she had burned all of Harding's love letters to her. Yet many observers were convinced that her tale was essentially true. [16]

In 1964 a packet of some two hundred letters, all indisputably in Harding's handwriting, turned up among the effects of a deceased widow in Marion, Ohio. They provide irrefutable evidence of the future President's infidelity. The lady in question, Mrs. Carrie Phillips, was the beautiful wife of one of Harding's fellow townsmen and friends, and the illicit affair ran its amorous course from 1910 to 1920. [17]

One of the worst smudges on Harding's reputation was the widely heralded story that his wife had burned all his papers. Suspicious souls concluded that there was much more scandal to be hidden. For reasons not known, Mrs. Harding evidently destroyed some material,

---

[15] Harry M. Daugherty, *The Inside Story of the Harding Tragedy* (1932), p. 3. The allegation that Harding was a creature of Daugherty rather than vice versa will not stand scrutiny, although Daugherty did play an important role in the preconvention campaign of 1920.

[16] Another book that blackened the President's reputation was Gaston Means's *The Strange Death of President Harding* (1930). Although enjoying an enormous sale, it was the ghost-written work of a man who was a swindler, a perjurer, and an ex-convict.

[17] Harding's heirs successfully brought suit to prevent the publication of these letters, and agreement was reached in 1971 that they would be sealed until the year 2014. *The New York Times*, Dec. 31, 1971.

perhaps trivia, but the great body of the papers remained intact, kept in the possession of the Harding Memorial Association. In 1964 the entire collection of some 350,000 items was turned over to the Ohio Historical Society for the use of scholars. Harding's reputation would have been better served if the custodians of these manuscripts had not kept them under lock and key for some forty years.[18]

WAS HARDING A COMPLETE FAILURE AS PRESIDENT?

Historians have traditionally given Harding a failing grade. Their views have been colored by the financial scandals of his administration, by the snickering charges about his sex life, by his admitted lack of intellectual sophistication, and by the conservative and isolationist bent of his administration. Any fair evaluation has also been clouded by the writings of jaundiced journalists and others who, lacking the Harding papers, based their accounts largely on rumor, legend, inference, and newspaper headlines. Many of these writers merely copied lurid tales from one another.

As for the "woman scrapes," the only documented one occurred before Harding became President. The unprovable one involving Miss Nan Britton evidently terminated before he became President, or shortly thereafter. In any event, these affairs did not have any demonstrable relation to his effectiveness in office.[19]

Harding was not a big enough man for the presidency — few if any men are — and he not only was aware of his shortcomings but was often acutely unhappy about being out of his depth. Much of his trouble, like that of some other Presidents, came from untrustworthy appointees whom he trusted. Yet his administration ended the war, negotiated treaties with the defeated foe, and carried through a difficult era of reconstruction, including overcoming a depression. Harding was not under the thumb of the Senate. He did not attempt to take America into the League of Nations — indeed, he had opposed it in his electoral campaign — yet he made some significant moves in the direction of disarmament and international cooperation, notably the Washington Con-

[18] For detailed information about the Harding Papers see the parallel articles by Kenneth W. Duckett and Francis Russell, "The Harding Papers," *American Heritage,* XVI (Feb. 1965), 24–31, *et passim.* The first author deals with the papers generally; the second with the letters to Mrs. Carrie Phillips.

[19] The tongue of scandal has connected other Presidents with sexual irregularities, including Jefferson, Jackson, and particularly Cleveland, who in effect admitted siring an illegitimate child while a bachelor. Mrs. Longworth wrote: "Harding was not a bad man. He was just a slob." Alice Roosevelt Longworth, *Crowded Hours* (1933), p. 325.

ference. (If the taxpayers were unwilling to build up to authorized naval strength, that was not his fault.) He did successfully urge the Senate to vote accession to the World Court, and this recommendation took considerable courage, even though Senate reservations ultimately killed adherence. He probably went as far in cooperating with the League of Nations as an isolationist public opinion and the Senate "irreconcilables" would permit. He markedly improved relations with Latin America, and in this respect became one of the godfathers of the future Good Neighbor Policy.[20] His administration refused to recognize the Soviet Union, although sending extensive famine relief in 1921–1923; yet nonrecognition had been inaugurated under Wilson and was continued under Coolidge and Hoover.

As time went on, Harding developed more confidence and worked harder at his desk than most predecessors. Since his mind did not operate with lightning speed, he conscientiously overburdened himself with excessive detail. But at the end he thought he was doing a fairly good job. He had insisted on the high-quality appointments of Hoover and Hughes to his Cabinet (despite considerable opposition in the Senate). His administration, under multimillionaire Secretary of the Treasury Mellon, substantially liquidated the financial burdens of the war and took significant steps toward collecting the huge Allied war debts.[21] Under Harding the national debt was dramatically reduced, as it was to be every year through 1930. Taxes were scaled down (especially for the rich), the Bureau of the Budget was established, and a decade of pulsating prosperity was inaugurated.

Significantly, the legislative output of Congress was substantial. A new emergency immigration law was passed in 1921 to stem the influx from war-torn Europe; a new tariff was enacted in 1922 (Fordney–McCumber), which in many respects was better than the Hawley–Smoot Act to be passed under Hoover in 1930. The humane eight-hour day was substituted for the 12-hour day in the steel industry, largely through Harding's personal intervention. This list could be considerably lengthened, and under any other President would be regarded as praise-

---

[20] In 1921 the Senate approved a treaty granting an indemnity of $25 million to Colombia for the loss of Panama, thereby acknowledging wrongful treatment, and in 1923 Washington recognized the revolutionary government of President Obregón of Mexico, thereby paving the way for a renewal of diplomatic relations.

[21] In February 1922 Congress established the World War Foreign Debt Commission, designed to make arrangements for payment of the Allied war debts, and in June of the following year Great Britain agreed to pay her debt of $4,600,000,000 over sixty-two years at rather heavy 3.3 percent interest. The agreement was the most favorable to the United States of the series of pacts thus negotiated. See H. G. Moulton and Leo Pasvolsky, *War Debts and World Prosperity* (1932).

worthy. But the damning scandals hang over the administration like an oily smudge.

After sifting through the voluminous Harding papers, recent writers have come up with more favorable assessments.[22] They emphasize the point that the Republican policies inaugurated under Harding, both domestic and international, were carried forward under Coolidge and Hoover in the golden 1920s. In his lifetime Harding was one of the most popular of Presidents, and his death elicited an awesome outpouring of grief. His renomination and reelection were widely regarded as foregone conclusions. If he had lived and had cleaned house, posterity would think much better of the affable Ohioan.

ADDITIONAL GENERAL REFERENCES

John D. Hicks, *Republican Ascendancy, 1921–1933* (1960); W. E. Leuchtenburg, *The Perils of Prosperity, 1914–1932* (1958); P. W. Slosson, *The Great Crusade and After, 1914–1928* (1930); H. U. Faulkner, *From Versailles to the New Deal* (1950); F. L. Allen, *Only Yesterday* (1931); Thomas H. Buckley, *The United States and the Washington Conference, 1921–1922* (1970); J. C. Vinson, *The Parchment Peace* (1956); Merze Tate, *The United States and Armaments* (1948); Burl Noggle, *Teapot Dome: Oil and Politics in the 1920's* (1962); J. L. Bates, *The Origins of Teapot Dome* (1963); Andrew Sinclair, *The Available Man* [Harding] (1965); Francis Russell, *The Shadow of Blooming Grove* [Harding] (1968); R. K. Murray, *The Harding Era* (1969); Randolph C. Downes, *The Rise of Warren Gamaliel Harding, 1865–1920* (1970); G. H. Soule, *Prosperity Decade, 1917–1929* (1947).

[22] See Andrew Sinclair, *The Available Man* (1965), and especially the more scholarly Robert K. Murray, *The Harding Era* (1969). Much less favorable is Francis Russell, *The Shadow of Blooming Grove: Warren G. Harding in His Times* (1968). Harding was born in Blooming Grove, Ohio, and the shadow was the rumor of his alleged Negro ancestry.

31

Coolidge and Pseudoprosperity

Upon the unexpected death of Harding, in August 1923, Vice President Calvin Coolidge shouldered the presidential burden. The supposedly closemouthed New Englander, after belatedly cleaning up the scandalous mess inherited from his predecessor, basked in the continuing prosperity of the "Roaring Twenties." Catching the popular fancy, he was overwhelmingly elected in his own right to a full term in 1924.

As the prototype of a hardheaded businessman, Coolidge made a persistent but only temporarily successful effort to collect some of the war-loan money owed by the European debtors. Although he continued to shun the League of Nations officially, he cautiously recommended adherence to the World Court, supported the Kellogg–Briand pact outlawing war, and improved dangerously embittered relations with both Nicaragua and Mexico.

A clever yet unobtrusive politician, Coolidge came to be regarded as both the symbol and guardian of prosperity. He probably could have been reelected in 1928 if he had not enigmatically eliminated himself from the presidential sweepstakes. The Great Depression that descended shortly after he left office ultimately dampened the esteem in which he had been held. Yet seldom in American experience have the President and his times chimed together so harmoniously.

WAS COOLIDGE A STRONG, SILENT PRESIDENT?

If Coolidge had any one asset that stood out from the others, it probably was good luck. A shrewd hack politician who kept his hand shyly but firmly on the rail of the political escalator, he had risen gradually from low office to the governorship of Massachusetts. He managed to get off a ringing declaration after the Boston police strike was broken, and this fortunate stroke overnight made him a national figure and subsequently the Republican Vice President. Luck next brought Coolidge to the presidential chair when Harding died on August 2, 1923.[1]

The prosperity that revived in 1922 under Harding continued unbroken during the Coolidge years, except conspicuously for the farmers, and the tight-fisted President became a highly popular figure. As the son of a small storekeeper, he had absorbed the viewpoint of businessmen and was highly regarded by them. "The business of America is business," he sententiously declared in 1925.

Coolidge's philosophy was to avoid trouble by ducking the "big problems": *laissez-faire* and *status quo* were his twin idols.[2] This idolatry may explain in part why he was so notoriously laggard in cleaning house after the Harding scandals; he delayed about six months before authorizing an investigation of the malodorous Teapot Dome scandal.

The pinch-faced but popular Coolidge could easily have been reelected in 1928, but when he chose not to run, Herbert Hoover was nominated instead. "Coolidge luck" held to the end; the Vermonter left office in March 1929, seven months before the crash struck Wall Street, inaugurating the Great Depression. Coolidge had not discouraged the orgy of speculation; rather he had encouraged it. He may not have glimpsed what was coming, but he was doubtless shrewd enough to realize that prosperity had never been permanent.

Coolidge was not a strong presidential leader. Congress ignored many of his recommendations, rejected two of his major appointments, passed into law unpalatable tax and immigration bills, and overrode his veto of the soldiers' bonus bill. Yet three of his major vetoes stood.

---

[1] The Coolidge image of simplicity was greatly enhanced when the new President took the oath of office at 2:47 a.m. in a Vermont farmhouse by the light of an oil lamp. He was then visiting his father, a notary public, who officiated. Advised by the Attorney General that the first ceremony was probably illegal because the father was not a federal official, Coolidge privately retook the oath in Washington at the hands of a federal judge. Donald R. McCoy, *Calvin Coolidge* (1967), pp. 148–151.

[2] In 1924 Coolidge told a press conference: "A great many times if you let a situation alone it takes care of itself. I mean that if I let this situation alone somebody may take care of it better than I can." Howard H. Quint and Robert H. Ferrell, eds., *The Talkative President* (1964), p. 9.

Nor was Coolidge always close-mouthed, the "Silent Cal" tradition to the contrary. He could be embarrassingly, even boorishly, uncommunicative at White House dinners and other state occasions. But in private he flashed considerable dry Yankee wit and at times was positively voluble. A subtle master of self-advertising, he gave the press an extraordinary number of interviews, which in themselves belie his alleged taciturnity.[3] Radio was coming into its own, and his platitudinous pronouncements, delivered in a Yankee nasal twang, were probably heard by more Americans than the remarks of any previous President.

Coolidge was what Americans have come to prize as a "character." As a sober antidote to the "flapperized" 1920s, he appealed to many older voters with his nineteenth century virtues of honesty, thrift, conscientiousness, and morality. The dour, pinchpenny Vermonter may not have been strong and silent, but "Cautious Cal" he certainly was.[4]

WAS THE ELECTION OF 1924 A VOTE FOR GRAFT?

When the Teapot Dome scandal burst, the Democrats were in high fettle; they were certain they could oust the G.O.P. in 1924. But unhappily for their fortunes, a large number of leading Democrats became enmeshed in the oily mess. Doheny, the oil-man briber, was a prominent California Democrat. He testified under oath that he had employed four ex-members of Wilson's Cabinet, including the able lawyer and former Secretary of the Treasury, William G. McAdoo, Woodrow Wilson's son-in-law. Doheny also revealed that he had paid McAdoo $50,000 a year for a total of $150,000. The recipient of this sum was a leading candidate for the Democratic nomination, and his connection with the oil scandals, though probably only indirect, hurt him politically. Teapot Dome was a prime factor in McAdoo's convention deadlock with Governor Alfred E. Smith during the Madison Square Garden meeting in 1924 that ran to an unprecedented 103 ballots.

[3] Coolidge held scantily attended bi-weekly press conferences, but many more than any of his predecessors. The newsmen were required to submit questions in advance, and Coolidgean caution further prescribed that the answers could be attributed only to "the White House Spokesman." About one-sixth of the stenographic transcripts have been published in book form by Howard H. Quint and Robert H. Ferrell, who find him "almost garrulous" on occasion. He appears to have been reasonably well informed about what was going on and determined to mind his own business. Although no isolationist, he had no desire to travel abroad, because there were so many places in the United States he had never seen. See Quint and Ferrell, eds., *The Talkative President*, pp. 19, 253.

[4] Mrs. Alice Roosevelt Longworth denies having originated the quip that Coolidge looked as if he had been "weaned on a pickle," but she enjoyed repeating it. *Crowded Hours* (1933), p. 337.

Instead of McAdoo, who might have defeated Coolidge, the exhausted convention turned to a less appealing candidate, John W. Davis. This compromise choice was a conservative Wall Street lawyer whose legal connections suggested involvement with big oil companies. Teapot Dome may have actually aided Coolidge by helping to eliminate a formidable Democratic rival, McAdoo, and enabling the closelipped President to shine more brightly as a Puritan in a corrupt era.

A third party Progressive group,[5] with Senator Robert M. La Follette as its presidential candidate, hammered vigorously on the Harding scandals. It certainly drew some strength away from both Democrats and Republicans, but not enough to jeopardize Coolidge's lead. Actually, the Teapot Dome transaction in itself was hardly a debatable subject in 1924: neither Republicans, Democrats, nor Progressives favored it. Corruption in government was much discussed, but the Republicans pointed with pride to Coolidge's (belated) housecleaning.

If the Republicans had defended Teapot Dome, one might argue that they had received something of a mandate to go on stealing. But since both Democrats and Republicans were tarred with the same oily brush, the so-called issue was badly blurred, and the masses had become weary of the whole mess. Nor can one claim with certainty that corruption was the leading concern of the voters.[6] Such issues as prohibition, farm relief, taxation, and foreign policy also demanded attention. If anything, Coolidge's lopsided election was probably a vote for continued prosperity, which benefited Republicans, Democrats, and Progressives.

WERE THE ALLIED WAR DEBTS VALID DEBTS?

The Republican 1920s were more or less an entity with regard to foreign relations, and Coolidge carried on unbroken the general policies of his predecessor (and his successor). Among his most vexing problems were the Allied war debts. Congress in 1922 had established the World War Foreign Debt Commission for collecting them, and in 1923 Great Britain, the chief debtor, had been induced to come to terms. The Coolidge administration was left to deal with most of the other borrowers.

During the fighting phase of the recent war, Washington had advanced to 10 of its Associates over $7 billion. The overwhelming percentage of this sum, principally in credits, was expended in the United

---

[5] Officially known as the Conference for Progressive Political Action.

[6] See J. L. Bates, "The Teapot Dome Scandal and the Election of 1924," *Amer. Hist. Rev.*, LX (1955), 303–322; Burl Noggle, *Teapot Dome: Oil and Politics in the 1920's* (1962), Ch. 8.

States, primarily for military supplies that were consumed in the common cause. Each of the Allies provided what it could. Cuba, for example, supplied sugar, Liberia rubber, and the United States credit dollars, while hastily raising an army.[7]

Many misinformed Americans believed that the Treasury had shipped billions of gold dollars overseas to the Allies. Actually, little gold had left the country. When in later years Americans demanded that their dollars be "sent back," they were asking for hard money that the debtors had never seen. Certainly few citizens were asking for the return of what had actually been shipped: such items as motheaten blankets, spent cartridge cases, and other consumed or damaged materiel.

War loans — as contrasted with much of the $3 billion in post-Armistice grants for restoration and rehabilitation — were not productive loans in the ordinary sense. A banker lends money to a manufacturer who builds a factory in the expectation of repaying his obligation from profits. As far as the Allies were concerned, the war-spawned loans were a dead horse.

WERE THE WAR DEBTS ALL ALLIED DEBTS?

The total sum involved in the so-called war debts was over $10 billion, yet of this figure somewhat less than one-third was loaned after the Armistice of November 1918, principally in the form of commercial credits and nonmilitary supplies. America's clash with the Central Powers did not technically end until formal terms of peace were concluded in 1921, but for all practical purposes the post-Armistice figure was a peace debt rather than a true war debt.

Ten of the foreign borrowers were America's ex-Allies or Associates, but somewhat less than $400 million, or about 4 percent of the total sum of $10.3 billion, went to nations that were not technically Allies at all. Hence the generic term *Allied* war debt is misleading. Relatively small sums were advanced to four small countries carved out of former Russian territory: Estonia, Latvia, Lithuania, and Finland. A larger amount was lent to six nations erected from former enemy territory: Poland, Czechoslovakia, Yugoslavia, Austria, Armenia, and Hun-

---

[7] Some Europeans argued that if the Americans had entered the war when they should have, say 1915, it would have ended sooner and the Republic would have saved more money than it loaned to the Allies. This argument was given additional force when many Americans conceded during the conflict that the cause was so righteous that they should have become involved from an early date. Some Americans even declared that the credit dollars should be provided as gifts, not loans.

gary. All of these six new states had been created out of areas formerly held by Germany or by Germany's allies, Austria–Hungary and Turkey.

The Finnish war debt was a special case. Oppressed Finland had torn herself away from Russia, and in so doing had become associated to a considerable degree with the German cause (as she was again to be in 1941–1944). Her "war debt" to America was strictly a post-Armistice commercial loan and it was relatively tiny: $8.2 million as compared to $4.2 billion for Britain, the heaviest debtor. Finland was the first nation to come to terms, in 1923. The frugal and energetic Finns won great acclaim in the United States for continuing to pay their installments in the 1930s, after the other (and much greater) obligations of the principal European debtors had fallen into default in the depression-cursed 1930s. Finland was able to continue payments largely by husbanding her dollar exchange, and this objective she attained by selling goods to America and cutting down on purchases from America. Hence payments on the Finnish debt were substantially paid for by American manufacturers out of lost profits. Most citizens were not aware of this circumstance; hence "Brave Little Finland" was extravagantly praised for "showing up" the "welshing" former Allies.[8]

WOULD CANCELLATION OF WAR DEBTS HAVE BEEN WISE?

Cancelling the debts was certainly feasible economically because the United States did not get the bulk of the money back and obviously never will. But politically such a course was impossible, primarily because a host of voters strongly opposed it. Anyone understanding elementary economics could reason that if the borrowers did not remit their obligation to the Treasury, the American taxpayer would be asked to foot the bill.[9] Politicians repeatedly argued that if the debtors did not pay up, faith in international borrowing would be destroyed. Would the Americans be naive enough to advance more credits in future conflicts? [10]

After World War I ended, Great Britain, which had loaned large

---

[8] Finland kept up her payments regularly until 1941–1945, when she became involved in war with both Russia and Germany. Congress thereupon granted postponement. Payments began again on January 1, 1945, and have continued since then toward the sixty-two-year goal.

[9] When the debts were finally adjusted, the interest rates ranged from 3.3 percent to 0.3 percent, while Washington was paying its citizens 4.25 percent interest on the Liberty Bonds that had raised much of the money.

[10] Congress in 1934 passed the Johnson Act forbidding any person or private corporation from lending money to a government that was in default to the United States.

sums to the French, herself proposed an around-the-boards cancellation
of debts. As an exporting nation, she had done this at the end of the
Napoleonic wars on the sound principle that prosperous customers were
preferable to impoverished debtors. Such a course in 1919 would probably have lightened the reparations burden on Germany, eased the tax
load of impoverished countries, revived home economies and international trade, and reduced the animosity that the debtor always feels
toward the hard-fisted creditor.

The French, who had been bled white of manpower, were especially bitter about repayment. But they and other debtors were finally
forced to come to terms, particularly after the State Department frowned
on loans by American bankers to delinquent countries. The French
employed strong arguments. They had sacrificed tens of thousands of
men in holding back the German hordes while the Americans were slowly
raising and readying an army. America provided money; France provided
men. The French were not asking for their blood back, and neither, they
felt, should the Americans ask for their dollars back. Besides, the credits
that France spent in the United States had enriched America's economy,
caused war industries to reap immense profits, and enabled the Treasury
partially to repay itself through high income taxes and excess profits
taxes. So ran the French argument.

There were only three effective ways by which the money could
be paid back: in gold, in goods, or in services, such as shipping and
tourism. The debtors could not easily spare the necessary amounts of
gold: what they had was generally needed, so they claimed, to protect
their own currencies. They hoped to sell goods to America to build up
dollar balances, but they were handicapped by the tariff barriers hastily
erected by Congress in 1921 and further increased in 1922 and 1930.
Moreover services, such as shipping, could not provide nearly enough
money, even though tourists were often gouged.

When the Europeans complained that they could not remit because of the difficulties interposed, the American taxpayers responded
by saying in effect, "Pay anyhow." President Coolidge, with his corner-
grocery-store philosophy, reportedly complained, "They hired the money,
didn't they?" Although this statement cannot be documented, it not
only is in character but squares with Coolidge's deep concern for reducing the national debt and keeping a balanced budget.[11]

As time passed, America became increasingly critical of her
debtors. Prohibitionists insisted that these wicked foreigners wasted too
much money on alcohol that should have gone into repayment. Europe's

---

[11] See Quint and Ferrell, eds., *The Talkative President*, pp. 102, 176.

heavy expenditures for armaments also came under increasing fire, especially loans by France to satellite nations for arms. But the French felt insecure, largely because the United States had "welshed" on its moral commitment to the abortive Security Treaty and the League of Nations. No municipality will ever disband its police force and fire department to pay off its bonded indebtedness.

DID THE U. S. CANCEL ANY ALLIED WAR DEBTS?

Between 1923 and 1929 most of the debtors came to terms with Washington and arranged for their payments in installments, principal and interest. Bolshevik Russia openly repudiated the obligation incurred during the "capitalistic" war, but her debt of $192 million was relatively small, though fifth in size on the list.

The loans had originally been made with the understanding that they would bear interest at 5 percent, then the common rate. This figure was plainly too high, and in every case the terms were negotiated downward, largely on the basis of presumed capacity to pay. The highest percentage was 3.3, agreed to by five debtors, including heavily obligated Great Britain. The largest concession to a major nation was to Italy, 0.4 percent.

In no case did Washington consent to a reduction of the principal, but it did spread the repayments out over sixty-two years (Austria excepted). This arrangement meant a burden on two generations, one unborn. Would they be willing to pay for the follies of their fathers? The total interest payments, if made, would more than double the original obligation.

Yet in a significant sense the United States did cancel about half of all the debts that were renegotiated.[12] By figuring on the basis of the 5 percent interest originally current, and spreading the payments of principal and interest over sixty-two years, France, the second largest debtor, received a forgiveness of 60.3 percent. Italy, the third largest, was granted an astonishing 80.2 percent. (The rising Benito Mussolini had many admirers in the United States.) In short, Uncle Sam was not nearly so hard-fisted as a superficial glance would indicate.[13]

[12] See H. G. Moulton and Leo Pasvolsky, *War Debts and World Prosperity* (1932).
[13] Much of America's determination to get the money back was rooted in disenchantment with the Allies. They had shown much greed and quarrelsomeness during the peace negotiations at Paris and later. Moreover they had received partial recompense for their losses by transfers of enemy ships, oil-rich mandates, and other benefits.

WERE WAR DEBTS AND REPARATIONS UNRELATED?

The policy consistently pursued by Washington was that, as far as it was concerned, there was no connection whatever between debts and reparations. American officials remained unmoved by suggestions that if the obligations owed to the United States were cancelled, the Allies could scale down the enormous reparation burden imposed on Germany — initially $32 billion, plus mountainous interest. The French and Belgians were counting on indemnification from Germany to pay off their borrowings from Washington. But the American public and government continued to argue that reparations and debts were two separate problems, and that the Europeans would have to work them out without expecting Uncle Sam to be the "sucker." But merely saying that the twain were not connected did not disconnect them.[14]

American private bankers loaned some $2.25 billion to Germany from 1924 to 1931. The ex-Allies paid to the Washington government about $2.60 billion, which represented less than half of Germany's reparations payments to them. In effect, the United States merely transferred funds from Wall Street to the Washington Treasury by way of Europe.

After the Great Depression descended in 1929, loans from Wall Street to Germany dried up; payments of German reparations to the Allies dried up; and remittances of the Allied debtors to Washington dried up. Faced in the early 1930s with oppressive economic problems, some of the European nations sought to avoid outright repudiation by making token payments on their obligation. But Washington insisted that such a practice did not suffice. By the mid-1930s all of the principal debtors had defaulted. Payments were naturally not revived when an even more catastrophic world war engulfed Europe in 1939, and the burdens of the old conflict were eclipsed by those of the new.

On paper the obligation of the debtors, with accrued interest, had mounted from the original $10.3 billion to over $16 billion on the Treasury books by 1970, and was still mounting. When the French President De Gaulle in the late 1960s was putting pressure on the dollar by draining off American gold, voices were raised in America demanding

[14] President Hoover insisted, at least in public, that debts and reparations were unrelated. This is surprising because he had served on the World War Foreign Debt Commission established in 1922, and was fully cognizant of the problem. Moreover in 1925 the United States became *directly* involved when it agreed to accept 55 million gold marks per annum of Germany's reparations to defray the cost of occupying Germany, as well as of other claims. *Foreign Relations of the United States, 1925* (1940), pp. 149–150.

that France pay up. But since all the other debtors (except Finland) were also in arrears, this kind of demand would have been regarded as spitefully discriminatory.

DID AMERICA'S ECONOMIC POLICIES HELP HITLER?

As we have seen, the failure of the United States to ratify the Treaty of Versailles turned it into a harsher peace, which Hitler used as one of his strongest arguments during his meteoric rise to power.

Specifically, the failure of America to approve the treaty and hence exercise a moderating influence on the Reparations Commission led to the imposition on the Germans of an astronomical reparations burden of some $32 billion, plus interest. Already prostrated by a war that had cost them much more than that figure, they recoiled from paying this kind of tribute to the victor. In the end, they remitted only about one-seventh of the original assessment in money, not counting interest. If they had initially received a bill of $8 billion or so, they might have made an honest effort to shoulder the burden.

The French in particular were determined to extort reparations, partly to restore devastated areas and to pay off their debt to Britain and America. When the Germans proved obstinate, France in 1923 moved troops into the Ruhr Valley, the industrial heart of Germany. Berlin's response was to resort to runaway inflation, thus ruining the German middle class, which might have been an effective bulwark against Hitlerism. Hitler himself complained loudly of the tribute drained away by the victors.

Germany's reparations burden was eased substantially by the Dawes Plan (1924) and the Young Plan (1929),[15] but by this time the Great Depression was descending. In 1932 America's debtors met at Lausanne, Switzerland, and agreed to lower the original reparations bill of $32 billion to a modest $714 million, which was virtually cancellation. But the joker was that Uncle Sam would have to consent to a downward revision of the war debts. With consistency worthy of a better cause, the depression-bedeviled Washington government, reflecting public opinion, would have none of this "sucker" scheme. If "Uncle Shylock" would not cancel while his budget was in the black, he certainly would not do so when it was in the red. Faced with the alternatives of cancellation or of simply not getting the money, Washington stood pat and forced a general default.

[15] The Young Plan reduced the original $32 billion to $9 billion, plus $17 billion interest.

It is clear that the war debts were substantially cancelled, first by the reduction in interest by the United States, and second by the refusal of the debtors to pay more than a fraction of the total obligation. With the wisdom of hindsight, an observer can now see that if Washington had consented to an around-the-boards cancellation of war debts proposed by the British, the world (and America) would have been spared a vast amount of frustration, bitterness, and economic dislocation.

Hitler was a child of the Great Depression, to which the nationalistic economic and foreign policies of the United States substantially contributed.

WAS HUGHES TO BLAME FOR JAPANESE EXCLUSION?

Immigration was closely related to the debt-reparations problem, for the United States excluded not only European goods by means of high tariffs but also many impoverished Europeans by means of immigration quotas. In 1924 the emergency immigration law of 1921 was about to expire, and Congress was undertaking to strengthen the old one with more permanent legislation.

Under an exchange of notes with Washington known as the Gentlemen's Agreement, the Tokyo government had bound itself in 1907–1908 to withhold passports from coolies hoping to emigrate to the mainland of the United States. This arrangement on the whole had worked satisfactorily. But Congress was in an anti-Japanese mood, heightened by the demagoguery of certain California members; and it was considering legislation that would flatly exclude all Japanese, while putting most other prospective immigrants on a quota basis.

Secretary of State Hughes was aware of Japan's sensitivity to slights, and he labored to head off offensive discrimination. He finally suggested to Japan's envoy in Washington, Ambassador Hanihara, the desirability of preparing a statement for transmittal to Congress expressing Tokyo's understanding of the Gentlemen's Agreement. The worried envoy, in cooperation with the State Department, responded to Hughes' invitation with a temperate and able survey, which unfortunately added an explosive paragraph. It warned America that denying Japan her proper but tiny annual quota of 146 nationals would result in "grave consequences" — a phrase which, in the understated language of diplomacy, strongly suggested war.[16]

[16] *Papers Relating to the Foreign Relations of the United States, 1924* (1939), II, 369–373.

Secretary Hughes realized that the tactless expression was fraught with trouble. But time was growing short, Congress was about to act, and embarrassments would result from asking Hanihara to re-write his statement. Congress might overlook or discount this one slip in an otherwise friendly note, in which case Hanihara's statement would do more good than harm.[17]

Knowing the outcome, we can now see that the offensive protest should have been returned to Hanihara for revision, or not sent on to Congress at all. Many Congressmen believed or professed to believe that the sovereign United States was being threatened. The result was an angry reaction which blocked all possibility of even the tiniest quota for Japan. The sensitive Japanese were deeply insulted, and their subsequent exclusion had a direct relation to the state of mind that led to the violent assault on Pearl Harbor in 1941.

It seems evident that the ordinarily statesmanlike Hughes blundered in this instance. Perhaps Congress would have flatly excluded the Japanese anyhow, but the Hughes-inspired note of Hanihara had a highly incendiary effect. President Coolidge, who announced that he opposed the abrupt exclusion of all Japanese, considered vetoing the entire bill. But new legislation was urgently needed to slow down the influx from war-torn Europe; besides, the anti-Japanese feeling already generated in Congress was so strong that a veto probably would have been overridden.

DID KELLOGG ORIGINATE THE KELLOGG-BRIAND PACT?

President Coolidge was worried, and the navy men were alarmed, by the race in constructing noncapital ships that had not been restricted by the Washington Conference in 1922. Evidently hoping to duplicate Harding's somewhat hollow triumph, Coolidge rather hastily arranged for a conference of the five leading naval powers at Geneva, Switzerland (1927).

Obviously the Conference was hampered at the start by the refusal of Italy and France to attend. The chief differences arose be-tween Britain and America over the size of large cruisers, while the politely bowing Japanese attempted to serve as mediators. With high-paid lobbying by the arms manufacturers adding to the confusion, the

[17] Details from my interview with Mr. Hughes in May, 1937, and from his autho-rized biography, Merlo J. Pusey, *Charles Evans Hughes* (2 vols., 1951), *II*, 512–516.

Conference broke down in complete futility after six weeks of wrang-ling.[18]

Meanwhile public pressure had built up in the United States for a more direct approach: namely, outlawing wars rather than limiting arms. Secretary of State Kellogg showed scant enthusiasm for a bilateral treaty with France to achieve this end, but he finally yielded to an over-whelming public outcry and developed considerable enthusiasm for a multination approach. On August 27, 1928, the Pact of Paris, popu-larly known as the Kellogg–Briand Pact, was signed by fifteen powers, and ultimately approved by almost all of the remaining nations.

Somewhat inconsistently, the new treaty formally outlawed war as an "instrument of national policy" but permitted defensive warfare. This was a loophole that made a mockery of the whole movement, for there has seldom been a conflict that militarists could not justify as offensive self-defense, including Hitler's attack on Denmark in 1940. One result was that the numerous conflicts fought after hostilities were formally abolished in 1928 became defensive "incidents." The greatest success of the Kellogg–Briand Pact was in outlawing declarations of war rather than outlawing war itself. Such ill-founded hopes as did remain were completely shattered by the coming of World War II in 1939.

But the Kellogg–Briand Pact, which was widely heralded as ushering in the millennium, cast a brighter glow on the prosperous Coolidge administration. The initially reluctant Kellogg, who had been prodded into immortality by an aroused public opinion, was awarded the Nobel Peace Prize in 1929. The hardheaded and practical-minded Coolidge had been skeptical of "outlawry" from the outset.[19]

DID COOLIDGE LAUNCH THE GOOD NEIGHBOR POLICY?

Franklin Roosevelt's widely heralded Good Neighbor Policy had many earlier authors,[20] including his predecessor, President Hoover. The clos-ing years of the Coolidge era, which experienced a dramatic improvement in dealings with Latin America, helped pave the way for the new day.

By 1927 official relations with Nicaragua and Mexico were about

[18] A revelation in 1929 of the activities of W. B. Shearer led to a highly publicized Senate investigation. The charges of Charles A. Beard that the Navy League was effective in promoting naval armament in the 1920s and 1930s are refuted in Armin Rappaport, *The Navy League of the United States* (1962). The League was more active than it was influential.

[19] McCoy, *Calvin Coolidge*, Ch. 34.

[20] For evidence that President Wilson's last Secretary of State substantially im-proved relations with Latin America, see D. M. Smith, "Bainbridge Colby and the Good Neighbor Policy, 1920–1921," *Miss. Valley Hist. Rev.*, L (1963), 56–78.

as embittered as they could be, short of a complete rupture. Coolidge had an army of several thousand Marines in Nicaragua fighting his "private war" in support of a conservative regime. At the same time, tensions with Mexico had almost reached the breaking point, largely because of the expropriation of American-owned oil properties.

Coolidge luck — or was it good judgment? — came to the rescue. In 1927 the President dispatched Colonel Henry L. Stimson, Hoover's future Secretary of State, to troubled Nicaragua. There he was able to arrange for a fair election that was acceptable to the rival parties. Coolidge next had the happy inspiration to send to Mexico his former Amherst College classmate, the wealthy Wall Street banker and amateur diplomat, Dwight W. Morrow. Adopting a friendly and sympathetic approach, he was able to thresh out a series of understandings. To assist him in his public relations he arranged for a good-will visit by the famed aviator, Charles A. Lindbergh, the recent west-to-east solo conqueror of the Atlantic and his future son-in-law.[21] As far as Latin American relations were concerned, the Coolidge administration ended on a relatively high note.

DID SACCO AND VANZETTI RECEIVE A FAIR TRIAL?

In August 1927, late in the Coolidge era, two Italian anarchists, Nicola Sacco (a shoemaker) and Bartolomeo Vanzetti (a fish peddler) were electrocuted by the State of Massachusetts. They paid with their lives for the alleged murder of a paymaster and his guard seven years earlier, in 1920. When arrested, both were carrying revolvers and told numerous lies, but they had none of the holdup money in their possession and neither had a criminal record. The two were tried in 1921 on rather flimsy evidence that connected them with the crime. The jury in Dedham, no doubt influenced by the anti-Red hysteria then convulsing the country, was probably prejudiced against the defendants from the outset. They were aliens, radicals, conscientious objectors in the recent war ("draft dodgers"), ill-educated (they spoke broken English), and relatively friendless. The presiding judge reflected an ultraconservative bias.

The case was soon whipped up into an international scandal, with increasingly violent demonstrations by radicals at home and abroad.

---

[21] Lindbergh was an unusually skilled aviator, not just a stunting "Flying Fool"; he was the first man to fly solo across the Atlantic, New York to Paris. This achievement had occurred in 1927, although as early as June 1919, two men (Alcock and Brown) had flown from Newfoundland to Ireland nonstop. The next month a British dirigible with a crew of 27 flew from Scotland to New York and back.

On appeal, the Supreme Court of Massachusetts upheld the original verdict and denied a new trial. Petitions were then addressed to the governor, who appointed an advisory committee of three prominent conservatives. Although new evidence had come to light, they recommended against clemency, whereupon the execution went forward as scheduled. Sacco and Vanzetti became enshrined as martyrs, not murderers, in the worldwide "class struggle."

Whether the two defendants committed the crime as charged will long be debated. Ballistic evidence made public some three decades later indicated that the revolver found in Sacco's possession was used to murder the guard.[22] But the fairness of the procedures was another issue. Although the necessary legal forms were preserved, there is ample reason to believe that a new trial in a saner atmosphere and under different auspices might have resulted in a lesser penalty, if any penalty at all. Certainly much of the evidence used to secure a conviction was subsequently discredited. America's image would have been improved by a new trial or, at worst, a commutation of the sentences to life imprisonment. Death precluded the possibility of belated justice.

DID COOLIDGE PREFER NOT TO RUN IN 1928?

President Coolidge served out a year and a half of his predecessor's term, plus four years of his own. Would the unfinished stint of Harding count as a whole administration in determining a violation of the two-term tradition? Theodore Roosevelt had so interpreted the unwritten law when he bowed out in 1909. If Coolidge had received a second nomination in his own right, had been elected, and had served out the new term, he would have been President longer than any of his predecessors, nearly ten years.[23]

Prosperity was so potent and Coolidge was so popular that he almost certainly could have won the nomination in 1928 if he had wanted it and had nodded his assent. But evidently in an attempt to quiet speculation, he issued a cryptic statement in August 1927: "I do not choose to run for President in 1928."

Far from ending speculation, Coolidge increased it, and it continues to this day. Did he mean that in no circumstances would he accept the nomination of his party? Or did he mean that, while he did not *wish* to run, he would do so if his party chose to "draft" him? Perhaps a world crisis or some other emergency would cause him to become "an

[22] Francis Russell, *Tragedy in Dedham: The Story of the Sacco–Vanzetti Case* (1962).
[23] The Senate, which contained various rivals for the presidential nomination, reaffirmed the no-third-term tradition on February 10, 1928, by a vote of 56 to 26.

indispensable man." But Coolidge, who seems to have enjoyed the game, kept people guessing. His silence certainly had a practical side, because rivals for the nomination, especially members of the rather uncooperative Congress, would be more deferential as long as the uncertainty was prolonged.[24]

If Coolidge had wanted the nomination, he did not need to issue any kind of statement, negative or positive. Politicians would have assumed that his hat was in the ring. The probabilities are — though the positive evidence one way or the other is scanty — that Coolidge meant what he said in his quaint New England idiom.[25] He probably did not want the burdensome office for four more years. A "draft" would have been a compliment, but it could have been declined, as Theodore Roosevelt declined the nomination of the Progressive party in 1916. The country was still prosperous, and there is much to be said for quitting gracefully while one is ahead. Coolidge's health was not good (he may have suffered a minor heart attack while President); he was greatly saddened by the death of a beloved son; and four more years on the demanding job were not inviting. If he had been elected for a second time, he probably would not have lived out his term, for he died of a heart attack on January 5, 1933, two months short of the constitutional four years.

Coolidge was somewhat like the man who was lucky enough to miss the airplane that crashed. Herbert Hoover received the nomination, overwhelmingly defeated his Democratic opponent, and was in turn overwhelmed by the Great Depression.

DID CATHOLICISM DEFEAT AL SMITH IN 1928?

A tradition long persisted in American politics, until John F. Kennedy won in 1960, that a Catholic could never be elected President. None had ever been, and the immensely popular Democratic vote getter, Governor Al (Alfred E.) Smith of New York, was badly defeated in 1928, presumably because of his Catholicism.

---

[24] A clearer-cut declination than Coolidge's would have been possible. Lyndon Johnson's renunciation of a second elected term on March 31, 1968, left no doubt when he said that he would not "seek" or "accept" a second nomination by his party. General W. T. Sherman sent a famous telegram to the Republican convention in 1884 which has been popularly paraphrased to read, "If nominated, I will not accept; if elected, I will not serve." This has come to be known in politics as a "Sherman statement," or "pulling a Sherman." William Safire, *The New Language of Politics* (1968), p. 397.

[25] The evidence is marshaled pro and con in McCoy, *Calvin Coolidge*, Ch. 35. See also Cyril Clemens and A. P. Daggett, "Coolidge's 'I Do Not Choose to Run': Granite or Putty?" *New England Quar.*, XVIII (1945), 147–163. The joint authors conclude that the renunciation was "genuine."

Actually, Smith's worst handicap was not his Catholicism but his affiliation with the minority party. There simply were not enough Democrats, and even these had been further divided by the convention donnybrook of 1924, with the Southern wing being pro–Ku Klux Klan and pro-prohibition. Moreover Smith was running against a formidable Republican candidate, Herbert Hoover, the beneficiary of Republican prosperity. The "Great Humanitarian" was not only a household word but something of an idol of the masses, though not with the professional politicians, through whose ranks he had never come.

Born on an Iowa farm to a Protestant (Quaker) family, and early orphaned, Hoover worked his way through Stanford University. He then became a fabulously successful mining engineer, fed the Belgians after the German invasion in 1914, headed the Food Administration during the war ("Hooverizing" became a synonym for nonwaste), saved millions of Europeans from starvation after the Armistice, and then served as a brilliantly successful Secretary of Commerce. No living American was more honored or respected abroad, where the "Great Engineer" had lived much of his life. Backing the prohibition of alcohol, as authorized by the 18th Amendment in 1919, he seemed to be the embodiment of sobriety, efficiency, economy, respectability, and continued prosperity.

Al Smith, despite his liberal record as four-time governor of New York, suffered from fatal handicaps. Though of humble background like Hoover, he had not come up in the tradition of the log cabin and farm boy, but from the sidewalks of New York and the Fulton Fish Market. Owing to the early death of his father, he had left school at age fifteen; and educational and cultural polish were somewhat lacking, as the "snob element" was quick to point out. In addition, Smith was of foreign background (both maternal grandparents had been born in Ireland), and his upbringing on asphalt and concrete did not seem quite "grassrootish." The revived KKK, strong in the Solid South, was anti-foreign as well as anti-Negro, and Smith was anti-Klan.

Governor Al ("cohol") Smith was also avowedly and drippingly "wet," and his "rum-soaked" stand on prohibition antagonized not only the "drys" everywhere but the "drys" within his own party, especially in the normally Democratic South.[26] Though reputed to be personally honest, he was a member of the Society of Tammany — the notoriously corrupt Tammany machine. Finally, he was a Roman

[26] After his nomination, Smith sent a sensational telegram to the Houston nominating convention in which he repudiated the somewhat evasive liquor plank in his platform by avowing that he favored modification (rather than outright repeal) of the 18th Amendment and the Volstead Act. He would return liquor control entirely to the state governments and outlaw its consumption in "any public place" (i.e., the saloon).

Catholic in a predominantly Protestant country; and bigots were quick to charge that the Pope would control the White House.[27]

But some of Smith's handicaps helped him as well as hurt him. His sidewalk upbringing endeared him to many urban voters, for he carried the twelve largest cities in the country, many of them normally Republican strongholds. His foreign background appealed to immigrants, while his "wet" stand on prohibition attracted the thirsty, especially among European newcomers in the metropolitan areas. His Catholicism no doubt handicapped him in the Protestant and dry Solid South, for there he lost five ordinarily sure states of the eleven that had seceded in 1860–1861. But his religion evidently helped him in Catholic strongholds such as Massachusetts and Rhode Island, both of which the Democrats had not carried for many years. Smith's Catholicism had obviously not proved fatal when he was four times elected Governor of New York, thrice against Protestant rivals. Yet in the 1928 campaign against Hoover he rather narrowly lost his home state. His enormous metropolitan vote in the North foreshadowed the long-lived coalition under Franklin Roosevelt of the normally Democratic Solid South and the newly won urban North.[28] Previously Democratic strength had concentrated largely in the agrarian South, plus the agrarian West — and in the West the voting population was relatively sparse.

It is impossible to determine whether Catholicism hurt Smith more than it helped him. He might have lost some of the South on the wet–dry and anti-Klan issues alone. Many Southerners rejected him, not because of his religious views, but because the Catholic Church was favorable to the desegregation of Negroes. General prosperity was hard to beat, and it largely explains why Hoover netted an enormous 58.2 ~rcent of the popular vote — a percentage exceeded only three times ⁷972, when Nixon polled over 60 percent.[29]

---

out that the nonfighting tenets of the Quaker faith would ⸺onstitutional capacity as Commander-in-Chief of the armed

⸺d Smith by a margin of 21,430,000 to 15,016,000; yet, as com- ⸺loover won only 5,673,000 more Republican votes, while Smith ⸺00 votes for the once badly-divided Democrats, or a gain over his ⸺ne million. But claims that an "Al Smith Revolution" ushered in ⸺ Revolution" seem to be exaggerated. See J. H. Clubb and H. W. ⸺Cities and the Election of 1928: Partisan Realignment?" *Amer. Hist.* ⸺(1969), 1205–1220.

⸺on in 1964 (61.1), Roosevelt in 1936 (60.8), and Harding in 1920 (60.3). ⸺lemoirs, Hoover acknowledges the potency of prosperity, but blames Smith ⸺ving brought the religious issue "out into the open." Actually the issue had ⸺. brought dramatically into the open at least as early as April and May of 1927, ⸺.en the *Atlantic Monthly* featured an attack by a critical lawyer followed by a ⸺ebuttal from Smith. *The Memoirs of Herbert Hoover: The Cabinet and the Presidency, 1920–1933* (1952), p. 208; Edmund A. Moore, *A Catholic Runs for President* (1956), Ch. III.

ADDITIONAL GENERAL REFERENCES

J. D. Hicks, *Republican Ascendancy, 1921–1933* (1960); W. E. Leuchtenburg, *The Perils of Prosperity, 1914–1932* (1958); H. U. Faulkner, *From Versailles to the New Deal* (1950); P. W. Slosson, *The Great Crusade and After, 1914–1928* (1930); G. H. Soule, *Prosperity Decade, 1917–1929* (1947); F. L. Allen, *Only Yesterday* (1931); D. R. McCoy, *Calvin Coolidge: the Quiet President* (1967); C. M. Fuess, *Calvin Coolidge* (1940); W. A. White, *A Puritan in Babylon* (1938); Andrew Sinclair, *Prohibition* (1962); Charles Merz, *The Dry Decade* (1931); Marvin Barrett, *The Jazz Age* (1959); G. H. Knoles, *The Jazz Age Revisited* (1955); L. E. Ellis, *Frank B. Kellogg and American Foreign Relations, 1925–1929* (1961); R. H. Ferrell, *Peace in Their Time: The Origins of the Kellogg–Briand Pact* (1952); J. C. Vinson, *William E. Borah and the Outlawry of War* (1957); E. A. Moore, *A Catholic Runs for President* (1956); Oscar Handlin, *Al Smith and His America* (1958); Alfred E. Smith, *Up to Now* (1929); Richard O'Connor, *The First Hurrah: A Biography of Alfred E. Smith* (1970).

32

Hoover and the
Great Depression

Herbert Hoover, a Republican, entered the White House in 1929, al-
though as late as 1920 politicians doubted whether he was a Democrat or
a Republican. Enemies accused the "Great Engineer" of being a political
babe in the woods, yet no man can be elected President who is wholly
without political instincts. His great task was to perpetuate so-called
prosperity. But unfortunately a country that is burdened with un-
prosperous farmers and transient workers is not wholly prosperous.

Hoover, though not a charismatic leader, was a gifted and re-
sourceful administrator with an extraordinary grasp of domestic prob-
lems. He shone as a social engineer. The Superman of popular fancy
never existed, and when the Depression descended he revealed himself
to be a frustrated and irritated mortal. Far from letting problems drift, he
exercised presidential powers to an unusual degree, conspicuously after
the stock market crashed in 1929. He appointed commissions; sum-
moned conferences; showed great concern for health, housing, and child
welfare; reorganized the government along more efficient lines; promoted
merit in the civil service; urged the voting of government money for use-
ful public works; and in various other ways tried to combat the Depres-
sion. But the economic sickness was unprecedentedly severe, and many
of his meritorious measures did not go far enough soon enough.

As far as the Washington government was concerned, Hoover
advocated a balanced budget, strict economy, lowered taxes, the gold
standard, and no direct government doles to sap the moral strength of
needy citizens. He modified his views substantially as the Depression

deepened, in recognition of the stark truism that no government can safely permit its people to starve in a land of plenty. And there can be no doubt that some did starve, despite White House denials, for people who are not desperately hungry do not fight like animals over garbage.[1] *Hoover's conversion to the principle of more adequate help for the needy was belated and rather halfhearted; he had seriously overestimated the soundness of the economy and his capacity to deal with the crisis.*

DID HOOVER CONTRIBUTE TO THE GREAT DEPRESSION?

When the Great Depression came in 1929, President Hoover was widely blamed for having caused it. What is the truth?

Ever since the national government was launched in 1789, cyclical financial panics or business depressions had occurred about every twenty years. The last sharp downturn had occurred on Wall Street during 1907, and the historical weather vane indicated another in the mid-1920s.[2] It came in 1929, perhaps delayed by the rather severe secondary depression of the early 1920s.

Aside from its seeming inevitability, the Great Depression was doubtless caused in part by the economic dislocations resulting from the Great War of 1914–1918, including the tangle of international debts and reparations. The tinsel prosperity of the 1920s, encouraged by a wild speculative boom on Wall Street and elsewhere, probably helped trigger the crash and worsen it.[3]

Hoover was Secretary of Commerce when the speculative bubble neared the bursting point, and he has been often censured for not having restrained it. Although he did protest against the easy-money policies

---

[1] Shivering men sold apples for five cents each on street corners, and about 6,000 were thus employed at one time in New York City. Such tactics were good merchandising by the apple growers, and did provide some employment. But one may doubt Hoover's claim that "Many persons left their jobs for the more profitable one of selling apples." *The Memoirs of Herbert Hoover: The Great Depression, 1929–1941* (1952), p. 195.

[2] The years of the major panics under the Constitution are as follows:

	Year span	Party in power
1819		Democratic-Republican
1837	18	Dem.
1857	20	Dem.
1873	16	Rep.
1893	20	Dem.
1907	14	Rep.
1929	22	Rep.

18.3 year average

[3] See J. K. Galbraith, *The Great Crash* (1955), pp. 94–95.

of the Federal Reserve Board, we must remember that he was neither President nor Secretary of the Treasury during this period. President Coolidge and Secretary of the Treasury Mellon encouraged rather than discouraged the feverish speculation; indeed Coolidge was rather tickled when an incautious word of his caused the stock market to rise or fall. Hoover, of course, was President from March to October 1929, and while he was aware of the seriousness of the speculative fever, he had no direct authority to control the New York Stock Exchange or the Federal Reserve Board. His rather muted warnings against heavy speculation were generally ignored.

Probably Hoover would have been less savagely blamed for fathering the Depression if he had not been guilty of overoptimistic statements during the presidential campaign of 1928. In his speech of acceptance, he smugly assured his huge audience in the Stanford University football stadium that "the poorhouse is vanishing from among us" and that "We in America today are nearer to the final triumph over poverty than ever before in the history of any land." He seemed to guarantee that he and his Republican policies would bring perpetual prosperity. Not surprisingly, a favorite slogan of his followers was "A chicken in every pot and two cars in every garage." [4]

Such overconfidence was a reckless challenge to the gods. The party that takes credit for the sunshine must also take discredit for the floods. If the Republicans could willfully create prosperity, they must be no less able to create depression. Consequently, the Democrats originated the myth that the Republican party is the party of depression, while the Republicans later stressed the countermyth that the Democratic party is the party of war. [5]

DID THE DEPRESSION BEGIN ABROAD?

President Hoover and his apologists argued that the Depression did not really begin with the Wall Street collapse of October 1929, but that a number of foreign countries were already suffering from depressed conditions which reacted unfavorably on the United States.

In the sense that World War I was the basic "cause" of the

---

[4] This catchword is often incorrectly attributed to Hoover, who did say (October 22, 1928), "The slogan of progress is changing from the 'full dinner pail' to the full garage."

[5] There have been as many major panics under Democrats as under Republicans, partly because the Democrats are a much older party. More major foreign wars have occurred under the Democrats than under the Republicans, although counting the Civil War, more American lives have been lost during Republican administrations.

Great Depression, one can say with some confidence that the economic malaise started in Europe. But hard times in America are customarily dated from the stock market collapse.[6] One of the triggering influences seems to have been the raising of London money rates to 6.5 percent, which caused a heavy withdrawal of European capital from the American market. But if other countries were suffering from depressed conditions, America was also hurting in certain sectors, especially agriculture. In the summer of 1929 production in steel and automobiles began to fall off.

A new and more ominous phase of the Great Depression occurred in May 1931, when a prominent Austrian banking house collapsed, thereby dramatically worsening conditions internationally. By this time there was no doubt that the economic catastrophe was a worldwide phenomenon. Nations do not live in vacuums; indeed there has been no major depression in the United States that was not in some degree "caused" by developments abroad.

DID THE HAWLEY-SMOOT TARIFF CAUSE THE DEPRESSION?

During the presidential campaign of 1928, the politically inexperienced Hoover was pressured into promising to call Congress into special session for a "limited" revision of the tariff, with emphasis on the needs of the farmers. The resulting Hawley–Smoot Act was a logrolled monstrosity which boosted the tariff substantially higher, largely in response to the demands of industrial interests. What finally emerged was the highest "protective" barrier in United States history.[7]

Hoover, who had often sought the advice of experts but who became distrustful of academicians, received a petition from more than 1,000 economists and other prominent figures urging him to veto the bill. But such a rejection would damage the Republican party; besides, he had fought for and secured a flexible provision. This would enable him, on the recommendation of the Tariff Commission, to raise or lower

[6] One reads that "everybody" in 1929 was speculating by buying common stocks on margin. About 16,000,000 of the 120,000,000 or so Americans owned stocks. Probably most of these investors were not speculating, and many of those who did gamble were not buying on margin.

[7] Republican tariff advocates, ignoring the accepted shibboleth that competition is the life of trade, long argued that America's great prosperity since the Civil War years (except for periodic depressions) was due to protective duties. The case is difficult to prove because prosperity may have been due primarily to a combination of other factors, including marvelous natural resources. Individual manufacturers no doubt benefited from protection, but even in periods of so-called prosperity, large segments of the economy were suffering, notably the farmers in the 1920s.

specific duties by as much as 50 percent. In this way he could correct some inequities.

Not content with signing the bill, Hoover defended it vigorously, partly because he believed in the principle of protection. He argued that the tariff was really a moderate one, and he reached this astonishing conclusion by a juggling of statistics.[8] He also stressed the rather hollow concessions made to farmers, who actually needed little protection because they could generally outproduce foreign competition. Many of the tariff changes hurt rather than helped agriculture, principally by cutting off the purchasing power of foreigners.

Hoover and his supporters were correct in denying that the Hawley-Smoot tariff had "caused" the Depression. The downward lurch had begun with the Great Crash of October 1929, some eight months before the passage of the controversial bill. But there can be little doubt that this ill-advised legislation deepened the Depression by inviting severe tariff reprisals from foreign nations, by cutting off foreign markets, by reducing foreign purchasing power in the United States, and by prompting more American factories to move to Canada or other foreign countries.

While it is true that the Hawley–Smoot enactment did not cause the Depression, the earlier Republican Fordney–McCumber Act of 1922 cannot wholly escape blame. It was a high tariff, with rates on dutiable goods averaging about 40 percent, and as such hampered the European nations in paying their war debts. It evidently played some role in inducing these countries to start raising retaliatory barriers even before Hoover's distressing experience with the Hawley–Smoot provocation.

WAS HOOVER A DO-NOTHING PRESIDENT?

Lack of success in battling the Great Depression gave birth to the misconception that Hoover was a do-nothing President — a "fat Coolidge" — who let conditions slide from deplorable to desperate. An examination of his basic philosophy does much to explain his policy.

Born in 1874, in the heyday of the second Grant Administration,

---

[8] The usual way of reckoning tariff levels is to compute them on the basis of the average annual rates on goods that are charged duties, exclusive of items on the free list. By this standard the Hawley–Smoot rates ran to about 59 percent. But if one lumps together the value of imports on the free list with those requiring duties, as Hoover did, one comes out with a modest figure of 16 percent. On this basis, if Congress erected a prohibitively high rate on all dutiable items, then the average tariff on all imports would be zero. See Harris G. Warren, *Herbert Hoover and the Great Depression* (1959), pp. 91–92; Herbert Hoover, *The Memoirs of Herbert Hoover: The Cabinet and the Presidency* (1952), pp. 297–299.

Herbert Hoover was essentially a child — an orphan child — of the nineteenth century. After working his way up from poverty to the status of a millionaire mining engineer, he believed that others should pull themselves up by their own bootstraps, using intelligence, thrift, hard work, and courage. Although not claiming authorship of the phrase "rugged individualism," he believed devoutly in it and used the term repeatedly.[9] He clearly abhorred collectivism in all its forms, including socialism and communism.

Hoover did not believe that the federal government was a charitable institution designed to help out needy individuals: if they were given handouts from Washington, such traditional virtues as self-reliance and thrift would be undermined, with a consequent enfeebling of the nation's fiber. To this extent he was schooled in the basic philosophies of Presidents Jefferson, Jackson, Van Buren, and Cleveland. They, like their fellow Americans, believed that people should sweat out depressions as best they could, with the help of relatives and local charities.[10] Faced with overwhelming unemployment after the Great Depression developed, Hoover reluctantly accepted the principle that the human budget is substantially more important than the Washington budget.

Before coming to the White House, Hoover was universally recognized as a humanitarian: probably no other man in history has saved more people from imminent starvation. He was deeply sensitive to the criticisms that while he was able to feed hungry foreigners, he could not feed starving Americans, and that he favored government loans to provide feedstuffs for pigs but not foodstuffs for people. The prospect of a direct dole shocked him: it would undermine the national character while unbalancing the budget.

In short, Hooverian philosophy held that government might properly help people indirectly, especially by aid to business through devices such as bankers' loans and the protective tariff, but not directly. The "Great Engineer" vetoed the Muscle Shoals Bill, precursor to the Tennessee Valley Authority, because he did not believe that the government should enter into competition with private electric power companies. But he supported other schemes for useful public works that would

[9] Hoover evidently did not fully realize that his support of the tariff (government help to manufacturers) and of prohibition (government interference with individuals' private lives) ran counter to "rugged individualism."

[10] In 1887 President Cleveland vetoed a bill appropriating $10,000 to provide seedgrain for Texas drought sufferers. The Texas legislature could easily have met this need, and the veto message declared that "though the people support the Government the Government should not support the people." President Hoover in 1930 specifically referred to this precedent.

employ large numbers of men, notably the Hoover Dam (originally Boulder Dam), begun on the Colorado River in 1930.

Hoover was far from being a do-nothing President.[11] He actively bestirred himself to inaugurate measures that would alleviate the Depression. Critics subsequently complained that he did not start soon enough or go far enough, but few men in 1930–1932 could have foreseen the length and depth of the crisis. If he had not gone as far as he did, his successor would have had much more difficulty in launching the sweeping measures of the New Deal. Some admirers have gone so far as to claim that Hoover was the real father of the New Deal, and although he bitterly disclaimed any such paternity, there was an element of truth in this observation. After all, Hoover reversed the hands-off approach of nineteenth-century Chief Executives and finally accepted the principle that, when local remedies failed, the welfare of the masses was a direct concern of the national government. He was not so much a do-nothing President as one who was unable to do anything really effective to overcome the Great Depression.

WAS THE RECONSTRUCTION FINANCE CORPORATION A SUCCESS?

Despite his aversion to involving the government in private business, Hoover rather belatedly recommended the Reconstruction Finance Corporation (R.F.C.), which Congress established in January 1932. This scheme had the additional merit in his eyes of avoiding a direct dole by providing huge interest-bearing loans from the Treasury to troubled banks and related institutions. Benefits would "dribble down" to the masses, while individualism would be protected by barring loans to individuals. The assumption was that these large borrowers could not obtain the money elsewhere and that their salvation was in the public interest.

The basic idea for the R.F.C. seems to have grown out of the War Finance Corporation of World War I, which Hoover had reason to remember. Much of the initiative for the new institution came from Eugene Meyer, a governor of the Federal Reserve Board.[12] Because the scheme squinted toward socialism, Hoover supported it with a notice-

[11] Contrary to some critics, Hoover was not completely wedded to a doctrine of *laissez-faire* or governmental hands-off. J. S. Davis, "Herbert Hoover, 1874–1964: Another Appraisal," *South Atlantic Quar.*, LXVIII (1969), 309. Dr. Davis knew Hoover personally.

[12] Gerald D. Nash, "Herbert Hoover and the Origins of the Reconstruction Finance Corporation," *Miss. Valley Hist. Rev.*, XLVI (1959), 455–468.

able lack of enthusiasm. Yet the Reconstruction Finance Corporation turned out to be the most successful anti-Depression agency created during his administration, so much so that one wonders whether the worst of the economic paralysis might have been averted if Hoover had backed it earlier and on a more generous scale.

Unhappily, the establishment of the R.F.C. was attended by conflict of interest. General Charles G. Dawes, its first president, resigned in mid-1932, and shortly thereafter the Corporation granted a loan of $92 million to a near-bankrupt Chicago bank in which he was deeply involved. Critics were quick to point to possible collusion, and to charge that the R.F.C. was a "millionaire's dole."

Hoover, with his skill in manipulating figures, later responded that 90 percent of the loans went to small banks and related financial institutions. This was true of the number of transactions but not of the quantity of money involved. The great bulk of the funds under Hoover benefited the larger financial entities that were in trouble — a process popularly known as "bailing out the bankers."

Despite such accusations, the R.F.C. survived for nearly twenty-two years, earning millions of dollars on its interest-bearing and pump-priming loans. Formally abolished by Congress in 1953 amid charges of political favoritism, it closed its books with fewer than five percent of its loans unliquidated. All told it had disbursed some $12 billion to promote peacetime activities.

SHOULD THE BONUS ARMY HAVE BEEN EVICTED?

In the summer of 1932 about 20,000 unemployed veterans of World War I converged on Washington to pressure Congress into paying them forthwith the soldiers' "bonus" (adjusted compensation) [13] not due them until 1945. They set up improvised quarters in vacant buildings and in a shantytown "Hooverville" on the Anacostia mud flats, near the Capitol. The lack of sanitary and other facilities created the likelihood of widespread disease. When Congress voted down the desired "bonus" legislation, several thousand of the petitioners quietly departed, many of them with loans granted by Congress against the scheduled "bonus" payments.

---

[13] Veterans' groups resented the use of the word "bonus" and preferred "adjusted compensation," which was designed to pay them a sum that would at least partially reimburse them for the wages they would have earned in civilian life. The bonus bill of 1924 (passed over Coolidge's veto) involved about $3.5 billion. A measure permitting loans against this obligation, at 4½ percent interest, was approved and passed in 1931 over Hoover's veto.

Thousands of the remaining ex-soldiers just hung around, some of them joined by families. Their continued presence created fears of violence against the vulnerable White House, as well as increased apprehension among the public health officials. The few outspoken Communists in the Bonus Army, scorned and even roughly handled by their non-Communist comrades, were eager to precipitate a riot that would cost lives. Such disturbances were finally triggered, and the police, some of them suffering injuries from brickbats, overreacted by killing two men on July 28, 1932.

Officials of the District of Columbia, understandably feeling that their police force was not adequate to handle the defiant veterans, called upon the President for federal assistance. Under the command of General Douglas MacArthur, some 600 troops, including both cavalrymen and infantrymen, were speedily assembled, supported by a machine gun squadron and six tanks. The veterans were given forty-five minutes to evacuate the vacant buildings near the Capitol, and when they responded with brickbats, stones, and clubs, thereby injuring some of the soldiers, they were ejected with bayonets and tear gas. MacArthur's detachment then proceeded to the main encampment at Anacostia, where it halted and gave the occupants an hour in which to leave. By this time darkness had fallen, and the soldiers were ordered to ignite several of the shanties so as to provide light for the operations. The fleeing occupants evidently set fire to others.[14] The Bonus Army — men, women, and children — was completely dispersed.

President Hoover claims in his *Memoirs* that the federal troops used more force than anticipated, for he had not contemplated wiping out the Anacostia encampment. He further declares that "not a single person" was injured, even though some soldiers were hurt by brickbats, and many of the veterans (and soldiers) were gassed and burned by the gas bombs. Hoover also alleges that the riffraff thus evacuated contained few genuine veterans but a large number of Communists, criminals, and ex-convicts.[15] The Communists themselves have exaggerated their role by claiming credit for having sparked the heavy-handed dispersal. But because the testimony of these ex-Communists is suspect, and because they were about the only ones who stood to gain from this discreditable episode, their version has probably received undue emphasis.

No doubt the Bonus Army should have been disbanded, either by persuasion or force. In a democracy, legislation should not be de-

[14] General Douglas MacArthur, in *Reminiscences* (1964), p. 95, refers only to the incendiary work of the marchers, although there is abundant photographic evidence of the part played by the soldiers.
[15] *Memoirs of Herbert Hoover: The Great Depression*, pp. 225–232.

bated under the threat of mob action, and no great municipality should permit dangerously unhealthful conditions to exist for two months during a hot and humid summer. Since the Bonus Army was unarmed, except for bricks and clubs, it certainly could have been forced out with less brutality.[16] This eviction was clearly a case of overzealousness on the part of the regular army, and while we credit Hoover's statement that he did not anticipate such ruthlessness, we must concede that he grievously damaged his image as the "Great Humanitarian."

A second and smaller Bonus Army came in May 1933, and President Roosevelt "killed it with kindness." Not only did he provide an army camp, with plently of food, coffee, and entertainment, but he conferred with the leaders (Hoover had refused to do so) and sent his wife out in the mud to commune with the veterans. They departed with a good taste in their mouths. Such tactics helped to explain why Roosevelt was President and Hoover was not.

WAS PROHIBITION A "NOBLE EXPERIMENT"?

As if the Depression were not enough, the problems of prohibition continued to bedevil Hoover throughout his harassed four years.

By 1917 the prohibition of alcoholic beverages had been voted through in most of the United States, whether by state legislatures or by community action (local option). Shortly after America entered the war against Germany, Congress enacted legislation restricting the diversion of grain for intoxicants. Such self-denial was rendered the more palatable by patriotic fervor and by the association of prominent German names with the traffic in alcohol, especially beer. Americans were becoming accustomed to Spartan legislation.

On December 18, 1917, Congress overwhelmingly passed the prohibition amendment (18th) to the Constitution; the certainty of such action had been virtually assured by the Congressional elections of November 1916. By January 16, 1919, the requisite number of states had ratified. The amendment was then implemented by the loopholed Volstead Act, passed by Congress in October 1919.[17]

---

[16] No shots were fired by the soldiers and they killed no one, although an eleven-week-old "bonus baby" allegedly died from exposure to tear gas. Separate investigations by the F.B.I., the police, and the Army concluded that the child suffered death from natural causes. The author is indebted to a Master's thesis at Stanford University by Stuart G. Cross based on the Hoover Papers, "The Bonus Army in Washington, May 27–July 29, 1932" (1948). See also Roger Daniels, *The Bonus March* (1971).

[17] A long-standing grievance of the American soldiers who went to France during the war, some two million strong, was that prohibition was "put over" on them while

Contrary to a prevalent misbelief, alcohol was not completely banned. Its manufacture, sale, and transportation were made unlawful, but the citizen might buy liquor, consume private stocks, and make wine or cider on his own premises for private consumption. He might secure alcohol on a doctor's prescription from his druggist. The brewers might even continue to produce "near beer" lawfully, provided that the alcoholic content did not exceed one-half of 1 percent, as compared to the usual 4 percent.

In the early 1920s, before illicit booze and attendant gangsterism created a national scandal, prohibition did substantially prohibit intoxicants. But by the late 1920s, enforcement was plainly breaking down. Disregard for unpopular legislation — a national trait which prohibitionists failed to recognize — had reached alarming proportions and was undermining respect for all authority.[18]

Hoover felt no great enthusiasm for prohibition, but he was nominated by the Republicans on a "dry" platform. Referring to the attempt to abolish alcohol by legislation, he declared in his speech of acceptance: "I do not favor the repeal of the eighteenth amendment. Our country has deliberately undertaken a great social and economic experiment, noble in motive and far-reaching in purpose. It must be worked out constructively." In popular parlance this statement was reduced to "The Noble Experiment," much to Hoover's annoyance. In the eyes of most "wets," there was nothing "noble" about an "experiment" that involved so much lawlessness and encroached so heavily on their private lives and thirsts.

In the view of "drys," the "experiment," though "noble" in eliminating the odious saloon and saving the poor workingman's wages, was not an "experiment" but rather a fixture. Prohibitionists regarded the dry era as an overdue Progressive reform now permanently written into the Constitution. By late 1928 the restriction was about a decade old, and this was more than a period of "experimentation." People did not refer to the Negro-citizenship "experiment" (15th Amendment) or the woman-suffrage "experiment" (19th Amendment), so why speak of the prohibition "experiment"?

---

they were abroad fighting for their country. There was an element of truth in this charge, although the crucial Congressional election of November 1916, had taken place when few of them were in uniform. In view of the relatively speedy ratification by the states, one may doubt that their presence in America would have made a great deal of difference in the end result.

[18] The "drys" argued that unless prohibition was enforced, the nation would learn not only disrespect for the law but for the Constitution. Actually the South had made a mockery of the 14th Amendment (civil rights for Negroes) and the 15th Amendment (the vote for the Negroes) since their inception in 1868 and 1870.

WHY DID PROHIBITION ENFORCEMENT BREAK DOWN?

The 18th Amendment was repealed in December, 1933 primarily because the American people were fed up with this "ignoble experiment."
They concluded that the evils spawned by prohibition were worse than
those that had previously existed. The fanaticism of the "drys" in
securing the amendment was matched by the fanaticism of the "wets" in
repealing it.[19] All previous experience had shown that Americans, from
the days of smuggling under the British Navigation Acts and the Jeffersonian embargo, could not be forced to obey laws where a majority or a
large minority regarded them as unwise or intolerably restrictive.[20] From
the outset there were numerous communities where public sentiment
was against prohibition, notably in the great urban centers, where
immigrant populations had brought with them drinking habits from
the Old Country.

What led to the overall collapse of this reform? Congress failed
to vote adequate enforcement funds, while the overburdened states and
localities frequently washed their hands of the problem. Dirty politics,
bribery, corruption, and other forms of chicanery hampered the relatively few enforcement officials. Juries (often with drinkers among
their members) were frequently loath to convict bootleggers. Defiance
of the law became a status symbol among the middle and upper classes:
forbidden fruit is usually sweeter. Many women were imbibing who
previously had not drunk, and much hard liquor, especially gin, was
consumed because it was easier to conceal and transport than bulky,
low-alcohol beverages. Finally, the Great Depression and the unbalanced
budget were potent factors; they added force to "wet" propaganda that
repeal would provide countless jobs for the unemployed and hundreds
of millions of dollars in tax revenues. The nation would drink its way
back to prosperity.

WAS PROHIBITION A FAILURE?

Some "drys" argued that prohibition did not fail because it was never
really tried. Reliable figures are hard to obtain, but it appears that
people consumed less liquor, especially during the early years of

[19] See Andrew Sinclair, *Prohibition* (1962), Ch. 21.
[20] From the days of the Whiskey Rebellion (1794) onward, there have always been
illicit stills in the hills concealed from revenue collectors.

prohibition, for per capita consumption evidently fell. There was less drinking among the working classes, which had formerly drunk cheap beer, because only the more affluent could afford a quality bootlegged product. In this sense, prohibition was "class legislation," and for that reason especially abhorrent to the poor, who increasingly felt the need to drown their sorrows during the Great Depression. Certainly the corner saloon disappeared, with its inviting swinging doors and its capacity to sponge up the wages of weak-willed workers. Yet in a sense it had been the only club that poor men could patronize; its place was taken by the grill-doored speakeasy, which could be entered only by those patrons who had money or influence.

There is reason to believe that the national health improved during the prohibition era, except for those who died or went blind from poisonous alcohol or adulterated "rot gut." Certain statistics point to a decline of alcoholism and mental disturbances, as well as to an increase in savings accounts. Yet prosperity may have been more influential than prohibition in swelling bank balances.

The argument is also advanced that there was no true crime wave, if one excepts open defiance of an unpopular law which many people did not feel could be regarded as a crime. The machine-gun tactics of the feuding gangsters in Chicago were not typical of the nation, nor even of many other cities.[21]

But whatever the reasons, the prohibition amendment simply did not abolish alcohol, except in some degree for the poor classes. It probably could never have been made to work in America for a protracted period, even under the best possible conditions. Prohibition not only ran counter to human desires but to nature itself; alcohol is one of the easiest of chemicals to produce. Under favorable conditions it is self-manufacturing.

WAS THE REPEAL OF THE 18TH AMENDMENT DESIRABLE?

"Drys" had unwisely credited prohibition with the prosperity of the "Golden Twenties" — unwisely, because when the Depression came the "wets" could blame them for it. Just as an avalanche of "dry" propaganda had insured the enactment of prohibition, so a deluge of "wet" propaganda by the liquor lobbyists helped to engineer its repeal.

Conspicuous among "wet" agencies was the Association Against

21 See J. C. Burnham, "New Perspectives on the Prohibition 'Experiment' of the 1920s," *Jour. of Social History*, II (1968), 51–67.

the Prohibition Amendment, which capitalized on the Depression with the promise of more jobs and more revenue from revived industry. Repealists made much of the invasion of basic rights by overzealous enforcement officers. This argument was reinforced by the occasional shooting of innocent citizens, to say nothing of scores of the guilty. Such distressing incidents further caused the stigma of complete failure to be attached to the "noble experiment" and to be widely accepted as an article of faith. One by one, many of the states repealed their "little Volstead Acts" and on February 20, 1933, nearly two weeks before Hoover left office, Congress had enacted the 21st Amendment, which repealed the 18th. It was approved by the requisite number of states in December 1933.

Few fair-minded observers could deny that conditions in 1933 had become intolerable, given the halfhearted attempts at enforcement, and that outright repeal or substantial modification was imperatively needed. Many repealists were willing to legalize light wines and beer, but not spirits. Others in addition wanted restrictions written into the new 21st Amendent that would bar the flow of liquor into those states that wished to remain dry. Still others felt that some kind of rational liquor sales under federal auspices, as in certain European countries, might be desirable. But such was the national disgust and such was the Depression-spawned mood that Congress simply washed its hands of the whole wretched business and turned the regulation over to the states and localities.[22]

Saloons promptly returned, though seldom called by that earthy name. Alcoholism gradually rose to an appalling level, thus becoming one of the nation's major killers. One of the strongest arguments used by the "drys" in their early drive for prohibition was that in a machine age the dangers resulting from befuddled wits, whether in the factory or on the highway, were too great to be tolerated. If the Congressmen who had repealed prohibition with such abandon had been able to look ahead, they might have been more willing to impose certain safeguards. By the 1970s about half of the 50,000 or more fatalities resulting annually from automobiles were drink-connected.

DID HOOVER SCORE A SUCCESS IN DISARMAMENT?

Difficulties spawned by the Depression, unemployment, the tariff, prohibition, and other problems were paralleled by perplexities abroad. As

[22] See Sinclair, *Prohibition*, p. 393.

a peace-loving and economy-minded Quaker, Hoover was especially disturbed by the costly naval race in the smaller craft, such as cruisers and destroyers, which had not been curbed by the Washington Conference in 1922. In this deadly competition the United States, which had lagged far behind, would have to expend an enormous sum if it hoped to catch up.

In 1930, after preliminary negotiations between Hoover and the British, a five-power naval conference assembled in London. A treaty finally emerged which in its entirety was signed by only the three leading powers. It placed an upper limit on *all* categories of ships, not just capital ships and aircraft carriers. The United States was granted parity with the British in all categories, if it chose to build up to those levels. Japan was left with the small end of a 10-10-6 ratio in capital ships, but improved this ratio somewhat in destroyers and cruisers, while securing parity in submarines. Italy and France subscribed to only relatively unimportant clauses of the treaty. As a consequence, the other signatories would be released from their commitments if they felt their security threatened by a French or Italian building program.

The chief fly in the ointment was that the United States, to attain the parity that it was granted on paper, would have to spend about a billion dollars on cruisers and other smaller craft. But Hoover, anxious to win some acclaim for his floundering administration, hailed the results as a signal victory for disarmament. Ever resourceful with figures, he argued that the nation would save a huge sum; that is, if one used the higher standards that had been discussed but rejected at the abortive Geneva Conference of 1927.[23]

With a jittery world in no mood to disarm, Hoover achieved even less success when he tried to arouse the World Disarmament Conference, meeting in Geneva in 1932. He dramatically proposed that existing land armaments be reduced by approximately one-third, and that certain offensive weapons be abolished. The one-third proposal was unrealistic; the defense-weapons concept was unworkable. There are practically no "offensive" weapons that cannot be used defensively in certain circumstances. A tank is generally used to attack, but an immobile tank can be used defensively with lethal effect. An aerial bomber is ordinarily classed as an offensive weapon, but if used to bomb factories that are manufacturing bombers for one's enemy, it becomes a defensive weapon.

---

[23] Hoover estimated that this saving to the three signatory powers would be 680,-000 tons of warships. *Memoirs of Herbert Hoover: The Cabinet and the Presidency,* p. 351.

DID HOOVER ORIGINATE
THE HOOVER–STIMSON DOCTRINE?

As a Quaker, Hoover had no stomach for becoming involved in a Far Eastern war to restrain Japan's imperialistic ambitions. Although his Secretary of State, Henry L. Stimson, was an internationalist, Hoover was not. Despite unusually wide contacts with the outside world, or perhaps because of unhappy experiences there, he was at heart an isolationist.[24] He managed to keep a tight rein on interventionist proclivities of the energetic Stimson.

In 1931 the Japanese imperialists, in a well-planned campaign, overran China's spacious Manchuria, and proceeded to set up a puppet state called Manchukuo. This act of aggression, a curtain-raiser for World War II, was a flagrant violation of the Nine Power Pact of 1922 and the Kellogg–Briand Pact of 1928, as well as the Covenant of the League of Nations. If the League had taken resolute action, it might have halted the Japanese. But it backed off, partly because the United States was not a member and American support was problematical. There is no truth in the myth that Washington proposed anti-Japanese boycotts which the British and French rejected. Actually, Secretary Stimson rebuffed such overtures from the League, though indicating that the United States Navy "probably" would not interfere with an embargo.

A peace-loving Hoover was completely opposed to any boycotts, for to him the word spelled "bombs." He did, however, support a statement by Secretary Stimson to the effect that America would refuse to recognize the fruits of any aggression contrary to the Kellogg–Briand Pact. To the very end Washington declined to sanction the puppet state of Manchukuo.

This doctrine of not recognizing disagreeable realities in the hope that they would go away did not demonstrably halt the Japanese invaders. It was a cheap but ineffective substitute for resolute action. Popularly called the Hoover–Stimson nonrecognition doctrine, it soon raised the question of authorship. Hoover recalls that he first suggested the idea in a Cabinet meeting but concedes that he was indebted to a statement by Secretary Bryan in 1915 for the basic idea.[25] One can

---

[24] Hoover's antipathy to foreigners, especially the Russians and French, seems to have grown out of efforts of their governments to thwart his famine-relief activities during and after World War I.

[25] On May 11, 1915, Bryan had broached the concept in a note to Japan protesting Tokyo's Twenty-One Demands on China. *Papers Relating to the Foreign Relations of the United States* (1924), p. 146. See also Hoover, *Memoirs of Herbert Hoover: The Cabinet and the Presidency*, pp. 372–373.

understand Hoover's desire to claim this bit of credit for an administration that was so generally discredited, but the application of moral suasion proved to be so impotent that the problem of authorship seems hardly worth disputing.

In 1932, when the Japanese brutally attacked China's Shanghai, Secretary Stimson approached London with the aim of instituting cooperative economic sanctions. But the British, previously rebuffed by Washington during the Manchurian coup of 1931, preferred to work within the League of Nations rather than with a power outside it. In any event, Hoover almost certainly would have vetoed any such involvement as liable to lead to a shooting war.

WAS THE ONE-YEAR MORATORIUM TO HOOVER'S CREDIT?

In June 1931, while Europe was wallowing in the acute phase of the Depression, President Hoover proposed a year-long moratorium on the payment of reparations and intergovernmental debts, including those due Washington. At the same time he reaffirmed his opposition to the ultimate cancellation of the war debts, or to any linking of German reparations with them.[26]

Hoover erred in not consulting Paris in advance, for the French were determined to secure their indemnity from Germany. They grudgingly acceded to the moratorium after a delay of two weeks, during which the economic crisis greatly worsened. Public opinion in America favored the one-year Hoover holiday, especially those investors who stood a better chance of collecting their private debts from Europe if the public debts were suspended.

When Congress reassembled in December 1931, it approved the moratorium by large majorities. At the same time it spurned a recommendation by Hoover that the war debts be reexamined in the light of the current international emergency. By this time the Treasury was running a heavy deficit, and if the national government would not cancel the war debts when it enjoyed a surplus, it almost certainly would not do so when it was in arrears. When the year-long Hoover Holiday ended, six debtors defaulted outright. By June 15, 1934, after another year had passed, all the others had done likewise except "brave little Finland."

President Hoover was extravagantly praised in Republican circles for his statesmanship in engineering the moratorium. Although it no

---

[26] Hoover privately believed in a more lenient treatment of the debtors than he publicly announced. Davis, "Herbert Hoover," *South Atlantic Quar.,* LXVIII (1969), 304–305, 315.

doubt eased Europe's distress, it had no dramatic effect in stemming the Depression in America. The irony is that Hoover, who to the end unrealistically avowed that debts and reparations were not interconnected, set the machinery in motion for outright default, which, in effect, amounted to cancellation. The moratorium probably helped European recovery, but cancellation was not what Hoover had aimed at or wanted. He continued to insist that the "war debts" could and should be paid.

DID HOOVER INAUGURATE THE "GOOD NEIGHBOR" POLICY?

No one person can claim exclusive credit for coining the phrase "good neighbor" or inaugurating the policy associated with that term. It received its greatest acclaim during the era of Franklin Roosevelt, but a substantial improvement in relations with the republics to the south occurred in Mexico and Nicaragua during the last months of the Coolidge administration. Hoover carried on from there.

To demonstrate his interest and concern, President-elect Hoover embarked upon a seven-week trip to Latin America shortly after his electoral triumph in 1928. He visited about half of the Latin American republics, and there received a series of welcomes that were spotty in their enthusiasm. These good neighbors remembered all too well the armed interventions in the past under the Monroe Doctrine, as well as the continued presence of American bayonets in Haiti and Nicaragua.[27]

Yet Hoover did make progress in improving relations. He adopted a more restrained interpretation of the Monroe Doctrine, withdrew the last American troops from Nicaragua, and negotiated a treaty with Haiti for a similar purpose. Although it was rejected by the Haitians, the path was paved for the final evacuation in 1934. A policy of withdrawal was spurred by the Depression, for sour Yankee investments in Latin America had wiped out hundreds of millions of dollars, and there were fewer dollars for Dollar Diplomacy to protect.

The gains in goodwill achieved under Hoover were substantially wiped out by the bitter reaction among Latin Americans to the Hawley–Smoot tariff. This partial closing of Yankee markets to their exports was regarded as a viciously unfair blow below the trade belt by good neighbors already suffering from the worldwide depression.

[27] Alexander DeConde, *Herbert Hoover's Latin–American Policy* (1951), Ch. II.

WAS ROOSEVELT'S NOMINATION IN 1932 A SURE THING?

By 1932 President Hoover was clearly the most unpopular man in the country, thanks to the Depression and other baffling problems. His defeat for reelection was probably inevitable, but the nomination of his rival, Franklin D. Roosevelt, was much less of a certainty.

Former Governor Al Smith of New York — defeated in 1928 by bigotry, snobbery, aridity, and prosperity — felt that he was entitled to a second chance, now that the Great Depression had seemingly guaranteed the election of almost any respectable Democrat. His most formidable rival was New York's Governor Franklin D. Roosevelt, a protégé of Smith. Despite a commendable record as a Depression governor, Roosevelt had developed the reputation of being debonair, airy, vague, evasive, and weak-willed. The journalist-pundit Walter Lippmann, early in 1932, had publicly declared that Roosevelt was "a pleasant man who, without any important qualifications for the office, would very much like to be President." [28]

When the Democratic convention met in Chicago, Roosevelt quickly amassed a majority of the votes but fell about 100 short of the necessary two-thirds. For several anxious hours the danger loomed that a compromise coalition might be formed against him. But Speaker of the House Garner, a rival for the nomination, threw his bloc of votes to Roosevelt, and the nomination was clinched. What motivated Garner, who was rewarded with the vice presidency, has long been a subject of controversy. Why any man should want to yield the powerful position of Speaker of the House for such a back seat is difficult to comprehend. The answer to the riddle seems to be that Garner made the sacrifice as a good party man. He evidently feared that a disruptive fight over a compromise candidate would ruin all chances of a Democratic victory, as it had in 1924.[29]

WAS THE 1932 ELECTION
A MANDATE FOR THE NEW DEAL?

After being nominated, Roosevelt flew to Chicago to accept the prize in person — the first future President to make such a personal appearance. He was eager to display his radiant personality and his physical vigor,

[28] Quoted in Frank Freidel, *Franklin D. Roosevelt: The Triumph* (1956), p. 249.
[29] William E. Leuchtenburg, *Franklin D. Roosevelt and the New Deal, 1932–1940* (1963), p. 8.

despite the paralysis of his lower limbs suffered in 1921. At the end of a fighting speech, he declared, "I pledge you, I pledge myself, to a *new deal* for the American people." The phrase gradually caught on and the Rooseveltian program ultimately came to be known as the New Deal.

Roosevelt, though overwhelmingly victorious in November, received no mandate for the New Deal simply because the famed New-Dealer-to-be had no such clearly shaped program in mind when the campaign began and when it closed. Although he advocated some of the schemes that came to be earmarks of the New Deal, there were many that he did not stress or even mention, including heavy deficit spending, gigantic federal works projects, and massive relief outlays. Hoover's fact-filled campaign speeches, though gloomily delivered, were judged by many to have won the public debate.

One of the ironies of the anti-Hoover campaign of 1932 is that the Democratic platform and orators condemned Hoover for unbalancing the budget and squandering too much money. "Throw the spenders out" was a slogan of those Democrats who were soon to show the country what spending really was. At Pittsburgh, on October 19, 1932, Roosevelt promised to balance the budget, though leaving an escape hatch to provide for "starvation and dire need."

Roosevelt's landslide majority in 1932 was almost certainly more a vote of no confidence in Hoover than of confidence in the Democratic candidate. The overwhelming blight of the Depression and the administration's inability to bring it under control counted heavily against Hoover, who fell victim to a "national grouch." Having come in on a landslide in 1928, he went out on one. Billed as a demigod and miracle man, he was baffled by a phenomenon that probably was beyond the grasp of any mortal man.

Hoover himself argued, and evidently died believing, that the country was pulling itself out of the Depression in mid-1932. Then the shock to public confidence caused by Roosevelt's nomination, campaign, and election plunged the nation deeper into the abyss. This allegation cannot be proved one way or the other. But such gain as had been achieved was so slight, and the subsequent depression was so deep, that one may question Hoover's self-justifying analysis.[30]

---

[30] *Memoirs of Herbert Hoover: The Great Depression*, p. 40; Warren, *Hoover and the Depression*, pp. 269–270. Hoover states that if the New Dealers had carried out his policies, "we should have made a complete recovery in eighteen months after 1932, as did all the dozen other nations with a free economy." The first part of this statement is unprovable and the second part is demonstrably untrue, particularly in the case of Britain, France, and Austria.

DID F.D.R. REFUSE TO
COOPERATE WITH LAME-DUCK HOOVER?

Roosevelt was elected on November 8, 1932, but he could not take office until March 4, 1933, nearly four months later. During this critical period the Depression sank into one of its worst phases, highlighted by the wholesale closing of banks throughout the country.

In such a crisis, close communication between the President-elect and the President-reject was considered imperative. Two meetings were arranged between Hoover and Roosevelt, but no agreement emerged. Roosevelt was loath to assume responsibility for decisions, including the fate of the war debts, that he would have no authority to implement.

Hoover and many Republicans believed that Roosevelt refused to cooperate during these lame-duck months because he wanted the Depression to worsen dramatically. Then he would take the helm and claim political credit for having saved the nation from complete disaster. This is a charge that we cannot readily document, although it is what a cynical politician, insensitive to the public welfare, might have done.

On February 17, 1933, President Hoover sent Roosevelt a letter which the latter's Democratic advisors regarded as "cheeky." The President-elect was urged, among other things, to give "prompt assurance" that he would balance the budget, preserve government credit, and refuse to tamper with or inflate the currency. When Roosevelt failed to respond affirmatively, Hoover was further confirmed in his belief that the incoming Democrats were determined to deepen the Depression.

But Hoover did not come into court with completely clean hands. Three days after urging the issuance of such a public affirmation, he wrote in a "confidential" memorandum, "I realize that if these declarations be made by the President-elect, he will have ratified the whole major program of the Republican Administration; that is, it means the abandonment of 90 percent of the so-called new deal." [31]

In politics the winner, not the loser, dictates the terms, and one should not be surprised that Roosevelt refused to tie his hands. He had not received a clear-cut mandate from the electorate for a specific New Deal, but he clearly was chosen by voters who wanted new remedies, vague though they might be, for the old Depression. Hoover was less than fair in making accusations of noncooperation.

[31] W. S. Myers and W. H. Newton, *The Hoover Administration* (1936), pp. 338–341.

WAS HOOVER A FAILURE AS PRESIDENT?

Before he left office, Hoover was the most booed man in American history. Because his name became synonymous with depression and with an unwillingness to feed hungry Americans directly, he continued to suffer condemnation by the Democrats. In a certain sense, the shadowy Hoover ran again in the next half-dozen or so presidential elections. Personally shy and too thin-skinned to be a highly successful politician,[32] he was so deeply humiliated by his repudiation in 1932 that he spent much of the next three decades condemning the New Deal and its Democratic successors. In this sense he was fighting the campaign of 1932 all over again; and if he had only kept his peace, his failures might have faded sooner from the public mind.

Gradually much of Hoover's tarnished prestige returned, as he became the elder statesman of his party, living to age 90 (narrowly outlived only by John Adams among the Presidents). After World War II he returned to public service by helping to feed the destitute in thirty-eight countries. He next headed two important commissions that made extensive recommendations as to the reorganization of the federal government. In 1951–1952 he published three volumes of Memoirs, which suffer from a wounded ego, excessive self-justification, and a tendency to manipulate facts and figures in such a way as to refurbish his image.[33] Historians, many of whom had branded him a complete failure as President, now became more charitable and were disposed to rank him as an "average" Chief Executive. A part of this reassessment was probably due to troubled consciences among those who suspected that they had judged him too harshly.

Hoover suffered from serious handicaps that do much to explain what happened. He had been oversold as a wonder worker, and he evidently developed a belief in his near-infallibility. Accustomed all his life to running his own show and giving orders to subordinates, he was not an up-from-the-ranks politician, as was customary. Failure was

---

[32] Hoover, who was unduly sensitive to criticism, bitterly accused the publicity director (Charles Michelson) of the Democratic National Committee of running a deliberate "smear" campaign against him in 1932. Memoirs of Herbert Hoover: The Great Depression, pp. 219ff. This charge is doubtless true but the President's record contained so much valid ammunition that "smear" tactics were probably not necessary to defeat him.

[33] This tendency to present a distorted picture is evident in Hoover's favorable account of his early mining activities in Australia; he exaggerates his successes and plays down his failures. Geoffrey Blainey, "Herbert Hoover's Forgotten Years," Business Archives and History (Sydney), III (1963), 53–70.

largely a stranger to him. He had started politically from the top, much to the annoyance of many of the old professionals, for whom he notoriously had scant respect, whether they sat in Congress or not.

It is true that Hoover began with a nominal Republican majority in the Senate. But he never had a reliable majority because the Republican insurgents ("Sons of the wild jackass," in Senator George H. Moses' phrase) repeatedly combined with the Democratic minority to harass him. In the second half of his term the Democrats won control of the House, and while they cooperated with him better than might have been expected, they were hardly a part of an effective team. Certain critics charge that Hoover's failures in dealing with the tariff, the farm problem, and prohibition were so pronounced before the Depression broke that even without this economic disaster he would deserve low marks.

People spoke of the "Coolidge luck" but not of the "Hoover luck." If the Great Humanitarian had been President from 1924 to 1929, he almost certainly would have been highly regarded as a Chief Executive. Then came the Depression. And as if that were not bad enough, it was accompanied by the nation's worst crop-destroying drought, complete with dust bowls.[34]

Hoover was one of the most industrious and fact-crammed of the Presidents; he labored at a killing pace and wrote his own speeches in longhand. He provided active but not effective leadership, notably in connection with the Hawley–Smoot tariff. To bolster public morale, he understandably issued cheery statements about prosperity being just around the corner — only it was not, with the consequent development of a serious "credibility gap." He was too much concerned with balancing the fiscal budget at the expense of the human budget. Although a superior man, he was no superman.

Yet, given the unprecedented severity and longevity of the Depression, who else would have done better? The political reputation of every other major democratic leader was blighted by hard times, whether in Britain, France, or Germany. Franklin Roosevelt needed some eight years, a $20 billion deficit, and a Hitlerian holocaust to overcome the Depression. Hoover's great sin was his failure to preserve the pseudo-prosperity of the Coolidge era — a prosperity which he had seemingly promised to perpetuate and for which he had been elected. If he had led the people to expect less, they would have forgiven him more when he failed to do the seemingly impossible.

[34] Dust storms had occurred on the Great Plains as early as the 1880s.

ADDITIONAL GENERAL REFERENCES

J. D. Hicks, *Republican Ascendancy, 1921–1933* (1960); W. E. Leuchtenburg, *The Perils of Prosperity, 1914–1932* (1958); F. L. Allen, *Since Yesterday* (1939); G. H. Soule, *Prosperity Decade, 1917–1929* (1947); Edward R. Ellis, *The Great American Depression, 1929–1939* (1970); Jordan A. Schwartz, *The Interregnum of Despair: Hoover, Congress, and the Depression* (1970); Dixon Wecter, *The Age of the Great Depression, 1929–1941* (1948); G. V. Seldes, *The Years of the Locust* (1933); Broadus Mitchell, *Depression Decade* (1947); Gene Smith, *The Shattered Dream: Herbert Hoover and the Great Depression* (1970); A. M. Schlesinger, Jr., *The Age of Roosevelt: The Crisis of the Old Order, 1919–1933* (1957); H. G. Warren, *Herbert Hoover and the Great Depression* (1959); A. U. Romasco, *The Poverty of Abundance* (1965); R. H. Ferrell, *American Diplomacy in the Great Depression* (1957); E. E. Morison, *Turmoil and Tradition: a Study of the Life and Times of Henry L. Stimson* (1960); D. M. Dozer, *Are We Good Neighbors? Three Decades of Inter-American Relations, 1930–1960* (1959).

33

The New Deal and the New Neutrality

Radiating optimism in an atmosphere of despair, Franklin Roosevelt declaimed before an inauguration throng on March 4, 1933, "The only thing we have to fear is fear itself." [1] *The next day he proclaimed a holiday for all banks, including those that had not yet closed their doors, preparatory to reopening them on a sounder basis. He then drove his initial New Deal program through the "Hundred Days Congress," which he had called into special session and which hurriedly enacted an unprecedented pile of legislation.*

Like a triple-headed monster, the New Deal lurched forward uncertainly on three fronts simultaneously: recovery, relief, and reform. Under attempted recovery, one must list banking legislation; an abandonment of the gold standard and a devaluation of the dollar; the ill-fated National Recovery Administration (N.R.A.) for business; and measures for creating jobs on public works and other projects. Under relief, Congress provided the Civilian Conservation Corps (young men to work on conservation projects); various direct relief appropriations; assistance to agriculture; and aid to homeowners and bankrupts. Under reform, Congress curbed bankers and stockmarket operators; established the vast Tennessee Valley Authority for flood control, navigation, soil preserva-

---

[1] The phrase was not completely original with Roosevelt or his numerous ghost writers; it goes back to Francis Bacon, who wrote in 1663, "Nothing is terrible except fear itself." Roosevelt's concern for the "forgotten man," as expressed in his preconvention campaign in 1932, may have derived from Professor William G. Sumner's famous essay of 1883, "The Forgotten Man."

*tion, and electric power; authorized reciprocal tariff-lowering agreements
with various countries; improved the status of labor through the Wagner
Act and the Fair Labor Standards Act; enacted the epochal Social Security
Act; subsidized the construction of housing; restrained public utilities;
and passed a red-letter law for reorganizing the executive arm of the
national government.*

*The New Deal officially continued from March 1933, to Decem-
ber 1943, when Roosevelt publicly abandoned "Dr. New Deal" in favor
of "Dr. Win-the-War."* [2] *Some historians have seen in his gigantic program a First New Deal and a Second New Deal — a distinction which
adds only confusion to a confused undertaking because there are at least
three differing definitions of the two so-called New Deals. Since the
intertwined goals of recovery, relief, and reform were kept in view
throughout, efforts to discover subcategories within the overall program
are somewhat like hunting for seams in a seamless garment.* [3]

HOW NEW WAS THE NEW DEAL?

As a phrase, "New Deal" was already common currency in American
politics, and can be traced at least to Carl Schurz (1871) and Mark Twain
(1889). It had been more recently used by Woodrow Wilson, Robert M.
La Follette, and David Lloyd George (in England).

From one point of view, the New Deal was a logical progression
from the reformist demands of the Populists and Muckrakers at the turn
of the century, followed by the Progressive movement. Then came
Theodore Roosevelt's Square Deal and New Nationalism, and Woodrow
Wilson's New Freedom. The extent to which the New Deal marks a
sharp divergence from the evolutionary past is a matter of dispute among
scholars. There can be little doubt, however, that World War I interrupted Wilson's economic and social reforms, and that a postwar setback
also occurred during the conservative Republican era of Harding,
Coolidge and Hoover.

When Franklin Roosevelt became President in 1933, America
was clearly lagging behind certain nations of Western Europe in legislation for improving the welfare of the masses, such as health care, un-

---

[2] James M. Burns, *Roosevelt the Soldier of Freedom, 1940–1945* (1970), p. 423.

[3] See William H. Wilson, "Two New Deals: A Valid Concept?" *Historian*, XXVIII
(1966), 268–288. Much of the confusion grows out of the assumption that the Second
New Deal came in 1935, when the program became (a) more radical or (b) less
radical.

employment insurance, and old age benefits. In a sense the legislative program known as the New Deal was catch-up reformism, rather than a radical departure from anything known to America or to the more progressive countries of the Western world.

Conservative critics of Roosevelt condemned his radicalism, and during his lifetime and shortly thereafter one frequently read of the "Roosevelt Revolution." With the lengthening of perspective, historians began to label him more commonly as a progressive rather than a radical. In possibly saving American democracy by a relatively mild injection of socialism, he may have averted a violent overturn and thus saved the capitalistic system. He may have headed off collectivism by major doses of reformism.

Writers of the radical New Left have downgraded the extent of Rooseveltian reform. In particular they have stressed the opportunities for socialistic change that were not pushed, and have written off the New Deal as a holding operation for American capitalism. More specifically, critics charge that Roosevelt short-changed the "forgotten man," especially the sharecroppers, tenant farmers, migratory workers, farm laborers, unemployed blacks, unskilled workers, and slum dwellers. It is indisputable that all of these unfortunates benefited to some extent from New Deal schemes, but not enough to please most humanitarians. Few can deny that Roosevelt introduced sweeping reforms; the dispute centers on whether he went as far as he should have gone.[4]

WAS ROOSEVELT A SUPERIOR ADMINISTRATOR?

Born to a patrician family and inheriting wealth, Roosevelt had attended the best schools. With his Harvard-Groton accent and his rather supercilious manner, he could hardly have been regarded as the future champion of "the forgotten man." But poliomyelitis felled him in 1921, the year after he ran unsuccessfully for the vice presidency, and by putting steel braces on his legs it may have added more steel to his backbone. This point is only conjectural, for there is evidence that he was highly ambitious politically before the dread disease struck. In any event, paralysis prostrated this aristocrat and reduced him to hobbling mobility, thereby bringing him down nearer the level of the common man and probably increasing his political appeal. Physical disability seems also

[4] See B. J. Bernstein, ed., *Towards a New Past* (1968), pp. 263–288. For a critique of recent literature, see J. S. Auerbach, "New Deal, Old Deal, or Raw Deal: Some Thoughts on New Left Historiography," *Jour. of Southern Hist.*, *XXXV* (1969), 18–30.

to have added to his courage, buoyancy, and optimism, for he once remarked that after a man has spent many months trying to wiggle his
big toe, he can accomplish anything.

In the conventional sense, Roosevelt was not a good administrator. Known as the "gay improviser," he outwardly reduced much of his
office to chaos. He believed, like a resourceful quarterback, in discarding
the "game plan" if the one being used did not work. He would unexpectedly and daringly abandon solemn campaign promises if he felt that
the public interest required a shift, notably in increasing deficits, unbalancing the budget, and multiplying the bureaucrats. Like Hoover and
other Presidents, he created a wide "credibility gap." Hating to fire
people, he would keep appointees in office who were quarreling with
one another, or appoint competing commissions. He evidently hoped that
the clash of personalities and ambitions might strike off the sparks of
fruitful new ideas. He was especially successful in attracting brainy
young men to the public service, more so than any of his predecessors.[5]

Some admirers of Roosevelt, conceding that in routine matters
he was a poor administrator, argue that overall he was an "administrative
artist." He kept his eye on the mainstream and got schemes adopted,
even though they may not have worked out well. He induced Congress
to authorize a sweeping reform of the executive branch in the Reorganization Act of 1939, under which he set up the large-scale Executive
Office. This innovation in itself is regarded as the greatest single administrative achievement of any President.[6]

Roosevelt's management of World War II, in collaboration with
Winston Churchill, demonstrated an unusual capacity to grapple with
large problems. Whatever his administrative faults, F.D.R. "thought
big." He was a gifted leader who inspired many voters with the feeling
that he knew where he was going, although he often had no clear idea
as to what path he was taking. After Hoover's failure to bring results,
Roosevelt's daring leadership struck a responsive chord.

WAS ROOSEVELT AN ECONOMIC ILLITERATE?

Various unorthodox maneuvers by Roosevelt, such as devaluing the
dollar, going off the gold standard, and torpedoing the London Economic

[5] The so-called "Brain Trust" (initially "Brains Trust") was formed in 1932 when
F.D.R. was still governor of New York. It consisted of a small group of experts,
mostly college professors, whose brains he picked for New Deal ideas and who,
with shifting personnel, served as a kind of Kitchen Cabinet. See R. G. Tugwell, *The
Brains Trust* (1968). Tugwell was a member.

[6] Clinton Rossiter, *The American Presidency* (1956), p. 100.

Conference, have led critics to charge that he was not only erratic but downright ignorant in dealing with financial problems.

Roosevelt had a good undergraduate grounding in economics at Harvard, as well as considerable experience in business during the 1920s, plus four years as governor of New York, a state with one of the largest budgets in the country.[7] Although never "bookish," he had a remarkably retentive memory for statistical data relating to the economy. The President ordinarily attains his high office as a result of his political rather than his fiscal skills, and in Roosevelt the public perhaps got somewhat better than it might have expected.

President Hoover had followed economic orthodoxy with scant success, and Roosevelt, with his joy in experimentation, could hardly be blamed for trying new expedients. The unorthodox economic theories of John M. Keynes, the brilliant British theoretician, were coming into vogue, but were not published in full-blown form until 1936. Roosevelt, like Keynes, favored combating a depression with heavy deficit expenditures on projects like public works; they in turn would maintain a high level of employment and purchasing power. In the light of subsequent events we may surmise that Roosevelt was on the right track but not on a large enough scale. A cutback in spending triggered the recession of 1937–1938, and a heavy increase of overseas war orders after 1939 eased and then ended the unemployment crisis. The supreme irony is that a war-bent Adolf Hitler, rather than a free-spending Franklin Roosevelt, unwittingly provided the extra stimulus that pulled the nation out of the Great Depression.

WAS THE "GOOD NEIGHBOR" PHRASE OR FACT?

As earlier observed, the United States was moving in the direction of improved relations with Latin America during the 1920s, conspicuously in the last months of the Coolidge administration and the four years of President Hoover. During his goodwill tour of Latin America after his election in 1928, Hoover thrice referred to the "good neighbor" or "good neighbors" during his first speech, that in Honduras.[8]

In his inaugural address, Franklin Roosevelt declared, "In the field of *world policy* [italics inserted] I would dedicate this nation to the policy of the good neighbor." The most spectacular application of this

[7] See Daniel R. Fusfeld, *The Economic Thought of Franklin D. Roosevelt and the Origins of the New Deal* (1956). Roosevelt first introduced his "fireside chat" radio technique while governor of New York.

[8] Alexander DeConde, *Herbert Hoover's Latin American Policy* (1951), p. 18.

pledge involved Latin America, and hence obscures the fact that Roosevelt was extending it to the entire globe.

Secretary of State Cordell Hull labored earnestly to implement the Good Neighbor policy. His most useful work was performed in a two-way reduction of tariffs through a series of bilateral treaties under the Reciprocal Trade Agreements Act, passed by Congress in 1934. Latin America, which had been badly bruised by Hoover's Hawley–Smoot Act of 1930, was pleased with this opportunity to reduce tariff barriers. The Republican "outs" were less happy with the whittling down of "protection" by individual treaties, but they should have remembered that Secretary of State Blaine, a Republican, was one of the earliest and warmest advocates of reciprocity.

What rankled most with Latin Americans was the interventionist twist given to the Monroe Doctrine by Theodore Roosevelt, a fifth cousin of Franklin Roosevelt. They particularly resented the occupation of the Caribbean republics by American Marines. In 1933 Roosevelt revived a Hooverian proposal to evacuate Haiti, and the next year the Marines sounded taps and departed. For the first time in many years, no U. S. troops "profaned" Latin American soil.[9] Late in 1933 the Washington government approved a declaration adopted by a Pan-American Conference in Montevideo, which had declared, "No State has the right to intervene in the internal or external affairs of another." Following words with deeds, the United States released Cuba in 1934 from the shackles of the Platt amendment of 1901, under which the Yankees could intervene to restore order.

Roosevelt's nonintervention pledge was greeted with great rejoicing south of the border. One of the prettiest ironies of history is that the interventionism of the first Roosevelt was swept away by the second Roosevelt. Yet despite the improved atmosphere the new Good Neighbor policy failed to remove the basic conflict between Latin American nationalism and overweening Yankee power.[10]

DID F.D.R. TORPEDO THE
LONDON ECONOMIC CONFERENCE?

In June 1933 a sixty-six nation conference assembled in London to work out international remedies for the economic sickness caused by the Great

[9] None were to return until 1965, when President Johnson ordered the temporary Dominican intervention.

[10] See David Green, *The Containment of Latin America: A History of the Myths and Realities of the Good Neighbor Policy* (1971).

Depression. The three most pressing problems were tariff barriers, the debts-reparations tangle, and the stabilization of currencies. Roosevelt flatly ruled out any discussion of tariffs and debts, but agreed to a consideration of currency stabilization.

Discussions in London were creaking along slowly when the gold-bloc nations attempted to commit America to a currency-stabilization program. Roosevelt had only recently taken the nation off the gold standard, and his tinkering with the currency had been followed by some feeble blushes of recovery. Even these were showing signs of fading in the light of the stabilization proposal from London.

Roosevelt believed that prosperity, like charity, begins at home. In choosing currency-manipulating recovery in his own country rather than recovery abroad, he would have to halt a move toward international currency stabilization. Such a course was dictated for Roosevelt by political as well as economic motivations. He finally dashed off a radio message to the Conference, scolding it for concentrating on currency stabilization to the exclusion of "fundamental economic ills." In view of the fact that he had excluded consideration of such "fundamental economic ills" as the tariff and war debts, while agreeing in advance to consider currency stabilization, this tactlessly worded bombshell outraged the delegates. The Conference lingered on for several more weeks, and then broke up without having solved any major problems.[11]

Apologists for Roosevelt argue that so widespread were the economic ills throughout the world that agreement on fundamental problems would never have been reached in any event. F.D.R., the argument goes, merely administered euthanasia to a conclave that was painfully dying. Even so, the same result could have been achieved by a diplomatically worded message; it would have enabled the delegates to bury the conference under harmless platitudes. Roosevelt's brusque and seemingly impulsive decision, not untypical of the early New Deal, did nothing to cushion the worldwide depression. It dealt a heavy blow to international cooperation, while hastening the ominous drift toward isolationism, big-navyism, and extreme nationalism. There was a growing spirit of every-nation-for-itself-and-the-devil-take-the-hindmost.

[11] The only concrete achievement of consequence was an international agreement favorable to silver, which Senator Key Pittman of the silver-producing state of Nevada managed to secure despite drunken antics with a bowie knife in his hotel. A. M. Schlesinger, Jr., *The Coming of the New Deal* (1959), pp. 211, 229–230. See also Fred L. Israel, *Nevada's Key Pittman* (1963), pp. 91–92.

WAS NONRECOGNITION OF THE U.S.S.R. JUSTIFIED?

Ex-President Herbert Hoover and other conservatives of like mind repeatedly charged that Roosevelt's recognition of the Moscow regime in November 1933 was a colossal blunder.[12] Many of them believed that the added prestige thus given to the usurping Bolshevik minority enabled it to hang on and fix its shackles permanently on the Russian masses.

From 1917 to 1933 nonrecognition of Russia had been a policy of both Democrats and Republicans, from Woodrow Wilson to Herbert Hoover.[13] The chief objections to recognition were that the new regime had repudiated Tsarist debts owed Washington, refused to compensate American private interests for confiscated property, and promoted world revolutionary propaganda in the United States. Moreover Americans distrusted and feared Bolsheviks, who had not only seized private property of Russian citizens but had enthroned atheism after dethroning the Greek Orthodox Church. The establishment of diplomatic relations is ordinarily not a seal of approval but merely recognition of an established government. Yet many Americans mistakenly believed that official intercourse would indicate endorsement of a hated Communist regime.

By the end of 1933 the Great Depression had changed the atmosphere. If the Russians did not pay their debts, they were now in distinguished company: Britain, France, and Italy were also in default or were about to be. Even the levels of the minor prewar commerce with Russia had fallen. In the desperate attempt to revive business and relieve unemployment, Roosevelt was willing to explore the possibility of lucrative dealings with the Soviets. Russian spokesmen spoke glibly of a billion-dollar trade — although Washington subsequently learned that they were counting on this sum in loans or credits from the United States.

Other arguments for recognition were advanced. The Bolsheviks had abandoned communism in 1921 in favor of a form of state socialism, which they continued to retain under a relatively small minority of

[12] Hoover's innate aversion to any form of collectivism was strengthened by a number of disagreeable experiences with the suspicious Russian officials when he administered the gigantic Russian relief program, 1921–1923. H. H. Fisher, *The Famine in Soviet Russia, 1918–1923* (1927), p. 48.

[13] The traditional recognition policy of the United States prior to the Wilson administration, with a few exceptions, had been to recognize firmly established governments routinely, whatever their origins. Wilson undertook to withhold recognition, especially in the case of Mexico, from regimes of which he disapproved. Subsequent administrations generally returned to the traditional policy, except notably in the cases of Communist Russia and Communist China. Since recognition was withheld from these governments primarily on the grounds of disapproval, belated recognition seemingly involved a species of approval.

so-called Communists. Other great nations had recognized Russia without demonstrably ill effects, and the nonrecognition by America or any other nation had not perceptibly undermined the Moscow regime. Moreover Hitler was on the rise in Europe, as were the Japanese militarists in East Asia, and the United States, the argument ran, should do what it could to strengthen the Soviets as a counterforce. Finally, the absurdity of the old policy was obvious — nonrecognition of a nation of 160,000,-000 people who occupied one-sixth of the earth's surface.

WAS RECOGNITION OF RUSSIA A BLUNDER?

The New Deal, championed by the avowedly liberal Roosevelt, seemed to call for a new approach to the Kremlin. Negotiations were opened in Washington with the Soviets, and a much-disputed agreement resulted late in 1933. The United States would formally recognize the Moscow regime, which in turn bound itself to permit freedom to worship for Americans in Russia and to discontinue Communist propaganda in the United States. Further negotiations over claims, debts, and loans were postponed to a later date but were never satisfactorily worked out.

This belated recognition agreement unfortunately led to much disagreement. Soviet-directed Communist propaganda continued in the United States under the Communist International, which was intimately connected with official Moscow. Denial by the Kremlin officials of any responsibility rang hollow: they could have stopped their campaign promptly if they had chosen to do so. For their part, the Soviets claimed that they had been tricked into believing that they would receive immense loans from America. But the Russians were such poor credit risks that these assurances were probably never given, and in any event the already inconsequential trade with the Soviet Union further declined. Both Americans and Russians claimed that they had been deceived.

Was recognition a mistake? Roseate hopes of trade and other benefits were dashed, but the acceptance of a reality was achieved. As the subsequent nonrecognition of Red China from 1949 on proved, there are certain disadvantages in not being able to communicate directly and officially with one's diplomatic adversary. In any event, the recognition of Moscow seems to have had little effect in either strengthening or weakening the Communist regime. The Roosevelt administration merely faced up to what was probably inevitable.[14]

[14] See Robert P. Browder, *The Origins of Soviet–American Diplomacy* (1953); Donald G. Bishop, *The Roosevelt–Litvinov Agreement* (1965).

DID ROOSEVELT BETRAY THE DEMOCRATIC PARTY?

Franklin Roosevelt's Democratic party dated its heritage back to Thomas Jefferson and Andrew Jackson. Both of these earlier giants became "forgotten men" to the Rooseveltians, who in effect created a New Deal party. New Dealers largely abandoned the Jeffersonian concepts of strict construction, a weak central government, decentralization, a small bureaucracy, states' rights, a modest public debt, bare-boned economy, and a balanced budget. All these Democratic principles were now embraced by the Republicans, who increasingly were forced into the position of conservatism and obstructionism.

In one conspicuous respect, the nominal Democratic party remained true to Jeffersonian principles. It retained its appeal to the common man, in contrast with the more affluent Republicans. To the end, the New Dealers remained anti-big business, anti-big banking, anti-monopoly, and anti-high tariff.

Jefferson remarked in 1813, "The earth belongs to the living, not to the dead." Had he been alive and faced with hungry millions of men, he probably would have favored many of the non-Jefferson devices of the New Deal. He had often reversed himself while living, and he could hardly have objected to being reversed when dead, especially in the light of drastically changed circumstances. Ironically, the New Dealers refurbished Jefferson, whose early advocacy of nullification in the Kentucky resolutions of 1799 had hurt his "image" after the Civil War. And as if to do penance for having taken such liberties with his principles, in 1938 the Rooseveltians began building the imposing Jefferson Monument in Washington to his memory.

WAS THE NEW DEAL PRO-NEGRO?

Black Americans had traditionally supported the Republican party — the party of the freedom-giving Abraham Lincoln. As "the last hired and the first fired," they suffered acutely during the Hooverian phase of the Depression, yet they loyally voted for Hoover in 1932. But in the Congressional elections of 1934, many of them moved over into the Democratic camp. By 1936, feeling that they had paid their debt to Abraham Lincoln, they bolted bodily into the Rooseveltian ranks and remained with the Democrats.

This shift is not difficult to explain. Although outrageous discriminations continued, many of the agencies set up under the New Deal extended limited benefits to Negroes. They were clearly enjoying a larger measure of relief than they had received under the Hooverites.[15] In addition, Roosevelt made a determined effort to appoint competent blacks to positions of responsibility, albeit minor offices, but even this recognition was a noteworthy change.

Oddly enough, not a single piece of significant civil rights legislation was enacted during Roosevelt's four terms. The Southern members of Congress were in a position to jeopardize New Deal legislation if the hot issue of Negro rights was raised, and President Roosevelt, ever the political realist, decided to play the race problem in low key. Hence the new Democratic party consisted of the Solid South, plus the urban North, with the workingmen and the Negroes playing an essential part in the mix.

WAS F.D.R. JUSTIFIED IN ATTACKING THE SUPREME COURT?

In 1936 the Democrats renominated Roosevelt, who staged a bare-knuckle campaign against ex-President Hoover and the moneyed interests. The Republicans chose the rather colorless Governor Alf Landon of Kansas, an ex-Bull Mooser who was more liberal than generally supposed but who was somewhat restrained by the wealthy conservatives of his party.

Roosevelt won in a landslide, contrary to the prediction of the *Literary Digest*, which was, until then, successfully conducting the most famous national straw vote.[16] The outcome of the election was not a mandate, as sometimes supposed, to pack the Supreme Court. Roosevelt and his party had not even raised that issue during the recent campaign.

[15] See Raymond Wolters, *Negroes and the Great Depression* (1970).

[16] The *Literary Digest*, then the most prominent weekly newsmagazine, had mailed out millions of straw-vote ballots, primarily to promote subscriptions and incidentally to forecast the presidential elections of 1920, 1924, 1928, and 1932. It guessed the winner in all four. In 1936 it predicted a Landon victory on the basis of its returns, which were 1,293,669 to 972,897. When Roosevelt triumphed in a landslide, the journal confessed that it did not know what went wrong. One common explanation is that the names on its mailing list were taken from telephone books and local directories, and that during the Depression the "forgotten man" who voted for Roosevelt often did not have a telephone or own a home. Yet in 1932, when the Depression was acute, the magazine used exactly the same techniques and predicted the winner within less than a 1 percent margin of error. See *Literary Digest*, Nov. 14, 1936, p. 7. More sophisticated polling techniques, based on carefully selected samples of the population, came to the fore in the late 1930s.

But the Democratic victory in a broad sense was a mandate from the electorate to continue with the changes or attempted changes sponsored by the New Deal.

Yet the Supreme Court was not listening to the people's voice. Heavily weighted with aged conservatives, it had been handing down a series of Old Deal decisions, including invalidation of the National Industrial Recovery Act (NIRA) and the Agricultural Adjustment Act (AAA). It had also declared unconstitutional a minimum wage law adopted by the state of New York, while seeming to be sharpening its judicial hatchet for the prolabor National Labor Relations Act (Wagner Act) of 1935 and the epochal Social Security Act of 1935. In view of the Court's hostile attitude, not only was the established New Deal in jeopardy but the remainder of the program seemed to be facing a hopeless roadblock.

Roosevelt was understandably in a mood to strike back. He felt that since America was presumably a democracy in which the citizenry ruled, the Court ought to line up with the will of the voters as broadly expressed in three successive "free" elections.[17] These were Roosevelt's defeat of Hoover in 1932, the Democratic landslide in the Congressional elections of 1934, and Roosevelt's "Landonslide" victory in 1936.

DID ROOSEVELT ATTEMPT TO PACK THE SUPREME COURT?

For about two years Roosevelt had been pondering some scheme that would make the Court more responsive to the people, and at one time he considered but rejected the idea of "packing" that body. Then on February 5, 1937, about two weeks after his second inauguration, he sprang his proposal on Congress without previously consulting any of its leaders or any member of his Cabinet, except his Attorney General. Rather deviously declaring that the federal court system had fallen hopelessly behind in its homework because of too many old and enfeebled members, Roosevelt carefully avoided saying that he was acting because of distaste for the notorious anti-New Deal bias of the berobed oldsters. He proposed that after a Justice of the Supreme Court had served 10 years and had reached the age of seventy without retiring, then the President might nominate an additional member, up to the number of six. A total of forty-four judges might thus be added to the lower federal courts on the same basis.

There seems little doubt that Roosevelt was under strong com-

---

[17] Cynics wondered aloud how "free" the elections were when relief checks for the voters arrived in large batches on the eve of balloting.

pulsion to act and that his scheme was constitutional, for Congress had on several previous occasions changed the number of Supreme Court justices. But the "slick" manner in which he attempted to tamper with what had become a sacred cow provoked a furious reaction that he, a master politician, ought to have anticipated. About the best that his defenders could say was that he was trying to "unpack" the Court by adding new blood that would offset the reactionary blood of the "senile" members.

The steam was taken out of Roosevelt's scheme by several surprises. Chief Justice Hughes was able to present conclusive evidence that the Court was not behind in its work. Then in a series of memorable 5 to 4 decisions the Court upheld a Washington State minimum wage act (resembling the one it had recently overturned), the National Labor Relations Act (Wagner Act), and the Social Security Act. Many people related this change of heart, as was probable, to the club that Roosevelt was holding over the Court.[18] Moreover, during the prolonged fight one of the oldest members retired, to be replaced by Mr. Justice Black, a strong and long-lived liberal. Roosevelt now had his safe New Deal majority, and during the two and one-half years after the struggle began he replaced five members of the nine-man bench.

WHO WON THE COURT FIGHT?

Roosevelt lost his battle to "pack" or "unpack" the Supreme Court after a fight in Congress that lasted 168 days. A watered-down version of the original proposal was finally adopted which embodied only procedural, not personnel, reforms in the lower courts.[19] But Roosevelt won his battle in the sense that his attack, whether coincidentally or not, was followed by a change of heart and of vote on the Supreme Bench. Admirers, who praised his fighting zeal,[20] insisted that while losing the battle he won the war.

[18] The "swing man" in these crucial 5 to 4 decisions was Justice Roberts, who had voted against the New York minimum wage on a technicality. His support for the next minimum wage act was recorded *before* Roosevelt's "court packing" message. He may have been influenced in subsequent rulings by the threat to the Court; his shift gave rise to the quip "A switch in time saves nine." Merlo Pusey, *Charles Evans Hughes* (2 vols., 1951), II, 757.

[19] One innovation earlier passed by Congress (approved March 1, 1937) was that a justice could retire at age seventy with his full salary. This change was obviously designed to encourage retirements and weaken F.D.R.'s more sweeping scheme.

[20] Roosevelt, who on occasion got his "Dutch up," was so genial and so disinclined to hurt people's feelings by saying "no" that he described himself as a "softy." The impression took root that he was not a fighter, but his protracted, head-on battle with Congress over the Court, when he might have beaten a retreat, should correct this misconception.

But did Roosevelt win the war? In struggling to secure adoption of his scheme, he so antagonized the more conservative members of his own party in Congress that they joined hands with the Republican minority to insure that virtually no major New Deal measures would pass after the summer of 1938. Roosevelt now had a Court disposed to uphold his program, but he also had a Congress that was indisposed to enact his reformist proposals. In this sense he lost both the battle and the war. Moreover, the suspicions aroused by the court-packing proposal created a vast amount of distrust for Roosevelt's interventionist foreign policies.[21]

In retrospect we can see that Roosevelt probably would have secured his New Deal Court within a short time without a disruptive fight. Perhaps he should have been a little more patient. But he had no advance assurance that a majority of the Court would change its stance; some of the oldest members seemed to be hanging on primarily to block New Deal reforms. A major portion of his program, already enacted or about to be enacted, seemed to be in jeopardy. We can understand why he should have sought some way out of the impasse, other than a time-consuming constitutional amendment of uncertain fate. Roosevelt believed that the Court, not the Constitution, needed changing.

WAS THE NYE MUNITIONS INVESTIGATION USEFUL?

In 1933 Hitler abruptly withdrew Germany from the League of Nations; in 1935 he announced that he would openly rearm, in defiance of the restrictive Treaty of Versailles. The next year, taking advantage of Mussolini's imperialistic grab of Ethiopia, Hitler marched his troops into the German Rhineland, as France and Britain irresolutely wrung their hands. World opinion was increasingly fearful of a dictator-spawned world war.

In this explosive atmosphere a phobia developed in America against the munitions manufacturers — the so-called "Merchants of Death." During 1934–1935 a veritable avalanche of condemnatory books and articles poured from the press exposing existing malpractices and demanding curbs. The assumption was that the arms makers, backed by the bankers, had dragged the United States into World War I; consequently a demand mounted for legislation that would properly

[21] See William E. Leuchtenburg's perceptive essay, "Franklin D. Roosevelt's Supreme Court 'Packing' Plan," in Harold M. Hollingsworth and Williams F. Holmes, eds., *Essays on the New Deal* (1969), pp. 69–115.

control this nefarious traffic. A popular slogan ran, "Keep America out of the Blood Business."

Responding to an aroused public opinion, the Senate created an investigating Committee, under the chairmanship of Senator Gerald P. Nye of North Dakota, an isolationist. Munitions makers and bankers were haled before the Committee, and they confessed — what was already common knowledge — that they had made fabulous profits during World War I. Many suspicious citizens leaped to the conclusion that somehow these soulless profiteers had dragged America into the inferno to protect their ill-gotten gains.

Subsequent scholarship indicates that the impact of the Nye Committee has been overplayed. On the whole the probers conducted fair hearings, and they failed to prove that arms manufacturers conspired to cause wars. Chairman Nye was far less sensational in the Committee room than he was out on the platform, where he voiced a number of extravagant charges that helped to give his investigation a bad name. The influence of this group in bringing about the passage of the subsequent neutrality legislation by Congress may have been exaggerated. With the public mind already inflamed by the press, such laws probably would have been enacted in any event. The Nye Committee gave a further push to a movement that had already gained impressive momentum.[22]

WERE THE NEUTRALITY ACTS UNWISE?

Fearful of involvement in a second world war and spurred by Mussolini's invasion of Ethiopia, Congress passed the first of the neutrality laws in 1935. It stipulated that *whenever the President formally declared that a state of war existed,*[23] he could forbid the sale or transportation of munitions to those nations involved. He was also empowered to *warn* American citizens that they could travel on belligerent passenger ships, like the ill-starred *Lusitania* of 1915, only at their own risk. Roosevelt signed the bill with reluctance; he and his advisors much preferred a more flexible arrangement that would deny munitions to the aggressor while making them available to the victims of aggression.

The next year, 1936, Congress tightened the law, notably by

22 See John E. Wiltz, *In Search of Peace: The Senate Munitions Inquiry, 1934–1936* (1963).

23 When Japan invaded China in 1937, Roosevelt refrained from declaring a state of war. To have done so would have been to deny arms to both China and Japan, and an unneutral America wanted China to win.

forbidding loans to the belligerents, except for ordinary commercial transactions. Early in 1937, with the Spanish civil war in the headlines, all these restrictions were extended to internal conflicts. In May 1937 Congress reenacted the general limitations on the traffic in arms, on loans to belligerents, and on involvement in civil wars, while making travel on belligerent ships unlawful, rather than at the passenger's risk. Commodities such as copper and oil were as essential to waging war as munitions themselves, but rather than deny American producers juicy profits, Congress compromised. It permitted such sales, provided that the purchasers took them away in their own ships and paid for them in cash. This "cash-and-carry" provision was to last two years.

Taken as a package, the neutrality laws were obviously designed to profit from the "lessons" of history and keep the United States out of a conflict such as World War I. In other words, if this legislation had been on the books in 1917, the likelihood of America's direct involvement would have been greatly reduced if not eliminated.

It is fashionable to condemn the neutrality laws of the 1930s as foolish, purblind, and ineffective. But their basic weakness was that they were too effective, especially after the fall of France in 1940. They tied the hands of a United States that wanted to help the Allies win a war which many Americans felt had to be won in the nation's own interest. If France had held the line, America's entry into the conflict might have been averted, while the two camps of belligerents fought to a stalemate, without the necessity of repealing the neutrality legislation. The fundamental fault of the new laws was that they were tailored for a different war — the one that had been fought twenty years earlier.

The claim is often made that Hitler was encouraged by this self-shackling neutrality legislation to attack Poland and start World War II. One may doubt if America's attitude greatly affected his calculations, for he must have known that what a legislative body passes it can also rescind. Indeed, several months before Hitler struck in 1939, Congress had heatedly debated the question of repeal, with the House (but not the Senate) passing a modification, 200 to 188. Moreover, Hitler was counting on lightning victories, which he achieved. He evidently concluded that if he succeeded, the Americans could not possibly wipe out their neutrality legislation and ship over enough munitions in time to make a significant difference.[24]

Paradoxically, the early neutrality laws were not completely neutral. The Act of 1936 provided that, as a means of upholding the

[24] W. L. Langer and S. E. Gleason, *The Challenge to Isolation, 1937–1940* (1952), p. 147.

Monroe Doctrine, arms could be exported to any Latin American state at war with a non-American nation. This was favoritism in both the national and hemispheric interest.

DID F.D.R. BETRAY LOYALIST SPAIN?

The democratic "Loyalist" government of Spain, following its harsh persecutions of the Catholic Church, provoked a rebellion led by General Franco, a pro-Catholic and ultraconservative General Franco. This bloody and brutal conflict, costing about a million lives, ground on from July 1936 to March 1939.

United States policy during civil wars, conspicuously in Latin America, had generally been to make arms available to the established regime. On this basis America should have sold munitions in quantity to the Madrid government. But numerous isolationists, fearing to involve the United States, raised loud objections. An arms embargo in time of international war, though not civil war, had already been authorized by the Neutrality Acts of 1935 and 1936. The British and French, seeing advantages in noninvolvement, were determined to stand on the sidelines. Moreover, the Catholic Church, understandably horrified by the atrocities of the Spanish Loyalists, was pro-Franco, as were many Catholics in America. Subsequent research has shown that about two-thirds of Catholic laymen in the United States did not follow their leaders, and that F.D.R. mistook the voice of the clerics for that of their flocks.[25]

President Roosevelt had signed with misgivings the inflexible Neutrality Acts of 1935 and 1936. But in the case of the Spanish civil war, he took the initiative in urging Congress to bracket internal conflicts with external conflicts in imposing a ban on exporting munitions. Congress responded favorably in January 1937, with only one dissenting vote in either house.

Thus the Western democracies stood with arms folded as Hitler and Mussolini poured troops and materiel into Spain for the support of Franco. Communist Russia, for its part, sent less conspicuous aid to the Loyalists, in weapons and personnel, and infiltrated their camp to a substantial degree in an effort to halt fascism. The very presence of Communists in Spain did much to chill whatever sympathy the Ameri-

---

[25] J. D. Valaik, "Catholics, Neutrality, and the Spanish Embargo, 1937–1939," *Jour. of Amer. Hist.*, LIV (1967), 73–85. See also Richard P. Traina, *American Diplomacy and the Spanish Civil War* (1968).

cans may have had for the Loyalist cause. As a result, the legitimate Madrid government was pounded into submission in a kind of dress rehearsal for the weapons and techniques of World War II.[26] Possibly American arms would only have prolonged the agony.

Roosevelt, at heart pro-Loyalist and anti-Franco, later acknowledged in private his mistake in pursuing a hands-off Spanish policy.[27] The subsequent success of the dictators was but one more step up the ladder to the outbreak of World War in 1939. If F.D.R. had been privileged to see far enough ahead, he might have tried to exercise decisive leadership in favor of the Loyalists, who became the victims of unneutral neutrality. But he was too much concerned about the Catholic vote, about the upcoming presidential election of 1936, about the disruptive power of the isolationist elements in Congress, and about the dangers of jeopardizing the passage of the remainder of his New Deal measures.

WAS THE REACTION TO QUARANTINE SPEECH NEGATIVE?

Early in October 1937, several months after Japan had opened her undeclared war with China ("the China incident"), Roosevelt journeyed to Chicago, the so-called isolationist capital of America, to make a sensational speech. Obviously alluding to the Japanese militarists in China and to the intervention of Hitler and Mussolini in Spain, he referred to the disease known as "international anarchy" which threatened to spread to the Western Hemisphere. Just as a physician quarantines the victims of an epidemic, so must the United States "quarantine" the aggressors with "positive endeavors," at which Roosevelt only hinted.[28]

This electrifying speech was well received by the audience, but isolationist elements, in Congress and out, emitted a loud outcry of protest against meddling abroad and thus forsaking neutrality. "Positive endeavors" strongly suggested economic sanctions against Japan. Roosevelt, with his politician's instincts, recoiled somewhat in the face of this

[26] Parallels to the American Civil War suggest themselves, but in this case Britain and France sold arms impartially to both rebels and Unionists.

[27] See Claude G. Bowers, *My Mission to Spain* (1954), p. 418. Bowers was the strongly pro-Loyalist U. S. Ambassador during these critical years, and his testimony is not completely reliable.

[28] There is evidence that F.D.R. was thinking of an Anglo–American naval quarantine by July 1937, but by February 1938, his hopes were dashed by American isolationism and British noncooperation. John M. Haight, Jr., "Franklin D. Roosevelt and a Naval Quarantine of Japan," *Pacific Hist. Rev.*, XL (1971), 203–226.

outburst. Henceforth there was little talk about "positive endeavors," whatever they may have meant.[29]

To say that Roosevelt was forced to back down because of the popular uproar is to put the case too strongly. There is evidence that he exaggerated the angry response of the isolationists and underestimated the surprising amount of popular approval. Moreover, he had no specific plan with which to implement his bold words — at least none that he was willing to announce. In the circumstances, he was willing to drift. "It's a terrible thing," he later remarked, "to look over your shoulder when you are trying to lead — and to find no one there."

Some two months after the bold Quarantine Speech, Japanese aviators, flying in broad daylight, bombed and sank a gunboat, the U. S. S. *Panay*, on China's Yangtze River. Two Americans were killed and some thirty were wounded as the escaping survivors were repeatedly machine-gunned. The Tokyo Foreign Office promptly presented profuse apologies and an offer of a large indemnity, which was accepted. Neutrality-minded America breathed a sigh of relief. The circumstantial evidence is strong that the attack was engineered by hotheaded Japanese officers who were defying the civilian government, but there is a possibility that the *Panay* was thought to be a Chinese gunboat disguised with American flags.[30]

WAS MUNICH A COMPLETE SURRENDER?

In March 1938 Hitler seized German-speaking Austria. Later in the year he began beating the drums for annexation of the German-inhabited part of Czechoslovakia known as the Sudetenland. The Czechs had a strong and well-equipped army, as well as an alliance with France (but not with Britain). Yet Hitler seemed determined to strike, despite the protests of his generals that they were not ready.[31]

President Roosevelt sent last-minute appeals to Hitler and to his Italian ally, Mussolini, urging restraint. Whether influenced by these pleas or not, Hitler consented to a four-power Conference in Munich, Germany in September 1938 to discuss the Czech crisis. Russia was not

[29] T. B. Jacobs, "Roosevelt's 'Quarantine Speech,'" *The Historian*, XXIV (1962), 483–502.
[30] Manny T. Koginos, *The Panay Incident: Prelude to War* (1967), p. 129.
[31] When Hitler sent his armies into the Rhineland in 1936, he did so against the advice of his generals and in readiness to beat a retreat if the French, who then had a better army, responded aggressively. But the British and French were divided as to what course they should take, and consequently Hitler successfully bluffed them.

invited. Stalin was later quoted as declaring that this snub was a determining factor in persuading him to clasp hands with Hitler in the
ill-starred Russo–German pact of 1939, which made inevitable World
War II.[32]

France and Britain were much less well prepared for war than
Hitler, whose superior aerial bombing fleets could presumably have
devastated their cities. Paris and London consequently responded to
their fears, to divided counsels, and to the somewhat specious argument
of self-determination for all Germans. The upshot was the controversial
Munich agreement, which stipulated that Czechoslovakia would be shorn
of her Sudetenland, thus making the Czechs even more vulnerable to
an attack from Germany. This sacrifice came to be known as "appeasement" — the hope that by appeasing Hitler's lust for conquest the
democracies would head off future territorial grabs and a new world war.

An annex to the Munich agreement contained a proviso, signed
by Hitler, Mussolini, and the representatives of Britain and France,
guaranteeing the newly established frontiers of Czechoslovakia against
"unprovoked aggression." Three days earlier, Hitler had declared in a
Berlin speech, "The Sudetenland is the last territorial claim I have to
make in Europe." Less than six months later, in March 1939, he
shattered remaining illusions by seizing the remainder of Czechoslovakia,
which was clearly non-German. He had no difficulty in claiming that
his action was "provoked" by the alleged disintegration of the new
Czech government.[33]

WAS THE MUNICH APPEASEMENT A TOTAL LOSS?

Munich was a compromise, though a one-sided one. Hitler got what he
wanted from Czechoslovakia, in return for an explicit pledge not to take
more. Contrary to a common misconception, the immediate reaction in

[32] Stalin was not one in whose word one could repose complete confidence.
Moscow also declared that it was prepared to honor its mutual assistance pact with
the Czechs if, as the terms provided, the French should honor their alliance with
Czechoslovakia. Russia was not contiguous to Czechoslovakia, and since the Poles
and the Rumanians presumably would not have permitted Russian troops to cross
their soil, Soviet offers of assistance rang hollow. Poland was unfriendly to Czechoslovakia and shortly after Munich forced a cession of a part of Czech territory, as
did Hungary. See Adam Ulam, *Expansion and Coexistence: The History of Soviet
Foreign Policy* (1968), Ch. V.

[33] The text of the Munich Agreement, accompanied by documents, may be conveniently found in Monica Curtis, ed., *Documents on International Affairs, 1938*
(1943), *II*, 289–290.

much of the Western world was relief and rejoicing.[34] Prime Minister Chamberlain returned to London, umbrella and all, to be acclaimed by cheering crowds and to announce that he had achieved "peace for our time." Less than a year later World War II erupted.

The Munich agreement failed, but Britain, France, and the United States all gained a year of grace in which to ready their arms, even though they did not put the time to as good use as they might have.[35] Perhaps more important, these nations became better prepared psychologically. If Britain and France had gone to war because Hitler wanted the three million Germans of Czechoslovakia to be united with the Germans of Germany on the basis of "self-determination," the moral cause of the Western allies would have been somewhat vulnerable. But after Hitler seized the remainder of mutilated Czechoslovakia and stormed into Poland, the eyes of many once-indifferent spectators were unglued, and World War II essentially became a struggle to halt what was regarded as mad-dog aggression.

Although Munich was designed to appease Hitler, it merely whetted his appetite for more. The mere mention of any major compromise agreement since that day has routinely raised cries of "appeasement," "Munich," and "surrender on the installment plan." There have been numerous instances since 1938, especially in the 1960s during the earlier stages of the Vietnam War, when reasonable compromise stood some chance of success. But in every case official Washington was chilled by the inevitable outcries of a Munich surrender. Some scholars have even suggested that the later equating of Munich with all compromise solutions — "the Munich syndrome" — has actually done more harm than the original Munich agreement itself.[36]

DID HITLER CAUSE WORLD WAR II?

In the year following the Munich capitulation in 1938, Hitler seemed bent on war with Poland to secure the once-German city of Danzig and

[34] A Gallup poll in the U.S. (Oct. 1, 1938) favored the Munich surrender rather than war, 59 percent to 41 percent. At the same time the respondents felt that Hitler's demands for the Sudetenland were not justified (77 percent to 23 percent). Hadley Cantril, ed., *Public Opinion, 1935–1946* (1951), p. 1165.

[35] The British installed radar and built up their fleet of high-class fighter planes. These two precautions saved them in the aerial Battle of Britain during the summer of 1940.

[36] Arthur M. Schlesinger, Jr., *The Bitter Heritage* (1967), pp. 89, 91. The United States, fearful of mounting charges of "Munich," refused to approve the Geneva settlement of 1954 regarding Vietnam.

the once-German Polish corridor separating Germany into two parts.[37] Many people, especially in Britain, fearing both Hitler and Stalin, openly expressed the hope that the two menaces would neutralize each other. Especially comforting to the Western world would be a lethal war between the two giants that would bleed both to death and leave the "peace-loving" nations to pursue their quiet paths.

Hitler and Stalin were fully aware of such ill-concealed desires. In the summer of 1939 the British and French were engaged in fateful negotiations with Moscow, hoping to work out some kind of mutual defense arrangement that would protect all parties against the rising might of Germany. Soviet Russia was holding out for a guaranteed position of dominance or control in Finland, the Baltic States, and eastern Poland, but Britain and France were unwilling to go this far. After Moscow had appeared to be coming to terms with the two Western powers, Stalin suddenly reversed the tables. On August 23, 1939, he concluded a nonaggression pact with Germany that would give Hitler the green light to attack Poland and the West. A part of the agreement, then kept secret, cleared the way for Germany to seize western Poland and for Russia to grab eastern Poland, as both nations soon did.[38]

The cynical nature of Stalin's bargain is evident. By giving Hitler a free hand to assault Poland, he became a co-conspirator in triggering World War II. He evidently hoped to confound his ill-wishers in the West by turning Hitler against Poland and then France, where he hoped that the Germans would bleed themselves white in assaulting France's famed Maginot Line. Then Stalin not only would have removed his only feared rival but would bestride the continent like a colossus.

But in 1940 the German assailants outflanked the uncompleted Maginot Line and knocked France out of the war in a few weeks. The next blow would presumably be an invasion of Britain. Stalin was now confronted with a triumphant and unweakened rival, unchecked by the West.[39] Hoping to put as much territory as possible between himself and his partner in aggression, he promptly seized the three Baltic states

[37] In 1934 Hitler had signed a ten-year nonaggression pact with Poland.

[38] The nonaggression pact between Stalin and Hitler was to last ten years, or longer, but before two years had elapsed Hitler had launched a devastating surprise attack on his co-conspirator. Stalin had proved unwilling to give Hitler sufficient control in the Baltic and the Balkans, and the Soviets remained a menace on Germany's flank. See R. J. Sontag and J. S. Beddie, eds., *Nazi-Soviet Relations, 1939–1941* (1948), pp. 78, 226–254.

[39] Nikita Khrushchev, who was with Stalin when the news arrived of France's capitulation, records that the dictator "let fly with some choice Russian curses and said that now Hitler was sure to beat our brains in." *Khrushchev Remembers* (1970), p. 166. It is evident that both Hitler and Stalin tried to "outsmart" the other. Stalin would buy time to prepare for a German onslaught: Hitler would secure his rear while attacking the West. *Ibid.*, p. 128.

and also Rumania's Bessarabia and Northern Bukovina. These buffers were not enough to restrain Hitler when he struck Russia in June 1941.

Adolf Hitler was the primary aggressor in the attack on Poland, although Stalin must fully share the blame for having encouraged him to attack and for having seized his share of territory from the nutcrackered Poles. Hitler loudly maintained that not he but the British and French had caused World War II. He regarded his assault on Poland as a localized affair, designed in part to regain some German territory (self-determination again) which the Poles had stubbornly refused to yield. But Britain and France declared war against Germany on September 3, 1939, three days after Hitler's attack, in response to their well-publicized treaty obligations to Poland. If these two powers had only been willing to call it quits after Hitler and Stalin had divided Poland, then there would have been no World War II. Hence, according to Hitler's line of reasoning, Britain and France were to blame.[40]

Any attempt to shift the primary responsibility for a shoot-out from the bank robbers to the teller who refused to yield his money is not convincing. Reviewing Hitler's career, one has only to remember his paranoid thirst for war, his seemingly insatiable appetite for neighboring territory, his blatant disregard of treaty obligations, his repeated breaking of his plighted word, his mastery of the double cross, and his genocidal zeal. The evidence indicates that he was a mentally unbalanced and fanatical conqueror who would have to be stopped before he became powerful enough to jeopardize the liberties of all men.[41]

ADDITIONAL GENERAL REFERENCES

W. E. Leuchtenburg, *Franklin D. Roosevelt and the New Deal, 1932–1940* (1963); A. M. Schlesinger, Jr., *The Coming of the New Deal* (1959), and *The Politics of Upheaval* (1960); J. M. Burns, *Roosevelt: The Lion and the Fox* (1956); E. E. Robinson, *The Roosevelt Leadership, 1933–1935* (1955); Basil Rauch, *The History of the New Deal, 1933–1938* (1944); John M. Blum, *From*

[40] The British historian, A. J. P. Taylor, in *The Origins of the Second World War* (1961), blames Allied leaders for their weakness, incompetence, impracticality, stupidity, and tardiness. The Anglo–French pledge of military support to Poland (March 31, 1939), he argues, was an unrealistic and provocative act of futility.

[41] A Gallup poll (Oct. 10, 1939) found the American people rejecting Hitler's claim that Britain and France had no real reason for continuing the war once the Polish question was settled. The vote was 79 percent to 9 percent, with 12 percent without opinion. Cantril, ed., *Public Opinion*, p. 1165.

the Morgenthau Diaries: Years of Crisis, 1928–1938 (1959), and Years of Urgency, 1938–1941 (1965); R. G. Tugwell, FDR: Architect of an Era (1967), and The Brains Trust (1968); Otis L. Graham, Encore for Reform: The Old Progressives and the New Deal (1967); Raymond Moley, The First New Deal (1966); T. H. Williams, Huey Long (1969); D. F. Drummond, The Passing of American Neutrality, 1937–1941 (1955); W. L. Langer and S. E. Gleason, The Challenge to Isolation, 1937–1940 (1952); R. A. Divine, Roosevelt and World War II (1969); R. E. Sherwood, Roosevelt and Hopkins (1948); Bryce Wood, The Making of the Good Neighbor Policy (1961); R. A. Divine, The Illusion of Neutrality (1962); W. S. Cole, Gerald P. Nye and American Foreign Relations (1962); Manfred Jonas, Isolationism in America, 1935–1941 (1966); F. J. Taylor, The United States and the Spanish Civil War (1956); Dorothy Borg, The United States and the Far Eastern Crisis of 1933–1938 (1964); A. A. Offer, American Appeasement: United States Foreign Policy and Germany, 1933–1938 (1969).

34

America as a Nominal Neutral, 1939-1941

For about nine months after Hitler precipitated World War II, the United States maintained a reasonably neutral posture, though unabashedly favoring the democracies. But the collapse of France before Hitler's mechanized might, followed by the aerial battering of Britain, presented a dramatically different picture. Roosevelt's transfer of fifty obsolescent U. S. destroyers to the British navy in September 1940 was a flagrant violation of old-style neutrality. The Lend–Lease Act of March 1941, which pledged American resources for the defeat of the aggressors, came close to being a declaration of war.

The shipment of lend–lease materials to Britain inevitably raised the issue of convoying merchant vessels with American warships. From April 1941 to December 1941 the U. S. navy was waging a small-scale but undeclared war with Nazi submarines in the North Atlantic.

In the Far East, America was attempting to halt Japanese expansion, primarily in the interests of its own long-range security. After Washington had imposed economic embargoes designed to bring Japan to her knees, the Japanese burst out of what they regarded as an encirclement with a devastating surprise attack on Pearl Harbor, December 7, 1941. Tokyo regarded the encirclers as the ABCD powers — Americans, British, Chinese, and Dutch.

Beyond question the United States repeatedly violated both its neutral obligations and international law during the so-called neutrality period. But since the dictators had already flouted solemn agreements, Washington would have been muddleheaded indeed if it had played the

*game by the ancient rules while its adversaries were evidently bound by
none. Confronted with the menace of a new totalitarianism, Roosevelt
opted for an unneutrality designed to thwart the dictators.*

WHY WAS TRUE NEUTRALITY IMPOSSIBLE?

A prominent public opinion poll, taken shortly after Hitler invaded
Poland in September of 1939, reported that 84 percent of Americans were
pro-Ally, 2 percent were pro-German, and 14 percent were without opinion.[1] Hitler's rapacity and ruthlessness, especially in seizing neighboring
territory and in viciously persecuting the Jews, had already alienated
the American public. In marked contrast with 1914–1917, any appreciable pro-German sentiment was virtually nonexistent.

Yet the American people had no desire to become involved, disillusioned as they were by the aftermath of World War I and feeling that
their entrance into that conflict had been a mistake. Public opinion
polls revealed that while the respondents overwhelmingly hoped that
the Allies would win, by a comparably wide margin these same citizens
desired to stay out.[2] As events developed, the American people were
finally prepared to render unneutral help at the risk of war, but on the
very day of Japan's surprise attack on Pearl Harbor they still wished
to remain on the sidelines.

There was good reason to believe that World War II would be
something of a carbon copy of World War I, with America omitted.
Great Britain, boasting superior naval strength, would again apply her
slow strangulation blockade. Hitler's armies would batter vainly against
the "impregnable" concrete-and-steel Maginot Line on the French border,
and finally would surrender in exhaustion, as they had in 1918.

This grand strategy did not work out. Until June 1941, when
Hitler turned furiously upon Stalin, Germany had a backdoor access
to supplies from Russia, thus offsetting in large degree the British
blockade. The Maginot Line might have proved impregnable if the
Germans had attacked it frontally, as they were supposed to do. But by
outflanking it from the north, they reduced it to impotence. With France
knocked out of the war and Britain in grave danger of invasion, America
awakened to her peril and gradually forsook all pretense of neutrality.

Two highly vocal pressure groups formed. One was the America
First Committee, which deplored any involvement in the overseas con-

---

[1] Gallup Poll (October, 1939), *Public Opinion Quarterly, IV,* 102.
[2] Gallup Poll (October 4, 1941), *ibid., VI,* 164. The count was 79 percent against
entering the war.

flict and which featured as its most famous spokesman the hero-aviator, Colonel Charles A. Lindbergh.[3] The other leading organization was The Committee to Defend America by Aiding the Allies. Its name implied that by sending supplies to the democracies the United States would keep the war on the other side of the ocean and thus insulate the Republic from involvement in it. Both groups professed to want to stay out of the conflict, but a considerable number of aid-the-allies zealots, secretly or openly, favored direct participation.

DID THE NEUTRALITY ACTS FAIL?

In the summer of 1939 President Roosevelt had attempted to induce Congress to repeal the arms embargo so that America could send aid to the threatened democracies. Hitler, though rattling the saber, had not yet begun war, so the legislators felt under no strong compulsion to act. After the Germans invaded Poland, on September 1, 1939, Roosevelt summoned Congress into special session, which convened on September 21. In his ringing message he called for a "return" to neutral rights under "international law" because embargoes, such as President Jefferson had used, could backfire dangerously. They had caused the British to invade Washington in 1814, F.D.R. alleged, and burn the Capitol building in which Congress had then sat.[4]

Roosevelt was inclined to be devious in his various attempts to persuade Congress and the public to act in what he regarded as the national interest. The ban on munitions imposed by the Neutrality Act of 1937 had nothing to do with "abandoning" international law and little to do with neutral rights. If a sovereign nation wishes to embargo munitions (as Presidents Taft and Wilson had embargoed shipments of arms to the government of Mexico), it may do so, whether as a national policy or as a means of conserving scanty supplies. Moreover, Roosevelt's reference to the War of 1812 was not aptly chosen,[5] although some listeners were no doubt impressed by it.

---

[3] Lindbergh had visited Germany and had been deeply impressed by Hitler's air force. He argued that the Allies could not win, that America could coexist with a victorious Hitler, that Jewish elements in America were promoting interventionism, and that the Allies could never hope to secure control of the air. He proved to be completely wrong in this last judgment, the area in which he had the greatest expertise. Thirty years later, he had changed his views remarkably little. See the Introduction to *The Wartime Journals of Charles A. Lindbergh* (1970).

[4] *Cong. Record*, 76 Cong., 2 sess., pp. 10–12 (Sept. 21, 1939).

[5] Jefferson's embargo was repealed in 1809, to be followed by more limited economic sanctions which forced the British to announce a repeal of their odious Orders in Council. Economic sanctions, rather than causing the war, almost averted it.

After a prolonged debate, Congress passed the Neutrality Act of 1939. The embargo on exports of war supplies was lifted, but the purchasers would have to come and get their cargoes on a cash-and-carry basis. American ships were forbidden to enter the proclaimed danger zones, which had proved so deadly before the nation went to war with Germany in 1917. The revised law also renewed restrictions on loans to the belligerents and on travel in their ships.

The Neutrality Act of 1939 was unneutral in the sense that it changed the rules after the game had started. If it had been passed a few months earlier, it might have acted as a brake on Hitler, though this is doubtful. The Germans could not send merchant ships to America under the guns of the British navy; hence the new law operated to Germany's disadvantage and to the advantage of her enemies. In this sense the statute was unneutral, and was designed to be so. On the other hand, it worked to the advantage of the Japanese militarists in their aggression upon China, begun in 1937, because Japan could send ships to the United States for war supplies, and did. The hard-pressed Chinese Nationalists, with whom most Americans sympathized, could obtain few arms under the revised Neutrality Act.

In 1917 the United States declared war on Germany after she had sunk a number of unarmed freighters flying the Stars and Stripes in the danger zones. Before the Japanese attacked Pearl Harbor in December 1941 no American merchant ships were sunk by German submarines in the proclaimed war zones, primarily because such merchantmen could not lawfully be there.[6] The neutrality legislation of the 1930s, as earlier noted, worked not too poorly but too well. It was finally modified late in November 1941, and then virtually abandoned because it barred unneutral help to those countries, especially the democracies, whose preservation Americans regarded as in the national interest.

WAS THE BASES-FOR-DESTROYERS DEAL LEGAL?

Following the collapse of France and the escape to England of some 330,000 British and French troops in the "Miracle of Dunkirk,"[7] Great

[6] On May 21, 1941, a German submarine commander, possibly misinterpreting orders, brutally torpedoed (with warning) an American freighter, the *Robin Moor*, in the South Atlantic, not in a war zone. No lives were lost, but the survivors suffered hardships in open boats. The Germans claimed that the vessel was carrying contraband of war to British South Africa. Some two weeks before Pearl Harbor, the Neutrality Act of 1939 was amended to permit American merchantmen to transport munitions into the danger zones.

[7] A legend has sprung up that Hitler deliberately held back his forces to promote an amicable peace settlement with Britain. His motivations were evidently complex

Britain was in grave danger of a cross-Channel invasion. Her shipping losses were such that she desperately needed for antisubmarine work several dozen overage but still highly serviceable American destroyers left over from World War I.

In September 1940 President Roosevelt daringly concluded an executive agreement with Prime Minister Churchill which authorized the transfer to Britain of fifty reconditioned American destroyers. The British, for their part, agreed to lease or transfer to the United States for ninety-nine years eight base sites on their territory, continental or insular, ranging from Newfoundland to British Guiana. Two of these leases were to be outright gifts; the other six were in exchange for the warships.

After the fall of France in June 1940, Washington had made available to the British large quantities of obsolescent rifles and other war supplies. Such acts of favoritism were generally arranged through private parties or otherwise cloaked so as to keep within the strict letter, if not the spirit, of neutrality. But the destroyer deal marked an open abandonment of any pretense. This transfer of serviceable naval vessels directly from a presumably neutral nation to a belligerent was a violation of neutral obligations and also of pre-Hitler international law. The trading away of public property by the President was presumably a violation of domestic law as well, even though Roosevelt's Attorney General prepared a labored defense, much of which hinged on the placement of a comma in the relevant statute.[8]

Isolationists in Congress and out, particularly Republicans, were outraged. They declared that such transfers of warcraft needed for America's defense should have been approved by Congress. But a formal authorization would have aroused prolonged debate, at the end of which Britain would have been in even more critical shape. Public opinion polls found citizens favorable to the transaction by about a two-to-one margin, and a grudging Congress finally approved indirectly by voting money for erecting bases on the leased sites. The President displayed considerable political courage in engineering the swap during a

---

and are still debated, but basically he appears to have sought to conserve his tanks by relying on the air force to finish off the enemy. B. H. Liddell Hart, *History of the Second World War* (1971), pp. 83–84.

[8] A recently enacted law had provided that destroyers could not be transferred to Britain unless the navy certified their uselessness for America's defense. Naval officials had testified otherwise. Moreover, if Hitler vanquished Britain, the fifty warships might be used against the United States. But pro-Roosevelt legalists argued that the British bases were more valuable for America's defense than the vessels in question, and that consequently the dubious transaction met at least the spirit of the law.

heated election campaign, in which he was running for an unprecedented third term.

Roosevelt publicly likened the destroyer deal to the Louisiana Purchase of 1803. In the sense that Jefferson's bargain was designed in large part to keep foreign (French) militarism from the nation's back door, this comparison made sense. If Britain fell to the trans-Channel invader in 1940, as seemed entirely possible, the possession of these bases would serve to fend off European aggression.

WAS THE TWO-TERM TRADITION THE ISSUE IN 1940?

In June 1940, several days after the formal collapse of France, the Republicans nominated for the Presidency the dynamic and magnetic Wendell L. Willkie, a former public utilities executive. A recent convert to Republicanism, he had voted for Roosevelt in 1932. The legend quickly gained currency that he was chosen because the galleries in Philadelphia, chanting "We Want Willkie," overbore the delegates. The truth is less simple: the nomination came largely as the result of hard work, adequate finance, and skillful management.[9]

Would Roosevelt meet this formidable challenge by making a frontal assault on the no-third-term tradition? He was evidently torn between a desire to return to the quiet of his New York estate and a reluctance to relinquish the levers of power, especially since France had fallen and Britain was in grave danger. Could the President in good conscience deny to his fellow citizens his experienced hand during these desperate days for democracy?

It is possible that Roosevelt would not have run again if the French collapse had not drastically changed the complexion of the European war. In the absence of an overseas crisis, he might not have defeated the personable Willkie, who polled a much larger percentage of the popular vote (44.8) than either of Roosevelt's previous two opponents. Many Democrats who opposed a third term in principle supported their President because he was evidently the only man who could defeat the Republican nominee.

Roosevelt's reelection in 1940 was hailed by many politicians and some historians as a mandate to abolish the no-third-term tradition. This issue was clearly a factor in the campaign, but only one of a num-

[9] Hugh Ross, "Was the Nomination of Wendell Willkie a Political Miracle?" *Indiana Mag. of History*, LVIII (1962), 79–100. Full-length studies are Warren Moscow, *Roosevelt and Willkie* (1968) and Herbert S. Parmet, *Never Again: A President Runs for a Third Term* (1968).

ber, including the widely held isolationist fear that the President was about to send American "boys" off to foreign wars.[10] Most of the voters who objected to another four years for Roosevelt were Republicans who, in many cases, opposed him primarily on grounds other than the two-term tradition. The burning issue appears to have been, "Shall the nation keep an experienced professional at the helm in a period of deepening international crisis or turn to an inexperienced amateur?" There is good reason to believe that Roosevelt was reelected in spite of the two-term tradition, and the outcome cannot properly be regarded as a mandate on this issue or on any other.

Various public opinion polls taken in 1939, before the fall of France but after the outbreak of war against Poland, are revealing. They indicate that the general public, Republicans and Democrats alike, opposed a third term by a margin of approximately two to one. After the fall of France only one-third were willing to say that under no circumstances should a President be elected for a third time.[11]

The only real mandate on the third-term issue came in 1947–1951, when, by action of two-thirds of Congress and three-fourths of the state legislatures, the two-term limit was written into the Constitution as the 22nd Amendment. Republicans, slapping at the memory of the dead Roosevelt, were more favorable to this limitation than the Democrats, but many of its supporters were Democrats.[12] Ironically, the Republicans thus unknowingly barred their own future candidate, Dwight D. Eisenhower, from running for a third term in 1960.

WAS LEND–LEASE AN UNNEUTRAL SUBTERFUGE?

With the election safely behind him, President Roosevelt unveiled his historic lend–lease scheme to the newsmen (December 17, 1940), even though it had not been an issue in the recent campaign. The democracies,

---

[10] Stung by Willkie's vehement attacks, Roosevelt declared in a memorable Boston speech (October 30, 1940), "I have said this before, but I shall say it again and again and again: Your boys are not going to be sent into any foreign wars." He had previously qualified such affirmations with the phrase "except in case of attack," and when asked why he did not this time, he replied, "It's not necessary. If we're attacked, it's no longer a foreign war." James M. Burns, *Roosevelt: The Lion and the Fox* (1956), pp. 448–449. When American boys were sent abroad to many foreign theaters in World War II, critics recalled Roosevelt's unqualified pledge.

[11] Hadley Cantril, ed., *Public Opinion, 1935–1946* (1951), pp. 652–653.

[12] Certain key Democratic legislatures turned the tide for ratification in 1951. The Korean War had broken out in 1950, and the fear was prevalent that President Truman, unpopular in many quarters, would use his wartime powers to help insure reelection. The 22nd Amendment did not bar him from running again, but it imposed a moral barrier. Hence it was a slap at both Truman and Roosevelt.

especially Britain, were in urgent need of money, materiel, and ships to continue the fight. Roosevelt, who had unpleasant memories of the quarrels over Allied war debts, devised his lend–lease proposal. He would lend or lease to those nations resisting aggression vast quantities of arms and military supplies, with the understanding that these hand-outs would be returned or replaced with equivalents when the conflict was over.[13] He would "get rid of the silly, foolish old dollar sign." At this same press conference, Roosevelt gave categorical assurances that lend–lease cargoes would not have to be convoyed by American war-ships, and that such shipments would not involve a greater danger of direct participation in the war than letting the existing overseas crisis worsen.[14]

Administration spokesmen in Congress did a skillful job. They contrived the number 1776 for the lend–lease bill, with its suggestion of a war for liberty. They defended the proposal, not as a measure that would ultimately involve the Republic, but as one that would keep the conflict away from America's shores and doors. The bill was given not only a patriotic number but a reassuring title, "An Act Further to Promote the Defense of the United States." It would authorize Roose-velt to lend "defense•articles" to those governments "whose defense the President deems vital to the defense of the United States."

During the subsequent debate in Congress over lend–lease, the issue of convoying inevitably arose. If the nation was going to send shiploads of arms abroad to fight America's battles, why stand by and watch them being sunk en route by German submarines? Would not the United States have to use its warships to escort these merchant vessels to their destination? Lend–lease would lead to convoy; convoy would lead to shooting; and shooting would lead to war. But admini-stration spokesmen, understandably but rather disingenuously, soft-pedaled or shunted aside the issue of convoys: one thing at a time and the first things first. Nevertheless, the final version of the bill read, "Nothing in this Act shall be construed to authorize or to permit the authorization of convoying vessels by naval vessels of the United States." In short, Roosevelt might use his presidential power to convoy, but the lend–lease act did not authorize him to do so.

Lend–lease was subjected to prolonged debate in Congress and throughout the land. Public opinion polls indicated strong popular

[13] Actually the dollar sign was not eliminated; it was used in settling accounts with some forty nations, in sums that were small when compared to those of World War I. Difficulties with Russia continued into the 1970s.

[14] James M. Burns, *Roosevelt: The Soldier of Freedom* (1970), p. 26; Samuel L. Rosenman, comp., *The Public Papers and Addresses of Franklin D. Roosevelt, 1940 volume* (1941), pp. 606–612.

support, and the bill finally passed by comfortable margins in both houses. Citizens dimly perceived that this scheme meant one step closer to war, yet most of them seemed to feel that such aid would be more likely to keep the conflict from American shores than do-nothingism.[15] Roosevelt and many of his supporters realized that lend–lease would lead the nation nearer to the conflagration, and perhaps inevitably to direct participation in it. But most Americans were evidently willing to take that risk, while still hoping to remain aloof.

Lend–lease was one of the most momentous measures ever to pass Congress. Under it some $50 billion in military supplies was ultimately disbursed, and it played a crucial role in winning the war against the Axis powers. It was in effect a declaration of hostilities, and as such abandoned all remaining pretenses of neutrality. Short of actual shooting, what could be a more warlike act than for one great nation to commit in unlimited measure its economic resources to help one side against the other, and then deliver on that pledge? [16]

WAS IT FOLLY TO SEND AID TO RUSSIA?

The two most dramatic turning points of World War II, until Japan's Pearl Harbor attack in 1941, were the fall of France in June 1940, and Hitler's assault on Russia in June 1941. Although warned by American and other sources of the impending onslaught, Stalin was caught by surprise and lost hundreds of thousands of men. Hitler evidently wanted to dispose of an untrustworthy rival at his rear, avert a dangerous two-front war by a lightning invasion, and then have a free hand to finish off Britain.

It will be recalled that in the summer of 1939, on the eve of the fateful Hitler–Stalin pact, many people in the Western world were outspokenly hoping that the two dictators would bleed each other white in lethal embrace. Instead they clasped hands, with the consequent partition of Poland and the defeat of France. When Hitler suddenly turned

[15] See Cantril, ed., *Public Opinion, 1935–1946*, pp. 409–410. Relevant assurances of Roosevelt and administration supporters regarding lend–lease are presented in Charles A. Beard, *President Roosevelt and the Coming of the War, 1941* (1948). This book is notably untrustworthy on the pre-Pearl Harbor crisis. For a scathing review, see Samuel E. Morison, *By Land and By Sea* (1953), Chapter XV ("History through a Beard"). In justifying Roosevelt's breaking of his word, Morison states that "all promises have implied predicates," and that pledges by public officials "imply no important change of conditions that will make their implementation contrary to the public interest" (p. 336).

[16] The story is fully told in W. F. Kimball, *The Most Unsordid Act: Lend-Lease, 1939–1941* (1969).

on his co-conspirator nearly two years later, the ill-wishers of the two dictators had their prayers answered. The pair of cutthroats would presumably exhaust each other in a bloody stalemate, while the democracies could relax and enjoy greater security.

But could they? Suppose that Hitler overran the Soviet Union? In this case he would be stronger than ever and in a better position to crush Britain and menace America. The bleed-white thesis had much to commend it, provided that both sides bled about equally, but what assurance was there that they would?

At the outset, few military experts in the Western world gave Russia much of a chance to hold the line; at best she might resist for several months. The morale of the Russian army had been shattered by the trumped-up purge trials of 1936–1938, following which thousands of Russian officers, including high ranking generals, were executed. Overconfident Soviet troops had performed most unimpressively in the Winter War of 1939–1940, during which tiny Finland, though finally crushed, inflicted stinging defeats and tens of thousands of casualties on the Russian invaders. Hitler must have concluded from this face-losing exhibition that the Soviet Union would be easy pickings.[17] Not only did he have the advantage of surprise, but he had amassed the most terrifying striking force the world had yet seen, as demonstrated by his recent invasions of Poland and France.

President Roosevelt's immediate response to Hitler's astonishing blow was to promise the Russians assistance, and he soon made available a limited quantity of funds and military supplies. He did not immediately authorize substantial lend–lease aid but waited four and one-half months.[18] Meanwhile his agents reported that there was a fair chance that the USSR might be able to take full advantage of "General Mud," "General Frost," and "defense in depth." If so, they might halt the invader, despite an initial series of near-catastrophic defeats.[19]

WAS LEND–LEASE HELP TO RUSSIA DECISIVE?

Critical decisions on the battlefield can almost literally turn on a hair. If Hitler had only seized Moscow before winter fell with a vengeance (he

[17] Nikita Khrushchev describes the Finnish debacle in terms unflattering to the Soviets. His guess of a million Russian dead seems much too high. *Khrushchev Remembers* (1970), pp. 150–157.

[18] See R. H. Dawson, *The Decision to Aid Russia, 1941* (1959), p. 284.

[19] Many Russians, including Ukrainians, greeted Hitler as a deliverer from Stalin's tyranny, but he brutally drove the "Mongol halfwits" back into the arms of their oppressor. This shortsightedness may have cost him victory.

did reach its outskirts); if he had only captured Leningrad, which stood after the most incredible large-scale siege in history (some 600,000 people starved to death); if he had only taken Stalingrad in the winter of 1942–1943 — if, if, if — the story of World War II might have been dramatically different.

All told, the United States shipped some eleven billion dollars worth of lend–lease ("Lenin-lease") aid to Russia. An appreciable amount of assistance had flowed to the Soviets by the time Stalingrad was teetering, and it may have turned the tide. By American calculations, from 1941 to 1945 Uncle Sam provided a substantial share — perhaps 10 percent — of all Soviet military supplies. Certain postwar Russian spokesmen, conceding at the most only 3 or 4 percent, have downgraded the quantity and quality of this support, and have insisted that they would have won anyhow — though perhaps a little later — if American aid had never come. In any event, American capitalists, the charge went, waxed fat from lend–lease profits.

No people likes to praise other nations for having won its battles for it; elementary textbooks in the United States do not go overboard in crediting French help with a major role in winning the War of Independence. But even if American percentages are discounted, one must remember that bare statistics of aid to Russia do not tell the whole story. A vast amount of lend–lease came in the form of tanks, trucks, jeeps, and other automotive equipment, which the Soviets desperately needed for mobility. Without it they might not have reversed the German assault, at least not as soon as they did.

Ex-Premier Nikita Khrushchev, who had a considerable hand in managing this war, is surprisingly generous in his alleged memoirs. He concedes that the equipment, ships, and supplies (including food and warm clothing) received from America "greatly aided us in waging the war." He goes on to say, quite correctly, that such assistance was provided, not out of any idealistic regard for Russia or the Communist system, but out of a realistic desire to overcome the common foe.[20]

DID THE ATLANTIC CHARTER
ALLY THE U. S. WITH BRITAIN?

One of the most important documents of World War II, comparable in many respects to Wilson's ill-fated Fourteen Points, was the Atlantic Charter, August 1941. It grew out of a historic meeting on a British

[20] *Khrushchev Remembers*, p. 226.

battleship in Newfoundland waters between President Roosevelt and Prime Minister Churchill, each statesman attended by numerous military and civilian advisors. The document that finally emerged was not formally signed by the two men, like a treaty, but was issued in the form of a press release. It was nevertheless an official statement of their joint views and was recognized as such.

Actually the Charter in itself was a kind of afterthought.[21] Roosevelt and Churchill were primarily concerned with lend–lease, a common defense against Nazi aggression, and a stiff policy against further Japanese expansion in East Asia. After spending so much of their time on war aims, the conferees decided to issue a statement outlining their peace objectives. These were rather hastily drafted and given to the world as the Atlantic Charter. Less specific than Wilson's Fourteen Points, the document set forth such principles as self-determination for subject peoples, freedom of trade, freedom of the seas, disarmament of the aggressors after "the final destruction of Nazi tyranny," and a new organization for collective security. These ideals gave much hope to conquered peoples (like the Poles), and provided a foundation for the United Nations Alliance of 1942 and the United Nations Organization of 1945.

Critics of the Atlantic Charter wondered why so many people had journeyed so far at such grave risk to turn out such a collection of platitudes. Some commentators hinted at ominous secret commitments of a major nature.[22] Some isolationists accused the two leaders of having entered into an alliance, of which the Atlantic Charter was the only visible fruit. What right, critics asked, did a neutral United States have to meet with the representatives of a belligerent nation to contrive measures for defeating another belligerent nation? Such isolationist outcries missed the point. The United States was no longer a neutral; it had pledged itself to send (and was sending) enormous quantities of lend–lease to Britain; it was already engaging in acts of belligerency against German submarines while patrolling the North Atlantic. For all practical purposes, America was already a quasi-ally of Great Britain. The meeting in Newfoundland waters brought the two nations to an even closer understanding, and in this sense the Atlantic Charter repre-

---

[21] William L. Langer and S. E. Gleason, *The Undeclared War, 1940–1941* (1953), p. 677.

[22] Churchill reported to the War Cabinet, as recently released documents reveal, that Roosevelt promised to look for an incident that would justify his opening hostilities with Germany. *The New York Times*, Jan. 2, 1972. Roosevelt's subsequent handling of the *Greer* incident provides some confirmation.

sented the sealing of an informal alliance that was to be official before another six months had passed.[23]

DID F.D.R. DELIBERATELY
PROVOKE HOSTILITIES WITH HITLER?

The fateful Lend–Lease Act was signed on March 11, 1941, after which the inevitable happened. German submarines began sinking British freighters laden with the arms provided by American taxpayers. Roosevelt responded in April 1941 by exercising his presidential powers to establish naval "patrols," whose responsibility was to radio the position of lurking submersibles to nearby British warships and bombers. As early as April 10, 1941 an American destroyer (*Niblack*), while picking up survivors from a torpedoed Dutch merchantman, dropped depth bombs on or near a menacing submarine, supposedly German.

Another lurch toward the abyss came in July 1941, when Roosevelt assumed responsibility for protecting Iceland, which had been cut loose from Denmark by Hitler's invasion of the mother country. As commander-in-chief of the navy, the President followed his Icelandic coup by ordering American warships to escort convoys of lend–lease cargoes to Iceland, whether carried by vessels of British, neutral, or American registry. From Iceland, British warships would shepherd them to England. Roosevelt felt that the critical plight of Britain justified his turning his back on previous public assurances that there would be no convoying. Opinion polls revealed that the citizenry rather strongly supported this critical decision, even though it was somewhat devious and not clearly understood.[24]

Hitler, although provoked, was fully occupied with the invasion of Russia. Above all he did not wish to push the United States into the conflict at this juncture; as a corporal in the German army during World War I, he had vivid memories of how fresh manpower from the aroused Western giant had helped crush the Fatherland. The orders that he issued to his U-boat commanders were to avoid fighting unless endangered by aggressive American action.

Further ugly incidents were inevitable. On September 4, 1941, the Iceland-bound destroyer *Greer*, reacting to two menacing torpedoes fired by a German submarine, dropped a number of depth bombs. A

---

[23] See T. A. Wilson, *The First Summit: Roosevelt and Churchill at Placentia Bay, 1941* (1969).

[24] Cantril, *Public Opinion, 1935–1946*, pp. 1127–1129.

week later Roosevelt took to the radio to announce that henceforth United States warships would follow shoot-on-sight orders within American defensive areas in the North Atlantic. Details of the affair, as revealed somewhat later by the Navy Department, cast the German submarine commander in a much less aggressive light. The *Greer* had been trailing him for three and one-half hours, while provocatively radioing his position to nearby British air patrols, one of which dropped four depth charges. Finally, the U-boat turned and attacked, evidently not knowing the nationality of its pursuer.[25]

DID WAR BEGIN IN THE ATLANTIC?

In October 1941 the U. S. destroyer *Kearny* was damaged by a German torpedo south of Iceland, while involved in a furious battle in support of British warships. Again the U-boat commander could not be sure of his foe's identity. Upon learning that eleven American lives had been lost in the attack, Roosevelt lashed back with a speech in which he declared "the shooting has started." Later that same month, the destroyer *Reuben James*, in waters southwest of Iceland, was torpedoed and sunk with the loss of about one hundred lives.

Recognizing these ugly realities, Congress responded in November 1941 with a partial repeal of the already watered-down Neutrality Act of 1939. The twin bans on loans to belligerents and travel on their ships were retained, but two significant changes were added. Henceforth American merchantmen could be armed, and all American merchant ships, whether armed or not, could legally sail into the danger zones with cargoes of munitions or other supplies.

By Roosevelt's own admission an undeclared war with Germany had begun at least in the early autumn of 1941. When the Japanese, allies of Hitler, attacked Pearl Harbor on December 7, 1941, they were waging on a large scale a shooting conflict with America that had started unofficially on a small scale in the Atlantic some months earlier.

Roosevelt clearly used uncandid but legal methods in his efforts to bring the American people to an awareness of what he regarded as their peril.[26] Believing that the bolstering of Britain was imperative for

[25] For a temperate discussion of Roosevelt's devious procedure see Langer and Gleason, *The Undeclared War*, pp. 747–748. The authors do not excuse Roosevelt for publicly exploiting the attack on the *Greer* before having in hand a detailed report from the Navy Department.

[26] During the presidential campaign of 1944, Congresswoman Clare Boothe Luce charged Roosevelt with having "lied us into a war because he did not have the political courage to lead us into it." The present writer, in an incautious moment,

the defense of the United States, he was willing to risk war to achieve that end.[27] By late 1941 the opinion polls indicated that most Americans were willing to support him in his main objective, while fervently hoping that a full-dress clash would not ensue. They wanted to have their cake and eat it too; to engage in belligerent acts while preserving official peace.

DID F.D.R. ERR IN "APPEASING" JAPAN?

American public opinion and official policy during the 1930s were definitely anti-Japanese and pro-Chinese. These attitudes were crystallized by Nippon's takeover of Manchuria in 1931, by her assault on Shanghai in 1932, and by her invasion of China in 1937 and subsequent years. Although Japan had been a traditional friend of the United States, her bare-fisted aggression aroused much sympathy for the Chinese underdog, especially among church groups in America that supported schools, churches, and other missionary endeavors in China.

Washington's policy toward Japan was obviously not based primarily on an attempt to uphold the Open Door in East Asia for American merchants. Trade with the Chinese was relatively minor, while the two-way Japanese–American commerce, which would be ruined by an armed clash, was enormous. The State Department was indeed concerned with commercial enterprises in East Asia generally, but far more compelling were strategic considerations. If Tokyo pursued its aggressive policies in Asia to their logical conclusion, in conjunction with Hitler and Mussolini, she would pose an intolerable threat to American holdings in the Eastern Pacific, especially the Philippines. The security of the United States seemed to dictate a firm stand against further Nipponese expansion.

Tokyo, for its part, insisted that if the Japanese were only

wrote in 1948 that "because the masses are notoriously shortsighted, and generally cannot see danger until it is at their throats, our statesmen are forced to deceive them into an awareness of their own long-run interests. This is clearly what Roosevelt had to do. . . ." What I intended to say was that "This is clearly what Roosevelt *felt* he had to do. . . ." See T. A. Bailey, *The Man in the Street* (1948), p. 13. Charles A. Beard, in his controversial *President Roosevelt and the Coming of the War* (1948), exposes F.D.R.'s devious conduct in regard to lend–lease and convoying, but he handpicks the evidence to support the conclusion that Roosevelt wanted to goad the Japanese into attacking in December 1941. The record reveals that Roosevelt did not want war with Japan at that time, even though he was prepared to risk it.

27 Roosevelt, with memories of World War I, evidently expected to limit such involvement, if it came, to naval and aerial aid, plus a minimum of ground forces. W. Averell Harriman, *America and Russia in a Changing World* (1971), p. 15.

permitted to take over China and bring order out of chaos, then American and other Western nations would share in a much larger trade than they had previously enjoyed ("The Greater East Asia Co-Prosperity Sphere"). But Washington had no faith in such assurances.

When Japan opened full-scale war on China in 1937, Roosevelt showed his favoritism for the Chinese by making loans available to them and by refusing to invoke the Neutrality Act. These concessions meant that a trickle of war supplies could go to the victims of aggression, while the Nipponese aggressor would continue to receive vast quantities of scrap iron, oil, aviation gasoline, and other essentials necessary to sustain his war machine. Roosevelt hoped that by a "soft" policy he would please the moderates in Japan, and that they in turn would restrain the militarists who seemed bent on pursuing far more aggressive goals.

Then came the fall of France in 1940, followed by the orphaning of French Indochina. Roosevelt attempted, without success, to curb Nipponese advances upon that rice-rich land by placing partial embargoes on shipments of war materials to Japan. When these proved ineffective, he administered a severe jolt on July 25, 1941, by freezing Japanese financial assets in the United States. This stroke, in association with the British and Dutch, inaugurated a virtually complete embargo on all war supplies, especially petroleum products. Japan then had oil reserves that would sustain her for only twelve or eighteen months of prospective wartime consumption.[28] Seemingly all Washington had to do was to wait for the oil gauge to drop, and then the Japanese would have to pull out of China and retreat to their overcrowded islands.

Roosevelt was severely criticized for not having cut off these war sinews sooner. But he feared that to do so would precipitate hostilities with Japan by forcing her to turn southward to the Dutch East Indies for oil. He did not want such a two-ocean war, which would almost certainly involve the British, who were desperately resisting Hitler. A diversion of American strength to a conflict with Japan would reduce the flow of supplies going to Britain (and later Russia) under lend–lease. Moreover, the United States was badly prepared for hostilities with the Japanese. For many years American experts had written off the Philippines as certain to fall to Japan (as they did). But recently, with the development of the long-range bomber, American military men had concluded that the islands might possibly be defended — that is,

[28] See Louis Morton, "Japan's Decision for War," in K. R. Greenfield, ed., *Command Decisions* (1959), pp. 63–87.

if many more months were afforded them in which to build up aerial and ground strength.

Subsequent events seemed to prove that Roosevelt was correct in his fear that an end to "appeasing" Japan might force the Japanese to strike toward the oil of the Dutch East Indies. Such a thrust would involve America and Britain in an all-out two-front war, for which both were grossly unprepared. Whether he should have "appeased" longer or not at all is a question for endless debate.

WAS JAPAN OR AMERICA THE AGGRESSOR?

From the standpoint of Tokyo the Americans were the aggressors; all that Japan wanted was to be let alone to take over neighboring China, Indochina, and other areas in Southeast Asia of strategic or economic value. Such expansion was in response to what the Nipponese militarists regarded as their Manifest Destiny. America, they noted, had achieved her Manifest Destiny at the expense of her neighbors, including Mexico, so why should she interfere with the Japanese? The Americans had even taken the Philippines in 1898–1899, strategically situated in Japan's backyard, yet Tokyo had not protested.

Negotiations with Tokyo preceding Pearl Harbor sank on the rocks of China, where the invading Japanese were still vainly seeking to achieve their "New Order." In Secretary Hull's firm and final note of November 26, 1941, Washington proposed that Japan clear out of both China and Indochina in return for certain commercial concessions that suggested a bribe. Tokyo backed off. After waging inconclusive warfare against the Chinese for four and one-half years, at a cost of some 160,000 men, the Japanese would suffer an intolerable loss of face if they should now abandon, under pressure from America, what they then held. From the point of view of Tokyo, there were only two alternatives: knuckle under or burst out. Japanese military planners realized that they were challenging a colossus with a productive capacity some ten times their own, but they were hoping for good luck and quick victories rather than a war of attrition. They would have to win quickly or lose slowly.

There was a third alternative, namely some kind of face-saving compromise concerning China. The Washington officials were evidently willing to "string along" the negotiations by discussing some such modus vivendi, even though they had positive proof that the Japanese, by late November 1941, were not negotiating in good faith. But the Chinese Nationalists protested bitterly against being made the sacrificial goat in such a scheme, and the Japanese military could scarcely afford further delays. The oil gauge was dropping too rapidly; the time bomb was ticking too ominously; and unfavorable winter weather was too imminent.[29] In short, deadlock came primarily because America was unwilling to offer, and Japan was unwilling to accept, a mutually satisfactory compromise on the China tangle. Diplomats on neither side wanted to be charged with having negotiated a Far Eastern Munich. Ironically, some kind of compromise might have been possible if the Japanese had only known that the Americans, in demanding a withdrawal from China, were not including Manchuria. Though still technically a part of China, it was nominally the puppet Japanese state of Manchukuo.[30]

From the vantage point of Tokyo, a ruthless Uncle Sam assumed the role of the aggressor when he issued the crippling freeze order of July 25, 1941, in response to Japan's takeover of southern Indochina. America's press was quite outspoken in its predictions that within a few months the Japanese would have to yield or die of anemia. Nippon's rulers chose neither course: they believed that they were resisting an iron encirclement.

From the vantage point of Washington, the Japanese "aggressors," like Hitler, had brutally challenged law, order, treaty commitments, peaceful processes, democratic procedures, and territorial integrity. Japan's expansionist tactics were believed to pose an intolerable threat to the long-run security and other basic interests of the United States.[31] As in dealing with Hitler, the American people were willing to take an uncompromising stand that risked war, all the while hoping that war would not come. If the Japanese felt that they were bursting out of an iron ring, the Americans believed that "mad-dog militarists," whether in Europe or Asia, should be restrained and contained in the interests of national security.

---

[29] If the U. S. had pressed for its *modus vivendi* with Japan, or had held out some hope for compromise in its final note, the Japanese might have delayed several weeks or postponed their planned strike until the following spring, by which time Hitler's invasion of Russia would have been stalled and the defeat of the Axis would have been predictable.

[30] See John Toland, *The Rising Sun* (1970), pp. 144–145.

[31] Except for the sinking of the *Panay* in 1937, for which apologies and indemnities were speedily forthcoming, the Japanese had done little *direct* damage to United States interests, except to destroy some missionary property in China and mistreat some American citizens.

WHY WAS THE U. S. SURPRISED AT PEARL HARBOR?

Shortly after sunrise on Sunday, December 7, 1941, swarms of bomb-carrying Japanese warplanes, operating from aircraft carriers some 275 miles to the north, struck devastating surprise blows on the American fleet in Pearl Harbor, Hawaii, and on neighboring installations. Six of the eight big battleships were grounded, destroyed, or sunk, while numerous other vessels and aircraft were demolished or severely damaged. Total casualties on the American side ran to over 3,500 men.

About a year earlier American cryptographers had broken the main Japanese diplomatic code, and had begun to intercept and decode the secret messages being sent from Tokyo to Japan's representatives in the United States.[32] These "Magic" intercepts revealed that meaningful negotiations had completely broken down following Secretary Hull's stand-firm-on-China note of November 26, 1941; that the Japanese were stalling the discussions along to cover some momentous action; and that the blow was scheduled to fall somewhere on or about December 7.

President Roosevelt dismissed the idea of a preemptive strike by the United States; he felt that a democracy could not take such unethical action.[33] After many months of tension, he and some of his top associates were visibly relieved when all uncertainty was removed by the assault on Pearl Harbor. Secretary of War Stimson was somewhat consoled, for he, along with General MacArthur and others, initially believed that the attackers had been bloodily repulsed by the "alerted" and well-armed defenders.

Why were the Americans caught completely napping? For one thing, they did not believe that the Japanese would be rash enough to attack so formidable a bastion as Pearl Harbor, risk a costly repulse, unite a divided nation, and throw the overwhelming might of an angry Uncle

[32] Although properly decoded, these intercepts were badly translated by "experts" who caused Japan to appear in a more bellicose light than she intended. Toland, *The Rising Sun*, pp. 133–135, gives some arresting examples. Further adverse complications were introduced by an inadequate command of oral English by the Japanese ambassador in Washington. See R. J. C. Butow, "The Hull–Nomura Conversations: A Fundamental Misconception," *Amer. Hist. Rev.*, LXV (1960), 822–836.

[33] At a meeting of the "War Cabinet" in the White House on November 25, 1941, Roosevelt was reported by Secretary Stimson to have said that the problem was how to "maneuver" the Japanese into firing the first shot without undue damage to the United States. "Maneuver" was an unfortunate word, later seized upon by F.D.R.'s critics, although perhaps Stimson did not report his precise language. Like Lincoln on the eve of the attack on Fort Sumter, Roosevelt did not want war but perceived that if the foe struck first, he would have a moral advantage. See R. N. Current, "How Stimson Meant to 'Maneuver' the Japanese," *Miss. Valley Hist. Rev.*, XL (1953), 67–74. Wanting one's adversary to strike first, if there must be an attack, is not the same as wanting an attack.

Sam into a war that had been dragging on in East Asia since 1937. Other advisors were convinced of Japan's technical inability to mount such an assault. Still others reasoned convincingly that if Japan moved at all, she would slowly absorb British Malaya (with its tin and rubber), Thailand, or the Dutch East Indies (with their abundant oil). If such cautious procedures had been followed, Roosevelt would have found it difficult, if not impossible, to wring a war declaration from Congress.

During the two weeks before the blow at Pearl Harbor, American intelligence operatives reported many Japanese troopships moving down the coast of Southeast Asia, headed presumably for Thailand, British Malaya, or the Dutch East Indies. If one has secret intercepts foretelling an attack, and if he has indisputable proof of enemy troops massing in the most logical theater, he would naturally expect the assault to come there. Instead it came at a place where the American mind could not believe such a bold stroke to be either physically possible or strategically profitable.

Japanese strategists merely planned to immobilize the United States fleet so that it could not interfere with a speedy conquest of their objectives in Southeast Asia. This thinking partly explains why they did not land a few troops in Hawaii, as they could easily have done, and why the main thrusts fell on Southeast Asia, as Roosevelt had expected. Ironically, the American fleet did not have sufficient auxiliary craft and other resources to mount a formidable attack some 4,500 miles away for many months to come.

DID F.D.R. DELIBERATELY EXPOSE THE FLEET?

Certain "revisionist" historians have come to conspiratorial conclusions.[34] Since Roosevelt knew from the decoded ("Magic") intercepts from Tokyo that an onslaught was imminent, and since he did not specifically warn the commanders at Pearl Harbor that it was going to occur there on December 7, he must have planned to lure the Japanese into an attack by deliberately exposing the battleship fleet, all the while withholding essential information from the defenders. The argument further alleges that since he wanted so desperately to help Britain against Hitler, and

---

[34] For an analysis of the literature, see Louis Morton, "Pearl Harbor in Perspective: A Bibliographical Survey," *U.S. Naval Institute Proceedings*, LXXXI (1955), 461–468. Extremists charged that Roosevelt not only deliberately exposed the fleet but did so to insure his reelection in 1944 and divert attention from his failure to relieve unemployment. Yet by December 1941, the unemployment problem was virtually licked.

since he had been unable to provoke Hitler into lashing back, then the Machiavellian solution was to enter the war through the Asiatic "back door" by inviting an assault from Japan. If he had not plotted to destroy the fleet, so his critics say, he certainly would have pulled it back to the Pacific Coast, where it would have been "safe." (It would have been even safer in the Chesapeake Bay; but as the conventional muscle of diplomacy, it was kept in Hawaii to exert pressure on Japan.)

The fantastic theory of deliberate exposure presupposes that Roosevelt was both a murderer and a madman. He loved ships, especially those ships; he had been Assistant Secretary of the Navy when some of them were built. He yearned to halt the aggressors and, once war came, he naturally hoped to go down in history as the President who won it. When a nation is already short of adequate naval strength for a two-ocean conflict, it does not scheme to have its Pacific fleet shattered on the first day of the war. If this kind of insanity had existed, it almost certainly would have manifested itself during the subsequent conflict, which Roosevelt conducted with an extraordinary grasp of strategic realities. Moreover a Pearl Harbor plot would have required the collaboration of a half-dozen or so highly placed military and naval officials who were known to be honorable men and who could hardly have concealed the secret for decades.

Roosevelt did not welcome war with the Japanese, whom he hoped to "baby along," as he put it, pending the building up of adequate military and naval strength in the Pacific. He simply did not have, as he complained, "enough navy to go around." He wished above all to help the British overcome Hitler, and an idiotic way to do that would be to bait the Japanese into a Far Eastern war. Such a conflict would spread thin existing American forces and almost certainly involve the British, who already had one war too many. Even so, Prime Minister Churchill was so desperately anxious to have America as a fighting ally that he welcomed this "back door" involvement as better than none at all.

As is so often the case, the simple and nonconspiratorial explanation of how Roosevelt was surprised is evidently the correct one.[35] The Japanese themselves were hardly less astonished to find Pearl Harbor, the Gibraltar of the Pacific, so completely off guard when they struck.

---

[35] The familiar thesis of so-called deliberate destruction of the *Maine* in 1898 and the *Lusitania* in 1915 has already been discussed. For the unproved rumor that the British had warned F.D.R. of the attack on Pearl Harbor three days in advance, see R. T. Ruetten, "Harry Elmer Barnes and the 'Historical Blackout'," *The Historian,* *XXXIII* (1971), 202–214.

WAS PEARL HARBOR ADEQUATELY WARNED?

It appears that just about every American in authority, from Roosevelt on down, was in some degree obtuse, confused, careless, bungling, inefficient, asleep, or looking the wrong way.

Japan's warlords chose early Sunday morning for their sneak attack because they logically reasoned that many of the victims would still be sleeping or somewhat groggy from their Saturday night celebration.[36] The extent of such befuddlement has probably been exaggerated; the defenders surprised the enemy by rallying quickly. They ultimately shot down enough Nipponese planes — about 30 or nearly 10 percent of the attackers — to discourage renewed assaults. The allegation that Pearl Harbor was defenseless is insupportable: it not only *was* hotly defended but was never captured by the Japanese. It represented, with the fleet, one of the greatest concentrations of military might in the world.

Certain essential facts point up the incredible luck of the attackers, who had made meticulous preparations over many weeks, and the carelessness and unperceptiveness of the defenders.

American strategists had long assumed that in the event of war with Japan the enemy would try to hit Hawaii. In the "war games" as early as 1932, an American naval force representing the Japanese staged a successful attack on Hawaii with carrier-based aircraft *on a Sunday morning.*[37]

Six of the attacking Japanese aircraft carriers were ominously lost to American naval intelligence for about a week prior to Pearl Harbor.

Japan's consulate in Honolulu, under instructions, was sending home much detailed information as to the location of the American warships in Pearl Harbor. But these intercepted messages, having a low priority, were not all decoded and translated until too late.[38]

---

[36] Despite war warnings from Washington, weekend passes and liberty were routinely granted. Some of the men returned to their posts the day after (Monday morning), not realizing that an attack had occurred.

[37] Much has been made of the fact that Ambassador Grew routinely reported (Jan. 27, 1941) from Tokyo a "fantastic" rumor, picked up from his Peruvian colleague, that the Japanese were planning an all-out surprise attack on Pearl Harbor. *Foreign Relations of the U.S.: Japan, 1931–1941* (1943), II, 133. But the State Department files are filled with rumors of events that never occurred; besides, at this date the Japanese had not decided to make the attack. The final decision came on December 1, 1941, subject to an eleventh-hour reversal if the Americans made acceptable concessions.

[38] Toland, *The Rising Sun*, pp. 176, 185, 189, 192–193.

In Washington and elsewhere in the United States, the Japanese Embassy and consulates were observed burning their papers just prior to the open rupture.

Four hours and thirteen minutes *before* the onslaught, an enemy midget submarine was sighted off the mouth of Pearl Harbor. One hour and ten minutes *before* the assault, such a submarine was sunk in the same area. But in neither case was this information relayed to the commanders or acted upon by them in time for defensive action.

Fifty-three minutes before the bombs fell, a primitive radar screen picked up the aircraft coming from the north, but the blips were dismissed by higher authority as of no significance. They were thought to represent incoming aerial reinforcements, which were due to arrive from the *east*, not the north.

The top military and naval commanders in Hawaii, General W. C. Short and Admiral H. E. Kimmel, were emphatically warned by Washington on November 27 that negotiations had "ceased" and that Japan might launch an attack somewhere "within the next few days." In response, General Short reported the precautions he had taken against sabotage by local Japanese, but he received no reply advising him to be looking primarily for attacking aircraft. Washington evidently assumed that its recent "war warning" was sufficient. Both commanders complained that they should have been informed more specifically of the imminent blow. They would have appreciated knowing where the Japanese were going to attack, with what, and at what time of what day. They were not so informed because Washington did not know: not one of the numerous "Magic" intercepts that were translated in time referred specifically to an attack on Pearl Harbor.[39]

WHO WAS TO BLAME FOR THE PEARL HARBOR DEBACLE?

There were eight official investigations, which in some degree were marred by interservice rivalry, partisanship, hysteria, and contradictory testimony. The first one found General Short and Admiral Kimmel guilty of dereliction of duty; the later ones, not untinged with politics,

---

[39] The last warning, dispatched from Washington when the "Magic" intercepts indicated that relations with Tokyo would be broken in about an hour and a half, was delayed in transmission by incredible mixups. Finally sent by commercial cable, it was delivered to Pearl Harbor by a Japanese–American on a motorbike some seven hours *after* the attack. Yet even this admonition did not hint at an attack on Hawaii: "Just what significance the hour set may have we do not know but be on the alert accordingly." Quoted in Hans L. Trefousse, ed., *What Happened at Pearl Harbor?* (1958), p. 67.

spread the responsibility over to Roosevelt and other highly placed Washington officials, military and civilian. Some critics were disposed to blame the American public for not providing more ships for defense and more airplanes for reconnaissance. Perhaps so, but it is probable that, given the devastating blow, more ships and planes would have meant more destruction.

A basic difficulty was that the authorities had so much information from "intercepts" as to be confused. They also fell into the trap of thinking that the enemy thought as they did.[40] If the American commanders had read history, they might have remembered that the Japanese were not bluffers, contrary to a common belief, and that hitting without warning was an old Nipponese custom: in 1894, in the Sino–Japanese War; in 1904, in the Russo–Japanese War; in 1931, in Manchuria; and in 1941, at Pearl Harbor. Declarations of war had gone out of fashion, notably when Hitler struck Poland in 1939 and Russia in 1941.[41]

General Douglas MacArthur, commanding in the Philippines, was promptly advised of the disaster at Pearl Harbor by telephone. Yet when dawn came some *eight hours later*, Japanese aircraft bombed his installations and severely damaged his precious fleet of long-range bombers, lined up in neat rows for the slaughter. In his *Memoirs*, he states that he had not been warned of the crushing nature of the Japanese attack on Hawaii (he thought the enemy would be beaten off with heavy losses); and he shifts the responsibility for his reverse to a subordinate.[42] If MacArthur had not become a hero in the subsequent defense of the Philippines, he probably would have been made a scapegoat, along with the commanders in Hawaii.

In view of MacArthur's setback, one wonders if Pearl Harbor would have been any less of a shocker if Japan had officially declared war

[40] See Roberta Wohlstetter, *Pearl Harbor: Warning and Decision* (1962). If one reads the last chapter of a detective novel first, one can more easily recognize relevant clues. Maxwell M. Hamilton, then chief of the Division of Far Eastern Affairs, Department of State, later told the present writer that in rereading the high-level "Magic" intercepts he found not even the hint of an imminent attack on Pearl Harbor.

[41] The Tokyo government, hoping to avoid the opprobrium of striking without warning, planned to deliver the note declaring negotiations at an end a few minutes *before* the attack, too late for the defenders to get ready. Because of decoding delays in Washington, the so-called ultimatum was not presented until more than an hour after the assault. Yet this note did not formally break off relations or declare war — that action came from Tokyo two days later. The document merely said that the Japanese government "cannot but consider that it is impossible to reach an agreement through further negotiations." Such a notice was unlikely to alert the defenders of Pearl Harbor any more than they had already been alerted. See Trefousse, ed., *What Happened at Pearl Harbor?*, p. 236; *The Memoirs of Cordell Hull* (2 vols., 1948), *II*, 1095–1097.

[42] Douglas MacArthur, *Reminiscences* (1964), pp. 117–120.

on the United States twenty-four hours or even eight hours in advance. Many Americans still felt that the Japanese, with their thick spectacles, were unable to build or fly airplanes, much less operate them with deadly precision.

WAS PEARL HARBOR AN UNMITIGATED DISASTER?

In many respects Japan conferred an immense favor on the United States by her devastating hit-and-run raid, even though a beaten-off attack would have served about as well. Overnight the Americans, previously divided by angry debate between isolationists and interventionists, united in an outburst of outrage. With only one dissenting vote in either House, Congress speedily passed a declaration of war against Japan. If the Japanese had moved slowly into Southeast Asia, Roosevelt might not have been able to get a war resolution through Congress, or if so, only after bitter and divisive debate. Why shed American blood for British and Dutch imperialism in the Far East?

A declaration of war on Japan, without a Pearl Harbor, would almost certainly have been followed by an outcry of "On to Tokyo." [43] The American battleship fleet, after months of delays in preparing for operations so far from its base, might then have sailed out to the Far East. There it probably would have been demolished by Japanese aerial bombers in deep water, as the British battleships *Prince of Wales* and *Repulse* were destroyed off the Malayan coast three days after Pearl Harbor. The loss of American life almost certainly would have been many times that in Hawaii, where the battleships were sunk in shallow water. Several of these behemoths were ultimately reconditioned and employed usefully in combat operations against Japan.

Many of the American warships lost in Hawaii were obsolescent, and ultimately were more than replaced by modern units. A previously economy-minded Congress promptly voted immense appropriations. The great oversight of the Japanese attackers was not to destroy the Hawaiian drydocks, fuel tanks, repair shops, and submarine facilities, all of which were vital during the later war in the Pacific. [44] Fortunately for the Americans, their three priceless aircraft carriers were not present on

[43] When General MacArthur was cornered at Bataan in the Philippines, a public cry arose to send out a fleet to succor him, but there were no ships to spare, especially after Pearl Harbor.

[44] So great was the demoralization on December 7 that a few regiments of Japanese troops probably could have captured the main Hawaiian island (Oahu), but since occupation of the archipelago was not a part of the Japanese plan, no transports were brought along.

that "day of infamy." This fortuitous fact has been seized upon by "revisionists" to support the thesis of deliberate exposure by Roosevelt.[45]

DID HITLER GOAD JAPAN INTO ATTACKING?

A common assumption during the ensuing war was that Hitler had prodded his Japanese ally — allied under the Axis pact of 1940 — into bombing Pearl Harbor. This is far from the truth. Hitler had in essence given the Japanese a firm promise of blank-check support, hoping for favors in return. But he was not advised of the impending attack; indeed he was more surprised than Roosevelt, who knew that a blow was going to fall somewhere. Yet Hitler loyally backed his ally; and four days after Pearl Harbor, Germany declared war on the United States, as did Italy.[46]

Again Congress was spared an agonizing and disruptive debate, for the decision was taken out of its hands. A declaration of war on Germany and Italy, even after Pearl Harbor, would not have come easily, unless preceded by an enemy declaration. Millions of Americans were prepared to wage a private war of revenge in the Pacific; so why weaken the nation's strength by involvement in a strictly European conflict? In promoting national unity, America's three antagonists conferred a great boon on her by declaring war first.[47]

The Soviet Union and the Western democracies were not the most cooperative of associates during World War II, but in this regard they were models as compared to Japan. Instead of coordinating their blows with Hitler's, as faithful allies should have done, the Japanese ran their own show in East Asia and the Pacific. If they had only struck at Russia's Siberian back door, they probably could have knocked the Soviet Union out of the war, as Hitler vainly urged them to do. They would also have cut off American lend–lease supplies flowing to Siberia. But the Russians had a strong army in icy Siberia, as well as submarines and a bomber fleet that presumably could have laid waste Japan's bamboo cities. Russia seemed to be collapsing anyhow,[48] and perhaps the

[45] The commanders in Hawaii further explained their surprise by noting that on the eve of the attack various ships had been ordered away that would have been kept there if an assault had been imminent.

[46] See H. L. Trefousse, *Germany and American Neutrality, 1939–1941* (1951), pp. 147–153.

[47] The three U. S. counterdeclarations of 1941 all used the familiar formula that war had been "thrust" upon America. The war declarations of 1846 (against Mexico) and 1917 (against Germany) had also employed this formula.

[48] The Soviet Union was evidently caving in and Nazi invaders were at the gates of Moscow when the attacking Japanese task force left home waters for Hawaii. Two

two European menaces would bleed each other white, leaving Japan supreme in the Far East.

So the Japanese took the seductive path southward, where there was oil, to say nothing of other easier pickings. And they wound up on the losing side.

WAS HITLER A MENACE TO AMERICA?

One argument used most effectively by the interventionists prior to Pearl Harbor was that Hitler, if he won, would cross the ocean and enslave the American people.

Hitler was not a normal person, and what went on in his head would baffle the psychiatrist, let alone the historian. He evidently wavered between visions of ultimately attacking the United States and refraining from provocations. He had no clear-cut plans for invading America, or even Britain, when he lashed out at Poland. But this does not mean that he could not have devised blueprints if both Russia and Britain had quickly collapsed, as they came perilously near doing. With Japan supreme in the East and Hitler victorious in the West, with the British navy and the workshops of a captive Europe in German hands, and with Hitler preparing secret weapons (including the atomic bomb), the United States would have faced a formidable menace. If the blow had fallen, it probably would have come indirectly by way of Latin America. Both there and in the United States the Nazis had been pursuing an active program of infiltration.[49]

America was inadequately prepared to meet an immediate threat of this nature in two oceans. To be sure, peacetime conscription had been adopted in September 1940; and in August 1941, it was renewed for eighteen months by a margin of one vote in the House of Representatives. Incredibly, the Army thus narrowly escaped evisceration some three months before Pearl Harbor.

An immense body of isolationists did not believe that the dictators posed any real threat to the United States. This attitude explains why, prior to the downfall of France in 1940, Congress viewed

---

days *before* Pearl Harbor, the Russians launched a surprising counteroffensive which halted the invader. Their success was due largely to the transfer of 20 divisions from Siberia, after their master spy in Japan, Dr. Richard Sorge, had informed them of Tokyo's decision to strike southward. Toland, *The Rising Sun*, pp. 121–122.

[49] See Alton Frye, *Nazi Germany and the American Hemisphere, 1933–1941* (1967); G. L. Weinberg, "Hitler's Image of the United States," *Amer. Hist. Rev.*, LXIX (1964), 1006–1021.

with such indifference Roosevelt's repeated appeals for military and naval appropriations. The President, instead of exercising his dynamic leadership for preparedness, finally felt compelled to "do good by stealth," as in the destroyer-bases deal and the lend–lease scheme. He probably underestimated the capacity of the American people to face harsh realities; perhaps he should have appealed to them more vigorously and more often.

A Hitler who was speedily victorious over both Russia and Britain might never have tried conclusions with America, directly or indirectly. Strict neutrality on the part of the United States might have kept the Republic on the sidelines, ultimately to face a fearsome foe. But the American people were unwilling to take that chance, even though they risked war. If they guessed wrong, they would invite catastrophe or, at best, life in an armed camp.

The Nazi–Fascist threat was replaced after 1945 by the menace of Communist Russia, but the United States since then has occupied a powerful defensive position with nuclear weapons — a position stronger by far than it would have held if Britain and Russia had been quickly overrun in 1941–1942. And both of these nations might well have gone under if America had not lifted the arms embargo and sent desperately needed aid, followed by active participation.

ADDITIONAL GENERAL REFERENCES

James M. Burns, *Roosevelt: The Lion and the Fox* (1956); and *Roosevelt: The Soldier of Freedom, 1940–1945* (1970); W. L. Langer and S. E. Gleason, *The Challenge to Isolation, 1937–1940* (1952) and *The Undeclared War, 1940–1941* (1953); R. E. Sherwood, *Roosevelt and Hopkins* (1948); J. W. Pratt, *Cordell Hull, 1933–1944* (2 vols., 1964); R. A. Divine, *The Illusion of Neutrality* (1962) and *The Reluctant Belligerent: American Entry into World War II* (1965); Manfred Jonas, *Isolationism in America, 1935–1941* (1966); M. L. Chadwin, *The Hawks of World War II* (1968); D. F. Drummond, *The Passing of American Neutrality, 1937–1941* (1955); R. H. Dawson, *The Decision to Aid Russia, 1941* (1959); W. L. Neumann, *America Encounters Japan* (1963); P. W. Schroeder, *The Axis Alliance and Japanese–American Relations, 1941* (1958); R. J. C. Butow, *Tojo and the Coming of the War* (1961); Herbert Feis, *The Road to Pearl Harbor* (1950); Roberta Wohlstetter, *Pearl Harbor: Warning and Decision* (1962); Leonard Baker, *Roosevelt and Pearl Harbor* (1970); James V. Compton, *The Swastika and the Eagle: Hitler, the United States and the Origins of World War II* (1967).

35

The United States
in World War II

Mobilizing the home front for an all-out war effort was a gigantic task in the dreary months after Pearl Harbor. Priorities were established; various substitutes were created (for example, synthetic rubber); essential commodities were arbitrarily rationed for the first time in American experience; prices, wages, and rents were controlled; workers were "frozen" to their jobs; labor disturbances were kept to a minimum; and manpower was drafted for the armed services.

Overall military strategy, as adopted by Washington, was primarily concerned with throwing America's enormous productive power into the scales as soon as possible and winning a speedy victory. President Roosevelt also had plans for postwar peace, insofar as he could square idealism with harsh realism. But the British and Russian leaders often seemed much more preoccupied than the Americans with the probable long-range political effects of their military decisions.

Large-scale contacts with the enemy came first in the Pacific and Far Eastern theaters, although a get-Hitler-first strategy had been worked out with the British early in 1941. Japanese forces, as expected, invaded the Philippines. Filipino and American troops under General MacArthur retreated, also as expected, to the bottleneck Bataan Peninsula, thus buying time by delaying the invader before surrendering. Prior to the end MacArthur, under orders from Washington, transferred operations to Australia, where he took command of the Allied forces in the Southwest Pacific defending against Japan's invasion of New Guinea and the Solomon Islands. There the Americans painfully turned the tide in the six-month battle for Guadalcanal. With the indispensable support of the navy, General MacArthur gradually fought his way back up the ladder of islands and redeemed the Philippines early in 1945.

Meanwhile, in June 1942, a powerful Japanese fleet, stealthily advancing toward Hawaii, suffered a smashing defeat from a numerically inferior American force at the crucial battle of Midway. The clash featured carrier-based aircraft. The United States was able to concentrate what strength it had left in the Pacific for this engagement because it was decoding Japanese secret messages.[1]

By "island-hopping" — that is, bypassing many of the Japanese strong points in the Pacific — the American forces ultimately captured staging areas in the Marianas (Tinian, Saipan, Guam) in mid-1944. From these bases long-range bombers mounted devastating incendiary raids on Japan's bamboo cities. The noose tightened as the Americans captured two strategic islands nearer Japan, Iwo Jima[2] and Okinawa, despite severe losses to warships at Okinawa from Japanese suicide (kamikaze) aircraft. The stage was thus set for the climactic kill with atomic bombs in August 1945.

American strategists believed that the way to win the war quickly and avert a Russian collapse was to launch an overwhelming cross-Channel invasion from England against the Hitler-held coasts of France. British reluctance to risk such a venture prematurely led to a side-issue invasion of French North Africa in November 1942, followed by the conquest of Sicily and a thrust into Italy. To Stalin's acute dissatisfaction, the long-awaited D-day invasion of Hitler's Europe did not come off until June 1944. This tremendous operation proceeded with sensational success, although during the landing and for several anxious weeks thereafter the issue seemed to hang in the balance. The Allied drive toward the Rhine River suffered a severe setback when the Germans mounted an incredible surprise offensive through the Ardennes region into Belgium, late in December 1944, only to be halted by the stubborn American defenders, notably in the "Battle of the Bulge." Hitler's last-card gamble, which depleted his reserves, proved costly in the end. Regrouped Allied forces continued their merciless drive deep into Germany, while the Soviets crashed forward from the east. Hitler committed suicide in a burned-out Berlin bunker, April 30, 1945,[3] and

---

[1] The story is told dramatically in Walter Lord, *Incredible Victory* (1967).

[2] Joe Rosenthal's famous staged photograph of four Marines raising the U. S. flag on Iwo Jima came three hours after the original flag raising. Richard Wheeler, "The First Flag-Raising on Iwo Jima," *Amer. Heritage*, XV (June 1964), 54–60, 102–105.

[3] As might be expected, the rumor spread that Hitler had escaped, and was living somewhere in exile, perhaps in Argentina. Not until 23 years later was the information published that a Soviet counterintelligence team had found his remains on May 5, 1945. *The New York Times*, August 2, 1968, 1:2.

the Germans yielded unconditionally on May 7. The Japanese, atomized
into submission, capitulated on August 14, 1945.

WAS THERE A UNITED NATIONS BEFORE 1945?

In World War I the United States had been one of the Allied and
Associated Powers, more commonly referred to as the Allies. In World
War II the United States was one of the United Nations, also sometimes
called the Allies. The subsequent United Nations Organization, established in the spring of 1945 after Germany had surrendered, was first
labeled the U.N.O. and then the U.N. or United Nations. Some American
right-wingers, antagonistic to the U.N. in the postwar years, resented the
use of the term United Nations in referring to the wartime allies. But
that was their official name.

On January 1, 1942, three weeks after Pearl Harbor, the so-called
Declaration of the United Nations was signed in Washington, after extended conferences among Roosevelt, Prime Minister Churchill, and
others. It pledged the signatories to abide by the principles of the
Atlantic Charter, to employ their resources to the full against the common enemy, and to make no separate armistice or peace.[4] This pact was
immediately signed by the representatives of the twenty-six countries
at war with the Axis powers; ultimately by a total of fifty-one.

The Declaration of the United Nations was not a treaty requiring approval by the Senate. It was an executive agreement, with the
binding force of a treaty internationally, legally drawn up and implemented by the President. In effect it was a firm alliance. It insured unity
during the war and collective security afterwards, for it formed the
nucleus of the yet unborn United Nations Organization. Beyond question, it must be ranked as one of the most significant documents in world
history.

COULD THE UNITED STATES HAVE LOST THE WAR?

After the half-sleeping American giant had been aroused and the war
was won, many citizens took victory for granted. One often heard that
the democracies were bound to win, once the United States, with its
enormous industrial capacity, entered the fray. This supposition does not
square with the facts.

America undoubtedly had the industrial capacity — about ten

---

[4] *Department of State Bulletin, VI* (1942), p. 3.

times that of Japan. But the problem was to convert it to military power, while there was yet time. Substitutes had to be found for the rubber, tin, and quinine of East Asia, now that the Japanese controlled these supplies. The race between disaster and the manufacture in quantity of synthetic rubber, under a $4 billion crash program, was perilously close. At the same time, the further deterioration of the battlefront had to be checked, whether in the Pacific, East Asia, North Africa, or Russia.

There was always the possibility that Hitler would produce secret weapons that would make his Fortress Europe impregnable and his power for offensive operations irresistible. Although he was more backward with perfecting the atomic bomb than Americans had feared, he had made alarming progress with the Snorkel submarine, the jet airplane, and the explosive-carrying rocket. A delay of another six months in the D-day invasion of France might have spelled the difference between victory and defeat.[5]

Losing a war means in effect losing control of a war — of not being able to impose one's will on the enemy. In this sense a nation can lose a conflict without suffering a crushing defeat. Japanese were counting on seizing control of coveted acquisitions in Southeast Asia and the Pacific, and then digging in and making reconquest so costly as to cause a war-weary Uncle Sam to give up the attempt. From their point of view a draw that would leave them in possession of their conquests would be essentially a victory. We have only to remember that in Korea in the 1950s and in Vietnam in the 1960s and 1970s the enemy dug in so deeply that America was willing to settle for stalemates, which many critics regarded as defeats. In neither case was the nation prepared to make the necessary sacrifices — including outraging world opinion — to win an "absolute victory" with all available weapons, including nuclear bombs. America was unable or unwilling to impose her will on the enemy; and the same result could have occurred in the conflict with Japan, 1941–1945.

Every great war is a war of lost opportunities; crucial decisions on the battlefield can turn on a hair. If the Japanese had attacked Russia's backdoor Siberia, if they had not assaulted Pearl Harbor, if Midway and Guadalcanal and other criticial engagements had gone the other way, Japan might have succeeded in her desperate gamble, as she

---

[5] On June 14, 1944, eight days after the D-day invasion of France, Hitler initiated the bombing of southern England with jet-propelled pilotless aircraft (V-1s). These "buzz bombs" were so slow that many were shot down. On September 7, 1944, some three months after D-day, the Germans fired the first of their speedy and relatively noiseless V-2 rockets on England. Since there was no defense against them, they caused fearful damage. They stopped functioning only when their launching sites were captured by the Allied invaders of Europe.

almost did. If, in the Western theater, Moscow, Leningrad, Stalingrad, and El Alamein (Egypt) had not held, if the Germans had not mishandled the aerial Battle of Britain, if the Allies had not won control of the air,[6] if the Allied feint to the north at the time of D-day had not worked, Hitler might have proved to be unconquerable.

WAS THE "RELOCATION" OF JAPANESE–AMERICANS DEFENSIBLE?

In the weeks following Pearl Harbor, hysteria swept the Pacific Coast of the United States. There was a widespread feeling, intensified by nighttime air raid warnings and blackouts, that the Japanese might engineer a sneak attack on the mainland. If they should land troops, they presumably would be aided, either directly or through espionage and sabotage, by the tens of thousands of Japan-born Japanese (*Issei*), especially in California. The problem was complicated by the fact that nearly two-thirds of the Japanese were American-born citizens (*Nisei*), as much entitled to all the rights of citizenship as President Roosevelt. Yet were they loyal to America or to Japan? How could one tell? Had not all Japanese been proved treacherous by Pearl Harbor? If the invaders came and were welcomed by people of their own race, how could one determine whether the welcomers were Japanese nationals or American citizens?

High officials in Washington, with Roosevelt's approval, finally decided upon drastic action, primarily as an act of military necessity. They were also prompted by an understandable anti-Japanese prejudice following Pearl Harbor, as well as by pressures from public opinion on the Pacific Coast. The army herded some 112,000 Japanese and Japanese–Americans into ten "relocation centers" — a polite term for concentration

---

[6] Allied bombing was most effective in knocking out enemy transportation, oil refineries, and aircraft facilities. Saturation attacks on cities failed to break civilian morale; in many instances such punishment increased the will to resist. Yet such attacks partially satisfied Allied desires for vengeance. Incredibly, German arms production continued to mount until mid-1944, despite declining morale, and then dropped at an increasing rate each subsequent month. Yet without bombing, the output of factories probably would have been even higher. One cannot say, as often alleged, that Allied aerial attacks were useless in a military sense; they certainly helped to shorten the war. This was especially true of the American daylight "precision bombing" as contrasted with the British nighttime "saturation bombing." But a greater concentration on strategic targets, rather than on civilian populations, almost certainly would have done more to justify the heavy expense and losses incurred, to say nothing of the moral opprobrium. See *The United States Strategic Bombing Survey: Over-all Report (European War)* [September 30, 1945], especially pp. 95–98.

camps — from California to Arkansas, where they could be of little assistance to a seaborne invader.[7] This hasty uprooting was accompanied by much hardship, including not only physical discomfort and emotional strain but property loss. The victims were forced to sell their automobiles, tractors, houses, land, and businesses at fire-sale prices to white Americans, who all too often greedily took advantage of the plight of their "treacherous" fellow citizens. In many cases the purchasers were glad to be rid of unwelcome competitors in farming or business.

In sober retrospect the treatment accorded a large mass of bona fide American citizens was outrageous; it could be justified only by presumed military necessity. On these grounds the Supreme Court in 1944 upheld the mass uprooting. After the war, the Washington government made belated and partial, but only partial, financial recompense for losses incurred in the hasty relocation. Even so, no amount of money could adequately compensate the sufferers for hardship, heartache, and accusations of disloyalty.[8]

Relocating the Japanese–Americans proved to be wholly unnecessary. Japan's warlords, having committed their troop strength to East Asia and the Western Pacific, were unable to mount a serious land invasion of the Pacific Coast.[9] The Japanese–Americans and the Japanese aliens in Hawaii, where martial law was proclaimed, did not reveal serious disloyalty during the war, and they were not herded into concentration camps. One compelling reason was that the relocation of so large a proportion of the population would have proved impracticable. Indeed Japanese–American troops from Hawaii, as if to prove their loyalty, fought with unusual distinction, particularly in the Italian campaign.

The harsh decision to evacuate these unoffending citizens on the Pacific Coast was understandable in the light of the existing hysteria. Precautionary measures of this nature often have to be made after assessing all available military information, some of it false, and calculating probabilities. If Japanese armies had invaded the Pacific Coast and had

[7] General John L. DeWitt has been unfairly blamed for being primarily responsible for the evacuation. He initially had in view moving *only* Japanese aliens, as well as German and Italian aliens, under less harsh circumstances than those ultimately employed under Roosevelt's authorization. His attitude toward the Japanese hardened with time. Stetson Conn, "The Decision to Evacuate the Japanese from the Pacific Coast (1942)," in Kent R. Greenfield, ed., *Command Decisions* (1959), pp. 88–109.

[8] See Bill Hosokawa, *Nisei: The Quiet Americans* (1969).

[9] What was then regarded as the mainland United States suffered only slight damage from balloon-carried explosives from Japan, and from shells from two submarines in 1942 off the coast of California and Oregon. In the same year the Japanese bombed Dutch Harbor and Ft. Mears, Alaska, and occupied two fog-girt islands in the western Aleutian chain, far from continental Alaska.

been assisted by people of their own blood, a storm of condemnation would have burst over the administration in Washington. This was probably a basic reason why President Roosevelt himself took an active and positive role in authorizing the mass evacuation.[10]

WAS "UNCONDITIONAL SURRENDER" A STATESMANLIKE FORMULA?

At the end of the Casablanca Conference of Allied leaders in North Africa, January 1943, Roosevelt issued a sensational statement to the press. It declared that the Axis powers would be forced to submit to "unconditional surrender," though this formula "did not mean destruction of the population." [11] The added qualification was largely lost sight of in the subsequent uproar.

"Unconditional surrender" was not a new concept: it appeared inferentially in Roosevelt's war message ("absolute victory"), following the attack on Pearl Harbor; it was implicit in the "complete victory" affirmation in the Declaration of the United Nations, signed by twenty-six countries early in 1942. The ruthless prescription had been discussed at considerable length in Washington as early as May 1942. Roosevelt, remembering "Unconditional Surrender" Grant of Civil War days, had mentioned the watchword to Churchill in private conversation. The British Prime Minister warmed to the phrase at once; he was the one who in the Casablanca Conference proposed that an announcement of the stern policy be given to the press.[12] In short, "unconditional surrender" was not a spur-of-the-moment brainstorm of Roosevelt, as often asserted.

There were indeed persuasive arguments for issuing the iron-toothed pronouncement. The Russian allies, dismayed by the failure of Britain and America to launch a second front, and suspicious of separate Allied "deals" with the French Vichyites, feared that the democracies might offer concessions to Hitler that would betray Russia. There was some talk of Stalin's coming to terms with Nazi Germany and dropping

[10] Conn, "The Decision to Evacuate the Japanese from the Pacific Coast (1942)," pp. 88–109. See also Audrie Girdner and Anne Loftis, *The Great Betrayal* (1969). Using harsher methods than the Americans, the Canadians evacuated some 22,000 Japanese, most of them Canadian citizens. *Ibid.*, pp. 424–425. See also D. S. Myer, *Uprooted Americans* (1971).

[11] *Foreign Relations of the United States: The Conference at Washington, 1941–1942, and Casablanca, 1943* (1968), p. 727. The traditional accounts erroneously credit F.D.R. with springing the policy upon a "dumbfounded" Churchill at a press conference.

[12] *Ibid.*, p. 635.

out of the war, as the Bolsheviks had done in 1918; [13] and Soviet armies were presumably needed to help crush Japan when Germany was prostrated. Not only would "unconditional surrender" reassure the Russians but it would inspirit subject peoples such as the conquered French and the Poles, as well as the partially conquered Chinese. The Allies, moreover, would be keyed up to greater sacrifices and unity. At the same time the democracies would avoid the divisive controversy that had followed the *conditional* surrender of Germany in 1918, and avert all talk of a victorious army having been stabbed in the back by Jews and other disloyal elements. Public opinion polls reveal that "unconditional surrender" was overwhelmingly approved by the American people — a fact that partly explains why Roosevelt clung stubbornly to it.[14]

DID UNCONDITIONAL SURRENDER PROLONG THE WAR?

A common objection to Roosevelt's fearsome phrase was that Hitler's propagandists used it to whip their people up to a last-ditch resistance, thereby lengthening the conflict and costing countless lives. Such uncompromising terms disheartened German liberals, who, the argument goes, might otherwise have overthrown the Nazi tyrants and made a negotiated peace.[15] But German liberals were few and timid, Hitler ruled with a bloody hand, and the few army officers who plotted against him were not disposed to surrender unconditionally. President Wilson had drawn a distinction in 1917–1918 between the German leaders, who would have to be eliminated, and their misled people, who would be granted an honorable peace. Early in World War II the Allies tried the

[13] Any fear of Stalin's making peace with Hitler at this stage was unrealistic; the Soviets were in the process of wiping out the German invaders at Stalingrad while the Casablanca Conference was being held. In retrospect, "unconditional surrender" seemed like a high price to placate Stalin, especially since he remained pathologically suspicious of a "sellout" to the very end. On the other hand, the controversial phrase helped to win the war by postponing many divisive political issues until after victory.

[14] For a book which strongly argues that Roosevelt was deeply concerned with political objectives, indeed sometimes more perceptively than Churchill, and that "Unconditional Surrender" was helpful if not indispensable in prosecuting and ending the war, see Raymond G. O'Connor, *Diplomacy for Victory: FDR and Unconditional Surrender* (1971).

[15] A logical corollary of the "Unconditional Surrender" formula was the Morgenthau plan, presented at the Quebec Conference in September, 1944, by the Secretary of the Treasury. It envisaged a de-industrialization and "pastoralization" of postwar Germany. Although Roosevelt and Churchill temporarily approved it, they subsequently dropped it, but not until it had leaked out and had been used with damaging effect by German propagandists.

same bait, but the Nazis understandably refused to bite a second time.

Italy was required to surrender unconditionally in 1943, with the tacit understanding that she would be treated leniently. She probably would have yielded sooner if formal concessions had been possible. The four to six weeks of delay enabled Germany to bring in reinforcements, which greatly prolonged the subsequent Italian campaign.

Japan might have surrendered sooner if Roosevelt had not proclaimed "unconditional surrender"; indeed, the war might have ended without the dropping of the two atomic bombs. Ironically, the Japanese did successfully gain one important "condition": the retention of their Emperor, for which they might have settled earlier.

"Unconditional surrender" was a negative policy which led to the elimination of the German government. It also facilitated the division of Germany (and Berlin) into four parts, ultimately into two — with a subsequent Pandora's box of perplexities. The victors, including the Americans, were woefully unprepared to assume the responsibility of governing the conquered Germans. The severe Allied policy, by insuring complete destruction of the enemy, also facilitated the top-dog ascendancy of the Soviet Union in Eastern Europe and the Far East, with a consequent upsetting of the balance of power.

"Unconditional surrender" as a concept had considerable merit, but as a phrase it was vague and easily misinterpreted. It left no room for bargaining. It encouraged "unconditional resistance," and hence came under fire from some of America's top military men. On balance, a softer term such as "Honorable capitulation" might have served better.[16]

DID F.D.R. OVERAPPEASE VICHY AND FRANCO?

After Hitler conquered France in 1940, he left roughly the southeastern half under a puppet government located at Vichy. This regime, headed by an aged war hero, Marshal Pétain, still controlled the overseas colonies, together with a considerable army and powerful units of the French navy.

Liberals and Communists in the United States were highly critical of any dealings with a Nazi-manipulated accomplice in Vichy. But a severance of relations would have ended all consular and diplomatic representation, which was essential in supplying information for the successful invasion of North Africa late in 1942. To collaborate with those

---

[16] In negotiating for the capitulation of the German armies in Italy, the Americans found "unconditional surrender" a real obstacle. Allen Dulles, *The Secret Surrender* (1966), p. 30.

who collaborated with the enemy was distasteful, but Washington regarded such conniving as a military necessity.

No less ticklish were relations with Franco in Spain. Openly friendly to Hitler and Mussolini, both of whom had aided him in his successful civil war, he had to be kept neutral. If driven into the arms of Hitler (he almost got there), he might have thwarted the invasion of North Africa, further blocked the Mediterranean, and delayed, even prevented, Allied victory.

The Allies kept Franco in line by "appeasement" — principally by permitting limited cargoes of petroleum and other supplies to be shipped to him. When the tide began to turn and Hitler appeared doomed, such acts of favoritism were substantially reduced or ended. America's ambassador in Spain, a prominent historian from Columbia University, Dr. C. J. H. Hayes, was bitterly criticized by Communists and other so-called liberals in the United States for "appeasing" Franco.[17] They evidently did not realize that the envoy was sent to Madrid for that purpose. Perhaps he appeased somewhat more than he had to, but how fine a line could he draw? It is better to be safe than sorry; better to appease somewhat more than necessary than to appease not quite enough to prevent catastrophe.

Critics of appeasement were hoping to promote liberalism and reform in the postwar world. Roosevelt was looking primarily to a destruction of totalitarian tyranny through a crushing military victory, achieved as speedily as possible. He is somewhat vulnerable to criticism for having concentrated so heavily on winning the war and for not having given even more thought than he did to winning the peace by securing viable political settlements. But driving Vichy France and Franco Spain into the arms of Hitler would have postponed victory, perhaps prevented it. And delay was to Hitler's advantage, largely because he had fearsome secret weapons in the making.

SHOULD THE SECOND FRONT HAVE COME SOONER?

Even before America's formal entry into the war, British and American leaders had agreed that in the event of hostilities the proper strategy would be to concentrate on destroying Hitler. The Japanese could be mopped up later. The logical assumption was that if Japan were crushed first, Hitler would still be a tough nut to crack, but that if Hitler fell,

---

[17] Hayes, a prominent Catholic layman, tells the story from his vantage point in *Wartime Mission in Spain, 1942–1945* (1945).

Japan would be doomed. This strategy was followed throughout, despite vengeful outcries in America for "getting Hirohito first." American naval and military commanders in the Pacific, notably General MacArthur, repeatedly and understandably complained that their needs were neglected in the interests of the European front.[18]

Soviet Russia, involved in "meat-grinder tactics," suffered far heavier casualties from the German invasion than did all of the Western democracies combined. Stalin repeatedly pleaded for the British and Americans to open a second front in western Europe so as to draw Nazi divisions off his back, but such a diversionary assault was slow in forthcoming. The Allies held out hope to him of a cross-Channel invasion in 1942, then in 1943. It was finally mounted in 1944.[19] The difficulties of landing a large and well-equipped army, supported by air power and naval units, were enormous. Moreover the British, who had lost hundreds of thousands of men in France during World War I, had no stomach for launching a direct invasion that might well be bloodily crushed. Prime Minister Churchill repeatedly argued for postponement, urged alternatives, and pressed for an invasion by way of the "soft underbelly" of the Balkans, which might not have proved so soft. On the other hand, such a thrust might have substantially rolled back Russian influence in that area.

Suspicious Soviets, who evidently thought that crossing the English Channel was somewhat like crossing a Russian river, had no sympathy with these delays. Ever distrustful of the capitalistic West, they concluded that the Americans and British were deliberately stalling so that the Soviet Union would be bled to death. This is probably what Stalin would have been tempted to do if the tables had been reversed. Communist agitators in the United States avowed that, in the absence of support from the West, the Soviets would either collapse or make a separate peace with Hitler, leaving the Allies in the lurch. Some American advocates of a second front declared that it should be launched forthwith, even if bloodily repulsed, to demonstrate the good faith of the democracies. This kind of talk was dampened by the costly small-scale Allied raid on Dieppe, France, in August 1942. The 6,000 attackers were bloodily repulsed, with more than half their force killed, wounded, or taken prisoner.

Instead of the cross-Channel second front in 1942, the Allies

[18] See Douglas MacArthur, *Reminiscences* (1964), p. 156.

[19] The shipping and war supplies sent to Russia under lend–lease diverted strength that could have gone into an earlier attempt at a second front. Some British spokesmen noted that Stalin provided no second front, in fact aided Hitler, when Britain so desperately needed one in 1940–1941.

settled for the North African invasion. It initially went off with gratifying success, thanks to the cooperation of the anti-Nazi French forces there. Blunders were made and painful lessons were learned which may have spelled the difference between victory and defeat when the D-day invasion of France occurred in 1944. Still Stalin clamored for a "genuine" second front, and again it was postponed in 1943. When it finally came in 1944, the Russians, instead of overflowing with gratitude, were prone to say, "It's about time." [20]

Whether or not a successful second front could have been launched in 1943 will long be disputed. If the Allies were better prepared in 1944, the German defenses were stronger. And one should emphasize that when the landings finally came, the beachhead hung in the balance for several weeks. Lady Luck was also with the invaders. The weather cooperated, while a successful feint to the north succeeded in drawing off German reserves.

WAS THE NORTH AFRICAN INCURSION SOUND STRATEGY?

The invasion of French North Africa with Allied troops, chiefly American, was one of the riskiest gambles of the war. Much depended on the weather, on the height of the surf, on the menacing German submarines, on the coordination of Allied military and naval units, on the resistance put up by the Vichy French army, on a possible flank attack by Franco from Spain or by Hitler through Spain. The ultimate success of the scheme, with light casualties, was a near miracle.

Most of the top American military men opposed the diversion of this large a force (850 ships and some 200,000 men) from the second front projected for 1943. They favored concentrating all available strength for a crushing blow across the English Channel at Hitler, whom no amount of "periphery pecking" could topple. But Roosevelt was adamant. Fearful of an abortive second front, as were the British, he desired to strike a blow at Nazi Germany and enhearten the Russians by demonstrating that he meant business. He was also eager to achieve some kind of success after the dreary string of losses to the Japanese in the Pacific. He hoped to have the victorious invasion under way on the eve of the Congressional elections of 1942, which would probably turn out more favorable to the administration if the Democrats could boast of a victory over the Germans. Understandably Roosevelt was much dis-

[20] See John R. Deane, *The Strange Alliance* (1947), p. 151. W. Averell Harriman recalls that Stalin spoke to him of the Allied landing in highly complimentary terms. *America and Russia in a Changing World* (1971), p. 71.

appointed when the blow, scheduled for late October at the latest, had to be postponed for military reasons until five days after the election.[21] Roosevelt could now be commended, as he was, for "rising above politics."

Churchill warmly backed the North African invasion; it would ease pressure for a cross-Channel second front and help clear the Mediterranean for British shipping. Stalin was somewhat pleased but not overjoyed, for the operation did not significantly reduce German pressures on the USSR, and he bitterly refused to accept it as a substitute for a second front in France.

Hitler reacted to the North African thrust by occupying the remainder of neutralized Vichy France in an attempt to seize the French fleet, which the prewarned crews were able to scuttle. The German–Italian army in eastern North Africa was ultimately nutcrackered between the Allies advancing from both east and west. But the success in Africa led to Sicily, and Sicily led to the Italian boot, up which the Allies had to struggle in one of the costliest and most frustrating campaigns of the war. Meanwhile Hitler's Fortress Europe remained redoubtable.

The North African stroke deeply involved Roosevelt in French political infighting and gave America an additional black eye. General Charles de Gaulle, who headed the Free French cause in England, was not informed of the assault in advance, presumably for reasons of security. American officials, in an effort to induce the Vichy French forces to cease resisting the invasion, successfully solicited the good offices of Admiral Darlan, a notorious Vichyite and collaborator with Hitler. Liberals, independents, and idealists in America were shocked by this dalliance with Vichy. But Roosevelt, ever the master of expediency, recalled the ancient Bulgarian proverb to the effect that in time of grave danger one may walk with the Devil until the bridge is crossed.

WAS F.D.R. DYING WHEN REELECTED IN 1944?

Once the two-term tradition was shattered in 1940, the argument against a fourth term was seriously weakened. With the war far from being won by mid-1944, President Roosevelt consented to run again, obviously with the intent of guiding Allied forces to victory. Hopeful Republicans nominated the young "racket-busting" governor of New

---

21 James M. Burns, *Roosevelt: The Soldier of Freedom* (1970), pp. 287, 290, 291; Dwight D. Eisenhower, *Crusade in Europe* (1948), p. 195. The Democrats suffered a severe setback but managed to retain control of Congress.

York, Thomas E. Dewey, whom Roosevelt snowed under at the polls in November. Many citizens evidently had little confidence that the inexperienced Dewey could do a better job than the experienced Roosevelt in first winning the war and then winning the peace. New plans for collective security were on the drawing boards, in the hope that they could succeed where the old League of Nations had failed; and the voters remembered that the Republicans were still generously tarred with the brush of isolationism.

Less than six months after his electoral victory, Roosevelt was dead of a cerebral hemorrhage. Many people concluded that he had perpetrated a hoax on the public, and that he must have known, as a semi-invalid since 1921, that he could not endure the heavy strain of the office for a total of sixteen years. No doubt Roosevelt himself felt some premonitions. It is significant that he arranged to "dump" the ultra-liberal Vice President Henry A. Wallace, who had much vociferous support, in favor of the little known Senator Harry S Truman, who was known to be much more conservative.

After twelve years in office, Roosevelt was clearly showing the burden of his weighty responsibilities. He limited the number of his formal campaign speeches, thus currying favor with the voters by appearing to devote his energies to winning the war rather than re-winning the Presidency. His most effective speech — that to the Teamsters in Washington — was delivered sitting down. The heavy steel braces on his legs were becoming less bearable. During the campaign the merciless eye of the camera portrayed him on several occasions as an exhausted and ailing man.

What the public did not know was that in a railway car in San Diego he turned white while his torso was convulsed in agony, and that during a speech in Bremerton (Washington) he had suffered severe chest pains (possibly angina pectoris). The agony went away but the speech itself, halting and rambling, left a most unfortunate impression.[22] Roosevelt was nearer the grave than most people suspected, including possibly himself.

WAS EISENHOWER A BRILLIANT GENERAL?

A graduate of West Point, Dwight D. Eisenhower had risen rapidly to high position. After commanding the invaders in the North African landings of November 1942, he became chief of all Allied forces in North Africa in 1943, and went on from there to direct the invasion of Sicily

---

[22] Burns, *Roosevelt: The Soldier of Freedom*, pp. 507–508. For F.D.R.'s high blood pressure and other symptoms, see below, p. 727.

and the initial landings in Italy. Subsequently he was named supreme commander of the Allied forces that were to assault the shores of France in June 1944.[23]

If one may judge by results, Eisenhower was a highly competent general, although not one of Napoleonic brilliance. His critics, especially in the British camp, have assailed him for not fighting the war the way they would have fought it, but we can hardly quarrel with success.[24] Military capabilities aside, there can be no question as to Eisenhower's captivating personality and his capacity to persuade reluctant allies to work together cooperatively, whether British, Canadian, French, or American. His well recognized talents as a conciliator, rather than any spectacular military gifts, largely account for his having been entrusted with high commands.

Eisenhower has been most savagely criticized for having held back his victorious armies, thus permitting the Russians to enter Berlin as conquerors and Prague as liberators. The claim is that if American forces had captured these key cities first, the Russian Communists would not have entrenched themselves there, and Soviet influence in Central Europe would have been rolled back nearer the borders of the Soviet Union.

The decision to halt at the Elbe River, made by Eisenhower on April 1, 1945, was a purely military one. He might or might not have been able to fight his way to Berlin before the arrival of the Russians, who were some thirty miles away, whereas he was about 100 miles distant. To have done so would have cost an estimated 100,000 American casualties, according to General Bradley. But, say the critics, would not the counteracting of Communist influence have been worth the price? Possibly so, if the Americans could have remained. But pursuant to arrangements worked out by the British and Russians in London, and agreed to by Washington on May 1, 1944, the Soviets were to have a zone in conquered Germany, with Berlin located deep within it.[25] In short, Eisenhower was bound to withdraw from Berlin, even if he had

---

[23] Roosevelt originally intended to back General Marshall for the post of supreme commander, but finally decided that Marshall's continued presence in Washington as Chief of Staff was indispensable. Eisenhower, *Crusade in Europe*, p. 207.

[24] The British General Bernard Montgomery long and bitterly complained that his grand strategy of a massive northerly drive toward Berlin should have been adopted, rather than Eisenhower's successful "broad front" concept. *The Memoirs of Field Marshall the Viscount Montgomery* (1958), Ch. 15. Montgomery's cautious management of his own command was less than brilliant. See B. H. Liddell Hart, *History of the Second World War* (1971), Ch. XXXI.

[25] *Foreign Relations of the U. S., 1944*, I, 211. For the whole story see William M. Franklin, "Zonal Boundaries and Access to Berlin," *World Politics*, XVI (1963), 1–31. The status of the British and American zones in Germany was not agreed upon until February 1945 at Yalta, where the Soviets permitted the British and Americans to create a French zone out of their jurisdictions.

sacrificed a substantial portion of his army to get there. And these men were presumably needed to crush Japan.[26]

WERE THE RUSSIANS COOPERATIVE ALLIES?

Although formally allied with the United States and other Western nations under the Declaration of the United Nations, the Soviets did not act like wholehearted comrades-in-arms. At times they appeared to be allies only in the sense that they were fighting on the same side as the Americans. There was never any overarching Allied command, such as was achieved under the French Marshal Foch in 1918. Admittedly the Soviets roughly coordinated several of their great drives in the east with the Allied blows in the west, notably after the second front was opened in June 1944, but self-interest was clearly involved on both sides.[27] The way to overthrow Hitler was obviously to force him to fight a relentless two-front war.

Themselves old hands at conspiracy, the Russians were highly suspicious of their Western allies, whose headquarters in Moscow they "bugged." The Kremlin had declared undying war on capitalism, and for years had been preaching violent world revolution. The Soviets resented the Allied delays in launching an all-out second front; they were suspicious of Americans who entered the Soviet Union to determine Russia's lend–lease needs; they were unconscionably slow in granting visas to Allied representatives and reluctant to provide lists of their requirements lest they reveal their weaknesses; they jealously guarded their military secrets while receiving much classified information from the Allies; they acted as though they were expecting to have to fight the capitalist nations, especially America, after they had disposed of Hitler; and they resented the lenient treatment accorded by the West to Fascist Spain, Argentina, and other neutrals. This is only a partial list of the annoyances experienced by the Western democracies.[28]

Particularly disturbing was the reluctance of the Russian leaders to attend top-level coordinating conferences. Stalin, who was directing

[26] See Forrest C. Pogue, "The Decision to Halt at the Elbe (1945)," in Greenfield, ed., Command Decisions, pp. 374–387; S. E. Ambrose, Eisenhower and Berlin, 1945 (1967).

[27] Stalin's honoring of his military commitments persuaded many American leaders that he would be cooperative after the war. Harriman, America and Russia, p. 31.

[28] The story is told in great detail by General Deane's The Strange Alliance (1947). General Deane was the chief American military liaison officer in Moscow during the critical war years. More broadly based is Robert H. Jones, The Roads to Russia: United States Lend–Lease to the Soviet Union (1969). Ironically, lend–lease enabled Russia to absorb much of Eastern and Central Europe.

the grand strategy of the Russian armies, flatly declined to confer at Casablanca, in January 1943. To achieve an imperative meeting with him, a crippled Roosevelt was forced to undertake the long and hazardous journey to Teheran (Persia). F.D.R. made the trip again in February 1945, this time meeting the Soviet leader on Russian soil, at Yalta, in the Crimea. Basically about all that the Russian Communists had in common with the West was a desire to remove the menace of Hitlerism and Japanese militarism.

Mistrust was mutual in the "strained alliance." Capitalist America from the beginning had abhorred Bolshevik Russia, with its bloody liquidation of the upper class, its unilateral dropping out of the war against Germany in 1917–1918, its repudiation of debts, its enshrining of atheism, its propaganda abroad for world revolution, its wiping out of dissenters, its stamping out of embryonic democratic processes, its breaking of agreements, and its trumped-up trials of traitors. Added to all of this, Stalin negotiated his fateful pact with Hitler (for defense purposes) which triggered World War II; seized his conspirator's share of Poland; attacked tiny Finland in 1939–1940; and following the fall of France extinguished (evidently for defensive purposes) the adjacent Baltic nations of Latvia, Esthonia, and Lithuania, plus two areas in Rumania. Few people were deceived when Moscow dissolved the Communist International (Comintern) in 1943. As suspected, it merely went underground, to emerge in reconstituted form in 1945.

WAS CHINA A GREAT POWER DURING WORLD WAR II?

During the war Roosevelt stoutly maintained that China was a great power. He managed to have her associated with the Big Three (U.S., USSR, Britain) as one of the Big Four; and ultimately this status gave her a permanent seat on the Security Council of the United Nations. Winston Churchill believed that categorizing China as a great power was "an absolute farce," but during the conflict he decided to humor the American President.

Roosevelt, with a soft spot in his heart for China, was fond of recalling how his grandfather Delano had made two fortunes in the China trade. Americans in general seem to have swallowed the myth that the Chinese, far from disliking all "foreign devils," had a special fondness for the United States.[29]

[29] A corollary myth was that the hundreds of millions of Chinese were about to become a vast market for American products and goods, especially if they would boost American textiles by adding an inch or two to their shirttails.

It will be remembered that concern for China in 1941 had led to a breakdown of negotiations in Washington and war with Japan. The Nationalist leader, Generalissimo Chiang Kai-shek, enjoyed the sympathy and limited support of the United States in his dual war against both Japan and the Chinese Communists. Like Stalin, he was not the ideal ally; his basic aims did not square with those of the United States. He fought with one eye on the Japanese and one on the Communists, against whom he diverted some of the few arms that the United States managed to send him.

In all fairness, Chiang had abundant reason to be unhappy over the inability of the United States to provide large-scale assistance after Pearl Harbor. Roosevelt was anxious to boost his morale and prevent him from caving in to his enemies, for American military men regarded China as the potential springboard for mounting the invasion of Japan. Partly for this reason, Chiang was accorded great power status in lieu of more substantial help.

WHY DID MYTHS DEVELOP ABOUT YALTA?

Early in February 1945 Roosevelt conferred at length with Premier Stalin and Prime Minister Churchill at Yalta, in southern Russia. Arrangements were made for coordinating the striking power of the Western Allies with that of Russia in forcing Germany to surrender unconditionally. Agreement was also reached on these subjects: the postwar zones of the victorious Allies in Germany; the launching of the United Nations Organization; the creation of a new Poland under "free elections"; "democratic" regimes in liberated Europe; and the restoration of Russian influence in the Far East. Premier Stalin, a shrewd bargainer, promised to hurl his armies against the Japanese forces in East Asia in return for the territorial and other concessions granted him in that area.

Myths and misconceptions soon attached themselves to the Yalta agreements.[30] The meetings were held behind closed doors, which naturally inspired many rumors and which increased when five different secret deals leaked out or were announced within two years. The most vital concealment related to Russia's pledge to enter the war against Japan within at most three months after Hitler's unconditional surrender. If the Japanese had known of this behind-the-curtains arrangement, they

[30] See A. G. Theoharis, *The Yalta Myths: An Issue in U.S. Politics, 1945–1955* (1970).

might have launched an attack on Russia's rear, thereby impeding the conquest of Germany. When Stalin's entry into the Far Eastern war was later deemed unnecessary, rumors multiplied as to the alleged one-sided nature of the bargain.

Compromise had to be reached on both sides at Yalta if there was to be agreement, and since the time allotted to the conference was short (seven days), the settlement of controversial issues tended to be cloaked in deliberately vague language. This was conspicuously true of the stipulations regarding "free elections" in liberated Central Europe — stipulations which later led to angry charges in the West that Stalin had broken solemn pledges.[31]

Photographs of the black-caped Roosevelt, taken at the time of the Yalta Conference, reveal a figure who was wan, weary, slack-jawed, and aging. On-the-spot observers noted that at times he looked gray, haggard, and ill. When he returned to Washington, he presented his report to Congress sitting down, and his rather fumbling delivery displayed little of the old fire. Two months after Yalta he died. His death at this time provided further basis for the rumor that a sick and exhausted President, with an enfeebled mind, had been tricked by a crafty Stalin into betraying America's basic interests.

No one can deny that at times during these weeks Roosevelt looked thin (he was dieting), tired, and unwell. Yet there is no evidence that at Yalta he showed signs of brain damage; and he held up his end of the negotiations creditably.[32] Moreover he had advisors at hand, including Secretary of State Stettinius and the Ambassador to Moscow, W. Averell Harriman. Winston Churchill, aided by Foreign Secretary Eden, was also there. Churchill not only participated in the discussions but signed the relevant agreements; and there seemed little question about the Prime Minister's mental vigor.

[31] The Yalta "Declaration on Liberated Europe" was not a flat guarantee of "free elections." The three powers merely agreed jointly to render assistance "when in their judgment conditions require" such help in holding "free elections" in accordance with "democratic principles." There was only an implied pledge of free elections; besides the Communist concepts of democracy and those of the so-called democratic nations have long been widely divergent; for example, "The Democratic [Communist] Republic of Vietnam." For the Yalta texts see *Foreign Relations of the United States: The Conferences at Malta and Yalta, 1945* (1955), pp. 966–987.

[32] Roosevelt had been unwell during much of 1944, afflicted with elevated blood pressure and a heart condition, among other ailments. His health was better at Yalta, though the blood pressure was still high, and rumors of "small strokes" then or before his death are unfounded. See the account of Dr. Howard G. Bruenn, "Clinical Notes on the Illness and Death of President Franklin D. Roosevelt," *Annals of Internal Medicine,* LXXII (1970), 579–591. Dr. Bruenn attended Roosevelt from March 1944, to the day of his death, and wonders how history might have been changed if modern methods for controlling hypertension had been available.

DID THE YALTA PAPERS REVEAL A BETRAYAL?

Negotiated by a Democratic administration, the Yalta agreements quickly came under partisan fire. The Republicans, who were naturally critical, redoubled their attacks as the compacts did not turn out as expected. Alger Hiss was there as an expert concerned with the yet unborn United Nations Organization; and when he was convicted in 1950 of perjury in connection with passing on confidential documents to Moscow prior to World War II, many citizens assumed that he had been largely responsible for the "betrayals" of Yalta. When the Republicans attained power under President Eisenhower in 1953, they pressed for publication of the documents relating to Yalta and for a repudiation of the accords.

Publication of the Yalta papers in 1955, after a curious leakage to the press, proved to be a keen disappointment to partisan Republicans. Alger Hiss appeared in an inconsequential role, and no new damning evidence of a "betrayal" was forthcoming. Since the Yalta arrangements were cast in the form of executive agreements, not subject to approval by the Senate, President Eisenhower could have repudiated them forthwith. Though urged to do so, he declined to act because the administration decided that the best interests of the United States would be served by letting them stand.[33] We must remember that all three parties at Yalta, including Stalin, made substantial concessions.

The first of Roosevelt's two conferences with Stalin had occurred at Teheran, late in 1943, nearly two years before the Yalta meeting, and at a time when the President's mental and physical vigor was not in question. Publication of the Teheran records in 1961 (six years after the Yalta papers) did not make much of a splash, but they did reveal that the two leaders had then agreed upon most of the essentials of the Yalta pacts. These included the partition of Poland, the entry (for a price) of the Soviet army into the war against Japan, the dismemberment of Germany, and the launching of a United Nations organization.[34]

---

[33] Efforts by Congress to pass repudiating resolutions all failed. Theoharis, *Yalta Myths*, Ch. XI.

[34] See William M. Franklin, "Yalta Viewed from Teheran," in Daniel R. Beaver, ed., *Some Pathways in Twentieth Century History: Essays in Honor of Reginald Charles McGrane* (1969), pp. 253–301.

WAS POLAND "SOLD OUT" AT YALTA?

The conferees at Yalta agreed that Poland should be refashioned. She would lose a large area on the east to Russia but gain a roughly equivalent area to the north and west from Germany. Despite the self-determination pledge of the Atlantic Charter, adhered to with reservations by Stalin, tens of thousands of Poles would fall under Soviet rule and tens of thousands of Germans under Polish rule. The conferees further agreed that a more "broadly based" and "democratic" government should be established in Poland and that it should be "pledged to the holding of free and unfettered elections as soon as possible on the basis of universal suffrage and secret ballot." [35]

A shell-shocked Russia, twice invaded by the Germans through Poland in one generation, was determined to create there a friendly and subservient buffer state in the interests of Soviet security.[36] The USSR proceeded to violate the "free election" assurances, not only in Poland but elsewhere in Eastern Europe, and began to create puppet regimes that would take directions from Moscow. As a consequence, Roosevelt was hotly accused of having betrayed the Poles, for whom World War II had begun in the first place.

Roosevelt at Yalta understood Russia's paramount interest in Poland, and he also knew that the Soviet armies were already there, as well as in other "liberated" countries of Eastern Europe. The United States, then fighting hard against the Germans on the western front, had no means of evicting the Russian troops, assuming that it was willing to do so. Roosevelt did not surrender Poland: that unhappy country was not his to surrender. He realized the necessity of wording the agreement about free elections somewhat vaguely, in the hope of interpreting it

---

[35] It will be observed that the Soviets did not guarantee "free elections"; the Big Three *pledged* the new government of Poland to hold them. The offense of the Soviets was to *interfere* with the implementation of this pledge. *The Conferences at Malta and Yalta*, p. 973.

[36] As "liberating" Russian armies neared the outskirts of Warsaw in August 1944, the anti-Communist Polish underground under General Bór rose against the German conquerors. The Soviets halted for several months, evidently deliberately, while the Germans methodically destroyed Warsaw and about 250,000 Polish men, women, and children. See Arthur B. Lane, *I Saw Poland Betrayed* (1948), Ch. III. Lane had become U. S. Ambassador to Poland in 1944. The argument that the Russians were forced to halt by strategic considerations does not explain why the Soviets refused to permit American bombers to succor Warsaw effectively with air-dropped supplies. B. H. Liddell Hart, *History of the Second World War* (1971), p. 583. The case for Stalin is presented in Gabriel Kolko, *The Politics of War* (1968), pp. 115–121.

later to the advantage of the Poles.[37] He perceived that if Stalin should later break his pledges (as he later did according to Western lights), then the onus would be on him. If Roosevelt had held out for firmer assurances, the Yalta Conference might well have broken up, with a body blow to Allied unity and morale, and with a death knell for the embryonic United Nations Organization.

We should remember that when Poland lost territory on the east to Russia, she gained an area to the west at the expense of Germany. Germans, though enemies, protested against this alleged betrayal of the Atlantic Charter. But we should also note that the Yalta arrangements (so far as then known) were generally praised *at the time* by the American public, except for numerous Polish–Americans and German–Americans.[38] Many anti-Communist Catholics in the United States also condemned this "appeasement" of Stalin.

DID F.D.R. PAY TOO MUCH FOR STALIN'S ARMY?

At the time of Yalta, the war against Hitler was far from won, although the German armies were again reeling backward following the temporary setback to American hopes by the surprise Ardennes offensive of December 1944. After crushing Germany, the Americans and British planned to mount an invasion of Japan, at a cost of perhaps a million casualties and eighteen months. When the Big Three met at Yalta, a majority of Roosevelt's military advisors, quite in contrast with some who spoke up later, were emphatic in declaring that Stalin's armies were imperatively necessary for the Far Eastern fighting.[39] The Nipponese had an estimated 2 million troops on the Asiatic mainland, and if the

[37] The myth that Roosevelt "sold out" Eastern Europe by making the Yalta agreements is vitiated by the pains that Stalin later took to break them. See Harriman, *America and Russia*, p. 35.

[38] In 1943, at Teheran, Roosevelt had agreed that eastern Poland should be given to Russia but that Poland should be expanded to the west (at the expense of Germany) even to the Oder River. He explained to Stalin that he could not publicize his views because he might have to run again in 1944, and he did not want to antagonize "six to seven million Americans of Polish extraction. . . ." *Foreign Relations of the United States: The Conferences at Cairo and Tehran, 1943* (1961), p. 594.

[39] The American intelligence reports available at Yalta evidently did not represent faithfully the near-prostration of Japan. More than five months after Yalta, President Truman journeyed to the Potsdam Conference in Germany. He later wrote that his "most urgent" reason for going was to get "a personal reaffirmation" of Stalin's agreement to enter the war against Japan. Unlike Roosevelt, the peppery Truman was not then accused of being feeble-minded. See *Memoirs of Harry S Truman* (1955), *I*, 411. At the time of Yalta, General MacArthur evidently favored Russia's entry into the war but later alleged that he had opposed it. M. F. Herz, *Beginnings of the Cold War* (1966), pp. 13–14.

Russians could engage them, the invasion of Japan would presumably be that much less costly. Moreover, the first testing of America's atomic bomb was months away, and no one could predict the success of this "professors' dream" with certainty.

Oddly enough, Soviet involvement in the Far Eastern war was a clear case of the old second-front issue in reverse. In 1942, 1943, and 1944 the Russians had begged the Allies to pin down as many German divisions as possible; in 1945 the Allies urged the Russians to divert as many Japanese divisions as possible. In the earlier case the Allies were in a position to drive a hard bargain if they had chosen to do so; but so desperate was their plight that keeping Russia in the war was compensation enough. By 1945 Stalin was in the driver's seat, and, in view of American eagerness, one is somewhat surprised that he did not ask for more.

In return for Russia's entering the war against Japan "two or three months" after the conflict in Germany had ended (Stalin came in exactly three months after the end),[40] the USSR would receive various concessions. The "lost fruits" of the Russo–Japanese War of 1904–1905 would be returned, including the southern half of Sakhalin Island. In China's Manchuria, the harbor of Dairen would be internationalized and Port Arthur would be leased to the Soviets as a naval base. Manchuria's railroads were to be jointly operated by the Chinese and Soviets, without removing China's sovereignty, and Outer Mongolia, once China's, would continue as a Communist satellite of Moscow. The strategic Kurile Islands, formerly partially Russian, were to be handed over entirely to the Soviets. All these arrangements affecting China required the assent of Chiang Kai-shek, and in an embarrassing secret pledge at Yalta, Roosevelt undertook to secure it.

One bargain Stalin kept was his pledge regarding the Far East, thereby shattering Tokyo's hopes of Russian mediation. Six days before Japan surrendered, his armies crashed into the depleted Japanese forces in Manchuria in the so-called "victory parade," which involved relatively light Soviet casualties. Reeling from two atomic bombs and the Russian declaration of war, Tokyo surrendered.

After Japan collapsed so unexpectedly, the dead Roosevelt was assailed for having paid too high a price, largely at the expense of his Chinese ally, for the services of an unneeded Russian army. Yet we

[40] The task of redeploying Soviet armies, equipment, and supplies across Siberia by rail was formidable and time-consuming. Stalin might well have taken longer (let the democracies do some bleeding!) if the collapse of Japan had not seemed so imminent. A highly favorable assessment of Stalin's stance is Diane S. Clemens, *Yalta* (1970).

cannot be completely sure that Soviet participation was altogether unnecessary; it may have tipped the scales for surrender. Americans who lived through those days remember the rejoicing that greeted Russia's entry: it would save the lives of countless American "boys." Moreover the Yalta agreement set specific bounds to Stalin's share of the loot; his armies were powerful enough to have taken all of Manchuria, Korea, and substantial parts of China proper as well.

It now seems clear that Stalin could not have been kept out of the Far Eastern war, bargain or no bargain.[41] He wanted specific spoils, and this was the surest way to get them. Roosevelt may or may not have paid an unnecessarily high price. But like all statesmen faced with critical decisions, he had to act in the light of circumstances as they appeared at the time, and in response to the advice of the experts in their respective fields.

WAS CHIANG KAI-SHEK KNIFED AT YALTA?

Roosevelt was also charged with having double-crossed Chiang, who was not even an ally of the Soviet Union, by promising Stalin important Chinese territory and other concessions. Some critics have insisted that Chiang, reeling from this "sellout" by the United States, lost his country to the Communists in 1949 because of Roosevelt's perfidy.

This alleged betrayal at Yalta, kept secret from Chiang temporarily for reasons of security, was clearly underhanded. But the truth is that no territory was taken from China; the Russians seized Manchuria from the Japanese and restored it to the Chinese, with a few strings attached. Outer Mongolia, already a Soviet satellite for some twenty years before Yalta, had already been alienated from Peking.

At Yalta, Stalin promised — another promise he kept — to negotiate a treaty of friendship and alliance with China for the purpose of wresting Manchuria and other Chinese territories from the Japanese invader. The war-ravaged Chinese Nationalists, though haggling over Outer Mongolia and Manchuria, were pleased with the boost to their prestige that would come from recognition by and assistance from the

---

[41] On two earlier occasions (Moscow Foreign Ministers Conference and Teheran) Stalin had promised the Americans to enter the conflict against Japan, evidently in the expectation of concessions in the Far East. Roosevelt reported that at Teheran he had discussed Dairen, Sakhalin, and the Kurile Islands. *Conferences at Cairo and Tehran*, p. 869. Stalin remarked at Yalta that he would have to justify the sacrifice of a war against Japan to his own people, who were already war-weary. *Conferences at Malta and Yalta*, p. 769.

Soviets. So anxious was Stalin to enter the Far Eastern war that he did not wait for signing the treaty with China, but concluded it six days *after* he had launched his assault.[42]

Bargain or not, Roosevelt almost certainly could not have kept the Soviet armies out of Manchuria. When they finally left in 1946, they stripped the factories of machinery, to replace that destroyed by the Germans in the East, but conveniently left large caches of captured Japanese arms. These fell into the hands of the Chinese Communists, who used them in their takeover in 1948–1949. The concessions regarding the Manchurian railroads and the two seaports had no lasting significance: they were formally abandoned by the USSR ten years later, in 1955.

Ambassador-designate to Moscow, Charles E. Bohlen, had been present at Yalta as an interpreter. In 1953 he testified before the Senate Committee on Foreign Relations: "I believe that the map of Europe would look very much the same if there had never been the Yalta Conference at all." [43] The same judgment would probably apply to the map of Asia.

WAS F.D.R. FOOLISH TO GAMBLE ON RUSSIA'S COOPERATION?

Ever since 1917 the Kremlin had repeatedly avowed unending hostility to the capitalistic system, while actively promoting propaganda to that end. Roosevelt realized that if the postwar world was to enjoy a durable peace under a new international body — the yet unborn United Nations Organization — an accommodation with the Kremlin was imperative. He reasoned that there was some possibility of weaning the Soviet Communists from their suspicious and uncooperative ways if he treated them with cordiality and generosity. This hope explains in part why he provided lend–lease aid to the Russians with such a lavish hand,

[42] The dropping of the two American atomic bombs on Japan in August and the impending surrender by Tokyo probably hastened Soviet entry into the war before the conclusion of the treaty with China. Tokyo had already sent out two peace feelers to Moscow, which at that time was still neutral. See Robert J. C. Butow, *Japan's Decision to Surrender* (1954), Ch. VI. At Potsdam, Stalin had told President Truman (July 17, 1945) that his armies would be ready for action by mid-August, but that prior agreement would have to be reached with China. *Foreign Relations of the United States: The Conference of Berlin (The Potsdam Conference), 1945* (1960), p. 1585.

[43] *Nomination of Charles E. Bohlen: Hearings before the Committee on Foreign Relations, U.S. Senate, 83rd Cong., 1 sess.* (1953), p. 34.

including some they did not need immediately and were evidently stock-piling for a future war, perhaps with the United States.[44]

Roosevelt had boundless confidence in his snake-charming per-sonality. He was eager to meet the man he called "Uncle Joe" Stalin, the hardened conspirator of the Kremlin, and woo him from his nasty Communist ways.[45] The record does not reveal that Stalin abandoned any basic Soviet desires or interests in response to this glad-handing. Such an approach probably aroused his suspicions, as did the overgener-ous American handouts during the war. Many Russians evidently wondered what Roosevelt was trying to "put over."

F.D.R., whose knowledge of Marxist philosophy was less than profound, was somewhat overtrustful in his long-shot gamble on Russian cooperation with capitalism after the war. But from one point of view his strategy was worth the risk. Any other course would have fully confirmed Soviet mistrust and guaranteed continued hostility, possibly open warfare.

DID F.D.R.'S DEATH INSURE FRICTION WITH RUSSIA?

The Myth of the Empty Chair has gained considerable currency. It is that if Roosevelt had only lived, a rift between postwar Russia and America would never have widened, and the Cold War would never have chilled the world. This view was advanced by Soviet propagan-dists, who were aware that Roosevelt, as an essential partner in victory, enjoyed popularity with the Russian people — or those of them who had some conception of what was going on. Many of them wept when they heard of his death.

Actually, Roosevelt died knowing, or strongly suspecting, that his gamble on Russian cooperation had failed. During the month before the end, alarming official reports reached him that the assurances of "free and unfettered elections" in Poland were being flouted, and that the Soviets were also creating satellite nations in Eastern Europe, notably Rumania, in violation of the "free elections" formula.

A highly disagreeable episode occurred in March 1945, the

[44] Writers such as George F. Kennan have argued that Roosevelt made a tragic mistake by not throttling down lend–lease aid by 1944, when the tide of battle had strongly turned in favor of the USSR. Yet continued Russian success in the east was essential for a successful D-day landing in France. To the end, Roosevelt clung to the policy of not attempting to extort concessions for lend–lease.

[45] After Stalin was attacked by Hitler in 1941, and particularly after he became an ally, the American press and other vehicles of propaganda, including the popular movie, *Mission to Moscow*, portrayed "Uncle Joe" as a benign, pipe-smoking, grand-fatherly gentleman.

month before Roosevelt's death. The American authorities in Italy were negotiating the preliminaries of a surrender by the German armies, without at that point consulting the Soviets, although advising Moscow what was going on. Alleging that German troops were thus being released for combat against the advancing Russian armies, Stalin sent off scorching protests to Roosevelt. He evidently feared a revival of the bleed-Russia-white strategy, for he bluntly accused the Americans of bad faith and double dealing. Roosevelt, a week before he died, indignantly rejected these accusations (April 5, 1945), and expressed "bitter resentment" against the "vile misrepresentations" of Moscow's informers. Stalin cooled down somewhat, but the incident revealed glaringly that the cordiality which Roosevelt had tried to promote was no more than skin deep.[46] On April 6, responding to a strongly anti-Stalin message from Prime Minister Churchill, Roosevelt agreed that the United States would have to take a tougher stance.[47]

WAS ROOSEVELT A GREAT PRESIDENT?

Roosevelt was undeniably a great President in the sense that he influenced great events greatly, whether through the New Deal or the global war. He may have saved both American capitalism and American democracy from threats, whether at home or abroad.

F.D.R. nevertheless had serious weaknesses. He was not, like Hoover, a talented administrator at the secondary or lower levels, although he grasped the overall picture. He was not a gifted stylist like Lincoln; he kept a whole stable of ghost writers. He was not a ruggedly granite character like Cleveland; he was more like the willow that bent with the wind.[48] He was not the powerful moral force of a Wilson, whose Fourteen Points had shaken the world, although he was coauthor of the Atlantic Charter and a chief architect of the United Nations Organization. Despite his proclaimed ideals, he was inclined to be devious and uncandid. He was not a dedicated democrat like Jefferson, who had profound faith in the teachableness of the masses. Roosevelt rather

[46] For the heated Stalin–Roosevelt interchange, see *Correspondence between the Chairman of the Council of Ministers of the U.S.S.R. and the Presidents of the U.S.A. and the Prime Ministers of Great Britain during the Great Patriotic War of 1941–1945* (2 vols., Moscow, 1957), II, 198–210. See also Harriman, *America and Russia*, p. 38.

[47] Text published in *The New York Times*, April 6, 1945.

[48] Roosevelt's long-term love affair with his wife's former social secretary, Mrs. Lucy Mercer Rutherfurd, was thought to be strictly platonic. She was visiting with him in Georgia the day he died. Burns, *Roosevelt: The Soldier of Freedom*, pp. 7, 199, 600, 606. See also Joseph P. Lash, *Eleanor and Franklin* (1971).

distrusted the people and undertook to deceive them on occasion for what he regarded as their own good.

Yet Roosevelt was a great man. He was a great personality; a great showman; a great actor; a great voice ("fireside chats" on radio); a great orator; a great optimist; a great hope-inspirer; a great politician (though he made his share of serious mistakes); a great vote-getter; a great phrase-maker (often with borrowed phrases); a great opportunist; a great humanitarian and liberal reformer (really a friend of the "forgotten man"); a great tradition-breaker and innovator; a great activist; a great war leader (if we overlook certain blunders). Although caught substantially unprepared because of the isolationism of his people, he managed the best fought of America's major wars. Bold and courageous, he worked effectively with Prime Minister Churchill, to whom one of his messages ran, "It's fun to be in the same decade with you." Yet the two men often had sharp disagreements, including those relating to the future of the British Empire. At times Britain was a more difficult ally than Russia.

Roosevelt was working on a Jefferson Day speech the day before he died. It contained the following admonition: "The only limit to our realization of tomorrow will be our doubts of today. Let us move forward with strong and active faith." The end came on the same note as the beginning, when he had proclaimed, "The only thing we have to fear is fear itself."

ADDITIONAL GENERAL REFERENCES

A. R. Buchanan, *The United States and World War II* (2 vols., 1964); K. S. Davis, *Experience of War: The U. S. In World War II* (1965); R. W. Shugg and H. A. De Weerd, *World War II: A Concise History* (1946); C. R. MacDonald, *The Mighty Endeavor: American Armed Forces in the European Theater in World War II* (1969); S. E. Morison, *The Two-Ocean War* (1963) [a condensation of his 12-volume work]; K. R. Greenfield, ed., *Command Decisions* (1959) and *American Strategy in World War II* (1963); W. L. Neumann, *After Victory: Churchill, Roosevelt, Stalin and the Making of the Peace* (1967); Gaddis Smith, *American Diplomacy During the Second World War, 1941–1945* (1965); J. M. Burns, *Roosevelt: The Soldier of Freedom, 1940–1945* (1970); Herbert Feis, *Churchill, Roosevelt, Stalin* (2nd ed., 1967); Gabriel Kolko, *The Politics of War: The World and United States Foreign Policy, 1943–1945* (1968); J. L. Snell, ed., *The Meaning of Yalta* (1956); Diane S. Clemens, *Yalta*

(1970); Anne Armstrong, *Unconditional Surrender* (1961); R. A. Divine, *Second Chance: The Triumph of Internationalism in America during World War II* (1967) and *Roosevelt and World War II* (1969); H. L. Stimson and M. Bundy, *On Active Service in Peace and War* (1947); E. E. Morison, *Turmoil and Tradition* (1960) [life of Stimson]; W. H. McNeill, *America, Britain and Russia: Their Co-operation and Conflict, 1941–1946* (1953); John L. Gaddis, *The United States and the Origins of the Cold War, 1941–1947* (1972).

36

Truman and the
Rift with Russia

After Japan was atom-bombed into submission, in August 1945, the titanic conflict ended. In subsequent months a cold war between the Soviet Union and the "free" world gradually broke into the open.

Friction between the Soviet Communists and the capitalistic societies began with the Russian Revolution of 1917. It has continued without interruption to the present, even though partially sublimated by the United Nations alliance during World War II. During this conflict, further suspicion developed between Moscow and the West over such controversies as the delayed launching of the second front, America's trafficking with fascist dictators, and the future of liberated Eastern Europe, especially Poland. A brief chronology of headline events will demonstrate how action triggered reaction in an ever-widening vicious circle.

In March 1945 American officials were shocked by evidence of a Communist takeover in Poland and Rumania, despite what Washington regarded as Stalin's pledges of "free elections" at Yalta. The Soviets were determined to interpret their commitments as guaranteeing friendly satellite nations on their borders, not only for security but also for economic exploitation, to the exclusion of the West. Spokesmen for Moscow repeatedly insisted that the United States, under the Monroe

Doctrine, had about a score of friendly "puppets" of its own in nearby Latin America.[1]

World War II had not yet ended when financial problems began to vex Soviet–American relations. In May 1945, shortly after Hitler's surrender, President Truman overhastily cut back on lend–lease shipments to the Russians, as well as the other Allies. More serious was the unwillingness of Washington to provide immense loans to the Soviets with which to repair some of the Hitler-wrought devastation. Opinion polls in America indicated that there was considerable support for such assistance to the brave Russian ally, but the Kremlin's alarming conduct following the overthrow of Germany chilled these impulses.

America's atomic bomb, first dropped in August 1945, also proved to be an apple of discord. To the Soviets, the United States seemed to be attempting to hold them in line with "atomic blackmail." A few irresponsible but highly publicized Americans, including ex-Governor George H. Earle of Pennsylvania, urged that the bomb be used on Russia in a "preventive war." Washington, through the Baruch plan in June 1946, offered to share the "secret" of the atomic bomb but under safeguarding terms that the suspicious Soviets felt would put them at a disadvantage. They realized, of course, that they were closer to making their own bomb than the Americans suspected. So a priceless opportunity slipped away and the superpowers entered upon a dangerous and costly race in nuclear weapons.[2]

A frightening showdown developed early in 1946 over the refusal of the Soviet occupation army to leave Iran, as formally bound to do. The Soviets were seeking oil concessions comparable to those enjoyed by the Anglo–American companies, but Washington, acting through the United Nations Organization, exerted extreme pressure, backed implicitly by the A-bomb. The Red Army left in May 1946.

THE COLD WAR: PHASE II

Early in 1947 President Truman, alarmed by the Communist threat to Greece and Turkey, came to their assistance by announcing the so-called

---

[1] The U. S. admittedly had a sphere of interest in the Latin American states, but they were all independent entities, except insofar as they were controlled by economic pressures from the north. There was no true parallel to Soviet-dominated Poland or Rumania.

[2] In 1949 the USSR detonated its first atomic bomb, followed by Britain in 1952, France in 1960, and China in 1964. After 1949 the U. S. pushed on toward the much more powerful hydrogen bomb, amid much dispute among American scientists as to the wisdom of this course, and detonated one in 1952. Fears that the USSR would do likewise were fully realized in 1953.

Truman Doctrine. Congress voted the necessary funds. This new policy was the curtain-raiser for America's sweeping Marshall Plan, proposed in June 1947 and designed to revive Western Europe economically by providing multibillion-dollar economic assistance. The Kremlin countered by binding its satellite neighbors together under the "Molotov Plan."

The Soviets were determined to convert their East German zone into a Communist puppet that would block the ever-present threat of a reunited Germany. In June 1948 they made a bold bid to squeeze the three Western powers (U. S., Britain, and France) out of four-sectored Berlin. The Russian blockade of all land and water routes almost succeeded. But the Americans and British reacted by mounting the famed Berlin airlift, which, after some close shaves, ultimately persuaded Moscow to back down in May 1949.[3]

Late in February 1948 the Moscow-manipulated Communists seized the government of democratic Czechoslovakia. This shocking coup further opened American eyes and helped to speed the languishing Marshall Plan appropriations through Congress. Five nations of Western Europe, including Britain and France, responded later the next month by entering into a defensive alliance under the Brussels Pact. This was enlarged by April 1949 into the 12-nation North Atlantic Treaty Organization, formalized in Washington and including the United States. The pact affirmed that an armed attack "against one or more of them in Europe or North America shall be considered an attack against them all."

Seeking further defense against Communist aggression, the Western nations proceeded to fashion their three zones of Germany into a rearmed West German Republic. It was formally admitted to the North Atlantic Treaty Organization (NATO) on May 9, 1955. Remembering the Germanic invasions of Russia during World War I and World War II, the Soviets responded five days later by creating the defensive Warsaw Treaty Organization. It consisted of the USSR and its puppets: Albania (later dropped), Bulgaria, Czechoslovakia, East Germany, Hungary, Poland, and Rumania.

Thus action produced counteraction, and most of Europe was lined up in two defensive armed camps, with a nuclear-armed West confronting a nuclear-armed East. The American people, generally approving Truman's "get tough" policy toward the USSR, elected him in his own right in 1948, in a confused and surprising four-way campaign.

---

[3] Some Americans were of the opinion that if the United States, still with its monopoly of atomic bombs, had bulldozed its way through the blocked roads, the Soviets would have yielded. See Robert Murphy, *Diplomat Among Warriors* (1964), p. 317. Yet if the Russians had not given way, there could well have been a new world war.

WAS THE ATOMIC BOMB NECESSARY?

Before the outbreak of World War II in 1939, German physicists, who had reached the front rank in science, had made considerable progress toward harnessing the atom. Scientists in France, Holland, Britain, and America had also been discovering the essential secrets of nuclear fission. Their ranks were swelled by refugees from vicious Hitlerian persecution, especially certain eminent physicists of the Jewish faith.

It is understandable that much of the pressure for pushing ahead with the atomic bomb should have come from these victims of Nazi tyranny.[4] Jewish scientists driven from Germany especially feared that Hitler would finish first in the nuclear race. If the Nazis added the atomic bomb to their arsenal before the democracies could produce it, Germany obviously would be in a position to enslave much of the world. Acting as the spokesman for exiled Jewish scientists in America, the famed Albert Einstein addressed an appeal to President Roosevelt on August 2, 1939, almost exactly a month before Hitler burst into Poland. Not until December 6, 1941, the day before Pearl Harbor, did Washington make the momentous decision to go ahead full throttle with the nuclear bomb. Roosevelt managed to secure from Congress blank-check appropriations of some $2 billion to carry through this top-secret "Manhattan Project."

Many of the refugee scientists who prompted action evidently had in view not using the bomb but holding it as a safeguard against atomic blackmail by a merciless Hitler. They could not even be sure that he did not have this frightful weapon when the Allies invaded Europe in 1944. They soon made the ironical discovery that the bomb was not needed for the primary purpose originally intended; the German physicists were lagging substantially behind the pace set by their enemies. Hitler, counting on a relatively short and victorious war, had given higher priority to missile development and other new weapons. Allied scientists clearly won "the battle of the laboratories."[5]

War with Germany ended in May 1945, but the practice had been accepted on both sides of gutting great cities with explosive or incendiary bombs. In principle, there was no essential difference between a block-busting bomb and a city-busting bomb, especially when the

---

[4] See Leo Szilard, "Reminiscences," *Perspectives in Amer. Hist.*, II (1968), 94–151, for the recollections of an influential refugee scientist.

[5] The bomb was a cooperative project. It involved a pooling of British and American industrial capacity and technical know-how, plus the indispensable skills of the European émigré scientists.

United States was eager to save the lives of its fighting men and end this incredibly costly war in a hurry. So the bomb was tested in New Mexico in July 1945, and then used in the following month to wipe out two Japanese cities, Hiroshima and Nagasaki.

The Japanese had been far from the minds of the exiled scientists who urged Roosevelt to make the atomic bomb. At that time Japan was engaged only in war with the Chinese. When the bomb fell on Hiroshima, Hitler had been dead for more than three months, and the Japanese paid dearly for his sins as well as their own.

Yet the highest officials in Washington, if we may believe President Truman and Secretary of War Stimson, regarded the bomb as a purely "military weapon." They never had any intention of withholding it in this war, even against Germany, if they completed it in time and concluded that it would help shorten the conflict.[6] A nation would be foolish indeed if, during an all-out contest, it were to divert an enormous amount of money, resources, manpower, and brains to making a lethal weapon of this type which it had no intention of using either as a destroyer or a threat of destruction.

WAS THE DROPPING OF THE A-BOMB IMPERATIVE?

Persuasive indeed were the arguments advanced by those who urged using the bomb against the Japanese. Top American strategists calculated that the conquest of Japan would take some eighteen months and cost a million or so casualties, not counting those of Japanese soldiers and civilians. Japan had some 2,000,000 troops defending her homeland, with about 3,000,000 abroad, plus some 5,000 bomb-laden *kamikaze* (suicide) airplanes, which could take a frightful toll.[7] The Japanese militarists were determined to make a last-ditch, hara-kiri stand, and only by the narrowest of margins was this mad course averted. First came the atomic bomb on Hiroshima, August 6; then the Russian declaration of war, August 8; and finally the second atomic bomb on Nagasaki, August 9. The Americans had evidently harnessed divine wrath, and the Japanese would not lose face unconscionably if they surrendered to a foe in league with the supernatural. Peace came only after the bombs had jolted Nippon into submission.

[6] Henry L. Stimson and McGeorge Bundy, *On Active Service in Peace and War* (1948), p. 613; *Memoirs by Harry S Truman* (1955), I, 419.

[7] The Japanese also had 7,000 *kamikaze* planes in storage or undergoing repair, and 5,000 young men training as their pilots. Samuel E. Morison, *History of United States Naval Operations in World War II* (1961), XIV, 352. *Kamikaze* planes inflicted grave damage on U. S. warships during the Okinawa campaign.

American decision makers were not too much concerned about compassion. The Nipponese had treacherously hit below the belt at Pearl Harbor, and they had meted out inhumane treatment to American prisoners. Anyhow, Japan had already suffered severely from fire-bombing raids on Tokyo — raids that had probably cost more lives than those taken by either of the two atomic bombs. By hastening the end of the war, so the argument ran, the United States would be conferring a favor on the Japanese — a kind of "mercy killing." A prolonging of conventional attacks, including aerial bombing, would take a terrible toll and perhaps leave even more lasting bitterness.

In later years a number of lower-echelon scientists claimed that the military used the bomb for lethal purposes over their protestations. But President Truman's close scientific advisors, in possession of the broad spectrum of the essential facts — technical, strategic, and political — were in unanimous agreement.[8] A list was made of the four Japanese cities most essential to war production, and Hiroshima and Nagasaki happened to be among them.[9] Little if anything was then known about the long-range effects of nuclear radiation, including possible genetic damage. In the light of the information then possessed by the key officials in Washington, the course adopted seemed entirely proper. Prime Minister Churchill agreed heartily, and President Truman repeatedly declared in later years that if he had to make the same decision again, he would not do differently. He was prone to remark that those who were shedding tears over the Japanese were not weeping over the Americans deceitfully done to death at Pearl Harbor.

WAS JAPAN SURRENDERING WHEN "ATOMIZED"?

As early as February 1945, the Japanese had sent out preliminary feelers to the Soviets in the hope of promoting mediation between America and Japan. Evidently not knowing that Stalin was bound by the Yalta agreements to attack the Japanese after Hitler's defeat, Tokyo tried again in July without success. Washington was not only aware of these overtures but was also informed of them by Stalin at the Potsdam Conference of July 1945.[10]

---

[8] The key advisory body was the Interim Committee, consisting of five top officials and civilians, plus four eminent scientists, all of whom were advised by four other top-level scientists.

[9] Hiroshima, in addition to war production, quartered the defensive Second Army, which was virtually wiped out. Morison, U. S. Naval Operations, XIV, 344.

[10] Foreign Relations of the U. S.: The Conference of Berlin (The Potsdam Conference) (1960), II, 1587–1588 (meeting of July 18, 1945).

There can be no doubt that by the summer of 1945 the insular Japanese were facing certain defeat. Their navy was shattered; their armies were riddled; their cities were being laid waste with fire bombs; their merchant marine was substantially wiped out by American submarines; and their industrial production was crippled. They were like a cut chrysanthemum, gradually fading and doomed to die.

Surrender by Japan was delayed by two principal obstacles. One was the face-saving, suicidal spirit of the militarists; the other was the inelastic policy of unconditional surrender. On July 26, 1945, the Allied conferees at the Potsdam Conference in Germany issued a manifesto to Japan: either she must surrender unconditionally or suffer "prompt and utter destruction." [11] Tragically, the Potsdam Declaration did not reveal that America then possessed an atomic bomb of unimaginable destructiveness that could be used to wipe out the Japanese.

Also tragic is the fact that subsequently Japan was granted conditions, at her request, of less than unconditional surrender; namely, the retention of her Emperor. With a millennium-long tradition of imperial succession, this concession meant more to her people than Westerners could realize. If the Potsdam ultimatum had shown a willingness to keep the Emperor, the Japanese might have saved enough "face" to surrender before the United States felt compelled to drop the atomic bomb. But making concessions to Japan was regarded as a species of "appeasement" that might be interpreted as a sign of military weakness and weariness, especially after heavy American losses in the recent Okinawa campaign. Even some staunch defenders of America's decision to resort to instant incineration blame the authors of the Potsdam Declaration for not having been more specific. The argument goes that the Japanese should have been bluntly informed of the atomic bomb — a weapon of unparalleled explosiveness — reinforced by photographs of the first nuclear cloud at Alamogordo, New Mexico. If this had only been done, the Japenese might have surrendered without having two of their cities destroyed, with a loss of some 100,000 lives at Hiroshima and some 75,000 at Nagasaki.

Such a conclusion is highly speculative. "Unconditional surrender" was still a major obstacle, and many Japanese leaders would have dismissed reference to an apocalyptic weapon as "Yankee bluff." In this case the bombs would have been dropped, but the Americans

---

[11] *Ibid.*, *II*, 1474–1476. The Potsdam proclamation was issued by authorization of President Truman, Prime Minister Churchill, and President Chiang of China. Chiang was not present but Premier Stalin was; Russia was not represented primarily because the USSR was not yet at war with Japan.

would have been in a stronger moral position after having more specifically warned their intended victim.[12]

As events turned out, Tokyo did not respond officially to the Potsdam ultimatum but unofficially announced a determination to "ignore it entirely. . . ." An unfortunate translation of this response as reported in the Tokyo press led to the impression that the warning had not only been rejected but rejected contemptuously.[13] Speaking informally some years later, President Truman reportedly remarked that all he got was a "snotty" answer, whereupon the United States let the "Japs" have it.

SHOULD THE U.S. HAVE DEMONSTRATED THE A-BOMB?

Critics of Truman's "inhuman" decision have argued that he should first have ordered a demonstration of the bomb in some desert area or in a thinly populated region of Japan. Once the Japanese had witnessed the incredible frightfulness of this monster weapon, they would surely have hoisted the white flag of surrender.

This possibility was thoroughly discussed in Washington, but the objections were so weighty that the proposed demonstration was rejected by the Interim Committee. First of all, the United States then had only two atomic bombs and was not scheduled to get a third until about ten days after the second one was dropped. Moreover, after elaborate arrangements for an exhibition, the bomb might not explode, and in this event the Americans would look like bluffers.[14] If a thinly peopled target in Japan should be announced in advance, what was to prevent the Japanese from sending up fighter planes or moving American prisoners of war to that spot? Finally, detonating the bomb in a desert area would wreak much less visible damage than on a city. The Japanese might not be sufficiently impressed; significantly, the two bombs that wiped out two Japanese cities did not budge the top military and naval men in Japan.[15]

If the decision makers in Washington had only known then what they were to know later, they might have staged a demonstration in spite of these objections. They were evidently not aware of long-run

[12] Herbert Feis, *The Atomic Bomb and the End of World War II* (1966), p. 201.

[13] Robert J. C. Butow, *Japan's Decision to Surrender* (1954), pp. 145–149; *For. Relations, Potsdam Conference, II*, 1293.

[14] The United States suffered much embarrassment in the 1950s and 1960s from pioneering space rockets that failed to function properly.

[15] Morison, *U. S. Naval Operations, XIV*, 351. Some critics condemn the use of the second bomb, contending that one would have served its purpose.

radioactive damage, of genetic harm, of the revulsion in much of the
civilized world, and of the alleged racism involved in dropping the bomb
only on yellow people. Yet, given the British bombing of refugee-
crowded Dresden (some 135,000 deaths) and attacks on other German
cities, as well as Hitler's earlier ruthlessness against Rotterdam and
London, there is little reason to believe that the perfected A-bomb would
not have been used on the Germans if deemed necessary. As events
turned out, Germany surrendered three months before the first bomb
was ready to be dropped.

WAS THE A-BOMB AIMED PRIMARILY AT RUSSIA?

In 1965 the sensational thesis was advanced in detail by a writer of the
New Left school that Truman used the bomb to show the Russians that
Uncle Sam had atomic muscle, and to warn them to be acquiescent in
American postwar policy or suffer possible destruction.[16] Such Machiavellian motivation is supported by inference rather than convincing
proof. It had much earlier been voiced by Russian propagandists and
others who cried "atomic blackmail." Soviet officials *at the time* publicly
expressed no such fears.

The Soviet Union had proved to be a suspicious ally during the
war and an untrustworthy one even before the fall of Hitler. Already
on record were the Russian takeovers of Eastern Europe, including
Poland and Rumania, in defiance of the "free election" pledges made by
Stalin at Yalta in February 1945. The desirability of keeping Russia
"in line" crossed the minds of some of the top decision makers, who
quite properly considered all possible angles when they decided to use
the bomb.[17] Some of them even thought that after spending about $2
billion on this supergadget, the American taxpayers ought to have some
fireworks for their money.[18] If the bomb had not been dropped and the
war had been prolonged bloodily, the voters would have been outraged
upon learning that this lethal atomic weapon had been kept on the shelf.

To argue that the bomb was dropped *primarily* to impress the
USSR ignores the hard fact that there were other and more pressing
reasons for devastating Japan. These boiled down to winning the Far
Eastern conflict in a hurry and saving American (and Japanese) lives in
the process. The Americans notoriously fought World War II without

---

[16] Gar Alperovitz, *Atomic Diplomacy* (1965).
[17] Feis, *Atomic Bomb*, pp. 194–195.
[18] W. D. Leahy, *I Was There* (1950), p. 441. Admiral Leahy reports that Truman
was aware of this motivation.

adequate attention to its political aftermath; otherwise they would have been more interested in snatching much of Central and Eastern Europe from the advancing Russians.

Although the Russians had been difficult allies, they were allies, and a great reservoir of goodwill still existed for them in America. There was still a lively hope of cooperating with them in the United Nations. The Japanese were not only enemies, but bitter enemies; atrocities were common on both sides; [19] and the Japanese often fought suicidal engagements rather than fall into the hands of the mayhem-minded Yankees. Critics are prone to forget that the atomic bombs were dropped on Japan, not simply because the Japanese were nonwhite, but because they were widely regarded as a subhuman foe from whom vengeance for Pearl Harbor must be exacted. Millions of Americans favored hanging the Emperor as a war criminal, with or without a trial.[20] There were otherwise decent citizens who regretted that the Japanese surrendered before the United States had an opportunity to obliterate a few more Japanese cities, including men, women, and children.

DID THE A-BOMB SAVE AMERICAN LIVES?

The argument that dropping the A-bombs in August 1945 saved the lives of hundreds of thousands of American "boys" has one basic weakness. The first landing of United States troops on Japanese soil was not scheduled until November 1945, and various delays such as those that had hampered the invasion of North Africa and France probably would have held up operations for at least several more weeks. Because all other serious ground fighting between the Japanese and Americans had ended, no heavy losses to U. S. troops could have occurred before Japan had been subjected to about three more months of blasting and fire-bombing from the air, plus blockading and bombarding from the sea.

It is conceivable that the Japanese could have continued their last-ditch stand in the absence of the A-bomb, which narrowly tipped the scales for surrender.[21] During such resistance, hundreds of thousands

[19] Colonel Charles A. Lindbergh gives gruesome details of atrocities, including the kicking in of gold-filled teeth for souvenirs. *The Wartime Journals of Charles A. Lindbergh* (1970), especially pp. 996–997.

[20] For a controversial journalistic book branding Hirohito the archconspirator in plotting war, see David Bergamini, *Japan's Imperial Conspiracy* (1971).

[21] The two bombs, plus Russia's entry and assurances that the Emperor might be retained, did not bring capitulation. Only by the personal intervention of the Emperor was surrender achieved, amid suicides, assassinations, and attempted assassinations. Morison, *U. S. Naval Operations, XIV*, 349–350.

of Japanese, including women and children, would probably have per-
ished from the "conventional explosives" of American bombers. If the
Americans and their allies had been forced to land with large bodies of
troops, they would have been subjected to severe losses, for the Japanese
possessed enormous quantities of weapons and ammunition.

Yet a delay of three months while waiting for Japan to surrender
was not pleasing to Americans. The war was appallingly costly in
dollars; the Allies were war-weary; the American troops, especially those
being redeployed from Europe, were eager to resume interrupted lives.
In view of these considerations and others, there was strong pressure
on Washington to end the war, in Secretary Stimson's words, "with
maximum force and maximum speed." The A-bombs probably contributed significantly to that end, even though questions of humanity
later took on larger dimensions. As events turned out, whatever moral
advantage America had gained from the Japanese sneak attack at Pearl
Harbor was more than wiped out by the nuclear bombing of a staggering
foe.

Even so, two fortuitous developments evidently flowed from
using the horrendous new weapon. As President Truman and his advisors hoped, the war ended suddenly, before the Soviets could get a
boot in the door of Japan. As a consequence, the occupying American
forces were able to create a democratic Nippon. The dropping of the
bomb, presaging vastly more horrible explosives, may have demonstrated
the terrible inhumanity of such devices so forcefully as to preclude their
use in future conflicts. World opinion certainly helped to restrain the
United States in the subsequent Korean and Vietnam Wars. Poison gas
had been used with lethal effect in World War I, but it was not employed
in World War II. Both sides had mutually intimidating stockpiles, but
this was a ruinous game that two could play.

DID RUSSIA "STEAL" THE A-BOMB FROM THE U. S.?

During the years immediately after World War II, many Americans
comforted themselves with the delusion that the "backward" Russians
could not possibly develop an atomic bomb within the near future.
Experts in the United States were speaking in terms of five to fifteen
years, even if captured German physicists helped the Soviets. Meanwhile
America could drastically reduce its costly military establishment, while
counting on its arsenal of nuclear weapons to keep the Russians "in line."
Winston Churchill expressed the opinion in 1949 that America's posses-

sion of this fearsome device was all that kept the victorious Russians from sweeping to the English Channel in the postwar years.

The bare facts are that Russian physicists had embarked upon theoretical studies of nuclear fission early in 1939; that the USSR had launched a crash program in June 1942, during some of the worst phases of the Hitlerian invasion; that early in 1945 Soviet plants were turning out quantities of processed uranium; that Russian scientists achieved their first chain reaction some eighteen months after Germany's surrender; and that they detonated their first atomic bomb in 1949, only four years after the war had ended in Europe.[22]

President Truman at Potsdam, shortly after the initial nuclear testing in New Mexico, "casually" informed Marshal Stalin that the United States had a "new weapon of unusual destructive force." [23] The Soviet leader seemed neither surprised nor greatly impressed. Russian intelligence operatives had already discovered that both Germany and the United States were engaged in urgent secret work in this area. The trial of Dr. Klaus Fuchs in England (1950) for passing on America's nuclear secrets to the Russians further proves that the Kremlin knew what was going on in America.[24] Stolen information probably facilitated Russian progress, but the Soviet scientists, with captured German physicists in their hands, probably would have come up with the A-bomb about when they did without "stealing" America's secrets. Americans do not like to contemplate what might have happened if the Soviets had accumulated a large arsenal of atomic bombs while the United States had none. In this case the world might well have witnessed genuine "atomic blackmail" in reverse.

WHO STARTED THE COLD WAR?

A cold war has been defined as the existence of intense political, economic, military, and ideological rivalry between two nations or blocs of nations, short of actual bloodshed. This term came to be applied to the tensions between the Communist bloc and the so-called free world (including dictators) after Hitler was crushed in 1945. The phrase "Cold War" seems to have been first used in 1947 by America's "elder

[22] Gordon Wright, *The Ordeal of Total War, 1939–1945* (1968), p. 105.

[23] *Memoirs by Harry S Truman, I,* 419.

[24] Dr. Fuchs, a German-born British subject, worked with the American A-bomb project from 1943 to 1946 and also in 1947. He pleaded guilty in England to four counts of betraying U. S. and British secrets. See *New York Times,* March 2, 1950, 1:1.

statesman," Bernard Baruch, although such friction had existed with the Soviets before, during, and immediately after the titanic clash with Hitler.[25]

In a sense, the phrase "Cold War" is a misnomer. Certain phases of it became extremely hot; in Korea and Vietnam the United States and its allies suffered hundreds of thousands of casualties, as did the other side. The shooting thus begun in 1950 in Korea continued for more than two decades, though often intermittent and on a small scale. In both Korea and Vietnam, Communist Russia and Red China morally supported and physically armed America's opponents, though the Soviets, unlike the Chinese in Korea, did not engage in any large-scale combat action.[26] Hence observers who refer to the Cold War are thinking of the absence of an all-out conflict between the United States and its ideological partners, on the one hand, and the Soviet Union and its ideological partners, on the other.

It is pointless to try to attribute exclusive blame for the Cold War to either the Communist World or the so-called Free World. Can we blame dogs for being hostile to cats, or water for being incompatible with oil, or fire for reacting violently to gasoline? Communism, by the very nature of its closed society, has a built-in hostility to open-door capitalism — a hostility that existed from the beginning and presumably will always exist as long as the two systems retain their basic identity and ideology. In this sense the Cold War has existed since at least 1917, when the Communists took over in Russia and proclaimed their undying hostility to the capitalist world. Basic frictions and suspicions were soft-pedaled during the anti-Hitler war, but they were always present; and circumstances in the postwar years intensified the friction as each side sought to promote its ideologically directed aims. If the West feared Communist world revolution, the Soviet leaders feared, or professed to fear, "capitalistic encirclement." The Cold War came so naturally that its avoidance would have been more remarkable than its occurrence.

If Communism had been confined to the Soviet Union, without being superimposed upon Tsarist imperialism, the so-called Free World would have had fewer misgivings. But Communism at this stage was an international, Moscow-directed, imperialistic conspiracy, dedicated to winning, by whatever means necessary, the rest of mankind to its ideol-

---

[25] Winston Churchill, in a speech at Fulton, Missouri (March 5, 1946), gave wide publicity to the "Iron Curtain" that Moscow had caused to clang down between East Europe and the West. The phrase in this context has been traced back to Hitler's propaganda minister, Dr. Josef Goebbels (Feb. 23, 1945).

[26] Red China assisted North Korea, 1950–1953, with hundreds of thousands of "volunteers." The Korean armistice was signed in 1953 but in many of the succeeding years there was some shooting or minor bloodshed near the line of demarcation.

ogy. In short, the United States had no intention of turning the USSR into a capitalistic state, but the Kremlin made no secret of its determination to communize America and the rest of the world.[27]

Washington undeniably made diplomatic mistakes during the postwar years that further aroused Soviet apprehensions. But the mutual antipathy was always there, and it basically accounts for the suspicions that developed a vicious circle during the era of the Cold War. The Communist dictatorship, which in essence had imprisoned its own people in a regimented and rationed police state, needed the bogey of an aggressive, capitalistic Uncle Sam. Otherwise the war-ravaged and war-burdened masses might overthrow their rulers rather than endure the prolonged sacrifice of liberties and basic consumer goods during the costly arms race attending the Cold War.

World War II, by spurring to the full America's productive capacity, pulled the nation out of the Great Depression. The Soviet leaders were evidently counting on peace, redeployment, and unemployment to bring back Hooverian depression, which in turn would soften up the Western world for Communist infiltration or takeover. Ironically, Soviet aggressiveness so frightened the Americans that they spent tens of billions of dollars on rearmament that probably averted the anticipated depression.[28]

DID THE SOVIETS WANT THE U. N.?

At Yalta Stalin had shown little interest in the projected United Nations Organization. He evidently reasoned that once Hitler was eliminated, Soviet military might and Moscow-controlled satellite states would safeguard Russia's interests. For reasons that may or may not have been valid, Stalin flatly rejected Roosevelt's request that the USSR send its high ranking Foreign Commissar Molotov to the San Francisco Conference, where the United Nations Organization was to be born in the spring of 1945. Only after the shock of Roosevelt's death did Stalin relent and dispatch Molotov.

The Russian delegation, which arrived in San Francisco with

[27] After Communist Yugoslavia broke away from the Soviet orbit in 1948, the U. S. sent some $2 billion in ten years in aid to that country in an effort to keep it independent. Americans clearly had less fear of homegrown communism than of the world-revolution Communist conspiracy.

[28] As evidence of nonaggressive intentions, the United States hastily reduced its army in Europe during a ten-month period from about 3,500,000 men to some 500,000, thereby creating a power vacuum. The Soviets had available a much larger striking force in Eastern Europe. Until 1949 the Americans, of course, were relying to a considerable extent on the A-bomb to deter the Soviets.

a conspicuously strong bodyguard, created a disagreeable impression from the outset. Molotov belligerently supported the interests of the Soviet Union. He urged representation at San Francisco for the new Polish government, which obviously was a pro-Communist creature of Moscow. He vehemently but unsuccessfully demanded that "fascist" Argentina, which had not declared war on the Axis by March 1, 1945, be excluded from the Conference in conformity with the agreement reached at Yalta.[29]

Molotov cavalierly brushed aside the rights of the small states, which had not borne the brunt of the fighting, if they had fought at all. He vainly attempted to secure a veto over even discussions in the proposed Security Council. A compromise was narrowly reached when the conferees agreed that the members of the Security Council might veto issues of substance but not procedural matters, while permitting debate on controversial issues. The framers of the United Nations Charter had assumed that the veto would be used sparingly in relation to issues of vital import; the Soviets proceeded to use it routinely. They had employed it more than 100 times by March 17, 1970, when the United States used it for the first time in nearly twenty-five years.[30]

Considerable misunderstanding exists about the veto. The American delegates, fully aware that the U. S. Senate would have a whack at their handiwork, were no less firm than the Soviets in their determination that this vital safeguard be retained by the United States.[31] The Russians realized that they were heavily outnumbered by the nations of the non-Communist world, and they did not have the slightest intention of sitting down at a Council table and seeing their interests voted away by unfriendly majorities.

It seems reasonable to suppose that the Soviets joined the United Nations Organization, unlike many of the other members, with no illusions about its guaranteeing permanent peace. As insiders, they could employ the veto and other weapons to head off moves that seemed inimical to their interests. Using the UN as a propaganda sounding board, which they repeatedly did, they could fight fascism and promote world communism more effectively.

[29] Argentina declared war on Germany and Japan on March 27, 1945, nearly a month late. Ironically Poland, over which World War II began, was not represented at San Francisco.

[30] The U. S. joined Britain in vetoing a proposal to use force against the all-white government of Rhodesia.

[31] In August 1946, when the Senate voted 60 to 2 in favor of joining the International Court of Justice under the UN, it exempted from "compulsory jurisdiction" all disputes involving domestic affairs, such as tariff and immigration. In short, the United States, under the so-called Connally Resolution, would be the sole judge of what was "domestic."

WHY DID RUSSIA TURN AGAINST AMERICA?

A major objective of Moscow's foreign policy was to establish friendly foreign states along Soviet borders for defense, especially against a rearmed Germany. Stalin may have intended to carry out his pledges regarding "free elections" in liberated Eastern Europe at the time of the Yalta Conference, but local hostility to the Russian "liberators" proved alarming. As between America's friendship and huge postwar loans, on the one hand, and puppet Communist regimes on his borders, on the other, he would choose the latter.

Stalin, ultimately with complete success, undertook to erect Communist regimes in Poland and Rumania as early as March 1945, shortly before a disillusioned Roosevelt died.[32] The Communist minority, defeated in what was alleged to be a fair election in Hungary, seized power in 1947. After elections in Bulgaria of dubious fairness, the Communists assumed control in 1946. Finland, having fought against Russia in World War II, was permitted to remain nominally independent as long as its foreign policy squared with Soviet interests. The Yugoslav Communists, under Tito, took over their country in 1945–1946, but in 1948, despite enormous pressure, broke away from Moscow-directed communism. In Greece, during the postwar years, Communist-supported guerrillas waged what amounted to a civil war.[33] In Italy and France there were Communist parties, both numbering millions of voters, that threatened a perfectly legal conquest at the ballot boxes.

The Soviets continued to nurse grievances against the United States while extending their control over most of Central Europe. Czechoslovakia held out only until 1948, but Greece, with American assistance, staved off Communist infiltration.

In May 1945, several days after Germany surrendered, President Truman hastily signed an order, which he later claimed he had not read, cutting back on lend–lease shipments to the Allies. Such a brusque step seemed to be required by Congressional legislation and by public opinion, which was feeling the cost of a war that had already ended in Europe. The distrustful Soviets, who had enjoyed unique privileges under lend–lease, were deeply offended by this abrupt cancellation. "Revisionist"

[32] The Soviets pointed out that the Allies had excluded the USSR from partial control of Italy after her surrender, and in Eastern Europe the shoe was on the other foot. The Soviets were also barred from effective postwar control over Japan, and this exclusion provided further justification for their treatment of neighboring satellites.

[33] This uprising ended in 1948, partly because Tito's Yugoslavia broke away from Moscow and cut off the flow of assistance.

writers have seen in the incident an attempt to coerce the USSR into following American postwar policies, especially in Eastern Europe, with a consequent impact on the beginnings of the Cold War.

Facts do not support this thesis, because the record shows no evidence of an intent to coerce. Truman's action was not discriminatory and it shocked and hurt the other Allies, especially Britain. The President promptly cancelled the order, and the ships at sea that had turned around were permitted to continue their original voyages. Soviet help was desired to fight Japan in the Far East, and consequently lend–lease shipments for the purpose of waging that war continued to flow uninterruptedly to the Russians. The unpleasantness was quickly patched up, and about a month later Stalin sent Truman his personal thanks for American aid. Although this episode was maladroitly handled, there is little reason to believe that it had an important bearing on the developing Cold War.[34]

DID LOANS AND TRADE CAUSE THE RIFT?

Russia had suffered enormous damage to her economy from the invader, and she was counting on repairing her losses by reparations from the Germans and loans from Washington. Reasoning that the Americans badly needed to sell their postwar surpluses to avert a depression, the Soviets requested a credit of $6 billion in January 1945. The Washington officials were aware of the Congressional act that barred certain types of loans to nations in default, as Russia was on the Tsarist obligation. They also realized that the war-torn Soviets were not the best possible credit risks, and that much opposition would be encountered in an economy-minded Congress. After prolonged delays and much haggling over interest charges and other stipulations, the negotiations collapsed completely.[35]

Some three months after Germany's surrender in May 1945 the Soviets asked for a billion-dollar loan. No response was forthcoming

[34] See George C. Herring, Jr., "Lend–Lease to Russia and the Origins of the Cold War, 1944–1945," *Jour. of Amer. Hist.*, LVI (1969), 93–114.

[35] The loan of 1945 ($3.75 billion) to Britain had never commanded majority support in the public opinion polls. America was already burdened with an enormous debt and heavy taxes. A Gallup Poll in October 1945 found the proposed $6 billion loan to the USSR opposed by a margin of 60 percent to 27 percent. *Public Opinion Quar.*, IX, 533. For the Soviet point of view, see T. G. Paterson, "The Abortive American Loan to Russia and the Origins of the Cold War, 1943–1946," *Jour. of Amer. Hist.*, LVI (1969), 70–92. The author is concerned with what *might* have happened if credits had been granted. Actually the mutual suspicions that blocked the loans were among the basic causes of the Cold War.

for some months; the unconvincing official explanation was that the request had been misplaced while certain documents were being transferred to the State Department.[36] Whether true or not, this excuse struck the Soviets as flimsy. Unable to arrange a substantial loan on their terms, they understandably undertook to secure partial reparation for their war losses by plundering or moving German factories in their zone of occupation. They might well have done so anyhow.

Many of the "revisionist" historians have blamed the United States for the Soviet rift because the Americans were seeking an open door for international trade in Central Europe. This accusation overlooks the ingrained antipathy between the two systems: the Soviet closed society and the democratic open society. The Soviets evidently placed a higher priority on friendly buffer neighbors than they did on trade; the United States, while hoping for a free-trade area, was much more concerned with Communist domination, which the Moscow-directed Communist International had long proclaimed. Moreover, prewar commerce with Eastern Europe was relatively small in America's overall total, and not worth anywhere near the expense of a Cold War.[37] The imports of Poland (and Danzig) in 1938 from the United States amounted to less than 1 percent of all American exports; with Bulgaria, Hungary, and Rumania thrown in, they accounted for slightly more than 1 percent.[38] One must remember that the United States, which has traditionally favored the Open Door, was much more concerned about British trade restrictions than those of Russia during these postwar years.

WERE THE NUREMBERG WAR CRIMES TRIALS FAIR?

The mass trial of more than a score of German "war criminals" at Nuremberg, Germany, during 1945–1946 was unique. The victors were determined to punish the Nazi leaders while establishing new international law that would deter future aggressors. Many of the Nazi officials had committed such brutal crimes against humanity, including wholesale

---

[36] Martin F. Herz, *Beginnings of the Cold War* (1966), p. 174.

[37] Harry Hopkins, on a special presidential mission to Stalin, assured the Soviet leader on May 30, 1945, that "the United States had no economic interests of substantial importance in Poland. . . ." *Foreign Relations of the U. S.: The Conference of Berlin, I,* 54.

[38] W. Averell Harriman, U. S. Ambassador to Moscow during World War II, decries two extremes: the concept of a Soviet dominated Communist monolith bent on enchaining the world, and the belief that the differences are only "a matter of economic theory. . . ." He spurns the view that "all we have to do is show love and affection for them and everything will be all right." *America and Russia in a Changing World* (1971), p. xvii.

murder and mutilation, that they could have been convicted as individuals in the courts of any civilized country. But the second category of guilt was waging aggressive warfare or conspiring to wage it, and this "crime against peace" had never hitherto been regarded as an offense that could be prosecuted under any known judicial processes.

America, by participating in the international Nuremberg trials, was accused of trying to establish *ex post facto* law, which is forbidden in domestic legislation by the Constitution. On the other hand, if society hangs a man for murder, why not execute an arch murderer like Hitler, who was responsible for launching an aggressive war that caused millions of deaths, even though there was no international law to cover his peculiar case? The Kellogg–Briand Pact, signed by almost all nations in 1928, had outlawed aggressive war but had not prescribed judicial processes or punishment for the offenders.

A peculiarity of the trials at Nuremberg was that one of the four judges was Russian, while the other three were British, French, and American. With no small measure of hypocrisy, the Soviet member of the panel undertook to convict the Germans of many of the same crimes that the Soviets had committed, conspicuously in making the fateful conspiratorial pact with Hitler and then invading Poland for their share of the loot.[39] But the Allied judges made clear that they were there to try the beaten foe, not themselves. The general results were a foregone conclusion, although the Soviet panelist and the American prosecutor were both outraged when three of the defendants were acquitted, only to be convicted later by a German tribunal and sentenced to relatively light prison terms. Twelve defendants were condemned to death. Another oddity was that the Soviets, in dealing with less conspicuous ex-Nazis, repeatedly condoned the war crimes of those who could be counted on to collaborate with them in reconstructing Germany along Communist lines.

Lesser German war criminals were prosecuted by the Americans, and subsequently by the German courts. More than twenty of the most blameworthy Japanese leaders were tried by an eleven-nation tribunal, after the fashion of Nuremberg, and seven were put to death, while the others received prison sentences. The United States Supreme Court refused to hear an appeal which alleged that the international court in Japan was unlawful.[40]

[39] In 1943 the invading Germans announced the discovery of a mass grave containing the corpses of some 4,250 uniformed Polish soldiers, mostly officers, in Russian-seized Poland. Moscow blamed the Germans for the massacre, but the weight of the evidence points toward the Russians. See J. K. Zawodny, *Death in the Forest* (1962).

[40] *In re* Yamashita (1946).

As the British General Montgomery cynically remarked, the results of the trials proved that the real crime is to wage war unsuccessfully. These "legal lynchings," whether for wholesale murder or "crime against peace," conveyed a scant moral message to the German people, who were convinced that revenge was the motive, especially when the Russians, with unclean hands, were both prosecutors and judges. Nor does the record show that the judgments of Nuremberg were conspicuously successful in restraining aggressive war. The aggressor almost invariably blames the other side for the provocation, as was notably the case in 1950 when the North Koreans attacked South Korea, and in 1956 when the Israeli, British, and French attacked Egypt. Ironically, Britain and France had been prosecutors and judges at the war crimes trials of the leading Nazis.

Precedents established at Nuremberg did not offer much comfort to Americans, whether civilian or military, should they ever be on the losing side. The United States was later accused of being the aggressor in Vietnam, although there is a hot dispute as to who aggressed against whom. Many critics of America's involvement in Indochina condemned the American leaders as war criminals, like the Nazis in the dock at Nuremberg. And when the U. S. army undertook in 1970–1971 to prosecute its own personnel for atrocities against Vietnamese civilians, one again heard the argument, so common during the prosecution of Nazis, that the defendants were only carrying out military orders from above.[41]

WAS THE TRUMAN DOCTRINE ILL-ADVISED?

In February 1947 the British, who had been giving the rightist Greek government military and financial assistance against Communist-backed guerrillas, informed Washington that Great Britain could no longer bear the burden. Unless the United States took it up, Greece might fall to the Communists, as might Turkey, on whom the Soviets were exerting pressure. If both nations gravitated into the Communist orbit, the Eastern Mediterranean, with its vital approaches to the Dardanelles and the Suez Canal, would be dominated by Moscow.

After hurried conferences with various advisors, President Truman decided that the time had come to "get tough" with the Soviets. Appearing before Congress on March 12, 1947, the peppery President

[41] See Eugene Davidson, "The Nuremberg Trials and One World," in George L. Anderson, *Issues and Conflicts* (1959), pp. 230–255; Telford Taylor, *Nuremberg and Vietnam: An American Tragedy* (1970).

declared that "it *must* be the policy of the United States to support free peoples who are resisting attempted subjugation by armed minorities or by outside pressures." He thereupon requested an initial appropriation of $400 million to provide military and economic succor to both Greece and Turkey. After a two-month debate, during which strong public support developed, Congress responded favorably by comfortable majorities.

The Truman Doctrine, which inaugurated a series of aggressive responses to Communist aggression, led by logical steps to the vastly more important Marshall Plan later in 1947 and to the North Atlantic Treaty Organization of 1949. Although hailed as a spectacular seizure of the diplomatic offensive in the Cold War, the Truman Doctrine was essentially defensive and was designed to implement the policy of "containment." The reputed author of this concept, the distinguished foreign service officer George F. Kennan, grew increasingly displeased with its heavy emphasis on military rather than political containment, and with its extension to the whole world, including Korea and Vietnam.[42] This latter point is often overlooked. Although initially applied to Greece and Turkey, the policy as proclaimed by President Truman was limited to no country or continent. As far as Communist aggression was concerned, whether direct or indirect, Uncle Sam would take on the backbreaking task of being Policeman of the World.[43] He would support established regimes, some of which were controlled by unsavory right-wing dictators. Kennan, on the other hand, would have concentrated on those several areas whose industrial capacity could provide major economic and military potential.

WAS THE MARSHALL PLAN ALTRUISTIC?

Americans have long preened themselves on their generosity in putting prostrate Western Europe back on its feet by an outpouring of some $12 billion, not as loans, but as gifts under the Marshall Plan. To be sure, compassion for an unfortunate Europe underlay the program, but considerations of national self-interest were dominant in making the final arrangements possible.

[42] See George F. Kennan, *Memoirs, 1925–1950* (1967), Chs. 13, 15. Realizing that a war-torn Russia was overextended, Kennan did not share the feeling of urgency about Greece, and was even less concerned about Turkey.

[43] Supporters of the UN criticized Truman for not calling on that body instead of going it alone. The basic explanation is that action on the Greece–Turkey crisis seemed urgent, and the Soviets would be certain to wield a crippling veto in the Security Council.

The name of the Secretary of State is imperishably attached to the Marshall Plan, although he was only the spokesman for a scheme that had been thrashed out behind closed doors by President Truman and his corps of advisors.[44] At the Harvard University commencement exercises in June 1947 Marshall proclaimed that if the nations of Europe would get together and hammer out long-range plans for economic recovery, with emphasis on self-help and mutual assistance, the United States would support them financially "so far as may be practical. . . ."

Washington placed no ban on participation by the Soviet Union and its satellites. As a consequence, representatives from the Soviet Union gathered in Paris later in June with delegates from other countries. The Russian contingent consisted of Foreign Minister Molotov and some 80 experts and clerks — a large enough group to indicate serious intentions. But after prolonged telephone conversations with Moscow and much bickering in Paris, the Russians quit the conference. If they had remained, they might have snarled up the deliberations to a point of complete disruption. What their motives were for leaving is a mystery locked in the Kremlin archives. Moscow evidently concluded that in the interests of its own security, as well as of the spread of Communist influence in Europe, it would do well not to get tangled up in this capitalistic scheme. Shortly after leaving Paris, the Soviets countered with their "Molotov Plan," embracing their satellites. These countries included a reluctant Poland and Czechoslovakia, both of which had expressed an active interest in the Marshall Plan.

The task of pushing the initial estimates of some $6 billion through Congress was formidable. Among the arguments in favor of the Marshall Plan were simple humanitarianism; the prosperity that would come from having a receptive customer for America's industrial and agricultural surpluses; [45] and the rescue of Western Europe from the Communist influence, which was feeding on near chaos. In short, the nation's security and prosperity seemed to require the Marshall Plan — motivations that were not completely altruistic. Prosperity was a potent argument, especially after the Great Depression of the 1930s, but security was undoubtedly a determining consideration. The first Marshall Plan appropriation was stalled in Congress when, in February 1948, the Communists took over Czechoslovakia in a brazen coup. The next month both houses of Congress voted the necessary funds, and on

---

[44] See Joseph M. Jones, *The Fifteen Weeks* (1955).

[45] In the years after 1945 the United States Congress appropriated well over $100 billion for foreign aid. The overwhelming percentage of the money was spent at home for goods and arms, thus reducing unemployment and sustaining prosperity. Otherwise such outlays would not have been approved by Congress.

April 3, 1948, President Truman signed the appropriation, ten months
after Secretary Marshall had electrified the world with his Harvard
address. Whatever the motives, the Marshall Plan was a resounding
success in putting Western Europe back on its economic feet and bolstering it against communism.

DID TRUMAN SUPPORT
ISRAEL FOR HUMANITARIAN REASONS?

In his memoirs Truman gives the impression that he favored a Palestine
homeland for the Jews primarily because of his humanitarian concern
for a persecuted people who had suffered so grievously from Hitlerism.
But his words and actions during this critical period strongly suggest that
he was largely, if not primarily, concerned with the fate of the Democratic party and his own election in 1948.

A displacement of the Palestinian Arabs by an influx of European
Jews was bound to offend the Arab world, which possessed the world's
largest known oil reserves. Many of Truman's key advisors in the
State and Defense Departments [46] repeatedly pointed out that America's
long-run interests would be badly served by antagonizing the tens of
millions of Arabs, and that the Western world had no right to make
them suffer for the sins of a paranoid Hitler.[47] Such counselors strongly
believed that some other solution for the Jewish homeland should be
sought.

In August 1945 Truman recommended that 100,000 Jewish
refugees be forthwith admitted to Palestine, which was still under a
British mandate. On October 4, 1946, a month before the Congressional
elections and on Yom Kippur (the most sacred Jewish day), the President
called for the partition of Palestine and the establishment there of a
Jewish state. On November 29, 1947, with support from the United
States, the United Nations Assembly approved partition by a narrow
margin.

[46] In July 1947 Congress legislated a coordination of the army, navy, and air forces
under a Secretary of Defense with Cabinet status. Opposition from the rival services
was intense, and the resulting "unification" left much disunity.

[47] Many Americans had a well-justified feeling that the Roosevelt administration
had been unduly lethargic about attempting to save some of the Jews liquidated by
Hitler. See A. D. Morse, *While Six Million Died: A Chronicle of American Apathy*
(1968); David S. Wyman, *Paper Walls: America and the Refugee Crisis, 1938–1941*
(1968); H. L. Feingold, *The Politics of Rescue: The Roosevelt Administration and the
Holocaust, 1938–1945* (1970). In defense of official Washington, one should note that
the American public — nativist, anti-Semitic, and job conscious — was overwhelmingly opposed to letting down the bars.

But early in 1948 Truman temporarily yielded to various pressures and backed away from the recently adopted scheme. America's ambassador to the United Nations, acting under instructions, urged that partition be abandoned in favor of a trusteeship for Palestine under the United Nations. Not only did this substitute receive insufficient support, but Truman's popularity plummeted among the Jewish voters.

With the presidential election only six months away, Clark Clifford, Special Counsel to the President, urged Truman to redeem himself with the Jewish electorate by a prompt recognition of the new State of Israel. On May 14, 1948, when the British mandate expired, the Israelis immediately proclaimed their new nation, and within eleven minutes Truman precipitately extended *de facto* recognition. His courting of the Jewish voter continued until the eve of the election, when, in both a statement and a speech, he promised strong support to the infant new nation.

It is easy to demonstrate statistically that Truman's margin of victory over the Republican Thomas E. Dewey in 1948 was due to a successful bid for the Jewish vote. The President failed to win New York, probably because the Progressive Henry A. Wallace diverted more than a half-million votes. But Truman did carry by a narrow margin three states with a substantial body of Jewish voters. The following table tells its own story:

	Electoral vote	*Shift of popular vote necessary to give electoral votes to Dewey*	*Estimated Jewish population (including minors)*
Ohio	25	3,554	153,000
California	25	8,933	430,000
Illinois	28	16,807	280,000

If Dewey had carried these three Northern states, he would have won in the Electoral College 267 to 225. As it was, he lost by a margin of 303 to 189, with 39 Southern votes going to J. Strom Thurmond, the Dixiecrat candidate. Because of these 39 votes, and the difficulty of securing a clear majority in the Electoral College, Dewey needed Ohio, California, and Illinois for a clean-cut win.

The subsequent explosive history of the Middle East suggests that some solution of the Jewish problem less offensive to the Arabs would have better served the long-range interests of the United States. Truman may well have been sincere in his sympathy for the Jews, but he was clearly much concerned about the Jewish vote. His prospects for reelection did not seem good, and there was no Arab vote in America worthy of the name. But the partition of Palestine aroused incalculable and enduring bitterness against the United States in the Arab world.[48]

WAS TRUMAN'S ELECTION IN 1948 A "MIRACLE"?

Political pundits and pollsters were so confident that the Democratic Harry S Truman would be defeated for the presidency in 1948 by the Republican Thomas E. Dewey that the astounding results were widely interpreted as something of a miracle.

In truth, the odds seemed to be overwhelmingly against Truman. As an "accidental President," he had been elected only to the vice presidency. The Democrats, entrenched in power for nearly sixteen long years, had made a host of enemies. If the two-party system was to retain its vitality, there would seemingly have to be a change. Public opinion polls, which by now had established an impressive record for accuracy, predicted that the Republican candidate, Thomas E. Dewey, would "win in a walk."

Truman's political liabilities were frightening. For the first time in eighteen years, the Republicans had won both houses of Congress in 1946 — an augury highly unfavorable to the party in power. After an abortive "dump Truman" move, the President was nominated without undue enthusiasm by his party, which was "stuck with Harry." The Southern bloc, normally a bastion of the Democratic party, nominated their own "Dixiecrat" candidate, J. Strom Thurmond, in protest against Truman's demand for civil rights for Negroes. Henry A. Wallace, the peace candidate, headed a fourth ticket, the Progressive.[49] Ordinarily a party is in grave trouble when it splits two ways, but a three-way split was widely judged to be lethal.

Yet Truman enjoyed valuable assets. He could count on the bulk of the Negro vote, the Jewish vote, and the farm vote (he had once been a dirt-farmer in Missouri and Dewey was a "city slicker"). Truman's futile veto of the Taft–Hartley ("slave labor") Act had won the plaudits of organized labor.[50] The internationalists applauded his support

[48] The above account has drawn heavily on John G. Snetsinger, "Truman and the Creation of Israel" (unpublished doctoral dissertation, Stanford University, 1969), which is based on Truman's Papers and more than a dozen other manuscript collections. Dean Acheson, Truman's admiring Secretary of State, absolves him of all political motivation in the Palestine solution. *Present at the Creation* (1969), p. 176.

[49] K. M. Schmidt, *Henry A. Wallace: Quixotic Crusade, 1948* (1960); see also Irwin Ross, *The Loneliest Campaign: The Truman Victory of 1948* (1968).

[50] The Taft–Hartley Act of 1947 was designed to equalize the bargaining position of management by placing certain restraints on organized labor. It was passed over

of the UN. The country, despite inflationary pressures, was still prosperous — and prosperity always helps the party in power.

Republican overconfidence, bolstered by the polls, played directly into Truman's hands. Candidate Dewey was cold, polished, smug, vague, platitudinous. Truman, for his part, played the game of politics with consummate skill. Shortly after his nomination, he summoned what he called the Republican "do-nothing" Congress [51] into special session and demanded that it enact some of the pressing legislation that the Republicans had promised in their recent platform. Unwilling to reflect any credit on the Democratic administration, Congress dithered for eleven days and then adjourned without passing anything of consequence.

Truman's greatest singe asset was himself. He went out on the stump and delivered hundreds of "give-em-hell" speeches to increasingly enthusiastic crowds. In keeping with tradition, the American people warmed to a "gutsy" underdog fighter. The pollsters, unduly sure of themselves, made their great mistake by winding up their returns about two weeks before the election, and during this period there was evidently a great upsurge for Truman. Polling techniques have since then been refined.[52]

Truman's victory was more than a fluke or a personal triumph; the Democratic party carried both houses of Congress, the House of Representatives by a landslide (263–171). Truman won 303 electoral votes to the combined vote of 228 for his three opponents. His margin of the popular vote over Dewey was 24,104,000 to 21,971,000. In accounting for his preelection confidence in victory, Truman pointed to the fact that a majority of the states had Democratic governors, and they strengthened their lead 30 to 18. The triumph was surprising but hardly miraculous. Nobody seemed to be for Truman except a great majority of the Democratic voters, who substantially outnumbered their Republican rivals.

Truman's veto, and various efforts to repeal it have failed. The progress of organized labor during the subsequent years would indicate that the epithet "slave labor" was something of an exaggeration.

[51] Truman's characterization of the 80th Congress as a "do-nothing" body was unfair; actually it passed an impressive amount of major legislation, including the Taft–Hartley Act and the appropriations for the Truman Doctrine and the Marshall Plan. See Susan M. Hartmann, *Truman and the 80th Congress* (1971).

[52] In Britain the Conservative Edward Heath overturned the Laborite Harold Wilson in a surprise election (1970) which caught the pollsters guessing wrong about as badly as those of 1948 in America. As in the case of Truman, they had not made allowances for an eleventh-hour swing to the winner.

ADDITIONAL GENERAL REFERENCES

H. S. Truman, *Year of Decisions* (1955) and *Years of Trial and Hope* (1956);
Dean Acheson, *Present at the Creation* (1969); J. F. Byrnes, *Speaking Frankly*
(1947) and *All in One Lifetime* (1958); Cabell Phillips, *The Truman Presidency*
(1966); Walter LeFeber, *America, Russia, and the Cold War, 1945–1966*
(1967); J. W. Spanier, *American Foreign Policy Since World War II* (1960);
E. F. Goldman, *The Crucial Decade: America, 1945–1955* (1956); William H.
McNeill, *America, Britain, and Russia, 1941–1946* (1953); J. A. Lukacs, *A
History of the Cold War* (1961); M. F. Herz, *Beginnings of the Cold War*
(1966); D. F. Fleming, *The Cold War and Its Origins, 1917–1960* (2 vols.,
1961); Louis J. Halle, *The Cold War as History* (1967); N. A. Graebner, *The
New Isolationism* (1956); R. E. Osgood, *NATO: The Entangling Alliance*
(1962); Herbert Feis, *The China Tangle* (1953) and *From Trust to Terror: The
Onset of the Cold War, 1945–1950* (1970); Tang Tsou, *America's Failure in
China, 1941–1950* (1963); G. F. Kennan, *Memoirs, 1925–1950* (1967); Lloyd
C. Gardner, et al., *The Origins of the Cold War* (1970); Lloyd C. Gardner,
Architects of Illusion: Men and Ideas in American Foreign Policy, 1941–1949
(1970); Joyce and Gabriel Kolko, *The Limits of Power: The World and United
States Foreign Policy, 1945–1954* (1972); B. J. Bernstein, ed., *Politics and
Policies of the Truman Administration* (1970).

37

The Korean Conflict and Its Aftermath

Inaugurated anew in January 1949, President Truman proclaimed a Fair Deal of social reform at home and a Point Four program of aid for backward countries abroad. Aware of mounting tensions in the Cold War and of alarming Soviet progress in nuclear science, he made the momentous decision, in January 1950, to press ahead with the production of a hydrogen bomb. This horrendous weapon would be immensely more powerful than the "primitive" atomic devices dropped on Japan.[1]

In June 1950 the forces of Communist North Korea burst into South Korea in a Soviet-backed effort to unite the entire country under communism. Truman reacted swiftly by arranging for American intervention under the banner of the United Nations, ultimately contingents from sixteen countries. Forced to retreat far to the south, the allied troops under General Douglas MacArthur staged a spectacular comeback, and were authorized to pursue the North Koreans across the dividing line of the 38th parallel. The seesaw began anew when the Chinese Communists unexpectedly entered the war and drove MacArthur's divided force southward again in a humiliating retreat.

The Korean conflict, though at first supported by the American public, settled down to a stalemate that was bloody, frustrating, and unpopular. General MacArthur, unwilling to fight while partially shack-

---

[1] A number of conscience-troubled American scientists did not favor developing the hydrogen bomb, but a persuasive argument was that if the United States did not get it first, the Soviets would. This turned out to be true: the first American hydrogen bomb was produced in 1952; the first Soviet hydrogen bomb in 1953.

led, became so unsympathetic toward Washington's efforts to localize the conflict that Truman abruptly removed him in April 1951. An uneasy armistice was not signed until 1953, after spokesmen for the new Republican administration of General Eisenhower had hinted darkly at the possible use of nuclear weapons.[2]

DID THE U. S. SEND SUBSTANTIAL AID TO CHIANG?

A revolutionary overthrow of the ancient Chinese Empire in 1911 inaugurated a decades-long era of internal turmoil. In 1921 the Chinese Communist Party was founded, and then entered upon a twenty-eight-year struggle to take over the central regime in Peking. Japan's seizure of China's Manchuria in 1931, followed by full-scale hostilities in 1937, weakened the Nationalist government of Chiang Kai-shek by confronting him with a two-front war: one with the Japanese invaders and one with the Communists. America's entrance into the conflict against Japan in 1941, precipitated largely by Washington's concern for China, did little or nothing to improve the position of Chiang's Nationalists.

Simultaneously with Japan's surrender in 1945, the Soviets negotiated a treaty of friendship with Chiang Kai-shek, but they clandestinely or openly supported the Communist rebels. The United States, for its part, provided substantial aid to Chiang's Nationalists, including the transportation of his troops to more favorable positions. It assisted in de-Japanizing occupied China. It supplied military and financial aid in the amount of about $2 billion from 1945 onward. It vainly attempted, through the abortive ambassadorial mission of General George C. Marshall, to induce the Nationalists and the Communists, highly incompatible yokefellows, to form a coalition government.

The Nationalist regime was gradually undermined by incompetence and corruption, combined with defections to the Communists. In 1948 the dam broke, and the next year Chiang fled with the remnants of his army to the offshore island of Formosa (Taiwan), there to impose his rule on the Taiwanese. For more than twenty years, bolstered with American money and military aid, he nursed the vain hope of reconquering the mainland.

[2] Dwight D. Eisenhower, *Mandate for Change, 1953–1956* (1963), p. 181.

WHO LOST CHINA?

American critics noisily charged that Washington lost China to the Communists by helping the Nationalists too little and too late.[3] This charge was buttressed during the McCarthy era in the 1950s by accusations that pro-Communist sympathizers in the Foreign Service and State Department recommended negative policies that played into the hands of the simple "agrarian reformers"[4] in China.

In retrospect it seems reasonable to conclude that America did not lose China because China was not America's to lose. China lost itself. The argument is not convincing that if Washington had only sent more arms to Chiang, the results would have been reversed. Vast quantities of American military equipment wound up in the hands of the Communists, through capture, sale by corrupt officers, or defections from the Nationalist camp. Larger amounts of military and financial aid, given sooner, probably would have only prolonged the agony. In August 1949 the State Department issued a formal White Paper blaming Chiang for the loss of the mainland and announcing a cessation of further aid to his cause.[5]

It is obvious that when the Chinese Communists took over in 1948–1949 Chiang's regime had lost the confidence of the masses. When conditions become bad enough, a people will turn to almost any alternative, including communism. Some experts have concluded that only the injection of large numbers of American troops into China could have bolstered up Chiang — even temporarily. But with a weary America already at the end of one world war, and with the "I Wanna Go Home" movement attaining irresistible momentum among overseas troops, no one in authority was publicly proposing the commitment of a single American soldier to war with Asia's teeming masses.

America's painful experience in tiny Vietnam during the 1960s and later provided some retrospective wisdom. The involvement of over 500,000 United States troops, plus overwhelming air and sea power, was barely enough to bolster a weak and corrupt Saigon government that did not enjoy the confidence of a large body of its people.

[3] One interesting observation is that the United States evidently sent to the Nationalists far more outright aid than the Russian Communists gave to the Chinese Communists during the critical years from 1945 to 1949.

[4] The phrase had Chinese origins, but was picked up by Americans, including Ambassador Patrick J. Hurley, who later became violently anti-Communist. Many people mistakenly assumed that the difference between the Communists and the Nationalists was comparable to that between Democrats and Republicans in America.

[5] L. P. Van Slyke, ed., *The China White Paper, August 1949* (1967), contains a reprint of the original.

WAS COMMUNIST CHINA
PART OF A COMMUNIST MONOLITH?

By 1949 the Communists had seemingly parlayed Lenin's 1917 suitcase into control of most of Europe and Asia, altogether about a billion people. This wave of the future was seemingly irresistible, and the impulse in America was to do something to prevent Moscow communism from realizing its avowed intention of taking over the whole world. A compulsion to halt the vast Communist juggernaut had much to do with Washington's "get tough with Russia" policy, followed by a shooting involvement in Korea in the 1950s and in Vietnam in the 1960s.

In truth communism was never an ideological monolith; it has always been beset with divergent ideals and objectives. We have only to recall the dramatic break between Stalin and Trotsky in the late 1920s, with the loser being exiled and ultimately murdered. Yugoslavia's Tito, splitting off from Moscow in 1948, developed his own brand of home-grown communism.

Peculiarly instructive is the case of Communist China. After the Russians had openly adopted the Chinese as their protégés following the collapse of Chiang in 1949, they devoted much money and expertise to the industrialization and strengthening of their new bedfellow. But by the early 1960s the Soviet Communists and the Chinese Maoists developed a violent split over their interpretation of Marxism, and the Russian tutors were withdrawn or expelled. Before long the Chinese and Soviet armies were involved in minor bloodshed over border disputes, and by the 1970s Peking was developing nuclear bombs and long-range missiles that could be used against its former benefactors. Once more the old story of creating a Frankenstein's monster was repeated.

The nagging question of who lost China should be addressed to the Kremlin rather than to Washington. To a far greater extent than was ever true of the United States, the Soviets once had China and then had let it get away.

America's policy of not recognizing the Peking Communist regime was based largely on the hope that nonrecognition would weaken the new government. It might even collapse and cease to be a part of the terrifying "monolith." Yet by thus departing from the traditional policy of recognizing *de facto* governments that were obviously entrenched in power, Washington did not perceptibly weaken the Communist regime. At the same time it denied itself useful contacts. American public opinion, long nurtured on the myth of a dangerous "monolith," had little desire to give aid and comfort to the Chinese dragon.

WAS THE KOREAN WAR NECESSARY?

Korea, once independent, was formally annexed by Japan in 1910. At the end of World War II, Russian troops occupied the area north of the 38th parallel, while Americans held the region to the south. The Soviets, after communizing and arming the North Koreans, nominally withdrew in 1948. The Americans, after partially democratizing and arming the South Koreans, pulled out in June 1949, leaving only a few technical advisers.

With Moscow's aid and encouragement, the North Koreans suddenly invaded South Korea in June 1950, obviously with the intent of uniting the entire country under their Communist dictatorship. The Soviets evidently did not expect an armed response by the United States.[6] They may have been partly misled by Secretary of State Acheson, who had pointedly excluded Korea as within the Far Eastern defense perimeter of the United States in a famous speech on January 12, 1950. But he had also declared — a fact often overlooked — that Korea was a responsibility of the United Nations, which had established the government of South Korea.[7]

Moscow clearly expected the nations of the Free World to stand aside with folded arms. A struggle for the unification of a once-united country could be legitimately regarded as a civil war, not within the jurisdiction of outsiders. Korea traditionally has been described as a strategic pistol pointed at the heart of Japan, and partly for this reason the Japanese had fought the Russians in 1904–1905. But conceptions of grand strategy had changed, and the Joint Chiefs of Staff in Washington had concluded as early as 1947 that Korea was not worth a war. This decision does much to explain why the raw American troops in Japan were badly unprepared to stem the tide in Korea, whether from the standpoint of numbers, equipment, or state of mind. As usual, America was grossly unprepared for war, partly because of a sharp cutback in

[6] Nikita S. Khrushchev is quite frank in stating that the North Korean Communists, without provocation, initiated the thrust with the backing of Stalin, and in the confident expectation that the U. S. would not intervene. *Khrushchev Remembers* (1970), Ch. 11. Ex-Ambassador W. Averell Harriman presents supporting evidence in *America and Russia in a Changing World* (1971), p. 56.

[7] Dean Acheson, *Present at the Creation* (1969), p. 357. Acheson notes that General MacArthur, in March 1949, had announced the same defense perimeter. Australia and New Zealand were also excluded.

the military budget, and partly because Washington was placing undue reliance on the atomic bomb for deterrence.

President Rhee of South Korea forthwith appealed to the United States for aid. President Truman, in a sharp reversal of policy, decided that the line of the 38th parallel would have to be held. He believed in the necessity of "containing" communism, in the folly of "appeasing" the aggressor (as at Munich in 1938), and in the desirability of preserving collective security. If the United Nations quailed before this naked aggression, as the League of Nations had before the Japanese in Manchuria in 1931, then the United Nations would presumably die and World War III would be inevitable.

Truman therefore encouraged the United Nations through the Security Council to call upon its members to resist this wanton attack.[8] Acting under U.N. authorization and his own prerogatives as commander-in-chief, Truman gradually committed American ground, aerial, and naval assistance to the South Koreans. Ultimately he received military support, most of it merely token, from fifteen other members of the United Nations.

Haste was so imperative when the North Koreans first struck that Truman avoided a long-winded debate in Congress by not asking for a declaration of war. He never got around to making such a request, and Congress never took the initiative, even though public opinion at first was favorable.

WHO WON THE KOREAN WAR?

Well-equipped North Koreans almost drove the South Korean armies and the United Nations forces out of the peninsula. But General MacArthur, appointed to the U.N. top command, finally held the line and then executed a daring flank attack at Inchon, September 1950. This stroke cut off the rear of the North Korean armies, and forced their remnants to flee northward across the 38th parallel. The first phase of the Korean War was clearly won by the United Nations and South Korean forces.[9]

South Korean troops, in hot pursuit, chased their foes across the 38th parallel. The U.N. Assembly, calling for the establishment of "a unified, independent and democratic Government in Korea," author-

---

[8] See *ibid.*, Ch. 44; Glenn D. Paige, *The Korean Decision* (1968). The USSR veto was not used because the Russian delegate was absent in protest against the presence of the delegate of Nationalist China.

[9] South Korea, thanks to a Soviet veto, was not a member of the U.N.

ized MacArthur to take "all appropriate steps" to attain this goal. This, of course, meant invading North Korea, and Washington dispatched more specific orders to that end. Peking issued clear warnings that a menacing invasion of North Korea would draw Communist China into the conflict, but the reaction in Washington was to dismiss these threats as mere bluff.

General MacArthur was confident that he could wind up the war by Christmas. Unwisely dividing his army in a rash dash northward, and not assessing properly reports that the Chinese were actually intervening, he was caught near the northern border by an inpouring of several hundred thousand Chinese "volunteers." His forces were driven southward 275 miles, in a headlong, frostbitten retreat, well below the 38th parallel. In subsequent months they fought their way up to near that dividing line.

General Ridgway, who became commander of the U.N. forces, later declared that his troops could have "pushed right on to the Yalu River on China's border in the spring of 1951. . . ." But he felt that the price "would have been far too high for what we would have gained. . . ." [10] His estimates were 100,000 of his men killed or wounded, and then he would be facing formidable Chinese armies — plus all of China — behind the broad Yalu River, with North Korean guerrillas swarming in his rear. The farther either side advanced in Korea, the longer its supply line became, with an inevitable slowing of progress.

After intermittent fighting and negotiating, an armistice line (roughly the battle line) was settled upon in 1953, but the war did not officially end. A formal peace lay many years in the future. If the U.N. and South Korean forces won the first phase of the conflict by expelling the invader, they definitely did not win the avowed objectives of the second — that is, the unification and democratization of all Korea. The United States and its allies stood about where the enemy had started from in 1950, hundreds of thousands of casualties later — on both sides. Nor can one say that the Americans, a part of a U.N. coalition, lost the war, even though they settled for less than they had sought when they began the counterinvasion of North Korea after Inchon. For that matter, the North Koreans had not attained their avowed objectives. In this sense, all parties had lost. Hence, as at the end of the War of 1812, a stalemate solution was indicated and finally adopted — in this case on a provisional basis.

Yet from one point of view the United Nations won. It had

[10] See Matthew B. Ridgway, *The Korean War* (1967), pp. 150–151.

shown that it could intervene to halt aggression, as the League of Nations had failed to do in the 1930s. It did not perish in the rice paddies of Korea.

SHOULD THE KOREAN WAR HAVE BEEN WIDENED?

General MacArthur, with his brilliant record in two previous wars, was a strong-willed and difficult subordinate. As during the Pacific war from 1941 to 1945, he felt that Washington was sending him inadequate military strength for the job. After Chinese "volunteers" massively entered the war in November 1950, he urged alarming proposals on the Joint Chiefs of Staff in Washington. He would unleash Chiang Kai-shek's ill-equipped armies for service in Korea and for guerrilla action or counterinvasion in China. He would have U. S. naval and air forces blockade the Chinese coasts and bombard or bomb China's vital centers, including the "privileged sanctuary" in Manchuria, from which the enemy was launching attacks.

Policy makers in Washington regarded the clash in Korea as a peripheral diversion, with the main foe being the Soviet Union in the European theater. Truman had no desire to fritter away strength in the Far East that might be needed by his NATO allies in Europe, and he strove to keep the limited war in Korea from widening into World War III. In this course he had the worried support of his U.N. allies.

Objections to MacArthur's proposals were numerous. Chiang Kai-shek's troops, whom the South Koreans feared, needed much more training and equipment. A blockade of China's ports would create friction with Britain (at Hong Kong) and with Russia in Manchuria (Port Arthur and Dairen). Besides, a naval blockade could hardly be crippling while supplies from Russia were pouring in through China's back door. As for strategic (nonnuclear) bombing,[11] it would be of dubious effectiveness. Moreover, a bombing of Chinese bases in the staging areas of Manchuria, near the Russian border, might well bring the Soviets into the conflict, in accord with the Sino–Soviet treaty of 1950. Finally, if the enemy enjoyed a "privileged sanctuary" in Manchuria, the United Nations enjoyed one to the south; by some kind of

[11] A nuclear bombing of China was presumably ruled out in Washington because of a desire to localize the war. Probably it was not employed in Korea because the results in that underdeveloped country would not be effective enough to offset an outraged world opinion, including that of America's allies, especially Britain. General Ridgway was convinced that MacArthur was seeking no less than a "preventive war" with China so as to weaken her as a future menace. Ridgway, *The Korean War*, pp. 143–144.

tacit understanding, the Communist aircraft did not bomb important military installations in South Korea or Japan.

DID MacARTHUR DESERVE SUMMARY REMOVAL?

Under the American democratic system, foreign policy and military policy, often intertwined, are formulated by the civilian officials in Washington, after seeking the advice of the Joint Chiefs of Staff and other counselors. Viewing the global problems from this vantage point, and with abundant intelligence available to them, the top policy makers arrive at judgments that take into account overall strategy. The commander in the field may express his own views in advance, but once the decision is made he must stifle his dissent and carry out his orders to the letter. If he cannot bring himself to do this, he is under obligation to resign.

MacArthur disagreed with Washington's overall policy, which kept him from winning the kind of smashing victory which he had come to expect. He indiscreetly made known his views to newspapermen and Congressmen. On March 24, 1951, he issued a virtual ultimatum to the Chinese and North Koreans to negotiate or suffer "doom." He not only had no authority to publish such a proclamation, but by jumping the gun he sabotaged a conciliatory overture that Truman was about to make to the enemy. By this time the President had had more than enough, and he summarily removed the five-star general from all of his commands.

MacArthur may or may not have been right in his prediction that Russia would not come into the war (he had guessed wrong on China) and that in the long run the nation's best interests would be served by crushing the Chinese. But that is not the point. His hostility to and repeated interference with policies carefully formulated in Washington clearly overstepped the authority of the commander in the field and jeopardized civilian control of military affairs — a principle sacred to the Republic.

Truman's abrupt dismissal of the General, to whom the country owed much, predictably aroused a storm of criticism. The President could better have shown MacArthur the elevator, rather than kicking him out the fifth story window.

IS THERE A SUBSTITUTE FOR VICTORY?

General MacArthur repeatedly declared, "There is no substitute for victory." [12] So spoke the military man, accustomed to heady successes.

One implication of this observation is that victory is permanent and that it settles all immediate problems. Yet victory has a tendency not to keep and to create more problems than it solves, whether long-run or short-run. Hence "preventive wars" are desperate solutions. A victory in World War I overthrew the Kaiser but did not keep Germany permanently enchained, while helping to give birth to Adolf Hitler and World War II. Instances could be multiplied.

General MacArthur objected, as was instinctive with a professional soldier, to fighting with shackles in a "limited," "no-win" war. His philosophy was to crush the enemy, force him to surrender, and then impose terms on him. But limited wars are common in human experience, especially in that of the United States. The Republic was clearly fighting for limited objectives when it warred with Britain in 1776 and 1812, Mexico in 1846, Spain in 1898, Germany in 1917, North Korea and China in 1950, and North Vietnam in the 1960s. Not one of these foes accepted unconditional surrender (except Italy in 1943 and Germany in 1945), and all of America's declared foreign wars (except those with Italy and Germany) ended in negotiated settlements.

Wars are normally fought to achieve political ends, not for the glory of the generals and admirals. There are substitutes for victory, and one is a negotiated settlement that reduces rancor and gives promise of promoting lasting amity. A classic example is the Treaty of Ghent, which ended the stalemated War of 1812 and which initiated more than a century and a half of unbroken peace with Britain.[13]

WAS THE U.N. WORTH SAVING?

One of Truman's major purposes in rushing to the defense of South Korea was to keep the U.N. from collapsing and thus to avert World War III. Possibly the new world organization was saved by dispatching troops, but many critics, expecting its ultimate demise, wondered if the

[12] This statement appeared in a letter from General MacArthur to Representative Martin, who read it in Congress, April 5, 1951. *Cong. Record*, 82 Cong., 1 sess., p. 3380.

[13] See Raymond G. O'Connor, "Victory in Modern War," *Journal of Peace Research* VI (1969), 367–384.

intervention was worth what it cost. Certainly the United States was hampered in its prosecution of the Korean War by disagreements with the other participating nations. Coalition warfare, so the axiom runs, is the most difficult of all to wage.

In truth the United Nations, initially oversold, has proved to be a bitter disappointment to those who had expected it to perform the miracle of preventing all future wars. The hope was that it would create a powerful police force which would compel misbehaving members, even the major powers, to toe the line. But no great nation, particularly the USSR and the U. S., was going to hand over control of its sovereign destinies in vital matters to armed foreigners. Hence the proposed constabulary was never formed.

Numerous other problems arose. The framers of the U.N. Charter had not anticipated a routine casting of the veto in the Security Council, but the Soviet Union, outvoted by the capitalist world, used this weapon with the greatest of freedom. Voting blocs quickly formed in the General Assembly, including Communist, capitalist, and racist, thereby complicating political machinations. The wholesale admission of ministates greatly bloated the General Assembly; tiny nations entered, such as the minute Republic of Maldives, which numbered some 108,000 souls. By 1970 the U.N. boasted 127 members, in contrast with 51 when the organization was formed in 1945. Some of the new countries could not boast the population of many modest-sized American cities, although they enjoyed a vote equal to that of the United States in the General Assembly. At the same time, Communist China, representing some 700,000,000 people, was excluded. Finally, the resolutions of the U.N. were repeatedly ignored or flouted by various nations, ranging in power from the USSR to tiny Israel. Some members exercised their "pocketbook veto" by refusing to pay authorized financial assessments for peace-keeping operations, notably those in the Congo in the 1960s.

Despite such drawbacks the U.N. has enjoyed considerable success in using its good offices to avert or limit small wars, which might have become vastly bigger. Most of these achievements have involved smaller nations, with several notable exceptions. The U.N. exerted substantial influence in dampening down the multipower Suez intervention of 1956 and particularly in heading off a nuclear holocaust at the time of the Cuban missile crisis in 1962.

The failure of the U.N. to form a potent international police force has been disappointing. But on occasion the organization has provided a neutral peacekeeping contingent, notably in policing the desert strip between Israel and Egypt, following the war of 1956. Significantly, the withdrawal of these troops in 1967, on the demand of Egypt, touched off the six-day Israeli–Arab clash.

Exaggerated expectations regarding the war-preventing role of the U.N. have obscured the fact that the organization has done much good in other areas.[14] Its functions have by no means been solely military and political; they have embraced problems ranging from social and cultural to economic and judicial. The U.N. has provided a forum for all countries, large and small, where they have ventilated their grievances and presented their points of view, including blatant propaganda. Nations have eagerly sought membership in the organization, in marked contrast to the old League of Nations in its declining years.

DID TRUMAN BRING ON McCARTHYISM?

During World War II the Roosevelt administration had made a commendable effort to exclude partisanship from foreign policy. Many citizens remembered that political infighting had contributed heavily to the defeat of the League of Nations in 1919–1920, and they were determined that the prospective United Nations Organization should suffer no such fate.

Bipartisanship in foreign policy worked reasonably well during World War II and in the Truman years immediately after it. The effort to rise above politics usually involved consultation by the administration with leaders of the opposition (Republican) party in Congress *in advance* of making important policy decisions. But the Republicans frequently complained that they were too often advised of a decision *after* it had already been made. They were not called in for the takeoff, they insisted, but only for the crash landing, when they could be asked to share the blame. Actually, a purely nonpolitical foreign policy in a democracy is a virtual impossibility. The party in power, in its appeal to the voters, will customarily claim credit for its achievements, and the "loyal opposition" will naturally criticize those same achievements.

Whatever remained of Truman's bipartisanship in foreign policy was badly shaken by the cataclysmic events of 1949–1950. Early in 1949, after China fell into the Communist camp, many Americans naturally began to look for pro-Communist scapegoats, especially in the Department of State. Late in 1949 came Russia's first atomic bomb, and this earth-shaking event, occurring years earlier than predicted, created

[14] See Ruth B. Russell, *The United Nations and United States Security Policy* (1968).

the suspicion that pro-Communist Americans must have passed on vital "secrets" to the "backward" Russians. The final shocker was the sudden incursion of the Communist North Koreans into South Korea in 1950, followed by Truman's "no-win" strategy. Many frustrated Americans concluded that policymaking in Washington was being subverted by Communists or Communist sympathizers.

President Truman, aware of charges that subversives were infiltrating the Executive Branch, promulgated an order in March 1947, inaugurating a loyalty check. To some extent, right-wing critics later charged, he helped to bring on McCarthyism by not exercising more vigilance and vigor in this inquiry.[15] When Alger Hiss, a former high-placed State Department official, was accused in 1948 of having passed on state secrets to Moscow in the 1930s, Truman lightly dismissed the investigation as a "red herring." After two sensational trials, Hiss was found guilty of perjury (1950) in connection with his denial of complicity in such subversion. In 1950 Judith Coplon and a Soviet accomplice were convicted of conspiracy and attempted espionage, and in 1950–1951, four persons were convicted of atomic espionage, two of whom were put to death — Julius and Ethel Rosenberg.

The prevailing atmosphere of dismay, frustration, suspicion, and fear was made to order for a demagogue, and a potent one appeared in the person of Senator McCarthy. Truman may not have been primarily to blame for his success, but conditions that developed — or were allowed to develop from 1945 to 1950 — got this Red-baiter off to a flying start.

DID McCARTHY ELIMINATE
COMMUNISTS FROM GOVERNMENT?

A freshman U. S. Senator from Wisconsin, Joseph R. McCarthy had been elected in 1946 as "Tail-gunner Joe." (He had served with the Marines in the recent war but had never been a tail-gunner, and his Purple Heart award did not result from enemy action.) Seeking an issue that would bring him notoriety and power, he seized upon Communists in government, although with highly dubious sincerity.[16] In an electrifying speech at Wheeling, West Virginia, February 12, 1950, he waved aloft a paper

---

15 For the controversial thesis that Truman helped bring on McCarthyism by over-stressing the Communist menace to win Congressional support for the Truman Doctrine and the Marshall Plan, see Richard M. Freeland, *The Truman Doctrine and the Origins of McCarthyism* (1972).

16 Richard H. Rovere, *Senator Joe McCarthy* (1959), pp. 58–59.

which he alleged contained the names of some 205 card-carrying Communists or sympathizers in the State Department who were influencing government policy. The list was never produced, and he finally pared the original figure to virtual nothingness. Nevertheless, McCarthy was made chairman of a Senate investigating subcommittee, which placed in his hands the power to make or break a large number of frightened citizens. He flatly accused the Democratic administration of "twenty years of treason."

McCarthy inaugurated an incredible witchhunt by his bullying, browbeating, scatter-gun accusations. He resorted to Hitler's big-lie technique and faked documents or photographs.[17] He was largely responsible for eliminating from the Senate at least eight members, and he tried to "get" others. He badgered Secretary of State Dulles, who wanted to live on good terms with Congress, into appointing a McCarthyite, Scott McLeod, as Personnel and Security Officer for the State Department. He terrorized the custodians of American overseas libraries into burning a few leftist books. He attacked the United States Army in an investigation during which he insulted officers and overexposed himself to a vast television audience during month-long hearings. The American people got a long look at his essential meanness and ruthlessness, and from then on his influence waned.

In December 1954 the Senate finally voted to "condemn" McCarthy (not "censure" as often stated) by a vote of 67 to 22.[18] The minority were all fellow Republicans, some of whom had been eager to capitalize on his former popularity. The charges against him were contempt of a Senate subcommittee, abuse of certain Senators, and insults to the Senate itself. These accusations overlooked such serious offenses as his besmirching the reputations of honest citizens under cloak of senatorial immunity, his causing many decent people to lose their jobs or to be blacklisted, his use of "guilt by association," his assumption that the accused were guilty until proved innocent, and his repeated use of fabricated or otherwise false evidence.

Ignored by the press and public, McCarthy was left a shattered man. His influence gone, he took heavily to drink and died in 1957. Ardent supporters claimed that the Communists had finally "got" him.

After all this uproar, McCarthy evidently did not succeed in personally uprooting a single card-carrying Communist from a sensitive

---

[17] McCarthy's successful campaign to defeat Senator Tydings for reelection featured a faked photograph showing Tydings conversing with the Communist leader, Earl Browder. *Ibid.*, p. 160.

[18] In Senate parlance, "condemnation" was less serious than "censure."

post in government, much less from the Department of State. There is, however, one instance of a *former* Communist who left his job when McCarthy stumbled onto his trail and then abandoned it.[19] A few other liberals or persons with pro-Communist leanings may have left government service rather than face possible defamation by McCarthy. Some had already been exposed.

DID McCARTHY HELP THE COMMUNISTS?

Senator McCarthy's chief contributions were of a negative order. He permitted the Republican administration of Eisenhower to negotiate a truce in Korea that he would almost certainly have condemned if the Democratic Truman had accepted it. Above all, the Senator opened the eyes of the American people by showing how vulnerable they were to the wiles of a dangerous demagogue.

The other side of the ledger reveals an overwhelming list of debits. McCarthy persuaded many citizens that honest or questionable mistakes of judgment by government officials were outright treason. He focused undue attention on the few Communists under the bed, rather than on the real Communist threat from abroad. He caused freedom of speech and thought to become captives in the Land of the Free. Countless Americans, while spying on neighbors, began to fear one another more than a foreign foe. McCarthy made a mockery of civil rights for the individual under the Constitution, thereby promoting a species of home-grown fascism. Liberals and nonconformists (in the tradition of those who had founded America) were equated with Communists; un-American investigative committees flourished; loyalty oaths were extorted from public servants; and official lists were compiled of proscribed organizations.[20]

McCarthy also brought democracy in America into grave disrepute at a time when the nation was desperately trying to check communism by promoting democracy abroad. This was notably true of Germany, which had recently experienced a bully-boy dictatorship, complete with book-burning. The Senator shattered the morale of the State Department not only by hampering its recruiting program but by discouraging candid reportage by foreign service officers abroad — the very information upon which sound public policy is based. Henceforth diplo-

[19] Rovere, *Joe McCarthy*, p. 160.
[20] See Robert Griffith, *The Politics of Fear: Joseph R. McCarthy and the Senate* (1970).

mats in the field would think twice before they reported views that might be exhumed by future McCarthys seeking to purge them from the service.

There was food for thought in the accusation by McCarthy's critics that he could not possibly have helped the Communist cause more if he had been on Moscow's payroll. Communists rejoiced as he tore the nation asunder. In effect, he attempted to burn down the barn to get rid of a few rats. He caused many worthy citizens to forget that if one gives up basic liberties to purchase security, one may wind up with neither liberty nor security.

WAS TRUMAN A NEAR-GREAT PRESIDENT?

A Missouri dirt-farmer, an ex-haberdasher, a small-time machine politician in Missouri, and then U. S. Senator, Harry S Truman fell heir to the presidency after serving only seven weeks as Vice President. He was almost completely unbriefed by President Roosevelt as to the earth-shaking commitments at Yalta and elsewhere. Yet this ordinary-appearing "average man's average man" plunged in with a will, did his homework, and displayed both courage and decisiveness in handling the unprecedented number of "gutty" decisions that had to be made at his desk. It bore the motto, "The Buck Stops Here." Truman was a great surprise, rather than a great President, in that he managed his office far better than most people had reason to expect. His appearance and manner to the contrary, he was far more than an "average man." [21]

Spunky Harry Truman was a fighter. He fought for the rights of labor (he vetoed the Taft–Hartley "slave labor" bill); he fought for civil rights for Negroes (thereby splitting off the Southern wing of his party in 1948); he fought to protect the Executive Branch of the government from legislative interference (thereby inviting the McCarthyite investigations); he fought to cover up for his political cronies when they were caught using their influence for pecuniary gain (the "Missouri gang"); he fought Congress (which overrode twelve of his vetoes); he fought vigorously and successfully for election to his office "in his own right"; and he fought during his second administration to achieve the social reforms — in public housing, social security benefits, rent control, and minimum wages — embraced in his program known as the Fair Deal.

---

[21] Former Secretary of State Dean Acheson, the controversial official whom Truman loyally supported, writes admiringly that "if he was not a great man, he was the greatest little man the author of the statement knew anything about." *Present at the Creation* (1969), p. 729.

Some of Truman's "great decisions," which were commended at the time, do not look so statesmanlike in the long view. Dropping the atomic bomb, though supported by his key advisors, could have been avoided. His abrupt cancellation of lend–lease was, by his own admission, a blunder. The creation and hasty recognition of Israel, partly for partisan purposes, foreclosed other alternatives which might have proved less harmful to America's long-run interests. The effort to persuade the Chinese Communists and Nationalists to form a coalition government was doomed from the outset, and the "dumping" of Chiang Kai-shek in 1949, though probably inevitable, was done with a brutality that is best explained by political motivations.

Intervention in Korea and its aftermath called for other controversial judgments. The decision to intervene was questionable, in view of its sudden reversal of established military policy — and the Korean problem dragged on for decades, despite enormous expense and bloodletting. The sacking of MacArthur was justified, though handled in anger and with all the finesse of a punch in the nose. When the administration authorized the General to go north,[22] it brought in China, which then established itself beyond doubt as a Far Eastern military power in fighting the Americans and their associates to a standstill. The emergence of Red China in turn led to American fears for Indochina, and in the spring of 1950 (a decision often overlooked) the Truman administration authorized the first of hundreds of millions of dollars to support the French against the rebellious Ho Chi Minh — a momentous initial step in the nation's Vietnam entanglement.

Critics of Truman, especially left-wingers, are prone to blame him for heating up the Cold War. But his reactions were part of a vicious circle for which no one in particular was to blame; conflict was inherent in the clash of two incompatible systems. The Truman Doctrine, which may or may not have saved Greece and Turkey, had much to commend it, but the President was less than far-visioned in making it applicable to the entire world, including Vietnam. The Marshall Plan, on the other hand, is generally accounted (in non-Communist circles) an enormous success and an act of genuine statesmanship. The Berlin airlift may have saved this key city for the West, and the entangling NATO alliance of 1949 provided a bulwark against further Soviet penetration in Europe.

One obvious moral of the Truman days is that policies cannot be properly assessed until events have run their course. Many historians, impressed with the surprising decisiveness of the peppery President and

---

[22] The orders of MacArthur were subject to certain conditions, including no evidence of China's intended entrance and the use of only South Korean troops near her border. MacArthur ignored both stipulations. Ridgway, *The Korean War*, pp. 44–50.

unduly concerned with immediate results, have classified him as a "Near Great." A more cautious judgment would be that he was unexpectedly competent, rather than great, but even this is a compliment.

ADDITIONAL GENERAL REFERENCES

Harry S. Truman, *Years of Trial and Hope* (1956); Cabell Phillips, *The Truman Presidency* (1956); Dean Acheson, *Present at the Creation* (1969); Herbert Feis, *The China Tangle* (1953); Tang Tsou, *America's Failure in China, 1941–1950* (1963); David Rees, *Korea: The Limited War* (1964); J. W. Spanier, *The Truman–MacArthur Controversy and the Korean War* (1965); Trumbull Higgins, *Korea and the Fall of MacArthur* (1960); R. H. Rovere and A. M. Schlesinger, Jr., *The General and the President* (1951); M. B. Ridgway, *The Korean War* (1967); R. J. Caridi, *The Korean War and American Politics* (1968); G. D. Paige, *The Korean Decision* (1968); C. A. Willoughby and J. Chamberlain, *MacArthur, 1941–1951* (1954); Courtney Whitney, *MacArthur* (1956); Douglas MacArthur, *Reminiscences* (1964); J. L. Collins, *War in Peacetime: The History and Lessons of Korea* (1969); Athan Theoharis, *Seeds of Repression: Harry S. Truman and the Origins of McCarthyism* (1971); Alan D. Harper, *The Politics of Loyalty: The White House and the Communist Issue, 1946–1952* (1969).

38

The Eisenhower
Interlude

*War hero Dwight D. ("Ike") Eisenhower was elected President in 1952
on the Republican ticket over Governor Adlai Stevenson of Illinois,
whom the Democrats drafted — one of the few cases in American history of a genuine presidential draft. The General, a middle-of-the-roader
who tended to be a strict constructionist of the Constitution, assembled
a Cabinet dominated by wealthy businessmen.[1] His first administration
was bedeviled by Senator Joseph R. McCarthy's ruthless drive against
alleged Communists in government, but this self-appointed prosecutor
finally overreached himself. Eisenhower consented to run for reelection
in 1956, despite a near-fatal heart attack in September 1955. The ensuing electoral campaign was complicated by an acute international
crisis growing out of Egypt's seizure of the Suez Canal, provoked in part
by the United States. Simultaneously the Soviets brutally suppressed
rebellious Hungary. With a war-experienced hand evidently needed at
the helm, Eisenhower defeated a warmed-over Governor Stevenson by an
even wider margin than before.*

*During his second administration, especially the last two years,
Eisenhower displayed unexpected energy. Presidential Assistant Sher-*

---

[1] Defense Secretary Charles E. Wilson, a former high official of General Motors,
was forced to dispose of his holdings in that company because of conflict-of-interest
defense contracts. He is supposed to have testified, "What's good for General Motors
is good for the country." What he actually said before the U. S. Senate Armed
Services Committee was: ". . . For years I thought what was good for our country
was good for General Motors, and vice versa." *Hearings Before the Committee on
Armed Services, U. S. Senate,* 83 Cong., 1 sess. (Jan. 15 and 16, 1953), p. 26.

man Adams was forced to resign under a cloud, in September 1958, and Secretary of State Dulles died of cancer in February 1959. The President was then compelled to assume more responsibilities and show more vigor, especially in foreign affairs.

Eisenhower was no crusader where civil rights were involved. He routinely backed the desegregation decision of the Supreme Court and finally intervened with federal troops in Little Rock, Arkansas, to protect a few black pupils. Despite a dampening business recession in 1958, he remained immensely popular to the end of his second term.

WAS EISENHOWER A TRADITIONAL MILITARY MAN?

After twenty long years of Democratic Presidents, the Republicans regained the White House in 1953 by capitalizing on the war-born popularity and glamorous grin of five-star General Dwight D. Eisenhower. The country was still prosperous but the voters were especially weary of professional politicians, of the so-called corrupt "mess in Washington," and of the unending "no-win" Korean War. Candidate Eisenhower won immense acclaim when he promised, if elected, to go to Korea and see what he could do to end the miserable affair. So great was his personal popularity that he made a far more impressive showing than the Republicans running for Congress on the same ticket; they narrowly won control of that body for only two of "Ike's" eight years.

Eisenhower was a West Point graduate, the former commander of victorious Allied armies in World War II, and a long-term professional soldier. But he was far from being cast in the same mold as other professionals such as General Zachary Taylor or General Ulysses S. Grant. Gifted as a coordinator, a conciliator, and an accommodator, he was a natural choice to command the multination Allied forces in North Africa and Western Europe. Diplomatic affairs had by now become so intimately intertwined with military affairs that Eisenhower soon gained unusual experience in dealing with many of the leaders of Europe, both military and civilian. His Republican backers also pointed out that he had been further "civilianized" by serving for two years as President of Columbia University after World War II. But many educators were critical, arguing that just as nations do not summon academicians to lead their armies, they should not call on generals to head their academies. Among both professors and politicians Eisenhower was not in his element; the impression deepened that the clean old general was above dirty politics.

Despite his presumed grasp of military affairs, the General–President pursued a defense policy vulnerable to criticism. Largely in the interests of economy, he cut back the conventional armed forces and relied heavily on "massive retaliation" with nuclear weapons ("More bang for the buck," the saying went). The difficulty with this approach was that without a "flexible response," involving some conventional forces, the nation could not deal effectively with small, brush-fire wars. The danger loomed that in a major crisis the choices would be holocaust or humiliation, a blowup or a backdown.[2]

Unlike military men who are accustomed to giving orders and having them obeyed with heel-clicking celerity, Eisenhower as President proved to be humble, modest, teachable, prudent, dignified (unlike Truman on occasion), capable of growth, blessed with common sense, and lacking a craving for power. He did not like to be bothered with the tedious background details of crucial decisions, and for this reason he delegated much authority under arrangements that resembled the staff system of the army. He much preferred to have the essentials of an important decision brought to him on a single sheet of paper. Not surprisingly, he unloaded much of his responsibility on Secretary of State Dulles and on Presidential Assistant Sherman Adams, who for nearly six years was one of the most powerful men in Washington, although not holding an elective office.

Eisenhower's Republicanism, at least at the start, was hardly more than skin deep: like Grant in 1868, he might have had the presidential nomination of either party. When he began singing the praises of the Republicans with high-sounding moralities, he seemed to be badly out of character. He became so discouraged with his attempts to force his liberal "Modern Republicanism" on the reactionary elements among his following that he gave serious thought to forming a new party.[3] To the end, he was still something of a military man, but his breadth of vision was highlighted when, in his farewell address of 1961, he warned the nation against the growing power of the vast "military-industrial complex." He warned more wisely than he knew.

---

[2] Incredibly, when the Soviets astonished the world in 1957 by firing into orbit their first Sputnik, Eisenhower dismissed this coup as a gimmick that should not cause "one iota" of concern.

[3] R. J. Donovan, *Eisenhower: The Inside Story* (1956), pp. 151–153. With the Democrats in power for twenty solid years, and with the two-party system in danger of disappearing, Eisenhower partially restored the balance. This may have been his greatest contribution to the nation; he was evidently the only winner whom the Republicans could have presented in the 1950s, so powerful was his appeal as a "father figure."

WAS PRESIDENT–GENERAL EISENHOWER A FIGHTER?

Despite his record as a professional fighter, Eisenhower did not distinguish himself as a fighting President. Having led the great *Crusade in Europe* (the title of his memoirs published in 1948), he had no desire to lead a great crusade in America. He was a tranquilizer rather than a stimulant. Remembering what his civics textbook had said about delicate checks and balances among the three branches of the government, he showed unusual deference to Congress, which was embarrassingly Democratic during the last six of his eight years. He leaned on that body perhaps as much as he led it, especially in the early months, when he was undergoing on-the-job training. Unlike Truman, he did not let fly with charges of a "do-nothing," "no-account" Congress. He had potent retaliatory weapons at his command, but he refused to get down "in the gutter" with "low-blow Joe" McCarthy, even when that Red-baiting demagogue was attacking Eisenhower's own Department of Defense. Critics frequently accused the President of abdicating moral leadership.

Eisenhower was a man of peace; he had seen enough carnage. One of his great regrets when he left office was that he had not insured world peace, although Republicans boasted (with exaggeration) that during his administration no American soldiers had been killed by enemy action on foreign soil.[4] Some of his problems were swept under the rug for later comers to the White House, but he did contrive to bring a shaky truce to Korea (on stalemate terms which President Truman would have been pilloried for accepting); he did restrain his more warlike advisors (including Vice President Nixon) from rushing into Vietnam when the French were collapsing in 1954 at Dien Bien Phu;[5] he did manage to avoid a clash with China while protecting Chiang on Taiwan from the Communist Chinese; he did contrive to uphold Allied rights in Berlin; he did refrain from backing the British, French, and Israelis in their war on Egypt in 1956; and he did resist the clamor to intervene on behalf of the Hungarian revolutionists against the Soviets.

---

[4] Actually the Korean armistice was not signed until after Eisenhower had been in office for more than six months, and in subsequent years American troops near the armistice line suffered a few fatalities from enemy fire.

[5] Eisenhower went so far as to instruct Secretary of State Dulles to draft a war resolution for Congress. It was dropped when Congressional leaders foresaw a rejection in view of the unwillingness of Britain to go along. Eisenhower subsequently gave substantial military aid to the anti-Communist government in South Vietnam, headed by Ngo Dinh Diem, and ultimately had some 700 American military advisors there. See *The Pentagon Papers, as Published by The New York Times* (1971), Ch. 1.

Another close call came in the eastern Mediterranean during 1958. Congress had given the President a blank check in 1957 (the Eisenhower Doctrine) which authorized him to use the armed forces to protect any nation in the Middle East that requested such assistance against "armed aggression from any country controlled by international communism. . . ." Responding to an urgent appeal from Lebanon, Eisenhower hastily landed some 14,000 men in July 1958. As the event proved, the Eisenhower Doctrine was not really applicable; the threat was an internal one, compounded by machinations from Egypt, which was not "controlled by international communism." Nevertheless, quiet was restored after many anxious days.

WAS EISENHOWER A REACTIONARY?

"Ike" was a split personality: he regarded himself as a moderate liberal in human relationships and international affairs, but as a moderate conservative in economic affairs, especially government finance. One basic reason why he consented to run for the presidency, despite strong inclinations to the contrary, was a desire to save his country from isolationism, particularly that favored by conservatives within his Republican party. As the business man's ideal, he had an obsessive concern for "fiscal responsibility" and balanced budgets. To his dismay the budget was out of balance for three of his eight years, for a total of about $20 billion in red ink.

Eisenhower Republicans found the various New Deal measures so deeply rooted that most of these changes could not be eliminated. Like the Jeffersonians of 1801, the victors not only accepted much of what they found, but even expanded some of it, including Social Security. Ironically, their clamor about the "corrupt mess" in Washington came home to plague them. As was inevitable, several cases of wrongdoing hit the headlines, conspicuously the case of Sherman Adams, the aloof and tough-fisted presidential assistant. His offense was to accept expensive personal gifts from a New England manufacturer, a longtime friend, and then make three brief inquiries on his behalf at federal agencies.[6] A

---

[6] See Sherman Adams, *Firsthand Report* (1961), Ch. 21. The manufacturer in question, Bernard Goldfine, subsequently pleaded guilty to income-tax evasion and was sentenced to prison. Eisenhower himself accepted expensive gifts for his Gettysburg farm. After his death the press revealed that he had deeded his Gettysburg holdings to the government as a national historic site. See D. A. Frier, *Conflict of Interest in the Eisenhower Administration* (1969).

telephone call from the White House usually carries considerable weight, even if routine, and Adams conceded that he had been imprudent. President Eisenhower reluctantly accepted his resignation after the administration continued to suffer political damage.

American Presidents roughly fall into two categories: the activists such as Jackson and the two Roosevelts, and the caretaker type such as Coolidge. After two major wars, the country wanted a breathing-spell President, and Eisenhower filled the bill. A frequent criticism was that with his immense popularity and ingratiating personality he should have developed a leadership of Congress that would have "made things happen." Instead, these critics charged, he "hoarded" his popularity and presided over the "Great Postponement," giving scant attention to various pressing domestic problems, including equality for Negroes. True, in 1957 he called out the federal troops to protect nine black children in their right to attend Central High School in Little Rock, Arkansas, but he did not act until the burning issue had caught up with him. The smouldering problems of the Middle East, Vietnam, Korea, Chiang's refugee China, Castro's Cuba, and others were put off to plague his successors.

WAS "IKE" A DO-NOTHING PRESIDENT?

In defense of Eisenhower one must add that he was hobbled by Democratic Congresses during six of his eight years, even though their leadership proved unusually cooperative. He was able to keep them reasonably well under control with the veto bludgeon. Moreover, he was not a well man much of the time. During a dark period about halfway through his eight years he suffered successively a near-fatal heart attack, a serious abdominal operation, and a mild stroke. When, in February 1956, he consented to run for a second term, some five months after his heart attack, he frankly told the American people that he could be only a part-time President. But so great was "the national love affair" that they elected him overwhelmingly on these terms, and despite a warning from candidate Stevenson (who died before Eisenhower did) that the President probably would not live out his term.

Largely for reasons of health, Eisenhower spent much time in rest and recreation, especially golfing ("eight long years of golfing and goofing," declared the Democrats). During his last two years, after Sherman Adams had been forced out and Secretary Dulles had died, he was compelled to take charge himself. During this period the "New

Eisenhower" provided more aggressive leadership than ever before.[7]   If he reigned too much and ruled too little, he did so with dignity, decency, and dedication. If he did not accomplish as much constructively as possible, at least he avoided rushing into situations that might have proved catastrophic. Some critics have concluded that his place in history is better assured by what he did not do than by what he did.

Many historians, predominantly Democrats, have not given Eisenhower especially high marks, ranking him in the same low average bracket with the impeached President Andrew Johnson.[8] But the voters held him in much higher regard. He may not have been a "great" President, but during his incumbency he was adored, even idolized, by more millions of American voters than any other occupant of the White House.

WAS THE DESEGREGATION DECISION OF 1954 CONSISTENT?

As far back as 1896, in the landmark case of Plessy v. Ferguson, the Supreme Court had decreed, by a vote of 7 to 1, that separate but equal facilities for Negroes traveling on railroads were permitted by the Constitution. Such was the legal support for separate schools for blacks.

In 1954, in the more famous case of Brown v. Board of Education of Topeka, the Supreme Court ruled, by a vote of 9 to 0, that separate but equal schools for Negroes were unconstitutional because, by being separate, they were "inherently unequal."

Countless Southerners, forced by the Court's ruling to desegregate their schools, were vehement in their criticism of this "sociological" decision. The Constitution in 1954 was the same as the Constitution of 1896, except for a few inapplicable amendments, yet what had been almost unanimously constitutional in 1896 had become unanimously unconstitutional fifty-eight years later. The Constitution had not changed but America and the outlook of the judges had; and the Constitution is what the Court says it is. By 1954 many sociologists and psychologists had concluded that statutory desegregation imposed a feeling of rejection, inferiority, and discrimination on the black child that warped his

---

[7] The Republicans had reason to regret their support of the kick-at-Roosevelt 22nd Amendment. Approved in 1951, it prevented Eisenhower, even if he had been willing, from serving a third term. He died in 1969, eight years after leaving office. Despite the predictions of many political scientists, his being a "lame duck" ineligible for reelection did not slow him down at all, during his last two years. Originally, he had opposed the 22nd Amendment; "long before" he left the Presidency he had come to regard it as "good for the nation." D. D. Eisenhower, *Waging Peace, 1956–1961* (1965), p. 643n.

[8] See T. A. Bailey, *Presidential Greatness* (1966), p. 24.

personality and impaired his capacity to learn. Hence separate schools, by their very nature, could not be equal, even when the physical plant and teaching were equal, which all too often they were not.

Little Rock, Arkansas became a storm center in 1957. In an effort to protect a few black pupils in their right to enter Central High School, Eisenhower was forced to dispatch federal troops, in a situation reminiscent of bayonet-enforced Reconstruction. The truth is that he never was a flaming champion of Civil Rights for blacks, and for various reasons he never publicly expressed support of the Supreme Court's decision of 1954, though later writing that he privately favored it.[9] Despite the successful Montgomery bus boycott by Negroes in 1956, to say nothing of numerous sit-ins, wade-ins, and pray-ins, Eisenhower evidently was not fully aware of the pressures that were building up for the Black Revolution. It burst in full fury during the administrations of his successors.

WAS DULLES A SUPERLATIVE SECRETARY OF STATE?

John Foster Dulles, an experienced diplomat and a distinguished international lawyer, served as Secretary of State during the six years from 1953 to 1959, when he was cut down by cancer. Upon his death, President Eisenhower, unable to choke back tears, declared that Dulles was not only the greatest Secretary of State he had ever known, but that he was one of the "truly great men of our time."

There can be little doubt that the elderly Dulles wielded more power than any other Secretary of State before or since. The primary reasons were that the ailing President leaned heavily on him in directing foreign affairs, and that the nation, with its immense nuclear arsenal, commanded more power than ever before. Yet Dulles proved to be, and remains, a highly controversial figure.

Determined at the outset to maintain good relations with the funds-granting Congress, Dulles permitted Senator McCarthy's inquisition to penetrate the State Department and the Foreign Service, thereby undermining the morale of those vital agencies. As a prominent Presbyterian layman, the Secretary preached high-sounding moralities which did not always square with stern realities. As frequently is true of loquacious men, he suffered from an advanced case of "foot-in-mouth" disease. He spoke of the "liberation" of Communist-captive peoples in Europe as more desirable than mere containment, with the result that

---

[9] Eisenhower, *Waging Peace*, p. 150.

the rebellious Hungarians and others were tragically led to expect American assistance. He was associated with "unleashing" Chiang for attacks on the Chinese mainland, when in fact Chiang was making only minor raids from Taiwan and did not have the strength to launch a major one. Dulles described the "art" of going "to the brink" of war, but not over the brink, in facing down an adversary — a process that the journalists called "brinkmanship." [10] (This is the kind of thing that statesmen have to do on occasion, but they are not statesmenlike when they talk publicly about it.) In line with Eisenhower's policy, Dulles further aroused anxieties by promising instant and "massive" retaliation against aggressors.[11]

Although proclaiming rollback and "liberation," Dulles soon found himself back on the old Truman road of containment, desperately holding the line. In so doing, he clung to frozen policies, such as the nonrecognition of Communist China and her nonadmission to the U.N., although one must concede that American public opinion strongly supported such ostracism. He also felt obliged to support dictatorial regimes, like that of Franco in Spain, in holding the dike against communism. Finally, he regarded neutralism, such as that of India, as immoral, even though America had pursued such a course for protracted periods.

Critics of Dulles who deny that he was a great Secretary of State cannot challenge his record as the greatest traveler among the Secretaries up to that time. Reluctant to delegate responsibility, he visited 46 countries and logged some 560,000 miles, or 22 times around the world, mostly in airplanes. Such visitations enabled him to maintain firsthand contact with pressing problems and foreign statesmen, while saving time. On the other hand, his appearance undercut the resident American ambassador, made for hurried decisions, and tended to stall the diplomatic machinery in Washington until he returned. His successors likewise used the airplane extensively.

Dulles did manage to keep the right-wing isolationists of his party from throwing overboard the new postwar internationalism. He helped negotiate the Soviet withdrawal from Austria in 1955; and in 1954, working through the Central Intelligence Agency (headed by his brother), overthrew a Communist-oriented government in Guatemala. He also helped to deter an invasion of Nationalist China (Taiwan) by the Communist Chinese. He added substantially to the number of defensive pacts which bound the United States to various nations, thereby increasing America's entangling commitments to 42 ("pactomania"). He

[10] See the Dulles interview in *Life*, XL (Jan. 16, 1956), 70–80.
[11] In a speech of January 12, 1954, Dulles referred to "massive retaliatory power," which in journalistic shorthand soon became "massive retaliation."

presumably strengthened America's posture in Eastern Asia by SEATO (Southeast Asia Treaty Organization) and in the Middle East by the Baghdad Pact (CENTO). Both combinations were weak, and the United States did not actually join the latter.

Above all, Dulles managed to keep the nation out of war. Yet he had narrow escapes in Vietnam in 1954; in Lebanon in 1958; and in Chinese waters in 1958, when Chiang was in jeopardy. Dulles' management of the Suez crisis brought the world to the brink of war, but luckily the worst was averted.

Dulles probably proved to be about as satisfactory a Secretary of State as could have been expected. He served when the might of Soviet Russia was on the rise, and merely to hold the line was something of a gain.[12]

WAS DULLES PRIMARILY RESPONSIBLE FOR THE SUEZ CRISIS?

Colonel Nasser, leader of poverty-cursed Egypt, had long dreamed of constructing a high dam at Aswan, on the upper Nile. Though estimated to cost about $2 billion and to take fifteen years, it would add perhaps one-third to Egypt's arable land and also supply an immense amount of electric power. Late in 1955, the United States and Britain, in collaboration with the World Bank, proposed to finance the initial steps. Both powers were interested in reducing poverty in Egypt and thus averting the possibility of a Communist takeover engineered from Moscow.

Nasser, after delaying acceptance of the British–American offer, came back with unrealistic counterproposals. Working both sides of the street, he strongly hinted that the Soviets, who had long coveted a power base in the Middle East, were prepared to treat him more generously. But Washington was in no mood to be "blackmailed" into pouring funds into unfriendly countries under the threat of their moving into the Kremlin's camp. Other nations, including those friendly to America, would be tempted to play this same game, with financial results that could ruin the Washington Treasury.

Congress was also becoming restive. Nasser had recently recognized Red China; he had been snuggling up too closely to the Soviet Union to please many Americans; he had mortgaged his cotton crops by making a huge arms deal with Soviet-dominated Czechoslovakia. Doubts multiplied as to Egypt's capacity to pay off a loan for the Aswan Dam.

[12] For a balanced appraisal of Dulles, see Gordon A. Craig, *War, Politics, and Diplomacy* (1966), Ch. 15.

Congressmen from the cotton-growing South saw no point in subsidizing the production of competitive cotton; Jewish voters opposed strengthening Nasser (Israel's implacable foe); and American voters were becoming increasingly uneasy about billion-dollar foreign aid. One significant result was that the Senate Appropriations Committee included in a report (July 1956) the stipulation that no funds voted under the Mutual Security Act could be used to finance the Aswan Dam, without prior approval of the Committee. But we should note that this was only a committee report, not an act of Congress, and that the door was left partially open.

After a silence of many weeks in Cairo regarding the offer of a loan, Secretary Dulles took action. He informed the Egyptian ambassador, on July 19, 1956, that in view of Egypt's lack of interest and her unacceptable counterproposals, Washington considered its proposal withdrawn, with Britain going along. President Nasser thereupon denounced the United States and eight days later nationalized the Universal Suez Canal Company, ostensibly to finance the Aswan Dam. He thereby triggered the most dangerous international crisis since World War II.

President Eisenhower concedes in his memoirs that Dulles' abrupt handling of the question may have been "undiplomatic." He further suggests that if Washington had dragged out the negotiations indefinitely, Egypt would have had less excuse to seize the Canal. Dulles, in his defense to the President, insisted that the Egyptian leader was well aware of the collapse of negotiations; that Nasser had been thinking (by his later admission) of seizing the Canal for about two years; that he had merely been seeking a pretext; and that "If I [Dulles] had not announced our withdrawal when I did, the Congress would certainly have imposed it on us, almost unanimously." [13]

This last statement is open to challenge. The adverse Senate report was only a conditional statement of dubious force. Negative action by both houses of Congress might well have consumed weeks, even months. By this time Nasser would have had to react without the provocation of a dramatic slap for all the world to see. A turndown by a legislative body, after many weeks of public discussion, would have been less humiliating. So many months of delay had already occurred that a few more probably would have been advisable.[14]

[13] Eisenhower, *Waging Peace*, p. 33. Chapters II and III are revealing of the crisis from the White House point of view.

[14] In the aftermath the Russians agreed in 1958 to help finance and engineer the Aswan Dam. Ten years in the building, it was completed in 1970, with the USSR receiving great acclaim, and with the Soviets visibly strengthening their military foothold in Egypt and elsewhere in the Middle East. Since 1959 the U. S. granted Egypt in foreign aid more millions of dollars than were embraced in the total offer to finance the dam in 1956 (U. S., Britain, and the World Bank combined). Herman Finer, *Dulles Over Suez* (1964), p. 503.

WAS EISENHOWER'S SUPPORT OF NASSER JUSTIFIED?

The Universal Suez Canal Company, most of whose stockholders were British and French nationals, was a private concern operating on sovereign Egyptian territory. Its expropriation by Nasser was supportable under international law, provided that fair compensation was paid to the owners. But all too often such adjustments prove to be unsatisfactory, although this case proved to be an exception.[15]

British shippers were the heaviest users of the Canal, and all of Western Europe was almost fatally dependent on it for vital oil supplies. Neither the British nor the French felt secure with President Nasser astride this life-giving waterway; Egypt had in fact barred Israeli shipping from the Canal since the war of 1948–1949. European technicians had been largely responsible for operating the Canal, and the British and French were certain that it could not function under Egyptian control. (It was in fact being operated without a hitch for weeks before the attempted seizure by Britain and France.)

Prestige was highly important to the two Western powers. The once-proud British Empire was fast shrinking (the last British troops had been forced out of Egypt earlier in 1956); the French Empire was also crumbling, with Nasser aiding France's Algerian rebels. Both Western nations remembered how they had faltered when Hitler seized the Rhineland in 1936, and they were determined to overthrow Nasser, the potential Hitler of the Nile, before he united the entire Arab world against them.

British and French leaders, allies of the United States in NATO, made it clear from the outset that they would resort to force, if necessary, to regain the Canal. They regarded such action as thoroughly justified by self-defense, as sanctioned under Article 51 of the United Nations Charter. But Eisenhower had other views. He realized that such an act of aggression, in reaction to a presumably legal expropriation, would flout America's nonaggression commitments under the U.N. and other international undertakings.[16] He did not believe that the United States could have one set of rules for its enemies, such as the North Korean aggressors, and another for its friends. He perceived that if the U.N. could be successfully overridden in this major instance, any real hope

[15] The stockholders received some $81 million in six installments, completed in 1962.

[16] In 1950 the U. S., Britain, and France had agreed to a Tripartite Declaration which pledged them to joint action to prevent violations of the Egypt–Israeli frontiers and armistice lines. Eisenhower, *Waging Peace*, p. 77n.

of peace through collective security would receive a shattering blow. Moreover, there was good reason to believe that an Anglo–French–Israeli aggression against Egypt would not even be sanctified by success, as it was not.

Committed to such views, Eisenhower attempted to work out compromise solutions through Secretary Dulles. None of them proved satisfactory or they fell under vetoes in the Security Council, wielded by the USSR (on behalf of Nasser) and by Britain and France (on their own behalf). The British and French quickly developed a deep distrust of Dulles, for they suspected that he was merely stalling while Egypt tightened its grip on the Canal. In any event, Washington's outspoken opposition to violence strengthened Nasser in his determination to stand pat.

WAS THE THREE-NATION ATTACK ON EGYPT A BLUNDER?

Fully aware that Eisenhower would oppose strong measures, the British and French decided to attack Egypt without notifying Washington in advance. For more than a week there was a blackout of news from London and Paris. On October 29, 1956, the superbly trained armies of Israel, aided by French aircraft and possibly French pilots, invaded Egypt and speedily penetrated to the Suez Canal. The Israelis were provoked by Egyptian raids, desirous of striking a preventive blow, and determined to open the long-closed Suez Canal and the Gulf of Aqaba. Two days later, British forces assaulted Egyptian centers after issuing an ultimatum that was spurned.

Attacks by Britain and France, though not well coordinated, came so soon after those of Israel as to suggest prior collusion, which the British and French leaders flatly denied. Ten years later the then French Foreign Minister, Christian Pineau, confessed that the three nations had made a definite mutual commitment in France on the eve of the assaults.[17]

Explanations by the British and French officials, then and later, declared that intervention was needed to keep the Canal open (which it already was), to separate the Israeli and Egyptian armies, and to prevent World War III. Yet the Egyptians were fully prepared to block the Canal with sunken ships, as they promptly did for five months. Moreover, the proposed separation of the Israeli and Egyptian armies seemed insincere

[17] See *Time*, Aug. 5, 1966, p. 32; Terence Robertson, *Crisis: The Inside Story of the Suez Conspiracy* (1965), p. 163; Anthony Nutting, *No End of a Lesson: The Story of Suez* (1967), Chs. 10–12.

because the British and French were clandestinely supporting the invasion and the Israelis had voluntarily pulled back from the borders of the Canal. As for preventing World War III, the British–French incursion came perilously close to triggering it.

Invading Anglo–French forces nearly won their immediate military objectives, but under various pressures London and Paris pulled back. A cease fire was arranged, and a U.N. peacekeeping force was established on the Israeli–Egyptian frontier. To this extent the invaders saved some face. The British in particular were restrained primarily by partisan criticism at home; by the alienation of world opinion, including that of the United States; by the threatened defection of key members of the Commonwealth; and by the shock to Britain's financial structure. Russian threats of nuclear annihilation are often credited with having tipped the scales, but we should note that such bomb-rattling did not come until after Washington had made clear that it would not support the British and French.

Numerous indeed were the repercussions of the Suez invasion. The NATO alliance, weakened by the refusal of Washington to support its allies, was almost fatally cracked. The Soviet Union emerged more than ever as the friend of colonial peoples and deepened its foothold in the Egyptian sands. Nasser came through stronger than before. Israel, forced to pull back on the basis of assurances from the U. S. and U.N., got neither security nor access to the Suez Canal. In 1967, eleven years later, the Israelis felt compelled to launch a "preventive war" in an attempt to secure them.

The irony is that, in the teeth of opposition from the United States, the strong-arm methods of 1956 were severely handicapped from the start. Nasser was bound to block the Canal, as he did; oil pipelines were bound to be disrupted by neighboring Arabs, as they were. The British in particular were not prepared militarily for a lightning invasion — the only kind that held out any real prospect of immediate success. The Kremlin may not have been bluffing when it threatened to pour in Russian "volunteers," and it almost certainly would have provided abundant arms, as it has since done. The Victorian age of gunboat imperialism had clearly passed.

SHOULD THE U. S. HAVE INTERVENED IN HUNGARY?

Eisenhower was especially annoyed when the British and French chose the last days of his 1956 campaign for reelection to present him with the embarrassment of an attack on Egypt. The Soviets were no less inconsiderate, for they simultaneously invaded Hungary and bloodily repressed a revolt in this unhappy Communist satellite. Moscow's intervention was peculiarly inopportune. While America was successfully restraining the assault by its French and British allies on Egypt, Eisenhower was in no position to curb the Soviet attack on Hungry or to force a withdrawal.

Stalin had died in 1953, and a successor, Premier Nikita S. Khrushchev, inaugurated a partial relaxation of Russia's iron-fisted dictatorship. In response to this freer atmosphere, serious disorders occurred in Poland in 1956, and then a full-fledged revolt in Hungary. Washington's official policy of "liberation" and "rollback," combined with appeals by U. S. sponsored radio broadcasts,[18] caused these oppressed peoples to increase their resistance and to expect a kind of aid that could hardly have been forthcoming.

Hungary was virtually landlocked, surrounded by neutral or unfriendly states. If an adequate American or United Nations force had been immediately available (which it was not), and if it could have moved with instant speed (which it could not), it would have had to force or fight its way through adjoining countries. Such an attempt would have meant delay and probably large-scale warfare. The United States could not in good conscience atom-bomb the Soviets in Hungary, but it might have threatened Russia with nuclear weapons. The Kremlin, with the victim so near, probably would have dismissed such a threat as a bluff. By 1956 the Soviets also had hydrogen bombs and presumably doubted that America would invite global incineration (including Hungary) on behalf of Hungarian freedom. Better, from Washington's point of view, that a nation should lose its liberty — perhaps temporarily — than that a planet should die.

A perplexed United States, despite bitter charges from the Hungarian freedom fighters and their relatives in America, did about all it could. It supported a condemnation of the USSR in the United Nations, sent aid to the refugees, and permitted a considerable number of them to enter its immigration gates.

DID THE U-2 AFFAIR RUIN THE SUMMIT CONFERENCE?

Worried about Russia's growing nuclear arsenal, the United States by 1960 had for several years been photographing Soviet installations from

---

[18] Radio Free Europe, allegedly sponsored by private American donations, was finally revealed in 1971 to be financed in part by the Washington government.

specially designed aircraft. These U-2s were then capable of flying above the range of antiaircraft missiles or interceptor airplanes, to the great annoyance of the Soviets. Using improved missiles, the Russians managed to shoot down an overflying U-2 and capture the pilot, Francis G. Powers, on May 1, 1960, some 1,200 miles inside Soviet territory. Moscow then trapped the Washington officials into making a series of denials that were proved to be lies before the whole world.[19] The image of America as an upright, truth-telling nation suffered a besmirching blow. President Eisenhower, seeking to make a clean breast of the whole affair, admitted full responsibility for authorizing the overflights. He then defended them as necessary in view of Premier Khrushchev's boasts of destroying America.

Espionage flights over another nation's territory were generally regarded as a violation of international law. Internal spying, depending on the tactics used, is ordinarily a violation of a country's domestic law rather than international law. The Soviets, in their appeals to the U.N. over the U-2 affair, plainly did not come into court with clean hands. All major powers engage in espionage, none more so than the secretive and suspicious Russians. Soviet embassies have traditionally been notorious spy centers, and this fact partially accounts for the reluctance of some nations to maintain diplomatic relations with the USSR. Soviet agents have repeatedly been caught operating in the United States; indeed, Francis G. Powers, the U-2 pilot, was eventually exchanged for a convicted Soviet spy in 1962. But nothing so sensational as the U-2 affair had occurred, and the humiliating public confession by the head of a state was not only without precedent but widely regarded as naive. Better than lying denials or defiant confessions would have been silence, or "We are investigating," or "Regrettable if true." The Soviets were so notorious for faking evidence [20] that the absence of a confession would have left many doubts.

A Paris summit conference had been scheduled for May 16, 1960, consisting of Premier Khrushchev, President Eisenhower, Prime Minister Macmillan of Britain, and President De Gaulle of France. But both Washington and Moscow had publicly taken such inflexible positions on the burning Berlin issue that any such gathering seemed doomed from the start. Khrushchev evidently seized upon the U-2 affair as the means of

---

[19] See David Wise and T. B. Ross, *The U-2 Affair* (1962).

[20] A photograph of the wreckage of the U-2 initially displayed by Premier Khrushchev was clearly that of some other aircraft. Eisenhower, *Waging Peace*, p. 550. See this whole chapter for a lucid account from the White House point of view. Eisenhower rejected the easy solution of blaming overzealous subordinates, lest he create the impression that proper presidential control was lacking. In view of common instances of such lack of control, this argument is not completely persuasive.

browbeating Eisenhower and breaking up the Conference before it could get off the ground. If the Kremlin leaders had wanted the meeting to continue, they could easily have used their police state methods to conceal the U-2 mishap. The fact that they did not do so, together with their failure to protest earlier overflights, is persuasive evidence that they either did not want the summit conference to be held or were sure that it would fail.

The U-2 espionage, though a diplomatic disaster, was actually a technological triumph. These high-soaring planes enabled the United States to adjust its arms program more realistically to that of the Soviet Union, while establishing the absence of a "missile gap" highly unfavorable to the United States.[21] The criticism that Eisenhower should have called off the last U-2 overflight earlier lest a mishap should jeopardize the foredoomed Paris conference overlooks one factor: the need for taking a calculated risk during photographically good flying weather. So many other previous overflights had gone off without mishap that taking another chance seemed justified.

WHO "LOST" CUBA?

Cuba had long suffered from a succession of heavy-handed dictators. The latest of them, Fulgencio Batista, enjoyed at least the tacit support of the United States, although Washington had cut off shipments of arms to him in 1958. American capital owned an extraordinary percentage of Cuba's utilities, mining properties, and sugar-producing facilities; and partly for this reason the United States government was willing to play along with the corrupt and dictatorial Batista.

So great was the distress among the depressed Cuban masses, in contrast to the upper classes, that agricultural reform was desperately needed. Then emerged Fidel Castro, a young left-wing revolutionary, who did not profess to be a Communist, although he had some Communist followers.[22] He parlayed a forlorn handful of men in 1956 into a force that took over control of the government on January 1, 1959, and compelled Batista to flee with his ill-gotten millions. Many Americans, recognizing the oppression of the Cuban people, were sympathetic to Castro and his presumed plans for agricultural reform; indeed, Wash-

---

21 *Ibid.*, p. 547n.

22 Khrushchev recalls that at the outset Moscow was for a considerable period in the dark as to whether Castro was a Communist. *Khrushchev Remembers* (1970), pp. 489–491. But it is difficult to prove, as sometimes alleged, that the United States drove Castro into the embrace of Russia by not being "nice" to him.

ington accorded him prompt recognition. After seizing control, he visited Yankeeland, where he evidently neither sought nor was offered substantial financial aid. He apparently was determined to have a real revolution, and he could not do so as long as he was constrained by the terms of assistance from the United States and restrained from seizing Yankee properties. Uncle Sam could serve as a rabble-rousing whipping boy.

Returning to Cuba, Castro launched sweeping reforms; expropriated the billion-dollar American holdings; tied himself economically to the Soviet chariot; avowed that he was a Marxist–Leninist; and became in effect a Communist puppet of Moscow ninety miles off the coast of Florida. Washington did not drive Castro into Moscow's arms; he deliberately betrayed the avowed principles of his revolution and threw himself into Moscow's arms.

But the United States did "lose" Cuba in the sense that the island had been first a political and then an economic satellite of the northern Republic. By cooperating with dictators, Washington condoned or fostered the conditions that caused the people to flock to Castro in such numbers that he was able to entrench himself. As in the case of Nationalist China in 1948–1949, when a regime becomes so corrupt that it does not enjoy the support of its people, it is in jeopardy. No one American can be singled out in assessing blame for what happened, but rather the policies that were shaped by the strategic and economic interests of the United States.

ADDITIONAL GENERAL REFERENCES

D. D. Eisenhower, *Mandate for Change, 1953–1956* (1963), and *Waging Peace, 1956–1961* (1965); M. J. Pusey, *Eisenhower, the President* (1956); R. J. Donovan, *Eisenhower: The Inside Story* (1956); Arthur Larson, *Eisenhower: The President Nobody Knew* (1968); Walter Johnson, *1600 Pennsylvania Avenue: Presidents and the People, 1929–1959* (1960); L. L. Gerson, *John Foster Dulles* (1967); J. R. Beal, *John Foster Dulles* (1957); Richard Goold-Adams, *John Foster Dulles* (1962); E. J. Hughes, *The Ordeal of Power* (1963); Sherman Adams, *Firsthand Report* (1961); R. M. Nixon, *Six Crises* (1962); R. F. Smith, *The United States and Cuba: Business and Diplomacy, 1917–1960* (1960).

39

Kennedy and the New Frontier

The Democrats in 1960 chose as their presidential candidate, John F. Kennedy, who ran under a banner of social and economic reform proclaiming the New Frontier. He barely succeeded in winning after a spirited campaign against Vice President Nixon, the Republican nominee. The new Chief Executive, vexed by a hostile coalition of conservative Democrats and Republicans in Congress, made disappointing progress in implementing his program. Perhaps his most significant legislative contribution was to help feed into the pipeline the bills for Medicare and other major legislation that passed under his successor. But Kennedy did wage a valiant fight against inflation, and angrily forced the steel companies to rescind (temporarily) price increases in 1962.

The most spectacular developments of these years occurred in foreign affairs, beginning with the Washington-supported but incredibly bungled invasion of Cuba by émigrés at the Bay of Pigs in April 1961. Kennedy, in his campaign for the presidency, had made much of the dangerous "missile gap" between the U. S. and the USSR. But upon reaching the White House he discovered that there was either no missile gap or that it was so small as to be no cause for alarm.[1] Such nuclear muscle no doubt was an important factor in enabling Kennedy to maintain American troops in Berlin, and particularly in forcing the Soviets to withdraw their nuclear missiles from Cuba during the fear-

---

[1] Roy E. Licklider, "The Missile Gap Controversy," *Pol. Sci. Quar.* LXXXV (1970), 600–615. Estimates of Soviet missile strength were largely guesswork.

some crisis of October 1962. In the more relaxed atmosphere that fol-
lowed this period of acute tension, Washington and Moscow agreed upon
a Nuclear Test Ban Treaty (1963), which barred all signatory nations
from further polluting the atmosphere with open-air testing. Yet this
overpraised achievement was offset by a deepening involvement in
Vietnam that boded ill for the future. What Kennedy would have done
in Southeast Asia no one can say with complete assurance; he was cut
down by an assassin in November 1963. The crisis that he left in
Vietnam was at least as alarming as the one he had inherited from
Eisenhower.[2]

WHO WON THE KENNEDY-NIXON "DEBATES"?

In 1960 the Democratic party nominated a United States Senator for
the presidency, a youngish (43) war hero from Massachusetts, John F.
Kennedy. He had made an excellent showing in the primaries, largely
as a result of his charm, eloquence, energy, organization, and abundant
finances. Surprisingly, he tapped as his running mate a presidential rival,
Lyndon B. Johnson of Texas, then the Senate majority leader. Kennedy
evidently suspected that Johnson would not give up his powerful Senate
post for the hollow honor of the vice presidency, but he realized that
such an overture would partially placate the Southern wing of the
Democratic party. To Kennedy's surprise, Johnson finally consented,
and the Kennedy camp grudgingly accepted him as the candidate most
likely to strengthen the party where strength was needed.[3]

The Republicans overwhelmingly nominated as their presidential
standard bearer Vice President Richard M. Nixon. He not only had
served under Eisenhower for nearly eight years, but had tactfully assumed considerable responsibility during the President's illnesses. The
highlight of the subsequent campaign was a series of four debates between the two major candidates, allegedly in the Lincoln–Douglas
tradition.

Comparing the hour-long Kennedy–Nixon encounters with those
of 1858 is rather pointless. In 1960 the contestants clashed on television
and radio, not in open air meetings three hours long. The first and fourth
contests featured opening and closing statements, in the manner of

[2] This is the judgment of the writers of the secret Pentagon Papers. *The Pentagon Papers As Published by The New York Times* (1971), p. 113.
[3] Arthur M. Schlesinger, Jr., *A Thousand Days* (1965), pp. 45–57. Johnson writes that he reluctantly accepted the nomination, primarily out of party loyalty. L. B. Johnson, *The Vantage Point* (1971), pp. 91–92.

a debate, followed by questions from a panel of journalists. The other two meetings were essentially press conferences, with each candidate answering questions posed by the newsmen and with his rival given an opportunity to answer. In the third "debate" the rivals were separated by a continent, with Nixon in Los Angeles and Kennedy in New York.

Nixon appeared to poor advantage in the first engagement: he was campaign-weary; he had lost about ten pounds as a result of a knee infection and subsequent hospitalization; his shirt collar hung much too loose; he presented a ghastly visage, with powder used to cover his dark "five o'clock shadow." (The baseless rumor began to circulate that he had been sabotaged by a Democratic makeup man.) A robust and ruddy Kennedy, crammed with facts and figures, made a better appearance and was generally judged to have won the first encounter. The radio audience, unable to see the rivals, was much more favorably impressed with the invisible than the visible Nixon. An estimated 80 million persons witnessed this first debate; considerably fewer viewed the remaining three, in which Nixon appeared to better advantage. Throughout all of them he was to some extent thrown on the defensive by having to support the record of two terms of Republicanism.

Nixon believed that, although he lost the first debate, he definitely won or at least drew the remaining three. Various public opinion polls gave Kennedy a substantial overall advantage.[4] We shall never know who came out ahead because there was no panel of expert and unbiased judges, as was customary in intercollegiate debating. Nor can we say that Kennedy prevailed because he won the subsequent election (as Douglas had over Lincoln for a Senate seat). The electoral contest was breathtakingly close, and turned on many "if" factors, including the debates.

Regardless of how well Nixon did in the exchange of arguments, in a sense he was bound to be the loser. He was then a much better known figure than Kennedy, and by consenting to share his larger audience with his challenger he made a fatal error. This was the same trap into which Douglas, better known than Lincoln in 1858, had fallen. But, like Douglas, Nixon evidently was confident that his skill and experience as a debater would enable him to overshadow his "inexperienced" rival. The televised debates gave Kennedy a vast amount of free publicity; caused him to appear as "mature" as the older Nixon; and almost certainly provided more than the margin of victory.

---

[4] The story is told from Nixon's vantage point in Richard M. Nixon, *Six Crises* (1962), Ch. 6; see also Theodore H. White, *The Making of the President, 1960* (1965), pp. 293–294.

DID CATHOLICISM HURT KENNEDY IN 1960?

John F. Kennedy was the second Roman Catholic to be nominated for the presidency by a major party, the first being Al Smith in 1928. Religious bigotry was bound to raise its loathsome head again, although the country evidently had become less concerned about a candidate's religion.

In 1956, when Kennedy was an unsuccessful candidate for the presidential nomination, his staff prepared and circulated a memorandum (used again in 1960) which argued that Catholicism would be more of an asset than a liability to a presidential candidate.[5] Many Catholics, traditionally Democratic, had been wooed away by the glamor of a war hero to become "Eisenhower Republicans," and they might be wooed back by a co-religionist. The Catholic voters were heavily concentrated in the urban areas of the North, such as New York, Boston, Philadelphia, Chicago, and Detroit, all of which were important for Kennedy's success.

Cleverly using reverse psychology, the Democrats harped on religious bigotry. Their leader repeatedly brought up the nasty subject and deplored the existence of a prejudice which barred the White House to tens of millions of citizens simply because they had been born into the wrong church. Kennedy undoubtedly won some backlash support from conscientious voters who did not want to be condemned as bigots. Nixon later complained of this heads-I-win-tails-you-lose strategy: Catholics were urged to vote for Kennedy because he was a Catholic; Protestants were urged to vote for him to prove they were not anti-Catholic.[6]

Kennedy lost a part of the normally Democratic Solid South, specifically Florida, Tennessee, and Virginia, largely because much of the Protestant, Bible-belt South could not stomach his religion. But these states had relatively few electoral votes, and he could afford to lose them. But the states of the populous North, with their large Catholic electorate, he had to carry, and did, including Illinois, Massachusetts, Michigan, New Jersey, New York, and Pennsylvania. Although there is evidence to support both sides, the presumption is that Kennedy's religion and the religious issue helped more than it hurt him.

[5] The text is published in *U. S. News & World Report*, XLI (Aug. 1, 1960), 68–72.
[6] Nixon, *Six Crises*, pp. 366–367. Kennedy proved that a Catholic would not be subservient to Rome; in fact he opposed federal aid to parochial schools. Mass was observed in the White House only once — on the occasion of his funeral services.

WHO INITIATED THE BAY OF PIGS INVASION?

After Fidel Castro began to "sell out" his revolution to communism in 1959, increasing numbers of Cubans fled to the United States, especially Florida. Many of them yearned to take up arms and overthrow the new dictatorship before it could become too deeply entrenched. To this end they received much encouragement. Helping revolutionists to win freedom was in the American tradition — in fact, it went back to Cuba of the 1850s and 1890s.

The Central Intelligence Agency (CIA), emboldened by its success in toppling a pro-Communist regime in Guatemala in 1954, urged the equipping and training in Guatemala of a small army of Cuba-bound exiles, ultimately numbering some 1,400 men. President Eisenhower sanctioned the formation of this force in March 1960, without making a definite commitment as to its use. This was the explosive legacy that he left on the doorstep of the incoming Kennedy administration.[7]

New on the job, Kennedy was undecided what to do about the tiny and poorly trained invasion army. To abandon it would create delicate problems and evoke criticism from anti-Communist elements. To back it would lay the Republic open to charges of violating not only international law but also its own domestic law, the U.N. Charter, the principles of the Organization of American States, and Franklin Roosevelt's nonintervention pledge of 1933. Yet Kennedy was assured by some advisors that the expedition, which was supposed to trigger a popular uprising, had an excellent chance of succeeding. Certainly the overthrow of Castro would delight many Americans. After much hesitation, Kennedy finally gave the order to go ahead but with one crucial restriction: there was to be no *direct* intervention by the United States.

WAS KENNEDY RESPONSIBLE FOR THE CUBAN FIASCO?

Just about everything went wrong with the invasion. The presence of the Cuban army-in-exile was advertised months in advance by the press

---

[7] During the fourth Kennedy–Nixon debate in 1960, Kennedy had proposed strong action against Castro, while Nixon, who was vigorously supporting the proposed invasion in private, took the opposite tack, largely because he did not want to betray the clandestine operation. Nixon was angry because he believed that his rival, already secretly briefed about the mission, was taking unfair advantage of him. Nixon, *Six Crises*, pp. 352–355. Pro-Kennedy sources state that Kennedy was not informed of the scheme until November 18, 1960, 10 days after his election. Schlesinger, *A Thousand Days*, pp. 226–227.

of Guatemala and the United States. Castro was fully alerted.[8] There
were to have been three air strikes from Nicaragua by obsolescent American aircraft, allegedly flown by Cuban pilots. Kennedy cancelled the
second one after the partially effective first one caused an international
uproar, during which Adlai Stevenson, representing America in the U.N.,
unintentionally lied in denying his country's involvement. After the
invading exiles had floundered into a desperate position, Kennedy
ordered *direct* supportive intervention with six unmarked carrier aircraft,
but they arrived an hour too late to provide the needed cover and hence
did not get involved. The pathetic invaders, though unofficially assured
of active American support, were destroyed or captured, and Castro
emerged stronger than ever.

America's moral position was gravely damaged, all the more so
because it was tainted with failure. There is an old saying that a thief
might as well be hanged for a sheep as a lamb, and since the United
States was so deeply involved there was much to be said for going all
the way and attempting to guarantee success. In retrospect, we can see
that Castro was too strong militarily (some 200,000 militia), and that
the anticipated uprising of the Cuban populace to greet the invaders was
based on wishful thinking.[9] Only open and massive intervention by the
United States could have brought even temporary success to this venture — and such drastic action could have triggered dangerous reactions, including a possible Soviet seizure of West Berlin.

In planning the operation, the Central Intelligence Agency
miscalculated and bungled. President Eisenhower should never have
allowed the little army to be trained; President Kennedy's advisors who
had doubts should have expressed them more forcefully; and the Joint
Chiefs of Staff, who wanted a landing at Trinidad (some distance to the
east), should have been less acquiescent. Finally, the President was misled in adopting a policy of half in, half out. As we see it now, he should
have played for keeps or not at all; his so-called *indirect* intervention
was so deep as to amount to *direct* intervention. A few Americans were
killed in the invasion attempt.[10]

An inexperienced Kennedy, less than three months in office,

[8] On April 7, 1961, 10 days before the invasion, the New York *Times* published
a front-page story about the proposed incursion but excluded the "imminence" of the
blow. For a detailed discussion of the responsibilities of a great newspaper in this
kind of situation, see Turner Catledge, *My Life and the Times* (1971), Ch. XXII.

[9] In 1850 and again in 1851, the Venezuelan adventurer, Narciso López, had led
two filibustering expeditions (700 men and 500 men) from American soil against
Spain's Cuba in the expectation that the oppressed masses would assist him. They
too failed to rise.

[10] Richard J. Walton, *Cold War and Counterrevolution: The Foreign Policy of
John F. Kennedy* (1972), p. 50. This journalistic appraisal is highly critical.

accepted responsibility for the humiliating fiasco. "Victory has a thousand fathers," he sadly remarked, "and defeat is an orphan." In this case, Kennedy was the one man who could have stopped the expedition or could have ordered full support for it. He did neither, and the responsibility was his. Having campaigned on the pledge to get the country "moving" again and to restore the nation's fading prestige, he had staged a sorry demonstration of leadership in his first big test and had grievously damaged the national image.[11] America had seemingly resurrected the old policy of gunboat dollar imperialism, only ineptly so.[12]

WERE THE RUSSIAN NUCLEAR MISSILES IN CUBA DEFENSIVE?

On October 14, 1962, an American U-2 reconnaissance airplane over Cuba, checking on many rumors, secured some shocking photographs. They showed unmistakably that the Soviets were feverishly emplacing about forty nuclear-tipped missiles in Cuba, some of them medium range (about 1,000 miles), others intermediate range (about 2,000 miles). As President Kennedy grimly informed the nation on television, these lethal weapons could wreak fearful damage as far north as the Hudson's Bay in Canada and as far south as Lima, Peru. (So could Soviet-based missiles already emplaced in Russia.)

Following the Bay of Pigs fiasco in 1961, the Soviets had shipped immense quantities of conventional arms to Cuba's Fidel Castro, who understandably feared another incursion. But even while busily preparing to emplace the nuclear missiles, the Soviets, including Premier Khrushchev, had insisted that the only weapons being sent the Cubans were short-range and for purely defensive purposes.

The line between an offensive and a defensive weapon is often difficult to draw, and from the viewpoint of both the Soviets and the Cubans the nuclear weapons *were* defensive. When they were properly positioned, the Americans would not dare to invade Cuba lest many of

[11] On the day after the Cuban fiasco, Kennedy ordered a quick review of the Vietnam situation with a view to taking more effective action against the Communists. The next month he secretly ordered the commitment of 500 special troops and advisors. *Pentagon Papers*, pp. 79, 88. Kennedy may have sunk deeper into Vietnam in an effort to refurbish his image as a decisive leader.

[12] Schlesinger's *A Thousand Days* has a valuable insider's account of the Bay of Pigs fiasco. The author concludes (p. 297) that Kennedy's failure in Cuba in 1961 contributed to his "success" in Cuba during the Soviet missile crunch of 1962. On the other hand, the President's indecisiveness in 1961 probably emboldened the Soviets to challenge him in 1962. For an opinion on this point see Elie Abel, *The Missile Crisis* (1966), p. 37.

their major cities be wiped out in retaliation. But from the standpoint of Washington these missiles, by about doubling Russia's first-strike nuclear-missile capacity, were so disturbing to the existing distribution of power as to constitute an intolerable offensive threat. The United States, moreover, would not be able to take a strong position on the explosive Berlin issue and other hot spots if it feared a shower of nuclear warheads from an island off its coast — an island whose fate had been of real concern to its security for more than a century.[13]

WAS THE NUCLEAR CRISIS OVER CUBA NECESSARY?

Why the American intelligence agents were caught short will probably always remain something of a mystery. For one thing, the hurricane season delayed aerial reconnaissance. For another, the Soviets moved with astonishing secrecy and celerity.[14] Moreover, as was true of the Japanese on the eve of Pearl Harbor, official Washington could not imagine that the Soviets would be that stupid: their national interest clearly did not call for so costly and reckless a military gamble in America's backyard, where their enemy would have the immense advantage of nearness in a prolonged war over Cuba.

Kennedy's pressing problem was how to induce the Soviets to back down during the scant two weeks between the discovery of their plot and the emplacement of the first missiles. If a substantial number became operational, the United States, he felt, would either have to fight, with terrible destruction to itself, or accept a permanent threat, and learn to live with it.

Kennedy's key advisors comprised what was known as the informal Executive Committee — about sixteen men all told — and during the critical thirteen days they threshed over all possible options. To the very end some of the members, both civilian and military, favored immediate action to clean out the menace, either by an aerial "surgical strike" on the missile sites under construction or a formidable American

[13] The presence of Soviet weapons, technicians, and troops (some 20,000) in Cuba was evidently a violation of the original Monroe Doctrine, for President Monroe had stated in 1823 that "we should consider any attempt on their part [the European powers] to extend their [political] system to any portion of this hemisphere as dangerous to our peace and safety." But Kennedy did not invoke this ancient Doctrine, which was a bad memory to the Latin Americans and which would have generated arguments as to its applicability. After all, the Russians were invited guests. Instead, Kennedy relied on the more elemental right of self-defense, plus the Rio Pact, which was supported by 19 of the 20 Latin American nations in the Organization of American States.

[14] Roberta Wohlstetter, in "Cuba and Pearl Harbor: Hindsight and Foresight," *Foreign Affairs*, XLIII (1965), 698, concludes that "the rapidity of the installation was in effect a logistical surprise comparable to the technological surprise at the time of Pearl Harbor."

army (some 100,000 men) or both. But an aerial "Pearl Harbor in reverse" would no doubt have killed and wounded hundreds of Russian technicians and troops, perhaps thousands, and the Soviets could hardly have failed to react by seizing Berlin or otherwise triggering a nuclear holocaust. Kennedy rejected the "surgical strike" while opting for a land invasion of Cuba, if necessary.

One debated solution was a diplomatic deal with the Soviets. They loudly complained that the "Yankee imperialists" had ringed the USSR with missiles in neighboring Turkey and nearby Italy. Then how could the Americans reasonably object if they in turn were partially ringed with nuclear missiles in Cuba? Oddly enough, the Washington authorities had already concluded that America's Jupiter missiles in Turkey and Italy were obsolete; and Kennedy had issued orders to withdraw them. But, to his anger, they were not carried out. It seems entirely probable that Khrushchev, seeking a face-saving exit once his daring scheme was exposed, would have jumped at this chance to work out some kind of swap; in fact, he proposed a mutual withdrawal of missiles from Turkey and Cuba, accompanied by a noninvasion guarantee for Cuba by the U. S. and for Turkey by the USSR.[15] But Kennedy, with the backing of his Executive Committee, rejected such a concession as an act of weakness that would dishearten Turkey, Italy, and the other NATO allies. He therefore pursued a hard line which came within a hair's breadth of a nuclear annihilation.[16]

The United States, if averse to a mutual swap, could in any event have "lived" with the Cubanized Soviet missiles, which would still have left the Americans with a heavy superiority in such weapons. Often overlooked is the fact that Soviet intercontinental ballistic missiles, supplemented by nuclear explosives that could be fired off American shores from Russian submarines, had been targeted on the United States for several years. Moreover the American people continued to live under a growing nuclear shadow that proved to be far more ominous than that projected by Moscow for Cuba.

Yet there can be no doubt that the nation's credibility as a party to some forty defense pacts would have been gravely weakened if Kennedy had backed down under the nuclear gun. Political considerations of an international and domestic nature, including the upcoming

[15] Robert F. Kennedy, *Thirteen Days: A Memoir of the Cuban Missile Crisis* (1969), pp. 199–200 (Khrushchev's letter of Oct. 26, 1962).

[16] There were many observers in England and the United States, including pundit Walter Lippmann, who strongly favored a mutual missile swap as a reasonable solution. Schlesinger, *A Thousand Days*, p. 827. Before Khrushchev yielded, the Soviet ambassador in Washington was quietly informed by Kennedy's brother that the U. S. was planning to remove the Jupiter missiles from Turkey and Italy, and in this sense Khrushchev received an informal *quid pro quo*. Kennedy, *Thirteen Days*, pp. 108–109.

Congressional elections, were in some respect more compelling than the military ones; taken together they explain why the President was prepared to go "to the brink" in squeezing the Soviet missiles out of Cuba.

WHY DID RUSSIA PROVOKE THE CUBAN CRISIS?

The response adopted by Kennedy was to establish a naval blockade of Cuba and warn off any Soviet vessels carrying "offensive" weapons or equipment. Because a blockade is normally an act of war, Kennedy chose the softer word "quarantine," thereby leaving his military options open and avoiding the moral odium of a sneak attack. The crucial question was: would the Soviets honor or challenge the American interdiction? Many of their oncoming vessels turned back; a few, not carrying offensive weapons, were allowed to go through.

Meanwhile, assisted by the mediation of the U.N., Khrushchev and Kennedy worked out a face-saving deal. The Russians would pull out their nuclear weapons from Cuba in return for an end to the "quarantine" and a pledge by the United States not to invade Cuba. America's acceptance of this arrangement was conditional upon U.N. inspectors personally verifying the withdrawal, but an angered and humiliated Fidel Castro refused them permission to set foot on Cuban soil. Technically the United States was thus released from its commitment, although it finally acquiesced in the settlement after verification by aerial reconnaissance. On November 20, some three weeks after the crisis had passed, the "quarantine" was lifted.

Moscow's official line at the time was that the Soviets had won a stunning triumph. Khrushchev heaps praise on himself in his purported memoirs for this "spectacular success," though conceding that he was "obliged to make some big concessions in the interests of peace "[17] He consistently claimed at the time and later that the Russians were only trying to save their good friends, the Cubans, from a "piratical" Yankee incursion. As soon as Moscow won its point by securing a no-invasion commitment from Kennedy, Khrushchev declared, it had no publicly avowed reason to keep the missiles in Cuba. So the Russians could withdraw, while posing as the champions of peace and rejoicing over their earth-shaking achievement.

This made-in-Moscow explanation is unconvincing.[18] So far as can be ascertained, the Soviets had not previously emplaced nuclear

---

[17] *Khrushchev Remembers* (1970), pp. 499, 504. There is conflicting testimony as to whether Castro or Khrushchev first proposed the missile scheme.
[18] Adam Ulam brands it "fantastic" and "mendacious." *Expansion and Coexistence: The History of Soviet Foreign Policy, 1917–1967* (1968), p. 669.

missiles in any of their European buffer satellites under the Warsaw Pact, or for that matter in adjoining China. (Perhaps they feared that such weapons might be turned around and fired the wrong way.) Cuba was not deemed essential to the defense of the Soviet Union, as were neighboring Poland, Czechoslovakia, and other nearby nations. For Moscow to incur grave risks and spend hundreds of millions of rubles to bolster a faraway and recent convert to communism that meant nothing to Russia's basic security bespoke a lack of realism uncharacteristic of the Kremlin.

Cuba was clearly in no real danger of invasion, at least not until this crisis developed — a crisis deliberately provoked by Moscow. The United States had its chance to overthrow Castro at the time of the Bay of Pigs, and burned its fingers while keeping hands off. But it did continue to use the weapon of economic boycott. During the subsequent year and one-half, Castro's army, the second largest in the Western Hemisphere, had been greatly strengthened with generous supplies of conventional Soviet weapons.[19] American military men estimated that some 25,000 to 40,000 casualties would be incurred by the invaders in the proposed invasion, which was only a day or so off when Khrushchev knuckled under.

The Soviets, caught with their missiles down, no doubt suffered a humiliating setback, as the skeptical Chinese Communists pointed out with malicious glee. An embittered Castro thought so too. Moscow's official line was the one best calculated to save face: the Soviets had undertaken to safeguard a "heroic little Cuba" and had accomplished this end. The probabilities are that they had set out primarily to strengthen their position in the Cold War by placing Uncle Sam even more menacingly under the threat of nuclear missiles. No other explanation makes much sense.[20] Two years later, when Premier Khrushchev was sacked

[19] In his correspondence with Kennedy, the Soviet Premier had referred to sporadic "piratical" attacks on Cuban shores by a few vessels evidently coming from the United States. If this was what really worried Khrushchev, the appropriate and inexpensive response would have been to provide Castro with some speedy defensive naval craft. A Soviet guarantee to defend Cuba with nuclear weapons would have served essentially the same end; in fact Khrushchev had publicly made such a promise earlier.

[20] The editor of *Khrushchev Remembers* refers to the chapter (20) on the Cuban crisis as "perhaps the most open, coherent, and circumstantial" part of these purported memoirs. He accepts Khrushchev's declaration of motivation — that is, to save Cuba from threatened invasion — and concludes that he "achieved what he set out to do." The following Khrushchev statements are either demonstrably false or highly dubious: that another Yankee-backed invasion was in the cards before the crisis developed; that enough of the missiles had become operational to destroy Washington, New York, Chicago, and other "huge industrial cities"; that the Russian people were kept "fully informed" about the crisis; that Robert Kennedy, "almost crying," feared a coup by the generals; that the United States demanded a U.N. inspection *after* Khrushchev agreed to withdraw the missiles; and that the United States bound both itself and all other nations not to invade Cuba.

and made an "unperson," one of the charges brought against him was that his reckless Cuban gamble had brought danger and humiliation to the Soviet Union.

WAS THE NUCLEAR TEST BAN TREATY EFFECTIVE?

For several years the Americans and the British, both stockpiling nuclear weapons, had been urging a ban on air-poisoning atmospheric tests. The Soviets had not warmed to such a pact, but in July 1963, Moscow expressed a desire to negotiate. What its motives were can only be surmised. Russian scientists had recently completed a series of exceptionally "dirty" tests, and the Kremlin may have felt that a ban on testing would bring strong moral pressure to bear on France, and particularly China, not to persist with their development of nuclear weapons. Communists and non-Communists both breathed the same air.

Negotiations proceeded rapidly in Moscow. In August 1963 the British, Americans, and Russians signed the partial nuclear test ban treaty. It was subsequently ratified, with considerable misgivings in the United States, by the three signatories and subsequently adhered to by many other nations.[21] By its terms the participating powers bound themselves not to test nuclear devices in the atmosphere, in outer space, or under the water. Underground testing, which presumably would not spew radioactivity into the air, was permissible, and any one of the signatories could back out after three months' notice if troubled by "extraordinary events."

The high hopes entertained for the treaty were disappointed. France and China, both of which refused to sign, pushed ahead with atmospheric testing, as the Americans, British, and Russians had previously done. Large-scale and accelerated explosions continued underground in Russia and the United States. Stocks of nuclear weapons were not destroyed or decreased; the fearfully costly race in armaments expanded. Other nations, if they had the will and the technical capacity, could join the nuclear club uninvited, as China did in 1964. About the only tangible result was that the atmosphere was less radioactive than it would have been if the signatories had not gone underground. This in

[21] The myth that the Soviets never keep an international agreement was a major argument against ratification. Although Moscow has broken a number of agreements (in its eyes with justification), it has honored many others from which it derived advantages. A Department of State memorandum listed 27. *Nuclear Test Ban Treaty: Hearings before the Committee on Foreign Relations, U.S. Senate,* 88 Cong., 1 sess. (1963), pp. 967–968.

itself was a substantial gain. But the diplomatic atmosphere between Moscow and Washington continued strained, even though the test-ban treaty was the first pact in 18 years that the West had been able to conclude with the Soviets regarding the control of nuclear weaponry.

WHO KILLED PRESIDENT KENNEDY?

On November 22, 1963, while riding in an open limousine in Dallas, Texas, Kennedy was killed by bullets fired from a telescopically equipped rifle aimed from the upper levels of a nearby building. The alleged assassin, Lee Harvey Oswald, was quickly seized, for the circumstantial evidence pointed overwhelmingly to him. Two days later, before Oswald could confess or explain the reasons for his crime, he was shot and killed by a self-appointed avenger, Jack Ruby, an emotionally unstable local nightclub operator with an unsavory reputation.

Rumors of a complicated conspiracy immediately began to circulate. Oswald, with strong leanings toward Marxism, had married a Soviet woman, had lived in Russia from 1956 to 1962, and evidently was connected with the pro-Castro Fair Play for Cuba Committee. Conspiratorial-minded people, both in America and abroad, could easily imagine that he was merely the hatchet man for the plotters of Moscow or Havana. Such suspicions were deepened by the counterassassination of Oswald by Ruby, who conceivably was acting under orders to silence Kennedy's killer before a confession could be wrung from him.

In these circumstances a thorough investigation by a prestigious body was called for, and President Lyndon Johnson appointed such a group a week after the assassination. Headed by Chief Justice Warren, it consisted of two prominent Senators (one Democrat and one Republican) and two prominent Representatives (one Democrat and one Republican), plus Allen Dulles, former head of the Central Intelligence Agency, and John J. McCloy, former Assistant Secretary of War. The investigation consumed nine months and resulted in a lengthy summary report, September 24, 1964,[22] supplemented by some twenty volumes of evidence (about 500 pages each) for possible later publication. Included was the testimony of eyewitnesses, of experts on firearms and ballistics, and of medical authorities. The main conclusions were that Oswald acted "alone and without advice or assistance," and that Jack Ruby was not

---

[22] *The Official Warren Commission Report on the Assassination of President John F. Kennedy* (1964).

part of "any conspiracy, domestic or foreign." The Commission, unable to find any satisfactory motivation for Oswald's crime, could present only suppositions.

Americans generally accepted the Warren Report, but many citizens and a host of foreigners retained their initial suspicions. The official explanations seemed all too simple. A number of books and articles were soon forthcoming to advance the thesis that Oswald was only the "fall guy" in an elaborate conspiracy and that rifle fire occurred simultaneously from different positions. The Warren Report was perhaps too hastily compiled, for there were some inherent inconsistencies. As is almost invariably true when there are many eyewitnesses, some will contradict others. It was all too easy to seize upon dubious testimony (rejected for good reason by the Commission) which seemed to prove the points critics were trying to make. Even so, the main conclusions of the Warren Report seem not to have been invalidated, despite the efforts of sensation mongers.[23]

WAS KENNEDY UNUSUALLY
SUCCESSFUL IN DOMESTIC AFFAIRS?

The tragic circumstances of Kennedy's death, as was true of Lincoln's, tended to maximize his successes and minimize his failures.

Despite much ballyhoo, the New Frontier program was not a resounding success. Kennedy prodded Congress rather than led it, and that body was refractory. Although the President had a nominal Democratic majority, the Democratic conservatives, generally from the South, joined hands with the Republican conservatives to defeat or delay much of his key social and economic legislation, including tax reform and Medicare. Much of what was actually passed had been largely re-written or watered down by Congress.[24] Ten days before Kennedy's death the New York *Times* concluded, "This has been one of the least productive sessions of Congress within the memory of most of the members." Yet an assassination-jarred Congress, under President Johnson's arm-twisting leadership, enacted an extraordinary body of legisla-

[23] There is a human tendency to reject the obvious explanation in such tragic affairs. One has only to recall the rumors that persisted regarding the escape of Lincoln's assassin and the death of Adolf Hitler. In 1969, Clay L. Shaw was brought to trial in New Orleans as an alleged part of the Oswald conspiracy; actually, the Warren Report was in the dock. The jury deliberated only fifty minutes before unanimously acquitting the defendant.

[24] Jim F. Heath, *John F. Kennedy and the Business Community* (1969), pp. 123–124.

tion, much of which no doubt would have been passed in due time without this tragic stimulus. And one must not forget that under Kennedy Congress enacted a respectable body of more or less routine measures. It also passed a few major bills, including the highly significant Trade Expansion Act (1962), which clothed the President with unusual powers to cut tariff rates.

Kennedy has been criticized for failing to anticipate the Black Revolution, which burst about his head, conspicuously with the riots at the University of Mississippi over the admission in 1962 of the first black student, James Meredith. Here again Kennedy was hampered by Congress. He dared not offend the Southern members by pressing for Negro rights — that is, if he hoped to secure the key reform measures of the New Frontier. But by executive action, which involved the appointment of a few blacks to federal office, he attempted to dampen some of the pressures that were developing.

DID KENNEDY SUCCEED IN FOREIGN AFFAIRS?

As a diplomatist, Kennedy compiled a spotty record. The immature young President got off to an incredibly bad start with the Bay of Pigs blunder. Later in 1961 he journeyed to Vienna for a meeting with Khrushchev, who sobered the youthful leader with his bellicose stand on most burning issues, including Berlin. When Khrushchev threatened to turn that controversial city over to the East Germans, Kennedy reacted — perhaps overreacted — by calling up the reserves. The next Soviet move was suddenly to erect a wall or barricade between East and West Germany, as a means of halting the exodus to freedom. Kennedy has been condemned for not having pushed the wall over with American tanks, but such a drastic response would almost certainly have provoked countermeasures that might well have touched off World War III.

When the Cuban missile crisis came in October 1962, Kennedy emerged with colors flying. But there might have been no such crisis if he had not impressed Khrushchev with his weakness at the time of the Bay of Pigs or if his administration had been more vigilant. As previously indicated, there were diplomatic alternatives to the reckless eyeball-to-eyeball confrontation. And Castro remained angry, defiant, and more deeply entrenched than before.

Kennedy was unsuccessful in his Grand Design for the commercial and military unification of Western Europe, with America as the senior partner. His plan probably would have been blocked in any event by the imperious and nationalistic President de Gaulle of France, but Kennedy's separate negotiations with Britain, to the exclusion of France, did nothing to mollify the touchy French leader.

America's deepening involvement in Vietnam boded ill for the future (see next chapter). Truman had sent financial aid to the French to help them fight their Vietnamese rebels; Eisenhower had provided military assistance, money, and some 700 military advisors; Kennedy, in fateful decisions reached in 1961, undertook to swell the American contingent, who numbered about 16,000 at the time of his death. Whether he would have sunk in as deeply as his successor, Lyndon Johnson, is a matter for debate.[25] But if the dam had begun to break, as it did in 1964–1965, he could not have easily turned tail with this many American military men involved. One should also remember that the hawkish advisers whom President Johnson had at his elbow — Secretary Dean Rusk, Secretary McNamara, McGeorge Bundy, Walt W. Rostow, and others — were the same men whom Kennedy had as his counselors. As events turned out, the alternatives were a humiliating retreat or a widening war.

WAS KENNEDY A "GREAT" OR "NEAR GREAT" PRESIDENT?

The untimely death of this handsome, charming, and idealistic young leader, cut down in his prime, led to an amazing outpouring of grief and affection, not only at home but all over the world. His "Thousand Days" (actually 1,037) were regarded as but a foretaste of finer things to come during the succeeding more than five years. His reelection in 1964 seemed reasonably certain, and he surely would have achieved a second term if Senator Barry M. Goldwater had been the Republican nominee, as he proved to be.

A legend of Lincolnian greatness and of outstanding achievement rapidly developed. Theodore C. Sorensen, Kennedy's intimate associate and major speech writer, wrote appreciatively that "the man was greater than the legend" and that he could not be ranked below "any of the great men who have held the presidency in this century." [26] (This would

---

[25] In November 1963, shortly after the assassination of President Ngo Dinh Diem of South Vietnam and shortly before his own assassination, Kennedy appeared to Arthur M. Schlesinger, Jr. as greatly depressed. He had handled Vietnam as "a political rather than a military problem. . . . No doubt he realized that Vietnam was his great failure in foreign policy, and that he had never really given it his full attention." Schlesinger, *A Thousand Days*, pp. 997–998. *The Pentagon Papers* (pp. 113–114) neither blame nor exculpate Kennedy for the deepening crisis.

[26] Theodore C. Sorensen, *Kennedy* (1965), p. 758. For the pitfalls involved in comparing presidential unlikes, see T. A. Bailey, *Presidential Greatness* (1966); for Kennedy, see pp. 328–331.

include Woodrow Wilson and Franklin Roosevelt, who served eight and twelve years respectively.) Arthur M. Schlesinger, Jr., a prominent historian and White House intimate, cautiously refrained from such dubious comparisons but boldly employed sweeping generalizations:

> Yet he had accomplished so much: the new hope for peace on earth, the elimination of nuclear testing in the atmosphere and the abolition of nuclear diplomacy, the new policies toward Latin America and the third world, the reordering of American defense, the emancipation of the American Negro, the revolution in national economic policy, the concern for poverty, the stimulus to the arts, the fight for reason against extremism and mythology.[27]

Upon careful analysis, this list is actually less impressive than it first seems. The "new hope for peace" was at best fleeting, and the Cold War continued to get hotter. "Nuclear testing in the atmosphere" was not eliminated: France and China continued with their dirty-air experiments. "Nuclear diplomacy" was not abolished; diplomacy continued to be backed by nuclear weapons, which have increased in number and potency every year since Kennedy took office. The "new policy toward Latin America" was the Alliance for Progress, which consisted of costly financial help in the interests of reducing poverty and inequity. This scheme fell far short of expectations primarily because the wealthy groups were unwilling to promote a redistribution of wealth. The "third world," including Latin America, clearly benefited from a Peace Corps consisting mostly of idealistic young American technicians and teachers who went out to "underdeveloped" countries to help the people improve their lot. Kennedy borrowed both the terminology and the idea,[28] which proved to be a resounding success, and a relatively inexpensive one at that.

Under Kennedy there occurred, as Professor Arthur M. Schlesinger states, a "reordering of American defense" by a shift from massive nuclear retaliation to a "balanced" military force capable of providing a "flexible response." But this meant that troops were available for Vietnam when the temptation grew strong to intervene. The American Negro was not "emancipated" and remains only partially free to this day. The "revolution in national economic policy" took place only in the sense that there were significant shifts, including a commitment to deficit financing by a reduction of taxes in the face of a heavily unbalanced budget. This legislation was not passed, however, until after the President's death. Kennedy no doubt had a "concern for poverty," but

27 Schlesinger, *A Thousand Days*, p. 1030.
28 For the origins see William Safire, *The New Language of Politics* (1968), pp. 325–326.

the expensive War on Poverty, begun on a large scale under Johnson, resulted in a victory for poverty. The New Frontiersmen certainly provided a "stimulus to the arts" and a "fight for reason against extremism," but the gains in both these areas were less than epochal.

This is not to say that there were not substantial achievements, including legislative. To have come out of the Cuban crisis of 1962 without nuclear incineration was, as events shaped up, to Kennedy's credit. The teletype "Hot Line" was subsequently established between Moscow and Washington to facilitate instant communication in critical situations. The program designed to put a man on the moon before the end of the decade, Project Apollo, was carried through with spectacular success in 1969, at a cost of some $24 billion.

Kennedy planted seeds of hope but did not live to reap the harvest. He was as much a promise of a President as he was a President; one fellow Harvard admirer wrote that he was great not for what he did but for "what he was about to do." A man of both ideas and ideals, he developed a distinctive "style" and grew visibly before his people. The personal and national tragedy lay in his being cut down after receiving his expensive on-the-job training and before he had a full opportunity to attain his far-reaching goals.

ADDITIONAL GENERAL REFERENCES

A. M. Schlesinger, Jr., A Thousand Days (1965); T. C. Sorensen, Kennedy (1965) and The Kennedy Legacy (1969); Roger Hilsman, To Move a Nation (1967); Tad Szulc and K. E. Meyer, The Cuban Invasion (1962); Elie Abel, The Missile Crisis (1966); R. F. Kennedy, Thirteen Days (1969); M. L. King, Jr., Why We Can't Wait (1964); William Brink and Louis Harris, The Negro Revolution in America (1964); Archibald Cox, The Warren Court: Constitutional Decision as an Instrument of Reform (1968); C. A. Bain, Vietnam: The Roots of Conflict (1967); G. M. Kahin and J. W. Lewis, The United States in Vietnam (rev. ed., 1969).

40

The Ordeal of
Lyndon Johnson

*Kept on a back seat as Vice President, Lyndon Johnson burst into full
view as President. As a skilled legislative leader with a social conscience,
he had an obsessive desire to attain the stature of the man he called his
political "daddy," Franklin Roosevelt. Applying unremitting pressures
on Congress, he secured the enactment of an impressive number of
measures that had been bottlenecked under President Kennedy.*

*In the presidential election of 1964, Johnson overwhelmed the
right-wing Republican candidate, Barry M. Goldwater, and won endorsement in his own right. Seeking a catch phrase like the "New Deal," he
seized upon "The Great Society"* [1] *for his program of social and economic
betterment. Congress, lopsidedly Democratic as a result of the recent
elections, responded to the lash of his leadership by turning out an impressive stack of bills. The frenzied pace slowed down to a walk after
1966, when the resurgent Republicans sharply narrowed the Democratic
majority in Congress.*

*Johnson's management of foreign affairs was much less satisfac-
tory. Politically sensitive to the cry of "soft on Communism," he hastily
landed troops in the revolution-torn Dominican Republic in 1965 in an
effort to avert a Castrolike coup. This reversal of noninterventionism,
as proclaimed in 1933 under Franklin Roosevelt, was a violation of*

---

[1] The phrase was evidently picked up by Richard Goodwin, a Johnson speech-
writer, who may have been influenced by a book, *The Great Society* (1914), published by an English Fabian Socialist, Graham Wallas. William Safire, *The New
Language of Politics* (1968), pp. 174–175.

various international commitments. It consequently aroused violent criticism among liberals in general and Latin Americans in particular. But the crisis soon passed and American troops were withdrawn.

Vietnam proved to be Johnson's undoing. Committed by his predecessors to support a dictatorial anti-Communist regime in South Vietnam, he gradually escalated the conflict to immense proportions in the hope of forcing the Communist enemy to the peace table. With antiwar or "dovish" sentiment in America growing more violent and disruptive, he declined to run again in 1968. On the eve of the election he announced a cessation of all bombing of North Vietnam, in the hope of starting meaningful peace negotiations. This last-minute concession was not quite enough to save the Democrats, whose nominee for the presidency, Hubert H. Humphrey, was narrowly defeated by the Republican challenger, Richard M. Nixon.

WAS NORTH VIETNAM
BOTH NATIONALIST AND COMMUNIST?

For about 800 unhappy years, commencing with the second century A.D., Chinese overlords imposed their rule on what is now Vietnam. Then, beginning about 939 A.D., and for approximately the next 900 years, the Vietnamese freed themselves from foreign control. Subsequent fears in the Western world that North Vietnam would throw itself into the arms of Communist China did not take fully into account the tenacity of Vietnamese nationalism and a millennium-long hatred for the Chinese. Some Western students of Southeast Asia concluded that a Communist Vietnam would add little or no strength to the Communist camp, but would create further dissension by providing a Yugoslav-type of Communist-nationalism (Titoism), subservient to neither Peking nor Moscow.[2]

New threats to Vietnamese independence came in the 1850s and 1860s, when imperial France, following the murder of some French Catholic missionaries, seized a substantial part of southern Vietnam. The intruders widened this foothold in the 1880s by establishing control over the northern area.[3] Resistance to French domination gained ground with the proclamation of self-determination, so eloquently advocated by Woodrow Wilson and others during World War I.[4] But the Vietnamese

[2] There was reason to believe that Moscow supported North Vietnam in the Vietnam War after 1954 partly in the hope of "containing" rival Peking.

[3] French Indochina at its peak embraced Vietnam, Laos, and Cambodia.

[4] Ho Chi Minh, later leader of North Vietnam, was in Paris in 1919 at the time of the Peace Conference. He addressed a memorandum to the Great Powers (including

uprisings of 1917 and the 1930s were ruthlessly crushed. Significantly, the most effective opponents of French imperialism were the Communists, into whose camp many Vietnamese nationalists naturally gravitated.

In 1940–1941, during World War II, the Japanese invaded Vietnam and forced the Vichy French regime to grant them valuable military privileges. The Vietnamese nationalist-Communists, led by Ho Chi Minh and taking the name of Vietminh in 1941, waged a sporadic guerrilla warfare against both the French and the Japanese. American agents not only encouraged the Vietminh to resist the common foe, but provided aid and led them to believe that the United States sanctioned their struggle for independence. Such assurances were bolstered by Roosevelt's declaration of self-determination in the Atlantic Charter and by American radio broadcasts.

When World War II ended in 1945, the Paris government, with General Charles De Gaulle as provisional president,[5] had an excellent opportunity to cut loose from its Indochina empire. (The British and Dutch, under pressure from Washington, liquidated vast holdings in Asia.) But the French decided to hang on, partly for reasons of prestige and economic gain, and partly for fear that independence would provide an incendiary example to their valuable holdings in North Africa. The Washington government, desiring a French ally in Europe to hold back Communist Russia, was reluctant to antagonize Paris by persistent demands for a free Indochina. With France thus determined to remain, a clash was bound to occur, as it did, amid charges of broken promises. War began on a full scale in November 1946, when the French fleet bombarded Haiphong, killing some 6,000 North Vietnamese civilians.

WAS SELF-DETERMINATION
THE U. S. CONCERN IN VIETNAM?

Before 1949 Washington had shown relatively little interest in Vietnam, other than urging the French to grant the Vietnamese their independence. But 1949 marked a turning point. Late that year the Soviets exploded their first large atomic device. In December the Communists completely engulfed mainland China, as Generalissimo Chiang Kai-shek fled to last-hope Taiwan. In February 1950 the Communist Russians and the Com-

the U. S.) urging that Wilson's principles of self-determination be applied to Vietnam. His pleas went unheeded.

[5] It is ironical that De Gaulle, himself largely responsible for the Indochina war, later condemned the United States for fighting in Vietnam.

munist Chinese concluded a thirty-year mutual defense treaty, and in June 1950 the North Korean Communists lunged into South Korea in a bold attempt to unite the entire country under their banner.

All this seemed to be proof of a great Communist "monolith" striving to take over the entire world. In May 1950, the month before the North Korean incursion into South Korea, the Truman administration authorized the first considerable economic aid to the French in Vietnam. On June 27, two days after the Korean onslaught, Washington announced the dispatching of a thirty-five-man Military Assistance Advisory Group (MAAG) to Vietnam, the first of a gradually increasing number, to instruct the anti-Communist Vietnamese in the use of American weapons. Such advisors were not formal combat units — these did not come until some fifteen years later — but they inevitably suffered casualties. Their first injuries were reported in October 1957; their first fatalities in July 1959. American financial grants to France for the war in Vietnam totaled hundreds of millions of dollars, and rose to over $1 billion for the fiscal year 1954, or about 80 percent of the current cost of the conflict to the French.[6]

Thus America's obsessive fear of the mythical Communist "monolith" led to a deepening involvement which flew in the face of tradition. The Americans had once been subject peoples, fighting to be free from imperial control, with the aid of French allies. The United States, with Woodrow Wilson and Franklin Roosevelt as eloquent spokesmen, had long been associated with self-determination and the end of colonialism. In Vietnam the United States, far from helping a colonial people to be free, was supporting with much money and a few men the efforts of France to subjugate some 25 million unwilling people. Ironical indeed is the fact that when the Democratic Republic of [North] Vietnam issued a declaration of independence in 1945, it followed the style of the American Declaration of 1776 and incorporated verbatim a part of its preamble. In the eyes of many Vietnamese, Ho Chi Minh was a George Washington.

WAS VIETNAM "PARTITIONED" AT GENEVA?

By 1954 the tide of battle was running heavily against the French in the Vietnam war. They had lost control of about three-fourths of the country, although they still maintained several hundred thousand men

---

[6] G. M. Kahin and J. W. Lewis, *The United States in Vietnam* (rev. ed., 1969), p. 32.

under arms, mostly loyal Vietnamese, and held a number of the most important cities. A crushing blow fell when some 12,000 men were trapped in a prolonged siege at Dien Bien Phu, in northwestern Vietnam, and forced to surrender, May 7, 1954.

Simultaneously a multipower conference was meeting in Paris for the purpose of ending the war. Ho Chi Minh's Vietminh were confident of controlling the entire country after another year of hard fighting, while the French were eager to cut loose and emerge without undue loss of face. Pressure was evidently applied to the Vietminh by their Communist friends, Russia and China, to accept a political rather than a military settlement. Continued fighting might well bring America into the war, as it ultimately did, and neither the Chinese nor the Russians, remembering Korea, welcomed this eventuality.

At Geneva in 1954 the French and the Vietminh (The Democratic Republic of Vietnam) formally signed a bilateral agreement to end hostilities and also approved the Final Declaration. In essence these two documents provided that the war should stop and that a *temporary* line of demarcation should be run about midway through Vietnam, roughly along the 17th parallel. (This was not a formal partitioning of Vietnam, as often stated, but a purely provisional division for withdrawals of troops and other administrative purposes, and was understood to be such.) The Vietminh troops would withdraw to the north of this line, and the French troops, with their loyalist allies, to the south, concurrently with the voluntary interchange of populations. (Some 900,000 refugees, mostly Roman Catholics, went south.)[7] "Free general elections by secret ballot" were to be held in July 1956, to determine the political composition of *all* Vietnam under one government.[8]

In addition to signatories France and the Democratic Republic of [North] Vietnam, the understandings at Geneva in 1954 were agreed to orally by the USSR, Red China, Britain, Laos, and Cambodia. Official Washington, alarmed by these gains for the Communist juggernaut and fearing the adverse effects of a "Munich" on the Congressional elections of 1954, declined to approve the Geneva Agreements. A similar course was followed by the State of [South] Vietnam, already erected by the French under their weak puppet Bao Dai, with his capital at Saigon. But

---

[7] A considerable number of Catholics remained, while some Vietnamese in the south moved north. The Catholic newcomers to South Vietnam, many of whom had fought for the French against the Vietminh, were widely regarded as carpetbaggers and caused much resentment when they secured influence and position in the government disproportionate to their numbers. Marshal Ky, a Catholic and later Premier and Vice President, had fought for the French.

[8] One should note that "North Vietnam" and "South Vietnam" never became the official names of the Democratic Republic of Vietnam and the Republic of Vietnam.

the official American spokesman at Geneva formally declared that the United States would "refrain from the threat or use of force to disturb" the agreements. Nevertheless, he asserted, Washington would view with "grave concern" any renewal of aggression.[9]

WHY WERE THE 1956 ELECTIONS NEVER HELD?

The so-called *Pentagon Papers*, filched from the Pentagon in Washington and sensationally published by *The New York Times* in 1971, reveal that the National Security Council viewed the Geneva settlement as a "disaster" for the free world. Official Washington, despite its hands-off pledge, regarded Vietnam as two nations, contrary to the specific intent of the Geneva Conference. Moreover, American policy actively supported the emergence of the Republic of [South] Vietnam with money and military aid. "South Vietnam," the anonymous writer for the Pentagon concluded, "was essentially the creation of the United States."[10]

Far from refraining from force, as pledged, Washington began secret operations against the Vietminh in June 1954, while the Geneva Conference was still in session. A team of special agents contaminated the oil supply of buses in Hanoi, the capital of North Vietnam, so that the engines would be ruined, and also sabotaged a railroad.[11] If it is true, as probable, that the North Vietnamese were engaged in similar clandestine activity while the Geneva Conference was in session, then both sides were performing acts of aggression even before the agreements were ever whipped into final form and accepted.[12]

The Vietminh clearly felt that they had won at the Geneva conference table what they could have won by another year or so of warfare. Otherwise they would not have consented to these terms. They were counting on "free general elections" being held in July 1956, as stipulated, for they seemed certain to win. They already controlled the populous North; they had a popular war hero and liberator (Ho Chi

[9] In September 1954 Secretary of State Dulles, seeking to counter the gains of Communism at Geneva and fearing the political repercussions of the outcry "Who lost Indochina?" fashioned the Southeast Asia Treaty Organization (SEATO) as a weak defensive shield. Included were the U. S., Britain, France, Australia, New Zealand, the Philippines, Thailand, and Pakistan. Later the United States dubiously interpreted SEATO as obligating the United States to come to the military aid of South Vietnam, but three of the signatories did not: Britain, France, and Pakistan. Kahin and Lewis, *The U. S. in Vietnam*, pp. 61–63.

[10] *The Pentagon Papers As Published by the New York Times* (1971), p. 25.

[11] *Ibid.*, pp. 15–16.

[12] *Ibid.*, p. 67.

Minh) to put up against the flabby Bao Dai. President Eisenhower later wrote that if the elections had occurred *at the time of the Geneva Conference*, the Communists would have received 80 percent of the vote.[13]

The elections were never held, primarily because the government in South Vietnam feared they would not be "free" but more likely because they were almost certain to be won by the Communists. Washington, still attempting to hold the dike against communism, encouraged the anti-Communist Saigon government in its refusal and provided heavy financial support.[14] The Hanoi regime in North Vietnam naturally felt betrayed; and this largely explains why thereafter it showed scant interest in another Geneva Conference.

HOW BINDING WAS THE
U. S. COMMITMENT TO SOUTH VIETNAM?

Late in 1954 an unexpectedly strong anti-Communist leader emerged in South Vietnam as prime minister, Ngo Dinh Diem. The next year he managed to depose Bao Dai, the Chief of the State of [South] Vietnam, and become president of the newly named Republic of [South] Vietnam, on the basis of an obviously rigged election (98.2 percent favorable). As a Roman Catholic strongly backed by Washington, Diem flatly rebuffed all attempts to hold the unification elections of 1956 or even to negotiate about them.[15] He argued that his recently created country had not approved the Geneva Accords, and that conditions for genuinely free elections must be demonstrated first by North Vietnam.

On October 1, 1954, responding to an appeal from the then Prime Minister Diem for help, President Eisenhower wrote a memorable letter in which he promised assistance, contingent upon "needed reforms" being undertaken. (They were never satisfactorily achieved under Diem.) The wording of the letter was rather ambiguous, and it contained no clear-cut promise of military support. But Eisenhower

[13] Italics inserted. D. D. Eisenhower, *Mandate for Change, 1953–1956* (1963), p. 372. Many readers have doubted this statement because they were thinking of Ho being pitted against Bao Dai's more popular successor, Ngo Dinh Diem.

[14] *Pentagon Papers*, pp. 21–25.

[15] Ngo Dinh Diem, of a prominent Roman Catholic family that had supported the French regime, fell into political disfavor and spent the years 1950 to 1954 abroad, mostly in the United States. He lobbied for American support, met Senator John F. Kennedy, and won the enthusiastic backing of Cardinal Spellman. How influential Catholic pressure proved to be in determining subsequent American intervention cannot be determined, but there can be no doubt that much concern was felt in the United States for those hundreds of thousands of Catholics in Vietnam who faced possible liquidation by victorious Communists. See Kahin and Lewis, *The United States in Vietnam*, p. 66n.

undertook to dispatch large quantities of military hardware and a few more military advisors, ultimately about 700, to help train the South Vietnamese army. Secretary Dulles, contrary to the spirit of the Geneva Accords, questionably invoked his brainchild, the Southeast Asia Treaty Organization, to support South Vietnam.

President Kennedy, at one stage acting secretly, fatefully expanded the commitment of his predecessor in 1961; by the time of his assassination in 1963 he had increased the American noncombat contingent to about 16,000 men. But the Communists continued to gain. In the same month as Kennedy's own assassination, President Diem and his brother were murdered in a military coup brought on by nepotism, corruption, greed, police-state repression, lack of needed reforms ("Diemocracy"), opposition by the numerous Buddhists, and growing resistance by Communist South Vietnam guerrillas known as the Viet Cong. Washington was so visibly relieved to be rid of Diem as to arouse suspicions, fully supported by the documents, that it had aided and abetted the coup.[16] Then came a musical-chairs succession of governments, all told eight more during the nineteen months following Diem's death. Finally, in June 1965, another military coup brought in General Thieu as head of state and Air Vice-Marshal Ky as premier.

COULD THE U. S. HAVE HONORABLY WITHDRAWN?

In later years the argument was often heard that the United States would lose too much face if it withdrew its troops from Vietnam. It had allegedly made a solemn commitment to win a complete victory, and if it reneged, its forty or so allies under various defense pacts could thereafter repose no confidence in it. Actually, the initial Eisenhower pledge of support was contingent on reforms that were not introduced. The original assurances were given to a government long since overthrown, and they never envisaged fighting the battles of corrupt military dictatorships until crushing victory over the Vietnamese Communists was achieved. Nor had such commitments contemplated, when made, sending an American army of some 550,000 men to fight the war for an undemocratic South Vietnamese regime. The bill for assistance finally mounted to over $100 billion, over 45,000 American combat deaths, and over 200,000 wounded, to say nothing of the sick, including numerous

---

[16] *Pentagon Papers*, Ch. IV. Although Washington may not have wanted Diem to be murdered, a coup always involved that possibility.

drug addicts. America's allies could hardly complain that the United States had fallen short of a determined attempt to honor its word.[17]

President Johnson clearly went much beyond his predecessors when, on January 1, 1964, he publicly assured the Saigon military government (soon overthrown), "We shall maintain in Vietnam American personnel and material as needed to assist you in achieving victory." [18] But critics argued that he had no constitutional authority to bind the nation to a never-ending war. Moreover, they charged that his repeated campaign pledges not to send American boys to fight Asia's wars involved a higher commitment than any he could have made to the military regime of South Vietnam.[19]

One disturbing fact is that after the Communist "monolith" was revealed as no monolith, following the Moscow–Peking rift in the 1960s, the basic reason for American intervention had disappeared. But by that time the nation was so deeply involved that such considerations as national honor and credibility of commitments argued against withdrawal. The official "line" proclaimed that the United States was fighting so that these people could freely determine their own destinies without outside interference. If applied consistently all over the world, this philosophy would soon bankrupt even a superpower.

WAS THE VIETNAM CONFLICT A CIVIL WAR?

As often noted, Washington in 1950 could have regarded the Korean conflict as an internal upheaval: an attempt by the north to reunite the entire country under Communist leadership. In its beginnings the Vietnam War was basically a civil war.[20] One must continue to remember that the Geneva conferees had regarded Vietnam as one country, with the 17th parallel line of demarcation as only temporary.

When the shooting stopped in 1954, many of the Vietminh fighters returned to their homes in the North, whereas a considerable number returned to or remained in their homes in the South. When the

[17] The United States has been known to dishonor its commitments when the national interest presumably would be best served by doing so. Notable examples are America's separate negotiations with the British enemy in 1781, at the expense of France, and Johnson's flouting of the nonintervention pledge in regard to the Dominican Republic in 1965.

[18] Public Papers of the Presidents: Lyndon B. Johnson, 1963–1964 (1965), I, 106.

[19] From time to time some of the less "hawkish" top advisors in Washington, including Robert F. Kennedy, proposed disengagement as an acceptable option. Pentagon Papers, pp. 174, 175, 387.

[20] Ibid., Ch. II.

elections of 1956 were not held and Diem not only failed to carry through land reforms but mercilessly persecuted dissenters, these ex-Vietminh finally resorted to organized guerrilla warfare against their own government after 1956. In 1960 the rebels, popularly known as the Viet Cong, set up their own central authority, the National Liberation Front (N.L.F.). Rather belatedly they were encouraged and then substantially aided by the North Vietnam regime in Hanoi, which by 1959 undertook to provide a flow of men and supplies. In the circumstances this delay was surprising.

If one accepts the Geneva Accords as the true basis of judgment, the conflict actually did begin as a civil war. The Chinese and Russians aided North Vietnam with war materiel, while the United States aided the seceding Saigon regime in the south with money, military supplies, and advisors. Ultimately hostilities spread to Laos and Cambodia, and military contingents of varying size (mostly token and temporary) were sent to South Vietnam from Thailand, South Korea, New Zealand, Australia, the Philippines, and Taiwan. Support for the Republic of [South] Vietnam thus turned the clash into an international conflict, but that was not how it began.[21]

Washington, with its politically ingrained fear of dealing with any brand of communism, steadfastly refused to negotiate any terms with the Viet Cong, even though these guerrillas were South Vietnamese. Yet there is an elementary rule that if one wishes to bring about an end to a conflict, one must deal with the parties who are fighting it.

WHO WERE THE AGGRESSORS IN VIETNAM?

The successful attempt of the temporary South Vietnamese regime to set up a separate state could be regarded as one phase of an internal civil war. When the Viet Cong arose and ultimately won the support of North Vietnam, the parties most directly involved were all Vietnamese, except for a handful of American military advisors.

Viewed by the North Vietnamese, the United States was the aggressor, especially after Washington began bombing North Vietnam in 1964–1965 and sending large contingents of troops onto South Vietnamese soil to fight the Viet Cong and the North Vietnamese. When the

[21] There is a rough parallel to the American Civil War, when a seceding South fought a unionist North for independence, with each side enlisting manpower from the other and with each securing arms from Europe. The parallel would be closer if Britain, France, and other European nations had provided large bodies of troops for the Confederacy.

Americans proposed to end their bombing of the North if the Hanoi Communists would stop their aggression (which consisted of supporting fellow Vietnamese), the reply was that this was not true reciprocity. The United States, Hanoi argued, was the real aggressor, while the South Vietnamese were only fellow countrymen in rebellion. If the North Vietnamese had been bombing American soil, a reciprocal stoppage of bombing would make sense, but not otherwise.

Washington resolutely maintained that the real aggressor was North Vietnam, backed with arms by Red China and Red Russia. The South Vietnamese, exercising their right of self-determination, had declared their independence of North Vietnam and wanted to live in peace, as was true of the South during the American Civil War. The Viet Cong, to be sure, had resorted to guerrilla warfare, as had the Loyalists in the American Revolution. But, declared the United States, the North Vietnamese assumed the role of aggressor when they (belatedly) "invaded" South Vietnam in support of the guerrillas. Much depended on what facts were emphasized.[22]

WERE THE TONKIN GULF
INCIDENTS DELIBERATELY PROVOKED?

According to official reports received in Washington, North Vietnamese torpedo boats twice attacked U. S. destroyers in the international waters of the Gulf of Tonkin early in August 1964. These clashes may have been cases of mistaken identity,[23] for small South Vietnamese gunboats, contributed by the United States and directed by American officers, had recently engaged in hostile action in this area.

The first incident, which occurred in bright daylight on August 2, 1964, involved the U. S. destroyer *Maddox*, then allegedly on "routine patrol" but actually on an electronic eavesdropping mission. After allegedly venturing within the twelve-mile limit claimed by the North Vietnamese, this warship was pursued outside territorial waters by three speedy, menacing torpedo boats. The *Maddox*, omitting warning shots, fired directly at its pursuers, who fled after harmlessly discharging torpedoes and inflicting one half-inch bullet hole. One North Vietnamese torpedo boat evidently sustained heavy damage.

Despite this warning of grave trouble, the *Maddox* was not only

---

[22] The secret Pentagon study states that Washington's official view of the war as one imposed on South Vietnam by aggression from Hanoi is "not wholly compelling." *Pentagon Papers*, p. 67.

[23] This was the theory of the anonymous analyst in the Pentagon. *Ibid.*, p. 259.

ordered to remain but was reinforced by the U. S. destroyer *Turner Joy*. Two days later, during the dark and overcast night of August 4, 1964, these two warships allegedly experienced torpedo attacks by unknown assailants during a furious two-hour battle. Two of the enemy were reported sunk. The American destroyers suffered no damage whatever, and the unknown foe left no debris that was discernible the next day. If there were strange vessels present, they could have been North Vietnamese torpedo boats or fishing craft,[24] or even Chinese ships of some kind. Tricky weather effects, faulty sonar or radar, strange engine noises, or plain nerves may have touched off the fusillade. The two American ships may have mistaken each other for the enemy.[25] The North Vietnamese denied having made such an attack, although acknowledging that they had chased the "intruding" *Maddox* two days earlier.

Within a few hours after the second reported attack, President Johnson hastily announced on television and radio that he had ordered a retaliatory aerial bombing of North Vietnamese warships and naval installations along 100 miles of the coast. (Altogether sixty-four sorties were flown.) Oddly enough, Johnson proclaimed the strikes before they had actually occurred, to the possible jeopardy of American airmen. Cynics charged that he wanted to extract the maximum political advantage during his current campaign for election against "bomb-happy" Senator Goldwater. Johnson states in his memoirs that since both North Vietnamese and Chinese radar would pick up the attacking planes, he wanted all parties to know precisely the nature and limited objectives of the attack.[26]

Johnson's two-fisted response electrified red-blooded Americans and provided the President with enthusiastic public support. The alleged attacks and the retaliatory responses were significant in two respects. They heralded the initial bombing of North Vietnam by the United States — a small-scale effort indeed compared with the deluge to come. They provided Johnson with an excuse to ask Congress for a blank-check resolution to prosecute the war in Southeast Asia. Passed with only two dissenting votes in Congress three days after the second alleged attack, this authorization came to be known as the Tonkin Gulf Resolu-

---

[24] For example, on the night of October 21, 1904, a Russian fleet destined for Japanese waters fired upon English fishing vessels in the North Sea under the illusion that they were enemy Japanese torpedo boats. This Dogger Bank incident, which involved the sinking of a British trawler and the killing of two men, nearly precipitated war but was settled by an international commission.

[25] Testimony to this effect was presented by two participants on CBS television, March 16, 1971. See also Eugene G. Windchy, *Tonkin Gulf* (1971), p. 207. This author interviewed a number of participants. He concludes (p. 292) that the second attack was "improbable" though not impossible.

[26] Lyndon B. Johnson, *The Vantage Point* (1971), p. 117.

tion. It clothed the President with power (which he probably had already as Commander-in-Chief) "to take all necessary measures to repel any armed attack against the forces of the United States and to prevent further aggression." Unknown to Congress, top Washington officials had already prepared a draft of this resolution more than two months earlier, and had selected possible targets for aerial strikes.[27]

DID JOHNSON OVERREACT TO THE TONKIN GULF INCIDENTS?

Senator J. W. Fulbright, Chairman of the Senate Committee on Foreign Relations, had supported the Tonkin Gulf Resolution, trusting to the President's assurances that the two attacks were "deliberate" and "unprovoked." Gradually becoming a bitter foe of the Vietnam involvement, he conducted hearings on the incidents in 1968. Among various revelations, the American commander of the two destroyers had urged that he be allowed time to reevaluate evidence of the second attack before drastic action was taken. Defense Secretary McNamara testified that the officer's later reevaluation (under pressure) was positive.[28] But this statement had been vigorously challenged.[29] The Pentagon additionally claimed the interception of North Vietnamese radio messages which reported the battle in progress and the loss of two Vietnamese boats.[30]

The Fulbright hearings more than suggested that the administration had been guilty of overstatement and deception, and that its response had been overhasty and disproportionate to the alleged offense. As the secret Pentagon Papers later confirmed, the Americans had been supporting South Vietnamese operations in this area, possibly with the

[27] Pentagon Papers, pp. 234–235, 249. Critics of President Johnson charged that the Maddox was a deliberately provocative "pigeon," designed to provoke an incident that would justify a Tonkin Gulf Resolution. The Pentagon Papers, published by the New York Times in 1971, provided abundant proof of Johnson's secretiveness and his proneness to tell the public one thing while doing something else. But the extent of the double-dealing has probably been exaggerated. Many of the Pentagon Papers are proposed contingency plans drawn up by subordinates; many are recommendations that were not adopted or were subsequently reversed by the authors; many are repetitious pleas for more troops by commanders who were plunged in over their depth. Nor was the total picture available to the editors, particularly the official files of the Central Intelligence Agency, the Department of State, and the White House.

[28] The Gulf of Tonkin: The 1964 Incidents. Hearings before the Committee on Foreign Relations of the U. S. Senate, 90th Cong., 2 sess. (1968).

[29] Windchy, Tonkin Gulf, p. 286.

[30] Pentagon Papers, p. 263. There is some reason to believe that these intercepts related to the admitted attack two days earlier. See Anthony Austin, The President's War (1971), Ch. XVI.

intent of provoking a response that would justify punitive bombing. If there had been less of a determination in Washington to bomb North Vietnam, possibly for electioneering purposes, the incident might have been settled peacefully. Other and more serious international offenses, before and after, have been amenable to diplomacy, notably the *Pueblo* affair in 1968 involving North Korea.[31] In short, if Congress had been in full possession of the facts, it almost certainly would not have acted so quickly or so near-unanimously.

DID JOHNSON DECEIVE THE VOTERS IN 1964?

President Johnson was nominated in his own right in 1964 on a middle-of-the-road platform that called for peace, prudence, and concern for the public welfare. The Republican conservatives committed "political suicide" by engineering the nomination of an extreme right-winger and bellicose anti-Communist, Senator Barry M. Goldwater of Arizona. Because the Republicans were the minority party, this alienation of their moderate and liberal majority guaranteed a vast amount of "bolting" to the Democratic candidate, with Goldwater's defeat a foregone conclusion. About the only uncertainty was the size of Johnson's popular majority, which turned out to be 61.1 percent, the largest in American presidential history.

Goldwater appeared to be the war candidate. Outspokenly opposed to Communist expansion, he condemned the "no-win" strategy in Vietnam. He not only favored a heavy bombing of North Vietnam, but he chilled much of the American public by proposing that the use of tactical nuclear weapons be left to the discretion of the field commanders. To many voters his proposal seemed like triggering World War III. The impression that Goldwater gave was one of impulsiveness, irresponsibility, and recklessness.

[31] On January 23, 1968, the North Koreans seized the U. S. intelligence ship *Pueblo*, allegedly operating in their territorial waters, with the loss of one American life. They not only kept the ship but subjected the crew of some eighty men to inhumane treatment for nearly a year before releasing them. On April 15, 1969, the defiant North Koreans shot down an American military aircraft, supposedly over international waters, with the loss of all thirty-one men aboard. In both instances, despite an American outcry for strong measures, the incidents were closed after protracted negotiations. Hostilities were avoided largely because America, with the costly Vietnam conflict on its hands, had no desire to reopen the Korean War. In the first case, severe retaliation might well have cost the lives of the American prisoners; in the second case, the dead could not be brought back to life by sacrificing countless more men, probably in vain. President Johnson claims that the *Pueblo* incident was part of a Communist plot to divert American strength to Korea from Vietnam on the eve of the Tet offensive by the North Vietnamese. Johnson, *The Vantage Point,* p. 535.

Johnson presented himself as the peace candidate. Echoing Franklin Roosevelt's Boston speech of 1940 (see p. 687), he repeatedly spoke against a deeper involvement in Vietnam. At Akron, Ohio, October 21, 1964, he declared, in one of about a half-dozen such public pledges, "But we are not about to send American boys nine or ten thousand miles away from home to do what Asian boys ought to be doing for themselves." [32] After the two alleged attacks on American destroyers in the Gulf of Tonkin, he authorized a limited one-shot, tit-for-tat, retaliatory bombing of North Vietnam.[33] But he assured the voters (August 4), "we still seek no wider war." This resolute exhibition of Americanism proved to be good electioneering: a Gallup poll found that popular approval of Johnson's handling of the Vietnam imbroglio shot up from 38 percent to 71 percent.

A sensational revelation of the *Pentagon Papers* related to a "general consensus" at a White House meeting (September 7, 1964) that large-scale bombing of North Vietnam would "probably" have to be launched "early in the new year." [34] We should note that this was only a "contingency plan" and not a firm decision; even so, it causes Johnson's campaign promises during the ensuing two months to appear in a less candid light. Yet the record reveals that he backed off from a firm decision for more than three months after the election. On February 13, 1965, following destructive raids by the Viet Cong, he authorized heavy and sustained bombing of important centers in North Vietnam. This was done despite repeated warnings of the Central Intelligence Agency that such attacks would not break the morale of a semiprimitive agricultural people.[35]

WAS THE ELECTION OF 1964 A MANDATE ON VIETNAM?

Did Johnson receive a firm mandate from the voters to avoid a heavy aerial bombardment and a deployment of ground troops in Vietnam? Is it true that the electorate voted for Johnson but got Goldwater?

Vietnam was not the only issue in the campaign, and it was not clear-cut. Goldwater took the ultraright position on many issues. The

---

[32] *Johnson Public Papers, 1963–1964*, II, 391. In his memoirs, Johnson claims he meant that American boys would only help "Asian boys" and not fight their battles for them. Johnson, *The Vantage Point*, p. 68.

[33] There was a third Tonkin Gulf attack on American destroyers, September 18, 1964, but Johnson chose to ignore it. *Pentagon Papers*, p. 316.

[34] *Ibid.*, pp. 310, 343.

[35] *Ibid.*, Ch. 8. Heavy bombing of industralized Germany in World War II had not broken the will to resist — in fact for a time had increased it.

only way to get a genuine mandate on a question of this kind is to poll the American people on that issue alone, and present clear-cut alternatives. Moreover, most promises, especially campaign promises, have implied conditions; and circumstances alter cases. Johnson never sought a declaration of war from Congress, but he had the blank-check Tonkin Resolution of August 7, 1964, approved during the presidential campaign.

By March of 1965, despite stepped-up American bombing of North Vietnam, the Vietnam dam was about to break, jeopardizing some 22,000 United States noncombat military personnel. The administration judged that the national interest then required the dispatch of a modest contingent of Marines to protect American installations. Landing on March 8, 1965, they proved to be the initial contribution to these gluttonous quicksands.[36] Opinion polls showed that the public, including anti-Johnson voters, strongly approved such action as in the national interest. If the people had been opposed, the charge of betraying campaign promises would have carried greater weight.

WAS THE VIETNAM WAR UNCONSTITUTIONAL?

The Constitution specifically confers on Congress the power to declare war, and since that body never formally took such action regarding Vietnam, critics repeatedly charged that America's involvement was illegal. A few irate citizens demanded that the President be impeached.

In past experience, as in 1917, Congress had passed a joint resolution by a simple majority vote, declaring that a state of war existed. This measure was signed by the President. If he had vetoed it (something that has never happened in American experience), Congress could have overridden him by a two-thirds vote.

The simple truth is that while Congress alone may declare war, the President can make war, provided that Congress will sustain him by voting the necessary funds. On scores of minor occasions the Chief Executive has ordered the Marines and other forces to fight in foreign countries, or he has engaged in undeclared wars, as in 1798–1800 with France, in 1917 and 1941 with Germany (in the Atlantic), and in 1951–1953 in Korea (though sanctioned by the U.N.).

In the case of Vietnam, Congress in 1964 passed the open-ended Tonkin Gulf Resolution, under which the President was given a free hand

[36] On April 1, 1965, Johnson secretly decided to use the American troops offensively, yet a day earlier he denied that any new far-reaching strategy was being suggested or promulgated. *Ibid.*, pp. 382, 400.

in Southeast Asia. Many members of Congress subsequently deplored their decision, for none of them evidently suspected that they were authorizing a conflict of major magnitude.[37] Indirectly they sanctioned the war by continuing to vote appropriations for its prosecution; in fact, they could have brought America's participation to a halt by withholding funds. But until the conflict became highly unpopular in the late 1960s, few Congressmen were willing to risk political suicide by supporting such a course.[38]

The Supreme Court thus far has refused to declare the Vietnam War unconstitutional; on October 12, 1971, it declined to act on a federal case appealed to it which upheld the government. But we may be reasonably sure that the Founding Fathers would never have clothed the President with the power to squander American fighting strength and money abroad on this scale if they could have peered into the future. A conflict involving over 45,000 American battle deaths and several hundred thousand wounded is more than a simple "police action" to be embarked upon at the discretion of a President.

HOW VALID WAS THE FALLING DOMINO THEORY?

In the 1950s various American spokesmen, including President Eisenhower, expressed grave concern over "falling dominoes" in Southeast Asia. This concept meant that if one of the states of Indochina fell, its neighbors would also be engulfed by communism, and there was no telling how far the repercussions would be felt. The fear that the Communist steamroller would be strengthened by the addition of a row of fallen dominoes took deep root.[39] It was used as a morale-booster with the American troops in Vietnam, who were told that if they did not halt communism in Southeastern Asia, they would ultimately be defending

[37] The administration feared, among various reasons, that a formal declaration of war might bring in China and Russia under treaty commitments to North Vietnam.

[38] Not until January 14, 1971 did President Nixon sign into law a repeal of the Tonkin Gulf Resolution. But the wound-down war continued. Windchy, *Tonkin Gulf*, p. 336.

[39] The secret *Pentagon Papers* show that practically all of the top policy makers in Washington subscribed to the domino theory from 1950 to the late 1960s, except for the Central Intelligence Agency. It reported (June 9, 1964) that no nation in Southeast Asia, "with the possible exception of Cambodia," was likely to succumb "quickly" if both Laos and South Vietnam fell. It also believed that heavy bombing of North Vietnam would be ineffective (as it proved to be) and that the real strength of the Communists lay in South Vietnam. The prognostications of the C.I.A., often startlingly correct, were largely ignored by higher-ups. See *Pentagon Papers*, particularly pp. 254–255, 331–332.

American freedoms on the shores of Hawaii or even the coast of California. Better to fight in the jungles of Vietnam than on the beach of
Waikiki.[40]

The domino theory ran counter to certain stubborn facts. First
of all, China, the biggest domino of all, had fallen to the Communists in
1949.[41] Yet it had not overwhelmed any of its neighbors and had even
failed to conquer Taiwan. North Korea, bordering China, had shown
remarkable independence of both Peking and Moscow. Neighboring
North Vietnam, with its centuries-long hatred of the Chinese, had been
willing to accept Peking's military assistance but not domination. Moreover, there was always the possibility of nationalist-Communist regimes
rising among the fallen dominoes, and these would bring even greater
disunity to the so-called "monolith."

One surprising fact is that the nations nearest the teetering
dominoes seemed much less concerned than the United States. Strong
criticism of American policy was voiced in Japan and India, while
Australia, New Zealand, the Philippines, Thailand, and Taiwan provided
little more than token military manpower, in some cases in response to
American money. South Korea supplied some 50,000 men, for which its
government received compensation from Washington.

One oddity about the military implications of a Communist
Vietnam is that the United States showed relatively little interest in the
fate of Indonesia, which the Communists almost took over in 1967. Yet
Indonesia was much more important in terms of population and natural
resources, though perhaps less important strategically.

WAS THE VIETNAM
INVOLVEMENT IN THE NATIONAL INTEREST?

The litmus test of any foreign policy is the national interest. If a given
course of action brings more disadvantages than advantages to the
United States, it should ordinarily be modified or abandoned.

Several misapprehensions were responsible for America's gradual
and inexorable involvement in Vietnam. One, as repeatedly noted, was
the fear of a nonexistent Communist "monolith," with the corollary

[40] Late in 1964, several months after the Tonkin Gulf incident, a Gallup poll
sought the reasons for the American presence in Vietnam. A total of 49 percent
replied "stopping the spread of [monolithic] communism"; 6 percent stressed a
moral obligation to the free world; 3 percent mentioned security; and 2 percent
referred to the legal commitment. A surprising 31 percent were unable to give a
reason. Gallup Release, December 2, 1964.
[41] The seizure of Tibet by the Chinese Communists in 1950 was the regaining of
territory over which China had earlier held suzerainty.

dogma of falling dominoes. Another was the idea of World Policeman, implicit in the Truman Doctrine of 1947. America, President Truman had declared, must "support free peoples who are resisting attempted subjugation by armed minorities or by outside pressures." This formula seemed to fit South Vietnam perfectly, especially after the French had left. America was to learn the hard way in both Korea and Vietnam that even its capacity to engage in global police work against communism was severely limited, especially in faraway Hungary in 1956 and even in nearby Cuba in the 1960s.

One argument of the militant "hawks" regarding Vietnam was that if the Communists seized control, there would be a blood bath, including the butchering of many tens of thousands of Roman Catholics. After sacrificing so many American lives on behalf of these luckless people, so the argument ran, the United States would be guilty of unforgivable inhumanity if it pulled out and left them to the mercy of the Communists.[42]

Undeniably Viet Cong guerrillas had committed incredibly brutal atrocities against their foes, in pursuance of a policy of terror and intimidation. They had demonstrated vengefulness, cruelty, and scant regard for human lives, as had both sides, including American soldiers. The chances were indeed alarming that thousands of South Vietnamese would be butchered if their cause lost. But, as the American "doves" pointed out, hundreds of thousands of Vietnamese civilians on both sides had already been killed, many by United States bombing, and the longer the war ground on, the more would be killed. Americans were destroying Vietnam in their efforts to save it, and at the same time they were demoralizing their own army and their own country. The United States, critics declared, had more than fulfilled any commitment to help the Vietnamese, who had shown a distressing reluctance to help themselves. In the process, the United States, the great champion of democracy, had become enmeshed in supporting unsavory military regimes in Saigon. Many South Vietnamese, perhaps a majority, hoped that the Yankees would go home before their country was irreparably ruined.

During the Senate hearings of 1966, George F. Kennan, a former foreign service officer and reputed author of the policy of containment, declared emphatically that if the Americans were not already in Vietnam, he could think of "no reason why we should wish to become so involved. . . ."[43] Obviously what kept the United States there was pride, prestige, patriotism, fear of communism, a sense of obligation, concern

---

[42] Ex-Ambassador Harriman argued that a peace settlement guaranteeing no reprisals would be honored by both sides. W. Averell Harriman, *America and Russia in a Changing World* (1971), pp. 144–145.

[43] J. W. Fulbright, ed., *The Vietnam Hearings* (1968), p. 108.

for the fate of the defeated (especially Catholic refugees),[44] a determination to prove that "aggression" should not pay, and a feeling that there should be something to show for the sacrifice of so much American blood and treasure. In the later stages of the war Uncle Sam was evidently more concerned with saving face than saving South Vietnam.

WHO PREVENTED PEACE IN VIETNAM?

One nation can provoke a war, but ordinarily two or more adversaries have to agree on terms of a truce or peace.

In the earlier stages of the Vietnam War, Hanoi apparently indicated that a negotiated settlement might be possible, but for various reasons the Americans, confident of winning, were unwilling to grant acceptable terms. After mediatory efforts had failed early in 1965, the U.N. Secretary General U Thant indicated that the United States was to blame.

By 1968, if not before, it became evident to Washington that the Communist enemy could not be crushed by any force that America was willing to employ. North Vietnam could have been turned into a desert with nuclear bombs, but such a holocaust would have outraged humanity and left the Viet Cong in the South. Once the North Vietnamese perceived that they could outlast their foe, they refused to negotiate unless America ceased all bombing and withdrew all its forces. In a military sense the war came to be essentially a draw, and a nation cannot expect to win at the peace table what it cannot win on the battlefield.

The United States by 1968 had become so deeply involved, with more than 500,000 troops and supporting units, that it could not face withdrawal. Such a humiliating course presumably would weaken its military credibility ("a paper tiger") and would undermine the reliance of its allies on its determination to meet commitments. Neither President Johnson nor President Nixon wanted to preside over what they erroneously believed was the one major war in the nation's history that the Americans had not won.

Yet America's military might, as the "doves" repeatedly argued, was hardly in dispute. The Vietnam conflict was in large part a guerrilla war that could not be won with conventional tactics; and no one doubted the overwhelming nuclear capability of the United States. America would lose face in some quarters by pulling out, but it would gain in-

[44] The cold-blooded massacre of hundreds of South Vietnamese civilians in Hué by the Communists at the time of the Tet offensive (1968) deepened fears of bloody reprisals.

calculably more moral face with those peoples throughout the world who regarded as obscene the attempt to defoliate, napalm, and smash a weak backward people into submission. The French in 1954 were humiliated by being forced to relinquish Indochina after defeat on the battlefield, but President De Gaulle ultimately restored much of his nation's tarnished prestige, despite this loss to the Vietnamese insurgents and the even greater loss of Algeria to its rebels.

As for destroying the faith of America's allies, the "doves" believed that disengagement from this war would quiet the condemnation of many foreigners. Such disapprobation deepened after the shocking, face-losing revelation of wholesale atrocities by American soldiers, at My Lai and elsewhere, involving the torture and butchering of Vietnamese men, women, and children. Many of the Allies in the NATO Pact prayed that the Republic would cease wasting its substance abroad and tearing itself apart at home so that it could present a stronger front to potential Communist aggression in Europe.

Washington repeatedly offered what it regarded as fair and honorable terms. The Vietnamese as repeatedly rejected them and demanded a complete American pullout. In a situation of this kind the recalcitrant party is the ultimate judge of what is honorable and fair, and if it dissents, the war goes on.

WHY DID JOHNSON "ABDICATE" IN 1968?

Political pundits had confidently assumed that President Johnson, a landslide winner in 1964, would actively seek a second elective term in 1968. He evidently loved power (this he denies in his memoirs); he was not one to quit under fire; and he presumably would relish credit for bringing the dreary Vietnam War to an honorable conclusion. Despite formidable nationwide demonstrations against the Vietnam involvement (which no doubt encouraged Hanoi to hold out), the Pentagon was recommending that some 200,000 more troops be sent to Vietnam, in addition to the 535,000 already there. The Communists, though finally repulsed, had revealed unexpected strength in the widespread Tet offensive of early 1968.[45]

Johnson cleared the air with a memorable television appearance on March 31, 1968. He announced that thereafter he would unilaterally restrict the aerial bombing of North Vietnam to its less populated south-

[45] President Johnson and administration spokesmen publicly dismissed the Tet offensive as a great failure for the enemy, but privately they were shocked and disillusioned. *Pentagon Papers*, p. 592.

ern sector, and that he would send only a nominal 13,500 reinforcements, rather than the talked-about 200,000. Then he exploded a bombshell when he emphatically declared that he would not accept another nomination for the presidency. He indicated that he was taking this step to expedite peace and bring unity to his country, torn as it was by the clash between the "hawks" and the "doves."

These may well have been major considerations in Johnson's decision not to seek reelection, but the circumstantial evidence is strong that other factors were present as well. The "dovish" Senator Eugene McCarthy of Minnesota, backed by antiwar young people of college age, had entered the Democratic primary in New Hampshire. He polled an incredible 42 percent of the vote, although Johnson gathered 49 percent as the beneficiary of an organized write-in campaign.[46] Four days following this evidence of a potent anti-Johnson sentiment, Senator Robert F. Kennedy, the dead President's popular brother, announced his candidacy, after earlier refusing to become involved in a seemingly hopeless challenge. (He subsequently made an impressive showing in the primary elections, during which he was assassinated.) Private polls indicated that McCarthy would carry the Wisconsin primary against Johnson, and this he did after Johnson's withdrawal.[47] In fact, public polls revealed that only 26 percent of all voters favored the President's handling of the Vietnam War and only 36 percent approved his overall stewardship.

In short, the indications were that Johnson would have to fight for a second nomination, with probable success, but that he might well lose to the Republican candidate, who proved to be Richard M. Nixon. Why not avoid a disagreeable struggle, which entailed the possibility of defeat, and work for peace and national unity? Why not run for a high place in history rather than another term in high office? Johnson was also concerned, as were members of his family, about the state of his health (he had suffered a near-fatal heart attack in 1955), about his strenuous five years in the White House, and about the hopelessness of the Vietnam morass. He later declared that his "abdication" had been in contemplation for several years, but the announcement, coming so soon after McCarthy's surprise showing in the New Hampshire primary and Robert Kennedy's announced candidacy, caused skeptics to believe that it was related to his plummeting popularity.[48]

[46] McCarthy won about 20 of the 24 delegates, owing to a split vote among the pro-Johnson candidates.

[47] In Wisconsin, McCarthy defeated Johnson, whose name was on the ballot (unlike the race in New Hampshire), 412,160 to 253,696. Johnson's announced withdrawal no doubt lessened his vote.

[48] Johnson argues in his memoirs that these last-minute developments, particularly the New Hampshire primary, were only coincidentally related to his earlier decision

Vice President Hubert H. Humphrey received the Democratic nomination with President Johnson's blessing and supported his chief's policy of keeping the war going until the enemy made reciprocal concessions that would lead to an honorable peace. The antiwar elements in America were growing in such numbers that this stance no doubt hurt Humphrey, who softened his views perceptibly later in the campaign. Then, on November 1, 1968, President Johnson ordered a unilateral cessation of all bombing of North Vietnam, not merely the southern part. The Hanoi regime, which had sent delegates to Paris following the March 31 announcement of a partial bombing halt, now expressed a willingness to discuss peace terms seriously.

This last-minute concession by Johnson, only five days before election day, evidently boosted Humphrey's stock. But his prospects were hurt by the refusal of South Vietnam to go along with the peace discussions in Paris — at least, as events turned out, until after the election.[49] Nixon, the Republican candidate, won by an extremely narrow margin.

WAS JOHNSON A FAILURE AS PRESIDENT?

Lyndon B. Johnson had got off to an impressively fast start after Kennedy's murder. As if to "show up" his predecessor, he galvanized Congress into action with an impressive display of cajoling and arm-twisting. Various measures bottled up in the Kennedy Congress came popping out — notably the tax-cut scheme, the Civil Rights Act of 1964, and the antipoverty legislation.

So great was Johnson's popularity in 1964 and so weak the Republican opposition that the "Accidental President" was overwhelmingly elected in his own right. At the same time he won strong support for his rather vague Great Society in Congress. This advantage enabled him to push through a remarkable budget of legislation that is roughly comparable to the record of Franklin Roosevelt's Hundred Days Congress. Included were important measures involving Medicare, voting

---

to withdraw. See Johnson, *The Vantage Point*, Ch. 18. Yet Johnson, who liked to keep his "options open" to the last minute, could have changed his mind while still on the air.

49 Johnson believes that Humphrey's softening of the hard line regarding bombing in Vietnam cost him the election, although it almost certainly won him many votes. The Johnson view is that the South Vietnamese, suddenly distrustful of Humphrey, purposely delayed going to Paris, and that their foot-dragging dampened hopes of a negotiated peace while insuring the election of hard-liner Nixon. *Ibid.*, p. 548. Harriman subscribes to this view. *America and Russia in a Changing World*, p. 136.

rights, housing, immigration, poverty, and aid to education, both elementary and secondary. Some of these schemes, especially those relating to housing and poverty, did not work out well.

If it had not been for foreign affairs, Johnson might be reckoned one of the near great or even great Presidents today. But he was shipwrecked on the reef of Vietnam. Losing not only his popularity but his credibility, he wound up with an aura of failure hanging over his entire five years. Committed by Presidents Truman, Eisenhower, and Kennedy to support anti-communism in Vietnam, he was aware that "containing" communism was politically popular and that "losing" Indochina would be damaging to the administration. He was evidently persuaded by military advisors that a "cheap" victory could be won with airpower. Encouraged to believe and to declare that victory was just around the corner, he sank ever deeper into a jungle war. The results were frustration and humiliation on the battlefront; the loss of tens of thousands of American lives and hundreds of thousands of Vietnamese civilians; a further unbalancing of the budget; a demoralization of the army; the besmirching scandals of American atrocities; a growing opposition to the draft; the exacerbation of racial tensions in the army and in the ghettoes; a mounting inflation at home; and a general sickness of American society. The war not only brought ruin to Vietnam but also blighted the United States, while causing Uncle Sam to appear as a big bully — and an ineffective one at that.

The Johnson administration proved less than candid in its efforts to softpedal bad news from the battlefront and cover up the shortcomings of the Saigon military regime which it was supporting in the name of democracy. So many misleading statements emanated from Washington as to create what journalists called the Credibility Gap.[50] Opposition to the Vietnam involvement became so violent among the nonviolent dissenters that, like Jefferson in the days of the unenforceable embargo, Johnson felt the very foundations of government shaking under him. Like Jefferson, Johnson found that Vietnam in his second term tended to erase from the public mind the many solid achievements in his earlier years. Historians may yet deal with the tall Texan more kindly than the voters, many of whom regarded his "abdication" as the most popular act of his presidential years.

---

[50] The Credibility Gap was nothing new, though the specific name was. Politicians are naturally under pressure to put the best possible face on events that discredit them or their party. Many Presidents have with reason been accused of deliberate falsification, conspicuously Polk ("Polk the Mendacious") and Franklin ("Double-crossing") Roosevelt.

ADDITIONAL GENERAL REFERENCES

Lyndon B. Johnson, *The Vantage Point* (1971); Eric Goldman, *The Tragedy of Lyndon Johnson* (1969); Rowland Evans and Robert Novak, *Lyndon B. Johnson: The Exercise of Power* (1966); T. H. White, *The Making of the President, 1968* (1969); P. L. Geyelin, *Lyndon B. Johnson and the World* (1966); John B. Martin, *Overtaken by Events* (1966) [the Dominican intervention]; Theodore Draper, *The Dominican Revolt* (1968); Jerome Slater, *Intervention and Negotiation: The United States and the Dominican Revolution* (1970); G. M. Kahin and J. W. Lewis, *The United States in Vietnam* (rev. ed., 1969); Robert Shaplen, *The Lost Revolution* (1965); Bernard Fall, *Two Viet Nams: A Political and Military Analysis* (2nd rev. ed., 1967); G. W. Ball, *The Discipline of Power* (1968).

41

Nixon and Resurgent Republicanism

As a minority President, Nixon was hampered by a Democratic majority in two successive Congresses, 1969–1973. He therefore could expect to secure little more than routine legislation, while using his veto to curb objectionable measures. But he did manage to give a more conservative cast to his administration and the Supreme Court. Bedeviled by simultaneous inflation and recession, he strove unsuccessfully for more than two and one-half years to bring back prosperity by deliberate deflation and calculated unemployment — "Nixonomics." Then, late in 1971, he suddenly switched his "game plan" to the "New Economic Policy," [1] which involved abandoning or reversing many of his conservative Republican principles.

Nixon had won the presidency by proclaiming that he had a secret plan to "end" the war and "win" the peace. In pursuance of his "Nixon Doctrine," he undertook at the outset to turn Asia's wars over to the Asians, beginning with the "Vietnamization" of South Vietnam. Intimately related to the aim of disentangling from Southeast Asia was Nixon's conciliatory new approach to Red China and the Soviet Union. It led to improved relations with Peking in 1971, while paving the way for China's admission to the United Nations and for the simultaneous expulsion of Nationalist China, later in 1971.

In February 1972 Nixon flew to Peking for air-clearing "sum-

---

[1] It is ironical that the Russian Bolsheviks, finding that their brand of communism did not work, abandoned it in 1921 for the "New Economic Policy" (N.E.P.).

844

mit" talks with the Chinese Communists. Although he could report few tangible results, he did reach a higher level of accommodation. Probably as a partial result of this overture, an apprehensive USSR was glad to receive President Nixon in May 1972. He concluded in Moscow, as the final fruits of negotiations that had been going on for many months, a series of agreements designed to promote better understanding and to slow down the mad race in nuclear weapons.

Peking and Moscow, now more friendly to the United States, evidently applied pressure to North Vietnam to end the war. On the eve of the presidential election of 1972 the White House could proclaim that a negotiated cease-fire was imminent. Further strengthened by this announcement, Nixon defeated Senator McGovern, the left-leaning Democrat, in a landslide of almost unprecedented proportions.

WAS VIETNAMIZATION A DELUSION?

Nixon's announced policy of Vietnamization was neither new nor clear cut. It had formerly been known as "de-Americanization"; it did not involve turning the war over at once to the South Vietnamese and withdrawing unconditionally. Nixon declared that American troops would be brought home gradually, and that he would not pull out all American ground strength until the South Vietnamese had at least a "reasonable chance" to hold their own. Meanwhile limited aerial bombing could continue. If the North Vietnamese initiated large-scale attacks (as they finally did in 1972), Washington would feel free to step up the war to any necessary lengths. In any event, American support for Saigon would continue, whether naval, aerial, financial, or logistical, plus a "residual" contingent of troops, not unlike the units maintained in South Korea since 1953. In short, Vietnamization came closer to meaning protracted war than immediate peace.

If Nixon's primary goal was to end America's participation in the conflict at once, he presumably could have attained it by setting a firm date for speedy and complete withdrawal. But he made "perfectly clear" in a series of nationally televised speeches that he was concerned about national honor, about previous commitments, about not being the first President to lose a war, and (inferentially) about his reelection in 1972. In other words, his basic goal was not a withdrawal but a slow-motion de-escalation which would enable the South Vietnamese to emerge victorious or at least hold the line. In this case, the United States would not have an outright defeat to blot its prestige.

Allegedly to lessen American casualties while withdrawing, Nixon authorized limited but highly criticized American thrusts into Cambodia (1970) and an American-supported South Vietnamese drive into Laos (1971). This one failed miserably. In both cases enemy sanctuaries and supply lines were temporarily disrupted, and additional time was probably purchased for Vietnamization. But these incursions, though justified on narrow military grounds, had the effect of spreading the fighting to other parts of French Indochina. This extension may have come anyhow, but such were the immediate results of trying to shorten the conflict by widening it. The "Johnson war" slowly became the "Nixon war" as the President sought a cautious middle course between outright defeat and complete victory. But unlike many "doves," he still believed that the national interest required keeping Southeast Asia from Communist clutches.

By mid-November 1972, nearly four years after taking office, Nixon was still fighting a reduced war, with the loss in his administration of thousands of American lives. Yet he had brought home about 500,000 troops, leaving some 30,000 noncombat personnel. His promise to "end" the conflict had fallen considerably short of the expectations he had aroused in his campaign for the presidency in 1968, but public opinion evidently supported the slow-motion withdrawal.

WAS THE STUDENT UNREST OF THE ERA UNIQUE?

Throughout the nineteenth century, and even earlier, riotous disturbances intermittently convulsed college campuses. For the most part such outbursts were triggered by poor food, harsh living conditions, and stern regulations. But these flareups, unlike many in contemporary European universities, were primarily nonpolitical.

The pattern had changed drastically by the 1960s, when the emphasis had shifted conspicuously from ordinary "hell raising" and spring "panty raids" to protest for social and economic reform. Student demonstrations crested in the years following 1964, when the University of California at Berkeley was wracked by mass disorders. Many of the participants were nonstudents, including "street people" and high school pupils. The demonstrators invariably comprised only a minority of the entire student body, though often a substantial minority. The "silent majority" that did not participate were involved to the extent that they commonly opposed punishment for the disrupters. A sprinkling of permissive professors, notably younger faculty members, supported the demonstrators, actively or passively.

Often overlooked is the fact that student uprisings in America were part of a worldwide phenomenon. Even more violent riots were occurring in a number of foreign countries, conspicuously in France, Mexico, and particularly Japan. The revolution of youth was one of the most significant movements of the century.

Why the student unrest? The new generation in America, reared on television violence, was the product of unusual parental permissiveness. Organized opposition naturally developed, even in the high schools, to the restrictions imposed by "The Establishment," whether personal, educational, governmental, or economic. Contempt for law led to disdain for its enforcers (the "pigs"), who in turn were provoked into overreacting with "police brutality." A "generation gap" developed ("trust no one over 30") between the young people, who were disenchanted, and their parents, who had "messed up" the world. The elders, for their part, were "turned off" by the "hippie" type youths, with their dirty clothes, long hair, bare feet, filthy speech, raucous music, mind-blasting drugs, and promiscuous sex. The students, in turn, felt that much of their impersonalized mass education was "irrelevant" to current problems. This view was widespread among underprivileged black students, who demanded a fair share of the educational pie, including courses on their African heritage taught by blacks. Both blacks and whites were acutely unhappy over the Vietnam War, the inequitable draft, and the intimate tie-in of many universities with the military arm in ROTC programs and defense contracts. Pacifists added to the clamor with their appeal, "Make love, not war." Youthful Communists, some of them nonstudents or professional agitators mysteriously financed, worked feverishly to radicalize the nation's social and economic structure, beginning with the colleges and universities.

The new student demonstrators of the 1960s were unquestionably unique in that many of them were seeking broad social, political, or economic goals. They were also unique in the scale and fury of their violence. As a special presidential commission concluded, the 1st Amendment fully protected orderly protest meetings, peaceful picketing, quiet vigils, and nonviolent demonstrations and marches. But the same investigators found wholly unacceptable the disruptions of classrooms, the shouting down of unpopular teachers and speakers, vandalism, arson, terrorism, and physical assaults on people. In many cases such tactics were not only disruptive but felonious.[2]

Shortly after President Nixon's announcement of the American incursion into Cambodia, April 29, 1970, protests erupted nationwide, notably at Kent State University in Ohio and at the predominantly

---

[2] See *Report of the President's Commission on Campus Unrest* (1970).

black Jackson State College in Mississippi. At Kent State four young people were killed and nine wounded by gunfire; at Jackson State two were killed and twelve wounded. The bombing of a building at the University of Wisconsin in August 1970 cost the life of one senior researcher and injury to four other persons. Such bloody incidents brought on revulsion, and the campuses began to simmer down. Contributing to this improved atmosphere were concessions to black demands, overdue reforms in curriculum and administration, more effective security measures, the enactment of punitive legislation, a lessening of the military connection with the universities, a more equitable draft law, and a reduction of the voting age from twenty-one to eighteen by Congressional statute and then by constitutional amendment (1971).

WERE THE 1970 ELECTIONS AN ENDORSEMENT OF NIXON?

To the embarrassment of President-elect Nixon, both houses of his first Congress contained a clear majority of the opposition Democratic party. The lineup in the House was 243 Democrats to 192 Republicans; in the Senate, 58 Democrats to 42 Republicans. Seeking greater support for his legislative program, Nixon was naturally eager to obtain a working majority of his own party. In his inaugural address he had urged fellow citizens to lower their voices and to "stop shouting at one another." Yet in the 1970 midterm elections he campaigned far more vigorously and provocatively than the incumbent usually does, concentrating his fire in the twenty-one states in which there were elections for governor or senator or both. Concerned with the shocking rise in crimes of violence, he stressed law and order. Democrats played up his unsuccessful efforts to halt inflation by deflationary measures that were bound to increase unemployment.

When the votes were counted, Nixon had not secured a majority in either house. The Republicans added only two seats in the Senate, leaving the total at 54 Democrats and 44 Republicans, plus one Conservative and one Independent. The Democrats won nine additional seats in the House.

The Republicans loudly claimed a moral victory, for the party in power normally loses something like thirty or forty seats in the midterm elections. Nixon had gained two in the Senate and had lost only a surprisingly small contingent of nine in the House. On the other hand, the Democrats insisted that these increases were really losses. The Republicans had started with relatively small minorities in both houses of Congress, and their candidates could have been expected to improve their position much more than they did. But heavily damaging to Republican claims of victory was the outcome of the gubernatorial contests. The Democrats won the bulk of these contests, thus reducing a Republican advantage in governors (32 to 18) to a Democratic superiority (29 to 21). This sharp shift augured well for a Democratic presidential victory in 1972.

It is entirely possible that the Republicans would have lost by a wider margin if Nixon had not campaigned so vigorously. But this assumption can neither be proved nor disproved, even though the Republicans suffered severe setbacks in some of the states in which the President made personal appearances. There less than a majority of the Republican candidates for Senator or governor gained victories, even after the President had laid his prestige on the line. Even so, Nixon claimed an "ideological majority" in the Senate, where, he insisted, most of the members, regardless of party labels, would now espouse his conservative philosophy.[3] There was something to be said for this allegation, but its force was weakened by the President's increasing departures from conservative Republican principles.

WAS NIXON A CONSERVATIVE?

Upon reaching the White House, President Nixon was generally regarded as a stalwart Republican who could be counted on to steer a conservative course. He initially continued his party's time-honored policies by battling for a sound dollar and a balanced budget while opposing deep tax cuts and price or wage controls. Pursuant to his campaign pledges, he appointed a conservative Cabinet, as well as justices of the Supreme Court who were known to be strict interpreters of the Constitution.

Nixon's most surprising trait proved to be his capacity to spring unexpected reversals — "government by surprise." At the risk of further unbalancing the budget, he early proposed (with generally indifferent success) such schemes as sharing federal revenue with the states, thorough welfare reform, a family assistance plan, improved health programs, and needed antipollution measures. He tried desperately and stubbornly to check inflation by cutbacks that reduced the number of jobs. When this brand of "Nixonomics" produced both simultaneous inflation and recession — a contradictory economic nightmare — he

[3] See Nixon's statement of Nov. 4, 1970, *Weekly Compilation of Presidential Documents*, Nov. 9, 1970, *VI*, 1543–1544.

shocked the nation on August 15, 1971, by unveiling his New Economic Policy. It involved a heavily unbalanced budget (the biggest deficit in the nation's peacetime history), a deep cut in taxes (to stimulate business recovery), limited controls on prices, wages, rents, and dividends (to halt inflation), a temporary 10 percent surtax on imported goods (to improve the adverse balance of payments), and a modest devalution of the dollar by international agreement (to encourage exports). The threat to foreigners posed by the surtax forced an upward revaluation of their currencies late in 1971, to the advantage of American foreign trade.

Nixonian inconsistencies also appeared in foreign affairs. Earlier notorious for his "hawkish" tendencies, Nixon seemed to be cooing with the "doves" as he partially wound down the Vietnam War, despite the temporary incursions into Cambodia and Laos. Famed as a foe of Communists, he unexpectedly extended a welcoming hand to Red China. Critical of "summitry" when out of office, he set new presidential records by journeying long distances to meet with numerous heads of state.

Some critics branded Nixon as inconsistent and treacherous; others praised him as realistic and flexible, arguing that when bad policies do not work, they ought to be changed. If, as Emerson observed, "A foolish consistency is the hobgoblin of little minds," Nixon had a highly expansive mentality. He was clearly willing to abandon the "game plan" in the hope of winning the game.

WAS THE WOOING OF RED CHINA PREMATURE?

Nixon angered the right-wingers of his own party by displaying a surprising cordiality toward Communist China — a move that was the more remarkable because he had early won his reputation in public life as a relentless anti-Communist. Preliminary overtures toward a better understanding included an easing of trade bans and the acceptance of an invitation from Peking in April 1971, for a visit by an American table tennis team, later reciprocated. This venture into "ping-pong diplomacy" was facilitated by Communist China's well-known and quickly demonstrated superiority in that indoor sport.

Then, on July 15, 1971, Nixon startled the world by announcing his acceptance of an invitation to visit Peking, some time "before May" 1972 (the eve of the presidential nominating conventions in America). His declared purpose was to secure a "normalization of relations," but not "at the expense of old friends." This stunning declaration seemed to foreshadow a diplomatic recognition of Peking and a seating of

Communist China in the United Nations, with a consequent expulsion of Chiang Kai-shek's Nationalist China (Taiwan). The Soviets, their relations with Peking already strained, evidently suspected that America and Red China were about to "gang up" on them. The Taiwanese cried betrayal. The Japanese, inadequately forewarned, lost much face. The South Vietnamese and South Korean governments feared ultimate abandonment by Uncle Sam. Conservative Republicans were aghast at this sudden shift: one suggestion was that the date of the projected visit to Peking should be Benedict Arnold's birthday.

In his formal announcement of the trip to China, Nixon had declared that there could be no "stable and enduring peace" without the People's Republic of China, now numbering some 750,000,000 people.[4] Red China not only possessed nuclear weapons but was reported to be developing intercontinental rockets to carry them. Some kind of accommodation between the two giants seemed to be urgently needed. To insist that the rump government of about 13,000,000 people on the offshore island of Taiwan properly represented or spoke for mainland China was an obvious absurdity. Whatever the motivations for Nixon's visit, the immediate reaction in America was overwhelmingly favorable. One prominent poll found 68 percent supporting the President's overture and only 19 percent opposed. Many Americans regarded the new relationship as overdue rather than premature.

Nixon's unexpected friendliness toward Peking no doubt facilitated Red China's entry into the United Nations, as conservatives had feared, together with the simultaneous expulsion of Nationalist China (Taiwan). The United States, while favoring the admission of Peking, opposed the ouster of Taiwan, but was outvoted by a substantial margin, October 25, 1971. Ultraconservatives in America were more than ever determined to pull the U. S. out of the U.N. and throw the U.N. out of the U. S.

WAS NORTH VIETNAM THE AGGRESSOR IN 1972?

Any hope that Nixon's new cordiality toward Communist China would result in effective restraints on Communist North Vietnam were dashed late in April 1972. Powerful units of the North Vietnamese army, unexpectedly spearheaded by Soviet-built tanks and other weapons, came crunching into South Vietnam through the demilitarized zone (DMZ),

[4] For Nixon's announcement of July 15, 1971, see *ibid., VII,* 1058.

capturing key outposts and driving panicky South Vietnamese troops before them. By this time the United States had reduced its army of some 500,000 men to about 60,000.

This overpowering Communist incursion was profoundly disturbing to Washington. It marked not only an open thrust into the temporary demilitarized zone established at Geneva in 1954, but it was also the first time that North Vietnamese troops had avowedly entered South Vietnam in large numbers. Washington was also shocked by the alleged violation of the "understanding" which President Johnson had presumably reached with Hanoi on October 31, 1968, when he called for a bombing halt in return for a cessation of aggressive action by North Vietnam. But such an "understanding" may have been the result of unjustified assumptions by the United States.

President Nixon, confronted as he was with the collapse of "Vietnamization," responded energetically to the "aggression" of the North Vietnamese. On April 26, 1972, he ordered a heavy escalation of the bombing of North Vietnam and increased bombardment by American naval units. Two weeks later (May 8), with the South Vietnamese defenses crumbling and with some remaining American combat units endangered, he went sensationally further. He announced that he would mine the ports of North Vietnam, in addition to bombing the supply lines from China. All this would be done in an effort to cut off the inflow of war materiel from the Soviet Union and China. Expressing his determination to uphold the nation's honor and credibility, while presumably saving American lives, Nixon was prepared to provoke the powerful Communist nations helping Hanoi rather than see the American-supported Saigon government crumple.

Defenders of the North Vietnamese argued that the so-called aggression through the demilitarized zone was merely a phase of the long-term civil war. The conferees in Geneva in 1954 had never intended to divide the country into two parts. The North Vietnamese were merely attempting to secure by force what the intruding Americans — viewed in North Vietnam as the aggressors — had not permitted at the ballot box in 1956. On the other hand, a nation such as the Republic of South Vietnam, which had existed as an independent government for nearly twenty years, albeit with foreign support, certainly had plausible grounds for claiming that an all-out armed invasion from the north was an act of aggression.

DID NIXON RECEIVE A MANDATE IN 1972?

While negotiations for a cease-fire in Vietnam were still in progress, President Nixon swamped his Democratic rival, Senator George McGovern, in the presidential election of November 1972. The margin of victory was awesome: Nixon garnered about 61 percent of the popular vote and carried all the states except Massachusetts (and the District of Columbia).

The Republicans obviously did not receive a mandate to press ahead with any of the programs proclaimed in their platform. Although Nixon won, his party lost when the Republicans failed to win control in either house of Congress. The Democrats even gained two seats in the Senate as well as a majority of the governorships. In a sense, while McGovern lost, his party won.

McGovern proved to be the "Goldwater of the left." The right-wing Goldwater in 1964 had alienated the left and much of his party's center; McGovern alienated the right and much of his party's center. Both aspirants suffered disaster. McGovern, with his leftist following, drove out of the party about one-third of its membership as "ticket-splitters," many of whom campaigned as "Democrats for Nixon." The President, unlike his rival, was clearly in tune with the middle-of-the-road mood of the country.

Countless voters held their noses and voted for what they regarded as the lesser of two evils. Probably more feared McGovern than loved Nixon. Only about 56 percent of the eligible electorate bothered to vote, partly because the public opinion polls had early predicted a Nixon landslide. Many citizens who had not approved of the Vietnam War, McGovern's chief issue, were reassured by the White House announcement on the eve of the election that "we believe that peace is at hand."

Many voters were impressed by Nixon's having "wound down" the war (on land but not on sea or in the air), and by the promised imminence of a cease-fire. McGovernite responses were that the cease-fire was only an election ploy, and, if achieved, should have come nearly four years earlier. Even so, the electorate seemed to favor fighting for "peace with honor" under Nixon rather than yielding "peace with surrender" under McGovern. The Senator, who had shown indecisiveness in action and indiscretion in speech, seems to have been an issue as much as a candidate.

Nixon, who barely campaigned at all, received no clear mandate to do anything. One of the few observations that one can make with certainty is that he polled many more votes than the ultraliberal Mc-Govern, who in Nixon's view was doomed the day he was nominated. Only the future could reveal what the victorious President would do with a defiant North Vietnam, which he was still bombing heavily, and with a distrustful Democratic Congress, which was eager to investigate charges of Republican corruption in the recent campaign.

ADDITIONAL GENERAL REFERENCES

Rowland Evans, Jr. and Robert D. Novak, *Nixon in the White House: The Frustration of Power* (1971); Richard M. Nixon, *Six Crises* (1962); Jules Witcover, *The Resurrection of Richard Nixon* (1970); Earl Mazo and Stephen Hess, *Nixon: A Political Portrait* (1968); Ralph De Tolendano, *One Man Alone: Richard Nixon* (1969); Richard Wilson, ed., *Setting the Course: The First Year: Major Policy Statements by President Richard Nixon* (1970); Garry Willis, *Nixon Agonistes: The Crisis of the Self-Made Man* (1970); John Osborne, *The Second Year of the Nixon Watch* (1971); Reg Murphy and Hal Gulliver, *The Southern Strategy* (1971); Leon E. Panetta, *Bring Us Together: The Nixon Team and the Civil Rights Retreat* (1971).

INDEX

Garfield, Pres. James A., 433, 444–45, 456

Garner, John Nance, 651

Geneva Accords. *See* Geneva Conference (1954).

Geneva Conference (1927), 647

Geneva Conference (1954), 822–25, 827–28

Geneva Tribunal (1872), 436–38

Gentlemen's Agreement (1907–1908), 624

German–Americans, 564

Germans, alleged atrocities of, 535

Germany, and World War I, 530–50, 552–57, 560–64, 566–67, 569–70, 571–73, 583–84, 586; and World War II, 675–79, 681–82, 689–94, 706–708, 710, 712, 715, 718–20

Gladstone, William E., 534

Goebbels, Josef, 750n

Gold currency, problems of, 470, 473

Gold standard, 443, 464

Goldfine, Bernard, 787n

Goldwater, Sen. B. M., 510n, 816, 832–33, 853

Gompers, Samuel, 520, 595

Good Neighbor Policy, 626, 650, 661–62

Goschen, Sir Richard, 532n

Gould, Jay, 435, 457

Grant, Pres. U. S., 434–36, 439, 444

Graves, Gen., 575

Great Depression, 459, 614, 622–23, 629, 634–37, 645, 664, 751

Greater East Asia Co–Prosperity Sphere, 696

Greeley, Horace, 438–39

Greer, battle with German submarines, 694

Gulflight, 546n

Griffith, D. W., "The Birth of a Nation," 402

Guadacanal, battle of, 710, 712

Guam, acquired by the U. S., 476

Guiteau, C. J., assassin of Garfield, 444–45

Haiti, Marines sent to, 524

"Half-Breeds," 444–45

Hanihara, Japanese Ambassador, 624–25

Hanna, Mark, 471, 477, 496

Harding, Pres. Warren G., 579, 593–97, 599, 604, 608–12

Harriman, W. Averell, 720n, 727, 755n

Harrison, Pres. Benjamin, 434, 441, 455–57, 465

Harvey, George, 526, 594

Hawaii, revolution of, 464–65; annexation of, 485

Hawley-Smoot Tariff Act (1930), 612, 636–37, 650, 665, 662

Hearst, William R., 477, 481

Hepburn Act (1906), 506n

Hay, John, 476–77, 487, 492

Hay–Poncefote Treaty (1901), 521–22

Hayes, C. J. H., Ambassador to Spain, 718

Hayes, Pres. Rutherford B., 433, 440, 442–45, 473

Hindenburg Line, breakthrough of, 570

Hiroshima and Nagasaki, bombed, 741–43

Hiss, Alger, 728, 777

Hitler, Adolph, 494, 532, 601, 604, 623–24, 626, 665, 670, 672–79, 681–83, 689, 693, 706–708, 710

Ho Chi Minh, 781, 821, 822

Hoover, Pres. Herbert, 604n, 629–30, 633–34, 638, 650, 654, 661, 664

Hoover Dam (Boulder Dam), 639

Hoover–Stimson nonrecognition doctrine, 648

House, Col. E. M., 593, 597n

Howard, Gen. O. O., 416

Huerta, Pres. of Mexico, 514, 525–28

Hughes, C. E., 550–51, 604, 624–25

Hull, Cordell, 662, 697, 699

Hungary, Russian suppression of (1956), 783, 797

Hurley, Patrick J., 767n

Iceland, Roosevelt's protection of, 692

Immigrants, German, 447n; "New," 447; I. W. A., 499

Immigration, 447–48

Smith, Gov. Alfred E., 616, 629–31, 651, 804, 824*n*

Smith, Gen. Jacob, 490

Snorkel submarine, Hitler's, 712

Social Security Act (1935), 668–69

Socialism, American forms of, 496

Southern historians of Civil War, 402

Soviet NEP policy, 664

Soviets, advocates of world revolution, 724

Spain, Loyalists in civil war, 673

Spanish-American War, 476, 480–90, 492–93, 565

Stalin, pact with Hitler, 676, 678–79; U.S. aid to, 689–91; 725; and Second Front, 720; and Yalta, 726–33, 746; 751; and Truman, 749

"Stalwarts," 445–47

Standard Oil of New Jersey, 498, 498*n*

Stanford, Leland, 460–61

States' rights reaffirmed in the South, 430

Stephens, A. H., 367*n*, 410

Stettinius, 727

Stevens, J. L., 465

Stevens, Thaddeus, 413–14

Stevenson, Adlai, Sr., 451, 783

Stimson, Henry L., 648, 699, 699*n*, 742, 748

Strike, the right to, 595

Stryker, L. P., on Johnson, 509

Submarine warfare in World War I, 529, 530–31, 542–49, 552–54, 557, 561, 564, 605; in World War II, 692–94

Sudetenland, Hitler's seizure of, 676

Suez Canal, 775, 783, 795

Summit conference at Paris (1960), collapse of, 799

Sumner, Sen. Charles, 412–13, 435–36

Supreme Court, liberalization of, 667, 670

Sussex sunk, 548–49, 552–54

Taft, Pres. W. H., defeated Bryan (1908), 495; presidency of, 498; and Theodore Roosevelt, 505–506, 509–510; achievements of, 507–508; as Chief Justice, 508; and "Dollar Diplomacy," 508–509; on Panama, 522; on treaties, 590; on arms embargo, 683

Taiwan, Nationalist China, 766, 791, 821, 851

Tammany Hall, Society of, 511, 630

Tampico affair, 527*n*

Tariff, Cleveland on, 451–52

Taxes in postwar South, 419

Teapot Dome scandal, 607–608, 615–17

Teheran Conference (1961), papers published, 728

Teller Amendment, 482*n*

Tennessee Iron and Coal Co., 509

Tennessee Valley Authority, 638–39, 657

Tenure of Office Act (1867), 473

Third-Term presidencies banned by Senate (1928), 628*n*, 686–87

Thurmond, Sen. J. S., 430

Tilden, S. J., 433, 440, 473

Tito, 440, 473, 753

Tolls exemptions, Panama Canal and, 521

Tonkin Gulf Resolution, 829–31, 833–34

Travel, American, in wartime, 547–48

Treaty of Ghent (1812), 774

Treaty of Paris (1899), 476, 491

Treaty of Versailles, 516, 532, 579, 588ff, 623

Treaty of Washington (1871), 436–38

Treaty with Columbia (1846), 501

Triple Entente, 531

Trotsky, Leon, 573–74

Truman, Pres. Harry S, 435, 722, 743, 753–54, 757–58, 760–63, 765, 770, 773, 776–77, 780–82; his Fair Deal, 519; at Potsdam Conference, 730, 733*n*, 749; lend-lease shipments cut back by, 739; decision to bomb Japan, 743; re-election, 763; and Vietnam, 816, 822

Truman Doctrine, 740, 781, 837

Trust busting, 498, 508

Tsar Nicholas, execution of, 574

Tsarist regime, debts of, 574